THINKING THROUGH

THE BIBLE

THINKING THROUGH
THE BIBLE

By John Mc Nicol

KREGEL PUBLICATIONS
GRAND RAPIDS, MICHIGAN 49501

Library of Congress
Catalog Card Number 76-25079
ISBN 0-8254-3214-6

First Edition 1944
Kregel Publications edition 1976

Printed in United States of America

CONTENTS

SUPPLEMENTARY NOTES

FOREWORD

For some years, *Thinking Through the Bible* has been out of print. The series has become a collector's item, as serious students of the Bible have "searched the scriptures" for the revealed mind and purposes of God.

Perhaps the uncertainty and confusion of the present period has caused this more serious Bible study. And as people have been confronted with the unknown, uncertain future, the committed Christian is "looking for that blessed hope and the glorious appearing of the great God and our Saviour, Jesus Christ" (Titus 2:13).

Dr. John McNicol, for over 50 years the teacher of Bible at Ontario Bible College (then Toronto Bible College), always taught his students to "think through the Bible", not to accept theories or doctrinal positions propounded by men, but to seek out what God has said.

This volume is the distillation of a half century of teaching. Some may not agree with Dr..McNicol's position, which he described as "historical premillenialism." But as this gracious and scholarly Christian teacher leads the reader step by step down what he calls the four highways: "The Highway of Promise and Prophecy, The Highway of Sacrifice and Worship, The Highway of Aspiration and Longing, The Highway of Fulfillment — Jesus Christ Himself," it proves to be a journey into truth.

Ontario Bible College is interdenominational and seeks to present to its students the several interpretations of *The Scriptures* so that each one might discover truth for himself. Scripture is of "no private interpretation." It is in such a scriptural climate that the student can show himself "approved unto God, a workman that needeth not to be ashamed, rightly dividing the word of truth."

It is for this purpose that we share in the reissuing of the unabridged *Thinking Through the Bible* in one volume. May it be an enrichment to the life and study of all who read; may it be used for the glory of God and to accomplish His work in the world.

As one who sat at Dr. McNicol's feet, translated his books into Hausa, and subsequently returned to the College to share with him in the ministry of training young people for the service of Jesus Christ, I have a particular joy in assisting in this venture.

Ontario Bible College   Douglas C. Percy

PREFACE

For over forty years the author of this book has been teaching the Bible to classes of young people preparing for Christian work in the Church and throughout the world. His method has been to lead his students straight through the Bible, book after book, from the beginning to the end. Critical questions have been dealt with only so far as it was necessary to clear the ground. They have not been allowed to occupy the field. The aim has been to enter the inner shrine of the Scriptures and discover the spiritual world in the Bible, the world that makes it the Word of God.

For this purpose the approach has been mainly exegetical and devotional. Other methods of approach have not been ignored. Whatever light could be gained from them has been used in the process of teaching. But the teacher has always reserved the right to judge for himself on the evidence submitted when subjective theories were proposed. He is not ignorant of the modern scientific approach to the Bible and its methods of analysis. But he does not forget that the scientific analysis of a rose does not explain the rose. More is needed than the scientific method to understand the Word of God.

The method that has been followed takes the Bible in the form in which we have it—the form in which it has come down through the Church and made its impact upon the world. It allows the Bible to stand upon its own feet, to speak for itself, and, wherever possible, to be its own interpreter. As a result the Book rises up in its living unity and bears its own self-evidencing witness to the majestic march of Divine revelation down through the ages which its pages record. It unfolds itself as the Word of the living God.

The Scripture quotations to be used throughout this new edition will be taken by permission from the American Standard Edition of the Revised Version. Our noble King James Version (A.V.) is the most suitable English Bible to use for the purpose of devotion and worship.

The first section deals with the historical part of the Old Testament—the books that contain the records of God's dealings with Israel as a nation. There, book by book, His redeeming purpose for mankind was seen to come out from the early ages of the world into the patriarchal and Mosaic eras, and then to move down through the centuries of Israel's national life. In that part of the Old Testament we have the historic background on which God's approach to man was first made.

The second section deals with the rest of the Old Testament—other kinds of books, in which the redeeming purpose of God is manifested in other ways. In the Poetical Books, we are shown first the heart of humanity in its deep need reaching out after God and searching for His approach. Then we are taken into the inner religious life of the devout Israelites, who responded to the Divine approach which they found in the revelation of the Law.

In the Prophetical Books, we are introduced to the highest form in which Divine revelation appeared in Israel. Here are heard the unmistakable accents of that voice which spoke "unto the fathers in the prophets" (Heb. 1:1). Here all the lines of the preparatory revelation of redemption which had been coming down through the ages are seen to converge directly toward the final revelation in the Lord Jesus Christ. Thus the Old Testament leads us, through the Prophets, to the threshold of the New.

True Christianity is essentially the **religion of redemption**; and it is the **story of the beginnings of the human race as described in the Old Testament that provides the necessary ground and reason for its message of redemption. Most of the ideas connected with the redemption explained in the New Testament get their real significance from the Old Testament system of worship and from the preaching of the Old Testament prophets. Without this background the Christian faith is left hanging in the air.**

That God was in Christ reconciling the world unto Himself, is the message of the New Testament. That He was in history beforehand preparing the way for Christ, is the meaning of the Old Testament. This has been the belief of the historic Church from the beginning. In this light the essential unity of the Bible stands out, the supernatural element in the Scriptures is explained, and the difficulties raised by subjective criticism fade away. The temple of God's Word is seen to rise up as the work of the Holy Spirit through the ages, guiding the writers to begin with, and afterwards presiding over the Church as she gathered the Scriptures together into her sacred Canon.

This is the belief held by the author, and this is his method of approach. The longer he has used this approach in teaching the Bible, and the more widely he has observed its results, the more profoundly he believes in its truth. In the present volume, which deals with the Gospels and the Acts, he continues this method of "thinking through the Bible" by carrying the lines of the Old Testament revelation into the New Testament. He finds them converging, in the Gospels, upon the central Figure of the whole Book, the Redeemer of mankind. And then he sees them beginning to spread out, in the Acts, into world-wide Christianity.

The section, which deals with the Epistles and the Book of Revelation, completes the series on "Thinking through the Bible". In this part of the Scriptures, and especially in the Epistles of Paul, the final purpose of the whole Biblical revelation comes to light and the unity of the Bible is manifested.

It was the special mission of the great Apostle, not only to carry the Gospel out into the Gentile world, but also to explain the real nature of Christianity. The mind of the former Pharisee had been steeped in the Old Testament; and when the light of the glory of God in the face of Jesus Christ broke in upon his soul, then the inner meaning of the old dispensation dawned upon him. With this background of training and experience, he gained an understanding of the new Christian system which was beyond that possessed by any of the other Apostles. His remarkable intellectual gifts, quickened as they were by Divine inspiration, enabled him to expound it with great clearness and fulness. For this reason his Epistles occupy a place of peculiar importance in the Word of God.

What Paul had come to see was, that the Old Testament had its consummation in Jesus Christ. The Law had been given for a temporary purpose and was to have a subsequent development. The religion of the Old Testament was concerned with salvation from sin and moral guilt, and this salvation had finally been achieved through the Cross of Christ. The Kingdom of God, which the prophets had foretold as the hope of Israel, belonged to the realm of moral and spiritual life. It was meant to have a supernatural character and to belong to a heavenly order. It was not to compete with human kingdoms by the use of worldly power, but was to be a source of light and blessing for all mankind. All this had now come into actual realization through Jesus Christ.

The essential reality in Christianity, as Paul saw it, is a new creation which is not of this world. The Gospel is not a code of ethics or a theory of religion. It is the way into a new life which transcends the old life and belongs to another world. This new world is not less real for being spiritual and invisible. It is not a subjective creation, due to the change that takes place in the heart and mind of the believer. It cannot be apprehended by the senses, but that does not mean that it belongs to the realm of abstract ideas. That zeal for the Gospel, that passion for Christianity, which throbs all through Paul's Epistles, was no mere enthusiasm for an abstract ethical ideal, no mere subjective conception of religious principle. It arose from an overmastering conviction of the new thing God had done when, in Christ, He reconciled the world unto Himself. Paul was possessed of a profound sense of the reality of the new creation which lies at the heart of Christianity.

This part of the Bible also reveals the essential nature of the Person of Christ. The Gospel which the Apostles preached was based on the historic facts of His life on earth; but the Saviour whom they presented in the Gospel was the living Christ, the ascended Lord, who now occupies the most exalted place in Heaven. A manifest glow comes into their Epistles when they refer to the exalted state of their Master. Paul frequently goes off at a tangent when he mentions the name of the Lord, seeking for words with which to express his sense of the glory of Him whom he had seen in the Damascus vision. The Book of Revelation, which is also a kind of Epistle, draws aside the veil and discloses the Son of Man occupying the heavenly throne. Then it brings the whole series of Epistles, and the whole Biblical revelation itself, to a splendid close. Over against the first heaven and the first earth, into which sin entered, it sets the new heaven and the new earth, in which sin is found no more. And in the midst of this beatific vision, "the Lamb is all the glory".

He who approaches this part of the Bible across the outer court of scientific criticism must take his shoes from off his feet when he enters here. Otherwise he cannot see the wealth that lies within. A reverent heart and a spiritual mind are the primary requisites for the apprehension of the revelation it contains. The scientific method can no more discover it than the botanist can explain to us the secret of a flower.

The critical and scientific approach to the sacred Canon of the Christian faith, which has occupied so much of the scholarly thinking of the Church during the past generation, has its own value. But how little it has really contributed to the understanding of Divine truth, or to the spiritual forces of Christianity! What the Bible needs most of all, in order to bring out its value for the cause of Christ in the world, is that devotional and exegetical approach which enters into the inner shrine of the Scripture revelation and summons all the resources of the human mind to the reverent study of the redemption that is in Christ Jesus. There can be no higher science than this. It is the occupation of those angelic intellects in Heaven unto whom "the manifold wisdom of God" is being displayed through the operation of His redeeming grace on earth (Eph. 3:10). It evoked from the heart of the greatest of the Apostles in the profoundest of his Epistles his wondering and adoring praise: "O the depth of the riches both of the wisdom and knowledge of God! How unsearchable are his judgments, and his ways past tracing out! For of him, and through him, and unto him, are all things. To him be the glory for ever. Amen" (Rom. 11:33, 36).

J. McN.

I

APPROACHING THE BIBLE

THE way to approach the Bible is to take it first as a whole and as it stands, to read it in its own light without prejudice and to allow it to speak for itself. It professes to contain the record of a historic revelation which God has given to man.

This revelation was given in various ways and by progressive stages down through the ages until it was consummated at last in His Son (Heb. 1:1-2). It was recorded from time to time, as it was made, by men inspired of God for the purpose, and the Bible is composed of the Scriptures they have written (2 Tim. 3:16; 2 Pet. 1:19-21). For this reason, and in this sense, the Bible claims to be the Word of God. Through these men God spoke to the people of their own time and revealed His mind and will regarding the human race and the world in which we live. In these Scriptures, which they have written and handed down, His Spirit now speaks, and through them He makes known His mind and will to us.

It becomes us, therefore, to read the Bible through with reverent and earnest attention, that we may know its contents and understand its spirit. Only thus can we properly test its claim to be the Word of God, and give it a fair opportunity to prove its claim to us. A reverent and earnest approach means that we bring to bear upon it, as we read it, all the active powers of our minds and all the light we have, and that we also summon our hearts to respond in faith to the truth which it reveals to us.

The principle that Jesus laid down for those who would test His own divine authority was this: "If any man willeth to do his will, he shall know of the teaching, whether it be of God, or whether I speak from myself" (John 7:17). The same principle is true of the Scriptures. A devout attitude toward God, and a readiness to do His will as we come to know it, are the essential conditions for recognizing the voice of God in the Bible. The secret of the Lord is with them that hold Him in reverence, and it is only in His light that we can really see light (Psa. 25:14; 36:9).

Approaching the Bible in this way, we seek first to understand the plain and literal meaning of its language. Then we discover that behind the literal sense of Scripture there is a spiritual and religious meaning. We find a new world in the Bible, the world from which God speaks. Thus the Scriptures establish their own authority for us. Through them we come to know the mind of God and learn to look upon our world as He would have us see it.

II

THE TWOFOLD STRUCTURE OF THE BIBLE

THE structure of the Bible bears witness to the character of the revelation which it contains. Its two parts, the Old and the New Testaments, are complementary to each other and stand together. They are two successive stages in the one progressive unfolding of the divine plan. But the difference between them is not merely one of order and sequence. There is a difference also in the kind of revelation contained in each. The relation that exists between them has been expressed by two of the early Church Fathers in concise statements which cannot be improved upon: "The Old Testament anticipates the New, and the New interprets the Old" (Chrysostom); "The New Testament lies hidden in the Old; the Old Testament stands open in the New" (Augustine).

The Old Testament is a book of outward forms, which embody and enshrine inward principles not yet in active operation. It contains types and prophecies of a coming Saviour, laws and ceremonies foreshadowing another dispensation. The history itself that is recorded there has a typical significance (1 Cor. 10:11). The New Testament, on the other hand, is a book of inward principles, which create and develop, by their own inherent spiritual power, the outward forms of life and worship foreshadowed in the old dispensation and now realized in the Christian dispensation.

The Apostle John, referring to the essential difference between the two dispensations, declares: "The law was given through Moses; grace and truth came through Jesus Christ" (John 1:17). In these words he is not contrasting law and grace as contrary methods used in different ages, but pointing out the two different stages of the one progressive plan of redemption. The Old Testament system, based upon the Law, prepared for the New Testament system, based upon the Gospel. The Law was imposed from without by the human agency of Moses as a formal system of life and worship. The Gospel brought the grace and truth that lay behind the Law into actual manifestation through the life and work of Jesus Christ. The writer of the Epistle to the Hebrews has the same idea in mind when he describes the Mosaic system of the Old Testament, in its relation to the Christian system of the New, as "having a shadow of the good things to come, not the very image of the things" (Heb. 10:1). The shadow became substance and reality in the revelation of the Lord Jesus Christ.

In taking the Bible as a whole, therefore, its two parts should be kept in their proper relation to each other, and should be considered in the light of it. The Old Testament is the necessary preparation for the New, and the New Testament is the necessary sequel and fulfilment of the Old. The setting in which the Christian revelation of the New Testament was given cannot be properly understood without the approach through the Old Testament revelation. Both parts of the Bible combine to form the Christian Scriptures. Both make up the Word of God, and both are needed for a true and full understanding of the historic revelation which God has given to man.

III

THE TWO TESTAMENTS

THE two stages of the Divine revelation which the Bible contains are centred in two Covenants. This fact accounts for the titles that have been given to its two parts. The word "testament" in these titles is due to the early Christian way of rendering the Greek word for "covenant" in Latin. In 2 Cor. 3: 14 Paul refers to the Mosaic Books of the Law as "the old covenant" (A.V. "the old testament"). Hence the name came to be used for all the Jewish Scriptures, which deal with the dispensation of the Law. It followed, as a matter of course, that the title "New Testament" should be given to the other Scriptures, which deal with the dispensation of the Gospel. The expression was used by Jesus when He instituted the rite that was to commemorate His death (Matt. 26:28; Mark 14:24; Luke 22:20; 1 Cor. 11: 25). The New Covenant had been foretold in the Scriptures of the Old Covenant (Jer. 31:31-34). The use of this term by the Lord links the two Testaments together, and indicates the essential relation that exists between them.

The two Testaments, as they stand in the Bible, are symmetrical in their arrangement. Each of them begins with a historical narrative in which the basis is laid for the subsequent books. This narrative contains the special revelation that marks the dispensation and is developed in the course of it. Each Testament ends with a prophetic outlook upon the consummation of the dispensation. The books contained in each of them fall into four groups in the same progressive order, thus showing the symmetrical development of the two dispensations.

The order of the books in the Old Testament differs from their arrangement in the Hebrew Bible, but in both cases the order begins with the Books of the Law. The rest of the Old Testament proceeds from the revelation of the Law and develops out of it. The thirty-nine books, as we have them, are arranged in the following four groups.

I. The Books of the Law: From Genesis to Deuteronomy. They tell of the origin of Israel and of the way this people was chosen by God to be the medium of His revelation to the world. Their central theme is the proclamation of the Law and the establishment of the Old Covenant.

II. The Historical Books: From Joshua to Esther. They record the history of God's dealings with Israel from the time of their entrance into the land of Canaan until their return and re-establishment there after the Babylonian captivity. Their central theme is the manifestation of the Law in the corporate life of the nation.

III. The Poetical Books: From Job to the Song of Solomon together with Lamentations. These books deal with various aspects of the religious life and experience of the people of God under the old dispensation. Their main theme is the realization of the Law in the life of the righteous man.

IV. The Prophetical Books: From Isaiah to Malachi. The writings of the prophets have to do with Israel's outlook upon the future and upon the nations around them. Their general theme is the consummation of the Law in the Kingdom of God in the world.

The New Testament also falls into four parts, which are parallel with the four divisions of the Old Testament. It begins with the books that contain the Gospel, and the rest of the New Testament proceeds from the revelation of the Gospel and develops out of it. The twenty-seven books are arranged in the following divisions:

I. The Gospels: From Matthew to John. These four books are not four different gospels, but four accounts of the one Gospel. The Gospel corresponds to the Law as the basis of the new dispensation. In it the grace of God, which was behind the Law, came to light in the revelation of Jesus Christ and in the establishment of the New Covenant.

II. The Acts. This one historical book deals with the manifestation of the Gospel in the world through the rise and spread of the Christian Church.

III. The Epistles: From Romans to Jude. These writings have to do with the realization of the Gospel in the life and experience of individual Christians and in the life and fellowship of the Christian Church.

IV. The Revelation. This one prophetical book, the last book of Scripture, looks forward to the consummation of redemption and the final triumph of the Gospel.

IV

THE UNIFYING THEME OF THE BIBLE

ALTHOUGH the Old and the New Testaments differ in character and are separated by a historic gap of four hundred years, yet they fit into each other in such a way as to give the Bible a living and unbroken unity. The sixty-six books of Scripture which compose the Bible are marked by great diversity, but they are linked together by a single theme which runs through them from the beginning to the end. This theme is the gradual development through the ages of God's plan for man's redemption.

The plan of God is brought to a head in the Person of the Redeemer. The Saviour of the world is the central figure of the whole Book. All the lines of the Old Testament converge toward Him; but they do not find their goal until, in the New Testament, He stands revealed.

The Old Testament in itself is incomplete; it ends in an unfinished way. It leads us from the creation of the world down through the stories of the patriarchs and the history of Israel, on through psalms and prophecies, till at last the road breaks off and disappears. If there were nothing more in the Bible we should be left in the dark. There are three different roads that can be followed through the Old Testament revelation, each of which ends in this way.

First, there is the highway of promise and prophecy. It begins in the Garden of Eden with the announcement that the seed of the woman should bruise the serpent's head (Gen. 3:15). This is a promise of some One who was to arise among men and destroy the power of Satan. This prophecy takes one form after the other as it goes on through the Old Testament, deepening in its significance and narrowing in its scope. In the age of the patriarchs it is passed on through Abraham (Gen. 22:18), and Isaac (Gen. 26:4), and Jacob (Gen. 28:14), till it is deposited with the tribe of Judah (Gen. 49:10). In the time of the monarchy in Israel it is taken up again and settled upon the house of David (2 Sam. 7:12-13; 1 Chron. 17:11-12).

The prophets carry on the announcement about David's son and expand it into the Messianic hope. "For unto us a child is born", declares Isaiah, "unto us a son is given; and the government shall be upon his shoulder"; and then he goes on to describe the nature of the coming Ruler and the character of his reign (Isa. 9:6-7). He is to be not only a triumphant King; he is to be the patient Servant of the Lord and a lowly sufferer as well (Isa. 42:1-4; 53:1-3). As we pass on through the Prophets, one feature after another is added to the picture. He is to be a Priest upon his throne, uniting the priestly with the kingly office (Zech. 6:13). But when we arrive at the end of the Old Testament, the coming One has not appeared; the promise is left unfulfilled.

We go back to the beginning again to take another road, the highway of sacrifice and worship. Immediately after the human family start their life outside the Garden of Eden, we find them bringing offerings to God (Gen. 4:3-4). Abel's offering is accepted because he sacrifices the firstlings of his flock. From this time on the worship of God through sacrifice appears again and again in the historic record. When Noah comes out upon the renewed world after the Flood, his first act is to build an altar and offer sacrifices thereon (Gen. 8:20). When Abraham becomes a sojourner in the Land of Promise, he builds an altar wherever he pitches his tent (Gen. 12:8; 13:18).

The children of Israel are brought out of their bondage in the land of Egypt under the sprinkled blood of the passover lamb, which has been sacrificed for their deliverance. At Mount Sinai the ransomed people enter into a covenant relationship with the Lord God, and the covenant is sealed by a sacrifice (Exod. 24:4-8). After that a whole system of sacrifices and offerings is organized. A tabernacle is prepared and set up in which they are henceforth to be offered, and one of the tribes is set apart to minister in the tabernacle and carry on the sacrificial system of worship. The ceremony of the altar has been developed into an elaborate ritual.

This goes on throughout all the history of the nation in their own land. Sacrifices are to be offered daily, and special sacrifices are required on specific occasions. The temple at length takes the place of the tabernacle, and hecatombs are offered at its dedication (1 Kings 8:62-63; 2 Chron. 7:4-5). The sacrificial shedding of blood is the heart of all the worship of God in tabernacle and temple alike. No other way of approach to God is provided for Israel.

And yet the devout Israelite knew that what God wanted was not the sacrifice itself or the blood of the victim. "Sacrifice and offering thou hast no delight in", says the psalmist (Psa. 40:6). "Will I eat the flesh of bulls, or drink the blood of goats?" (Psa. 50:13). The prophets denounced sacrifices when they were carried on with insincerity. "Bring no more vain oblations", cried Isaiah (Isa. 1:13); they were of no value without righteousness of life and conduct. "What doth Jehovah require of thee", asked Micah, "but to do justly, and to love kindness, and to walk humbly with thy God?" (Micah 6:8). The message of the prophets emphasized the ethical character of the Mosaic Law as its essential feature; yet they did not repudiate the sacrificial system of worship.

The most notable religious revivals in Israel, which involved the restoration of the temple services of sacrificial worship, occurred in the reigns of Hezekiah and Josiah, when such outstanding prophets of ethical righteousness as Isaiah and Jeremiah were preaching in Jerusalem. The one way of return to God after backsliding and apostasy was through the Levitical system of sacrifices. There was some vital reason, therefore, for all these ceremonies; there was some deeper significance in this ritual of blood. But the Old Testament comes to a close without giving us any explanation.

There is still a third road that can be traced through the Old Testament—one which is not so clearly marked as the other two but is there nevertheless- -, the line of aspiration and longing. Soon after the banishment from Eden, when the human race had only begun to develop in the earth, we read: "Then began men to call upon the name of Jehovah" (Gen. 4:26). Even as early as that it was found that the world could not satisfy the heart of man, and he began to turn back to God.

Abraham set out from his early home in response to a Divine call which appealed to an unsatisfied longing in his soul. He was looking for a city with deeper foundations than Ur of the Chaldees, a city "whose builder and maker is God" (Heb. 11:10). Jacob revealed the deepest desire of his heart at Peniel, when he cried out in the struggle with his Heavenly antagonist: "I will not let thee go, except thou bless me" (Gen. 32:26). At the end of his long life, when he was pronouncing his final prophecy over his sons, he paused in the midst of it, as though weary with the world, and turned to God with this cry: "I have waited for thy salvation, O Jehovah" (Gen. 49:18).

The elemental aspiration of the heart of man breaks out most fully in the story of Job. There its deepest depths are sounded. The whole book is a cry for God out of the darkness and mystery of suffering. It is all summed up in the words: "Oh that I knew where I might find him!" (Job 23:3). The same cry runs as an undertone through the Book of Psalms. "As the hart panteth after the waterbrooks, so panteth my soul after thee, O God" (Psa. 42:1). "Out of the depths have I cried unto thee, O Jehovah" (Psa. 130:1).

On through the writings of the prophets this line still runs, for we find them basing some of their most eloquent appeals upon the unsatisfied desires of the human heart; as when Isaiah cries: "Ho, every one that thirsteth, come ye to the waters" (Isa. 55:1). But again, the Old Testament comes to a close, and there is no indication given us as to how these aspirations are to be realized.

So the Bible leaves us there, facing the great gap between the Testaments, with Divine promises given but unfulfilled, with sacrificial ceremonies of worship required but unexplained, and with desires of the human heart awakened but unsatisfied. All the roads by which we have come thus far seem to end in the dark.

The moment we pass into the New Testament, light begins to break. On its very first page we find the words, "that it might be fulfilled" (Matt. 1:22). A child comes into the world at Bethlehem, of the family of David; and prophecy begins to come to pass. He grows up in a poor and humble home, "as a root out of a dry ground". He leaves the obscurity of Nazareth and goes down to the Jordan for a special anointing, and John the Baptist points Him out as the One that was to come (John 1:29). From that time on He goes about teaching and preaching and doing good; and prophecy is seen unfolding about Him as a flower unfolds to the rising sun.

In the meantime John has been cast into prison, and his faith begins to falter. He sends to ask Jesus if He really is the One that should come, or if someone else is to be looked for. John is the last in the long line of the prophets of the old dispensation; and the message Jesus sends back to comfort and assure him is simply this, that in the very character of the ministry now being carried on among the poor and needy people of the land, the words of the prophets whom John represents are being fulfilled (Matt. 11:2-5). Here then we find the first of the roads by which we have travelled through the Old Testament taken up again and reaching its goal in the New. In the life and ministry of Jesus Christ among men, the prophecies of a coming Saviour are finding their fulfilment.

The second road also soon appears. There came a time in the life of Jesus when He told His disciples that He must go to Jerusalem to suffer and be put to death. They sought to dissuade Him from this purpose, but He would not be turned aside. He steadfastly set His face to go to Jerusalem. In the upper room there He gathered His disciples about Him and instituted an ordinance that was to commemorate His death and set forth its significance: "This is my blood of the covenant, which is poured out for many unto remission of sins (Matt. 26:28). Then He went out to Gethsemane and on to Calvary. When He died, the veil that hid the innermost sanctuary in the temple was rent in twain; there was no longer need for it. On the Cross something had happened. A way of access was now open into the presence-chamber of God. The sin of the world that barred the way to God had been removed. The long line of ceremonial sacrifices was at last explained. Their meaning was fulfilled when Jesus Christ put away sin by the sacrifice of Himself (Heb. 9: 26).

And what about the aspirations of the Old Testament? During His ministry Jesus appealed to the yearnings of men and claimed to be able to satisfy them. In Galilee He looked out upon the multitudes and said, "Come unto me, all ye that labour and are heavy laden, and I will give you rest" (Matt. 11:28). In Jerusalem He stood among the throngs in the temple courts and cried, "If any man thirst, let him come unto me, and drink" (John 7:37). But the meaning of these invitations was not understood till after His death. When He arose and ascended into Heaven and sent back the Holy Spirit, then the full meaning of these great words was realized by His disciples. Their lives became flooded with a wealth of joy and blessing they had never known before. At Pentecost He had come back again to abide with them.

From this point onward the New Testament unfolds the significance of this great fact and shows how the living and ascended Lord, who had been dead but was now alive for evermore, meets all the needs and satisfies all the longings of the heart of man. As it draws to a close, we are shown the beatific vision of a numberless multitude out of all the races of men gathered round the Lamb upon the throne, of whom it is said, "They shall hunger no more, neither thirst any more" (Rev. 7:16).

And so it is that all the lines of the Old Testament revelation lead on into the New Testament and meet in the life and death and resurrection of the Lord Jesus Christ. He is the key to the whole Bible. Its central theme is not so much the plan of redemption as it is the Person of the Redeemer. The Scriptures all speak of Him; "the testimony of Jesus is the spirit of prophecy" (Rev. 19:10). His shadow falls across the pages of the Old Testament, and we can find Him there when we read it in the light of the New. The New Testament has a deeper and richer meaning when we read it in the light of the Old. When we see Christ in this way in all the Scriptures as their unifying theme, the Bible becomes for us, in the deepest and truest sense, the Word of the living God.

THE OLD TESTAMENT
BOOKS OF THE LAW

THE BOOKS OF THE LAW

THE first five books of the Old Testament form a group by themselves to which the term Pentateuch ("of five books" or "five-fold") has been given. They were originally regarded as one book and are always so referred to in the Bible. They are called "the law", "the book of the law", "the book of the law of Moses", or "the book of the law of God" (Josh. 1:8; 8:31, 34; 24:26; 2 Kings 22:8; Neh. 8:1-3). These titles indicate the general theme of the Pentateuch. The revelation which God gave to Israel at Mount Sinai in proclaiming His law to them and establishing His covenant with them is the central feature of these books. This revelation is the basis of the whole Old Testament dispensation, and all the later books rest upon it.

The Pentateuch is referred to also as "the book of Moses", or simply under the name of "Moses" alone (Ezra 6:18; Luke 16:29; 24:27). It professes to have come originally from his hand. Moses kept a record of God's dealings with the people whom he had led out of Egypt, and he was instructed from time to time to write therein (Exod. 17:14; 34: 27; Num. 33:2). It is also stated that "Moses wrote this law", and when he had finished "writing the words of this law in a book", he gave it to the Levites and instructed them how to have "this book of the law" preserved in Israel (Deut. 31:9, 24-26).

The book which Moses left behind was the beginning of the Bible. It was edited by other sacred writers, whose task was to preserve, transcribe, and hand on Moses' work. Marks of later hands are to be seen in Gen. 36:31, Num. 15:32, and Deut. 3:14, where notes are put in which were evidently written after Moses' day. The account of Moses' death at the end of Deuteronomy was probably written by Joshua. The last three or four verses were evidently added long afterwards.

Moses occupies a unique place in the Books of the Law. They make him a personal witness of the revelation which they record, and so link their Mosaic origin inseparably with the Divine character of the Old Testament dispensation. They represent him as the mediator of the Covenant between God and Israel, and the agent establishing the worship of Jehovah as the God of Israel. The monotheistic belief of the Hebrews and their national system of worship did not arise from a discovery of God reached by themselves, for their history shows that they were by nature prone to idolatry. The religion of Israel was the result of a supernatural revelation in which God Himself took the initiative, and these books tell the story of it. "He made known his ways unto Moses, his doings unto the children of Israel" (Psa. 103:7).

The claim of a Mosaic origin which the Pentateuch makes for itself is supported by other evidence of a cumulative character, which may be summed up as follows:

1. The unanimous tradition of the Jewish race throughout the ages ascribes these books to Moses. The Pentateuch forms part of their own national literature, and it was never doubted in Israel that it contains the true story of their origin and the true account of their religion. A uniform belief such as this, which is more deeply and solidly rooted than the traditions of any other people and has powerfully influenced the character and destiny of the race, cannot be lightly dismissed. Only an adequate cause can account for it. That cause could not have been an invention imposed upon the nation in the course of its history.

2. The internal evidence of the books themselves points to the age of Moses. The language reflects his age, and much of it would be unsuitable for a later age. The accounts of Joseph and the Israelites in Egypt correspond in the minutest details with what is known of that ancient country from other sources. The story of Israel's sojourn in the wilderness bears signs of having been written by an eye-witness. The narrative throughout the Pentateuch has an air of simple truthfulness. This evidence is not invalidated by the presence of double narratives or signs of different documents, for there were records of the past in Moses' time which he could use. Nor is it affected by the occasional references to later times, for they could have been inserted by the editors of Moses' work.

3. Archæology supports the historical character of these books. It has dispelled the critical doubts that were formerly cast upon the Genesis account of the patriarchs. Its more recent discoveries have thrown a flood of new light upon the time of Abraham, and also upon the later Mosaic era. In no case have they shown the Biblical record to be erroneous in any particular, or raised any doubt about it.

4. The Lord Jesus Christ took these books for what they claim to be. He referred to them and quoted them as the work of Moses (Mark 12:26; Luke 24:44; John 5:45-47). His testimony cannot be dismissed by saying that He accepted the traditional view about them that was current in His own day; for He did more than that. He regarded them as having Divine authority and as revealing the mind of God. He met the assaults of Satan in the wilderness by quoting from Deuteronomy with the statement, "It is written", thus showing what He thought of the authority this book carried (Matt. 4:4, 7, 10; Deut. 8:3; 6:16; 6:13). If its claim to have come from Moses had been false, it could not have had such authority for Him. The infallible spiritual insight of the Son of Man recognized the Word of God. He who "came out from the Father" (John 16:28) could not have been deceived about His Father's voice.

NOTE: Modern subjective criticism denies the Mosaic authorship of these books and substitutes for it an elaborate documentary theory. It regards them as a compilation of material from various sources put together long after Moses' day. It assumes that there were two original documents containing the traditions of the Hebrew people. One was the J Document, which used the name "Jehovah" for God. The other was the E Document, which used the name "Elohim" for God. To these was added the P Document, which was the work of the priests giving symbolic significance to the history. Finally came D, our Deuteronomy, which was "the book of the law" professedly found in the Temple in the reign of Josiah (2 Kgs. 22:8; 2 Chron. 34:14-15). This is the key to the whole critical theory. The book had been prepared secretly by unknown authors as a basis for moral reform and to support the preaching of the prophets. Its authorship was ascribed to Moses in order to give the work the greatest authority and the widest influence. Nothing dishonest should be seen in this; so it is declared. It was justified by the motive behind it and the standards of the time.

Such, in substance, is "the documentary hypothesis" of modern Biblical criticism. It has never been accepted with unanimity, for there always have been critical scholars who rejected it. The Christian Church as a whole, with a sound spiritual instinct, treats it with only academic interest, and simply passes it by. The common sense of Christians in general still continues to take these Books of the Law at their face value.

THE BOOK OF GENESIS

GENESIS, as its name implies, is the book of "beginnings". It goes back to the beginnings of the world, but it deals especially with the beginnings of redemption. This theme is manifest in the structure of the book. It is composed of ten separate sections, introduced by similar headings, and arranged in such a way as to show how God's purpose of redemption moved down through the early ages of the world by a selective process among men till it rested at last upon Israel. The structure may be shown as follows:

Introduction: The Creation of the Heavens and the Earth (1:1—2:3)
1. The Generations of the Heavens and the Earth (2:4—4:26)
2. The Book of the Generations of Adam (5:1—6:8)
3. The Generations of Noah (6:9—9:29)
4. The Generations of the Sons of Noah (10:1—11:9)
5. The Generations of Shem (11:10-26)
6. The Generations of Terah, the father of Abraham (11:27—25:11)
7. The Generations of Ishmael (25:12-18)
8. The Generations of Isaac (25:19—35:29)
9. The Generations of Esau (Ch. 36)
10. The Generations of Jacob (Chs. 37—50).

There is evidence of purpose in this arrangement. The word "generations" means the posterity of the persons named or the progress of events relating to them. It refers in each case to the history that follows. As we follow this plan through the book, we notice that the side branches of the race are always taken up first and cut off before the main branch, through which God's redemptive purpose runs, is carried onward. The history of Cain and his line in chapter 4 precedes that of Seth and his line in chapter 5. The generations of the sons of Noah precede the generations of Shem. The generations of Ishmael and of Esau precede those of Isaac and of Jacob respectively. With the generations of Jacob we arrive at last at the origin of Israel.

For purposes of study the Book of Genesis is best divided into two main parts: Chapters 1-11, which cover long ages of the world's early history, the narrative being given in bare outline, and Chapters 12—50, which deal with the age of the patriarchs alone, the narrative being amplified in greater detail. The first part may be summed up under four great themes, and the second part under four great names. This gives us the following working outline of the book:
I. The Beginnings of the World—Chs. 1-11
  1. The Creation (Chs. 1-2)
  2. The Fall (Chs. 3-5)
  3. The Flood (Chs. 6-9)
  4. The Nations (Chs. 10-11)
II. The Beginnings of Israel—Chs. 12-50
  1. Abraham (Chs. 12-23)
  2. Isaac (Chs. 24-26)
  3. Jacob (Chs. 27-36)
  4. Joseph (Chs. 37-50)

THE CREATION
(Chs. 1-2)

The Creation is described in these chapters from two different points of view. In the first account man comes at the end, as the crowning work of the Creator and as His final purpose in the material order. In the second account man comes at the beginning, as the starting point of human history and the preparation for a spiritual order.

1. A General Account of the Creation of the World (1:1—2:3). The Bible begins with a fitting prologue; it brings us to God at once. This account of the origin of the world is sublime in its majesty and simplicity. It has the unmistakable marks of a primitive revelation, broken fragments of which are found in the mythological accounts of Creation. It transcends science; but it does not conflict with science. It is not so much an account of the Creation as a revelation of the Creator. Its purpose is not to give information as to the way the world was made, but to reveal God at work in the making of the world.

The events of Creation are described as if they were seen by an observer on the earth while the handiwork of the Creator develops in progressive stages around him. The making of the world goes on, not as a process of evolution up an inclined plane, but as a series of steps up a stairway, each brought about by a creative act of God. Each period of creative activity is characterized by a higher grade of life than the preceding period; and each period is also the preparation for a still further advance introduced in the one following.

These progressive periods are represented as

"days", each with an "evening" and a "morning", a beginning and a culmination of its own particular form of life. The Hebrew day began in the evening and came to a head in the morning. After an introductory statement in which the earth is described as "waste and void" (vs. 1-2), these "days" or cycles of time begin. They form two great eras of three days each. In the first three days (vs. 3-13), that which was "waste" was given order and arrangement. In the next three days (vs. 14-31), that which was "void" was given fulness and life. At the end of the first era plants were created, introducing the element of organic life. At the end of the last era man appeared as the crowning work of creation, made "in the image of God", with a spiritual nature capable of fellowship with Him.

The seventh day follows as the period in which God "rested" from His creative work (2:1-3). It is not described as having an evening and a morning, for though it has had a beginning, it has not yet reached its consummation. "God blessed the seventh day and hallowed it", as the age for the spiritual development of the human race. It was the Creator's purpose that His highest creature should share His Sabbath rest by worship and fellowship with Him. This purpose, frustrated for a time by the fall of man, is now attained through the redemption of Christ (Heb. 4:9). Hints of the coming "morning" occur in such passages as Psa. 49:14; Isa. 60:1-3; and Rom. 13:11-12.

2. A Particular Account of the Creation of Man (2:4-25). Having told of the origin of the heavens and the earth, the story now takes up their "generations", or the history that proceeds from their creation. It goes back into the sixth day and deals with that part of the earth where man was placed (vs. 4-6). A suitable abode was being prepared for him. The reference is not to the vegetation of the world as a whole, but to that which requires human oversight and cultivation. The story of the human race is about to begin. Reminiscences of Eden linger in the ancient mythologies which tell of a garden of bliss and a golden age in the far past. They point back to the primeval truth which Genesis here records.

The conditions of man's original state as he came from the Creator's hand are set forth in pictorial form. We are shown that he had a dual origin, linking him with both the physical and the spiritual world (v. 7), and that he was placed in an ideal environment, perfectly suited for his enjoyment and the development of his nature (vs. 8-14). The locality of Eden, where human history began, was evidently known when this account was written. The description of it indicates that it was somewhere in the Mesopotamian plain. Throughout the account the Lord God is represented as the friend and instructor of man, giving him work to do and a purpose for his life (v. 15), and providing for the development of his whole nature.

Special provision was made for the development of man's moral nature. He was to learn to know the difference between good and evil, not by experimenting with them, but by following the expressed will of his Creator as the guiding principle of his life (vs. 16-17). His mental nature was trained, and his own peculiar social need discovered, by reflection on the nature of the animal world around him (vs. 18-20). His social nature was finally and fully provided for, and marriage instituted, when God "made a woman and brought her unto the man" (vs. 21-25). This is represented as the final step in God's creation of man. Adam's words mark the crowning point in man's primitive development: "This is now — ." They express his joy at finding his nature fully satisfied at last. The family was thus made the unit in the constitution of the human race. Manhood and womanhood together make humanity.

NOTE: A new name for the Creator is used in the special account of the creation of man. The two Divine names which occur throughout the Old Testament, "Elohim" (God) and "Jehovah" (represented in the English Version by the word Lord in capital letters), are here combined into "Jehovah God", or "the Lord God". The combination is continued to the end of chap. 3, that is, throughout the story of the creation and fall of man. This does not mean that another document is being used by the writer for his material, but that another idea is being introduced into the record. The "documentary hypothesis", which assumes that the two different Divine names come from two different documentary sources, fails to take account of the special significance of the names.

These two names are not used at random in the Hebrew Scriptures. They both designate the Supreme Being, but they represent Him under different aspects. Elohim is the common name for the Deity. It is the term used when His relation to all mankind is in view, and so it occurs alone in the general account of the creation of the world in chap. 1. Jehovah is the proper name of the God of Israel. It is the name by which He made Himself known to His chosen people as their covenant God. It implies the idea of redemption. The revelation of redemption in the Bible really begins with the story of man in the Garden of Eden, and so the new name is properly introduced here. The Creator of the world is also the Redeemer of men.

THE FALL
(Chs. 3-5)

The fact of the Fall is the pivot of the whole Bible. Without it the message of redemption would be meaningless. Something happened at the very beginning of man's history which perverted his nature and turned the stream of human life in the wrong direction. This section begins with a story which explains the nature of the event, and goes on to trace its consequences as they began to develop in the course of human history.

1. The Beginning of Sin (Ch. 3). The pictorial form in which the story is told does not mean that it is mythical or unreal. It should not be forgotten that our natural faculties themselves have been so altered and circumscribed by the Fall that the conditions of human life before that event are beyond the reach of our present experience and cannot be conveyed to our understanding in common speech. The life of man in Eden reached out into the unseen spiritual world, and from that world man has fallen. A similar reason exists for the symbolic language of Scripture describing the heavenly life which is still beyond our ken. The story in this chapter sets forth the facts in such a way as to show us how human sin originated and how Divine grace came out to meet it.

(1) Human sin. The serpent hides a mystery; behind it looms a dark evil intelligence, the real source of sin, who used the serpent as his instru-

ment. The shadow of Satan is seen here, the great enemy of God and man (Rev. 12:9; 20:2). From him came a temptation to doubt the love and question the will of God (vs.1-5). The act of disobedience which Eve and Adam committed (v. 6) consisted in turning aside to self-will instead of following God's will as the rule of life. Eve was deceived by the suggestions of the tempter, but Adam acted deliberately (2 Cor. 11:3; 1 Tim. 2:14).

That act of his put the permanent bias of self-will upon the original free will of man, and turned his whole nature in the direction of self-interest. This is the essence of sin. The immediate result of eating the forbidden fruit was a sense of shame before each other (v. 7), a sense of fear and guilt before God (vs. 8-10), and the rise of the ugly spirit of self in both the man and the woman (vs. 11-13). They had the knowledge of good and evil now, but they had obtained it by taking evil into their own being; it was incorporated in their own will and experience.

In pronouncing judgment God addressed the serpent, the woman, and the man, each in turn (vs. 14-19). A curse was to lie upon the serpent above all the animal world, aggravating its natural state to become the very symbol of evil. The woman's function of motherhood was to be accompanied by pain and sorrow, and she should become subject to her husband. Because of Adam's moral failure in yielding to his wife and disobeying God, the ground producing his food was to be cursed, and the race was to be condemned to an existence of painful toil. The world of nature would deteriorate and resist man's efforts to cultivate and subdue it. Man's life was doomed to end in death, and he was to go back to the dust from which he came.

(2) Divine grace. Even in pronouncing judgment, God manifested His grace and gave the guilty pair ground for hope. His redeeming purpose was implied in the judgment upon the serpent, which contains the first announcement of redemption for the race (v. 15). There was to be perpetual enmity between the serpent and the woman, that is, between Satan and the human race; and between the seed of the serpent and the seed of the woman, that is, between those who inherit the wickedness of their father the devil and are his spiritual children (Matt. 13:38; 23:33; John 8:44; Acts 13:10; 1 John 3:8-10) and those who are the children of God through the woman, born of God through the woman's seed. This is the only case in Scripture where the word "seed" is used of the posterity of the woman. In the statement that the seed of the woman should bruise the serpent's head and the serpent bruise his heel, there is a foreshadowing of the mystery of the Incarnation, the suffering of the Cross, and the ultimate triumph of Christ over Satan (Rom. 16:20; Rev. 12:9-10; 20:2-3, 7-10).

Adam showed his faith in the promise of God by the name he gave his wife as the mother of the coming seed (v. 20). God's grace is further seen in the provision of coats of skin to clothe the nakedness of Adam and Eve (v. 21). This involved the slaying of animal victims and probably had something to do with the institution of sacrifice, for the event antedates the permission of animal food (9:3).

Finally God proceeded to expel Adam and Eve from the Garden of Eden out into the world beyond (vs. 22-23). They were shut out from fellowship with God and lost their right to the tree of life. Thus the fall of man was not only a fall into sin, but also a fall from the spiritual world, the world that transcends the natural and visible order. For that world man was created, and now he could no longer have access there. But God's grace followed him still.

Supernatural symbols of God's presence were placed at the east of the garden, to keep and mark the way to the tree of life (v. 24). These gave man hope of an ultimate return to the fellowship of God, and in the meantime provided a way of worshipping Him. "The flame of a sword which turned every way", means a flame of fire in constant motion, living fire. It is the first appearance of the Shekinah in the Old Testament. Fire continues to be the symbol of the Divine presence and activity down through the Old Testament dispensation until the Day of Pentecost, when the Holy Spirit descended and sat upon each of the disciples in tongues, "like as of fire" (Acts 2:3).

2. The Growth of Sin (4:1-15). When Adam and Eve went out from the Garden of Eden, they carried with them God's promise of a Redeemer. The fundamental difference in the character of their two sons, Cain and Abel, was due to the attitude of each toward this redeeming purpose of God. It was shown, not in their different occupations (vs. 1-2), but in the offerings they presented to Him in worship (vs. 3-5). Cain's occupation was a higher and more important one than Abel's, for he continued the work God had given man to do at his creation. The two brothers are chosen out of Adam's family, which must have become very large by this time, as representative of the two classes of men, the seed of the serpent and the seed of the woman. The New Testament makes this distinction between them (1 John 3:12; Heb. 11:4). The age-long conflict was now beginning.

Man's worship of God would take place at first before the symbols of the Divine presence at the east of the Garden of Eden (3:24). There Adam's family would gather every Sabbath day. The phrase rendered "in process of time" is literally "at the end of days", and probably means, at the end of every weekly period. Week after week Cain brought the fruit of his own toil, but nothing else, showing no sense of sin. Abel brought a sacrificial victim, confessing thereby his need of redemption. Abel's sacrifice is described in Heb. 11:4 as "more excellent", literally "fuller", than Cain's. He added the sacrificial victim to his other offerings. His was the worship of faith, while Cain's was the worship of self-will. The Lord "had respect unto Abel and to his offering" by having the flame of fire consume it while Cain's was left unconsumed. It was thus, the writer of Hebrews means, that Abel "had witness borne to him that he was righteous"—that he was right with God.

The Lord met Cain's anger and resentment by explaining the merciful provision made for worshipping Him (vs. 6-7). Apparently God still maintained direct communication with men. The language of the passage is involved and its meaning is obscure. The word for "sin" is the technical term for "sin-offering" in the Mosaic sacrificial system, and in the light of that v. 7 may be paraphrased as follows: "If thou doest well (dost not sin), shall not thy offering be accepted? and if thou doest not well (dost commit sin), a sin-offering lieth at the gate of Eden. It is under thy hand, ready for thy use". But Cain persisted in his sullen self-will. Sin in him developed rapidly into hatred, and finally into murder, deliberately planned (v. 8). Something has dropped out of this verse in the Hebrew, for the word rendered "told" means "said unto" and requires an object. The Greek Septuagint, which was translated from the Hebrew in the third century B.C., has this: "And Cain said unto Abel his brother, Let us go into the field." This exactly suits the context and was probably in the original Hebrew text.

Then God called Cain to account; blood shed by man cries to God for justice. It was a judicial enquiry and probably took place when the time for worship came round again. It exposed Cain's heart; self-will had at last destroyed natural affection in him (vs. 9-10). He was doomed to live under a curse which was to spring from the ground in retribution against him. The ground would be barren under his hand, and he should be a wanderer in the earth (vs. 11-12). Cain shrank under the judgment of God, haunted by the memory of his crime and apprehensive of vengeance; and God gave him some kind of assurance of personal security before he went away from the presence of the Lord and the immediate vicinity of Eden (vs. 13-15).

3. The Progress of Man (4:16-26). The powers of the human race were first developed by the descendants of Cain. The beginnings of a progressive civilization are here described, but it was inspired by self-will and pride. Cain himself started it in the second generation by building a city in honour of his son and giving rise to architecture (vs. 16-18). In the seventh generation, Lamech violated the Creator's constitution of the family by introducing polygamy (v. 19). His sons were men of enterprise and genius. From them sprang pastoral pursuits, the basis of commerce and trade in primitive times (v. 20), music and the fine arts (v. 21), and the industrial and mechanical arts (v. 22). Lamech himself composed the first piece of poetry recorded in the Bible (vs. 23-24). It is a war song, in the parallel structure of Hebrew poetry, which he sang to his two wives, boasting of a murder he had committed. It casts a vivid light on the moral condition of the Cainite family. In the seventh generation from Adam, the self-willed spirit of Cain had developed into bold defiance of God and confident pride in human power.

In the meantime another son had been given to Adam and Eve in the place of Abel, to maintain the true worship of God and the spiritual development of man (vs. 25-26). In the same generation in which Cain was building a city to establish himself in the world, Seth was discovering that the world could not satisfy the heart and was leading men to seek the Lord. He became the head of a God-fearing line through whom the redeeming purpose of God was to be carried down through the ages.

The names of the three sons of Adam and Eve in this chapter are evidently intended to be significant. They seem to reflect the faith and religious experience of Eve, who gave them. She called her first-born Cain, saying, "I have gotten a man with the help of Jehovah", playing on the word for "get" which has a similar sound in the original. This would indicate a thought in her heart that Cain was the promised seed. When he disappointed her, she called the next son Abel, "a breath", or "vanity". This name expressed that disappointment, and also indicated the kind of experience she was meeting with in the world. When Seth was born she gave him a name which means "placed" or "put", believing that God had "appointed" him instead of the godly Abel to be the head of the line in which the promised seed should appear.

4. The Reign of Death (Ch. 5). The record now leaves the line of Cain and follows that of Seth. Ten generations are recorded from Adam to Noah. The results of the Fall work themselves out even in the godly line. Death now reigns. The phrase, "and he died", rings down the record like the tolling of a bell. There is one striking exception in the seventh generation (vs. 21-24). The translation of Enoch indicates what would have been the end of man's earthly life had there been no Fall; he would have passed on into the heavenly world without dying. The long lives of these antediluvian patriarchs bear witness to the vital powers with which man's physical nature was endowed in his original creation.

There are three statements in this chapter which deserve notice: (1) Adam begat a son "in his own likeness" (v. 3). The bias of self-will introduced into man's nature by the Fall was transmitted to the whole human race; every child of Adam is born with it. (2) Enoch "walked with God" (v. 22). This expression is unique in Scripture. Except in the case of Noah (Gen. 6:9), it occurs again only in connection with the priests' intercourse with God in the Temple (Mal 2:6). It means a peculiarly intimate and personal converse with the Lord, the kind of fellowship man was originally intended to have with his Creator (Heb. 11:5-6). (3) Lamech's reason for calling his son Noah ("rest"). "This same shall comfort us", or "give us rest" (v. 29). Evidently he felt the burden of toil upon an earth which was under the curse of man's sin, and he looked forward in faith and hope to the fulfilment of the Divine promise of deliverance.

THE FLOOD
(Chs. 6-9)

The development of sin resulted at last in such universal corruption that it brought on a judgment of God in which He destroyed the old world and made a new start with man under new conditions.

1. The Corruption of the Race (6:1-12). This came about when the line of Seth ("the sons of God") mingled with the rest of the race by following their own self-willed choice in marrying the "daughters of men" (vs. 1-2). The flesh had overcome the spirit even in the godly line, and the Lord determined to shorten the duration of human life (v. 3). The mingling of the two lines had resulted in a great development of the powers of the race, but also in great wickedness and the corruption of man's whole inner nature (vs. 4-5). The purpose for which God created man was being completely perverted; and, for the very preservation of the race, Divine justice required the destruction of its present representatives (vs. 6-8). In the midst of this universal wickedness there was one righteous man who "walked with God", and the record makes a new beginning with him (vs. 9-12).

2. The Making of the Ark (6:13-22). God's purpose of judgment, which has been already stated, was now revealed to Noah. God gave him instructions for the building of an ark for the preservation of himself and his house, and promised to establish His covenant with him, thus carrying on through him His design for the race. The narrative emphasizes Noah's complete obedience to the Divine instructions in all the preparations for the Flood (6:22; 7:5, 9, 16). He did the will of God in faith,

while all the rest of the world went on in their own wicked, self-willed way (Heb. 11:7).

3. The Saving of Noah (7:1—8:19). The story of the Flood is told with majestic simplicity and restraint. It was caused by an uprush of waters from the seas as well as a deluge of rain from the skies: "All the fountains of the great deep were broken up, and the windows of heaven were opened" (v. 11). In describing the course and duration of the Flood, the narrative is amplified and reads like a log-book. It marks out the week before it began (7:1-5), the day Noah entered the ark (7:6-10), the forty days of rain (7:11-17), the hundred and fifty days when the waters prevailed on the earth (7:18-24), the gradual subsiding of the waters till the tenth month when the tops of the mountains were seen (8:1-5), the sending out of the raven and the dove (8:6-12), and finally Noah's leaving the ark at the command of God (8:13-19).

4. The New Beginning (8:20—9:29). The new conditions under which the human race made a new start in its history are set forth in the incidents recorded in this section.

(1) Noah's sacrifice (8:20-22). His first act on coming out of the ark marked his faith in God. The way of approach to God was still by the altar of sacrifice. The Lord accepted the sacrifice, admitted the fact of universal sinfulness, thus taking account of it in His subsequent government of the world, and promised never to interrupt the course of nature again.

(2) The blessing of Noah (9:1-7). The blessing given to Adam was renewed, with several significant changes. Man's dominion over the animal world now became one of fear and dread. Animal food, blood excepted, was to be allowed, marking a coarsening of man's physical nature. Authority to punish crime, formerly forbidden to any private person because reserved for God Himself (4:15), was now delegated to man. Thus was instituted the principle of civil government suited to man's fallen state.

(3) The covenant with Noah (9:8-17). The promise not to destroy the world again by a flood was put in the form of a covenant, including in its scope both the human race and the animal world. The rainbow was made the token of this covenant and given a spiritual meaning. Nature thus became a symbol of spiritual truth.

(4) The prophecy of Noah (9:18-27). Noah's three sons were to become the heads of a three-fold division of mankind as they spread over the earth. His prophecy regarding his sons foreshadowed the destiny and character of these three branches of the race. Embodied in the prophecy is a hint that the purpose of redemption was to be carried down through the line of Shem. In a peculiar sense the Lord was to be the God of Shem (v. 26).

Noah's age at his death classes him with the long-lived antediluvians (vs. 28-29). After this, human life was shortened from age to age down to the time of the Hebrew patriarchs, when its limit was less than two hundred years. This is shown in the generations of Shem as recorded in ch. 11: 10-32.

THE NATIONS
(Chs. 10-11)

After the Flood the world was peopled by the descendants of Noah. National divisions among mankind began with the institution of authoritative human government (Rom. 13:1).

1. The Origin of the Nations (Ch. 10). Seventy nations are mentioned in the list, which is evidently intended to be symbolical rather than complete, representing all the races of mankind. The unity of the human race is set forth in this roll of the nations (Acts 17:26), which is God's final review of them before the sacred record takes up the story of the chosen nation, through whom the Redeemer of all the nations was to come.

The sons of Japheth are mentioned first (vs. 2-5). They produced the colonizing peoples and spread westward over the isles and coast-lands of the Mediterranean. The sons of Ham come next (vs. 6-20). They were the first to found powerful kingdoms, spreading through Mesopotamia and on into Africa. The sons of Shem come last (vs. 21-31). They apparently did not spread far from their original home.

2. The Rebellion of the Nations (11:1-9). This was the first manifestation of organized rebellion against God. Formerly human sin had been manifested as individual corruption and violence; here it broke out into united and centralized defiance of God. Self-will had now developed into corporate presumption, pride, and ambition (v. 4). It took the form of a godless political and national federation. It was visited by a Divine judgment, which confused the speech of men and caused them to scatter abroad over the earth. Thus do God's judgments confound the self-willed purposes of men (Psa. 2:4).

3. The Origin of the Chosen Nation (11:10-32). The nations having failed, God began to prepare a nation for Himself, through whom He could carry out His plan of redemption for the whole race. This section carries the record from Shem down to the time of Abraham. It closes with the migration of the family of Terah, the father of Abram (his name at that time), from Ur of the Chaldees in the southern part of Mesopotamia to Haran in the upper Euphrates valley. It prepares the way for the calling out of Abraham.

ABRAHAM
(Chs. 12-23)

With Abraham, who was born about 2000 B.C., a new stage of revelation begins. He was separated from the line of Shem at the call of God to live by faith. He was known as "the friend of God" (2 Chron. 20:7; Isa. 41:8; Jas. 2:23). No higher title was ever given to any man. Paul calls him "the father of all them that believe" (Rom. 4:11). His history illustrates the life of faith. It may be divided into four periods, each beginning with a special revelation from God and marked by a special response of faith on his part.

1. The Call and the Promise (Chs. 12-14). The Lord appeared to Abraham when he was still in Ur of the Chaldees, and called him to set out for a land which He would show him (Heb. 11:8). Migrating from Mesopotamia, he stopped at Haran and dwelt there till his father died (Acts 7:2-4). He was seventy-five years old when he took a further step in obeying the call of God and came into Canaan (12:1-5). There the Lord appeared unto him and gave him the definite promise of the land (12:6-9). This is the first mention of any "appearance" of the Lord. Hitherto Divine communications seem to have been direct. After this the Angel of the Lord appears in the narrative again and again as the Divine messenger.

The promise given to Abraham in connection with his call was threefold: (1) His name should become great and his seed should become a great nation. (2) They should be given Canaan as a special land of their own. (3) Through him and his seed a blessing should come to all the nations of the world. All this had in view the preparation and separation of a people through whom the Saviour of the world would come.

Abraham showed his faith by sojourning in the Land of Promise and building an altar to the Lord wherever he dwelt. His faith weakened during a time of famine, when he went down to Egypt and deceived Pharaoh about his wife (12:10-20). It revived again when he returned to Canaan and, to avoid strife among brethren, allowed Lot, who had accompanied his uncle from Haran, to choose the best of the land for himself (13:1-13). He was rewarded for this magnanimous act of self-sacrifice and faith by a new assurance of the Lord's own promise of the land (13:14-18).

When Abraham rescued Lot from the foes who had captured him in their plunder of Sodom (14:1-16), he gave further evidence of his faith by refusing to receive anything from the king of Sodom (14:17-24). Melchizedek appears upon the scene at this point as one of those who still carried on the primeval worship of the one true God. He is a witness to the fact of an original revelation. Abraham recognized him as a true priest of the Most High God and "gave him a tenth of all". The tithe seems to have come down from primitive times; it was man's recognition of the goodness of his Creator and his dependence upon Him.

2. The Promise Made a Covenant (Chs. 15-16). After this another revelation came to Abraham, and for the first time the specific expression is used which is so often repeated afterwards: "The word of Jehovah came". It met the particular need the patriarch would feel after the events related in the preceding chapter by first giving him an encouraging assurance: "Fear not, Abram". Then it gave him the promise that he should have a son of his own and an innumerable seed (15:1-6). The faith which he placed in the Lord on this occasion is used three times in the New Testament as an illustration of the faith that justifies the sinner: "He reckoned it to him for righteousness", that is, with a view to righteousness (Rom. 4:3; Gal. 3:6; Jas. 2:23). Abraham's faith in the Lord was such an attitude of entire trust that God could accept him as a righteous man.

God then renewed the promise of the land in the form of a covenant; and in so doing He revealed to Abraham the long period of affliction through which his seed should pass before they would be given the land. The wickedness of the inhabitants was not yet ripe for the judgment of God (15:7-21). After being ten years in the land, Abraham's faith weakened again. He took another false step at Sarah's suggestion, and Ishmael was born to him of Hagar, Sarah's handmaid (ch. 16).

3. The Covenant Sealed by Circumcision (Chs. 17-21). Abraham had to wait till he was ninety-nine years old before the Lord appeared to him again. This time it was to reveal Himself as the Almighty God, the One who is All-sufficient, besides whom Abraham needed none else to help him (17:1). Then the Lord renewed His covenant promise, and as a pledge of its fulfilment, changed the patriarch's name from Abram, "exalted father", to Abraham, "father of a multitude" (17:2-8). He also commanded Abraham to institute the rite of circumcision in his family as a sign and seal of the covenant (17:9-14). He added a blessing for Sarah also, promising to establish His covenant with a son whom she should bear to Abraham and whom he was to name Isaac (17:15-21). Abraham then proceeded to carry out the instructions now given to him (17:22-27).

During this period of his life three mysterious visitors came to Abraham's tent one day, and he entertained them with the generous and gracious hospitality of an oriental host. One of them was none other than the Lord Himself, coming with two heavenly attendants to call upon His earthly friend. He gave Sarah the promise of a son in her old age, meeting her incredulity with the question: "Is anything too hard for Jehovah?" (18:1-15). He then disclosed to Abraham the purpose of His visit. It was to reveal the imminent judgment of the wicked city of Sodom to the man whom He had chosen for the ultimate blessing of the world: "Shall I hide from Abraham that which I do?" (18:16-21).

The patriarch immediately began to intercede with the Lord in behalf of the righteous who might be in the city. His nephew Lot was there, but he does not mention him. His plea is based upon the righteousness of God, the fundamental quality of the Divine character: "Shall not the Judge of all the earth do right?" (18:22-33). The whole story of this chapter illustrates the believer's fellowship with God, and his ministry of intercession for the world. The answer to Abraham's prayer was the saving of Lot out of the judgment as recorded in the next chapter (19:29).

The visit of the two angels to Sodom for the rescue of Lot was followed at once by the destruction of the cities of the Plain (19:1-28). His wife, lingering behind, was involved in their doom. Through his daughters he became the ancestor of Moab and Ammon, nations which caused great trouble to the Israelites in the course of their history (19:30-38). The state of life in Sodom, as revealed by the story in this chapter, gives some idea of the wickedness for which the Canaanites were afterwards condemned to destruction at the hands of Israel.

Another lapse of Abraham's faith occurred when he was sojourning in the south; he deceived Abimelech king of Gerar as he had deceived Pharaoh (ch. 20). At last, when Abraham was a hundred years old, the child of promise was born to him, and he called his name Isaac (21:1-7). Soon after that, on Sarah's insistence, Abraham had to cast Hagar and Ishmael out of his home (21:8-21). At that time Abraham made a covenant with Abimelech at Beersheba and continued to sojourn there (21:22-34).

4. The Covenant Confirmed by the Oath of God (Chs. 22-23). The supreme trial of Abraham's faith came when he was dwelling in Beersheba. God commanded him to offer up Isaac as a burnt offering on Mount Moriah (22:1-8). This story is to be read in the light of the fact that human sacrifice was demanded by the false religions of the nations around. Could Abraham stand the same test when required by his God? His obedience in this case was rewarded by God's provision of a sacrifice in place of Isaac (22:9-14). The story is told with the calm and objective detachment that marks the style of the inspired writers of Scripture. The heart of the whole scene is depicted in the twice-repeated words: "They went both of them together".

The experience brought to the heart and mind of the aged patriarch a new revelation of God. This was no doubt what Jesus referred to when He declared that Abraham "rejoiced to see my day; and he saw it, and was glad" (John 8:56). The whole incident was a typical foreshadowing of the sacrifice the Lord God Himself was to make through the offering of His only begotten Son, that He might fulfil the covenant He had made with His friend Abraham. Abraham's faith having now been proved and perfected, the Lord confirmed all His promises to him in a peculiarly solemn way: "By myself have I sworn" (22: 15-18; Heb. 6:13-18).

When Abraham returned to Beersheba, he heard news of the family of his brother Nahor whom he had left in Haran (22:19-24). After this Sarah died at the age of a hundred and twenty-seven, and was buried in the cave of Machpelah at Hebron, which Abraham purchased as a burying place from Ephron the Hittite in the presence of the people of the land (ch. 23).

ISAAC
(Chs. 24-26)

Isaac was the longest-lived of the patriarchs (35: 28-29); yet his life was the least eventful. His character was gentle and peace-loving; he is an illustration of the meek who inherit the earth (Matt. 5:5). He followed in the wake of his father, doing the things his father did. His life was spent in the south among the wells that Abraham had digged.

This section tells how Abraham sent his trusted and faithful servant to seek a wife for Isaac among his own kindred (24:1-9); how the servant, seeking the Lord's guidance in the matter, met Rebekah at the well, was entertained by her brother Laban, and won her consent to come back with him (24: 10-60); and how Isaac received her and brought her into his mother's home (24: 61-67). The story goes on to tell of the death and burial of Abraham at the age of a hundred and seventy-five (25:1-11), and to record the generations of Ishmael (25:12-18). Then it takes up the family of Isaac and tells of the birth of his twin sons (25:19-26). The difference in their character, as they grew up, is manifested in Esau's sale of his birthright to Jacob, showing his lack of any sense of the unseen and the spiritual (25:27-34). He was a "profane person", a man of this world alone (Heb. 12:16). The birthright carried with it the inheritance of the Divine promise.

Isaac followed his father's footsteps in going down to Abimelech during a famine, and he fell into the same sin of deception (26:1-11). He became very prosperous and was envied by his Philistine neighbours. But he refused to fight for the wells which they took from him (26:12-25); and at last Abimelech made a covenant of peace with him (26:26-33).

On two occasions the Lord appeared to Isaac and renewed with him the promises He had given to Abraham (26:2-5, 23-25). On the second occasion Isaac built an altar to the Lord—the only time this is recorded of him. In the meantime, Esau brought grief into the peaceful family of Isaac and Rebekah by marrying women of Canaan (26:34-35).

JACOB
(Chs. 27-36)

In Jacob's character there was a conflict between two natures. His natural character was cunning and deceitful, but behind this was an appreciation of the unseen and a capacity for the spiritual. In the course of the discipline of life through which God led him, Jacob ("the self-reliant") finally became Israel ("one who has power with God"). His history as recorded in these chapters may be considered in four stages, each of which was marked by a crisis in his experience.

1. The Vision at Bethel (Chs. 27-28). In Isaac's old age Jacob obtained the patriarchal blessing from his father by deceit, at the instigation and under the direction of Rebekah (27:1-29). The incident brings out the characteristic faults of all the four parties in the story. Jacob thereby incurred the hatred of his brother Esau for whom Isaac had intended the blessing (27:30-45). He was sent away from home to seek a wife among his mother's kindred at Haran (27:46-28:9). At a certain place on the way, as he lay asleep, the Lord appeared to him in a dream, renewing the promises made to Abraham and Isaac, and giving him a special promise of personal care (28:10-17). In response to this promise Jacob marked the spot with a memorial stone, calling the place Bethel, "the house of God", and made a solemn vow, dedicating himself to the Lord (28:18-22).

2. The Discipline at Haran (Chs. 29-31). During a long exile, in which Jacob served his uncle Laban for twenty years, he married Leah and Rachel, and became possessed of a large family and great wealth in flocks and herds (chs. 29-30). Incurring the enmity of Laban and commanded of God to return to the land of his birth, he departed with his family and flocks without Laban's knowledge (31:1-21). Laban, when told of this, pursued after Jacob and overtook him in Gilead; and there the two men had an angry dispute (31:22-42). It ended in their making a covenant and setting up the watchtower of Mizpah as a witness of separation between them (31:43-55).

3. The Blessing at Peniel (Chs. 32-33). As Jacob went on his way, the angels of God met him, and he recognized in this incident a sign of Divine help and protection (32:1-2). As he approached the land where Esau lived he sent him a message of conciliation, but when word came back that his brother was coming to meet him he became greatly alarmed and took precautions against his possible vengeance. Then he turned to God in a humble and earnest prayer (32:3-12). At the same time he went on with his own devices and made an elaborate plan to appease Esau with presents (32:13-21).

When about to cross the border into his brother's territory, the Angel of God met him in the lonely night and wrestled with him, opposing his further progress. His confidence in his own strength was at last broken down, and he clung to the One whom he found to be stronger than himself (32:22-26). As a token of the new spirit of reliance on God which arose in him that night, his name was changed to Israel, "powerful with God"; and, as a token of the new blessing he had received, he called the place Peniel, "the face of God" (32:27-32).

Jacob soon found that his carefully laid scheme was not needed, for Esau came to meet him with a generous welcome (33:1-16). Jacob went on into Canaan and encamped at Shechem, purchasing a piece of ground and erecting an altar there (33:17-20).

4. The Return to Bethel (Chs. 34-36). Jacob had settled down too near the city of Shechem, and his family became defiled with the sin and shame of the Canaanites, who sought to intermarry with them (ch. 34). At the command of God, he purified his household of idolatry, and went up to Bethel and built an altar there where God had first met him in the time of his need (35:1-8). There God appeared to him again, reminding him that his name was no longer Jacob but Israel, and renewing His promise. Then Jacob renewed the vow he had made at Bethel before (35:9-15). Jacob had not been living up to his new name, but after this he is more often called by his new name in the narrative.

Jacob journeyed on farther south, and near Bethlehem Rachel died in giving birth to Benjamin, the last of Jacob's twelve sons. Then the names of them all are given (35:16-26). Jacob reached his father at Hebron, and there Isaac died at the age of a hundred and eighty and was buried by his two sons (35:27-29). At this point the narrative pauses to record the generations of Esau (ch.36), before going on with the rest of Jacob's life, which is henceforth taken up mainly with the story of his son Joseph.

JOSEPH
(Chs. 37-50)

Joseph's life is interesting and instructive from two points of view. (1) It is an illustration of the ways of Providence. Joseph had none of the Divine revelations granted to the three preceding patriarchs. The course of his life was governed by the over-ruling providence of God through seemingly fortuitous events. (2) It was a foreshadowing of the experience of Jesus Christ. Joseph went down into deep humiliation, and was exalted to be a prince and saviour of his people. His history may be taken in three parts, showing three stages in the providential ordering of his life.

1. Events Leading Joseph to Exaltation in Egypt (Chs. 37-41). Jacob's partiality for Joseph roused the hatred of his brothers, and this was increased when the ingenuous boy told them of the dreams he had—dreams which foreshadowed his future greatness (37:1-11). When they were tending their father's flock in Shechem, Jacob sent Joseph from Hebron to visit them, and, after plotting his death, they sold him to a caravan of merchants travelling down to Egypt (37:12-28). Then they sent back Joseph's coat, blood-stained, to deceive their aged father, who wept for Joseph and refused to be comforted (37:29-36). In the meantime the story of Judah and his family reveals the moral corruption which threatened the children of Israel through contact with the Canaanite life around them (ch. 38).

In Egypt Joseph was bought as a slave by Potiphar, a high officer of Pharaoh's, and served in his master's house. There his administrative ability was discovered (39:1-6) and his moral purity was tested and proved (39:7-12). He was cast into prison on a false accusation, and there he won the favour and confidence of the keeper of the prison, who discovered his capacity for governing men (39:13-23). The narrative points out that in all these experiences "Jehovah was with Joseph" (vs. 2, 21), and "made all that he did to prosper" (vs. 3, 23).

After this two state prisoners, Pharaoh's chief butler and chief baker, were put under Joseph's special care, and he had an opportunity to interpret dreams which they had, and his interpretation was verified in each case (ch. 40). Two years afterwards, the chief butler, who had forgotten Joseph all this time, spoke to Pharaoh about him when the king had two dreams which the magicians could not interpret (41:1-13). Pharaoh sent for Joseph at once and told him his dreams. Disclaiming any credit for the interpretation himself, Joseph said that God had revealed to Pharaoh in these dreams what He was about to do. There would be seven years of great plenty in Egypt and then seven years of famine. Joseph followed up his interpretation of the dreams with a practical suggestion for dealing with the matter (41:14-36).

Pharaoh had the insight to recognize Joseph's practical wisdom and administrative genius, and he appointed him to a position of supreme authority in Egypt to prepare for the coming famine (41:37-45). Joseph was only thirty years old when he was promoted to this post. He was given an Egyptian name and an Egyptian wife and two sons were born to him. The narrative goes on to give an account of his wise administration (41:46-57). The story of Joseph's career in these chapters is one of the most remarkable in all human history.

2. Events Leading Jacob to Settle in Egypt (Chs. 42-47). When the famine reached the land of Canaan, Jacob sent his ten oldest sons down to Egypt for grain. Joseph recognized them and proceeded to test them by treating them as spies (42:1-17). He kept Simeon behind till they should bring down Benjamin. Then he had their money put back into their sacks and provisions given them for their journey home. His conference with them was carried on through an interpreter, and he was deeply affected when he heard them talking among themselves about their old sin against their young brother. His discipline of them was having its effect (42:18-25). Then comes an account of their journey home, their report of the treatment they had received, the finding of their money in their sacks, ending with Jacob's determination that Benjamin should not go down to Egypt (42:26-38).

When their grain was exhausted, the sons refused to go back to Egypt without Benjamin, and Judah finally secured their father's consent by pledging himself to be surety for him. Jacob commended them all to the mercy of "God Almighty", and also showed his characteristic quality in sending a present to secure a favourable reception from "the man" (43:1-15). When they arrived Joseph commanded his steward to take them to his own house where they should dine with him at noon. They were alarmed and tried to explain themselves to the steward, who set their minds at rest by telling them that their God and the God of their fathers had been caring for them. He also restored Simeon to them. The words of the steward throw light on the religious influence that Joseph exerted over his own household (43:16-25).

When Joseph arrived and enquired for his father and greeted Benjamin he was deeply affected, and had to retire in order to recover himself. Then he entertained his brethren at a feast, during which Benjamin was given a special mark of honour. He was thus testing his brothers to see whether they would envy Benjamin as they had formerly envied him. They gave no sign of envy but entered fully into the enjoyment of the feast (43:26-34).

Next day, when they were sent away, Joseph applied his last test of their feeling for Benjamin. He had his steward put their money in their sacks as before, and also put his own silver cup into Benjamin's sack. Then he sent the steward after them to search for the missing cup. To the alarm and consternation of them all it was found in Benjamin's sack (44:1-12). They returned at once to the city and prostrated themselves before Joseph as penitents appealing to his mercy. Judah proved himself the noblest character among them by the way he acted as their leader and spokesman. He made a pathetic and eloquent plea for Benjamin in behalf of his aged father—one of the noblest pleas in all literature (44: 14-34).

Joseph could restrain himself no longer. He gave expression to all his pent up emotions and made himself known to his brethren with manifest tokens of deep affection. He assured them that God had sent him before them and made him a ruler of Egypt in order to preserve their lives. Then he urged them to bring their father back and promised to nourish them all in the land of Goshen during the remaining five years of famine (45:1-15).

Pharaoh heard of what had happened and added his invitation to that of Joseph. He commanded Joseph to provide wagons for his brothers and have his father and all his family brought down to Egypt. When the brothers returned to Canaan with the wagons and the news about Joseph, Jacob was overwhelmed and the spirit of the old man revived (45: 16-28).

Before leaving Canaan Jacob offered sacrifices to the God of his father Isaac at their old home in Beersheba. Then God appeared to him again, bidding him not to fear to go down to Egypt and renewing the old promises of the covenant. Encouraged by this Divine assurance, Jacob and all his family went on their way into Egypt (46:1-7). A list of their names is then given, seventy souls in all (46:8-27). This is followed by an account of their arrival in Goshen and their reception by Joseph. He instructed them to tell Pharaoh that they were shepherds, so that they might be given the land of Goshen to dwell in and thus be saved from mixing with the native Egyptians who disliked shepherds (46:28-34).

Joseph announced their arrival to Pharaoh and presented five of his brothers to him. Pharaoh gave them a welcome to the best of the land. Joseph then brought in his aged father, and the patriarch blessed the king (47:1-12). The narrative goes on to give an account of Joseph's administration in Egypt while the famine continued (47:13-26). Jacob lived seventeen years longer in Egypt and the children of Israel began to multiply greatly. As the time of his death drew near he secured a promise from Joseph to bury him with his fathers in Canaan (47:27-31).

3. The Last Days of Jacob and Joseph in Egypt (Chs. 48-50). When Joseph learned that his father was sick, he went to visit him taking his two sons, Manasseh and Ephraim, with him. Jacob gathered his strength to meet his son, told him of the blessing that "God Almighty" had given him at Bethel, and handed it on to Joseph and his sons (48:1-7). Then Joseph brought his sons before his father, and the patriarch blessed them both, but gave the blessing of the first-born to Ephraim the younger one. Thus Joseph received a double portion of the patriarchal blessing in the family of Israel, and two of the tribes that formed the nation sprang from him (48:8-22).

Jacob uttered a prophecy over his own sons, forecasting the destiny of the twelve tribes of Israel (49:1-27). In the midst of it he handed on the promise of the coming Redeemer to Judah (v. 10), and also gave expression to a momentary prayer which came from the deepest desire of his heart (v.18). When he was dying, he gave instructions to his sons to bury him with his fathers in the cave of Machpelah (49:28-33). After a touching exhibition of love for his father, Joseph had his body embalmed, and obtained permission from Pharaoh to bury it in Canaan (50:1-6). Accompanied by a splendid procession of Egyptian officials and elders of Israel, which passed around to the eastern side of the Jordan and aroused the wonder of the Canaanites, Joseph and his brethren buried their father in the cave which Abraham had purchased as a burying place (50:7-14).

When Jacob was dead, Joseph's brethren feared that he might now take vengeance upon them and they besought his mercy. He gave them a comforting assurance and continued his kindness to them. He lived to the age of a hundred and ten years, and at his death he assured them that God would yet visit them and bring them into the land which He had promised to their fathers, and he had them take an oath that they would carry up his bones with them (50:15-26).

* * * *

THE PROMISE OF A REDEEMER

The promise of a Redeemer begins in Eden and runs through Genesis, becoming more specific as it is passed down from age to age. In the light of the New Testament it may be drawn out as follows:

1. The Redeemer was first announced as the Seed of the woman (3:15). He was to belong to the human race. He would suffer in the conflict with Satan, but would be victorious over him and destroy his power (Luke 22:53; John 14:30; Rev. 12:3-5; Rom. 16:20).

2. He was to belong to the race of Shem (9:26). This is implied in the nature of the blessing pronounced on Shem. Through Shem the knowledge of the Lord God was to be preserved and made known to the world. The Redeemer would be the revealer of God.

3. He was to come from the family of Abraham (22:18), and Isaac (26:4), and Jacob (28:14). In their seed all the nations of the earth were to receive a blessing. The Redeemer was to be the Saviour of the world (Matt. 1:1; Luke 1:73; Acts 3:25-26; Gal. 3: 14).

4. He was to belong to the tribe of Judah (49: 10). The phrase, "until Shiloh come", should be rendered "until he come whose it is" (see marg.). The Redeemer would come as the One to whom the sceptre belonged and who had the right to rule. He would win the obedience of the peoples of the world (Psa. 110:1-3; Ezek. 21:27; John 12:31-32; Rev. 5:5-6).

Here the Kingdom of God begins to appear on the horizon of prophecy. This aspect of the promise is seen again in Balaam's prophecy of "a Star out of Jacob and a Sceptre out of Israel" (Num. 24:17). The promise is finally deposited in the house of David (2 Sam. 7:12-13; 1 Chron. 17:11-12), where it remains till the coming of Christ Himself (Luke 1:32-33).

THE BOOK OF EXODUS

EXODUS continues the narrative of Genesis, but a long period of time intervenes between the two books. Genesis ends with the family of Jacob settled in Egypt; when Exodus begins, the family has become a nation. Instead of family records and biographies as in Genesis, we have now national history. The book records the first stage in God's fulfilment of His promise to the patriarchs regarding their seed. The name "Exodus" refers to the "going out" of the Israelites from Egypt. But the theme of the book is wider than this, for it includes both the nation's deliverance from Egypt and its separation to God at Mount Sinai.

On the basis of these two ideas, the book may be divided into two nearly equal parts and outlined as follows:

I. Israel's Deliverance from Egypt—Chs. 1-18
  1. The Preparation for Deliverance (Chs. 1-6)
  2. The Conflict with Pharaoh (Chs. 7-12)
  3. The Journey to Sinai (Chs. 13-18)
II. Israel's Separation to God—Chs. 19-40
  1. The Giving of the Law (Chs. 19-24)
  2. The Directions for the Tabernacle (Chs. 25-31)
  3. Israel's First Failure (Chs. 32-34)
  4. The Construction of the Tabernacle (Chs. 35-40)

THE PREPARATION FOR DELIVERANCE
(Chs. 1-6)

These opening chapters show how the children of Israel had sunk into servitude in Egypt and were coming to realize the misery of their condition and their need of deliverance, and how, at the same time, God was raising up a deliverer for them and was preparing to redeem them from their bondage.

1. The Egyptian Oppression (Ch. 1). After a reference to the great increase of the Israelites in Egypt (vs. 1-7), we are told of the changed attitude of the rulers of Egypt towards them after Joseph's time, and of the new policy of oppression, and how it only resulted in multiplying and spreading them (vs. 8-14). Even the attempt to destroy the men children among the Israelites failed: "The people multiplied, and waxed very mighty" (vs. 15-22).

2. The Training of Moses (Ch. 2). The great figure of the book now comes into view. Moses' parents belonged to the tribe of Levi. He was adopted by Pharaoh's daughter, who discovered the babe among the flags by the river's brink (vs. 1-10). His life falls into three periods of forty years each (cf. Deut. 34:7; Exod. 7:7; and Acts 7:23). During the first two periods he was being trained and disciplined for the great work of his life, first in Egypt and afterwards in Midian. All that is recorded here is his unsuccessful attempt to deliver his people by his own method and his consequent flight to Midian (vs. 11-15), and his subsequent sojourn with the priest of Midian, whom he served as a shepherd and whose daughter he married (vs. 16-22). In the meantime the children of Israel were crying to God in their extremity, and He was preparing to answer their cry (vs. 23-25).

3. The Call of Moses (Chs. 3-4). At length the Lord appeared to Moses, told him that He was the God of his fathers and had heard the cry of His people in Egypt, and announced His purpose to deliver them out of that land and bring them into Canaan, and then called Moses to undertake the task (3:1-10). Moses shrank from it at first and proceeded to make excuses. God gave him an assurance that He Himself would be with him in the mission on which He was sending him (3:11-12).

Moses raised the question, what he should tell the people when they asked for the name of the God of their fathers, and the Lord went on to explain the significance of His name "Jehovah". It is from the future of the verb "to be" or "to become", and means "the One who will be" (see marg.). Thus it carried an assurance to His people that He would fulfil the promises which He had made to their fathers. Although known and used before, it was now to become the covenant and distinctive name of Israel's God, "my memorial unto all generations" (3:13-15). Moses was to gather the elders of Israel and tell them that the Lord God of their fathers had appeared unto him, promising to bring them up out of their affliction in Egypt into the land of Canaan. Moses and the elders of Israel were then to request the king of Egypt to let them go out into the wilderness to sacrifice to the Lord their God (3:16-22).

Moses still hesitated, fearing that the people would not believe him, and God gave him authority to perform certain miraculous signs (4:1-9). Holding back still on the ground of lack of eloquence, and showing his secret reluctance by asking God to send some one else on such a mission, Moses incurred the Divine anger and was told that Aaron his brother, who was coming to meet him, would act as his spokesman (4:10-17). Thus Moses was deprived of part of the honour that might all have been his. Moses then set out for Egypt, met Aaron on the way, and told him of his call. The two brothers gathered the elders of Israel and told them how the Lord had begun to visit the people in their affliction (4:18-31).

4. The Mission to Pharaoh (Chs. 5-6). The first appeal of Moses and Aaron to Pharaoh met with the king's refusal and caused him to increase the burdens of the people (5:1-14). They accused Moses and Aaron of being the cause of their sufferings (5:15-21). Moses then turned to the Lord, who reminded him of His covenant with Abraham, Isaac, and Jacob, and renewed His promise of deliverance, grounding it on His own Divine character: "I am Jehovah . . . . I will bring you out . . . . and I will bring you in" (5:22—6:8). Moses passed the Lord's message on to the people, but they were sunk in anguish of spirit and Moses himself was discouraged (6:9-13). All this serves to bring out the character of the various parties in the story: the hardness of Pharaoh, ripe for judgment; the unbelief of Israel, needing discipline; and the weakness of Moses, needing encouragement.

The section dealing with the preparation for deliverance closes with a summary of the house of Levi, giving the genealogy of Moses and Aaron (6:14-27). The actual story of the conflict with Pharaoh begins with verse 28.

THE CONFLICT WITH PHARAOH
(Chs. 7-12)

This section tells of Moses' repeated demands upon Pharaoh in the name of the Lord to let Israel go, and of the series of Divine judgments that fell upon Egypt because of his stubborn refusal, which came to a head in a final judgment that broke the power of Egypt. The story is introduced by a summary of the instructions already given to Moses (6:28—7:7).

1. The Judgments of the Plagues (Chs. 7-10). There was order and progress in these judgments. They occurred in three series of three plagues each, the first of each series being introduced by a command to warn Pharaoh "in the morning" (7.15; 8:20; 9:13), and the last falling without any warning at all (8:16; 9:8; 10:21).

The first series—blood, frogs, and gnats (7:8—8:19)—fell upon the land of Egypt and the soil. The second series—flies, murrain, and boils (8:20—9:12)—fell upon the persons of the Egyptians and their cattle. The third series—hail, locusts, and darkness (9:13—10:29) — were great nature plagues.

The plagues became more severe in their effects as they went on. The first series brought the defeat of the magicians (8:18-19); the second ended with their inability to stand before Moses (9:11); and the third issued in Moses' final rupture with Pharaoh: "I will see thy face again no more" (10:28-29). Thus in solemn and deliberate procession the avengers of God marched upon the guilty land.

2. The Passover Night (Chs. 11-12). The Lord announced that He would bring one plague more upon Pharaoh and upon Egypt, and directed Moses to get the people ready for it. It would cause the death of all the first born in a single night (ch. 11). Instructions were given to Moses and Aaron instituting the Passover (12:1-14) and the feast of Unleavened Bread, to mark the beginning of the nation's history and to be observed as a memorial ever afterwards (12:15-20).

Moses then informed the elders of Israel that a lamb was to be slain for each house in which the people were gathered, and its blood was to be sprinkled around the door, and the whole household were to remain inside till the morning (12:21-28). The phrase translated "in the basin" (v. 22) also means "on the threshold", and might have been so rendered, indicating where the lamb was slain. Every household was sheltered by a symbol - a type of the crucified Lamb of God standing, as it were, at the door (1 Cor. 5:7; Rev. 5:6). At midnight the judgment fell, and the Egyptians, under the first shock of it, sent the Israelites away out of the land in haste (12:29-36). The children of Israel were followed by a mixed multitude as they travelled with their flocks and herds, thrust out of the land on a night to be observed as a watch-night ever afterwards (12:37-42). The section closes with some further instructions about the ordinance of the Passover (12:43-51).

NOTE: The date of the Exodus may be placed about 1440 B.C., for recent archæology tends to show that the fall of Jericho occurred about 1400 B.C. The time of the Israelites' sojourn in Egypt may be gathered from Paul's statement in Gal 3:17 that the Law came four hundred and thirty years after Abraham received the promise. Abraham was seventy-five years old when he entered Canaan, and twenty-five years afterwards Isaac was born (Gen. 12:4; 21:5). Isaac was sixty years old when Jacob was born (Gen. 25:26). Jacob was a hundred and thirty years old when he entered Egypt (Gen. 47:9). This makes a total of two hundred and fifteen years for the sojourn of the patriarchs in Canaan, the period between the receiving of the promise and the entering into Egypt. This would leave the same period of time for the sojourn of the Israelites in Egypt.

The period mentioned in Exod. 12:40 for the sojourn in Egypt may have originally included the preceding sojourn in Canaan. The Septuagint version of this verse reads: "The sojourning of the children of Israel which they sojourned in the land of Egypt and in the land of Canaan was four hundred and thirty years". Stephen's statement in Acts 7:6 is a quotation of the prediction in Gen. 15:13, where the four hundred years may refer to the whole period of sojourning as well as to the affliction of Israel.

THE MARCH TO SINAI
(Chs. 13-18)

These chapters describe the three months' journey of the Israelites from the night of the Passover until they arrived on the plain before Mount Sinai (cf. 12:51 and 19:1-2).

1. The Departure from Egypt (Chs. 13-14). The sparing of the firstborn of Israel meant that all the firstborn hereafter belonged to God and were to be set apart for Him (13:1-16). The people were led by a pillar of cloud and fire by day and by night, a symbol of the Lord's own guiding and pro-

tecting presence (13:17-22). The Egyptians pursued after them and caused a panic among them, which Moses stilled with the assurance that God would fight for them (14: 1-14). At the Lord's command, Moses lifted up his rod, and the waters of the Red Sea were driven back by a strong wind, making a way for the Israelites to pass over in safety. The Egyptian host, going in after them, were discomfited and destroyed (14:15-31).

2. The Stages of the March (Chs. 15-17). The march of the redeemed people began with the triumph song of Moses and Miriam (15:1-21). In the wilderness of Shur, they had a two-fold experience: bitter waters at Marah, and rest and refreshment at Elim (15:22-27). In the wilderness of Sin, quails were sent one evening and manna was spread upon the desert floor in the morning (ch. 16). Manna was henceforth their daily food till they arrived in the land of Canaan (Josh 5:12). In the valley of Rephidim, water was provided out of the rock (17:1-7). There also they met their first foe in Amalek, who fought with Israel, opposing their advance. Amalek was defeated by Joshua and doomed by the Lord to ultimate destruction (17:8-16).

At every stage of the journey the people murmured at something (15:23-24;16:2-3; 17:1-3, 7), and in every case God abundantly provided for their need. Thus early in the story we see the persistent unbelief and failure of Israel and the patient grace and mercy of God.

3. The Advice of Jethro (Ch. 18). The father-in-law of Moses came to meet him (vs. 1-12), and, seeing how he was wearing himself out in acting as judge for the whole people, he advised him to appoint assistant judges and divide the people into thousands, hundreds, fifties, and tens (vs. 13-23). This was the origin of the organization of Israel for judicial purposes , which Moses subsequently carried out (vs. 24-27; Deut. 1:9-18).

THE GIVING OF THE LAW
(Chs. 19-24)

This section contains the account of the manifestation of God on Mount Sinai and records the Covenant of the Law. It is the centre of the Old Testament revelation and the origin of the whole Jewish dispensation.

1. The Manifestation of the Lord (Ch. 19). Three months after leaving Egypt, Israel encamped in the wilderness of Sinai before the mount where God had revealed Himself to Moses (vs. 1-2; 3:12). Moses now became the agent of communication between the Lord and Israel. Through him God appealed to them on the ground of what He had done for them, and promised to make them His own people—"a kingdom of priests and a holy nation"— if they would obey Him and keep His covenant (vs. 3-6). They promised obedience, and Moses prepared them for the revelation which the Lord was about to give them (vs. 7-15). Then there came such an overwhelming manifestation of supernatural power as to impress them with the unapproachable glory and holiness of the Lord and prepare them for receiving His Law (vs. 16-25).

2. The Moral Law (Ch. 20). "And God spake all these words" (vs. 1). The Scriptural expression used hereafter to designate the Moral Law or the Ten Commandments is literally, "the ten words"

(marg. of Exod. 34:28, Deut. 4:13, and 10.4). Hence the term, Decalogue. They were spoken directly out of the mount in the hearing of the people (Deut. 5:23). The New Testament refers to the Law as having been "spoken through angels" (Heb. 2:2; Acts 7:53; Gal. 3:19).

The introductory statement (v.2) contains the basis on which the Law rests. The Divine Lawgiver presents Himself first as the Redeemer of Israel before He declares the Law. It was given on the basis of grace—not as the means of salvation, but as the standard of life for a people already redeemed.The Ten Commandments express in concise form the whole duty of man to God and to his fellow man (vs. 3-17). They are all summed up in love to God and love to man (Matt. 22:37-40, Luke 10:26-28). They are not to be interpreted as taking cognizance of external acts only, but as extending to the thoughts and intents of the heart.

After the Decalogue had been promulgated it was given to Moses inscribed on two tables of stone (24:12; 32:15-16, 19;34:1). These tables may have divided the Law according to the twofold relation of man to God and to his neighbour, but no indication is given as to where the division was made, whether after the fourth or after the fifth commandment. By applying to the Decalogue the principle of love, the ten commandments may be analysed as follows:

Love to God (vs. 3-11). First: worship should be given to the Lord God alone. Second: the mode of worship should recognize His essential nature as unseen Spirit. Third: His name, meaning everything by which He makes Himself known, should be treated with reverence. Fourth: the Sabbath, which commemorates His finished work of creation, should be set apart as the special day for worshipping Him.

Love to God and man (v. 12). Fifth: parents should be honoured as God's earthly representatives. This commandment links the two tables as being a kind of transition between them.

Love to man (vs. 13-17). This will ensure respect for all that pertains to one's neighbour. Sixth: his life. Seventh: his family. Eighth: his property. Ninth: his character. Tenth: the heart should be conformed to the Law as the test of love.

The manifestation on the mount and the voice from the midst of it had a profound effect upon the people. It inspired them with a reverential fear of the unseen God of heaven, and they appealed to Moses to become their intermediary (vs. 18-21; Heb. 12:18-21). Henceforth they were to approach God in worship by the use of no image, but only by an altar of earth or of unhewn stones (vs. 22-26).

3. The Civil Law (Chs. 21-23). These ordinances were given through Moses as the final preparation for the Covenant which was about to be ratified. They are various applications of the Law to the social life of the people. They relate to the rights of persons (21:1-32), the rights of property (21:33—22:15), the administration of justice (22:16—23:9), and the feasts of the Lord (23:10-19). The section closes with a promise that the Angel of the Lord would go before Israel and bring them into the land, and a warning to hearken to His voice (23:20-33).

4. The Ratification of the Covenant (Ch. 24). All was now ready for the final act in establishing the Covenant of the Law, and the most important transaction in Israel's national history is recorded in this

chapter. The people promised to obey all the commandments and ordinances of the Lord, and Moses recorded them in a book, called "the book of the covenant". He then built an altar at the foot of Mount Sinai, and set twelve pillars around it representing the twelve tribes of Israel. Then a sacrifice of oxen was offered, and half the blood was sprinkled on the altar of the Lord and half upon the people, representing the two parties in the Covenant (vs. 1-8).

By this one sacrifice, which was never repeated, Israel was formally set apart as the people of the Lord. It foreshadowed the one sacrifice of Christ, and marked the fact that expiation was needed to bring man into fellowship with God (Heb. 9:18-22). It was followed by a sacrificial meal, symbolizing that fellowship.   In this the people were represented by Moses and Aaron, Nadab and Abihu (the future priests), and seventy of their elders. It took place up on the mount, and some manifestation of the glory of God was granted them which gave them a sense of security in His immediate presence: "they beheld God, and did eat and drink" (vs. 9-11).

After this Moses was called up into the mount to receive the tables of stone with the Law written upon them. He took Joshua with him, and left Aaron and Hur in charge of the camp.   For six days a cloud covered the sides of the mountain, while the glory of the Lord was seen at the top in the sublime and majestic appearance of fire.   Moses went up into the midst of the cloud and remained on the mount for forty days (vs. 12-18).

THE DIRECTIONS FOR THE TABERNACLE
(Chs. 25-31)

These instructions were given by God to Moses during the forty days he spent in the mount (cf. 24:18 and 31:18).   The people were all to make a free-will offering for the construction of a sanctuary that God might dwell among them.   It was to be made according to the pattern that Moses was shown in the mount (25:1-9). This meant that it was to have an important typical and spiritual meaning. The New Testament explains it as standing for the spiritual world of heavenly and eternal realities (Heb. 8:1-5; 9:23-24).

1. Its Form and Furniture (Chs. 25-27). The most important sacred vessels of the sanctuary are described first: the ark (25:10-22), the table of shewbread (25:23-30), and the candlestick (25:31-40).   Then the curtains of the tent of the Tabernacle (26:1-14), its boards and bars (26:15-30), and its veil and screen (26:31-37). Finally the altar of burnt offering (27:1-8) and the outer court in which it stood (27:9-19).   Then follows a command to have pure olive oil for the light in the Tabernacle (27:20-21).

The plan of the Tabernacle was as follows: The actual sanctuary was a covered tent, thirty cubits long, ten cubits wide and ten cubits high.   (The cubit was about eighteen inches).   It had two compartments.   The first, called the Holy-place, was twenty cubits long, and contained the candlestick, the table of shewbread, and the altar of incense. The second, called the Holy-of-holies, or the Holiest-of-all, was a perfect cube, ten cubits each way, and contained the ark of the Covenant.   It was the innermost shrine, where the symbol of the divine Presence dwelt.

Around this tent was an outer court, one hundred cubits long and fifty cubits wide, surrounded with a wall of curtains five cubits high.   In this court, between the entrance and the tent of the Tabernacle, stood the altar of burnt offering and the laver of purification.

The Tabernacle set forth the presence of God in the midst of His people (25:8; 29:45), and provided a way for them to worship Him. This way of worship set forth symbolically the way of salvation, which was to be wrought out through the coming Redeemer.   The steps of approach to God were by the altar of sacrifice (the Cross) and the laver of purification (Pentecost), and then on through the Holy-place with its altar of incense (the ministry of prayer) to the Mercy-seat within the veil, the meeting place of God and man (Heb. 10:19-22).

2. The Institution of the Priesthood (28:1—29:37).   Aaron and his sons were to be set apart for the priesthood, and special garments were to be made for them—"holy garments . . . for glory and for beauty"—,which they were to wear when ministering in the priest's office (28:1-5).   Aaron's garments for the high priest's office comprised the ephod (28:6-14), the breastplate (28:15-30), the robe of the ephod (28:31-35), and a mitre with a golden plate for his forehead (28:36-39), besides the linen garments worn also by his sons as the ordinary priests (28:40-43).   Aaron and his sons were to be consecrated by a series of special sacrifices and offerings (29:1-37).

3. The Services of the Tabernacle (29:38—31:18).   Provision was now made for the daily burnt offerings, to keep the people in continual fellowship with the Lord (29:38-46), and for the offering of incense before the Mercy-seat every morning and evening (30:1-10), and for the payment of a personal tax by each Israelite as atonement money for the maintenance of the Tabernacle services (30:11-16).   Then follow instructions regarding the use of the laver (30:17-21), and the composition of the anointing oil (30:22-33) and the incense (30:34-38).

The Lord marked the importance of the Tabernacle by naming the master workmen to whom its construction was to be entrusted (31:1-11). A new significance was now given to the Sabbath as a sign of the Covenant between the Lord and Israel (31:12-18).

ISRAEL'S FIRST FAILURE
(Chs. 32-34)

The natural character of Israel is revealed in what happened in the camp while Moses was absent in the mount.   Instead of an inclination for spiritual religion, they showed a propensity for idolatry. This was their character throughout the whole Old Testament age.   They were "a stiffnecked people", an expression used here for the first time (32:9) and often afterwards, stubbornly resisting the grace of the Lord (Acts 7:51).

1. The Sin of the People (32:1-29).   Their request was for some visible symbol of God to take the place of the pillar of cloud and fire—"make us a god (v. 1 marg.) which shall go before us".   They did not mean to forsake the Lord at once, but rather to serve Him under the form of worship to which they had been accustomed in Egypt.   However, it

was a violation of their solemn promise to keep the Law, and Aaron showed his weakness in yielding to their demand. It revealed an inclination to idolatry and it resulted in an orgy of heathen worship (vs. 1-6). When the Lord informed Moses of the apostasy of His people and offered to make of him a great nation in their place, Moses showed his true greatness by interceding for them on the ground that they were God's own people because He had delivered them out of Egypt and His own honour was involved in their continued preservation (vs. 7-14).

When Moses came down to the camp and saw what the people were doing, he broke the two tables of the Law he had brought with him, destroyed the calf, and proceeded to deal with the sin (vs. 15-20). Aaron made a pitiful excuse and cast the blame on the people. He incurred the anger of the Lord, but was spared at Moses' intercession (Deut. 9:20). The Levites rallied to Moses' side and were commissioned to carry out a stern act of judgment (vs. 21-29).

2. The Intercession of Moses (32:30-33:16). Moses now offered to make atonement for the people's sin and his greatness as a man of prayer is seen again. He became a true intercessor, confessing the sin of the people and pleading for their pardon. But if God could not pardon them—then Moses would rather perish with them. The Lord's reply meant that Moses could not take upon himself the penalty for the sins of other men. However, God would spare the people under Moses' leadership but He would visit their sin upon them (32:30-35).

The Lord went on to command Moses to lead the people to the land which He promised to their fathers, and He would send one of His angels to go before them. He would not go with them Himself, for they were a stiffnecked people and would be consumed if He went into their midst. They were dismayed when they heard these evil tidings, and stripped off their ornaments and wore them no longer (33:1-6).

At this point the narrative tells how Moses pitched his own tent away off from the camp that he might have a place of retirement where He could meet God. When Moses entered this "tent of meeting" the pillar of cloud would descend from its place at the top of the mount and stand at the door while Moses communed with God. When the people saw the pillar of cloud at the door of Moses' tent they would stand at their own tent doors and worship (33:7-11).

It was in this tent that Moses renewed his supplication. He reminded the Lord of the favour that He had already shown him, and on this ground he pleaded with God to revoke His decision to send a mere angel and restore His own presence to them. How could it be known that Israel had been separated from all other people by the favour of God unless He went with them Himself? (33:12-16).

3. The Answer of the Lord (33:17-34:9). Moses' importunity was rewarded and his request was granted. Then he made a request on his own behalf: "Show me, I pray thee, thy glory." God could not grant this request in full, for no man could see God and live. But He promised to make all His goodness pass before Moses and proclaim His name before him. Moses was to take his place in a cleft of the rock, where he would be under the protecting hand of God, while a transcendent manifestation of the Divine glory would pass by leaving an afterglow which Moses would be allowed to see (33: 17-23).

Next morning, following instructions given him by the Lord, Moses went up alone into the mount with two new tables of stone to have the Law rewritten upon them, and then the Lord fulfilled His promise. He descended in a cloud and passed by before Moses, proclaiming His name. Moses received a new vision of God and a new revelation of His character as "a God merciful and gracious, slow to anger, and abundant in lovingkindness and truth." Moses bowed his head in humble and reverent adoration. Then he made his final appeal that the Lord would not only pardon the people and go with them, but also attach them permanently to Himself as His inheritance (34:1-9).

4. The Renewal of the Covenant (34:10-35). This is the Lord's answer to Moses' final prayer. A summary is given of the ordinances contained in chs. 21-23 which were set before the people when the Covenant was first ratified (vs. 10-26). Moses remained in the mount for another forty days, and the ten commandments were written on the new tables of stone which he had brought (vs. 27-28).

When Moses came down from the mount his face shone with the reflection of the glory of God, and he knew it not; but it produced a sense of awe among the people when he spoke to them. It remained hereafter a property of his countenance, and was the crowning mark of his Divine authority. He wore a veil to cover it, which he removed when communing with God or addressing the people (vs. 29-35; 2 Cor. 3:12-18).

THE CONSTRUCTION OF THE TABERNACLE
(Chs. 35-40)

Everything was now ready for carrying out the instructions given to Moses regarding the Tabernacle, and the last section of the book tells how this was done.

1. The Offerings of the People (35:1—36:7). In view of the work before them, Moses first reminded them of the law about the Sabbath rest (35: 1-3), and then called upon them all to bring their free-will offerings for the making of the Tabernacle (35:4-29). He named the men whom the Lord had called to do the work, and the offerings were given to them (35:30—36:7). The people had brought too much and had to be restrained from giving.

2. The Accomplishment of the Work (36:8—39:43). It was carried out exactly as the Lord had commanded: the curtains and framework (36:8-38), the sacred vessels of the sanctuary (ch. 37), the altar and the laver and the outer court (ch. 38), and the garments of the priests (39:1-31). When all was finished it was inspected by Moses and received his blessing (39: 32-43).

3. The Erection of the Tabernacle (Ch. 40). The Tabernacle was reared up just one year from the day of the Passover and the departure from Egypt (cf. 12:2 and 40:17). The instructions of the Lord are recorded first (vs. 1-15), and then Moses' fulfilment of them (vs. 16-33). When the work was finished the glory of the Lord filled the Tabernacle and the cloud abode upon it, thus symbolizing the dwelling of God in the midst of His people (vs. 34-38). A similar scene took place at the dedication of the Temple of Solomon (2 Chron.

5:11-14), which was built for the same purpose and had the same significance as the Tabernacle of Moses.

*   *   *   *

THE BASIS OF THE OLD TESTAMENT DISPENSATION

Three great events recorded in Exodus laid the foundation for the Old Testament dispensation and determined its character. These were the deliverance of Israel from Egypt by the Passover (ch. 12), the giving of the Law at Sinai (ch. 20), and the erection of the Tabernacle in the wilderness (ch. 40). In these events there was also foreshadowed the character of the Christian dispensation.

1. The Passover accomplished the redemption of the people from bondage and marked the beginning of Israel's national life. It typified the redemption of the world by the sacrifice of the Cross (1 Cor. 5:7), the event which introduced the New Testament dispensation.

2. The Law was given to Israel as God's standard of life for His redeemed people. It demanded obedience on their part. Under the Christian dispensation the Law is not abolished; its demands still remain; but they are fulfilled through the Holy Spirit in the power of the Resurrection (Rom. 6: 4; 8:4).

3. The Tabernacle provided a place and a way for Israel to worship the Lord their God. Thus they would express their love to Him. In the Christian system access to God is provided through the ascended Christ, who as the great High Priest has passed into the heavenly Tabernacle (Heb. 10: 19-22).

Thus do these three facts hold deep significance, not only in themselves as providing the basis for the Old Testament dispensation, but as enshrining the secret of the new spiritual dispensation that was to come. They anticipated the three transcendent facts on which Christianity is based: the Cross, the Resurrection, and the Ascension.

THE BOOK OF LEVITICUS

THE opening words of this book connect it closely with the preceding book. Exodus closes by telling us that when the Tabernacle was finished and set up the glory of the Lord filled it. Leviticus begins by telling us that the Lord called to Moses out of the midst of the Tabernacle and spoke the laws which it proceeds to record. These laws had to do with the worship of God. The title of the book indicates that it contains Levitical or priestly regulations. The Levites are mentioned only in one place, and there only incidentally (25:32-33), but the priests are referred to continually throughout the book. It prescribes the various ceremonies and services which they were to carry on in the Tabernacle as they led the redeemed people of Israel in the worship of the Lord.

The laws of worship may be divided into two groups: those that concerned the way of approach to God (Chs. 1-16), and those that concerned the life of fellowship with God (Chs. 17-27). The one group culminates in the Day of Atonement (ch. 16) and the other in the Year of Jubilee (ch. 25). Under these two divisions we may outline the book as follows.

I. The Laws of Approach to God—Chs. 1-16
    1. The Sacrifices (Chs. 1-7)
    2. The Priesthood (Chs. 8-10)
    3. The Worshippers (Chs. 11-15)
    4. The Day of Atonement (Ch. 16)

II. The Laws of Fellowship with God—Chs. 17-27
    1. The Law of Holiness (Chs. 17-22)
    2. The Holy Seasons (Chs. 23-24)
    3. The Holy Years (Ch. 25)
    4. Conclusion and Supplement (Chs. 26-27)

THE SACRIFICES
(Chs. 1-7)

This section contains an exposition of the ritual of sacrifice. The words "sacrifice", "offering", and "oblation", occur about 300 times in the book, and of these nearly 200 are in these chapters. The sacrifices had a two-fold significance. (1) They were acts of worship. They provided the way in which the Old Testament worshipper could approach God. (2) They were types. They prefigured the spiritual worship of the Christian dispensation. They have all been fulfilled and done away in "the redemption that is in Christ Jesus" (Rom. 3:24).

The first three sacrifices in the list (chs. 1-3) were free-will offerings, presented by the free-will of the worshipper. They are all described as offerings "of a sweet savour unto Jehovah". The other two (4:1—6:7) were prescribed for cases of sin and trespass among the people.

1. The Burnt Offering (Ch. 1). The victim was slain and its blood was sprinkled round the altar; and then the whole was burnt upon the altar. A choice of victims was allowed, so that even the poorest could present a burnt offering. The worshipper thus signified the consecration of his person to the Lord.

2. The Meal Offering (Ch. 2). It was composed of fine flour, cooked or uncooked, or of the first ears

of new grain, and was burnt upon the altar. The offerer thus signified the consecration of the fruit of his labour to the Lord.

3. The Peace Offering (Ch. 3). In this case the fat of the victim alone was burnt upon the altar, the best part, as it were, being given to God: "all the fat is Jehovah's" (v. 16). The rest of the flesh was eaten in a sacrificial meal of thanksgiving (7: 15). The fundamental idea of this offering was fellowship with the Lord.

4. The Sin Offering (4:1—5:13). This sacrifice was to be offered for sins committed "unwittingly" or "through error", that is, such sins as did not spring from a spirit of rebellion against God (4:1-2). For wilful and high-handed sin which set at nought the Law there was no provision of pardon (Heb. 10: 28). The victim was slain and its blood was presented before the Lord in the tent of the Tabernacle. The fat was then burnt upon the altar, and the rest of the flesh was burnt without the camp.

This offering brought into peculiar prominence the idea that in order to have sin pardoned there must be expiation of guilt by the sacrifice of a victim substituted for the sinner. In the different victims that were prescribed for the offering, there was a recognition of graded responsibility. The anointed priest (4:3-12) and the congregation of Israel (4: 13-21) must offer a young bullock. A ruler must offer a he-goat (4:22-26), and one of the common people a she-goat (4:27-31) or a she-lamb (4:32-35). Special instructions were added for sins of neglect or rashness (5:1-13) and less costly victims were allowed for the poor (5:7-13).

5. The Trespass Offering (5:14—6:7). This sacrifice was prescribed for sins where some wrong had been done to another involving a misappropriation of property or a breach of trust. Together with the offering of the victim which was to be a ram, restitution was to be made by the offerer with a fifth part added.

6. Supplementary Laws of the Offerings (6:8—7:38). A manual of additional directions for the guidance of the priests in offering the various sacrifices. The fire on the altar was to be kept burning continually; it was never to go out (6:9-13). Certain portions of the offerings were to be given to the priests (6:14-18; 7:8-10, 28-36). No fat or blood was to be eaten (7:22-27).

THE PRIESTHOOD
(Chs. 8-10)

This is a historical section, containing an account of the setting apart of Aaron and his sons to the priesthood and their entrance upon their holy office. The word "priest" does not occur in these chapters, though it is used very often in the rest of the book. The expression used here is "Aaron and his sons", or "Aaron's sons". Aaron himself was set apart to be the high priest, and his sons were to perform the ordinary daily service of the regular priesthood.

1. The Consecration of Aaron and his Sons (Ch. 8). Everything was done by Moses, acting for the Lord, in the presence of the assembled congregation. Aaron and his sons simply yielded themselves. The ceremonies consisted of washing, robing, and anointing (vs. 1-13), and sacrifices of a sin offering, a burnt offering, and a peace offering, called here a "ram of consecration" (vs. 14-32). The ceremonies lasted seven days, and Aaron and his sons were

commanded not to leave the sacred enclosure of the Tabernacle court during that period (vs. 33-36).

2. The Inauguration of the Tabernacle Services (Ch. 9). Aaron offered a sin offering and a burnt offering for himself and his sons (vs. 1-14), and a sin offering, a burnt offering, and peace offerings for the people (vs. 15-21). He then blessed the assembled people, and the glory of the Lord appeared when fire came forth and consumed the burnt offering and the fat upon the altar (vs. 22-24). Thus did the Lord indicate His acceptance of the sacrifices, and thus the worship of the Tabernacle was begun.

3. The Judgment upon Nadab and Abihu (Ch. 10). Their sin is described as offering incense before the Lord with "strange fire", fire not kindled on the altar of burnt offering (v. 1). Its essence consisted in following self-will in the worship of God and ignoring God's revealed will. It was punished by a signal act of God's displeasure, intended to overawe the people with a sense of His unapproachable holiness (vs. 2-5). Aaron and his other two sons, Eleazar and Ithamar, were commanded to show no outward signs of mourning (vs. 6-7). Thus they were to recognize the justice of the Divine judgment.

The prohibition of wine and strong drink, which immediately follows (vs. 8-11), was a warning against any fleshly excitement in the worship of God (Eph. 5:18), and may indicate the probable cause of the rash act of the two priests. It would also seem from 16:1-2 that they had dared to go into the Holy-of-holies within the veil. Further instructions were given by Moses regarding the priests' portions of the sacrifices (vs. 12-15). The incident which follows brings out the wholesome effect which the tragic event produced upon Aaron (vs. 16-20).

THE WORSHIPPERS
(Chs. 11-15)

This section is concerned with the laws regarding ceremonial cleanness. It is distinguished by the words "clean" and "unclean", which occur more than 150 times out of about 200 times in the whole book. These laws were intended (1) to promote the health and morals of the Israelites, and also (2) to keep them separate from other nations. Besides this they embodied deep moral and spiritual teaching.

The worshippers of Him who is holy should be holy themselves. They should keep their bodies free from defilement, even in the matter of eating (ch. 11). These laws also emphasized the fact that the very sources of human life have been infected by sin (chs. 12 and 15). The regulations about leprosy (chs. 13-14) set it forth in a striking way as a symbol of the corruption and defilement of sin. The leper in the midst of Israel was a living death, to be shunned and abhorred by all (13:45-46). Such was sin in God's sight.

THE DAY OF ATONEMENT
(Ch. 16)

The whole sacrificial system of the Mosaic Law culminated in the ceremonies described in this chapter, which took place on what was known as the annual Day of Atonement (23:27). They were performed by the high priest alone. It was the only occasion in the year when he could enter into the presence of the Mercy-seat in the Holy-of-holies. The conditions for doing so are first stated: the sacrifices he was to bring for himself and the garments he was to wear are described (vs. 1-4). He did not wear his ordinary official raiment, but only the white linen garments he had in common with the other priests.

The special and peculiar significance of the day lay in the sin offering for the congregation, consisting of two goats, which were first presented at the door of the Tabernacle and chosen by lot for separate purposes (vs. 5-10). One was for the Lord, to be offered for a sin offering; the other was "for Azazel", to be sent away alive into the wilderness "for a scapegoat" (A.V.). While they stood there before the Lord, the high priest made atonement for himself and his house to prepare himself for making atonement for the people (vs. 11-14). He then slew the goat chosen by the Lord's lot as a sin offering for the people, and carried its blood into the Holy-of-holies and sprinkled it upon the Mercy-seat (vs. 15-19). Next he confessed the sins of the nation over the head of the live goat and sent it away into the wilderness, where it was to be left in a place from which it could not come back again (vs. 20-22). The expression "for Azazel" describing this goat, rendered "for a scapegoat" in the A.V. and given literally in the R.V., is obscure. Most probably it means "for complete removal".

The ceremony of the two goats thus set forth symbolically a two-fold truth: the means of atonement in the sacrifice of life by the shedding of blood and the result of atonement in the removal of sin from the presence of God. After that the high priest bathed himself and changed his garments and offered the burnt offerings for himself and for the people, and the services of the day were brought to an end (vs. 23-28). These ceremonies were to be observed yearly, on the tenth day of the seventh month, for the purpose of making atonement for the sins of the year. It was to be a day of humiliation, when the sense of sin was deepened to its utmost in the mind of Israel (vs. 29-34).

The spiritual significance of these ceremonies is explained in the Epistle to the Hebrews (8:1—10:18). The work of the high priest in the Mosaic Tabernacle on the Day of Atonement was typical of the atoning work of Jesus Christ as the great High Priest in the heavenly Tabernacle.

THE LAW OF HOLINESS

(Chs. 17-22)

This section deals with the kind of life which the redeemed people were to live in maintaining their fellowship with God. It is marked by the words "holy" and "sanctify", which occur in one form or another about 80 times out of about 150 times in the whole book. Its key note is, "Ye shall be holy: for I Jehovah your God am holy" (19:2; 20:7, 26). The phrase, "I am Jehovah" or "I am Jehovah your God", occurs again and again. The section may be summarized as follows:

1. Holiness in Personal and Family Life. (Chs. 17-18). The slaughter of beasts for food was to be performed at the Tabernacle, and the eating of blood was forbidden (ch. 17). Heathen impurities were forbidden, and all forms of personal defilement (ch. 18).

2. Holiness in Social Relations (Chs. 19-20).

Rules were given about various matters of conduct towards God and man (ch. 19), and heathen abominations and unholy practices were forbidden (ch. 20).

3. Holiness in the Priesthood (Chs. 21-22). General precepts and laws of cleanness were prescribed for the priests. Some of these were intended to show that a special separation or a higher degree of holiness was expected on their part.

THE HOLY SEASONS
(Chs. 23-24)

Israel's religious festivals were occasions (1) for thanksgiving to God for the blessings of the soil and the harvest, and (2) for commemorating past events in their history. They had also (3) a spiritual significance as symbolically foreshadowing various aspects of redemption. A list of the holy seasons of the year, called "the set feasts of Jehovah", is contained in ch. 23. There are many references and allusions to them in the New Testament. They are as follows:

1. The Weekly Sabbath (vs. 1-3). The seventh part of time was God's. This was the basis of the whole system of sacred seasons.

2. The Passover (vs. 4-5). On the fourteenth day of the first month, commemorating the deliverance from Egypt and foreshadowing the sacrifice of Christ the Lamb of God (1 Cor. 5:7).

3. The Feast of Unleavened Bread (vs. 6-8). For seven days after the Passover, setting forth Christ as sustaining the life of His redeemed people (1 Cor. 5:8).

4. The Feast of First Fruits (vs. 9-14). On the first day of the week after the Passover, signifying the consecration of the harvest to the Lord and typifying Christ as the first-fruits of the resurrection (1 Cor. 15:20-23).

5. The Feast of Weeks or Pentecost (vs. 15-22). On the fiftieth day after First Fruits, a thanksgiving to God for the bounties of His providence and prophetic of the Church as the first-fruits of the new creation (Jas. 1:18).

6. The Feast of Trumpets (vs. 23-25). On the first day of the seventh month, ushering in the sacred month and consecrating it to the Lord. It was prophetic of the Messianic age and the triumphant appearing of Christ (1 Cor. 15:52; 1 Thess. 4:16).

7. The Day of Atonement (vs. 26-32). The tenth day of the seventh month, the only fast day in the whole year. It foreshadowed the atoning work of Christ as the great High Priest and was prophetic of the present age of grace and salvation.

8. The Feast of Tabernacles (vs. 33-44). It began on the fifteenth day of the seventh month and continued for seven days. It commemorated the sojourn in the wilderness and was a time of thanksgiving for the ingathering of the fruits of the year. It was typical and prophetic of the blessings of redemption and the final ingathering of the redeemed (Jno. 7: 37-39; Rev. 7:9-17).

Ch. 24 forms a kind of appendix to the laws of the set feasts It contains commands and instructions about three holy things connected with the worship of God: the holy oil for the candlestick (vs. 1-4), the holy bread for the table (vs. 5-9), and the holy Name, which must not be blasphemed (vs. 10-23). In these three holy things we have intimations of the three Persons of the Trinity in the worship of Israel, the Spirit, the Son, and the Father.

THE HOLY YEARS
(Ch. 25)

The system of sacred seasons culminated in the seventh or Sabbatic Year (vs. 1-7), and beyond that in the sacred fiftieth year or Year of Jubilee (vs. 8-55).

1. The Sabbatic Year (vs. 1-7). Every seventh year the land was to be allowed to rest. There was to be no tilling of the soil, no sowing or reaping, during that period. The land, originally given by God, was, as it were, given back to Him.

2. The Year of Jubilee (vs. 8-55). After seven Sabbatic periods the fiftieth year was called a Jubilee. The land was to be at rest as in the Sabbatic year, and liberty was proclaimed to all its inhabitants (vs. 8-12). Every man was to be restored to his original inheritance, and land that had been sold was to be restored to its original owners (vs. 13-34). Servants and all who had become bondsmen were to be given their original freedom, for all the children of Israel belonged to the Lord and were His servants (vs. 35-55). The Jubilee was a time of universal restoration and was a type and prophecy of the final "restoration of all things" (Acts 3:21).

The fundamental principle on which the whole legislation of this chapter rested was God's ownership of the land: "for the land is mine" (v. 23). All the soil belonged to the Lord, and all purchasers of land were leasehold tenants. It was not capitalism, under which the soil is owned by individuals in perpetuity. It was not socialism or communism, under which all the land belongs to the people or the state. It was the divine and unchanging fact that "the earth is Jehovah's and the fulness thereof" (Psa. 24:1).

CONCLUSION AND SUPPLEMENT
(Chs. 26-27)

The real conclusion of the book is ch. 26, which begins with a brief summary of the whole Law in its fundamental principles (vs. 1-2), and goes on to state the promises and threatenings attached to it. Ch. 27, which contains some supplementary laws, seems to have been added as an appendix (cf. 26:46 and 27:34).

1. Blessings upon Obedience (26:3-13). These included the fruitfulness of the soil, peace and prosperity in the land, victory over enemies, and the presence of God in the midst.

2. Judgment upon Disobedience (26:14-39). This is first stated in a general way (vs. 14-17). Then follow four series of threatenings, cumulative in severity, each conditioned by the supposition that the nation would not repent notwithstanding previous experiences of the Lord's judgment. These four series are vs. 18-20, vs. 21-22, vs. 23-26, and vs. 27-39. The whole passage is prophetic; it describes what has actually happened in the nation's history.

3. Restoration upon Repentance (26:40-45). This passage is also prophetic, for it declares that however severe the Divine judgment should be and however long Israel's impenitence should continue, the nation would never be utterly destroyed or pass out of existence. God promises to remember His covenant with their forefathers when the nation repents.

4. The Law of Vows (Ch. 27). Various instructions to be carried out by those making voluntary vows, including the vowing of persons (vs. 1-8), the vowing of domestic animals (vs. 9-13), and the vowing of houses and fields (vs. 14-25). The chapter goes on to specify three classes of property which could not be dedicated by a special vow, for they already belonged to the Lord (vs. 26-33). The book then closes with a formal declaration of the Divine authority and the Mosaic origin of the laws it contains (v. 34).

* * * *

THE RELIGIOUS SIGNIFICANCE OF THE
LEVITICAL RITUAL

The ritual laws of Leviticus embodied, in ceremony and symbol, fundamental truths which lie at the heart of New Testament Christianity.

1. The fact of sin. The structure of the Tabernacle and its whole system of worship were designed to show that man was separated from God by sin. Sin must be atoned for and put away before man could be restored to the fellowship of God. Salvation from sin is man's first and deepest need.

2. The need of mediation. Sinful man could not come to God himself. The priest must act for him. The high priest alone could appear for him in the presence of God. There is but one Mediator between God and men, the man Christ Jesus.

3. The method of redemption. The worshipper could draw near to God only by offering a victim whose life was given for his own. He died, as it were, at the altar, and could approach no farther. The only way back to God is through the Cross of Jesus Christ.

4. The condition of fellowship. Acceptable worship was offered to God, and communion with Him was maintained, only by holiness and cleansing. The redeemed people must be separated to God and sanctified. Salvation from sin involves sanctification of life.

THE BOOK OF NUMBERS

THIS book contains the story of the Israelites in the wilderness from the time the Tabernacle was set up to the time they reached the Jordan and were ready to enter the land of Canaan. It begins one month after the close of Exodus and extends over a period of thirty-eight years and nine months (cf. Num. 1:1 and Deut. 1:3). The book is named from the event with which it opens, the census taken at Mount Sinai. The word "numbers" occurs nearly one hundred times in the first four chapters. Its theme is the pilgrimage of Israel. The object in view throughout is the Promised Land, and towards this the nation is moving (10:29).

It may be divided into three parts, corresponding to the three stages of the sojourn in the wilderness. In the first part (Chs. 1-10), the Israelites are encamped at Mount Sinai, making preparations for the journey. In the second part (Chs. 11-21), they are journeying in the wilderness. In the third part (Chs. 22-36), they are encamped on the plains of Moab, making preparations to enter the Land. The first part covers twenty days (10:11), the second part somewhat over thirty-eights years (33:38), and the third part several months. On this basis we get the following outline of the book:

I. The Encampment at Mount Sinai—Chs. 1-10
  1. The Outward Order of the Camp (Chs. 1-4)
  2. The Inward Order of the Camp (Chs. 5-6)
  3. The Last Events at Sinai (7:1—9:14)
  4. The Movement of the Camp (9:15—10:36)
II. The Journey in the Wilderness—Chs. 11-21
  1. From Sinai to Kadesh (Chs. 11-14)
  2. From Kadesh to Kadesh Again (Chs. 15-19)
  3. From Kadesh to the Plains of Moab (Chs. 20-21)
III. The Encampment on the Plains of Moab—Chs. 22-36
  1. Attempts to Destroy Israel (Chs. 22-25)
  2. The New Beginning (Chs. 26-30)
  3. The Eastern Settlement (Chs. 31-32)
  4. Concerning the Western Settlement (Chs. 33-36)

THE OUTWARD ORDER OF THE CAMP
(Chs. 1-4)

These chapters tell of the arrangements made for organizing the host of Israel. In this book Israel is regarded as the army of the Lord, preparing for and going forth to war.

1. The Numbering of the Men of War (Ch. 1). This was done at the command of the Lord, and they were numbered from twenty years old and upward (vs. 1-3). Moses and Aaron were assisted by the heads of the tribes (vs. 4-19). The number of the men of war in each tribe is given separately (vs. 20-43), and then 603,550 is recorded as the total (vs. 44-46). The Levites, being set apart for the service of the Tabernacle, were not included in this census (vs. 47-53). They were numbered from a month old and upwards, and their number is given later (3:39).

2. The Arrangement of the Tribes (Ch. 2). They were encamped around the Tabernacle in four divisions, three tribes on each side. On the east was the camp of Judah with Issachar and Zebulun (vs. 1-9). On the south was the camp of Reuben with Simeon and Gad (vs. 10-16). On the west was the camp of Ephraim with Manasseh and Benjamin (vs. 18-24). On the north was the camp of Dan with Asher and Naphtali (vs. 25-31). According to Jewish tradition, the standard of Judah (v. 3) was a lion, the standard of Reuben (v. 10) a man, the standard of Ephraim (v. 18) an ox, and the standard of Dan (v. 25) an eagle.

The order of the march was as follows: The camp of Judah went first, and then the camp of Reuben. The Levites came next with the Tabernacle (v. 17). Behind the Tabernacle came the camp of Ephraim (Psa. 80:1-2), and in the rear the camp of Dan. Thus the host of the Lord was thoroughly ordered and organized both for the camp and for the march. The chapter closes with a summary of the census (vs. 32-34).

3. The Organization of the Levites (Chs. 3-4). The tribe of Levi, to which Moses and Aaron belonged, was taken for the special service of the Lord instead of the firstborn of all Israel (3:1-13; Exod. 13:2). They were to have charge of the Tabernacle, and were numbered from a month old and upward (3:14-20). They were organized according to the families of the three sons of Levi, and were encamped immediately around the Tabernacle. The Gershonites had charge of the drapery, and were encamped on the west (3:21-26). The Kohathites had charge of the ark and the sacred vessels, and were encamped on the south (3:27-32). The Merarites had charge of the framework, and were encamped on the north (3:33-37).

Moses, Aaron, and the priests were encamped on the east, in front of the Tabernacle, "keeping the charge of the sanctuary" (3:38). The number of the Levites was 22,000 (3:39), and the number of the firstborn in whose place they were taken was 22,273 (3:40-43). There follows an account of the redemption of the 273 firstborn that were over and above the number of the Levites (3:44-51). The various duties of the three groups of Levites are explained in ch. 4: the Kohathites (vs. 1-20), the Gershonites (vs. 21-28), and the Merarites (vs. 29-33). They served in the work of the Tabernacle from the age of thirty to fifty. There were 8,580 Levites of this age numbered (vs. 34-49).

THE INWARD ORDER OF THE CAMP
(Chs. 5-6)

Special laws were given for preserving purity and holiness in the fellowship of the camp (ch. 5), especially in the case of secret sins and hidden evil, "that they defile not their camp, in the midst whereof I dwell" (v. 3). The law of the Nazirite ("the separated one") was provided for those who wished to make a special vow of separation (6:1-21). The peculiar character of this vow was separation from the natural joys and sorrows of life which were quite legitimate for others.

After this comes the three-fold blessing which Aaron and the priests were commanded to pronounce over the children of Israel (6:22-27). It was a foreshadowing of the blessing of the Trinity, the Christian blessing of the New Testament Church (2 Cor. 13:14).

THE LAST EVENTS AT SINAI
(7:1—9:14)

Three final acts of worship before the departure of Israel from Sinai are here described.

1. The Offerings of the Princes (Ch. 7). The twelve princes of the tribes who had taken part in the census brought their gifts in six covered wagons with twelve oxen. The wagons were disposed of to the Levites, two to the Gershonites and four to the Merarites. The Kohathites did not require any, for they carried the vessels of the sanctuary upon their shoulders (vs. 1-11). The offerings of the twelve princes were brought on twelve successive days. They were all identical; yet each of the twelve is separately and fully recorded in the sacred narrative (vs. 12-83). Thus does the Spirit delight to record the gifts of God's people. They were the dedication gifts for the service of the altar and the worship of the Lord (vs. 84-89).

2. The Separation of the Levites (Ch. 8). After a brief direction was given to Aaron about the lighting of the lamps in the golden candlestick (vs. 1-4), Moses was instructed to set apart the Levites for the service of the Tabernacle by special ceremonies of cleansing and consecration and formally place them under the priests (vs. 5-19). When this was done the Levites entered upon their official duties. They were to serve in the Tabernacle from the age of twenty-five to fifty (vs. 20-26), probably engaging in the lighter parts of their office up to the age of thirty, when their full duties began (4:3, 23, 30). No separate law is recorded as to the age when the sons of Aaron began and ended their priestly service, probably because the same rule applied to them.

3. The Observance of the Passover (9:1-14). This was Israel's second Passover, and the first observed in the wilderness. It takes us back into the first month of the second year (cf. 9:1 and 1:1). New regulations were now added to make provision for members of the congregation who could not observe the Passover at the regular time.

THE MOVEMENT OF THE CAMP
(9:15—10:36)

This section describes the way the movements of the camp were controlled, and gives an account of the departure from Sinai. The march of Israel was by Divine appointment.

1. The Cloud (9:15-23). This symbol of the divine Presence presided over the host of Israel, resting over the Tabernacle when encamped and leading the tribes when journeying. The elaborate manner in which the movements of the cloud are described shows the great importance attached to the Lord's guidance of Israel (Psa. 78:14; Isa. 4:5). All this was typical of the guidance of the Holy Spirit in the Christian dispensation.

2. The Silver Trumpets (10:1-10). The instructions regarding the trumpets form a beautiful and fitting conclusion to all the preparations for the march. They were appointed to give all the signals for the congregation and for the movements of the various divisions of the camp (vs. 1-7). They were to be used in the Land also, down through the generations of Israel, both in time of war and in days of gladness (vs. 8-10).

3. The Departure from Sinai (10:11-36). On the twentieth day of the second month in the second year the march began. The cloud led them towards the wilderness of Paran, just south of Canaan (vs. 11-13). The order of the march is fully described (vs. 14-28). Hobab seems to have responded to Moses' second appeal though not to his first (vs. 29-32), for he is afterwards found among the children of Israel (Judg. 1:16; 4:11). He went with Israel because of the good he could do rather than because of the good he would get. The journey towards the Promised Land begins under the protecting care of the Cloud and the leadership of the Ark of the Lord (vs. 33-36).

FROM SINAI TO KADESH
(Chs. 11-14)

These chapters record the incidents of the journey from Sinai to the southern border of the Land at Kadesh-barnea (Deut. 1:2, 46), in the wilderness of Paran (10:12; 12:16), and then give an account of Israel's failure there and refusal to enter in. The story brings out the unbelieving and rebellious character of the people and the patient and faithful spirit of Moses.

1. The Murmuring of the People (Chs. 11-12). Their spirit of discontent and unbelief showed itself very early (11:1-3). "The people were as murmurers", doubtless because of the difficulties of the march (1 Cor. 10:10). The mixed multitude among them (Exod. 12:38) lusted for the things of Egypt (11:4-9). Moses in his grief and displeasure appealed to the Lord for help in carrying the burden of the people, and he was commanded to bring seventy of the elders of Israel before the Lord that He might put the Spirit upon them and so enable them to share the burden with Moses (11:10-30).

Quails were sent in such abundance that a plague broke out among the people as a judgment upon their lust for flesh (11:31-35). Even Aaron and Miriam in their criticism of Moses showed the same spirit that infected the camp (12:1-3). Moses was vindicated by the Lord in a special judgment upon Miriam, who had probably instigated the complaint against him (12:4-16).

2. The Mission of the Spies (Ch. 13). At the Lord's command, Moses sent twelve men, one from each tribe, to spy out and report upon the land of Canaan (vs. 1-20). After forty days they returned, bringing a good report of the fruitfulness of the Land but an evil report of the difficulties and dangers to be encountered in it (vs. 21-33).

3. The Rebellion of the Nation (Ch. 14). At this report the people broke out into insurrection against Moses and Aaron, and refused to listen to Caleb and Joshua, the two faithful spies, who urged upon them the Lord's promise to give them the Land (vs. 1-10). The Lord at once threatened to disinherit the people and make of Moses a greater and mightier nation. But Moses showed his greatness again by pleading with God to pardon them on the ground of His own character, and the Lord answered his prayer at once, but declared that those who had failed Him should not see the Land. They were now commanded to turn back into the wilderness (vs. 11-25).

Then the Lord solemnly pronounced His judgment upon them. All that generation over twenty years, except Caleb and Joshua, were condemned to die in the wilderness (vs. 26-38). When this was announced to the people, they went to the other extreme and made a presumptuous and futile attempt to enter the Land against Moses' warning and without the Divine leadership (vs. 39-45).

From Kadesh to Kadesh Again
(Chs. 15-19)

This section covers more than thirty-seven years of wandering. The development of Israel's history and the accomplishment of God's purpose had been put back a whole generation. The nation was simply marking time, waiting on death. The history of these years is summed up in a list of camping places, most of which are quite unknown (ch. 33). It is probable that during this period Israel became a nomadic people, the tribes being scattered up and down and the Tabernacle forming a kind of central camp. At the end of the period they were assembled at Kadesh again (20:1).

1. **Further Instructions for Canaan (Ch. 15).** The Lord gave Moses some supplementary laws regarding the sacrifices for the purpose of reviving the hopes of the new generation that was growing up and directing their minds to the Promised Land (vs. 1-21). The law of the sin offering was to apply not only to the children of Israel but also to the strangers sojourning among them. But the soul that sinned in defiance of the Law and despised any commandment of the Lord was to be cut off (vs. 22-31). The incident of the punishment of a man found breaking the Sabbath law is probably recorded here as an illustration of sinning, not in ignorance, but in defiance of the law (vs. 32-41).

2. **The Rebellion of Korah (Chs. 16-17).** This was a serious breach of the divine order in Israel, and it affected the whole congregation. Its motive was jealousy and disappointed ambition. It was directed against the leadership of Moses and the priesthood of Aaron (16:1-3). The Reubenites, Dathan and Abiram, who were associated with Korah in the movement, were jealous of the one, and Korah was jealous of the other. Moses referred the matter to the arbitrament of the Lord Himself (16:4-19).

The Lord vindicated His servants and punished the rebels by an act of judgment in which He made "a new thing": the ground opened and swallowed them up (16:20-40). The next day the whole congregation murmured against Moses and Aaron because of it. They were smitten with a plague, which was stayed when Aaron, at Moses' command, made atonement for them by carrying incense into their midst (16:41-50). The confirmation of Aaron's priesthood by the budding of his rod in the sanctuary sobered the people into a recognition of the righteous judgment of God (ch. 17).

3. **Instructions for the Priests and Levites (Ch. 18).** The confirmation of the priesthood of Aaron and his family is appropriately followed by special regulations concerning the official duties of the priests and Levites (vs. 1-7). Then an account is given of the revenues that were to be assigned both to the priests (vs. 8-20) and to the Levites (vs. 21-32).

4. **The Water of Purification (Ch. 19).** A special provision was made for purification from defilement by contact with the dead. A red heifer was to be sacrificed and burnt, and its ashes, mingled with running water, were to be used for the purpose (Heb. 9:13). The enactment of this ordinance at this time may have been due to the extraordinary mortality which the Israelites had suffered because of the rebellion of Korah (16:49).

From Kadesh to the Plains of Moab
(Chs. 20-21)

Thirty-seven years had passed away since the rebellion at Kadesh, and a new generation had arisen. The whole congregation of Israel were now brought back to the same place (20:1). At the point where the nation failed it was to take up its life again and make a new start. From this point they journeyed south of Edom round to the east of the Jordan and encamped on the plains of Moab (22:1). The main incidents of the journey are these:

1. **The Failure of Moses and Aaron (20:2-13).** In an outburst of anger at another complaint on the part of the people because of lack of water, they considered only their own position (v. 10), and failed to sanctify the Lord in the eyes of the people (v.12). As a judgment they were not given the honour and privilege of bringing Israel into the Promised Land.

2. **Edom's Refusal of a Passage (20:14-21).** This was the beginning of the bitter and implacable hostility which the Edomites, the descendants of Esau, always showed towards their brother nation Israel. Edom's doom was announced by the prophet Obadiah some centuries later.

3. **The Death of Aaron (20:22-29).** This took place on Mount Hor. At the command of the Lord, Moses solemnly stripped Aaron of his high-priestly robes and put them on Eleazar his son. Moses and Eleazar came back alone, showing that Aaron was dead and the office had passed on to another. The congregation mourned for Aaron for a month.

4. **The Sign of the Brazen Serpent (21:1-9).** Because of the continued murmuring of Israel on the difficult journey round the land of Edom, the Lord sent a plague of fiery serpents. When the people came to Moses and acknowledged their sin, he prayed for them, and at the Lord's command he provided a remedy in the form of a brazen serpent, to which they were to look in faith (John 3:14-15).

5. **The Journey to Mount Pisgah (21:10-20).** The route of the march up the eastern side of the Dead Sea through the borders of Moab is given with considerable detail, probably because of the increasing interest in approaching the Promised Land. Nothing is known of "the book of the wars of Jehovah" (v. 14) from which the bits of song in this passage are quoted. This collection of war songs and "the book of Jashar" (Josh 10:13; 2 Sam. 1:18) belonged to Israel's national literature, but were not included in their sacred Canon.

6. **The Defeat of Sihon and Og (21:21-35).** Their kingdoms comprised the country east of the Jordan, known afterwards as Gilead and Bashan. These were the last kingdoms that barred the way into Canaan. Sihon had refused a passage to Israel, and Og had come out against Israel.

Attempts to Destroy Israel
(Chs. 22-25)

The Israelites were now encamped on the plains of Moab preparing to enter the land of Canaan. They had come through the perils of the wilderness, but greater perils now threatened them. Balak, king of Moab, made attempts first to curse, and then to corrupt Israel.

1. **An Attempt to Curse Israel (Chs. 22-24).** Balak sent to Mesopotamia for the soothsayer Balaam and hired him to pronounce a curse upon the camp of Israel (22:1-20). On the way, Balaam received a warning from the Angel of the Lord to speak only the word that God gave him (22:21-40). Balak took him to one hill top after another from which to view the camp of the Israelites, but each time the Spirit of the Lord compelled him to utter a blessing upon them instead of a curse (22:41— 24:9).

Finally, after three such attempts on the part of Balak, Balaam uttered a prophecy that a king should arise in Israel and "smite through the corners of Moab" (24:10-25). This was a Messianic prediction, which was partially and typically fulfilled when David conquered Moab (2 Sam. 8:2).

Balaam was a gifted man and had a certain amount of enlightenment. He is a witness to the fact that fragments of the primitive revelation of God still lingered in the world at that time. But he was self-willed and had a greed for gain (2 Pet. 2: 15-16; Jude 11; Rev. 2:14). He perished soon after this in the slaughter of the Midianites (31:8).

2. **An Attempt to Corrupt Israel (Ch. 25).** Unable to curse Israel, Balaam advised Balak to invite the people to the idolatrous feasts of Moab and Midian (vs. 1-3; 31:16). This resulted in gross sin on the part of Israel, which the Lord commanded Moses to punish with a stern act of judgment (vs. 4-5). A plague followed which carried off a great number of the people, before it was stayed by an act of jealous zeal for the honour of the Lord performed by Phinehas, the grandson of Aaron, who was given a special promise because of it (vs. 6-15). Moses was then commanded to destroy the Midianites (vs. 16-18).

THE NEW BEGINNING
(Chs. 26-30)

The plague by which the sin of Israel was punished probably swept away the last of the old generation (26:1). A new start was now made with the new generation in preparation for entering the Land.

1. **A New Census (26:1-27:11).** A new numbering of the tribes was made in the same way as before (26:1-50). The total number of the men of war, as recorded on this occasion, was 601,730 (26: 51). These were the numbers of the new generation of Israel and it was among them that the Land was to be divided by lot in proportion to the size of the tribes (26: 52-56). The Levites were numbered separately as before, and their number was 23,000 (26: 57-62). All the men numbered at Mount Sinai had died in the meantime except Caleb and Joshua (26:63-65).

At this point an incident occurred which led to the enactment of a special law that the daughters of a man who had died in the wilderness without leaving any son should be given a possession in Canaan in order to preserve their father's family inheritance (27:1-11).

2. **A New Leader (27:12-23).** Moses, being warned of his approaching death (vs. 12-14), asked the Lord to appoint a man over the people, and was instructed to ordain Joshua as his successor before the high priest and the whole congregation (vs. 15-20). Joshua was to get his instructions from the Lord, not directly as Moses did, but through the high priest "by the judgment of the Urim" (v.21; Exod. 28:30). The Urim and the Thummim, meaning "the lights and the perfections", were objects of some unknown nature carried in the breast-plate of the high priest by which he was enabled to learn the Divine will on special occasions. Moses accordingly carried out these instructions and gave Joshua a charge (vs. 22-23).

3. **New Laws (Chs. 28-30).** In view of the coming settlement in Canaan, some new regulations were given regarding the various offerings for maintaining Israel's witness to the Lord in the Land, including the continual burnt offering (28:1-10), and the offerings at the set feasts throughout the years (28: 11-29:40). Some new laws were also given regarding vows (ch. 30).

THE EASTERN SETTLEMENT
(Chs. 31-32)

The last commission given to Moses was the execution of the judgment which the Lord had already pronounced upon the Midianites (25:16-18). A thousand men from each tribe were chosen for the purpose. In the battle that followed all the kings and all the male members of Midian were slain (31: 1-24). The spoil was divided equally between the men who had fought and the rest of the congregation (31:25-47). When the officers found that not a single man had been lost in the battle, they presented all the golden articles they had received as booty as an offering to the Lord (31:48-54).

Then the tribes of Reuben and Gad came to Moses and Eleazar asking that the conquered territory east of the Jordan be given to them because it was a suitable land for the cattle which they had (32: 1-5). Moses rebuked them at first for making such a request, but they promised to help their brethren to conquer the land west of the Jordan (32:6-19). Moses then granted their request, and the land which comprised the kingdoms of Sihon and Og was divided between these two tribes and half the tribe of Manasseh, and was settled by their families (32: 20-42).

CONCERNING THE WESTERN SETTLEMENT
(Chs. 33-36)

The final preparations were now made for the conquest and settlement of the country west of the Jordan.

1. **A Survey of the Wilderness Journey (33: 1-49).** This passage summarizes the forty years of Israel's wanderings in the wilderness. It begins with the day they left Egypt (vs. 1-4), and gives the stages of the march to Sinai (vs. 5-15). Then comes a list of the encampments from Sinai to Kadesh (vs. 16-36), and from there to Mount Hor where Aaron died (vs. 37-40), and finally from Mount Hor to the plains of Moab (vs. 41-49).

2. **Instructions for the Conquest (33:50-34:29).** Moses was now commanded of the Lord to tell the Israelites what to do when they crossed the Jordan. They were to drive out all the inhabitants of the Land and destroy all their idols and all the centres of their idolatry. Then they were to divide the Land by lot for their own inheritance according to

their families (33:50-56). Then follow specific directions as to the borders of the land of Canaan to be divided among the nine tribes and a half (34:1-15), and the names are given of the men from these tribes who were to make the division (34:16-29).

3. Cities for the Levites (Ch. 35). The Israelites were to give out of their inheritances forty-eight cities with their suburbs for the Levites to dwell in (vs. 1-8). Six of these were to be cities of refuge for the manslayer, and instructions were given for their appointment (vs. 9-15). The law was then stated for distinguishing between a murderer, who was to be put to death (vs. 16-21), and a manslayer who had killed some person unwittingly, who was to be given protection in a city of refuge (vs. 22-28). The Israelites must not allow the Land to be polluted by blood (vs. 29-34).

4. The Preservation of Inheritances (Ch. 36). Another deputation approached Moses on this matter, following the one already recorded in 27:1-11. He was then led to give instructions that heiresses were to marry within their own tribe, so that the original inheritance allotted to each tribe in Israel would be safeguarded and preserved intact.

* * * *

WILDERNESS TYPES OF CHRIST

The story of Israel in the wilderness is used in the New Testament to illustrate the experience of the Christian Church. The Apostle Paul regarded the events of the exodus from Egypt as having spiritual significance and as typical of the redemptive work of Jesus Christ. This is evident from 1 Cor. 10:1-4. In the same passage he goes on (vs. 5-12) to refer to the failure of the Israelites in the wilderness and to use it as a warning against backsliding in the present Christian dispensation. In Heb. 4:1-9, a warning of the consequence of unbelief in the Gospel is based upon the rebellion of the Israelites in the wilderness and the failure of that generation to enter the Promised Land.

It is clear, therefore, that the apostolic writers regarded this part of Israel's history as full of typical significance. Seven types of Christ, mentioned in the New Testament by direct reference or indirect allusion, are to be found in the book of Numbers: 1. The pillar of cloud and fire (9:15-23; Jno. 8:12). 2. The manna (11:7-9; Jno. 6:48). 3. Aaron's rod that budded (17:8-11; Heb. 9:4). 4. The red heifer (19:1-10; Heb. 9:13). 5. The rock that gave forth water (20:8; Jno. 7:37; 1 Cor. 10:4). 6. The brazen serpent (21:8-9; Jno. 3:14-13). 7. The cities of refuge (35:9-15; Heb. 6:18).

THE NUMBER OF THE ISRAELITES

The numbering of the Israelites as recorded in chs. 1 and 26 presents a difficulty. The total number of the men among the Israelites in the wilderness is mentioned five times. Exod. 12:37 gives 600,000 as the round number of those who left Egypt. Exod. 38:26, Num. 1:46 and 2:32 give 603,550 as the number at Mount Sinai. Num. 26:51 gives 601,730 as the number at the end of the forty years. If these figures were the numbers of the adult men, it would mean, according to the ordinary average of one man for every four or five persons, a total of between two and a half and three million for all Israel, including men, women, and children.

The total number of the firstborn males was 22,-273 (Num. 3:43). Allowing the same number for firstborn females makes 44,546 mothers in Israel. In a total of two and a half or three million, this would mean an average of between fifty and sixty persons in each family. This is so much out of all proportion that it is evident that something has gone wrong with the original numbers as they were handed down in the sacred record.

No explanation has been given which clears up all the difficulties; but the most likely key is found in Num. 1:16, where the R.V. margin reads "families" for "thousands". The Hebrew word translated "thousand" means also "clan", and is sometimes rendered "family". It has clearly this meaning in Jud. 6:15 and Micah 5:2. The tribes of Israel were divided into clans or "families", and in each "family" there would be many households, or families in our sense of the term.

Applying this key to the numbering of the tribes recorded in ch. 1, we get the following result: Reuben, 46 clans and 500 warriors (v. 21); Simeon, 59 clans and 300 warriors (v. 23); and so on through the chapter, till we get a total for the twelve tribes of 598 clans and 5,550 warriors. Applying the key in the same way to the numbering in ch. 26, we get a total of 596 clans and 5,730 warriors. The average in modern countries where conscription prevails is one man in every fourteen or fifteen of the population being available for war. According to this proportion, 5,730 men of war in Israel would make a total of about 85,000 for all the tribes, exclusive of the Levites.

Applying the same key to the numbering of the Levites in ch. 3, we get the following result: Gershonites, 7 clans and 500 males (v. 22); Kohathites, 8 clans and 600 males (v. 28); Merarites, 6 clans and 200 males (v. 34). This would make a total of 1,300 males in the tribe of Levi. If we allow the same number for the female members of the tribe, we get a total of 87,600 for all the tribes. If this should be the true explanation of the method of numbering the people, it would go to show that at the most, the whole host of Israel numbered not more than about 100,000.

THE BOOK OF DEUTERONOMY

DEUTERONOMY means "a second law". The book contains a repetition of the Ten Commandments and an exposition of the Law. A new epoch had arrived in the history of Israel and in God's dealing with the nation. Their wanderings were over and they were about to enter the Land of Promise. The leadership of Moses was coming to an end but the Covenant with God was to abide. A new generation had grown up who had not seen the theophany on Mount Sinai or heard the Ten Words uttered there. It was fitting, therefore, that before Moses departed he should review God's goodness to Israel and give the new generation a restatement of the Law of the Lord and enforce upon them the duty of obedience and consecration.

This is the theme of the book. Taken as a whole, it is an exposition of the great commandment: "Thou shalt love Jehovah thy God with all thy heart, with all thy soul, and with all thy might" (6:5). The expressions, "Jehovah our God" and "Jehovah thy God", occur about 300 times. It may be classed with the Psalms and Isaiah for its spiritual quality among the books of the Old Testament. When Jesus met the temptations of Satan in the wilderness by appealing to the Word of God (Luke 4:1-12), His quotations were taken from Deuteronomy (8:3; 6:13, 16).

The book is unlike any of those that precede it, although it rests upon them. It is composed of addresses delivered by Moses to Israel, together with an account of the closing events of his life. It can be divided into the following four parts:

I. Moses Reviewing the Way—Chs. 1-4
II. Moses Reviewing the Law—Chs. 5-26
III. Moses Renewing the Covenant—Chs. 27-30
IV. Moses' Farewell to Israel—Chs. 31-34

REVIEWING THE WAY
(Chs. 1-4)

Moses' first address contains a review of God's goodness to Israel during the sojourn in the wilderness and an earnest plea for obedience and loyalty to Him. The introduction to it, and to the book itself (1:1-4), marks the occasion as one for both warning and encouragement. A journey of eleven days, which might have led them into the Land of Promise, had been stretched into forty years. The recent conquest of the nations that had barred Israel's entrance into Canaan was a pledge of future victory.

1. The Guidance of God from Horeb to Kadesh (Ch. 1). Moses begins with the Lord's command to them to set out on their journey, and tells of his appointment of assistant judges over the people (vs. 5-18). Then he gives an account of the arrival at Kadesh-barnea, the sending of the spies at the request of the people and the rebellion that followed their return (vs. 19-33), the consequent anger of the Lord and the judgment He pronounced upon that generation, and their presumptuous attempt to go up after His warning (vs. 34-46).

2. The Guidance of God from Kadesh to Moab (Chs. 2-3). After thirty-eight years more in the wilderness they arrived at the border of Moab (2: 1-15). Heshbon, the kingdom of Sihon who refused Moses' request for a passage through his country, was conquered (2:16-37); and then Bashan, the kingdom of Og who came out to fight against Israel (3:1-11). The land thus taken was given to the Reubenites, the Gadites, and the half-tribe of Manasseh (3:12-22). Moses then tells of his own request of the Lord to be allowed to go in and see the good Land, and of the answer the Lord gave him (3:23-29).

3. Exhortation and Warning (Ch. 4). Moses follows up his review of God's goodness to Israel with an earnest exhortation to obedience: "Hearken that ye may do" (vs. 1-8); "Take heed lest ye forget" (vs. 9-24). Then he gives a solemn warning against apostasy (vs. 25-31), which he enforces by pointing out the wondrous grace of God to Israel (vs. 31-40). At the end of this address Moses set apart three cities of refuge for the east of the Jordan (vs. 41-43).

REVIEWING THE LAW
(Chs. 5-26)

In this address, which occupies more than half the book, Moses restates the Law that was delivered by the Lord on Mount Sinai, and then goes on to give an extended exposition and enforcement of it. It is introduced by the statement contained in 4:44-49.

1. The Ten Commandments (Ch. 5). Moses repeats the Ten Words of the Covenant made in Horeb, with some differences in the fourth and fifth (vs. 1-21). The ground of the Sabbath law as given here is the redemption of Israel. In Exodus it was the creation of the world. Thus the Jewish Sabbath had a two-fold significance: it was a memorial of creation and a witness of redemption. When it became the Christian Sabbath and was changed to the first day of the week, it took on a third significance as a mark of the new creation. Obedience to parents, enjoined by the fifth commandment, is enforced with a promise of prosperity added to that of long life. Moses then tells of the people's dread at hearing the voice of God and their appeal to him to be their intermediary (vs. 22-33).

2. Israel's Loyalty to the Lord (Chs. 6-11). These instructions are based on the first two commandments. Moses first appeals to the people to love the Lord with all their heart (ch. 6), and then commands them to separate themselves entirely from the heathenism of the land. The nations of Canaan were doomed to destruction because of the nature of their idolatry (7:1-5). Israel was a holy people, chosen by the Lord and set apart for Him (7: 6-16), and He would give them victory over these nations (7: 17-26).

They were to remember God's goodness in the discipline of the wilderness (8:1-10), as a warning against highmindedness and forgetfulness of Him amidst the blessings of the Land (8:11-20). As a warning against self-confidence and self-righteousness in the Land (9:1-5), they were to remember their own failures in the wilderness: their apostasy at Horeb (9:6-21), their rebellion at Kadesh-barnea (9:22-29), and the mercy of God in restoring the tables of the Law and hearkening unto Moses' intercession for them (10:1-11). Then Moses gives another exhortation to obedience, urging upon them the greatness of the Lord their God (10:12-22), His great works which they have seen (11:1-7), and the great blessings He has promised them (11:8-17). Therefore, let them lay up His words in their hearts and study them diligently (11:18-25), and consider the blessing and the curse of the Law (11:26-32).

3. Israel's Religious Life (12:1—16:17). These instructions are based on the third and fourth commandments. Monuments of idolatry were to be destroyed and one central sanctuary was to be maintained for the worship of the Lord (12:1-14). Directions were given regarding the sacrifices and the worship to be carried on at this central sanctuary (12:15-32). False prophets, dreamers of dreams, and any other enticers to idolatry, were to be put to death (13:1-11). If a city should fall into idolatry, it was to be destroyed (13:12-18). As a holy people, Israel was to avoid all heathen practices and eat no unclean food (14:1-21).

The law of the tithe was explained (14:22-29). Instructions were given for the release of debtors and bond-servants every Sabbatic year (15:1-18), and for the dedication of firstlings to the Lord (15: 19-23). At the three principal yearly feasts—the Passover, the Feast of Weeks, and Tabernacles—all the men of Israel were to appear before the Lord at the central sanctuary (16:1-17).

4. Israel's Civil Life (16:18—18:22). These instructions are based on the fifth commandment. Moses now commands the people about the appointment of judges and magistrates, and explains their duties and the principles of judgment for their guidance (16:18—17:7). Cases too hard for local judges were to be referred to the priests and Levites at the central sanctuary (17:8-13), who were to have charge of the written Law (31:24-26.) He goes on to instruct and warn them about the king they will want to set up. When on his throne, he is to make the Law of the Lord his life-long study (17: 14-20).

Further instructions are given regarding the provision to be made for the priests and Levites (18:1-8), and concerning the people's relation to the prophets. Divination and necromancy, such as the nations of the land carried on, were forbidden (18:9-14). The Lord would raise up a true prophet from among themselves, like Moses himself, who would speak the words of God (18:15-22). This was a prediction of the subsequent rise of the prophetic order. It had its complete and final fulfilment in Jesus Christ, the perfect Prophet (Heb. 1:1-2).

5. Israel's Social Life (Chs. 19-22). These instructions are based on commandments six to ten. They include the special laws regarding manslaughter and murder, which had to do with the cities of refuge (ch. 19), and the rules of warfare and exemptions from military service (ch. 20). These are followed by a long list of minor laws and regulations, applying the principles of the commandments to various matters in the domestic life of the people (chs. 21-22).

6. Supplementary Instructions (Chs. 23-26). These have in view the perfecting of Israel as the people of the Lord. They concern the congregation of the Lord: certain persons are to be excluded (23: 1-8). They have to do with the army of Israel when in camp (23:9-14), and with the life of the people when at home in the land (23:15—25:19). Direc-

tions are given for the offering of the first-fruits (26:1-11), and for the giving of the tithes (26:12-15). Moses then closes this address with another exhortation to obedience, reminding the people that the Lord has chosen them for His own possession to be a holy nation (26:16-19).

RENEWING THE COVENANT
(Chs. 27-30)

In this group of addresses, Moses gave instructions for setting up the Law in the Land, and then he renewed the Covenant of the Law with the generation that was entering the Land.

1. The Recording of the Law (Ch. 27). A monument of stone was to be erected on Mount Ebal with sacrifices of thanksgiving, and the Ten Words were to be written upon it "very plainly" (vs. 1-10). Thus the Law of the Lord was to be established as the law of the Land. The blessings and the curses of the Law were to be pronounced in the hearing of the tribes, while they stood on the slopes of Mounts Gerizim and Ebal during the ceremony (vs. 11-26). The great alternatives were to be put before them in the most impressive way. The actual fulfilment of these instructions is recorded in Josh. 8:30-35.

2. The Obligations of the Law (Ch. 28). Moses now described the blessed results of obedience (vs. 1-14), and went on to give warning of the disastrous consequences of disobedience (vs. 15-68). This long passage contains one of the most notable prophecies in the Old Testament. It depicts the actual sufferings that befell the people of Israel in their subsequent history because of their apostasy, including the blight and barrenness of the land (vs. 15-24),their subjection to foreign foes (vs. 25-46), the siege and capture of their city (vs. 47-57), and their dispersion and homelessness among the nations (vs. 58-68).

The fulfilment of all this came to pass, first, with the fall of Jerusalem at the time of the Babylonian captivity (586 B.C.), and finally, after their rejection of Christ, in the destruction of Jerusalem by the Romans (A.D. 70), and in the age-long tribulation of the Jews since that time.

3. The Renewing of the Covenant (Chs. 29-30). The Law having been reviewed and explained, Moses renewed the Covenant with the new generation of Israel (29:1). He appealed to them to keep the Covenant on the ground of all that the Lord had done for them (29:2-13), and warned them of His punishment if they failed to keep it (29:14-29). He promised that the Lord would restore them if they should repent and return to Him (30:1-14), and closed with a most solemn appeal to them to be faithful to Him (30:15-20).

MOSES' FAREWELL
(Chs. 31-34)

These chapters record Moses' final messages and narrate the closing incidents of his life. With the passing of the great lawgiver of Israel, the Books of the Law come to an end.

1. His Final Charges (Ch. 31). He addressed words of encouragement both to the people and to Joshua the new leader of Israel (vs. 1-8). His charge to both was, "be strong and of good courage—fear not". Having written the Law, Moses

delivered it to the priests and elders, and instructed them to read it every seven years in the hearing of the people (vs. 9-13).

The Lord then gave a charge to Moses in view of his approaching death, and to Joshua in view of his leading Israel into the Land (vs. 14-23). Moses charged the Levites with the care of the book of the Law, and commanded them to keep it beside the ark of the Covenant as a witness against the people when they should turn aside from the Lord (vs. 24-29).

2. His Farewell Song (Ch. 32). The Lord had instructed Moses to write this song and teach it to the children of Israel as His witness against them (31:19, 22, 30). Its theme is the unchangeable faithfulness of the Lord contrasted with the perversity of His faithless people (vs. 1-43). Moses uses the term "Rock" as a name for God several times (vs. 4, 15, 18, 30, 31), in order to emphasize the fact that He was the foundation of Israel's life.

In vs. 8-9 he declares that God had His purpose with Israel in view in the dispersion of the nations. They were so distributed and located in the world that each might have its opportunity of seeking the Lord in due season through contact with His people (Acts 17:26-27). When Moses finished the song, he made a final appeal to the people regarding the Law (vs. 44-47), and was summoned by the Lord to ascend Mount Nebo that he might see the Land before he died (vs. 48-52).

3. His Farewell Blessing (Ch. 33). This is Moses' final message. It is a poem in three parts: an introduction, describing the majesty of God as He revealed Himself to Israel (vs. 1-5); the blessings pronounced upon the various tribes (vs. 6-25); and a conclusion, describing the excellency of God as the Keeper and Helper of Israel (vs. 26-29). Moses uses the term "Jeshurun" as a name for Israel (vs. 5, 26). He had used it in the preceding chapter (v. 15), and it occurs again in Isa. 44:2. It means "the upright one", and represents God's ideal for Israel.

4. His Lonely Death (Ch. 34). The manner of Moses' exit from the world was the crowning of his life. This chapter records the fulfilment of the instructions given to him when he had finished his song (32:48-52). It is an appendix, and quite distinct from the rest of the book. It bears evidence of being written after the settlement of the tribes in Canaan. Joshua as Moses' minister may have accompanied him into the mount until the Lord removed him, and would thus be able to describe the particulars of the view which Moses was shown (vs. 1-4). The prospect spread before him of the far-stretching land towards which he had led his people was symbolical of the spiritual vision of the heavenly places which Christ was to prepare for His people (Eph. 1:3; Isa. 33:17).

A veil of dignified reserve is drawn over Moses' death and burial (vs. 5-8). He suffered death, it is declared, and was buried, but probably his body was not allowed to see corruption. The reference in Jude 9 to Michael contending with the devil over the body of Moses would seem to mean this. His presence with Elijah on the Mount of Transfiguration would indicate that he had been raised from the dead. These two men, representing the Law and the Prophets in preparation for the coming redemption, had been received into glory on the ground of, and in anticipation of, the work of the Redeemer.

When the days of mourning for Moses were ended, Joshua took up the task of leading Israel to which Moses had ordained him. The book then closes with a statement about the greatness of Moses which must have been written well on in Israel's history (vs. 9-12).

* * * *

THE GREATNESS OF MOSES

The massive character of Moses stands out in Deuteronomy, on the background of the previous books, in all its sheer greatness and grandeur. The book could not have been compiled from any traditional source. The addresses it contains ring with the voice and accents of reality. It was most natural that Moses should address the younger generation before his departure, and it would have been strange if his words had not been recorded. There was no difficulty about their being written down, for there were trained scribes and tenacious memories in those days, before man's memory was weakened by the habit of relying on written records. The framework of the addresses is probably due to a later hand, but their author is Moses. They reflect the vast variety of his greatness.

Moses towers above all other figures in the Old Testament. He is mentioned in the New Testament more often than either Abraham or David, the two great ancestors of the Redeemer. He was endowed by nature with intellectual gifts of the highest order, which were developed by the training he received as the son of Pharaoh's daughter, being "instructed in all the wisdom of the Egyptians" (Acts 7:22). He had a greatness of soul never surpassed. He combined comprehensiveness of mind and clearness of judgment with great promptness and energy of action. Stephen summed up his natural qualities in the concise statement that he "was mighty in his words and works". Above all this he was endowed with the Holy Spirit in a pre-eminent degree for the special work to which God had called him (Num. 11:17, 25). He was peculiarly "the man of God" and "the servant of Jehovah". These titles are applied to him again and again in the subsequent books of the Old Testament.

Moses occupied a unique place in Israel in three respects: (1) As leader. It was "by the hand of Moses" that God took His people out of Egypt and led them like a flock through the wilderness. (2) As lawgiver. "The law was given through Moses", not as originating it, but as mediating it, as explaining and expounding it, as enforcing and applying it in all relations of life among the people. (3) As prophet. No other prophet had the close and intimate intercourse with God that Moses enjoyed. The Lord knew him "face to face". Of him it is said more frequently than of all other prophets together, "God talked with him", or "God spake to him."

As the founder of the religion of Israel and the dispensation of the Law, Moses is the supreme Old Testament type of our Lord Jesus Christ. The mediator of the Old Covenant pointed the way to the New Covenant, and prepared the ground for the Redeemer of the world.

Moses was fitted to be a true mediator because of his two most notable qualities: (1) His absolute devotion to God. "My servant Moses", declared the Lord, "is faithful in all my house" (Num. 12:7).

He had the highest conception of the glory of God. The honour of the Lord was always the ground of his plea in prayer, and the goodness of the Lord was the ground of his constant appeal for loyalty on Israel's part. (2) His unfailing sympathy for the people. Though they continually murmured and repeatedly rebelled, yet he interceded for them on every occasion and patiently bore with them. Rather than that they should be destroyed and he should be chosen to found a new nation in their place, he would have God reject him and blot his name out of His book (Exod. 32:32). Thus Moses was a true type of the "one mediator between God and men", not only in the work he did, but also in the spirit with which he did it.

THE OLD TESTAMENT
HISTORICAL BOOKS

THE HISTORICAL BOOKS

THE twelve books from Joshua to Esther contain the story of the Israelites from the time they entered the land of Canaan to the time the Old Testament ends, a period of a thousand years. It was about 1400 B.C. when Israel crossed the Jordan (recent archæology places the fall of Jericho at that date), and Old Testament history closes shortly before 400 B.C.

It is not history in the ordinary sense that we find in these books. What they record is rather the dealings of God with Israel as His chosen people and the development of His redemptive purpose through their national life. They show us how the Law, which had been given to the redeemed people at Sinai, was manifested in the corporate life of the nation.

Israel's special function among the nations as the Lord's covenant people was to bear witness to Him as the true God. It was in order to fulfil this purpose the more effectively that Israel was placed in the land of Canaan, which was on the cross-roads of the ancient world. There the people were to live out their national life in the midst of the nations, not by developing a civilization of their own as the other nations were left to do (Acts 14:16), but by carrying out the will of God as revealed in the Moral Law given to them at Mount Sinai and in the social and economic system that was based upon it.

This accounts for the peculiarities of these historical books. It explains why large blanks are left in some periods, and why other periods are given such extensive treatment and some events are narrated with such elaborate detail. Old Testament history is a revelation of the mind and will of God as He moved down through the ages in Israel, while at the same time it exposes the nature and heart of man as seen in the character of the Israelites. The men who composed the historical sections of the Bible made a careful selection from the material available. They were co-ordinating historical events with divine revelation.

It is not known who the writers of these books were. None of them claims any specific authorship. Six of them are included under the general division of "the Prophets" in the Hebrew Bible, namely, Joshua, Judges, and the double books of Samuel and Kings. This indicates that they came from a prophetic source and were written from the prophets' point of view.

Statements occur which show that historical records were added from time to time to "the book of the law" which Moses had left. When Joshua made a covenant with the people shortly before his death, he wrote the words of it "in the book of the law of God" (Josh. 24:26). When the monarchy was established, Samuel explained the new constitution to the people, "and wrote it in a book and laid it up before Jehovah" (1 Sam. 10:25). The Books of Chronicles mention a number of prophets and seers as having written the acts of the kings from David onward (1 Chron. 29:29; 2 Chron. 9:29; 12:15; 13:22).

All this goes to show that inspired men belonging to the prophetic order were the original authors behind the historical books of the Old Testament.

More important than knowing the names of the writers is seeing the evidence which these books give of the presence of God in the history of Israel. The men who wrote them were manifestly led by the Spirit of God to record the history in such a way as to reveal His purpose of redemption moving on, even through the failure of Israel, towards the coming of the promised Redeemer.

The history of Israel in these books is recorded in two different ways. A break occurs at the end of Second Kings. Up to that point the books of the Old Testament fit into one another in chronological order. They contain a continuous story from the Creation to the fall of the kingdom of Judah and the beginning of the Babylonian captivity. The Books of Chronicles begin the record over again, and carry it down to the close of the captivity and the eve of the return.

The books from Joshua to Second Kings deal with the nation as a whole, and their story comes to an end with its failure and dispersion. The Books of Chronicles are concerned only with that part of the nation that remained faithful to the Covenant. The two subsequent historical books, Ezra and Nehemiah, deal with the remnant that returned from the exile. It was through this remnant alone that God continued to carry on His redemptive purpose in Israel. Esther, the last of the historical books, takes us back to the Jews that remained in the dispersion and gives us a glimpse of them before Old Testament history finally closes.

These twelve historical books fall into three progressive groups, according to the three successive epochs through which Israel passed during the thousand years which they cover. These epochs, dated in round numbers, are as follows:

I. **The Age of the Conquest and Settlement of Canaan (1400-1100 B.C.).** The Books of Joshua, Judges, and Ruth. During this era Israel was a theocracy. The tribes were under the direct government of God through judges raised up by Him from time to time.

II. **The Age of the Monarchy (1100-600 B.C.).** The Books of Samuel, Kings, and Chronicles. They deal with the rise of the kingdom of Israel in its united form, and with its decline and fall in its divided form. During this era Israel was a monarchy, ruled by kings whose duty was to carry out the will of God.

III. **The Age of the Dispersion of Israel and the Restoration of the Remnant (600-400 B.C.).** The Books of Ezra, Nehemiah, and Esther. Israel had now passed into the era of Gentile rule. The Historical Books close with a small remnant restored to the land to await the advent of the Messiah, and with the masses of the Jews scattered through the Gentile world.

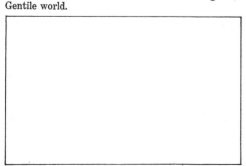

THE BOOK OF JOSHUA

THE theme of this book is the conquest and settlement of Canaan. This was accomplished under the leadership of Joshua, and from him the book gets its name. It bears evidence of coming from the generation in which the events took place (5:1; 6:25; 14:14; 24:26), although there are also signs of editing by a later hand (7:26; 15:63).

Joshua came first upon the scene in Exod. 17:9, without a word of introduction, as the captain of Israel in the fight against Amalek. His next appearance was at Sinai as Moses' minister or assistant when he went up into the mount (Exod. 24:13; 32:17). He continued to act in this capacity throughout the forty years in the wilderness (Exod. 33:11; Num. 11:28; Josh. 1:1). He represented his own tribe, Ephraim, among the twelve spies (Num. 13:8, 16). At the end of the forty years, he was appointed Moses' successor by the command of the Lord. Moses solemnly ordained him to that office in the presence of the whole congregation (Num. 27:15-23), and gave him a special charge (Deut. 31:7-8). Thus was Joshua prepared for the great task of his life, and after Moses' death the people at once recognized him as their leader (Deut. 34:9).

The book falls naturally into two equal parts, one dealing with the conquest of the land and the other with its distribution among the tribes. Thus we get the following outline:

    I. The Conquest of the Land—Chs. 1-12
        1. Entering into Canaan (Chs. 1-4)
        2. The First Campaign (Chs. 5-8)
        3. Completing the Conquest (Chs. 9-12)
    II. The Distribution of the Land—Chs. 13-24
        1. The First Allotment (Chs. 13-17)
        2. The Final Allotment (Chs. 18-22)
        3. Joshua's Farewell (Chs. 23-24)

ENTERING INTO CANAAN
(Chs. 1-4)

These chapters tell the story of the crossing from the eastern to the western side of the Jordan. By this way Israel passed out of the wilderness life into the Promised Land.

1. The Call to Advance (Ch. 1). The book begins with the Lord's call of Joshua to his new task and the Divine promise and assurance given to him (vs. 1-5), together with the conditions of success (vs. 6-9). This is followed by Joshua's charge to the people (vs. 10-15), and their promise of obedience (vs. 16-18). The words of Moses' previous charge to Joshua, "Be strong and of good courage" (Deut. 31:7), are repeated four times in the chapter.

2. The Mission of the Spies (Ch. 2). Two men, sent by Joshua to Jericho as spies to view the land, were received by Rahab and concealed in her house (vs. 1-14), and then secretly sent away (vs. 15-21). When they returned, they brought back a very different kind of report from that of the first spies (vs. 22-24; Num. 13:31-33). Rahab showed her faith by the way she received them (Heb. 11:31), by her confession regarding the Lord God of Israel

—"I know . . . . for we have heard"—, and by throwing in her lot with His people. She married into the tribe of Judah, and her name has a place in the genealogy of Jesus (Matt. 1:5).

3. The Crossing of the Jordan (Chs. 3-4). The narrative in these two chapters is composed of an introductory account of the preparation of the people for the crossing (3:1-6), and three sections, each commencing with a Divine command, which is followed by Joshua's communication of it to the people and an account of its execution. Each stage of the great event is thus directly connected with the Lord Himself.

(1) The bearing of the Ark into the Jordan (3:7-17). It was carried by the priests into the waters of the river ahead of the people, and they stood with it in the midst of the river till all the people passed over. It was the Ark, the symbol of God's presence and a type of Christ, that divided the waters. The miracle may have had a natural cause, but this was its spiritual significance.

(2) The placing of the memorial stones (4:1-14). Twelve stones taken out of the Jordan by twelve men, one from each tribe, were set up where Israel first encamped in Canaan, as a perpetual memorial of the great miracle (Psa. 114). They were also symbols of the nation. There were apparently two sets of stones, one placed in the bed of the river (v. 9), symbolizing the old Israel of the wilderness, the other set up in Gilgal (v. 20), representing the new Israel now ready for the possession of the land.

(3) The bringing of the Ark out of the Jordan (4:15-24). The Ark is prominent throughout the whole narrative; it is mentioned sixteen times in the two chapters. The people came up out of the Jordan and encamped in the land of Canaan on the tenth day of the first month, exactly forty years from the day preparations began for the first Passover (Exod. 12:3).

THE FIRST CAMPAIGN
(Chs. 5-8)

These chapters record the opening events of the war of conquest. They tell of the first victory and the first defeat.

1. The Preparation for the War (Ch. 5). The new generation was circumcised at the command of the Lord, marking them as His covenant people (vs. 1-8). Now that the Israelites were actually in the land which God had promised them when He redeemed them from Egypt, they were no longer under "the reproach of Egypt" (v. 9). The Egyptians could no longer cast ridicule upon them for their life in the wilderness (Isa. 25:8). The Passover was now observed for the first time in Canaan. The people partook of the old corn of the land, and the manna of the wilderness ceased (vs. 10-12).

Then Joshua was given a vision of the Prince of the Lord's host, who was none other than the Angel of the Covenant, now come to take command of the campaign (vs. 13-15). The wars of Israel in Canaan are always represented in the Old Testament as "the wars of Jehovah" (Num. 21:14). The conquest of Canaan was a Divine enterprise, in which the Israelites were the human instruments employed by God for executing His judgment upon the Canaanites.

2. The Fall of Jericho (Ch. 6). The first city in Canaan fell before the Ark of the Lord. The method of attack followed the Divine instructions, which were first given (vs. 1-7). The whole scene was an expression in symbolic action of the Lord making war upon Jericho: the seven days' march round the walls with the blowing of the seven trumpets (vs. 8-14), and the seven circuits of the city on the seventh day (vs. 15-19). The way the walls fell down showed that the Lord was giving the city to Israel. Their faith was manifested in their complete obedience to the Divine instructions (vs. 20-21; Heb. 11:30).

The city was "devoted" to the Lord as the first fruits of the conquest, only Rahab and her father's household being saved (vs. 22-25). A "devoted" thing was not to be employed for any man's use, but was either put away and destroyed to vindicate the justice of God, as the men and beasts in this case, or was consecrated to the special service of God, as were all the precious and useful vessels. A curse was laid upon the man that would rebuild Jericho, and Joshua's fame spread all over the land (vs. 26-27; 1 Kings 16:34).

3. The Trespass of Achan (Ch. 7). This consisted in taking for himself what belonged to God, and the secret sin of one man was the sin of the nation (v. 1). It resulted in the withdrawal of the Lord's blessing from Israel and their defeat at Ai (vs. 2-5). In distress and humiliation, Joshua cast himself before the Lord (vs. 6-9), and it was revealed to him that there was sin in the midst of Israel, which must be judged and put away before the Lord would be with them any more and give them victory again (vs. 10-15). The method of the Lord's judgment slowly drew the net of detection around the guilty man. His confession was worthless, for it was made only after he was discovered (vs. 16-21). The punishment of Achan was such as to be a warning to Israel ever afterwards (vs. 22-26; Hos. 2:15).

4. The Taking of Ai (Ch. 8). This victory was given to Israel after judging and putting away the wrong committed in the trespass of Achan, and was achieved according to Divine instructions (vs. 1-2). The story shows how Joshua made use of military strategy (vs. 3-29). Victory is given to those living in obedience to God; and obedience to God includes the use of reason and common sense.

The campaign closed with the building of an altar on Mount Ebal, and the recording and reading of the Law there (vs. 30-35), according to Moses' instructions (Deut. 27).

COMPLETING THE CONQUEST
(Chs. 9-12)

These chapters record the results of the subsequent campaigns, in which the whole land was finally subdued. The opening campaign had driven a wedge into the centre of the country, separating the north from the south. Joshua now proceeded to conquer the southern portion first and then the northern portion.

1. The Conquest of Southern Canaan (Chs. 9-10). This was brought about when Joshua went to the help of the Gibeonites, one of the southern nations, who had beguiled the Israelites into making a covenant with them.

(1) The covenant with the Gibeonites (ch. 9). While the kings of the Canaanites prepared for common action against Israel (vs. 1-2), the Gibeon-

ites sent an embassy to Joshua asking for an alliance (vs. 3-6). The Israelites were deceived by the wiles of the Gibeonites, because they "asked not counsel at the mouth of Jehovah" (vs. 7-15). Having made a covenant with them, they were obliged to keep it when they discovered the deceit. The Gibeonites were preserved from destruction but condemned to perpetual servitude (vs. 16-27). It is interesting to note that the binding nature of this treaty was recognized in the subsequent history (2 Sam. 21:1-6), and that the Gibeonites never seem to have had any corrupting influence upon the Israelites.

(2) The battle of Gibeon (10:1-28). Joshua responded to the appeal of the Gibeonites and came to their help against the southern confederacy of five kings who had attacked the city; and he utterly defeated them (vs. 1-11). The daylight was miraculously prolonged during the battle, enabling the Israelites to complete the destruction of their foes. This is the real significance of what happened. Its actual nature is unknown, and speculation about it is useless. The story is related in a passage quoted from the Book of Jashar (vs. 12-15), which was apparently a collection of national songs (2 Sam. 1:18). Joshua followed up his defeat of the confederate host and the five kings were all captured and destroyed (vs. 16-27).

(3) The extent of the southern conquests (10:28-43). Joshua followed up the victory at Gibeon by taking all the cities of the south and destroying their inhabitants (vs. 28-39). Then comes a summary of all the conquests of the southern part of Canaan (vs. 40-43). Nothing is said as to the length of time over which the events recorded here extended.

2. The Conquest of Northern Canaan (Ch. 11). A confederacy of northern kings, which was more formidable than that of the south because of their horses and chariots, gathered at the waters of Merom, and it was completely destroyed by Joshua (vs. 1-15). A general statement follows, describing the way Joshua completed the conquest of the whole land, even driving out the Anakim who had discouraged the spies at the first (Num. 13:33), till at last "the land had rest from war" (vs. 16-23).

The narrative emphasizes the fact that Joshua was carrying out Divine commands which he had received from Moses (vs. 15, 20, 23). The instructions given by Moses (Deut. 7) meant that the Canaanites were to be exterminated when the Lord delivered them up to the Israelites, and that all traces of their idolatry were to be destroyed. No covenant was to be made with any of them. This was stern treatment of conquered peoples, but its purpose is explicitly declared. It was not merely a judgment upon their abominable wickedness, of which Sodom was an example; but it was also necessary for the moral safety of the chosen people themselves, whom the Lord was now preparing for the ultimate salvation of the world.

3. A List of the Conquered Kings (Ch. 12). Here we have a summary of the conquests both east (vs. 1-6) and west (vs. 7-24) of the Jordan. From a comparison of 14:10 with Deut. 2:14, it may be inferred that the conquest of the land occupied seven years.

THE FIRST ALLOTMENT OF THE LAND
(Chs. 13-17)

This distribution was made while the headquarters of Israel were still at Gilgal (14:6). It comprised the central and southern conquests, which were divided among the tribes of Judah, Ephraim, and Manasseh. In each case the territory is described, its general features and boundaries being carefully laid down.

1. The Inheritances of the Eastern Tribes (Ch. 13). The chapter begins with the Lord's command to Joshua to divide the land that remained to be possessed among the nine and a half tribes (vs. 1-7). This is followed by a description of the territories which had been conquered east of the Jordan and were already given to the two and a half tribes (vs. 8-14). Reuben was given the southern section (vs. 15-23), Gad the central (vs. 24-28), and half Manasseh the northern (vs. 29-31).

2. The Inheritance of Judah (Chs. 14-15) There is first a statement of the way the land of Canaan was divided by lot among the nine and a half tribes (14:1-5). It was done by Eleazar and Joshua acting with the heads of the tribes. Eleazar the high priest is named first, because in the theocratic government established by Moses the priest had the legislative authority while the executive power rested with the judge (Num. 27:21; Deut. 17:8-9).

In the midst of the tribe of Judah came Caleb with his noble request for the hill country of Hebron to be given to him, that he might drive out the remnants of the Anakim (14:6-15). Then the territory of the tribe of Judah is described with its cities (ch. 15). In the course of it is an account of the way Caleb drove out the foes that were left in his inheritance (vs. 13-19), a passage which is repeated with slight variations in Jud. 1:10-15.

3. The Inheritance of the Children of Joseph (Chs. 16-17). After their territories had been allotted to the tribes of Ephraim (ch. 16) and Manasseh (17:1-13), they came to Joshua expressing dissatisfaction and received from him a characteristic answer (17:14-18). This is the first sign of the proud and arrogant spirit which Ephraim so often manifested in the later history.

Each tribe had the task of driving out the Canaanites that still remained in its territory, and in every case there was failure to do this (15:63; 16:10; 17:12-13).

THE FINAL ALLOTMENT OF THE LAND
(Chs. 18-22)

This distribution was made at Shiloh (18:1), where the Tabernacle had been set up to be the central place of worship for all the tribes. Here the headquarters of the nation were now established.

1. The Inheritance of the Remaining Tribes (Chs. 18-19). The land yet to be possessed was first surveyed by three men from each tribe and divided into seven portions (18:1-10). It was then distributed by lot among the seven remaining tribes: Benjamin (18:11-28), Simeon (19:1-9), Zebulun (19:10-16), Issachar (19:17-23), Asher (19:24-31), Naphtali (19:32-39), and Dan (19:40-48). A special inheritance was given to Joshua in the midst of Ephraim (19:49-51).

2. The Cities of Refuge (Ch. 20). These were to be a refuge for the manslayer who had killed

someone unwittingly (vs. 1-6), according to the law already given by Moses (Num. 35:9-15). The cities set apart for this purpose were Kedesh, Shechem, and Hebron west of the Jordan, and Bezer, Ramoth, and Golan east of the Jordan (vs. 7-9).

3. The Cities of the Levites (Ch. 21). The Levites, who received no inheritance in the Land like the other tribes, now applied for the cities that Moses had commanded to be given to them (Num. 35:1-8). The Israelites gave twenty-three cities to the Kohathites, thirteen to the Gershonites, and twelve to the Merarites (vs. 1-7). Then follow the names of the cities given to each group of families: the Kohathites (vs. 8-26), the Gershonites (vs. 27-33), and the Merarites (vs. 34-42), forty-eight cities in all, including the cities of refuge. The chapter closes with a statement that, in giving them possession of the Land, all the promises of the Lord to Israel had been fulfilled (vs. 43-45).

4. The Return of the Eastern Tribes (Ch. 22). Joshua commended the Reubenites, the Gadites, and the half tribe of Manasseh for helping their brethren in the conquest of Canaan, and then sent them away to their homes beyond the Jordan with a blessing (vs. 1-9). On their way they built a great altar in the region of the Jordan, and this caused offence to the rest of Israel, who feared they were turning away from following the Lord (vs. 10-20). The two tribes and a half explained that they had no such intention, but rather to erect a witness to the fact that their worship was identical with that of their brethren (vs. 21-34).

JOSHUA'S FAREWELL
(Chs. 23-24)

These chapters record the closing events of Joshua's life. On two occasions in his old age he called an assembly of Israel, that he might exhort them to obedience and renew their covenant with the Lord before he died.

1. His Charge to Israel (Ch. 23). He makes very little reference to himself. The burden of his message is the goodness and faithfulness of God to them in driving out the nations before them. Not one thing had failed of all the good things which He had promised them and now he warns them before he leaves them of the evil that will come upon them if they turn away from the Lord.

2. His Renewal of the Covenant (24:1-28). The second assembly was gathered at Shechem. Joshua traces the history of Israel from the call of Abraham to the present moment (vs. 1-13). He puts it in the form of an address of the Lord to the people, declaring His dealings with them. In the course of the short passage the Divine pronoun "I" occurs seventeen times. Everything of greatness in Israel's history is of God. Joshua then goes on to appeal to them to choose the Lord and serve Him, and shows his own devotion by the pledge he gives for himself and his house (vs. 14-15). The people give their promise, and the Covenant is renewed and a record of it made (vs. 16-28).

3. His Death and Burial (24:29-33). He died at the age of a hundred and ten, the same age as Joseph. The book closes with the record of the burial of the bones of Joseph, which had been brought up from Egypt in fulfilment of his wish (Gen. 50:22-26), and the death and burial of Eleazar the high priest.

* * * *

THE SPIRITUAL SIGNIFICANCE OF CANAAN

The Promised Land into which Joshua led the children of Israel is regarded in Heb. 4:1-9 as foreshadowing the "rest" which Christ gives to those who believe the Gospel. It was a type and symbol of Heaven, not as the future state of bliss, but as the spiritual world into which believers are introduced by their union with Christ (Phil. 3:20; Col. 1:13). It corresponds to "the heavenly places" of the Epistle to the Ephesians (1:3; 2:6).

The warfare of Israel against the Canaanites is an Old Testament counterpart of the warfare of the Christian Church against the spiritual hosts of wickedness in that world (Eph. 6:12). Israel was commanded by the Lord to wage that war, and there was to be no compromise in it (Num. 33:50-56). The driving out of the Canaanites and the destruction of their idolatry was not the arbitrary action of hatred and cruelty, but the deliberate execution of Divine justice. The Lord had waited long (Gen. 15:16), and now "the iniquity of the Amorite" was full (Lev. 18:24-28; Deut. 12:31). Recent archæology has brought evidence to light that their worship was most debasing and their morals were most corrupt. The Israelites clearly understood that it was because of their wickedness and abominable idolatry that these nations were to be exterminated. They were threatened with the same judgments themselves if they became guilty of the sins of these nations on whom they were executing the justice of God (Deut. 7:1-5; 8:19-20).

The land of Canaan, according to the borders described in Num. 34:1-12, was limited to the territory west of the Jordan. This was the Promised Land, and it was peculiarly fitted to serve God's purpose with Israel, both by its position and its nature. It was enclosed within natural boundaries on all sides, which gave it a secluded position and made it easier for Israel to be a separated people as commanded in the Law (Lev. 20:24-26). On the other hand, its central situation in the midst of the nations of the ancient world, and the great highways that led past its borders, gave a special advantage to Israel as God's witness to the other peoples of the world. The fertility of the land depended entirely upon the bounty of God's providence and His blessing upon the soil through the seasons of the year. This fitted it in a peculiar way for training Israel to trust in the Lord (Deut. 11:10-12).

THE BOOK OF JUDGES

THE Book of Joshua closed with the chosen nation established in the Land of Promise and renewing their Covenant with the Lord. The Book of Judges exhibits them in the first period of their life as a settled nation under the Law. They were given no king of their own such as the other nations had, for they were to look to God as their King. They were being trained in the obedience of faith. This was the significance of the discipline under which they were now to live. Would they keep the Covenant and live as the Law directed? While Joshua's influence remained they did so, and went on with the task of driving out the Canaanites. But before long backsliding began, and this characterized the whole age with which the Book of Judges deals.

It was an age of unfaithfulness and failure. The expression, "the children of Israel did that which was evil in the sight of Jehovah", occurs seven times in the course of the narrative (2:11; 3:7, 12; 4:1; 6:1; 10:6; 13:1). It is followed in each case by a statement that God delivered them into the hand of an oppressor. When they cried unto the Lord out of these oppressions, He raised up deliverers for them, who "judged" Israel in the sense of defending the national cause against foes. For this reason they are sometimes called "saviours" (3:9, 15; Ob. 21). These were the judges, and from them the book gets its name.

It was written after the commencement of the monarchy (19:1; 21:25), but before the reign of David (1:21; 2 Sam. 5:6-9). It stretches over nearly three centuries, covering the period between Joshua's death and Samuel's judgeship. It falls into three main parts:

I. Israel's Unfaithfulness to the Lord—Chs. 1-2
II. The Outward Result: National Servitude—Chs. 3-16
III. The Inward Result: National Corruption—Chs. 17-21

ISRAEL'S UNFAITHFULNESS
(Chs. 1-2)

The book begins by describing the state of Israel after Joshua's death, and goes on to show how unfaithfulness to the Covenant began, and then gives a general view of the times of the judges.

1. National Failure (Ch. 1). The Israelites made a good beginning: they "asked of Jehovah" (vs.1-2). They consulted the high priest at Shiloh to know the Lord's will, and under the leadership of Judah went at the work in earnest (vs. 3-10). One of their exploits is recorded in the story of Othniel and Achsah (vs. 11-15), which is repeated from Josh. 15:13-19. But gradually they weakened and let some of the Canaanites remain (vs. 16-28). This was true virtually of all the tribes (vs. 29-36). The statement, "did not drive out", occurs seven times in the chapter.

2. National Apostasy (Ch. 2). The nation was rebuked by a visit from the Angel of the Lord, who "came up from Gilgal to Bochim". This statement probably means that the Angel who had been sent to lead the host of Israel in the wilderness (Exod. 23:20-23), and who had appeared to Joshua when the camp was in Gilgal (Josh. 5:10, 13), now came to the new place of assembly in central Palestine. His words seemed to have made a deep impression upon the people (vs. 1-5), but this was only temporary, as the chapter goes on to show. A brief review of the time of Joshua (vs. 6-10) is followed by a summary of the times of the judges (vs. 11-23).

This passage traces the course of Israel's sin and God's method of dealing with it. Having allowed some of the Canaanites to remain, the Israelites soon forgot the Lord and fell in with the idolatry of their heathen neighbours (vs. 11-13). God's anger was kindled and He gave them over to the power of their enemies (vs. 14-15). Then He raised up judges to save them; but when the judges were dead they transgressed again (vs. 16-19). Finally God left a company of nations to prove Israel by using them for the chastening and discipline of His own people (vs. 20-23). A list of these nations follows in 3:1-6.

ISRAEL'S SERVITUDE
(Chs. 3-16)

The outward result of Israel's unfaithfulness consisted in a series of oppressions or servitudes. The book does not give a continuous history of the period, but contains the story of the men whom God raised up from time to time to deliver the nation out of these oppressions. These judges are not to be confused with the officers appointed by Moses for the administration of justice among the people (Exod. 18:21-26). They were raised up for a specific purpose and endowed with extraordinary powers. The peculiarity of their office lay in its entire dependence upon the authority of God. Four of them are mentioned among the heroes of faith in Heb. 11:32.

1. The First Group of Judges (Ch. 3). After a list of the nations left in the land to prove Israel (vs. 1-6), we have an account of deliverances by Othniel (vs. 7-11), Ehud (vs. 12-30), and Shamgar (v. 31). What is said of Othniel illustrates two things that were true of the judges as a whole. They were raised up (1) in answer to the cry of the people in the midst of their suffering, and (2) under the power of the Spirit of God. "The Spirit of Jehovah came upon" Othniel. This does not mean an abiding or sanctifying influence, but an extraordinary gift of power and enthusiasm for the occasion.

2. Deborah and Barak (Chs. 4-5). This story illustrates the helpless inefficiency of Israel's religious leaders during this period. There is no mention of the Tabernacle at Shiloh, which should have been the real centre of the national life. God raised up a woman to be prophet as well as judge. Her function was to inspire Barak with courage and enthusiasm for the battle of the Lord (4:1-16). The fact that Jael's deed was used for the destruction of Sisera does not mean that its moral quality was approved. It throws out into relief the moral darkness of the time (4:17-24).

Deborah's song is a grand outburst of impassioned poetry (ch. 5). It is a song of victory, consisting of a prelude (vs. 2-3), and three main sections: the significance of the victory (vs. 4-11), the muster and the battle (vs. 12-23), and the issues of the victory (vs. 24-31). The whole song breathes scorn for the foe who had oppressed Israel so long, and zeal for the Lord who had thus delivered His people.

3.   Gideon (Chs. 6-8).   He is the most important of the judges, and his history is full of moral and spiritual significance.

(1) His call (ch. 6).   The theocratic character of this early period in Israel's history is manifested in the way Gideon was called.   After seven years of Midianite oppression (vs. 1-6), in response to the cry of Israel, an unnamed prophet was sent to rebuke them for their disobedience and ingratitude to the Lord their God (vs. 7-10).   After that the Angel of the Lord appeared to Gideon, who had evidently maintained his loyalty to God in the midst of the prevailing apostasy, and, commending his devotion and zeal, summoned him to save Israel from the hand of Midian (vs. 11-18).   Gideon did not recognize the Divine character of the Angel till an offering presented to him was consumed by fire (vs. 19-24). That night, in obedience to a command of the Lord, Gideon broke down the altar of Baal that belonged to his father's household, and built an altar to the Lord and offered a sacrifice upon it.   Next day Joash saved his son from the wrath of the townsfolk by telling them that Baal should be allowed to fight for himself (vs. 25-32).   The fact that the vile Baal worship of the Canaanites was now practised amongst the Israelites shows how low they had sunk at this time.

When the Midianites and their allies invaded the land again, the Spirit of the Lord took hold of Gideon and he issued a rallying call to the men of the northern tribes (vs. 33-35).   Then he asked for a double sign from God, not because of any lack of faith, but because he knew his own strength was insufficient for the conquest of the foe and he wished to be assured that God would save Israel through him (vs. 36-40).

(2) The battle (ch. 7).   Gideon's army was reduced so that the people might have no occasion of boasting (vs. 1-3).   A simple test was used, which revealed those who were most fully devoted to the task in hand.   They lapped up the water with their hands while still on the alert with their faces to the foe; but the rest yielded to momentary self-indulgence and bowed down to drink (vs. 4-8).   The dream that Gideon heard related and interpreted in the camp of Midian prepared him for the victory. The interpretation was a natural one, for barley bread was the food of the poorest farming classes and fitly represented Israel while the tent fitly represented Midian (vs. 9-14).   Praising the Lord, Gideon returned to his little army, and prepared his men to attack the enemy without delay.   The victory was accomplished in such a way as to show that it was entirely from God (vs. 15-22).   The Israelites who had been sent away before the battle now pursued the Midianites, and Gideon sent word to the men of Ephraim to intercept the flying foe at the Jordan (vs. 23-25).

(3) The issues of the battle (ch. 8).   The tribal jealousy and local self-interest in Israel is revealed in Ephraim's complaint after the victory was won (vs. 1-3), and in the refusal of the men of Succoth and Penuel to give bread to Gideon's weary band of pursuers (vs. 4-9).   Gideon went on and captured the two kings of the Midianites and then returned and punished the two cities which had refused him food (vs. 10-17).   Then he sealed his victory over the Midianites by slaying their princes (vs. 18-21).

Gideon showed his loyalty to the Lord by refusing the kingship (vs. 22-23).   But, in usurping the function of the high priest and making his own city a centre of worship, he was yielding to the temptation to glorify himself and sowing the seeds of trouble (vs. 24-28).   His pretext may have been that the Lord had appeared to him directly; and, besides, the high priesthood at the central sanctuary seems to have sunk into insignificance.   After a statement about Gideon's family (vs. 29-32), the record goes on to say that Israel sank into Baal worship again when he was dead (vs. 33-35).

4.   Abimelech and his Successors (Chs. 9-10). The slow but sure working of Divine retribution is illustrated in the story of Abimelech, one of Gideon's many sons, whose mother belonged to Shechem.   He plotted with the men of Shechem, slaughtered his own brothers, and usurped the rule over Israel (9: 1-6).   Jotham, who had escaped the massacre, uttered a parable from the top of Mount Gerizim in the hearing of the men of Shechem, depicting the judgment that awaited both them and the king they had chosen (9:7-21).   After a short reign of three years, a conspiracy was formed in Shechem against Abimelech (9:22-29).   When he was informed of it, he captured and destroyed the city and slew its inhabitants (9:30-49).   But he was himself slain ignominiously when attacking a neighbouring city (9: 50-57).

After him Tola and Jair judged Israel twenty-three and twenty-two years respectively (10:1-5). After that came another period of idolatry and apostasy, which brought on an Ammonite oppression lasting eighteen years until Israel cried unto the Lord again (10:6-18).

5.   Jephthah and his Successors (Chs. 11-12). Jephthah had been cast out by his brethren and had become the head of a band of outlaws (11:1-3).   But when the Ammonites made war against Israel the people of Gilead sent for Jephthah and made him their head (11:4-11).   He seems to have been a true worshipper of the Lord God of Israel, for he had the agreement with the elders of Gilead ratified before the Lord, and in his subsequent message to the king of Ammon he showed a clear understanding of the Lord's dealings with Israel in the wilderness journey (11:12-28).   Under the Spirit of the Lord he won a great victory over the Ammonites (11:29-33).

The vow which Jephthah made before going forth to battle, and which caused him so much grief when he fulfilled it (11:34-38), did not result in the sacrifice of his daughter upon the altar, but in giving her up for life-long service at the Tabernacle (Exod. 38:8; Luke 2:37).   This meant that she could not marry; and, as she was his only child, it involved the blotting out of his family and the end of his hopes in Israel.   She "bewailed her virginity" because she would have to remain a virgin all her life. As long as she lived the daughters of Israel paid her a yearly visit to "celebrate" her self-sacrifice in fulfilling her father's vow (11:39-40).   The inspired historian who records this incident obviously implies that Jephthah was to be commended for not breaking his vow.   The inspired author of the Epistle to the Hebrews enrolls Jephthah among the heroes of faith (11:32).   All this is evidence against the idea that Jephthah offered a human sacrifice, which would have been abhorrent to the Lord, and was distinctly forbidden in the Law (Lev. 18:21; 20:2-5).

The civil war between Jephthah and the Ephraimites (12:1-6) was caused by the jealous temper of Ephraim, and reveals the national disintegration of Israel. Jephthah judged Israel six years, and after him came Ibzan, Elon, and Abdon in succession (12:7-15).

6. Samson (Chs. 13-16). The account of Samson is longer and more circumstantial than that of any other judge. In a sense he is the most representative of them all. He was a symbol of the nation itself, both in its strength and in its weakness, in its great possibilities and in its tragic failure.

(1) His birth (ch. 13). He could have had no better beginning. The Angel of the Lord came to announce his birth as a gift of God to his parents, who were apparently God-fearing people. He was dedicated to God from his birth. He is the first recorded instance of a Nazirite.

(2) His exploits among the Philistines (chs. 14-15). A Philistine oppression had been going on in the south west (13:1), apparently at the same time as the Ammonite oppression in the east (10:7). The Philistines were not Canaanites, but a foreign people who had migrated into Palestine in an early age. Samson grew up in the border of their territory, and the Spirit of the Lord began to use him against them by coming upon him in sudden, mighty impulses and giving him superhuman bodily strength (13:25; 14:19; 15:14). The Lord was with him as long as he kept his Nazirite vow. But the carnal element in his nature was very strong, and he yielded to it until at last it brought about his downfall. In the meantime the Lord used this conflict between the flesh and the spirit in him for the discomfiture of the Philistines.

(3) His fall, captivity, and death (ch. 16). Here we see the man of carnal lusts yielding up the secret of his strength and sinking into deep degradation and humiliation, and learning at last that without God he was nothing. In the midst of it he cried to the Lord for strength again (v. 28), and in his death he struck the heaviest blow at the oppressors of Israel (v. 30). With Samson the age of the judges comes to an end.

ISRAEL'S CORRUPTION
(Chs. 17-21)

These chapters form an appendix to the story of the judges. They disclose the depths of corruption and degradation into which the nation had sunk because of its unfaithfulness to the Covenant. Apostasy had brought on anarchy. "Every man did that which was right in his own eyes" (17:6; 21:25).

1. A Story of Religious Corruption (Chs. 17-18). An Ephraimite named Micah set up an image in his house and hired a Levite to be his priest (ch. 17). The tribe of Dan, on their way north to settle at Laish, stole Micah's image, took his priest with them, and set up image worship there (ch. 18).

2. A Story of Moral Corruption (Chs. 19-21). The infamous conduct of the men of Gibeah is related (ch. 19). The tribe of Benjamin refused to give up the evil doers, and all Israel made war upon it and almost exterminated it (ch. 20). Then measures were taken to restore Benjamin among the tribes of Israel (ch. 21).

* * * *

THE THEOCRATIC CHARACTER OF THE AGE
OF THE JUDGES

During the age of the judges there was no central government, but there was a theocracy. The tribes of Israel were settled in the Land as the people of God, and they were to look to the Lord as their King and obey Him. They were expected to seek His mind and will on specific occasions and enquire what He would have them do by consulting the high priest (20:27), who was equipped with the Urim and the Thummim for this special purpose (Exod. 28:30; Num. 27:21).

The theocratic character of the age is manifest in the way the judges were raised up as the agents of the Lord's rule (2:16). It is also brought out by the fact that the Angel of the Covenant appears on four occasions in the course of the book. He rebuked the people for their disobedience at the beginning (2:1-4). In the time of Deborah He pronounced a curse upon a city that had failed to come to the help of the Lord (5:23). He called Gideon to his great task (ch. 6). He charged the parents of Samson, before the birth of their child, to prepare him for the life of a Nazirite (ch. 13). He is mentioned some twenty times in the book.

The Book of Judges may be regarded as a historical commentary on the promises and threatenings of Deuteronomy. It illustrates the principles and methods of God's government in the life of a nation. It shows that religious apostasy brings moral degeneracy and national weakness, that national sin does not go unpunished, that the punishment of a nation is intended to bring it to a sense of its need of God, and that when a nation turns to God He works for its deliverance and blessing.

THE BOOK OF RUTH

THIS book is named from the chief person in the narrative. It is an appendix to the Book of Judges. It is a story of the best side of life in Israel during that period. It illustrates the truth that even in the darkest times God does not leave Himself absolutely without witness. There were children of faith living simple and beautiful lives in the midst of the strife and apostasy of the times of the judges.

The book also serves as a connecting link between the age of the judges and the age of the kings. Ruth the Moabitess was an ancestor of David (4:17). It is thus a step in the preparation for the coming of Christ. Ruth is one of the four women mentioned in the genealogy of Jesus (Matt. 1:3, 5, 6), which reminds us that He was a kinsman not of the Jews only, but of the Gentiles as well.

The keynote of Ruth's beautiful character was faith. She had come to trust in the Lord God of Israel (2:12). The story may be outlined as follows, showing four stages or aspects of her faith:

1. Ruth Choosing (Ch. 1). During a famine in the land, Elimelech of Bethlehem, with his wife Naomi and their two sons, went to sojourn in Moab, where the sons married Moabite wives. This way of seeking escape from trouble brought them no good, for all the men of the family died. Naomi, bereft of them all, prepared to return to Bethlehem and urged her daughters-in-law to remain in Moab. Orpah parted from her, but "Ruth clave unto her",

choosing to leave her own people and take her place with the people of God. The words in which she expressed her decision reveal the utter devotion of genuine love and faith (vs. 16-17). Their arrival at Bethlehem in their poverty moved the city with wonder, and Naomi confessed that the Lord had testified against her and afflicted her.

2. Ruth Serving (Ch. 2). It was the time of barley harvest, and Ruth went out to glean in the fields, as the poor were permitted by the Law to do (Lev. 19:9-10; 23:22). God's overruling care of her is marked by the fact that "her hap was to light" on the field of Boaz, a godly Israelite and noble character, who gave her a gracious and generous welcome. The daily life of Israel at its best is seen in the frank and friendly fellowship between Boaz and his men. When Ruth went back at even and told her mother-in-law of the day's experience, she learned that Boaz was one of their near kinsmen.

3. Ruth Resting (Ch. 3). Naomi now sought "rest" for Ruth by appealing to the law which laid a certain important obligation on a kinsman (Lev. 25:25-28; Deut. 25:5-6). This law was designed to prevent the extinction of any family in Israel and the alienation of any family inheritance. Naomi explained to Ruth how to make her approach to Boaz. When Boaz discovered her he addressed her with pious and fatherly tenderness and encouragement, and he promised to do the kinsman's part if a nearer kinsman, who should first be seen about it, refused to do it. Before Ruth went back to her mother-in-law he gave her a very generous supply of barley.

4. Ruth Rejoicing (Ch. 4). Boaz called the other kinsman to meet him at the gate of the city, where business was done, in the presence of ten of the elders. He presented the case, and asked him if he would redeem the field of Elimelech which Naomi had been obliged to sell and if he would marry Ruth. Being unable to fulfil the kinsman's part, he transferred the right of redemption to Boaz. The transaction was attested in the presence of the elders, according to the recognized custom. Boaz purchased the inheritance of the family and took Ruth to be his wife. The women of the city now rejoiced with Naomi, and Ruth had the joy of becoming a mother in Israel. Her son was Obed, the grandfather of David.

In thus recording the origin of David's family from Boaz of the tribe of Judah and Ruth the Moabitess, this book prepares for the transition from the theocracy to the monarchy, which is the theme of the next book.

THE FIRST BOOK OF SAMUEL

THE double Books of Samuel and Kings contain a connected history of the kingdom of Israel from its beginning in the days of Samuel to its end in the Assyrian and Babylonian captivities.

The two Books of Samuel tell of the rise and establishment of the monarchy. They are named from the man under whom this change in the nation's history was brought about. Their purpose is not to record a complete and continuous story, but to trace the dealings of God with Israel through this transition period of the nation's development. First Samuel tells how the kingdom was constituted, and gives an account of the way Israel passed from the direct rule of God under the judges to become a monarchy like the nations around. Second Samuel is concerned with the reign of David, the king of God's own choice, under whom the kingdom was finally established.

The First Book of Samuel may be divided into two parts under the names of Samuel and Saul respectively, giving us the following outline:

I. The Work of Samuel—Chs. 1-12
    1. Samuel's Early Life (Chs. 1-3).
    2. The Reformation in Israel (Chs. 4-7)
    3. The Origin of the Kingdom (Chs. 8-12)

II. The Reign of Saul—Chs. 13-31
    1. The Failure of Saul (Chs. 13-15)
    2. The Choice of David (Chs. 16-17)
    3. The Friendship of David and Jonathan. (Chs. 18-20)
    4. Saul's Persecution of David (Chs. 21-27)
    5. The End of Saul's Life (Chs. 28-31)

SAMUEL'S EARLY LIFE
(Chs. 1-3)

These chapters tell the story of Samuel's life up to the time when he came to be recognized throughout Israel as a prophet of the Lord. They take us back to the Tabernacle at Shiloh, which had become the national centre again after its long period of obscurity during the age of the judges. There Eli was both high priest and judge.

1. His Birth (Ch. 1). Samuel, whose name means "asked of God", was born in answer to the prayers of his mother Hannah, who dedicated him to the Lord as a Nazirite from his birth (vs. 1-20). His parents presented the child for service in the house of the Lord at Shiloh under the care of Eli the high priest (vs. 21-28). His father Elkanah was a Levite (1 Chron. 6:23, 27-28). The most majestic of the Divine names, "Jehovah of hosts", frequently used in the Prophets, occurs for the first time in this chapter (v. 3).

2. His Childhood (Ch. 2). Hannah's song of thanksgiving (vs. 1-10) has many echoes in the song of the Virgin Mary (Luke 2:46-55). The theme is the same in both. Samuel's growth as a child in the service of the Lord at Shiloh (vs. 11, 18-21, 26) was like that of Jesus in his home at Nazareth (Luke 2: 40, 52). In striking contrast with the life of the young Nazirite was the wicked conduct and unbridled self-indulgence of Eli's sons, the priests (vs. 12-17, 22-25). Eli's failure to restrain them brought a pronouncement of Divine judgment upon

his house, delivered by an unnamed prophet (vs. 27-36).

3. His Call (Ch. 3). "The word of Jehovah was precious in those days": it was rare, very seldom heard. "There was no frequent vision"—no vision spread abroad (v. 1). There was no publicly acknowledged prophet whose word came to all Israel. God revealed Himself to the child Samuel and sent a message through him to Eli about the doom that was to fall upon his house (vs. 2-14). Eli accepted the message, when told of it, with the passive submission of a weak character (vs. 15-18). He would submit to the will of God, but would not rouse himself to do it.

When Samuel grew up, it was recognized through all Israel that the word of the Lord was being revealed through him, and that he had been established as a prophet of the Lord (vs. 19-22). He was the first of the official prophets, who from this time continued in a long line of succession till the end of the Old Testament history.

THE REFORMATION IN ISRAEL
(Chs. 4-7)

This section tells of the great calamity that fell upon Israel in the Philistine war and brought the predicted judgment upon Eli's house, and of the subsequent reformation in the nation under Samuel's leadership.

1. The Loss of the Ark (Ch. 4). In a war with the Philistines, the Israelites had the Ark brought into their camp from Shiloh, thus revealing a mere carnal confidence instead of a spiritual trust in God (vs. 1-4). The result was a disastrous defeat, the capture of the Ark, and the death of Eli's sons who had come with it (vs. 5-11). The tragic news carried to Shiloh brought about the death of the aged high priest after a judgeship of forty years. The name given to his grandchild, who was born at the time, marked the significance of the tragedy (vs. 12-22). The destruction of Shiloh is referred to in Psa. 78:59-64, Jer. 7:12 and 26:9.

These events belonged to the Philistine oppression of Samson's time, which was still going on, for it lasted forty years (Jud. 13:1). Samson's judgeship had lasted half that time (Jud. 15:20; 16:31). It probably coincided with the last twenty years of Eli's judgeship at Shiloh, which would be the first twenty years of the oppression.

2. The Return of the Ark (Chs. 5-6). The Philistines placed the Ark in one of their temples, and learned that their God was powerless before the Lord God of Israel (5:1-5). They were also smitten with a great plague, which followed them when the Ark was sent from city to city among them (5:6-12). After seven months, the Philistines put it on a new cart drawn by two milch cows to see if it would return to its own territory. They did this as a supernatural test. If cows unaccustomed to the yoke drew the cart quietly, lowing as they went, deserting their calves, and without human guidance went straight to the nearest Israelite town, the conclusion must be that they were controlled by the God of Israel. And thus it happened (6:1-18).

But the Israelites, too, must be taught to reverence the holy symbol of the divine Presence; and the desecration of the men of Beth-shemesh was severely punished (6:19-21). Awed by this stroke

of Divine judgment, they had the Ark removed from among them to Kirjath-jearim, where it remained for twenty years (7:1-2). This period would coincide with the second half of the Philistine oppression.

NOTE: The statement in v. 19 that more than fifty thousand of the men of Beth-shemesh were slain presents a great difficulty, and that for two reasons. Such a punishment seems inconsistent with the character of God, and the population of Beth-shemesh could not have been as large as that number indicates. There is an unusual construction in the original Hebrew, which may be read as follows: "He smote of the people seventy men, fifty a thousand men". There is no "and" between the numbers. The most probable explanation of this peculiar expression is that it was intended to mean that seventy men were slain, and that this was done on the basis of fifty out of a thousand men. This would indicate that Beth-shemesh had a population of fourteen hundred.

3. The Nation's Return to God (Ch. 7). One of the greatest reformations in the history of Israel took place under the leadership of Samuel. The various steps in it are significant. It began with a national longing after the Lord (vs. 1-2). Then Samuel called upon them to repent and put away the idolatries they had been practising (vs. 3-4). An assembly of the people was held at Mizpah for national confession and for setting wrongs right among themselves (vs. 5-6).

While this was going on, the Philistines proceeded to make an attack. In the face of the peril, Samuel offered a burnt offering in token of the new consecration of the nation, and prayed to the Lord for them. The answer was a great thunderstorm, which discomfited the Philistines and led to their complete defeat at the hands of the men of Israel (vs. 7-11). Samuel set up a memorial to mark the event, and a period of peace followed (vs. 12-14), during which Samuel continued to act as judge in Israel (vs. 15-17).

THE ORIGIN OF THE KINGDOM
(Chs. 8-12)

The narrative now passes on to Samuel's old age (8:1), and describes the events which led to the appointment of a king and the establishment of the monarchy.

1. Israel's Request for a King (Ch. 8). Samuel's sons, whom he had appointed judges, were perverting justice, and the elders of Israel asked him to appoint a king for them "like all the nations" (vs. 1-5). This request was not wrong in itself, for the instructions given by Moses concerning the Law had made provision for a future king (Deut. 17:14-20). It was its motive and spirit that made it wrong.

Under the judges Israel was being taught to rely upon the Lord God as their unseen King, who raised up deliverers for them when they cried unto Him. They were being trained in faith. God had chosen them to be a people governed directly by Him, unlike the other nations. It was His purpose to teach them that their national life depended on a moral and spiritual order administered by their invisible King. While the misgovernment of Samuel's sons was the occasion for their request for a king "like all the nations", yet its real cause lay deeper. It was a rejection of God's invisible Kingship. Samuel took the matter to the Lord and was told to accede to their request, "for they have not rejected thee, but they have rejected me, that I should not be king over them" (vs. 6-9). Samuel then warned them of what was involved in having a king of this kind (vs. 10-18), but the people persisted and their demand was granted (vs. 19-22).

2. The Appointment of Saul (Chs. 9-10). These chapters contain a circumstantial account of the way Samuel was brought in touch with Saul, and they throw an interesting light upon the civil and religious life of the people at the time. Saul, the choicest young man in Israel in outward appearance, on a search through the country for his father's lost asses, came to consult the seer (9:1-14). Samuel, having been prepared by the Lord for the meeting, honoured him as the guest at a public feast, and then communed with him in his own house (9:15-27).

Next day Samuel anointed Saul privately as the ruler of Israel and gave him three signs, each with its own proper meaning, to assure him that God would be with him (10:1-6). Then he gave him specific directions for his conduct as king (10:7-8). When occasion arose to consult the will of God, he was to go down to Gilgal and wait for Samuel to perform the sacrifice. Gilgal was the religious centre of the nation at this time, and apparently the Tabernacle had been brought there from Shiloh (7:16; 11:14-15). Afterwards the Spirit of the Lord came upon Saul, and all the signs Samuel had announced came to pass (10:9-16). Samuel called the people together at Mizpah, and there Saul was publicly chosen by lot as their king (10:17-27).

3. Saul Confirmed as King (Ch. 11). Saul proved his ability as a leader and warrior by winning a great victory over the Ammonites, who had attacked Jabesh-gilead (vs. 1-11). This silenced all opposition to Saul. Samuel then called the people together at Gilgal, and there Saul was confirmed in the kingship with great rejoicing (vs. 12-15). Israel now had a king after their own heart. The age of the judges was at an end; that of the kings had begun.

4. Samuel's Farewell (Ch. 12). Samuel now solemnly laid down his office as judge (vs. 1-5), and then gave his farewell address to the people. He reviewed "all the righteous acts of Jehovah", from the deliverance of Israel out of Egypt up to the present time, and gave them a solemn warning against forsaking Him (vs. 6-18). He would still continue to exercise the office of prophet and would not cease to pray for them (vs. 19-25). Samuel was the first to apply the title, "Jehovah's anointed", to the king (v. 5), though the term had been used before prophetically in Hannah's song (2:10). This was the origin of the title Messiah applied to the promised Redeemer.

THE FAILURE OF SAUL
(Chs. 13-15)

It is not a history of Saul's reign that we have from now on, but an account of the events that revealed his wrong attitude toward God and led to his rejection. These events took place during a war with the Philistines (chs. 13-14) and a war against the Amalekites (ch. 15). As it was in war Saul had shown his strength, so it was in war he showed his weakness. The secret of his failure was persistence in self-will; he would not follow the will of God. Three qualities of his self-willed character

are revealed by the incidents that are recorded here.

1. His Impatience (Ch. 13). In the face of the peril from the Philistines and the panic that had taken possession of the Israelites (vs. 1-7), Saul could not wait to learn the counsel of God through the prophet Samuel as he had been instructed to do (10:7-8), but showed his impatience and self-assertion by offering the sacrifice himself (vs. 8-9). Samuel, arriving immediately afterwards within the appointed time, pronounced the Divine judgment upon his act. Saul had shown himself unfitted to be the representative of the invisible King. He should not be the founder of the kingdom; the Lord would appoint a man after His own heart (vs. 10-14). Saul's self-willed impatience availed nothing, and devastating raids by the Philistines continued to oppress Israel (vs. 15-23).

2. His Rashness (Ch. 14). Jonathan, Saul's son, performed an exploit of valour against a Philistine garrison (vs. 1-14). What seems to have been an earthquake occurred at the time and caused a terror of the supernatural among the Philistines (v. 15). This led to a battle in which the Israelites completely routed the Philistines (vs. 16-23). Saul was so intent upon his own selfish vengeance that he grudged his men the necessary time for rest and refreshment, and placed a curse upon any man who would stop for a moment to take food (v. 24). This resulted in an innocent transgression on Jonathan's part during the day (vs. 25-30), and the violation of the Law by the people under the stress of hunger at the end of the day (vs. 31-35). When the transgression of the vow was discovered (vs. 36-42), the people rescued Jonathan from Saul's attempt to carry it out to its fatal consequences (vs. 43-46). The chapter closes with a summary of Saul's wars; he was valiant in them all, but he failed to subdue the Philistines (vs. 47-52).

NOTE: The occurrence of the word "ark" in this chapter (v. 18) needs to be explained, for the Ark at this time was not with Israel, but was still in the house of Abinadab at Kirjath-jearim, where it remained till the reign of David (1 Sam. 7:1; 2 Sam. 6:1-3). The Septuagint rendering of this passage reads: "Saul said unto Abijah, Bring hither the ephod. For he wore the ephod in that day before Israel". This doubtless represents the original text. What Saul did was to summon the high priest, who was present "wearing an ephod" (v. 3), to enquire the will of God by means of the Urim and the Thummim for the occasion that had arisen. But when he saw the confusion among the Philistines increasing , he stopped the priest, saying, "Withdraw thy hand", and decided himself what to do. God's displeasure was revealed by His silence when, later on, Saul sought His counsel again (vs. 36-37).

3. His Disobedience (Ch. 15). Saul was commanded to execute the curse long before pronounced upon Amalek (Exod. 17:14-16); but instead of carrying it out fully, he spared the king and the best of the spoil for purposes of self-glorification (vs. 1-9). Samuel met him on his triumphal, vainglorious return journey, exposed his hypocrisy, and pronounced God's judgment upon him. He was now rejected from being king (vs. 10-23). Saul acknowledged his disobedience, but was not so much concerned about his sin against God as about the effect upon the people if Samuel openly disavowed him (vs. 24-31). Samuel himself carried out the judgment upon Agag, and from that day he came no

more to see Saul (vs. 32-35). Saul was no longer king of Israel in God's sight.

THE CHOICE OF DAVID
(Chs. 16-17)

The narrative now proceeds to show how God raised up a man of His own choice who would do His will, and how He prepared him for the kingdom.

1. David Chosen and Anointed (Ch. 16). While Samuel was mourning over the rejection of Saul, he was commanded of the Lord to go to Bethlehem and anoint as king one of the sons of Jesse (vs. 1-5). They were brought before him, and passed by one by one until the youngest was sent for, who had been keeping the sheep (vs. 6-12). David was chosen on a different principle from that on which Saul was chosen—not the outward appearance, but the heart. Samuel immediately anointed him, and from that day forward the Spirit of the Lord came upon David (v. 13).

A providential chain of events now began to prepare him for the throne, the first of which brought him into the court of Saul (vs. 14-23). Fits of melancholy had begun to seize the king, and David, being a skilful player on the harp, was appointed to play before him, and became his armour-bearer.

2. David Tried and Proved (Ch. 17). Another war with the Philistines provided the occasion that revealed the qualities of David's character. The challenge of the giant, Goliath of Gath, had dismayed Saul and the men of Israel (vs. 1-11). Young David, who had been sent by his aged father from his home in Bethlehem to visit his three eldest brothers in the camp, heard the giant's challenge, and enquired why he should be allowed to defy the armies of the living God (vs. 12-30).

Saul heard of David's words and sent for him. The interview brought out David's complete confidence in the Lord and his perfect naturalness. He undertook to fight the Philistine with the simple weapons he had learned to use as a shepherd lad (vs. 31-40). David entered the duel "in the name of Jehovah of hosts", confident of the issue, declaring that "the battle is Jehovah's"; and the disdainful and boasting giant was promptly overthrown. The death of their champion caused a panic among the Philistines, and they fled before the men of Israel (vs. 41-54). When David returned from the battle he was brought again into Saul's court (vs. 55-58). Here he was thrown into the company of Jonathan, and at once Jonathan's love for David began (18:1-2).

NOTE: The account of David's victory over Goliath is recorded in such a circumstantial way that it abounds in repetitions and appears to be inconsistent in some places with the last part of the preceding chapter. The Septuagint omits several parts of it in what seems to be an attempt to make a continuous story. The critical theory that the Hebrew text, from which our version is translated, is a compilation from two contradictory traditions reflects on the intelligence of the compiler and explains nothing. The real question has to do with the purpose of the writer. This event was the turning point in David's life and the first step on his way to the throne. Hence the story is told with such fulness of detail as to show that all the circumstances were overruled by God Himself. It is a peculiar characteristic of Hebrew narrative to pursue a leading idea to its ultimate issues and then go back and fill in the details. Thus the statement in 16:21 that David became Saul's armour-bearer probably refers to the position that David was given in Saul's court after his victory over Goliath.

THE FRIENDSHIP OF DAVID AND JONATHAN
(Chs. 18-20)

At this point David was thrown into the company of Jonathan, whose qualities of high courage and true faith have appeared in the narrative already (13:3; 14:6-7). Other qualities in his character, one of the noblest in all Scripture, are now to be seen in his unselfish and genuine devotion to David. His influence upon David was one of the chief means of refining and enriching the life of the young shepherd and preparing him for the kingdom. The story of Jonathan's love for David is all the more beautiful in being set against the dark background of Saul's jealousy of David. And yet through it all Jonathan never betrayed any disloyalty to his father.

1. Jonathan's Love for David (Ch. 18). The soul of Jonathan went out to David at once when he heard him being interviewed by his father. David was retained in Saul's service and the two young heroes entered into a covenant of friendship. David was given a post of command in Saul's army, and was sent on military expeditions. In all these he "behaved himself wisely", showing prudence and valour and winning the favour of the people (vs. 1-5).

Saul's anger was aroused by the public acclaim given David after his victory over the Philistine, and in a fit of madness he made an attempt on David's life as he was playing before him (vs. 6-11). When he saw that the Lord was with David he regarded him with fear and awe, and all the time David was gaining the affection of the nation (vs. 12-16).

Saul had promised to give his daughter to the man who would defeat Goliath (17:25), and now he proceeded to fulfil this promise with a crafty hope that making David his son-in-law would increase the chances of his death at the hands of the Philistines. David in his humility shrank from Saul's offer, but finally married his younger daughter Michal (vs. 17-27). In all the engagements with the Philistines David was the most successful of all Saul's servants, and his reputation kept growing (vs. 28-30).

2. Saul's Enmity to David (Ch. 19). Saul's fear of David at last settled into deadly enmity, and he gave orders to slay David. Jonathan warned David to hide himself while he interceded with his father on his friend's behalf. He succeeded by his earnest appeal in changing Saul's mind for the time being (vs. 1-7). But another great defeat which David inflicted upon the Philistines excited Saul to such a pitch of madness that he made another attempt on David's life. David had been playing before the king and at once slipped out of his presence. Saul sent messengers to his house to slay him there, but Michal saved her husband from them (vs. 8-17).

Then David fled to Samuel at Ramah and reported all that Saul had done. Samuel had established a school of the prophets there, and David dwelt with Samuel in the buildings which they occupied. (This is the meaning of the word, "Naioth"). When Saul heard that David was there he sent messengers to fetch him, but when they arrived and saw the company of prophets with Samuel at their head the spirit of prophecy took possession of them. When Saul was told of it he sent two other bands of messengers one after the other, and the same thing happened to them. Then Saul went himself and was seized and overcome by the spirit of prophecy so completely that he lay prostrate all day and all night (vs. 18-24). This experience should have taught Saul that in raging against David he was fighting against the Lord. But Saul went on hardening his heart against the Spirit of God.

3. David's Parting from Jonathan (Ch. 20). After that David left the school of the prophets and went to Jonathan and poured out his heart to his friend. He asked him why his father sought his life, and implored him to find out his father's intention at a feast of the new moon which Saul was to hold next day (vs. 1-10). The two friends went out into the open country to escape observation. Jonathan first renewed his covenant with David and then fixed upon a sign by which he would let David know the state of his father's mind (vs. 11-23).

When the new moon came David remained hidden in the open country and Jonathan made an apology for his absence from the king's table. Saul was so enraged by it that he hurled his spear at his son. When Jonathan saw that his father was resolved to put David to death he left the table in anger and grief (vs. 24-34). Next morning Jonathan went out into the country and let David know what had occurred by the sign agreed upon. Then the two friends had an affectionate meeting and farewell. They pledged themselves to each other in the name of the Lord, and then parted—David going away as a fugitive and Jonathan going back to his father's court (vs. 35-42).

SAUL'S PERSECUTION OF DAVID
(Chs. 21-27)

David now passed through a long period of discipline and trial at the hand of Saul. These experiences drew out his faith and patience, ripened his inner life, and helped to prepare him for his life-work as king. In the midst of this period, the aged prophet Samuel died (25:1), and David was thrown more than ever upon God alone. All this time David maintained his characteristic life-principle of seeking and following the will of the Lord (23:2, 9).

1. David as an Outlaw (Chs. 21-22). He sought refuge from Saul, first with Abimelech the high priest at Nob, where the Tabernacle was at the time (21:1-9), then with Achish the king of Gath (21:10-15). In the cave of Adullam he became the head of a body of men who gathered about him because of the distress which Saul's reign had caused among the people (22:1-2).

From there David took his parents over to the king of Moab, and then came back to the land of Judah (22:3-5). In the meantime Saul had been told by Doeg the Edomite, an enemy of David, how he had been received at Nob; and Saul had Abimelech and the priests slaughtered and Nob destroyed (22:6-19). Abiathar, one of Abimelech's sons, escaped and joined himself to David (22:20-23). He had taken the ephod with him, and David recognized him thereafter as the high priest (23:9).

2. David as a Freebooter (Chs. 23-25). David's great capacity for leadership was developed by the very situation into which Saul's persecution threw him. His band of men grew from four hundred to six hundred (23:13; 27:2; 30:9), and he used them for the protection of the cities of Judah against their foes and not for plunder, while all the time Saul kept on seeking his life.

We find him at Keilah, delivering it from the Philistines (23:1-13); in the wilderness of Ziph, where he and Jonathan met for the last time (23:14-29); in the wilderness of En-gedi, where David by a chance happening had Saul in his power but restrained his men from slaying him (ch. 24). The story of Nabal and Abigail (ch. 25) shows that David and his men were exerting a powerful influence, and that the devout and God-fearing people in Israel believed that David was the Lord's anointed on whom the kingdom should devolve.

3. David as a Man of Faith (Chs. 26-27). Still another experience of betrayal and persecution awaited David, another trial of his faith. He had come into the wilderness of Ziph again, and the Ziphites informed Saul, who at once went after him with three thousand men (26:1-5). David and his nephew Abishai stole into the camp by night and found Saul and all his men asleep. For the second time David had Saul in his power, and again he was presented with the tempting and plausible argument that God had thus delivered his enemy into his hand. But again he refused to take things into his own hand and serve his own interest by doing what he knew to be wrong; he left Saul's fate in the hands of the Lord (26:6-12).

David possessed that deep and patient faith which not only trusts in God's help, but also waits on God's time. By his subsequent actions that night he convinced Saul that he had spared his life, and moved Saul for the moment to acknowledge his folly (26:13-25). This was the last meeting of the two men. When David realized that it made no change in Saul's attitude toward him, his faith seemed to falter, and he went over among the Philistines out of Saul's reach altogether (27:1-4). Then he was given Ziklag to dwell in, and from there he made raids upon the foes that lay along the border of Judah (27:5-12).

THE END OF SAUL'S LIFE
(Chs. 28-31)

Saul's self-willed life ended in utter ruin and disaster during a final war with the Philistines (28:1-2), the events of which are recorded in these chapters.

1. Saul and the Witch of Endor (Ch. 28). This incident shows the utter spiritual darkness and despair into which he had sunk (vs. 3-7). The narrative indicates that Samuel really appeared, but that it was not the woman's necromancy that brought him forth, for she herself was startled beyond measure (vs. 8-14). Samuel brought God's last warning to Saul, and only confirmed the judgment already pronounced upon him by announcing the doom that was to fall upon him on the morrow (vs. 15-19). The result upon Saul was utter collapse. The man who had made self-will his rule of life had no power of will left (vs. 20-25).

2. David and the Philistines (Chs. 29-30). David and his men had accompanied the Philistine army in the invasion of the land of Israel, but the princes of the Philistines, distrusting him, had their king send him away (ch. 29). On returning to Ziklag, they found that it had been raided and destroyed

by the Amalekites (30:1-6). After consulting the mind of the Lord through Abiathar the high priest, David pursued the band of raiders with four hundred of his men, leaving two hundred behind (30: 7-10). He overtook them, scattered and destroyed them, and recovered all the captives and the spoil (30:11-20).

It was characteristic of David that he had the spoil divided with those who had been left behind on a principle of equality; and that became a law in Israel (30:21-25). He also distributed some of the spoil among the elders of the various cities in Judah that had sheltered and befriended him during his wanderings (30:26-31).

3. The Death of Saul (Ch. 31). Only a single verse is given to the battle of Gilboa; the narrative is concerned with the tragic death of Saul, which also involved the fate of the sons who had been faithful to him to the end (vs. 1-7). The gratitude which he had inspired among the inhabitants of Jabesh-gilead at the beginning of his reign by his relief of the city from the Ammonites (ch. 11), now led them to rescue the bodies of Saul and his sons and give their bones a respectful burial (vs. 8-13).

* * * *

THE GREAT FIGURES OF THE TRANSITION PERIOD

Three great figures stand out in the story of First Samuel, each of whom had special significance at this stage of Israel's history.

Samuel: He was the last of the judges, and the first of the prophets to be generally recognized by the nation (3:20). Hence it may be said that he established the prophetic office in Israel. The line of prophets, called of God to that office, continued from Samuel's time to the end of the Old Testament age. He founded the schools of the prophets, which appear in this book for the first time (10:5, 10-11; 19:20-21; cf. 2 Kings 2:3, 5, 7; 4:38; 6:1). The child of many prayers (1:10-11, 20, 27), Samuel lived a life of prayer and was known as a man of prayer (7:5, 8-9; 8:6; 12:19, 23; 15:11). This was the secret of his character and the source of his power and influence. He had no new truth to declare and no light to throw on old truths. His office was to preserve the truth taught by Moses, and to be God's representative in the last stage of the theocracy.

Saul: He was the kind of king the people asked for, who wanted Israel to be like the nations around them (8:4-5, 19-20). No more suitable man could have been chosen according to their standards. He had a commanding outward appearance (9:2; 10: 23), and he was a valiant soldier and an able leader in war (11:11). His character had elements of modesty (9:21; 10:21-22) and generosity (11:12-13). The secret of his failure was his persistent self-will. This brought on deterioration in his character and confusion in his kingdom. The tragedy of his life was all the greater because he dragged his loyal and noble-hearted son Jonathan in his own ruin.

David: He was the kind of man the Lord chose to found the kingdom of Israel, a man after God's own heart (13:14). He trusted God fully. That part of his history which is contained in First Samuel shows how God was training and preparing him for his life-work as king. The various elements in this training may be summed up as follows: (1) His boyhood as a shepherd lad. (2) His experience in the court of Saul. (3) His friendship with Jonathan. (4) His association with Samuel. (5) His exile and persecution at the hand of Saul. Instead of self-will as in Saul's case, the will of God was the ruling motive in David's life (Acts 13:22, 36). He was being prepared for the throne by learning to follow the will of God and not his own will through a long course of discipline and under all sorts of circumstances.

THE SECOND BOOK OF SAMUEL

THIS book contains the story of David's reign. It follows First Samuel without a break in the narrative. In First Samuel David was being prepared for the kingdom; in Second Samuel he is ruling upon the throne. The book does not give a complete history or a chronological account of the time. Much of the forty years of his reign is passed over in silence, and the events that are recorded do not all come in chronological order. It is not so much David's reign as King David himself that is the theme of the book.

David is one of the most important characters in the Bible. He stands with Abraham and Moses as one of the three pre-eminent figures in the Old Testament. Each of these men occupies a unique place. Through Abraham the covenant of grace was established. Through Moses the Law was introduced. Through David the Messianic kingdom was promised, in which both the covenant of grace and the Law were to be fulfilled. David is thus closely connected with the Lord Jesus Christ.

The book is in three main parts. The first part (Chs. 1-9) deals with David's rule as king, and gives the main features of his reign. The second part (Chs. 10-20) deals with his fall, and tells the story of his great sin and its tragic consequences. The third part (Chs. 21-24) records some of his acts, illustrating the theocratic character of his reign. From this we get the following outline:

DAVID KING OVER JUDAH
(Chs. 1-4)

The events recorded in the first main division of the book (Chs. 1-9) reveal the kingly qualities of David's character, and set forth the significance of his reign in the progress and development of God's purpose with Israel. After Saul's death the tribe of Judah anointed David king at Hebron, and he reigned there seven years and six months (2:11). The first four chapters cover these years, and the incidents they record bring out David's magnanimity.

1. His Grief over Saul and Jonathan (Ch. 1). When the news of their death was brought to him (vs. 1-10), the sorrow he showed was genuine (vs. 11-16). Its depth and sincerity are manifest in the lamentation he subsequently composed over them, which contains a very tender reference to the friendship between himself and Jonathan (vs. 17-27).

2. Made King in Hebron (Ch. 2). David's characteristic principle of life is manifested in his first act; he sought to know the Lord's will before taking any step (v. 1). When he went up to Hebron the men of Judah came, and there they made him their king (vs. 2-4). His large-hearted and sympathetic nature is revealed in the message he sent to the men of Jabesh-gilead, who had buried Saul (vs. 4-7).

The northern tribes, under the leadership of Abner, Saul's general, adhered to the house of Saul, and, apparently after some time had elapsed, made his son Ishbosheth their king (vs. 8-11). This brought on a conflict at Gibeon between a band of men under Abner and a band under Joab, David's general, in which Abner, though defeated, slew Asahel, Joab's younger brother, who had persisted in pursuing him after the battle (vs. 12-32).

3. Civil War in the Land (Chs. 3-4).A long war ensued between the house of Saul and the house of David, in the course of which Ishbosheth accused Abner of ambitious designs (3:1-11). Indignant at the charge, Abner sought to make a league with David, who demanded first the return of Michal his wife (3:12-16). He used his powerful influence with the elders of Israel, and was arranging with David at Hebron to bring them over to him, when he was treacherously slain by Joab in revenge for the death of Asahel (3:17-27). The grief and distress which David expressed over the murder of Abner was so manifestly genuine that it brought him still greater favour with the people (3:28-39).

After a reign of two years (2:10), Ishbosheth, Saul's son, was treacherously slain by two of his captains, who thought to win David's favour thereby (4:1-8); but David had them at once put to death (4:9-12).

DAVID KING OVER ALL ISRAEL
(Chs. 5-9)

David had made no attempt to force himself upon the other tribes, but waited on God to bring him to the throne of Israel. He had so commended himself to the people since the tribe of Judah had made him king that at last all the tribes of Israel came to David at Hebron. He made a covenant with them, and was anointed king of the whole nation. His reign continued for thirty-three years more (5:1-5). This section traces the growth of his kingdom and shows its real greatness.

1. Making Jerusalem his Capital (Ch. 5). David's wisdom and statesmanship were shown in choosing his capital. He captured the stronghold of Zion, which is mentioned here for the first time, and established his house and family in Jerusalem (vs. 6-16). He defeated the Philistines, who came up twice against him when they heard that he had been made king (vs. 17-25). David followed the same principle in his reign over Israel as in his reign over Judah; when some action had to be taken he first "enquired of Jehovah" (vs. 19, 23). He was founding his throne upon the will of God.

2. Making Jerusalem the Centre of Worship (Ch. 6). David now proceeded to make Jerusalem the religious centre for the nation by bringing up the Ark. The failure of the first attempt taught David a lesson: reverence was due to the symbol of the Divine Presence (vs. 1-11). After three months it was brought into the city of David, with manifestations of great rejoicing, in which the king took part (vs. 12-19). Michal, Saul's daughter, revealed her utter lack of sympathy with David's religious enthusiasm, and was justly punished by him (vs. 20-23).

3. Planning for a Temple (Ch. 7). When his wars were done, David planned to build a temple for the Ark of the Lord, and Nathan the prophet at first commended him for it (vs. 1-3). Afterwards the Lord sent a message through Nathan, telling the king that he was not the chosen instrument for this purpose (vs. 4-7). The Lord had raised him up to be ruler of His people, and would make his name great and establish his house (vs. 8-11). After David's death the Lord would set up his son and establish his kingdom; and his son should build a house for the Lord. Through him David's house and throne should be established for ever (vs. 12-17).

The separate details of this promise show that it was related primarily to Solomon, and had a certain fulfilment in him and his reign; but that it pointed beyond his time to the eternal continuance of David's posterity in Jesus Christ, and, beyond the earthly temple which Solomon was to build, to the spiritual temple of the Church which Christ would build (John 2:19; Eph. 2:19-22; 1 Tim. 3:15; 1 Pet. 2:5).

David accepted this message by going in before the Ark and offering a humble prayer of thanksgiving and praise (vs. 18-29). His prayer is recorded at length, and it shows that the Lord's promise had made a profound impression upon him. He evidently understood it as giving his house and his throne a peculiar place of everlasting continuance in the great purpose of redemption which God was carrying on through the ages.

The language in which David expressed his wonder at God's great goodness to him contains a remarkable utterance: "And this too after the manner of men, O Lord Jehovah?" (v. 19). The marginal reading is, "And is this the law of man, O Lord Jehovah?" Literally the words are: "And this the law of the man". No explanation of this obscure passage can account for the depth of feeling in David's heart which does not see here a reference to the coming Redeemer, the promised Messiah. The parallel passage in 1 Chron. 17:17 is also obscure, but it has the same implication. It may be rendered: "Thou hast looked upon me according to the order of the man that is from above", that is, "the man that is to come".

4. David's Conquests (Ch. 8). A summary of his various conquests is now given. His enemies were subdued on every side, and the borders of the kingdom were extended (vs. 1-14). The kingdom of Israel, which had fallen into confusion under Saul, was fully established under David. Twice the statement is made: "Jehovah gave victory to David whithersoever he went". The chapter closes with a list of his officers of state (vs. 15-18).

5. His Kindness to Jonathan's Son (Ch. 9). Success had not spoiled David, nor injured the tender qualities of his spirit. He enquired if any of Saul's house were left; and learning of Mephibosheth, a cripple, he restored Saul's lands to him and gave him an honoured place at his own table.

DAVID'S SIN AND REPENTANCE
(Chs. 10-12)

The Bible does not conceal or excuse the sins of its great men, even in the case of the man after God's own heart. It always paints sin in its true colours. David had been enjoying unbroken prosperity, and he began to take life more easily. During a war with Ammon, he sent Joab out to battle while he yielded to the indulgence of his palace (11:1). This was the beginning of his downfall.

1. Wars with Ammon and Syria (Ch. 10). David's ambassadors, carrying his greetings to the new king of the Ammonites, were treated with a cowardly insult (vs. 1-5). This brought on a war in which the Ammonites secured the help of the Syrians. Joab defeated the allied armies and drove the Ammonites into their capital (vs. 6-14), while David proceeded to bring the Syrians into subjection (vs. 15-19).

2. The Great Sin (Ch. 11). In the campaign of the following year, instead of taking his proper place in the field during the siege of the Ammonite capital, David tarried at Jerusalem, relaxed his watchfulness, and failed to enquire of the Lord as he had done in the past. He yielded to self-indulgence, and then there followed in quick succession covetousness, adultery, treachery, hypocrisy, and murder.

3. The Genuine Repentance (Ch. 12). The prophet Nathan, sent by the Lord to reprove David, brought his sin before him by means of a parable, and announced that it should have a series of dire consequences in his kingdom (vs. 1-12). David repented at once and acknowledged his sin. In this he differed from Saul, who stubbornly refused the Lord's correction. He sinned grievously, but he repented sincerely. His sin was at once forgiven, but its consequences were still to follow (vs. 13-14).

David's ready acceptance of the stroke by which God refused to answer his prayer regarding Bathsheba's child, shows both the sincerity of his repentance and the depth of his faith (vs. 15-23). This is followed by the record of the birth of Solomon, which was a token of David's restoration to the Lord's favour (vs. 24-25). In the meantime a message from Joab, implying a rebuke for his self-indulgence, called David to the field to complete the subjugation of the Ammonites (vs. 26-31). The last verse describes the kind of slavery under which David put the inhabitants of the city. He set them to work with saws and harrows of iron and axes of iron, and made them labour at brick-making.

SIN AND CRIME AMONG DAVID'S SONS
(Chs. 13-14)

Here begin the consequences of David's sin. The same sins he had committed reappear in his own family. Amnon's sin against Tamar, Absalom's sister (13:1-22), was followed by Absalom's murder of Amnon and his exile (13:23-39). Joab resorted to a device to secure Absalom's recall to Jerusalem (14:1-24), and, after two years, his reconciliation with the king (14:25-33).

Signs of weakness in David's character appear in the course of these incidents. When he learned of Amnon's sin he was wroth, but that was all. When he heard of Amnon's murder he was overcome, but made no attempt to punish Absalom or bring him to justice. He received Absalom back into favour with no sign of repentance on the part of the murderer.

NOTE: The meaning of 13:39 is obscure. The Septuagint reads: "King David desisted from going forth against Absalom". This is more consistent with the context and with the circumstances, and is probably the real meaning of the passage. David ought to have arrested and punished Absalom at once, but Absalom's flight made this difficult. Then as time went by, "David was comforted concerning Amnon". In accordance with this, the more probable meaning of 14:1 is that Joab perceived that "the king's heart was against Absalom". Otherwise his stratagem to obtain the fugitive's recall would have been unnecessary. Joab seems to have repeatedly interceded for Absalom (14:19-22).

THE REBELLION OF ABSALOM
(Chs. 15-18)

The consequences of David's sin reached their culmination in the temporary loss of his throne as a result of the rebellion of his own son. Both the weakness and the strength of his character are manifested in this story. No event in the Bible, except the crucifixion of Christ, is recorded with so much detail as is found here.

1. Absalom's Conspiracy (15:1-12). For four years he plotted with unscrupulous cunning to draw away the allegiance of the people from David to himself. Then he withdrew to Hebron on the pretext of paying a vow, and sent spies throughout all the tribes to be ready to proclaim him king. Ahithophel, the wisest of David's counsellors, was involved in the conspiracy.

2. David's Flight (15:13 - 16:14). These are the most pathetic scenes in all David's history. He went out accompanied by his friends and overwhelmed with sorrow; and yet he showed his faith in God by sending back the priests with the Ark,

and his foresight by sending back Hushai to defeat the counsel of Ahithophel (15:13-37). The cursing and shame heaped upon him by Shimei in the course of his flight was accepted by him as from the chastening hand of God, and he forbade his men to slay Shimei (16:1-14).

3. Absalom in Jerusalem (16:15 - 17:23). He entered the city with all his forces accompanied by Ahithophel, and was received by Hushai. Acting on the counsel of Ahithophel, Absalom established himself publicly in the king's household and in his father's place (16:15-23). Ahithophel urged further that an attack should be made upon David at once, but Hushai persuaded Absalom to reject this counsel as dangerous, for David was now "as a bear robbed of her whelps in the field". Let all Israel be gathered to Absalom first, and then he should lead them to battle himself (17:1-14). Thus Hushai secured time for David to escape over the Jordan; and Ahithophel, seeing his counsel rejected, committed suicide (17:15-23).

4. Absalom's Defeat and Death (17:24 - 18:33). David rallied his forces at Mahanaim, while Absalom gathered the men of Israel and led them over the Jordan into Gilead (17:24-29). David showed his military genius in the way he organized his forces, and his characteristic weakness in urging them, as they went forth into the field, to deal gently with his son (18:1-5). The battle, which spread over the country, came to an end with Absalom's death at the hands of Joab. David's stern and clearsighted general understood the king's weakness too well. He knew that with Absalom put out of the way the rebellion would collapse, and he called his men back from the pursuit (18:6-18).

When news of the victory reached David, he showed concern only for the fate of "the young man Absalom" (18:19-30). The results of his sin reached their culmination, and his sorrow reached its profoundest depth, in his agonizing wail (18:31-33). Five times in the course of it he repeats the words "my son": the father recognizes himself as reproduced in Absalom. And then comes the deepest cry of all: "Would God I had died for thee".

DAVID'S RESTORATION TO THE THRONE
(Chs. 19-20)

Joab reproved David for his excessive grief, which was affecting the spirit of his people, and recalled him to his duty as king (19:1-10). But David showed further weakness, and sowed seeds of later trouble, in secretly appealing to his own tribe of Judah alone to bring him back, and in seeking to displace Joab by the appointment of Amasa who had been Absalom's general (19:11-15). He showed the better side of his character in the way he received Shimei (19:16-23), Mephibosheth (19:24-30), and Barzillai (19:31-39).

The manner of his return caused a dispute between the men of Israel and the men of Judah (19:40-43), which gave occasion for Sheba, a Benjamite, to stir up a rebellion (20:1-3). This was the first attempt to divide the country, and it boded ill for the future. David called upon Amasa to rally the men of Judah; but Amasa delayed in carrying out the order, with the result that Abishai and Joab put down the rebellion; and, during the pursuit of Sheba, Joab treacherously murdered Amasa (20: 4-22). The section closes with a list of David's officers of state after he was restored to the throne (20:23-26).

DAVID'S THEOCRATIC ACTS
(Chs. 21-24)

The account of David's reign really ends with his re-establishment on the throne after the rebellion of Absalom. These chapters form a kind of appendix, intended to illustrate some features of his character and some aspects of his reign. Two incidents, those of the famine (ch. 21) and the pestilence (ch. 24), reveal certain principles of justice and retribution in the government of God, of which the kingdom of David was a type, and to which it was closely related. David's reign was really theocratic; his rule was under the direct government of God.

1. The Avenging of the Gibeonites (21:1-14). A famine which continued for three years led David to ask the Lord for the reason of it. It was because of the blood-guilt that Saul had brought upon the land in violating the covenant made with the Gibeonites in the days of Joshua (Josh 9:15). The nation was held accountable for the acts of its ruler. The crime was expiated by the execution of seven of the sons of Saul at the hands of the Gibeonites. This delay in the punishment of a sin that was committed back in Saul's reign emphasized the continuity of the nation's life and its continued responsibility before God from age to age.

2. David's Heroes (21:15-22). Some exploits are recorded here which David's warriors performed against the Philistines, showing the heroic spirit that he inspired in his men.

3. His Psalm of Praise (Ch. 22). This is the 18th Psalm in the Psalter with some variations. It is David's hymn of thanksgiving to the Lord for giving him victory in war and establishing him upon the throne. Here the deepest things in his character are revealed. The Lord is declared to be the source of all his strength. Everything of value in his life is traced back to God.

4. His Last Words (23:1-7). Following his great hymn comes this testimony of his confidence in the fulfilment of God's promise to him regarding his kingdom (7:12-16). It is a prophetic statement, indicating the spiritual bearing and import of his reign.

5. His Mighty Men (23:8-39). A list of the warriors of David's invincible army and some of their exploits. This passage illustrates one of the elements of his essential greatness. He could attach men to himself by strong personal ties and make heroes of them. He had the great gift of true leadership: he could inspire devotion on the part of his followers.

6. The Numbering of the People (Ch. 24). This was the final mistake of David's reign. He insisted on a census of the people, which Joab carried out under protest. Its motive was pride and vainglory, ambition to found a military monarchy (vs. 1-9). It was trusting in numbers instead of glorying in the Lord. When it was over, David realized his sin in the matter, and made confession and sought forgiveness (v. 10).

The prophet Gad was sent to offer him a choice of three evils as a punishment. David chose the stroke that came most directly from the hand of God, thus showing his faith and his submission to God's chastening (vs. 11-14). The fatal pestilence which swept through the whole land was stayed at the threshing floor of Araunah (vs. 15-17), and, at the command of God, David built an altar there, thus turning an occasion of judgment into one of worship (vs. 18-25).

All this happened because "the anger of Jehovah was kindled against Israel" (v. 1). Some national sin, probably the rebellion of Absalom followed by that of Sheba, was the reason why God allowed David to yield to national ambition and set those hidden forces in motion which bring national retribution. In the parallel account in 1 Chron. 21, Satan is revealed as the active agent inciting David's ambition (v. 1). But the sovereign God overruled it for His own purposes of righteousness and judgment.

* * * *

THE FOUNDER OF THE KINGDOM

This book is occupied entirely with King David. His story is given with a wealth of detail found in the case of no other Old Testament character. David was the national hero, the ideal ruler of Israel, who had no worthy successor except the Messiah Himself.

The qualities of his character which combined to make him so great a king were these: (1) His trust in God. He waited on God's time for coming to the throne. He enquired of God in making his plans and carrying them out. He regarded himself as God's servant, and his office as that of shepherding God's people. (2) His human sympathy. He had a large heart and a many-sided nature. He was tactful and generous in dealing with all kinds of men. He secured the personal devotion of all classes of his people. (3) His sincerity. His motives were not selfish, nor his purposes self-centred. There was no hypocrisy in his actions. His sorrow and grief, his joy and praise, were sincere; and his people knew this. (4) His contrition. After his great sin his repentance was deep and genuine. He accepted without rebellion the chastening judgment of God.

The Scriptures associate David in the closest way with the Lord Jesus Christ. Abraham and David form the two most important links in the ancestry of Jesus (Matt. 1:1). The promise to David regarding his seed (2 Sam. 7:12-16; 1 Chron. 17:11-14) looked forward to Jesus Christ as perpetuating for ever both his house and his throne. David's house was established for ever by the Incarnation, and his throne by the Resurrection and Ascension.

When Jesus was born in the family of David (Luke 1:27; 2:4), "the tabernacle of David", which had fallen down, was thus built again (Acts 15:15-16; Amos 9:11); and his posterity became eternal. The angel who announced the coming birth of Jesus declared that the Lord was to give unto Him the throne of His father David (Luke 1:32-33). On the day of Pentecost, Peter explained the promise about David's throne as having been fulfilled in the exaltation of Jesus Christ to the right hand of God (Acts 2:30-36). The throne of David was not the royal seat on which he sat, but the fundamental and constitutional principle by which he ruled: it was the administration of the will of God. He established his throne upon God's will (Acts 13:22, 36), and not upon his own will as Saul had attempted to do.

Jesus declared that He had come down from Heaven, not to do His own will, but the will of God who sent Him (John 6:36). He carried out this principle throughout His whole earthly life. By His resurrection and ascension to the right hand of God, He has been placed upon the Throne from which the will of God is administered in Heaven and on earth (Matt. 28:18). This was Peter's meaning, and Paul's teaching agrees with it. In 1 Cor. 15, where the Apostle explains the significance of the resurrection of Christ, he refers to His administration of the Kingdom, and declares that He shall continue to reign till all enemies are put under His feet (vs. 24-25). Thus the New Testament teaches that the promise to David has been already fulfilled in the Lord Jesus Christ.

THE FIRST BOOK OF KINGS

THE Books of Kings continue the history of the monarchy begun in the Books of Samuel, and carry it down to the fall and captivity of both the northern and the southern parts of the kingdom. They cover a period of more than four hundred years, from the accession of Solomon just before 1000 B.C. to the fall of Jerusalem in 586 B.C. While they tell the story of the kings of Israel and Judah, their purpose is not to record a complete history of these reigns, but to set forth the great struggle that went on during all this age between loyalty to the Lord on the one hand and apostasy and idolatry on the other. This explains why long periods and important reigns are often passed over with little notice, while other parts of the history are treated with elaborate detail. In First Kings the monarchy is seen in its glory and power; in Second Kings it is seen in its decline and fall.

The First Book of Kings begins with the accession of Solomon and the death of David, and carries the record down to the death of Ahab, under whom the apostasy of Northern Israel came to a head. It may be taken in two equal parts, the first part (Chs. 1-11) dealing with the reign of Solomon, and the second part (Chs. 12-22) with the divided kingdom. Thus we get the following outline:

I. The Reign of Solomon—Chs. 1-11
    1. Its Fair Beginning (Chs. 1-4)
    2. Its Crowning Work (Chs. 5-9)
    3. Its Clouded Close (Chs. 10-11)

II. The Divided Kingdom—Chs. 12-22
  1. The Disruption of the Nation (Chs. 12-16)
  2. The Ministry of Elijah (Chs. 17-22)

THE BEGINNING OF SOLOMON'S REIGN
(Chs. 1-4)

This section begins with an account of the events which led to Solomon being proclaimed king before the death of David, and then goes on to tell how his throne was established and to describe the special features of his reign.

1. Solomon's Accession to the Throne (Ch. 1). When David's strength was failing, Adonijah, a son whom he had always indulged, attempted to seize the throne with the support of Joab and Abiathar (vs. 1-10). Bathsheba and Nathan informed the king of the conspiracy (vs. 11-27), and David showed his old-time energy by issuing a royal command to have Solomon proclaimed and anointed king at once. This was carried out amid great public rejoicing (vs. 28-40). The conspiracy collapsed, and Adonijah, in fear of his life, sought refuge at the altar. Solomon treated him with royal clemency and dismissed him to his house with dignified authority (vs. 41-53).

2. Solomon's Throne Established (Ch. 2). Before his death, David gave a final charge to Solomon regarding the throne (vs. 1-4), together with some special commissions (vs. 5-9). After his death, Solomon was securely established on the throne of his father (vs. 10-12). He showed his royal qualities of fairness and decision in the way he dealt with Adonijah, who was showing further signs of ambition (vs. 13-25); with Abiathar and Joab, who were both involved in the conspiracy (vs. 26-35 and with Shimei, who had shown treachery to David (vs. 36-46). In his acts of judgment there was no vindictive vengeance, and yet no vacillating weakness.

3. Solomon's Gift of Wisdom (Ch. 3). Solomon showed devotion to the Lord early in his reign by a great sacrifice at Gibeon, where the Tabernacle was located at the time. There the Lord appeared to him with a special offer, and Solomon showed true humility in asking to be given the wisdom he needed for the administration of justice and judgment among his people (vs. 1-9). The Lord gave him that in a supreme measure, and riches and honour besides (vs. 10-15). The incident which follows illustrates the kind of wisdom given to Solomon; that intuitive discernment which goes at once to the heart of a matter (vs. 16-28).

4. Solomon's Glory and Greatness (Ch. 4). This chapter describes Solomon's system of government. It names the heads of the various departments of state (vs. 1-6), and the officers who presided over the twelve districts into which the country was divided and made provision for the king's luxurious table (vs. 7-19). It describes the peace and prosperity of the people and the splendour of the court (vs. 20-28), and the wisdom and fame of the king (vs. 29-34).

All this shows how thoroughly Solomon had organized the kingdom and how fully God had made good His promise to David. Now for the first time did Israel enter into full possession and enjoyment of the land promised to Abraham. The literal fulfilment of the outward and earthly promises was a pledge and assurance of the spiritual and heavenly realities of which they were the symbol and type.

THE CROWNING WORK OF HIS REIGN
(Chs. 5-9)

When Solomon's kingdom was established, he turned his attention to David's plan for the Temple of the Lord. These chapters are almost entirely concerned with the carrying out of this purpose, which was the great work of his reign.

1. The Preparation for the Temple (Ch. 5). His first step was to inform David's friend, Hiram king of Tyre, of his purpose to send to him for timber from Lebanon (vs. 1-6). Hiram gladly responded to Solomon's request, and the two kings made a trade league together (vs. 7-12). Solomon raised a levy out of all Israel to carry out the task of preparing the material for the building (vs. 13-18).

2. The Building of the Temple (Ch. 6). The date when the building began is given as 480 years after the exodus from Egypt (v. 1). The Septuagint reading here is 440 years, which would place this important epoch in Israel's history just about 1000 B.C. The chapter contains a general account of the erection of the Temple (vs. 2-10), the Lord's promise to Solomon concerning it (vs. 11-13), and a special description of the inner sanctuary (vs. 14-36).

This was on the same plan as the Tabernacle and was exactly twice its size. The Holy-place was forty cubits long, twenty wide, and twenty high. The Holy-of-holies, called here the Oracle, was twenty cubits every way. The walls, floor, and ceiling of the sanctuary were all overlaid with gold. The time taken to build the house was seven years (vs. 37-38). The process of building went on in impressive silence, fitly foreshadowing the building of its antitype, the spiritual temple (v. 7; Eph. 2:19-22).

3. The Furnishing of the Temple (Ch. 7). The account is interrupted here to tell of the building of Solomon's own house, which took thirteen years (vs. 1-12). Then the chapter goes on to give a graphic and elaborate description of the work of the artificer, Hiram of Tyre, in making the brazen furnishings for the Temple. The two pillars of brass set at the porch (vs. 13-22) were not for the support of the roof, but were probably free-standing columns with cressets at the top for holding fire and giving light. They may have been memorials of the pillar of fire.

The great laver, or "molten sea", stood on twelve oxen (vs. 23-26), and there were also ten smaller lavers of brass set on ten bases, five on each side of the court (vs. 27-39). The casting of all the brazen vessels and their ornaments was done in the plain of the Jordan, and no account was kept of the amount of brass used (vs. 40-47). Solomon had the furniture and the vessels used in the actual sanctuary itself all made of pure gold (vs. 48-51).

4. The Dedication of the Temple (Ch. 8). Solomon assembled the elders and representatives of all Israel for the consecration services in the seventh month. Throughout the ceremonies he acted alone, a type of the true "son of David". The Ark of the Covenant was brought up out of the city of David, and, when it was placed in the innermost shrine, the glory of the Lord filled the house (vs. 1-11). Solomon then blessed the assembled people, and told them that in the erection of the Temple the Lord's promise to David his father had been established (vs. 12-21).

Then followed his prayer of consecration as he stood before the altar with hands spread forth toward heaven (v. 22). For sublimity and comprehensiveness, for humility and faith, it has no parallel in the Old Testament. It is composed of an introduction recognizing the spirituality and omnipresence of God (vs. 23-30), and seven petitions, each heading up in the same repeated appeal: "Then hear thou in heaven thy dwelling place" (vs. 31-53). After his prayer Solomon blessed the assembly of Israel again (vs. 54-61). Then came the offerings and the feast; and the people returned to their homes full of joy and gladness (vs. 62-66). This ceremony, which took place in connection with the Feast of Tabernacles, was the crowning point of Solomon's reign.

5. Subsequent Events (Ch. 9). When Solomon had finished the Temple and his own palace, God appeared to him for the second time and repeated His promise to establish his throne, adding a warning lest he should turn away from the Lord (vs. 1-9). Solomon gave Hiram king of Tyre twenty cities in Galilee for the help he had received from him, but Hiram was not pleased with them (vs. 10-14). He built many cities for different purposes throughout his kingdom by compelling the remnant of the Canaanites left in the land to perform tributary service (vs. 15-25). He built a navy at Ezion-geber on the Red Sea in the land of Edom and got sailors from Hiram to man his ships (vs. 26-28). Throughout this chapter there is a subdued feeling that behind all the material prosperity of Solomon's reign there were elements of weakness and failure.

The Clouded Close of His Reign
(Chs. 10-11)

The increasing wealth and luxury with which Solomon surrounded himself turned his heart away from the Lord at last. His very fame led to his undoing.

1. Worldly Glory (Ch. 10). The widespread fame of Solomon brought a visit from the queen of Sheba in the south of Arabia, who was profoundly impressed by what she saw and heard. The story illustrates the magnificent splendour of the court and the wonderful wisdom of the king (vs. 1-13). It is followed by a more detailed account of the glory of Solomon (vs. 14-29). But it was the glory of this world alone.

2. Moral Failure (Ch. 11). Early in his reign Solomon made an alliance with Egypt and married the daughter of Pharaoh (2:1). Now we are told that he took many foreign wives, and that they turned his heart away from the Lord. He set up the abominations of idolatry as places of worship for his heathen wives (vs. 1-8). "His heart was not perfect with Jehovah his God . . . . He did that which was evil in the sight of Jehovah." The Lord was angry with Solomon for his apostasy, and announced, as a judgment upon him, the rending of his kingdom in the days of his son (vs. 9-13).

This judgment began to operate during his own life-time in a number of adversaries being raised up against him: Hadad the Edomite (vs. 14-22), and Rezon (vs. 23-25), and especially Jeroboam the son of Nebat, who had been one of Solomon's chief workmen. Jeroboam was an Ephraimite, and he had been told by the prophet Ahijah of the Lord's purpose to rend the kingdom of Solomon and give ten tribes to Jeroboam himself (vs. 26-40).

Solomon died after a reign of forty years, which closed in a cloud of God's displeasure (vs. 41-43). The most highly gifted man of Old Testament history in natural ability and worldly opportunity proved a failure in the end. The splendid and stately figure of Solomon, who is almost impersonal in his grandeur and magnificence, stands out in the sacred record as the supreme example of the peril of worldly prosperity and the insufficiency of human wisdom.

The Disruption of the Nation
(Chs. 12-16)

This section gives an account of the rebellion of the ten tribes and the origin of the northern kingdom of Israel, and then traces the results of this event in the corruption of the state down to the beginning of the reign of Ahab, a period of about sixty years.

1. The Rebellion of Jeroboam (12:1-24). Its immediate cause was the folly of the new king, Rehoboam, in taking the advice of the companions of his youth and rejecting that of the older and wiser men, and thus refusing the request of Jeroboam and the men of Israel to lighten the burdens imposed upon them in his father's reign (vs. 1-15). Behind it as a further cause was the long-standing jealousy of the northern tribes, especially Ephraim, over the rise and prominence of Judah. They rebelled against Rehoboam with the cry, "What portion have we in David?", and sent for Jeroboam to be their king (vs. 16-20). It was the Lord's way of carrying out the judgment He had foretold through Ahijah the Shilonite (v. 15). Rehoboam was forbidden of God through another prophet to fight against his brethren of Israel (vs. 21-24). From this time on the name "Israel" usually refers to the northern kingdom to distinguish it from the southern kingdom to which the name "Judah" is given.

2. The Sin of Jeroboam (12:25 - 13:34). This consisted in setting up high places at Bethel and Dan with a golden calf in each of them as an object of worship. He may have got the idea in Egypt where he spent some time after fleeing from Solomon (1 Kings 11:40), for calf worship prevailed there. His purpose was to keep the people of Northern Israel from going up to the Temple at Jerusalem at the stated feasts, and to make worship easy for them (12:25-33). Perhaps he did not intend to set up actual idolatry at once, but he abandoned the appointed way of approach to God with its significant symbolism, and established another "devised of his own heart". From this time he is described as, "Jeroboam the son of Nebat who made Israel to sin". All his successors followed in his steps, and Israel never returned to the house of the Lord in Jerusalem.

A warning of Divine judgment was sent him through a man of God from Judah as he was engaged in an act of worship at Bethel (13:1-10). The confusion introduced into the religious life of the nation by the disruption is revealed in the way this unnamed prophet was deceived by an old prophet of Bethel, and met his death through disobeying the instructions of the Lord on his way back to Judah (13:11-32). The warning failed to have an effect upon Jeroboam, for he went on in his evil way (13:33-34).

3. Warnings of National Judgment (Ch. 14). This chapter completes the account of Jeroboam's reign in Israel (vs. 1-20) and Rehoboam's in Judah (vs. 21-31). The sickness and death of Jeroboam's

son was the beginning of judgment upon his house. Judah also was turning away from the Lord into gross idolatry and sin, and Shishak's capture of Jerusalem and plunder of the Temple gave a warning to that kingdom.

4. The Course of National Apostasy (Chs. 15-16). These chapters cover the reigns of Abijam and Asa in Judah (15:1-24), and of Nadab, Baasha, Elah, Zimri, Tibni, and Omri in Israel (15:25 - 16:28), and carry the story down into the reign of Ahab (16:29-34). It was a dark period, filled with continual war between the two kingdoms, constant revolution and bloodshed in Northern Israel, and deepening apostasy until Ahab's marriage with Jezebel, the daughter of the king of the Sidonians, led to the vile worship of Baal being set up in Samaria, the new city which had been founded by Omri as the capital of the kingdom. It is declared that Ahab "did evil in the sight of Jehovah above all that were before him", and "did more to provoke Jehovah, the God of Israel, to anger than all the kings of Israel that were before him".

During his long reign of forty-one years in Judah, the good king Asa saw no fewer than eight kings of four rival dynasties on the throne of Israel, most of whom were military adventurers reaching the throne by the murder of their predecessors. There was a remnant in Jerusalem loyal to the Divine government (15:4), and this remnant held in check the development of evil in the southern kingdom (cf. 2 Kings 8:19).

THE MINISTRY OF ELIJAH
(Chs. 17-22)

In the midst of the darkest period of Israel's apostasy, the grand and rugged figure of the prophet Elijah suddenly appeared upon the scene. His mission was to rouse the nation from its sin and seek to bring it back to God. His character is revealed in the characteristic expression with which he made his prophetic announcements: "As Jehovah, the God of Israel, liveth, before whom I stand" (17:1; 18:10, 15). From this point onward the prophetic order holds the most important place in God's government of the nation.

1. The Great Drought (Ch. 17). The prophet's sudden appearance and dramatic announcement in the court of Ahab (v. 1) followed a period of fervent prayer on his part (Jas. 5:17), that the Lord would vindicate His own honour in the eyes of the nation by withholding the rain in fulfilment of the warning given in the Law (Deut. 11:13-17). During the drought the Lord provided for His servant, first in the solitude of the brook Cherith where he was daily dependent upon God (vs. 2-7), and then in the home of a poor widow at Zarephath, whose daily bread he shared and miraculously maintained, and whose son he restored to life (vs. 8-24).

2. The Contest on Carmel (Ch. 18). After three years Elijah suddenly reappeared and commanded Ahab to summon the prophets of Baal to Mount Carmel (vs. 1-19). Then there occurred one of the grandest and most spectacular scenes in Old Testament history. The story makes the false religious frenzy of the heathen prophets stand out in striking contrast with the calm, confident faith of Elijah. The Lord was triumphantly manifested in the fire that consumed the prophet's sacrifice (vs. 20-40). After this the rain came in answer to his prayer (Jas. 5:18), and he outran Ahab's chariot across the plain to Jezreel, a distance of about ten miles (vs. 41-46).

3. Elijah's Discouragement (Ch. 19). When Jezebel threatened his life, Elijah's faith and courage faltered under the great physical and spiritual strain through which he had passed, and he fled south to Beersheba, where he was strengthened by an angel, and on to Mount Horeb where the covenant of the Law, now broken by the people, had been given (vs. 1-8). There he received a fresh revelation from God, showing him that the destructive forces of judgment represented by the wind, the earthquake, and the fire were only preliminary to the real work of the Lord which was done by the gentle, silent ministry of the Spirit (vs. 9-14). He was sent back with a new commission, which indicated that judgment was still to continue; and he began to carry it out by calling Elisha as his servant and successor (vs. 15-21).

4. Ahab's Further Failure (Ch. 20). Ben-hadad, king of Syria, invaded Israel two years in succession, and on both occasions God gave the Israelites a remarkable victory. This was an opportunity for Ahab to manifest loyalty to the Lord, for he had received encouragement and warning from one of the prophets, who had told him on each occasion that the Lord would deliver the Syrians into his hand (vs. 1-30). But he failed again. Yielding to vanity, Ahab made an alliance with the man whom the Lord had devoted to destruction and put into his power for that purpose. For this disobedience his doom was announced by another unnamed prophet (vs. 31-43).

5. The Doom of the House of Ahab (Chs. 21-22). The story of Ahab's crime against Naboth brings out the utter selfishness of his character and the childish petulance of his behaviour (21:1-16). It brought Elijah again upon the scene, with the stern announcement of God's judgment upon the king and his whole house (21:17-26). The Divine mercy, which sought to follow Ahab all along, accepted his show of repentance and postponed the judgment beyond his reign (21:27-29).

Three years afterwards, in a new war with Syria, upon which Ahab entered for the recovery of Ramoth-gilead and in which he got the alliance of Jehoshaphat king of Judah (22:1-4), he showed his craving for the flattery of the false prophets and his unwillingness to consult a true prophet of the Lord (22:5-12). The baseness of his character was revealed in his mean treatment of the prophet Michaiah (22:13-28), and in his cowardly action toward his ally Jehoshaphat (22:29-33). Ahab went to his doom as Elijah had foretold (22:34-40), and Jehoshaphat went back to continue his righteous reign over Judah (22:41-53).

Throughout these chapters there is evidence that during Ahab's reign there were many faithful prophets and followers of the Lord in the land besides Elijah (18:3-4; 19:18; 20:13, 22, 35; 22:7-8). God has never left himself without witnesses, even in the darkest times.

```
┌─────────────────────────┐
│                         │
└─── THE SECOND BOOK OF KINGS ───
```

THE First Book of Kings ends with Ahab's son on the throne of Israel, continuing in the sins and apostasy of his father. The Second Book takes up the story and carries it down to the overthrow of the two kingdoms and the captivity of the entire nation. It is a story of national failure and Divine judgment. The great military empires of the age, Assyria and Babylon, were the instruments used of God in the chastisement of His chosen people. The northern kingdom was the first to fall, being destroyed by Assyria in 721 B.C. The southern kingdom fell finally at the hands of Babylon in 586 B.C.

Second Kings may be taken in three parts. The progress of apostasy and judgment was arrested for a time during the ministry of Elisha, which occupies the first part of the book (Chs. 1-10). The second part (Chs. 11-17) tells the story of the decline and fall of Israel, while carrying on the history of Judah also. The third part (Chs. 18-25) continues the story of Judah alone, and tells of its decline and fall. This gives us the following outline:

   I. The Ministry of Elisha—Chs. 1-10
      1. Elisha Succeeding Elijah (Chs. 1-2)
      2. Elisha's Beneficent Acts (Chs. 3-7)
      3. The Acts of Hazael and Jehu (Chs. 8-10)
  II. The Downfall of Israel—Chs. 11-17
      1. Reformation in Judah (Chs. 11-12)
      2. Iniquity in Israel (Chs. 13-15)
      3. The Assyrian Captivity (Chs. 16-17)
III. The Downfall of Judah—Chs. 18-25
      1. The Reign of Hezekiah (Chs. 18-20)
      2. The Reforms of Josiah (Chs. 21-23)
      3. The Babylonian Captivity (Chs. 24-25)

ELISHA SUCCEEDING ELIJAH
(Chs. 1-2)

Elisha continued the work which Elijah had begun, but carried it on in a different way. He lived and moved among the people and was in closer touch with the common life of Israel than Elijah had been. He was the prophet of mercy and grace, while Elijah had been the prophet of warning and judgment. As Elijah foreshadowed John the Baptist, so Elisha's work foreshadowed the ministry of Him who went about doing good. He must have continued in the prophetic office for about half a century.

1. The Last Acts of Elijah (Ch. 1). They were in keeping with his whole ministry. Ahaziah, the son of Ahab, had ignored the God of Israel by sending messengers to enquire of the Philistine god of Ekron in his sickness. Elijah met them with a message from the Lord that the king would surely die (vs. 1-8). Ahaziah went on to challenge the Lord by sending three captains in succession, each with a band of fifty soldiers, to arrest Elijah. The prophet called down fire from heaven upon the first two captains and their bands, but when the third approached Elijah with due reverence, he went with him and announced the Divine judgment to the king himself; and it was soon fulfilled (vs. 9-18). It was not because of any moral guilt on the part of the captains and their bands that they were destroyed, but because they were instruments of a will which opposed the will of the Lord.

2. The Translation of Elijah (2:1-14). The whole prophetic order was evidently aware that the removal of Elijah was about to take place in some supernatural way, as he made a farewell visit to one after another of the schools of the prophets over which he seems to have presided. Elisha persisted in accompanying his master till they passed over the Jordan, and then he requested a double portion of his spirit, that is, the portion of the first-born among the sons of the prophets, twice as great a share as any of the rest received. Elijah promised him this if Elisha should see him when he was taken from him into the unseen. And so it happened. Elijah was caught up into heaven in a way that was invisible to the common eyes of the sons of the prophets, but was visible to Elisha, who cried out as his master disappeared: "My father, my father, the chariots of Israel and the horsemen thereof". Thus he expressed what Elijah had been to the nation.

3. The First Acts of Elisha (2:15-25). When the sons of the prophets saw Elisha come back, dividing the waters of the Jordan as Elijah himself had done, they knew that the spirit of his master now rested upon him, and they recognized him at once as their head (vs. 15-18). The opening of his prophetic ministry was signalized by two miraculous acts, one of mercy (vs. 19-22), and the other of judgment (vs. 23-25). The "young lads" (not "little children", A.V.) on whom he invoked a curse showed a pagan irreverence towards the Lord God of Israel in their mockery of the prophet. They were old enough to be aware of the wickedness of their conduct. They reflected the apostate spirit of the nation.

ELISHA'S BENEFICENT ACTS
(Chs. 3-7)

Elisha's ministry was in many respects a striking contrast to Elijah's. Instead of appearing suddenly at critical moments with announcements of judgment, he moved up and down throughout the land, doing good and bringing blessing wherever he went. He was at the head of the schools of the prophets, and stood for the righteousness and honour of God against the wickedness and idolatry of the king. His influence overflowed the limits of Israel and extended into Syria.

Elisha's ministry was marked by an abundance of miracles, for it was a time of crisis in the history of Israel. Most of them were acts of mercy and helpfulness. The purpose of his prophetic office was to show that the Lord God of Israel was the living and true God, always able to help and save His people. The present section is composed mainly of a continuous series of Elisha's acts, comprising both public events and private and personal incidents.

The list is as follows: Providing abundance of water during a war against Moab and securing the defeat of the Moabites (ch. 3). Increasing the poor widow's supply of oil (4:1-7). Restoring the Shunammite's son to life (4:8-37). Healing the poisonous pottage and multiplying the loaves (4:38-44). Curing Naaman the Syrian general of leprosy, and smiting Gehazi, his own servant, with it (ch. 5). Recovering the axehead from the waters of the Jordan for one of the sons of the prophets (6:1-7).

Smiting the invading Syrians with temporary blindness (6:8-23).

A siege of Samaria by the Syrians had brought about a terrible state of famine in the city (6:24-31). The calm and strong faith of the prophet was manifest in his assurance of deliverance and in the word he sent to the king (6:32—7:2). His prediction was fulfilled next day when four lepers found that the Syrians had fled from their camp during the night in a great panic, leaving everything behind them (7:3-15). The record goes on to show how the event "came to pass as the man of God had spoken", both in the blessing that provided abundant food for the famishing people, and in the judgment that overtook the captain who disbelieved the words of "the man of God" (7:16-20). Thus did Elisha continually bear witness to the presence and power of the Lord God of Israel in the land.

THE ACTS OF HAZAEL AND JEHU
(Chs. 8-10)

When the Lord commanded Elijah to call Elisha as his successor, He also commissioned him to anoint Hazael as king over Syria and Jehu as king over Israel (1 Kings 19:15-16). These men were to be used as His instruments of judgment upon the house of Ahab and the apostate nation. The time was now come for the execution of judgment, and Elisha carried out the commission which God had given to Elijah in regard to both these men. These chapters tell how they came to their respective thrones, and how the Divine judgment began to operate through them.

1. The Preparation for Judgment (Ch. 8). The influence of Elisha at the court of Israel is seen in the restoration of the property of the Shunammite woman whose son he had raised (vs. 1-6). During a visit of Elisha to Damascus, the king of Syria sent Hazael to enquire of the prophet if he should recover from a sickness that he had. Elisha revealed his knowledge of Hazael's secret purpose to murder his master and his fore-knowledge of what he would do to Israel when he became king of Syria. Hazael carried out his treacherous design the next day, and thus usurped the throne of Syria (vs. 7-15). The rest of the chapter tells how the corruption which Ahab had brought upon Israel entered Judah after the reign of Jehoshaphat, through the marriage alliance of the royal house of David with the apostate house of Ahab (vs. 16-29).

2. The Fall of the House of Ahab (Chs. 9-10). The hour was now come for carrying out the sentence upon Ahab's house. Elisha sent one of the sons of the prophets to Ramoth-gilead to anoint Jehu, one of the captains of the army, as king of Israel, that through him the Lord might avenge the blood of His prophets whom Jezebel had slain (1 Kings 18:4), and destroy the whole house of Ahab (9:1-13). Jehu was a man of relentless character and swift action, and he headed a conspiracy which resulted in the death of both Joram king of Israel (9:14-26) and Ahaziah king of Judah (9:27-29). As he entered the gate of Jezreel, where Jezebel was living, she met the horrible doom that Elijah had foretold (9:30-37).

Jehu then proceeded to destroy all that were left of the house of Ahab (10:1-17), and all who worshipped in the temple of Baal (10:18-28). But Jehu followed the calf worship of Jeroboam, and, although the Lord commended his zeal in destroying Baal worship, He manifested His displeasure by allowing Hazael king of Syria to overrun the land east of the Jordan (10:29-36).

REFORMATION IN JUDAH
(Chs. 11-12)

After the death of Ahaziah king of Judah, the queen mother Athaliah, the daughter of Ahab and Jezebel (8:18), usurped the throne and destroyed all the royal princes, except the infant Joash who was hidden by his aunt Jehosheba (11:1-3), the wife of the high priest Jehoiada (2 Chron. 22:11). After seven years, a revolution was organized and carried out by Jehoiada, in which Joash was made king (11:4-12) and Athaliah was slain (11:13-16). Under Jehoiada's leadership the Covenant with the Lord was renewed and Baal worship was destroyed amid the rejoicing of all the people (11:17-21). This event is significant as showing that the Mosaic priesthood occupied a place of leadership in Judah at this time.

In the course of his reign of forty years, Joash (Jehoash) had the Temple of the Lord repaired and its worship restored, the money for the work being raised by voluntary giving (12:1-16). Before the end of his reign, Hazael king of Syria threatened Jerusalem, and Joash showed great weakness in buying him off with the sacred treasures of the Temple. A conspiracy among his own servants resulted in his assassination (12:17-21). The reformation of Joash's reign arrested the corruption and decline of Judah which had set in under the influence of Athaliah.

INIQUITY IN ISRAEL
(Chs. 13-15)

In the meantime the sin of the northern kingdom ran on through the reigns of Jehoahaz (13:1-9) and Jehoash (13:10-13) of the house of Jehu. In the reign of the latter occurred the death of the aged prophet Elisha, whose characteristic courage and confidence appear in the rebuke he gave the king in his last interview (13:14-21). In the same reign the Lord showed mercy and compassion to Israel in relieving them of the oppression of Hazael and giving them victory again (13:22-25).

When Amaziah, who had succeeded his father Joash on the throne of Judah (14:1-4), vaingloriously challenged Jehoash to come to battle (14:5-10), Judah was defeated and Jerusalem captured, and the treasures of the Temple and the king's house were taken to Samaria (14:11-16). Amaziah's reign ended, like his father's, with a conspiracy in which he was slain (14:17-22). During the long reign of Jeroboam II in Israel, the northern kingdom was extended to its widest limits and attained the height of its prosperity and power (14:23-29).

The kingdom of Judah enjoyed a long period of prosperity under the righteous reigns of Azariah, who is better known as Uzziah (15:1-7), and Jotham (15:32-38). But during the latter part of this period revolution and bloodshed prevailed in the kingdom of Israel. After the death of Jeroboam II, judgment overtook the house of Jehu (15:8-12). Then anarchy set in. Kings ascended the throne in quick succession through the murder of their predecessors (15:13-31). Of the five reigns in Israel recorded in this chapter, four ended in conspiracy and violence. The nation was fast hurrying on to its doom.

THE ASSYRIAN CAPTIVITY
(Chs. 16-17)

In the reign of Ahaz, who followed Jotham as king of Judah and introduced the abominations of idolatry into the land again (16:1-4), the kings of Syria and Israel combined to attack Jerusalem (16: 5-6). Ahaz paid tribute to the king of Assyria to get his help against them (16:7-9), and went to meet Tiglath-pileser at Damascus. There he saw a heathen altar which took his fancy, and he sent a pattern of it to the high priest at Jerusalem, and had it set up for the sacrifices in the Temple and the brazen altar set aside (16:10-16). Then Ahaz went on to spoil the Temple of its ornamental work in order to provide a present for the king of Assyria (16:17-20). This alliance with Assyria brought dire consequences to Judah at a later date.

In the reign of Hoshea, the last but not the worst of the kings of Israel, the judgment long threatened fell upon the apostate nation. Assyrian kings had already twice invaded the borders of Israel, exacting tribute (15:19), capturing many cities and taking away their inhabitants (15:29). Hoshea stopped paying tribute and conspired with Egypt, and thus brought the Assyrians upon the land again. After a siege of three years, the capital city Samaria was taken, and the whole nation was carried away into the eastern lands of Assyria (17:1-6).

At this point in the story the course of Israel's sin is set forth in a striking passage, in which the inspired writer points out the true cause of her downfall and doom (17:7-23). "It was so, because the children of Israel had sinned against Jehovah their God (v. 7). . . . Therefore Jehovah was very angry with Israel and removed them out of his sight" (v. 18). National disasters are due to moral and spiritual causes. Foreign people were brought in and placed in the land, and a mixed population grew up with a mixed form of worship (17:24-41). Thus originated the Samaritans of later days.

THE REIGN OF HEZEKIAH
(Chs. 18-20)

This was the crowning period in the history of Judah. Hezekiah was the best and greatest of her kings. He instituted at once a widespread and thorough religious reformation, and purged the land of idolatry (18:1-8). In the sixth year of his reign Samaria was taken and Northern Israel destroyed (18:9-12).

At a later period in his reign, Judah was overrun by the army of Sennacherib king of Assyria, and Hezekiah paid him tribute (18:13-16). Notwithstanding this, Sennacherib threatened to destroy Jerusalem and sent an army to demand its surrender. The city was delivered from this peril by a sudden intervention of the Lord. The story, which is told with elaborate detail, dwells upon the blasphemous and arrogant pride of the Assyrian general before the walls of Jerusalem (18:17-37), Hezekiah's devout appeal to Isaiah and the prophet's prediction of the fate of the Assyrian king (19:1-8), Sennacherib's further threatening message to Hezekiah and the king's humble prayer before the

Lord (19:9-19), the triumphant prophecy and assuring message of Isaiah (19:20-34), the sudden judgment on the Assyrian army and the subsequent assassination of the Assyrian king (19:35-37).

At another time Hezekiah was delivered from a serious illness and his life was prolonged, in answer to his tears and prayer (20:1-11). An embassy came from Babylon to congratulate him on his recovery, and Hezekiah, yielding to vanity, showed them the wealth and treasures of his kingdom (20: 12-15). This brought a rebuke from Isaiah and the first prediction of the Babylonian captivity (20: 16-21).

THE REFORMS OF JOSIAH
(Chs. 21-23)

During the long and wicked reign of Manasseh, who succeeded Hezekiah, Judah was plunged into the deepest depths of apostasy and iniquity. The abominations of Baal worship and other idolatries were introduced even into the Temple of the Lord (21:1-9). The prophets testified against him, but Manasseh went on in his wickedness (21:10-18). The conditions of his reign were continued through the short reign of Amon (21:19-26).

Josiah, the last of the good kings of Judah, was only a child of eight when he came to the throne (22:1-2). When he grew older he undertook a series of reforms, the first of which was to repair and restore the Temple in his eighteenth year (22:3-7). In the course of this work, the high priest Hilkiah discovered the Book of the Law. It was read before the king and had a profound effect upon him, because of its threatening of Divine wrath for national disobedience (22:8-13). He sent to enquire of the Lord through Huldah the prophetess, and received a message that these judgments would indeed fall upon the nation, but that he himself would be spared from seeing them and would die in peace (22:14-20).

Josiah gathered an assembly of the people to read the book to them and to renew the Covenant with the Lord (23:1-3). He had the Temple cleansed of all vessels that had been used for idolatrous purposes and rid of all idolatrous priests (23:4-14). He went through the land destroying all symbols of idolatry and all places of idolatrous worship, including Jeroboam's sanctuary at Bethel (23:15-20). Then the long-neglected Passover was again observed in Jerusalem (23:21-23). Josiah's reforms were more thorough-going than those of any other king (23:24-25).

But even this reformation, carried out with such great zeal and energy by Josiah, was too late to save the nation. The people were simply following the king's lead without any sense of penitence or any return to the Lord. They were too deeply sunk in depravity, too deeply affected with apostasy (23: 26-27). Josiah died in battle at Megiddo (23:28-30), and the kings who followed him went back to the ways of wickedness. His son Jehoahaz, after an evil reign of three months, was removed by the king of Egypt, who put another son, Jehoiakim, on the throne, and exacted a heavy tribute (23:31-37). Judah's doom was at hand.

THE BABYLONIAN CAPTIVITY
(Chs. 24-25)

The strokes of Divine judgment now fell in rapid succession. Jehoiakim submitted to Nebuchadnezzar king of Babylon, who had become the supreme world ruler by his defeat of Egypt at Carchemish in 605 B.C. During the evil reign of Jehoiakim the chastening hand of God was upon Judah, and bands of foreign foes kept invading and harassing the land (24:1-7). His son Jehoiachin succeeded him, but after three months Nebuchadnezzar a second time came to Jerusalem and captured the city. The king and ten thousand of the leading citizens, together with the treasures of the Temple and the palace, were removed to Babylon (24:8-16). Nebuchadnezzar left on the throne Zedekiah, the youngest son of Josiah; but he, too, at length rebelled (24:17-20).

And now the final judgment fell. Nebuchadnezzar came for the third time and laid siege to the city, which fell after a year and a half. The king sought to escape, but was captured, blinded, and taken to Babylon (25:1-7). Then followed the complete destruction of the city and the Temple, and the carrying away of the rest of the people, only the poorest being left behind (25:8-21). Nebuchadnezzar made Gedaliah governor of those who remained in the land; but he and his whole court were slain by conspirators, and all the people, in fear, moved down to Egypt (25:22-26). Night had fallen upon the land of Judah.

The book closes with a final glimpse of hope, an account of the favour shown to Jehoiachin after thirty-seven years of captivity in a Babylonian prison (25:27-30). It was a foreshadowing of the subsequent restoration of the house of David.

* * * *

THE KINGS OF ISRAEL AND JUDAH

The Books of Kings carry the history of Israel and Judah along together from the disruption to the fall of the northern kingdom, and then Judah remains alone to the end. There is much uncertainty in the chronology of the early part of this period, and the date of the disruption cannot be exactly determined. According to one method of reckoning, it may be placed at 965 B.C., which is about midway between the earliest and the latest possible dates. From this date the two kingdoms ran side by side till the fall of Samaria in 721 B.C. Judah continued for a further period of 135 years till the fall of Jerusalem in 586 B.C.

During the two centuries and a half of Northern Israel's history, nineteen kings belonging to nine different dynasties reigned over the ten tribes. During the 380 years of Judah's history, nineteen kings of David's dynasty sat on the throne, and one queen who usurped the throne for a time. The two kingdoms were usually at enmity with each other, but there was one period when an alliance was maintained through several reigns. The relation of the two kingdoms is set forth in the following chronological outline:

I. A period of early antagonism for some sixty years, down to about 900 B.C. (1 Kings 12:1—16:28; 2 Chron. 10-16).

Kings of Israel: Jeroboam (22 years), Nadab (2 years), Baasha (24 years), Elah (2 years), Zimri (7 days), Omri (12 years).

Kings of Judah: Rehoboam (17 years), Abijam (3 years), Asa (41 years).

II. A period of alliance for some eighty years, to about 820 B.C. (1 Kings 16:29—2 Kings 11:20; 2 Chron. 17-24).

Kings of Israel: Ahab (22 years), Ahaziah (2 years), Jehoram (12 years), Jehu (28 years), Jehoahaz (17 years).

Kings of Judah: Jehoshaphat (25 years), Jehoram (8 years), Ahaziah (1 year), Queen Athaliah (6 years), Joash (40 years).

Prophets in Israel: Elijah and Elisha.

III. A period of further antagonism for about one hundred years, to the fall of Samaria in 721 B.C. (2 Kings 12-17; 2 Chron. 25-28).

Kings of Israel: Jehoash (16 years), Jeroboam II (41 years), Zechariah (6 months), Shallum (1 month), Menahem (10 years), Pekahiah (2 years), Pekah (20 years), Hoshea (9 years).

Kings of Judah: Amaziah (29 years), Uzziah (52 years), Jotham (16 years), Ahaz (16 years).

Prophets in Israel: Jonah, Amos, and Hosea.

Prophets in Judah: Joel, Isaiah, and Micah.

IV. The period of Judah alone for 135 years, to the fall of Jerusalem in 586 B.C. (2 Kings 18-25; 2 Chron. 29-36).

Kings of the first reformation and subsequent decline: Hezekiah (29 years), Manasseh (55 years), Amon (2 years).

Prophets of the period: Isaiah and Micah.

Kings of the last reformation and final decline: Josiah (31 years), Jehoahaz (3 months), Jehoiakim (11 years), Jehoiachin (3 months), Zedekiah (11 years).

Prophets of the period: Nahum, Habakkuk, Zephaniah, Obadiah, and Jeremiah.

THE FIRST BOOK OF CHRONICLES

UP to this point the books of the Old Testament have followed one another in chronological order. They give a continuous history from Adam to the Babylonian captivity. The Books of Chronicles begin the record over again and are complete in themselves. They start with Adam, and carry the story down to the end of the captivity. The period from Adam to David is covered by genealogies, and the period from David onward by extended narrative.

The Books of Chronicles deal with the same period of Israel's history as the Books of Samuel and Kings, but from a different point of view. In Samuel and Kings God is revealed at work in the national life of His people. In Chronicles He is revealed at work in their religious life. This difference explains the omissions and additions in the narrative of Chronicles.

The special design of the Books of Chronicles is to show that, although the nation had failed, the purpose of God with the nation had not failed. The monarchy had been destroyed but the Covenant remained, and God's redeeming purpose was still being carried on to its fulfilment. In First Chronicles this purpose centres in the royal house of David, and in Second Chronicles in the Temple of the Lord.

These books are also interesting because of the things omitted in the earlier books but recorded in these. Twenty whole chapters and twenty-four parts of chapters are occupied with matters not found in the other books of Scripture. This accounts for the Septuagint title of the books, "Omissions". The title in our English Version is from the Vulgate, which gives a free rendering of the Hebrew title, "Words of Days", or "Diaries".

First Chronicles carries the story down to the death of David, and is in two unequal parts. The first part (Chs. 1-9) contains the genealogies, and the second part (Chs. 10-29) the record of David's reign. On this basis we get the following plan:

I. The Genealogies—Chs. 1-9
   1. The Line of Promise (Chs. 1-3)
   2. The Tribes of Israel (Chs. 4-8)
   3. The Remnant of Israel (Ch. 9).
II. The Reign of David—Chs. 10-29
   1. His Throne Established (Chs. 10-12)
   2. The Worship of God Established (Chs. 13-16)
   3. Preparations for the Temple Building (Chs. 17-22)
   4. Preparations for the Temple Services (Chs. 23-27)
   5. Final Directions Concerning the Temple (Chs. 28-29).

THE LINE OF PROMISE
(Chs. 1-3)

The line of the promised Redeemer is traced from Adam through Noah and the patriarchs, and on through the tribe of Judah down to David. It is then carried on to the return from exile, and for several generations beyond. Thus it leads onward toward Jesus Christ. These genealogies illustrate the sovereign choice of God in His procedure in history as He moves on toward the fulfilment of His purpose in the world.

1. The Patriarchs (Ch. 1). By a process of exclusion and elimination the lines are narrowed down to the separated race. The ten generations from Adam to Noah are named (vs. 1-4), and are followed by the descendants of the sons of Noah (vs. 5-23). Shem's line is then taken up, and the ten generations to Abraham are named (vs. 24-27), followed by the descendants of Abraham except those of Isaac's line (vs. 28-33).

The genealogy then returns to Isaac, names his two sons, and traces the descendants of Esau for several generations (vs. 34-42). Then come the names of the kings of Edom, the kingdom which Esau founded before the establishment of the kingdom of Israel (vs. 43-54).

2. The Tribe of Judah (Ch. 2). First, the twelve sons of Israel are named (vs. 1-2); and before proceeding to a survey of the twelve tribes, the record traces the genealogy of Judah, in order to prepare for the line of David which follows in the next chapter. The name used in Chronicles for the founder of the nation is not Jacob but Israel (1:34; 2:1), indicating that it is not the character of the man, but God's purpose in his life, that is in view. The genealogy of Judah as recorded here (vs. 3-55) shows that the tribe was composed of several divisions and that some alien clans were incorporated with it.

3. The House of David (Ch. 3). A survey of David's family is given (vs. 1-9), and then the royal line is traced through Solomon down to Zerubbabel, the leader of the return from Babylon, and for several generations beyond (vs. 10-24). The names which Zerubbabel gave to his sons (vs. 19-20) indicate that a spiritual revival was taking place in the nation just before the return: Hananiah ("the grace of the Lord"), Berechiah ("the blessing of the Lord"), Hasadiah ("the mercy of the Lord"), and Jushab-hesed ("mercy returns").

THE TRIBES OF ISRAEL
(Chs. 4-8)

Having traced the line through which the Messiah was to come, the record now gives a general survey of the genealogies of Israel as a nation.

1. The Tribes of the South (Ch. 4). Judah, the tribe to which the promise had been given, is taken up first (vs. 1-23). The list of names is interrupted to tell the significant story of Jabez (vs. 9-10). His name, which means "sorrowful", had cast the shadow of evil over his life, and by his prayer he had been delivered from it. Simeon follows next (vs. 24-43), because this tribe originally occupied part of the land included in the kingdom of Judah. Simeon did not grow like Judah (v. 27), and most of the tribe migrated elsewhere (vs. 42-43).

2. The Eastern Tribes (Ch. 5). The two tribes and a half that settled east of the Jordan are now surveyed. The religious lessons of their history are brought out in several comments (vs. 1-2, 20, 25-26).

3. The Tribe of Levi (Ch. 6). The line of the high priest is traced from Aaron to Jehozadak, who was high priest at the time of the captivity (vs. 1-15). The three branches of the tribe are then given as they sprang from the three sons of Levi (vs. 16-30). There follow the genealogies of the

three leaders of David's Levite choirs (vs. 31-48). The record then returns to the line of Aaron (vs. 49-53), and goes on to give a list of the Levitical cities where the priests and Levites dwelt (vs. 54-81).

4. The Tribes of the North (Chs. 7-8). After a survey of the remaining tribes (ch. 7), the tribe of Benjamin is taken up again (8:1-28), in order to trace the line of Saul, the first king of Israel (8:29-40).

THE REMNANT OF ISRAEL
(Ch. 9)

This chapter begins with a reference to the preceding genealogies and a statement about the Babylonian captivity (v. 1). Then it goes on to give a list of those who dwelt in Jerusalem after the return from captivity (vs. 2-34). With some variations, this corresponds to the list in Neh. 11:3-19. It was the restored community of Israel, with whom God made a new beginning after the Exile.

The prophets had foretold that a remnant should be preserved through the judgments of the Lord upon Judah and would return to the land after her fall and captivity (Isa. 1:9; 6:13; 10:20-23). With this restored remnant the Lord carried on His purpose in Israel till the coming of Christ. The list comprises heads of families, chiefly of Judah and Benjamin (vs. 3-9), priests (vs. 10-13), Levites (vs. 14-16), porters or doorkeepers and other classes of Levites (vs. 17-32), and singers (vs. 33-34). The chapter closes with a repetition of the line of Saul (vs. 35-44), in preparation for the story of the fall of his house in the next chapter and the establishment of the throne of David.

DAVID'S THRONE ESTABLISHED
(Chs. 10-12)

The record now passes from genealogy to narrative. The narrative begins with David, through whom the Divine purpose was being carried forward. The story of David's reign in Chronicles is almost wholly concerned with what he did to establish the worship of God in Jerusalem and to prepare for the Temple and its services. His great sin and its tragic consequences are passed over. It is the religious, not the political, aspect of his reign that is in view.

The present section tells how his throne was established. It begins with an account of Saul's last battle and death (10:1-12), and the reason why the Lord brought this judgment upon him and "turned the kingdom unto David" (10:13-14). Then comes a brief account relating how all Israel came to Hebron and made David king, and how he took Jerusalem and made it his capital (11:1-9).

Then we are told of the men who helped to strengthen David in his kingdom: his mighty men and their deeds of valour (11:10-47), the men who rallied round him in the days of his persecution at the hands of Saul (12:1-22), and the men who came to Hebron to make him king (12:23-37). The account closes by stating that all Israel "were of one heart to make David king", and describing the universal joy and gladness that marked the occasion (12:38-40).

THE WORSHIP OF GOD ESTABLISHED
(Chs. 13-16)

These chapters tell how David brought the Ark up to Jerusalem and established it there as the centre of Israel's religious life.

1. The Ark Removed from Kirjath-jearim (Ch. 13). David first used a human device instead of God's appointed method of carrying this sacred symbol (vs. 1-8). The tragic death of Uzzah was a warning of the holiness of the divine Presence in the midst of Israel (vs. 9-12). For three months the Ark remained in the house of Obed-edom, bringing blessing to it (vs. 13-14).

2. The Progress of David's Reign (Ch. 14). Before the next movement of the Ark is recorded, a survey is taken of David's house and family (vs. 1-7), and of his wars with the Philistines (vs. 8-17). The characteristic feature of David's rule, seeking and following the will of the Lord, is noted again and again (vs. 10, 14, 16).

3. The Ark Brought into Jerusalem (Ch. 15). This time the divine method was followed, and the Ark was carried on the shoulders of the Levites (vs. 1-15). It was brought up from the house of Obed-edom into the city of David with manifestations of great joy (vs. 16-29). This account has much more fulness of detail than the parallel account in 2 Sam. 6.

4. Plans for the Worship of God (Ch. 16). When the Ark was set in its place, a service of thanksgiving was held (vs. 1-3), and a psalm of praise was sung by the Levite choir (vs. 4-36), composed mainly of two portions of the Psalter (Psa. 105:1-15 and Psa. 96). Asaph was appointed to minister before the Ark in Jerusalem; and Zadok the high priest was appointed to minister before the altar of burnt offering in the Tabernacle at Gibeon, together with Heman and Jeduthun, who were appointed to conduct the service of song and praise (vs. 37-43). The worship of God in Israel was maintained in this way until the Temple was built and dedicated.

PREPARATIONS FOR THE TEMPLE BUILDING
(Chs. 17-22)

The presence of the Ark in Jerusalem created a desire in David's heart to provide a worthy dwelling place for it. This led to God's covenant with David regarding a son who should build a house for the Lord. For this Temple David now began to make elaborate preparations.

1. God's Promise to David (Ch. 17). David told Nathan what was in his heart, and through Nathan God revealed His purpose to David (vs. 1-15). The Lord promised to perpetuate the kingdom in David's line, and to raise up a son for him who should build the house of the Lord and whose throne should be established for ever. This covenant with David (vs. 11-14) was the basis of the Messianic predictions of the prophets; it looked forward to the coming and Kingdom of Christ. The humble and adoring prayer with which David responded to this promise (vs. 16-27) shows that he recognized its unique significance and the honour thereby placed upon him and his house (vs. 17-18). The promise to David has been more fully explained in the exposition of 2 Sam. 7, which is parallel with this chapter. See pages 188-189.

2. The Extension of the Kingdom (Chs. 18-20). These chapters give a general view of the wars and the victories by which David's kingdom was extended and its boundaries were made secure. His

victories were the direct result of God's blessing upon him: "Jehovah gave victory to David whithersoever he went" (18:6, 13). During his wars he gathered treasure and material for the house of the Lord (18:8, 11). The expression, "cut them with saws", in 20:3 should be read, "put them with saws", that is, put them to work with saws (cf. 2 Sam. 12:31, marg.). David placed the conquered Ammonites under this kind of servitude.

3. Choosing a Site for the Temple (Ch. 21). Yielding to a temptation from Satan and moved by pride because of his victories, David ordered a census of Israel that he might glory in the greatness of his kingdom; and he persisted in it notwithstanding the protest of Joab, until he saw that God was displeased (vs. 1-8). As a judgment upon him, David was offered, through the prophet Gad, the choice of three calamities; and he threw himself directly into the hands of the Lord (vs. 9-13).

A three days' pestilence then fell upon Israel, which was stayed just as the angel of the Lord, standing on Ornan's threshing floor, was about to smite Jerusalem with it (vs. 14-17). David, having acknowledged his own sin in the matter, was commanded to build an altar on the spot where the angel stood. He proceeded to purchase the place from Ornan and offer sacrifices there to mark his restoration to the favour of the Lord (vs. 18-27). Then David recognized that this was to be the site for the house of the Lord (21:28—22:1).

When this account of David's purchase is compared with the parallel account in 2 Sam. 24, it appears that there were two stages in it. David first bought the actual threshing floor and the oxen for fifty shekels of silver (2 Sam. 24:24). After having erected an altar there and offered the sacrifices, he purchased "the place", the whole hill top, for six hundred shekels of gold (1 Chron. 21:25), that he might secure it as a site for the Temple.

4. Preparing Material for the Temple (Ch. 22). David prepared abundant material for the Temple before his death (vs. 2-5). He gave to Solomon a special and earnest charge concerning the building of it (vs. 6-16), and to the princes of Israel a special command to help Solomon (vs. 17-19).

PREPARATIONS FOR THE TEMPLE SERVICES (Chs. 23-27)

In his old age David had Solomon appointed king, and he also had the priests and Levites organized for carrying on the worship of God in the Temple (23:1-2). The Levites were numbered and divided into courses according to the three branches of the tribe (22:3-23), and the duties of their office were prescribed (23:24-32). The two priestly branches of Aaron's family were divided into twenty-four courses for the priest's office (24:1-19). The rest of the sons of Levi were classified by lot (24:20-31).

David also made provision for the service of song and praise by setting apart the families of Asaph, Heman, and Jeduthun for this purpose (25:1-8). They were divided into twenty-four courses of twelve men each (25:9-31). Other Levites were designated for other duties: doorkeepers (26:1-19), keepers of the treasures (26:20-28), and officers and judges (26:29-32).

Then comes a survey of the military and civil administration of David's kingdom: the twelve divisions of the army and their captains (27:1-15), the twelve tribes and their rulers (27:16-24), the superintendents of departments (27:25-31) and the state councillors (27:32-34).

FINAL DIRECTIONS CONCERNING THE TEMPLE (Chs. 28-29)

David assembled the princes of the tribes and the officers and ministers of his kingdom, told them of his own desire regarding the house of the Lord, and of God's purpose regarding Solomon his son, and gave to them and to Solomon a solemn charge to serve the Lord and to carry out His purpose regarding the Temple (28:1-10). He then gave Solomon the pattern of the Temple and a final word of exhortation about it (28:11-21).

David dedicated his own treasures for the Temple, declaring, "I have set my affection on the house of my God", thus showing where the supreme interest of his life lay (29:1-5); and the princes and rulers made their offerings, doing it willingly "with a perfect heart" (29:6-9). David led the assembly in praise and prayer, and the people worshipped the Lord with sacrifices in abundance, "and did eat and drink before Jehovah on that day with great gladness (29:10-22). Solomon was made king anew, and his reign began with such manifestations of royal majesty as had not been seen before in Israel (29:22-25). The book closes with David's death and a general statement about his reign (29:26-30).

THE SECOND BOOK OF CHRONICLES

SECOND Chronicles continues the narrative of First Chronicles with the same theme and from the same point of view. It shows how the purpose of God was carried through Solomon's reign, down through the history of Judah, and on to the eve of the return from captivity. The history of Northern Israel is not recorded in Chronicles.

The real centre of Second Chronicles is the Temple, the house of the Lord, the place where He manifested Himself in the midst of His people. Solomon built it and established its services. The kings who repaired it and restored its services are given the largest place in the narrative. The decree of Cyrus for the rebuilding of the Temple brings the book to a close.

Second Chronicles may be divided into two unequal parts, the shorter part (Chs. 1-9) dealing with the reign of Solomon, and the longer part (Chs. 10-36) with the kingdom of Judah. The history of Judah, as recorded here, may be divided into four periods, each marked by a restoration of the Temple services after a time of apostasy, the last one ending with the final apostasy and the destruction of the Temple. This gives us the following outline of the book:

I. The Reign of Solomon—Chs. 1-9
II. The Kings of Judah—Chs. 10-36
1. From Rehoboam to Jehoshaphat (Chs. 10-20)

2. From Jehoram to Amaziah (Chs. 21-25)
3. From Uzziah to Hezekiah (Chs. 26-32)
4. From Manasseh to Zedekiah (Chs. 33-36)

THE REIGN OF SOLOMON
(Chs. 1-9)

The account of Solomon's reign in this book is almost entirely taken up with his work in building the Temple and establishing its services. There is no reference to the acts of judgment by which he punished offenders at the beginning of his reign, or to the Divine judgment which began to operate against him because of his sin at the end of his reign.

1. The Beginning of His Reign (Ch. 1). This is a much briefer account of the opening events of Solomon's reign than the account in First Kings. It records only his great sacrifice at Gibeon (vs. 1-8), his prayer for wisdom (vs. 7-13), and his royal wealth in horses and chariots (vs. 14-17).

2. The Building of the Temple (Chs. 2-4). These chapters correspond in the main with 1 Kings 5-7. There is no account of the building of Solomon's own house. Everything concerns the house of the Lord. The preparations for it are first described (ch. 2). These were the enlistment of a vast levy of labourers (vs. 1-2), a treaty with the king of Tyre for timber from Lebanon and for skilled workmen (vs. 3-16), and the organization of the labourers (vs. 17-18).

Solomon built the Temple house on Mount Moriah on the site which David had chosen (ch. 3). He began the building in the fourth year of his reign (vs. 1-2). Its dimensions and materials are described: the Holy-place (vs.3-7), the Holy-of-holies (vs. 8-14), and the pillars of the porch (vs. 15-17).

The making of the Temple furniture is described next (ch. 4): the brazen altar and the lavers (vs. 1-6), the candlesticks and the tables (vs. 7-10), the brazen vessels made by Huram (vs. 11-18), and the golden vessels for the sanctuary, all of which, it is emphasized, were "of pure gold", "of gold, and that perfect gold" (vs. 19-22).

3. The Dedication of the Temple (Chs. 5-7). These chapters correspond in the main with 1 Kings 8:1—9:9, but contain a somewhat fuller account.

(1) The bringing in of the Ark (ch. 5). The treasures dedicated by David were deposited in the Temple (v. 1). An assembly of the elders and rulers of Israel was gathered, and the Ark was brought up from the city of David and placed in the Holy-of-holies (vs. 2-10). Then the praise and worship of the Lord began, and His presence was manifested by the cloud which filled the house (vs. 11-14). The choir of Levite singers organized by David appears here for the first time. From now on the sacrifice of praise occupies a prominent place in the worship of God.

(2) Solomon's address and prayer (ch. 6). After his opening address to the people (vs. 1-11), he offered a solemn dedicatory prayer (vs. 12-42). The three closing verses of the prayer are not found in Kings. They express the idea that is most prominent in Chronicles of the Temple being the Lord's abode in the midst of His people and the source of all blessing for them.

(3) The sacrifices and the feast (ch. 7). The dedication of the Temple was confirmed by fire from heaven (vs. 1-3). The sacrifices followed (vs. 4-7),

and the feast of dedication, which lasted seven days (vs. 8-10). When all was finished, the Lord revealed Himself to Solomon with a promise of blessing for obedience (vs. 11-18), and a solemn warning of the destruction of the Temple for disobedience (vs. 19-22).

4. The Close of Solomon's Reign (Chs. 8-9). No reference is made in Chronicles to Solomon's fall. The account of his reign is brought to a close with a summary of his doings (ch. 8), the visit of the Queen of Sheba (9:1-12), and a description of the glory of his kingdom (9:13-31).

FROM REHOBOAM TO JEHOSHAPHAT
(Chs. 10-20)

After giving an account of the disruption of the kingdom which followed Solomon's death, the narrative leaves the ten tribes and proceeds to deal with the history of Judah alone. Chronicles is concerned only with the kings of David's line, for down this line the purpose of God was moving. The present section takes us from 965 to about 890 B.C.

1. The Reign of Rehoboam (Chs. 10-12). He began with an act of folly in taking the advice of his young companions instead of the mature counsel of his father's advisers, and so causing the revolt of the ten tribes and the disruption of the kingdom (10:1—11:4). Rehoboam then fortified the limited territory that was left to him (11:5-12). The priests and Levites throughout all Israel adhered to the house of David and settled in Judah and Jerusalem (11:13-17).

King Rehoboam married many wives and placed his many sons in fortified cities (11:18-23). He forsook the Lord and brought Divine punishment upon the nation through an invasion by Shishak king of Egypt and the loss of the treasures of the Temple (12:1-12). When the king and the princes humbled themselves at the preaching of the prophet Shemaiah, the Lord gave them some deliverance. Throughout Rehoboam's evil reign of seventeen years there was continual civil war between the two kingdoms (12:13-16).

2. The Reign of Abijah (Ch. 13). It lasted three years. He went to war with Jeroboam, appealing to the children of Israel to return to the worship of the Lord in Jerusalem (vs. 1-12). The men of Judah were ambushed by Jeroboam but were delivered by a Divine intervention (vs. 13-17). They prevailed, "because they relied upon Jehovah, the God of their fathers" (v. 18). Abijah enlarged and strengthened his kingdom by taking territory from Jeroboam, but he followed in the ways of his father (vs. 19-22).

3. The Reign of Asa (Chs. 14-16). He started well, cleared the land of idolatry and led Judah back to the Lord, with resulting peace and prosperity (14:1-8). In his days Judah was invaded by a great host under Zerah the Ethiopian; but in answer to Asa's prayer and appeal to the Lord for help, there came a Divine intervention and Judah was given a great victory (14:9-15). Encouraged by the preaching of Azariah (15:1-7), he restored the altar of sacrifice in the Temple and renewed the Covenant with the Lord (15:8-19).

Asa made a league with Ben-hadad king of Syria against an attack by Baasha king of Israel (16:1-6), and was rebuked by the prophet Hanani for not relying on the Lord, whose eyes "run to and fro throughout the whole earth, to show himself strong in the behalf of them whose heart is perfect toward him" (16:7-9). He resented the rebuke, and changed for the worse at the end of his reign of forty-one years (16:10-14).

4. The Reign of Jehoshaphat (Chs. 17-20). He sought the Lord and sent teachers of the Law throughout Judah (17:1-9), and established the kingdom in great power (17:10-19). He made an unhappy alliance with Ahab, the apostate king of Israel, and took part in the war against Syria at Ramoth-gilead, where Ahab was slain (ch. 18). On his return to Jerusalem he was rebuked by the prophet Jehu (19:1-3), and afterwards gave himself to the task of turning the people to the Lord throughout the land (19:4-7) and reforming the worship and service of the Lord in Jerusalem (19:8-11).

A great host of Moabites and Ammonites having threatened to attack Judah, Jehoshaphat led his people in seeking the help of the Lord (20:1-13). An assurance of Divine deliverance being given by Jahaziel, the king led his people in praise and thanksgiving, and immediately the Lord wrought a mighty overthrow of the foe (20:14-30). The mistake of Jehoshaphat's righteous reign was his continued alliance with the wicked house of Ahab (20:31-37).

FROM JEHORAM TO AMAZIAH
(Chs. 21-25)

Jehoshaphat's alliance with Israel bore its evil fruit in the introduction of Baal worship into Judah. The disastrous result of this apostasy upon the southern kingdom appears again and again in the history contained in these chapters, which take us to about 800 B.C.

1. The Corruption of the House of David (Chs. 21-22). Jehoram, the son of Jehoshaphat, had married Athaliah, the daughter of Ahab. When he came to the throne he murdered all his brothers and many of the princes (21:1-7). In his days the kingdom of Edom, which had been brought into subjection by David, revolted from Judah (21:8-10). Jehoram introduced idolatry into Judah, and received a written message from Elijah foretelling a Divine judgment upon him (21:11-15). This is the only mention of Elijah in Chronicles, and it is an evidence of the prophet's influence in the southern kingdom. The judgment came to pass when foreign foes overran the land, and after a reign of eight years Jehoram came to a miserable end (21:16-20).

He was followed by Ahaziah, who reigned for one year, and was slain in Samaria in the judgment which Jehu was executing upon the house of Ahab (22:1-9). Then came the usurpation of Athaliah and her attempt to destroy the royal house of David, and the hiding of the infant Joash from her by his aunt Jehoshabeath (22:10-12).

2. The Reign of Joash (Chs. 23-24). The high priest Jehoiada organized a movement among the Levites and the military captains, which resulted in putting Joash on the throne (23:1-11), and in slaying Athaliah and destroying her Baal worship (23:12-21). Joash was only seven years old when his reign of forty years began. He started well, and had the Temple repaired under Jehoiada by means of the renewal of the tax which Moses had laid upon the Israelites for the services of the sanctuary (24:

1-14; Exod. 30:12-16). After the death of Jehoiada, the aged high priest, Josiah was led away from the Lord by the princes, who stoned Zechariah, the son of Jehoiada, when he rebuked them (24:15-22; Matt. 23:35; Luke 11:51). This apostasy was followed by the disastrous invasion of a Syrian army and the assassination of the king at the hands of his own servants (24:23-27).

3. The Reign of Amaziah (Ch. 25). He followed the Lord at first, but "not with a perfect heart" (vs. 1-4). He carried on a successful war against the Edomites (vs. 5-13); but he brought back their idols and worshipped them, and brought upon himself a Divine warning through a prophet whom he refused to hear (vs. 14-16). He went to war with the king of Israel and met with a shameful defeat (vs. 17-24). His reign ended with his assassination as the result of a conspiracy against him (vs. 25-28).

FROM UZZIAH TO HEZEKIAH
(Chs. 26-32)

Judah now entered a long period of prosperity, during which the southern kingdom reached the height of its power. For the most part the nation was loyal to the Lord; only one of the four kings of the period turned to idolatry. The period extended throughout the eighth century B.C. and into the early years of the seventh.

1. The Reign of Uzziah (Ch. 26). He began his long and prosperous reign of fifty-two years by doing "that which was right in the eyes of Jehovah" under the guidance and counsel of Zechariah, a prophet otherwise unknown (vs. 1-5). He restored the military power of Judah, "and his name spread far abroad; for he was marvellously helped, till he was strong" (vs. 6-15). "But when he was strong, his heart was lifted up, so that he did corruptly". He usurped the priestly office by burning incense in the Temple in presumptuous defiance of the high priest's warning, and was smitten with leprosy (vs. 16-20). His son Jotham became co-regent until his death (vs. 21-23).

2. The Reign of Jotham (Ch. 27). He reigned with his father's equity, and refrained from his father's sin. He maintained the power and prosperity of Judah during the sixteen years of his reign. But a moral corruption which followed the prosperity of the previous reign was sapping the strength of the nation.

3. The Reign of Ahaz (Ch. 28). "He walked in the ways of the kings of Israel", during his reign of sixteen years, and introduced the worst abominations of idolatry (vs. 1-4). He was punished by a severe defeat at the hands of the kings of Syria and Israel (vs. 5-7). The captives who were taken from Judah to Samaria were restored at the command of the prophet Oded (vs. 8-15). Sending to Assyria for help, Ahaz only brought more trouble upon himself, and trespassed still more against the Lord (vs. 16-27).

4. The Reign of Hezekiah (Chs. 29-32). The best of the kings of Judah, he reigned twenty-nine years. He began a course of reformation in the first month of his reign, by calling the priests and Levites together and commanding them to cleanse the Temple (29:1-19). Then he had the Temple rededicated and its worship restored (29:20-36). He sent a proclamation throughout all Israel and Judah summoning the people to keep the Passover

(30:1-12) ; and a great assembly gathered in Jerusalem and kept the feast with great joy (30:13-27). This was followed by other reforms, the destruction of all heathen altars and idols throughout Judah, the reorganization of the Levitical services and the restoration of the tithes and offerings (ch. 31).

After this came Sennacherib's invasion of Judah, his threatened attack on Jerusalem, and his blasphemous defiance of the Lord (32:1-19), followed by the Lord's judgment on the Assyrian and His deliverance of Jerusalem (32:20-23). Hezekiah's heart was lifted up because of the honour and prosperity that came to him, and he incurred the displeasure of the Lord. When a deputation came from Babylon to visit him, "God left him, to try him, that He might know all that was in his heart". He was honoured by his people at his death, for he was a great and good king (32:24-33).

FROM MANASSEH TO ZEDEKIAH
(Chs. 33-36)

Hezekiah's good reign was followed by a long period of apostasy and sin; and the decline of Judah set in, from which the reign of Josiah, its last good king, could not save it. The period dealt with in this section begins in 695 and ends with the overthrow of the kingdom and the destruction of Jerusalem and the Temple in 586 B.C.

1. The Reign of Manasseh (Ch. 33). One of the worst of the kings of Judah, he introduced every form of idolatrous abomination, and his long reign of fifty-five years brought the nation into the depths of corruption and wickedness (vs. 1-9). He was punished by being taken in chains to Babylon, where he repented (vs. 10-13). He was restored to his kingdom, and attempted to bring back Judah to the worship of the Lord (vs. 14-20). But his son Amon, who followed him upon the throne for two years, went from bad to worse (vs. 21-25).

2. The Reign of Josiah (Chs. 34-35). Coming to the throne when he was only eight years old, Josiah began to seek the Lord in the eighth year of his reign; and in the twelfth year he began to purge the land of idolatry (34:1-7). In the eighteenth year he set about repairing the Temple, and in the process of this work Hilkiah the high priest found the Book of the Law (34:8-21). He consulted the prophetess Huldah about it, and she sent a message, both of judgment and of comfort, back to the king (34:22-28), who gathered an assembly of elders and people, and renewed the Covenant with the Lord (34:29-33). Then Josiah kept a great Passover, the greatest of all in the history of Israel (35:1-19). His death at the battle of Megiddo was greatly lamented by all the people (35:20-27).

3. The Last Kings of Judah (Ch. 36). The reigns of Jehoahaz (vs. 1-4), Jehoiakim (vs. 5-8), Jehoiachin (vs. 9-10), and Zedekiah (vs. 11-14) are briefly recorded. It is a story of rebellion and doing evil against the Lord all through. Judah had despised the warnings of the prophets and was ripe for judgment (vs. 15-16). God brought upon them the terrible scourge of the Chaldeans, who destroyed the Temple and the wall of Jerusalem, took the people away to Babylon, and left the land to enjoy its Sabbaths for the seventy years of Jeremiah's prophecy (vs. 17-21; Jer. 29:10; Lev. 26:34). The book closes with the decree of Cyrus for the rebuilding of the Temple, which prepared the way for the Jews to return from their exile (vs. 22-23).

THE PRESENCE OF GOD IN THE KINGDOM OF JUDAH

The fact of God's presence in the history of Judah is emphasized in Second Chronicles by the prominence given to the religious reformations carried on by its good kings, and by the record of several Divine interpositions which took place in the southern kingdom.

There were four periods of reformation in Judah, and the main feature in every case was a return to the worship of the Lord in the Temple by the restoration of the Levitical services. After backsliding and sin, the people were brought back to God by the way of the altar of sacrifice. Righteousness in Israel rested upon the worship of God as prescribed by the Law. Ethical conduct went hand in hand with the fear of the Lord.

The four reformations belonged to the reigns of the following kings: (1) Asa and his successor Jehoshaphat. In both reigns there was not only a renewal of the Temple services, but also a revival of interest in the Law. (2) Joash, who had the Temple repaired by the renewal of the original Mosaic tax. (3) Hezekiah, who had the Temple purified, repaired, and rededicated, and all its services of worship restored. He also had all Israel and Judah observe the Passover. (4) Josiah, in whose reign the Book of the Law, long neglected and forgotten, was discovered in the course of repairing and reopening the Temple. The king had the Covenant renewed and a great Passover kept. It was the last attempt at reform, but too late to avert the judgment which had long been threatened.

On five occasions of great peril in the history of Judah, Divine deliverances are recorded in the narrative of Second Chronicles. They are all said to have occurred in answer to prayer, or because the people turned to the Lord and relied upon Him. (1) In the reign of Rehoboam, the Lord gave "some deliverance" from Shishak's invasion, when the king and the princes "humbled themselves" (12:6-7). (2) In the reign of Abijah, the men of Judah were delivered from an ambushment of the Israelites, when "they cried unto Jehovah", and "because they relied upon Jehovah, the God of their fathers" (13:13-18). (3) In the reign of Asa, the huge army of Zerah the Ethiopian was smitten before the army of Judah, when the king cried unto God for help (14:11-12). (4) In the reign of Jehoshaphat, an invading host of Moabites and Ammonites was completely discomfited, after the king "set himself to seek unto Jehovah" and Judah "gathered themselves together, to seek help from Jehovah" (20:3-4). (5) In the reign of Hezekiah, Jerusalem was delivered from the Assyrian army of Sennacherib, when the king and the prophet Isaiah "prayed because of this, and cried to heaven" (32:20-21). All this is in line with the evident purpose of the Books of Chronicles to magnify the Lord in the history of His people.

THE BOOK OF EZRA

THE Book of Ezra continues the history of the Books of Chronicles, the last two verses of Second Chronicles being identical with the opening verses of Ezra. It tells the story of the return from the Babylonian captivity, and deals with the restored remnant of Israel.

A new historical background comes into view in this book. The Jews had now passed under the power of Persia, which had taken the place of Babylon as the great world empire of the time. Cyrus had captured the city of Babylon in 538 B.C., and had thus securely founded the Persian Empire. One of his first acts, after he became the supreme ruler in the Asiatic world, was to publish a decree giving the Jews liberty to return and rebuild their Temple. With this decree the book of Ezra opens.

The return and restoration of the Jews took place in two stages, and the narrative is confined to the work of these two periods. The first band of exiles returned in 537 B.C. under Zerubbabel, who belonged to the line of David; and in their time the Temple was rebuilt. Nearly eighty years later (458 B.C.), the second band returned under Ezra, who belonged to the line of Aaron; and under him the congregation was restored and purified. The book thus falls into two parts, one dealing with the restoration of the Temple (Chs. 1-6), and the other with the restoration of the congregation (Chs. 7-10). This gives us the following outline:

I. The Restoration of the Temple—Chs. 1-6
   1. The Return of the Exiles (Chs. 1-2)
   2. The Beginning of the Temple (Chs. 3-4)
   3. The Completion of the Temple (Chs. 5-6)
II. The Restoration of the Congregation—
     Chs. 7-10.
   1. Ezra's Expedition (Chs. 7-8)
   2. Ezra's Reformation (Chs. 9-10)

THE RESTORATION OF THE TEMPLE
(Chs. 1-6)

This section of the book deals with the return from the captivity of the first band of exiles under the leadership of Zerubbabel, one of the princes of Judah, and their work of rebuilding the Temple. It reveals God at work in history proceeding to fulfil His own word (Jer. 29:10; 33:7).

1. The Return of the Exiles (Chs. 1-2). The book opens with the decree of Cyrus, which is remarkable for its recognition of the Lord God of Israel as the true God (1:1-4). The immediate result of the decree is then recorded (1:5-11). Many heads of families were stirred up belonging to Judah and Benjamin, and they returned to Jerusalem together with a large number of priests and Levites. They took with them treasures that were given them and the sacred vessels of the Temple, which Cyrus had put in the hands of Zerubbabel, the leader of the expedition, whose Babylonian name was Sheshbazzar.

The register of those who returned is given next (2:1-63). The list follows a definite order: First the leaders associated with Zerubbabel (vs. 1-2), then the people (vs. 3-35), the priests (vs. 36-39),

the Levites (vs. 40-42), the Nethinim, who were probably descendants of foreign slaves, and other servants (vs. 43-58), and finally those who had lost the records of their lineage (vs. 59-63). The list is followed by a summary of the whole company, which numbered less than 50,000 altogether, and a statement of their arrival in Jerusalem and their voluntary gifts for the rebuilding of the Temple (2:64-70).

2. The Beginning of the Temple (Chs. 3-4). The returned exiles first settled in their own cities, and when the sacred seventh month approached they assembled with one accord in Jerusalem. They rebuilt the altar of God and restored the daily burnt offerings; "for fear was upon them because of the peoples of the countries" (3:1-3). This was their declaration of trust in the Lord in the face of their foes. The captivity had cured them of all hankering after idolatry, and they had returned to the land with the fear of God in their hearts. They observed the Feast of Tabernacles, and after that they restored the sacrificial system and the other set feasts of the Lord (3:4-6). Then they began to prepare material for the Temple with the grant that Cyrus had given them (3:7).

In the second year of the return the foundation of the Temple was laid with appropriate ceremonies and with praise to the Lord (3:8-11). But the joy of the people was mingled with weeping on the part of the old men, who had seen the glory of the former house (3:12-13). The adversaries of the Jews now began to show their hostility. They first appealed to Zerubbabel, seeking a share in the work. When this was refused them they began to hinder it in every way, attempting to frustrate the purpose of the Jews (4:1-5). The building of the Temple was discontinued for sixteen years (4:24).

These "people of the land" were a mixed race descended from the foreigners who had been settled upon the country by the Assyrians after the fall of the northern kingdom and had mingled with the Israelites left behind (2 Kings 17:24). They came to be known as Samaritans from the former capital of the land. At this point in the narrative an episode is inserted showing how they continued their opposition long after the Temple was built and attempted to stop the building of the walls of the city in the days of Nehemiah (4:6-23). The Persian kings mentioned in this section reigned after Darius. The thread of the narrative which was dropped at v. 5 is resumed in v. 24.

3. The Completion of the Temple (Chs. 5-6). In the second year of Darius (520 B.C.), under the preaching of the prophets Haggai and Zechariah, the work was resumed (5:1-2; Hag. 2:1-9; Zech. 4:1-10). Opposition was raised again, but it did not make the Jews cease. "The eye of their God was upon the elders of the Jews", and He wrought in their behalf (5:3-5).

The Persian governor wrote a letter to Darius, referring the matter to him (5:6-17). Darius had the archives searched and found the original decree of Cyrus (6:1-5). He sent back instructions that the Jews were to be allowed to go on with the building of the house of God, and were to be assisted in doing so (6:6-12). Then the work went on and prospered under the continuous preaching of Haggai and Zechariah, and the Temple was completed in the sixth year of Darius (6:13-15).

The dedication services were observed with great

joy (6:16-18), and after this the Passover was kept by the restored and rejoicing exiles (6:19-22). This is the last of six Passovers recorded in the Old Testament. The others took place in Egypt (Exod. 12), in the wilderness (Nùm. 9), at Gilgal in Canaan (Josh. 5), in the reign of Hezekiah (2 Chron. 30), and in the reign of Josiah (2 Chron. 35). The Passover at which the Lord was crucified was the seventh notable observance of this feast in the history of Israel.

THE RESTORATION OF THE CONGREGATION
(Chs. 7-10)

This section of the book deals with the return of the second band of exiles under the leadership of Ezra, and with the reformation carried on by him in restoring and purifying the congregation of Israel. Ezra was a priest of the line of Eleazar, and "a ready scribe in the law of Moses", who "had set his heart to seek the law of Jehovah, and to do it" (7:6, 10). His characteristic expression was "the good hand of Jehovah our God upon us".

1. Ezra's Expedition (Chs. 7-8). There is a gap of nearly sixty years between chs. 6 and 7. Ezra led a company of returning exiles in a four months' journey from Babylon to Jerusalem (7:1-10). The commission he received from the Persian king gave him authority to lead back to Jerusalem all who wished to go, to establish the observance of the Law of God in the land, to draw upon the king's treasury for supplies, and to appoint judges in Judah (7:11-26); and for this Ezra gave praise to God (7:27-28). A register of the heads of the families who returned with him is given, the whole company numbering about 1,500 men besides the other members of their households (8:1-14).

Ezra gathered them at Ahava to review them and prepare for the journey, and sent for the Levites and other servants of the Temple (8:15-20). He would not compromise the honour of God by asking an escort of soldiers from the king, but instead he proclaimed a fast to wait upon God for His guidance and protection (8:21-23). The gifts for the Temple were committed into the hands of the priests and Levites (8:24-30). The journey was made in safety—"the hand of our God was upon us". When they arrived in Jerusalem, they offered burnt offerings and sacrifices for all the twelve tribes of Israel (8:31-36).

2. Ezra's Reformation (Chs. 9-10). When Ezra arrived, he was informed that the people of Israel had been intermarrying with their heathen neighbours and had become corrupted with idolatry, and that the rulers were the chief offenders. He was greatly distressed and confounded (9:1-4). He poured out his soul to God in a prayer on behalf of the people (9:5-15). It is one long, impassioned confession. Ezra completely identified himself with the people, although not personally guilty.

The sincerity of his prayer produced an immediate result. The people gathered in a great assembly before the Temple, confessed their sin, and undertook to make a covenant with God to put away their foreign wives (10:1-4). Under Ezra's energetic leadership this reform was carried out, and the congregation of Israel was purified by complete separation from the heathen people of the land (10:5-15). Three months were occupied in examining the matter, which shows the care taken to do justice to the claims of the women put away (10:16-17).

The book closes with a list of the transgressors. They numbered only a hundred and thirteen, but they belonged to all classes—priests and Levites as well as the people generally (10:18-44). The significance of this feature of the reformation lay in the necessity for keeping the remnant of Israel free from defilement in order to preserve the holy seed. Through it God was working out His redeeming purpose, and from it the Messiah was to come.

THE BOOK OF NEHEMIAH

THIS book continues the story of the restoration which was begun in Ezra, and brings it to an end. It contains an account of the work of Nehemiah in rebuilding the walls of Jerusalem and completing the reformation begun by Ezra. It covers a period of twelve years (444-432 B.C.), from the twentieth year to the thirty-second year of king Artaxerxes of Persia (2:1; 13:6). It is the last in chronological order of the historical books and brings the Old Testament history to a close. It is written in the first person, and is obviously composed of memoirs left by Nehemiah, who occupied a high position in the Persian court.

The book is in two parts. The first part (Chs. 1-7) describes the restoration of the city, and the second part (Chs. 8-13) the restoration of the Covenant. From this we get the following outline:

I. The Restoration of the City—Chs. 1-7
    1. Nehemiah's Commission (Chs. 1-2).
    2. The Building of the Walls (Chs. 3-5).
    3. The Completion of the Walls (Chs. 6-7).
II. The Restoration of the Covenant—Ch. 8-13
    1. The Reading of the Law (Ch. 8).
    2. The Renewing of the Covenant (Chs. 9-10)
    3. The Dedication of the Walls (Chs. 11-12).
    4. The Last Reforms (Ch. 13).

THE RESTORATION OF THE CITY
(Chs. 1-7)

1. Nehemiah's Commission (Chs. 1-2). Nehemiah inquired of a party of Jews from Jerusalem who were visiting Shushan, the principal residence of the Persian court, and learned from them of the affliction and depression under which the remnant of Israel in Judah were living, and of the ruined state of the city walls (1:1-3). Greatly grieved about it, he fasted and prayed to the Lord (1:4-11). He confessed the sins of the people, pleaded the promise of God to Moses, and asked for favour in the eyes of the king.

Nehemiah's office of cup-bearer brought him into close personal contact with the king. Artaxerxes, noticing his sadness, inquired the reason of it; and Nehemiah told him of the desolate condition of Jerusalem (2:1-3). Asked by the king what request he had to make, Nehemiah "prayed to the God of heaven", and then asked and received from the king a commission to go to Jerusalem and rebuild the city (2:4-8). Nehemiah's characteristic habit of ejaculatory prayer is noted here for the first time.

When he arrived there and found that he would encounter opposition from the foes of the Jews in the land, he began cautiously and made a private inspection of the walls by night (2:9-16). Having ascertained the true state of affairs, he proceeded to arouse the people and encourage them to the good work of building up the walls of the city (2:17-20).

2. The Building of the Walls (Chs. 3-5). The work was thoroughly organized (ch. 3). Different groups of people built different sections of the wall, the general principle being, "every one over against his own house" (v. 28).

Opposition arose from their enemies without (ch. 4). First it was mockery and ridicule (vs. 1-6), then anger and plotting and open hostility (vs. 7-14). But the work went on, for "the people had a mind to work", and "we made our prayer to our God, and set a watch against them day and night, because of them". Nehemiah made careful plans for combining energetic work with vigilant defence (vs. 15-23). While some wrought in the work, others "held the spears from the rising of the morning till the stars appeared".

Difficulty then arose from within (ch. 5). The rich were oppressing their poorer brethren by usury (vs. 1-5). Nehemiah dealt with this in the same energetic fashion. The injustice was remedied, and the property of the poor was restored (vs. 6-13). Nehemiah himself set a noble example. For the twelve years during which he was governor he did not draw the official salary to which he was entitled (vs. 14-18). After recording this he adds a prayer that is characteristic of him: "Remember unto me, O my God, for good, all that I have done for this people" (vs. 19; 13:14, 22, 31).

3. The Completion of the Walls (Chs. 6-7). As the building of the walls proceeded, the enemies of the Jews resorted to stratagem, and made repeated proposals to Nehemiah to come out and meet them in a conference, but he resolutely declined (6:1-4); "I am doing a great work, so that I cannot come down". Then they sent an open letter slandering him and threatening to accuse him to the king. He denied the slander and turned to God for strength to go on with the work (6:5-9). Next they tried to terrify him by threats against his life. He scorned these threats and turned again to God. (6:10-14).

Thus Nehemiah went on with the work, and, under his energetic and inspiring leadership, the walls were finished in fifty-two days, with the result that fear came upon the nations around, "for they perceived that this work was wrought of our God" (6:15-16). This was achieved in spite of the fact that intrigues had been going on all the time between the nobles of Judah and the enemies of the Jews (6:17-19).

When the wall was completed and the gates were set up, Nehemiah organized the inhabitants into watchers for the safety of the city and for guarding the gates, "every one to be over against his own house" (7:1-3). But the city was very thinly populated (7:4). Nehemiah's first step toward increasing the population of the city was to get the register of the exiles who had returned at the first, and the list recorded in Ezra 2 is repeated here (7:5-73). Nehemiah begins this part of the record by saying, "My God put into mine heart". The step he took was decided upon because of what he recognized as a suggestion coming from the Lord (cf. 2:12). In the meantime the seventh month had come and, as they had done before (Ezra 3:1), the people gathered with one accord in Jerusalem for its sacred services (7:73-8:1).

THE RESTORATION OF THE COVENANT
(Chs. 8-13)

1. The Reading of the Law (Ch. 8). The narrative here goes on to tell the story of the reformation that followed the building of the walls. The seventh or sacred month of the year had come (7:73), and now Ezra appears in the book for the first time. Under his supervision the Law was read and expounded to a great assembly of the people which had gathered for the purpose (8:1-8). The Levites "read in the book, in the law of God, distinctly; and they gave the sense, so that they understood the reading".

This produced both grief and joy—grief on account of Israel's failure which the Law revealed, and joy on account of their return to the Law which they now understood (8:9-12). On the next day, the rulers and the priests and Levites gathered together to Ezra, "to give attention to the words of the law"; and they proceeded to put it into practice by observing the Feast of Tabernacles which they found enacted therein (8:13-18).

2. The Renewing of the Covenant (Chs. 9-10). Soon after the feast, in the same month, the people observed a day of fasting and humiliation, and separated themselves from all the heathen in the land (9:1-4). They were led by the Levites in a comprehensive prayer of confession and consecration (9:5-38), which included praise to God for His goodness to Israel in delivering the people from Egypt and revealing Himself to them in the wilderness (vs. 5-15), confession of their persistent sin against Him in the wilderness and in Canaan (vs. 16-31), and engagement to renew their covenant relation with Him (vs. 32-38).

The Covenant was then sealed by the people's representatives, whose names are given (10:1-27). The rest of the people all promised to walk in God's law, and to keep His commandments and ordinances (10:28-31), and also to maintain the services of the

Temple, and bring in the first-fruits and the tithes (10:32-39).

3. The Dedication of the Walls (11:1—12:43). Arrangements were now made for occupying the vacant spaces in Jerusalem, by transferring one tenth of the people from the other cities (11:1-2). Some volunteered to dwell in Jerusalem and were specially honoured by the people for doing so. It is called here for the first time "the holy city". The separation recorded in ch. 9, and the new consecration of ch. 10, gave it solemn significance.

The distribution of the population of Judah is then given: the rulers and officers who dwelt in Jerusalem (11:3-9), the priests and Levites and other ministers of the Temple who dwelt in Jerusalem (11:10-24), the people of Judah and Benjamin who dwelt outside Jerusalem (11:25-36). This is followed by a list of the priests and the Levites, arranged by periods from the first return to the days of Nehemiah (12:1-26).

After this the service of dedicating the walls was carried out with gladness and thanksgiving (12:27-30). Nehemiah organized two processions to go in opposite directions round the city walls (12:31-42). The rejoicing of the people that day was so great that "the joy of Jerusalem was heard even afar off" (12:43).

4. The Last Reforms (12:44-13:31). The walls having been built and dedicated, Nehemiah went back to the king in Babylon and remained there for some time (13:6). During his absence some abuses crept in, and when he returned he corrected them in his own energetic fashion. In the meantime certain men had been appointed to take charge of the portions prescribed by the Law for the priests and Levites (12:44-47), and all the mixed multitude had been separated from the congregation of Israel according to instructions found in the book of Moses (13:1-3).

During Nehemiah's absence from Jerusalem, Eliashib the high priest had given one of the chambers in the Temple to Tobiah the Ammonite (2:10) who was a connection of his. On his return Nehemiah cast out all Tobiah's belongings and had the chamber cleansed and restored to its proper use (13:4-9). He also found that the portions appointed for the Levites had not been given to them, and they had left their duties in the Temple in order to work upon their fields for their support. He had the payment of the tithes renewed and treasurers appointed to see that they were properly distributed (13:10-14). The Sabbath was being profaned by people working on that day, and also by self-seeking merchants who brought their wares to the gates of the city on that day. Nehemiah took measures to have the Sabbath properly observed (13:15-22).

He then condemned the mixed marriages which he saw some of the Jews had formed, drawing a warning from the fact that even the great king Solomon had been led into sin by his foreign wives. He proceeded to purify both the congregation and the priesthood of all heathen alliances (13:23-29). The book closes with a statement in which Nehemiah summarizes his work and utters his characteristic prayer: "Remember me, O my God, for good". It was thus he committed himself and his work to God, with no thought of personal fame (13:30-31). With these words Old Testament history ends, for the next book belongs to an earlier date.

THE BOOK OF ESTHER

THE Book of Esther has to do with the Jews who did not return to Judah at the time of the restoration. The great majority of the exiles had settled down in the land of their captivity, and were prospering in business and agriculture. The call to return found no response in their hearts. They were content to live outside of their land, away from their Temple, and apart from fellowship with the Lord their God. In this state the Book of Esther finds them. While Ezra and Nehemiah show how the Lord dealt with the Jews of the restoration, this book shows how He dealt with the Jews of the dispersion.

The Book of Esther is peculiar because the name of God does not appear in it. But this very fact helps to account for its place in the sacred Canon. It illustrates God's care of His people in the midst of the world. As in the providential government of the world God hides Himself, but rules and operates everywhere, so in this book His name is never used, but His hand is seen throughout. It contains the story of a great peril with which the Jews were threatened and a great deliverance that was wrought for them.

The events recorded in the book occurred in the interval between the time of Zerubbabel and the time of Ezra. They stretched over a period of ten years in the reign of Ahasuerus king of Persia (1:3; 2:16; 3:7), who is known as Xerxes in Greek history (485-465 B.C.). The whole story turns on a night when the king could not sleep (6:1), and the book may be divided at this point into two equal parts. The first part (Chs. 1-5) tells of the great peril, and the second part (Chs. 6-10) of the great deliverance.

THE GREAT PERIL
(Chs. 1-5)

These chapters show how a plot was laid to destroy all the Jews throughout the empire of Persia. As the story unfolds, the chief characters in the book come one by one into full view.

1. Ahasuerus the King (Ch. 1). The opening statement brings before us the vast extent of the Persian Empire and its great wealth and splendour (vs. 1-4). Then the first scene is presented. It is a public feast given by the king amid the gorgeous surroundings of his court and with all the license of a drunken revel (vs. 5-8). In the course of it he sends for Vashti the queen to be brought in, and her refusal to debase her womanhood at his command is the redeeming feature in this picture of Persian life and custom (vs. 9-12). In his drunken rage Ahasuerus appeals to his courtiers, and they incite him to depose the queen and put another in her place, because of this insult to his royal authority and to the honour of Persian husbands (vs. 13-22).

This feast, which he gave in the third year of his reign, was probably connected with the vast preparations Ahasuerus was making for his invasion of Greece which took place in 480 B.C. It reveals the real nature of the world empire throughout which the Jews were dispersed, and the vain and weak character of the king. Ahasuerus is mentioned by his title "king" nearly two hundred times in the book, but it is God who really reigns. He uses the drunken whim of Ahasuerus to prepare the way for making a Jewess queen.

2. Mordecai the Jew (Ch. 2). In the midst of the story in this chapter, which tells how Ahasuerus proceeded to choose a queen in the place of Vashti, Mordecai comes upon the scene (vs. 1-7). His cousin and adopted daughter, Esther, was finally chosen; but the fact that she was a Jewess was not made known (vs. 8-15). Esther was made queen in the seventh year of Ahasuerus (vs. 16-18). The occasion was probably in line with the way the king consoled himself after his humiliating defeat in Greece the previous year.

Mordecai's love and concern for Esther are shown in his daily frequenting the precincts of the palace. While sitting in the king's gate one day, he discovered a plot against the king's life, and revealed it to the king through Esther (vs. 19-23).

3. Haman the Agagite (Ch. 3). And now the enemy of the Jews comes upon the scene. Haman was a descendant of Agag, the king of the Amalekites upon whom the curse of God had fallen for their enmity to Israel (Exod 17:14; 1 Sam. 15:8). Ahasuerus promoted him to the highest position in the realm and commanded all to do him reverence. This reverence Mordecai persistently refused to give (vs. 1-3). Probably it involved an act of divine worship which Mordecai as a Jew would not give to any man.

The malice of Haman was so deep and bitter that he conceived a plot for the destruction, not only of Mordecai, but of all Mordecai's people (vs. 4-6). In the first month of the twelfth year of Ahasuerus, by the casting of the lot, Haman fixed on the thirteenth day of the twelfth month for the execution of his plot. He secured the king's consent by promising a great contribution to the royal treasury (vs. 7-11). The bribe was doubtless in line with the king's effort to replenish his treasury, which must have been exhausted by the Grecian expedition. A royal edict was accordingly issued and posted throughout all the provinces of Persia, that on that day the Jews were to be destroyed and their property was to be seized (vs. 12-15). A vivid light is cast upon the character of the two men and upon the bewilderment of the people by the last statement in the chapter.

4. Esther the Queen (Chs. 4-5). When this decree was published, Mordecai and the Jews throughout the provinces were filled with grief and dismay, and gave outward evidence of their sorrow (4:1-3). The news of this reached Esther in the palace, and she sent to Mordecai to learn the cause of it, and he sent back word charging her to supplicate the king on behalf of her people (4:4-8). The urgency of the case appealed to her, but the law of the court forbade her approach to the king except at his call, and she had not been called for a month (4:9-12). At the earnest request and warning of Mordecai she decided to make the venture, and appealed to her people to fast with her in preparation for it (4:13-17). "So will I go in unto the king . . . . and if I perish, I perish".

When Esther approached the king, he received her graciously, and promised to give her whatever she asked. Her first request was to invite the king and Haman to a banquet (5:1-4). When they came, she invited them to another banquet on the next day, saying that she would present her petition then (5:5-8). Haman was inflated with pride, and boasted of his wealth, advancement, and honour to his friends and his wife; but all this did not satisfy him while Mordecai remained in his way at the king's gate. On their advice, he had a gallows erected, intending to get the king's permission the next morning to hang Mordecai thereon (5:9-14).

THE GREAT DELIVERANCE
(Chs. 6-10)

The plot against the Jews had been perfected. By the laws of the Medes and Persians the king's decree could not be changed. Mordecai was in imminent peril. Haman was apparently on the eve of his triumph. But now, other forces, which Haman could not foresee or control, came into operation. Events began to move rapidly. The plot was frustrated; and instead of the Jews, it was their foes, who were destroyed. These chapters tell how all this took place.

1. The Elevation of Mordecai (Ch. 6). The king's sleepless night is the turning point of the story. To while away the time he had the records of the kingdom read to him, and there he discovered the forgotten service that Mordecai had rendered him, for which he had never been rewarded (vs. 1-3). As Haman came into the court next morning to request the hanging of Mordecai, Ahasuerus asked him what should be done to the man whom the king delighted to honour. Supposing that he himself was meant, Haman laid out a program of royal honours (vs. 4-9). At the king's command, Haman was obliged to proceed at once and bestow all these honours upon Mordecai (vs. 10-11). Leaving Mordecai again at the king's gate, he hurried back to his wife and friends in shame and consternation (vs. 12-14).

2. The Downfall of Haman (Ch. 7). In this state of mind he was called to the queen's banquet. There Esther presented her petition, pleading for her own life and the life of her people, and exposing Haman as their adversary and enemy (vs. 1-6). The king's wrath was roused. Haman's ruin came on apace. He was hanged on the gallows he had prepared for Mordecai (vs. 7-10).

3. The Rescue of the Jews (8:1—9:19). The mischief which Haman had wrought still remained. The day set for the destruction of the Jews was coming on. Esther now interceded with the king to have this device of Haman's frustrated. The king could not change his edict, but he gave authority to Mordecai, who had been promoted to Haman's place, to issue a counter-edict on the Jews' behalf (8:1-8). Accordingly a royal decree was prepared in the third month and published throughout all the provinces of the kingdom, granting the Jews the right to defend their lives and slay their enemies (8:9-14). The Jews everywhere were filled with gladness and joy, and many of the other people joined the Jews (8:15-17). A vivid light is cast upon the new situation by the statement: "The city of Shushan shouted and was glad". The people as a whole were evidently favourably disposed to the Jews.

When the fateful day arrived, the plot of Haman was completely reversed. The fear of the Jews was fallen upon all the other races in the empire, and the Jews smote their enemies, including the sons of Haman (9:1-10). By the king's permission they continued to carry out his decree during the next day, until the Jews "had rest from their enemies" (9:11-16). The restrained spirit in which the Jews executed this judgment on "them that hated them" is indicated by the thrice repeated statement: "But on the spoil they laid not their hand" (vs. 10, 15-16). The Jews celebrated their deliverance with a day of feasting (9:17-19).

4. The Feast of Purim (9:20—10:3). Mordecai urged the Jews to make this a yearly celebration (9:20-25). They accordingly established the Feast of Purim, or Lots, to commemorate their great deliverance from Haman's plot (9:26-28), and this was confirmed by Esther the queen (9:29-32). The book closes with an account of the greatness of Mordecai the Jew, under whose beneficent rule as the chief minister of king Ahasuerus the Jews continued to enjoy prosperity and peace (ch. 10). This is the ultimate end of the story: God's providential ways have a benevolent end.

The annual feast that Mordecai established, which the Jews still celebrate, marks the victory of God's providential government in a world which seems to be governed by chance. The whole book is a historical commentary on the text: "The lot is cast into the lap: but the whole disposing thereof is of Jehovah" (Prov. 16:33). Haman trusted in chance and worshipped the god of the Lots. Mordecai trusted in Providence and put his faith in the Lord God of Israel.

ISRAEL UNDER GENTILE RULE

In the last three historical books we see Israel occupying the position which the people were to hold, both in Palestine and in the Dispersion, until the coming of the Messiah. The nation was now definitely under the subjection of the Gentiles. Even in their own land, national independence was gone and Gentile power was in full control. The times of the Gentiles had begun (Luke 21:24).

The remnant that returned from Babylon had been cured of idolatry in the captivity, but the Restoration did not give them back all they had lost. There was no Ark in the Temple now, and no symbol of God's presence there. No miracle or miraculous intervention of God took place in Israel's history after the Exile. His presence and power were no longer manifested in any visible way. The dispensation was already waxing old and preparing to vanish away (Heb. 8:13).

Decrees of Gentile kings occupy considerable space in Ezra and Nehemiah. It was by such indirect means as these that God was now exercising His government over His people. When the New Testament opens, the same conditions remain. It was the decree of a Roman Emperor that brought Joseph and Mary to Bethlehem for the birth of the promised Redeemer there.

The Book of Esther shows that the Israelites had become known throughout the Gentile world as "Jews" (people of Judah). The name is used in the Scriptures only five times before the Exile (2 Kings 16:6; 18:26, 28; 25:25; 2 Chron. 32:18). In Ezra it occurs eight times, and in Nehemiah ten times. In Esther it is found throughout, occurring forty-five times. Evidently it was the name commonly applied to the Israelites among the other peoples of the world. It is the predominant name for the descendants of Abraham and Jacob throughout the whole New Testament.

THE OLD TESTAMENT
POETICAL BOOKS

JOB TO MALACHI

THE POETICAL BOOKS

THE five books from Job to the Song of Solomon, together with the Book of Lamentations, were written for the most part in poetical form. They deal mainly with the inward side of religious and moral life. The Historical Books have traced the development of the Law as it was manifested in the corporate life of Israel as a nation. The Poetical Books now set forth the development of the Law as it was realized in the life and experience of the individual Israelite.

Poetry is not so sharply distinguished from prose in Hebrew as in English. Some books are partly in prose and partly in poetry. In Job the narrative passages are in prose and the discourses in poetry. The elevated oratory of some of the Prophets, especially Isaiah, often glides into poetry.

The characteristic mark of Hebrew poetry is parallelism, pairs of lines corresponding in thought. The second line may repeat the thought of the first line in altered form, or add something so as to complete it, or state something in contrast with it. Occasionally the lines are grouped in strophes or stanzas, as in Psalms 42 and 43. Sometimes an acrostic structure is used, following the order of the Hebrew alphabet. This occurs in several Psalms, notably the 119th, and in the Book of Lamentations. This feature, of course, cannot be shown in translations of the Bible.

The King James Version of the English Bible (A.V.) does not distinguish poetry from prose, but the Revised Version sets out the poetical sections in their parallel lines. The rhythm which gives balance to the parallelism in the Hebrew cannot be represented in a translation. Fragments of poetry and several extended poetical passages occur in the preceding books of the Old Testament. Among these are two songs of Moses (Exod. 15:1-18; Deut. 32:1-43), Deborah's war song (Jud. 5), Hannah's song of thanksgiving (1 Sam. 2:1-10), and David's elegy over Saul and Jonathan (2 Sam. 1:17-27).

The Hebrews cultivated two kinds of poetry: didactic poetry, intended for teaching and appealing to the mind, and lyric poetry, intended for singing and appealing to the heart. The six Poetical Books contain both kinds. They can be classified accordingly in two corresponding groups: (1) Books of Wisdom—Job, Proverbs, and Ecclesiastes—which are didactic in character, and deal with the religious convictions. (2) Books of Devotion—Psalms, Song of Solomon, and Lamentations—which are lyrical, and deal with the religious affections.

THE BOOK OF JOB

THE theme of this book is the problem of pain in the providence of God, or the mystery of suffering in the lives of the righteous. Why do good men suffer? The subject is not dealt with in an abstract or theoretical way, but is wrought out in the living experience of a righteous man.

Job is mentioned in other parts of Scripture in such a way as to imply that he was an actual person and not an imaginary character (Ezek. 14:14, 20; Jas. 5:11). The story reflects the conditions of life in a pastoral age like that of the patriarchs. The Septuagint, which is the ancient Greek version of the Hebrew Scriptures, has a note at the end of the book identifying Job with Jobab, a descendant of Esau (Gen. 36:13, 33). This would place him in the age between Abraham and Moses, and near the time of the latter.

The date and authorship of the book are not known. It is clearly the work of a masterly mind. That it is very ancient, and was written before the revelation of the Law, may be inferred from the fact that in the entire discussion of God's moral government there is no reference to the Decalogue or the Levitical system of worship.

It is an attractive supposition, and not an unreasonable or improbable one, that Moses heard the story of Job and wrote the book when he was dwelling in Midian, during the years between his flight from Egypt and his call to deliver Israel (Exod. 2:15). This is more consistent with the internal evidence and the general character of the book than the theory of a late date, which is based on an evolutionary theory of religion and assumes that its ideas could not have been developed so early. There is no known writer in any age to whom it can be referred better qualified than Moses, or more likely to have written a book like this. The person who was capable of such an accomplishment could hardly have remained unknown to history.

The Book of Job is dramatic in form, and it may be divided into five progressive parts and analyzed as follows:

    I. The Afflictions of Job—Chs. 1-3
   II. Job's Controversy with His Friends—
        Chs. 4-31
      1. The First Round of Speeches (Chs. 4-14)
      2. The Second Round of Speeches
        (Chs. 15-21)
      3. The Third Round of Speeches (Chs. 22-24)
      4. Job's Final Speeches (Chs. 25-31)
  III. The Intervention of Elihu—Chs. 32-37
  IV. The Revelation of Jehovah—Chs. 38-41
   V. The Restoration of Job—Ch. 42.

THE AFFLICTIONS OF JOB
(Chs. 1-3)

The book opens with a series of scenes, alternating on earth and in Heaven, which reveal the source of Job's afflictions, describe their nature, and show how he bore them.

1. Job's Happy State (1:1-5). Job's life was right with God and man. His outward lot was marked by the special favour of God. The sacrifice which he offered habitually as the patriarchal head of the family was an evidence of his devotion to God and his care for the moral and spiritual welfare

of his children. His piety was so deep that it recognized the secret sins of the heart.

2. The First Council in Heaven (1:6-12). The veil is now drawn aside and the spiritual world is disclosed. The scene is described with restrained and simple dignity. The angelic agents of God's government present themselves before Him, and Satan comes among them. He has come from a restless and ceaseless survey of the lives of men upon the earth: "from going to and fro in the earth, and from walking up and down in it". (cf. 1 Peter 5:8).

The scene reveals the intimate relation between earth and Heaven. The righteous life of Job on earth had been honouring God in Heaven: "Hast thou considered my servant Job?" Satan has his retort ready. Job is pious because piety is profitable. Let his prosperity be taken away and his devotion to God will fail.

This charge against Job involves the honour of God. Satan insinuates that God is honoured only because of what He gives. There is but one way of refuting this charge, and that is to test Job. Satan is accordingly given permission to afflict him with adversity, but not to touch his person. Here we get the first light on the problem of suffering. Satan is the primary agent in the infliction of it, but God permits it, to prove the righteousness and piety of His servants on earth and so vindicate His own honour in Heaven.

3. Job Stripped of All (1:13-22). The scene changes to earth again, and events take place which have their springs in Heaven. The secondary instruments in the infliction of suffering now come into view. One day when Job's children were enjoying their usual happy family fellowship, four messengers came rushing into the father's presence in quick succession, and announced a series of calamities of which they were the sole survivors. In a single day he was stripped of all his wealth and bereft of all his children.

Job's actions manifest his deep and genuine grief, but his piety does not waver. He recognizes that he is now as poor as he was at his birth, but instead of finding fault with God's providence, he bows before Him in reverential worship and gives renewed expression to his faith in God.

4. The Second Council in Heaven (2:1-6). A considerable time must have elapsed before the next scene takes place. Job has stood the test long enough to prove his integrity and his loyalty to God. He has not only borne up under the first shock of disaster; he has endured the long strain of it afterwards. When the second council in Heaven opens, God claims the victory: Satan's accusation has been refuted. Satan, however, has another charge ready. With an insolent sneer he insinuates that Job cares only for his own skin. Let him be smitten in body and his devotion to God will fail. And now for the second time Job is put to the test. Satan may afflict his person, but is not allowed to take his life.

5. Job Among the Ashes (2:7-10). Satan goes forth to his malevolent work, and Job is subjected to the most searching of all tests, a loathsome and incurable disease. He is obliged to sit upon the ash-heap where the rubbish of the city is burnt, an outcast from his fellows, a pathetic and pitiful figure. The patience of his wife breaks down at last. She seems to have stood by Job in the first trial; but now, in the frenzy of her sympathetic anguish, she has lost her faith in God's goodness. But no word of complaint escapes Job's lips. There is no harshness in his reply to his wife, but rather a tender tone of pained surprise. She has not spoken with her usual wisdom: "What? shall we receive good at the hand of God, and shall we not receive evil?"

One purpose in Job's afflictions has now been achieved. Satan's attack on Job's character and God's honour has been foiled. It has been proved that righteousness and piety are not grounded in self-interest, and that God is worthy of being served and trusted for His own sake. Job's trial still goes on, however, for there is a higher purpose in it which has yet to be attained; but Satan appears in the book no more.

NOTE:—It is not to be inferred from these scenes that Satan appears in Heaven now as the accuser of God's people. He is still our adversary, but as our accuser he has been cast out of Heaven. Job lived under Old Testament conditions, before the redeeming work of Christ was done. As the death and resurrection of our Lord have made a change on earth, so His ascension has made a change in Heaven. By His atoning death on the cross He removed the ground of Satan's accusation against us. Just before His crucifixion He declared, "Now shall the prince of this world be cast out" (John 12:31). At His ascension He entered Heaven as our representative and advocate, and Satan had no longer any right to be there. The vision in Rev. 12: 7-12 symbolizes the casting out of Satan from Heaven as following immediately after the event described in the words, "her child was caught up unto God, and unto his throne" (v. 5). That is, Satan's expulsion from Heaven as the accuser of the saints was the immediate result of the ascension of the Lord. Instead of an accuser we have now "an Advocate with the Father, Jesus Christ the righteous" (1 John 2:1; cf. Rom. 8:33-39).

6. The Coming of Job's Friends (2:11-13). The three friends of Job were men of wealth and influence like himself. They have heard of his affliction and have come from distant places to condole with him. By this time a considerable interval must have elapsed. Job has had time to realize the full bitterness of his condition. The terrible disease that afflicts him has so changed his appearance that his friends do not recognize him. They are profoundly moved by their first sight of the sufferer. Their grief is deep and genuine. They do not inflict upon him the common platitudes of speech, but sit down with him in silence for seven days and seven nights. This is true sympathy and real friendship.

7. Job's Outcry (Ch. 3). In the presence of these companions of his former prosperity, Job's grief at last finds expression. No longer attempting to control himself, he breaks out into a passionate, pitiful cry for death. It is his response to the silent sympathy of his friends.

From this point to the middle of the last chapter, the book is composed of a series of addresses, which are all in poetical form. The present one containing Job's lamentation is in three parts, and it may be summed up as follows: "Oh that I had never been born" (vs. 1-10); "Oh that I had died at my birth" (vs. 11-19); "Oh that I might die now" (vs. 20-26).

This cry is very different from Job's first expressions of sublime faith, but it does not mean that he has renounced God or abandoned his integrity. It is to be remembered that Job has not been told why this evil has come upon him. He knows nothing of what has gone on in Heaven. He has not the New Testament light that we enjoy. He goes through his trial destitute of those grounds of consolation that suffering saints now possess. He has never heard that all things work together for good to them that love God. In the absolute darkness he trusts God still, and there can be no greater test of faith. But it is this very darkness that causes him at last to cry out. He has no clue to God's ways with him. He is "a man whose way is hid, and whom God hath hedged in" (v. 23). What is the meaning of life for a man when God has dealt with him so? The mystery of it has forced this cry from his lips.

This speech provides the basis for the discussion which follows. It leads the friends of Job to address him, and they begin at once to remonstrate with him about it. They have come to sympathize with Job and to comfort him, but they have their own theory about suffering, and they mean to apply it to Job's case. God sends suffering as a punishment for sin. Since Job suffers, sin must lie at his door. If he will confess it, and repent and turn to God, he will be delivered and all will be well. This is their belief, and it is the background of all the debate. Each man speaks in turn and Job replies to each. The debate goes round the circle three times.

THE FIRST ROUND OF SPEECHES
(Chs. 4-14)

The scene is still the ash-heap where Job is sitting with his friends around him (2:8, 13). The course of the discussion reveals the various characteristics of the three men. They press their arguments from different points of view. Eliphaz, who is perhaps the oldest because he speaks first, argues from what he has seen (4:8; 5:3; 15:17). He is the elderly man of experience and observation. Bildad is the learned man who refers to his authorities and appeals to the results of study and investigation (8:8-10). Zophar is the blunt man who has opinions of his own and prides himself on saying what he thinks (11:1-6; 20:2). Thus the wisdom of Eliphaz, the learning of Bildad, and the dogmatism of Zophar, are brought to bear on Job's case. The three men represent all that human philosophy has to offer on the problem of suffering. The real scene of the drama is the inner life of Job, and his speeches are the windows through which we see into his soul.

In their first speeches the friends deal mainly with the ways of God's providence. They argue that it is God's way to punish sin with suffering. In doing so Eliphaz emphasizes the goodness of God, Bildad the justice of God, and Zophar the wisdom of God.

1. Eliphaz (Chs. 4-5). He begins with a courteous apology for speaking at all, and proceeds to lay down the general law of sowing and reaping in the moral world (4:1-11). This was revealed to him once in a silent vision of the night (4:12-21). He describes a concrete case (5:1-7), and advises Job to seek God (5:8-16), promising him a happy result if he will submit to the chastenings of the Almighty (5:17-27).

2. Job (Chs. 6-7). He has been pained by the speech of Eliphaz. He protests that the greatness of his calamity has not been taken into account (6:1-13). He expresses deep disappointment at the attitude of his friends (6:14-23), and challenges them to show him wherein he has sinned (6:24-30). Then he renews his bitter cry, describing the misery of his life (7:1-10), and appealing to God to be left alone (7:11-21). This frank and open speech of Job, with all its terrible energy and depth of feeling, differs greatly from the pious moralizing of Eliphaz, with its utter lack of sympathy.

3. Bildad (Ch. 8). Less courteous than Eliphaz, he begins by reproving Job. He affirms that God's justice has been illustrated in the fate of Job's children, and tells him that it will be illustrated in his own restoration to prosperity and happiness if he will turn to God.

4. Job (Chs. 9-10). He admits the general truth of what his friends say: "Of a truth I know that it is so". And then he raises a far deeper question: "How can man be just with God?" He discusses this in the light of God's great power as contrasted with his own helplessness, and expresses the need of a daysman or umpire between himself and God (ch. 9). Then he makes a new appeal to God, seeking to discover why God should destroy the work of His own hands and why He will not leave him alone (ch. 10).

In this speech Job reaches the most agonized depths of doubt, and his words show how insoluble is the soul's problem on the lines of human righteousness. But from this point he reaches out to give expression to a great need. He utters the cry of the heart of humanity for a Mediator (9:33). It is really an aspiration: the Septuagint renders it, "Would that there were a mediator for us, who would hear the cause between us both". It shows that man was made for the Gospel by proving that the Gospel corresponds to the deepest craving of the human heart. Jesus is God's answer to Job's cry.

5. Zophar (Ch. 11). The third friend now breaks into the debate in a blunt, dictatorial way. He is perhaps the youngest of the three, and carries on the debate with hot-headed zeal and self-confidence. Reproving Job as a man "full of talk", he wishes God would speak to him. In the light of the wisdom of God, he exhorts Job to put away his iniquity and he will have a happy end.

6. Job (Chs. 12-14). He pours contempt upon the superior wisdom his friends assume, and shows that he knows more about God's ways than they do (12:1-13:2). He declares that his appeal is to God Himself (13:3-19). Then he begins to plead his cause with God (13:20-28). He describes the frailty of man's life, and raises the question: "If a man die shall he live again?" If he knew this was so, he could endure through all the days of his affliction till his release should come (ch. 14). This speech attains a high and noble tone. Job's suffering has developed in him sympathy with the human race. His faith reaches upward to the thought of a life for man beyond this one.

NOTE:—In this first round of speeches, each of the three friends has revealed his own character; and they have all applied their theory, each in his own way, to Job's case. Their view that suffering is sent as a punishment for sin is true so far as it goes, but it does not explain why a righteous man should suffer. The friends have failed to understand Job because they have not taken a sympathetic approach to his problem. Their addresses have been cold theoretical discussions of an abstract doctrine. They have brought the sufferer no help and no comfort.

Job's speeches, on the other hand, have been full of intense feeling. While he admits the general truth of what they say, he sweeps aside their application of it to his case and appeals to God Himself. What makes his affliction so heavy is, that he knows it has come from God and yet God leaves him in darkness about it and gives him no explanation. But Job never abandons his confidence in God. In the midst of his own sufferings he is learning to sympathize with all who suffer. He identifies himself with mankind in general, and so he discovers the deepest needs of the human heart. His cry is a cry to God from the heart of humanity, and his faith reaches out to God for an answer to that cry. Before this round of speeches has come to an end he has gained a presentiment of the Incarnation and of Immortality.

THE SECOND ROUND OF SPEECHES
(Chs. 15-21)

The friends now change their line of approach to Job and base their theory on the history of the wicked. Eliphaz argues that the wicked man has a terrible experience, Bildad that he has a disastrous end, and Zophar that he has but brief prosperity. All this describes Job's case, and therefore he must be a wicked man. The friends now become more violent and bitter in their attack upon him.

1. Eliphaz (Ch. 15). He rebukes Job for his last speech (vs. 1-16), and depicts the troubled conscience and the terrible experience of the wicked man (vs. 17-35).

2. Job (Chs. 16-17). His friends are miserable comforters (16:1-5). He pictures his disconsolate condition (16:6-17), and appeals to God as his witness and vindicator (16:18—17:5). He is sustained by an inward assurance that God will do him justice: "Even now, behold, my witness is in heaven, and he that voucheth for me is on high" (v. 19). Then he goes on to describe his helpless and hopeless state (17:6-16).

3. Bildad (Ch. 18). He rebukes Job (vs. 1-4), and describes the downfall and disastrous end of the sinner (vs. 5-21).

4. Job (Ch. 19). He reproaches his friends for their attitude toward him (vs. 1-6), laments his sufferings as proceeding from God (vs. 7-12) and from men (vs. 13-20), makes a pathetic appeal for sympathy (vs. 21-22), and then rises to the utterance of a lofty faith in God (vs. 23-29): "As for me I know that my Redeemer liveth, and at last he will stand up upon the earth: and after my skin hath been thus destroyed, yet from my flesh shall I see God" (vs. 25-26; marg.).

The original term for the word "Redeemer" in this passage is "Goel", which conveys something of the meaning of the word "Vindicator" also. The Goel was the man whose duty it was, in the law of that age, to buy back the property of a kinsman for him if he had lost it, or to purchase his freedom if he had become a bondslave, or to avenge his death if he had been unjustly slain. Job must soon die, but he grasps the thought that his Redeemer, his Goel, will live on after him. His faith anticipates a time when God Himself will vindicate his honour upon the earth, and restore, even in the flesh, the rights which he has lost. This is the highest and most wondrous flight of his faith. He has caught sight of the Resurrection.

5. Zophar (Ch. 20). He expresses his indignation at Job, and declares that the prosperity of the wicked is brief (vs. 1-11). Sin brings its own retribution, and the sinner cannot enjoy his prosperity (vs. 12-29).

6. Job (Ch. 21). He bids his friends be silent while he speaks (vs. 1-6), declares that the real mystery is the prosperity of the wicked (vs. 7-16), for it is no invariable rule that they are overwhelmed with calamity (vs. 17-26), and rebukes his friends for their false conclusion and vain comfort (vs. 27-34).

Job's replies in this round of speeches contain three strands of thought: (1) The terrible loneliness of sorrow. Job is a type of Him who was "a man of sorrows, and acquainted with grief". (2) The triumphant flight of faith. The noblest expressions of Job's trust in God occur in these chapters (16:19; 19:25). (3) The real mystery of life. It consists in the prosperity of the wicked being more manifest than their downfall (21:7-9, 17).

THE THIRD ROUND OF SPEECHES
(Chs. 22-26)

Having no further arguments to bring, the friends now charge Job directly with sin. Eliphaz makes the definite accusation, and Bildad follows it up with a brief speech. Zophar is silent altogether, showing that the attempt of the friends to convict Job has been exhausted. Job does not reply directly to the charge. He has maintained his innocence before, and he now deals mainly with the mystery of God's silence.

1. Eliphaz (Ch. 22). He charges Job with great wickedness (vs. 1-11), warns him that God takes note of his sin (vs. 12-20), and admonishes him to repent and return to God (vs. 21-30). This speech shows the effect of controversy on good men, and the length to which they will go for the sake of a theory. It is an impressive illustration of the fact that dogmas, however true in themselves, lose all their power for good unless they are inspired and maintained by love.

2. Job (Chs. 23-24). He wonders at the mysterious silence of God in his own case—"Oh that I knew where I might find him" (ch. 23)—and at the apparent absence of justice in God's government of the world (ch. 24). He points out instances of public wrong-doing (vs. 1-12), and secret sins (vs. 13-25), that go unpunished. This speech shows that Job's own misery has opened his eyes to the misery of his fellow men. What saddens him is that he cannot see any good end subserved in the wrongs and calamities that men have to endure.

3. Bildad (Ch. 25). He has only a few words left to say. God is too great and high for man to be pure in His sight.

4. Job (Ch. 26). He expresses sarcastic admiration of Bildad's words (vs. 1-4). He silences his friends by showing that he has a far more majestic conception of God's greatness than they have (vs. 5-13). He closes this round by indicating that the very greatness of God hides the mystery of man's problem (v. 14).

NOTE:—Throughout the debate, Job has not only been answering the arguments of his friends, but has also been searching for the light. He has been groping his way in the darkness. In his affliction he has been sounding the utmost depths of human need. He has expressed this need from time to time in the course of the debate in a number of cries out of the darkness. Each of these cries is either a profound question which he cannot answer, or the utterance of a profound faith in God. None of the cries is answered in the book itself, or even in the whole Old Testament. But each of them is met by the revelation of God in Jesus Christ, and its answer is found in the New Testament.

These cries of Job are the elemental aspirations of the heart of humanity. Thus "deep calleth unto deep"—the deeps of man's great need to the deeps of

God's great grace. Seven such cries may be found in the speeches of Job. They may be set forth with their New Testament answers as follows:

1. "How can man be just with God," (9:2).— "Being justified freely by his grace through the redemption that is in Christ Jesus" (Rom. 3: 24). "Because Christ also suffered for sins once, the righteous for the unrighteous, that he might bring us to God" (1 Pet. 3:18).

2. "There is no umpire betwixt us, that might lay his hand upon us both" (9:33).—"There is one God, one mediator also between God and men, himself man, Christ Jesus" (1 Tim. 2:5).

3. "If a man die, shall he live again?" (14:14). —"Our Saviour Christ Jesus abolished death, and brought life and immortality to light through the gospel" (2 Tim. 1:10).

4. "Even now, behold, my witness is in heaven, and he that voucheth for me is on high" (16:19).— "If any man sin, we have an Advocate with the Father, Jesus Christ the righteous" (1 John 2:1). "He is able to save to the uttermost them that draw near unto God through him, seeing he ever liveth to make intercession for them" (Heb. 7:25).

5. "As for me I know that my Redeemer liveth, and at last he will stand up upon the earth, and ..... from my flesh shall I see God" (19:25-26)— "Our citizenship is in heaven; whence also we wait for a Saviour, the Lord Jesus Christ" (Phil. 3:20). "We know that, if he shall be manifested, we shall be like him; for we shall see him even as he is" (1 John 3:2).

6. "Oh that I knew where I might find him" (23:3).—"No man hath seen God at any time; the only begotten Son, who is in the bosom of the Father, he hath declared him (John 1:18). "I am the way, and the truth, and the life: no one cometh unto the Father but by me" (John 14:6).

7. "He knoweth the way that I take; when he hath tried me, I shall come forth as gold" (23:10). —"I reckon that the sufferings of this present time are not worthy to be compared with the glory which shall be revealed to usward" (Rom. 8:18).

JOB'S FINAL SPEECHES
(Chs. 27-31)

The three friends have no more to say. Their theory that suffering is God's way of punishing sin may be true as a general principle of God's moral government, but it does not meet Job's case. Job never gives up his faith in the goodness and justice of God, but he also maintains that he is innocent of any conduct that would account for his suffering at God's hand more than others. He now makes his final reply, (1) closing the debate by establishing his innocence against the charge of his friends, and (2) reviewing his whole case to show that his sufferings must have a deeper cause than his moral conduct.

1. A Reply to his Friends (Chs. 27-28). He solemnly protests his innocence and integrity (27:1-12), and describes the treatment of the wicked at the hand of God as different from his own experience (27:13-23). Then comes a splendid chapter in which Job describes the unsearchableness of wisdom (ch. 28). Men penetrate into the bosom of the earth in mining operations and bring forth its treasures (vs. 1-11). But wisdom cannot be found, nor can it be purchased (vs. 12-22). God alone knows it (vs. 23-28). By wisdom Job means the secret of things, the solution of the problems of life,

the moral order of the world. The answer to Job's search for wisdom is found only in Jesus Christ.

2. A Review of his Case (Chs. 29-31). Now Job goes back in imagination over his own history. He recalls the happiness of his past life (ch. 29), and bewails the misery of his present experience (ch. 30). Then he solemnly and deliberately protests the innocence and integrity of his life (ch. 31). In doing so he reviews his personal life (vs. 1-8), his domestic life (vs. 9-15), his civil life (vs. 16-23), and his religious life (vs. 24-40).

In these chapters Job reveals himself more than anywhere else in the poem. There is both pathos and beauty in them. The story Job relates in ch. 30 bears a strange likeness to the path of the Cross trodden by the Son of God, and suggests that his history was not only a pattern of the ways of the Lord with His children, but also a foreshadowing of the experience of Christ. Here is the path of derision and contempt (vs. 1-8), of indignity and insult (vs. 9-15), of pain and distress (vs. 16-23), of loneliness and darkness (vs. 24-31). But while there is a striking similarity in their paths of suffering, there is a striking contrast in their endurance of suffering. Job's language is all full of self—self-vindication, self-pity, self-assertion.

In the three chapters the first personal pronoun occurs nearly 200 times. There is no expression of conscious weakness, no token of a broken and submissive spirit. How differently Paul dealt with his own justification (1 Cor. 4:4)! Job at last stands revealed. In vindicating himself he shows that he has needed the refining fire. Here we see, not a sinful man in whom sin needs to be punished, but a righteous man in whom self needs to die. This is the end to which the debate has led, and it prepares the way for the ultimate purpose of God in Job's affliction, which is worked out in the rest of the book.

THE INTERVENTION OF ELIHU
(Chs. 32-37)

The three friends have been put to silence, and Job himself has nothing more to say: "The words of Job are ended" (31:40). He relapses into silence, but the mystery still remains. A young man now comes into the discussion who has waited till the older men finished. He has been among the bystanders around the ash-heap listening to the debate. He speaks under the constraint of the spirit within him (32:17-18). He feels moved by "the breath of the Almighty" (32:8; 33:4). Thus he represents those who are enlightened by God and taught by His Spirit.

1. Elihu's Introduction (Ch. 32). The effect of the debate on Elihu is stated. He was indignant with Job, because he could only justify himself by accusing God; and indignant with the friends, because they could only justify God by accusing Job (vs. 1-5). Then he introduces himself and explains his reason for taking part in the discussion (vs. 6-22). Being young, he has listened with deference while his seniors were debating the question of Job's affliction. But he has come to see that years do not always bring wisdom, for their arguments have been unconvincing. There is a Divine spirit that gives true enlightenment to man, and because of this Elihu declares what he calls "mine opinion" (vs. 6, 10, 17), the conviction that has been wrought within him. He first addresses the friends (v. 6), and then turns to the bystanders (v. 15). Finally he begins to speak directly to Job himself (33:1).

2. His First Address (Ch. 33). He refers to Job's complaint that God was afflicting him without any cause (vs. 1-12), and then goes on to show that suffering is one of God's ways of speaking to man (vs. 13-22). God speaks in two ways (v. 14) : in dreams and visions (vs. 15-16), and in suffering and affliction (vs. 19-22). What man needs is "an interpreter" to explain God's righteous purpose (v. 23), and what God provides for man is "a ransom" (v. 24). God is gracious and uses suffering to keep man back from possible sin and danger (vs. 17-18), and also to give him new life and blessing after suffering has done its work (vs. 25-30). Elihu then closes his first address by challenging Job to answer him if he has anything to say (vs. 31-33).

Job's silence after this speech of Elihu's shows that he has been impressed by it. Elihu has brought a new view to bear on Job's case. Suffering is one of God's gracious methods of dealing with men. The sufferings of the righteous have a purifying purpose. They are sent of God to restrain men from self-righteousness and from possible sin, and to discipline the soul for a richer and fuller life.

NOTE:—The two ways in which, Elihu says, God speaks to man, correspond with His written Word brought home to our hearts by the Holy Spirit, and His providential dealings with us interpreted by His Word and Spirit. There was no written revelation in the days of Job. Dreams and visions were God's method of conveying His revelation in the days of the patriarchs. He no longer speaks in that way; His revelation is now conveyed through the Scriptures. God still speaks to us, however, through His providences, and through suffering and affliction. Elihu's idea of the "ransom" by which God accomplishes His purpose in dealing thus with men introduces the shadow of the Cross. Elihu does not explain it, but he makes two points clear: the ransom is provided by God and not by the sinner; and it is provided on the ground of his confession and repentance (vs. 23-28).

Considered in the light of the New Testament, Elihu's "opinion" is that suffering is the means God uses for helping His people to crucify self. The two strongest characteristics of the self-life are referred to in v. 17, namely, self-will and pride. Suffering helps the Christian to die to self, to reckon himself crucified with Christ and dead unto sin, to deny self and to take up his cross and follow Christ (Rom. 6:11; Gal. 2:20; 6:14; Col. 3:1-3).

3. His Second Address (Ch. 34). Job remaining silent, Elihu proceeds. He first appeals to the wise men around him, asking them to listen in order to try his words as he goes on to answer Job (vs. 1-4). He meets Job's complaint that God was afflicting him unjustly (vs. 5-9), by stating that God cannot do wickedness and that justice is shown in God's government of men (vs. 10-30). He then points out the true way to bear suffering: by penitent and patient submission to God, and willingness to learn what He would teach us (vs. 31-37).

4. His Third Address (Ch. 35). Job had questioned the advantage of serving God, and seemed to set up his righteousness as more than God's (vs. 1-3). Elihu now points out that man's sin does not hurt God, nor does man's righteousness add anything to Him (vs. 4-8). The reason why men do not find God is because they make no true devout appeal to Him (vs. 9-16). If God does not hear the afflicted, it is not because He does not care, but because they ask amiss. Their cry is only a cry for help and not a cry for God. Men should not cry out like the brutes simply because they are hurt. They should learn to trust in God as their Maker, and as One who can give them songs in the night (v. 10; Psa. 32:7; Heb. 12:11).

5. His Fourth Address (Chs. 36-37). Having answered Job's arguments, Elihu now begins his last address. He beseeches Job to listen for he has something to say on God's behalf (36:1-4). Then he proceeds to give an exalted description of God's character, and to explain the discipline of suffering in His providence (36:5-23). God's gracious wisdom is revealed in the way He uses suffering, for He has something to teach men which they can only learn through pain. It has different results according as men bear it in the right or the wrong way. His purpose is to lead the afflicted through their affliction out into a broad place of blessing.

Elihu then gives another description of God's greatness drawn from His wonderful operations in nature (36:24-33). A storm has been rising as the discussion progresses, and Elihu describes its approach as it gathers over the sky. Then the storm breaks, and in a vivid and splendid passage he magnifies the greatness and power of God as revealed in the mighty forces of nature (37:1-13). This storm is a fit symbol of the storm of affliction that has broken over the head of Job. Elihu appeals to Job to hear it, and to consider it, and to ask himself if he knows God (37:14-24). But the theme is too much for Elihu, and, in the presence of this overwhelming manifestation of God's power and majesty, he stops speaking. However, he has prepared the way of the Lord, for now Jehovah Himself begins to speak to Job out of the whirlwind (38:1).

THE REVELATION OF JEHOVAH
(Chs. 38-41)

When the voices of men have all ceased, the voice of God is heard speaking home to the heart of Job out of the storm. He speaks in reply to Job's repeated cry that God would appear and solve the mystery of his sufferings (13:22; 31:35). The answer is altogether unlike what Job had expected. The Lord does not refer to Job's particular case at all, nor does He say a word about his sufferings. In a series of splendid pictures from the material world and the animal creation, He makes the glory of His power and wisdom pass before Job. The sufferer's thoughts are turned away from himself altogether, and they are fixed on the greatness and goodness of God. In the midst of his sufferings, Job receives such a revelation of God's character as he has never had before. In the light of this vision he is completely humbled, and he is brought to understand his own littleness and imperfection.

1. Jehovah's First Address (Chs. 38-39). Beginning with a challenge to Job to gird up his loins like a man and answer Him (38:1-3), God proceeds to put a number of questions to him. The whole speech is a series of questions which make the magnificent panorama of creation to pass before Job. First, there is unfolded a view of the inanimate world of earth and sea and sky (38:4-38). Then comes a survey of the animal world (38:39—39:30). In all this sublime description of the universe God is suggesting His own complete understanding of it and joyous sympathy with it, and the perfect ease of His own activity through it all. At the heart of it there is a redeeming tenderness. The end in view is not to crush Job into submission, but rather

to lead Job to realize the true character of God and the deeper needs of his own life before God.

2. The Effect Upon Job (40:1-5). Now comes a pause in which the Lord asks for an answer from Job. The answer shows that he is beginning to learn the required lesson: "Behold, I am of small account."

3. Jehovah's Second Address (40:6—41:34). The voice of the Lord, still speaking out of the storm, goes on to challenge Job again. Let Job clothe himself with majesty and assume the reins of government in this world of God's with its vast variety of mystery. Let him bring down the proud and overthrow the wicked. When Job can do this, then God will acknowledge that his own right hand can save him (40:6-14).

Finally the Lord brings before Job two of the great creatures He has made, and suggests that Job should exercise his power and authority over them. Behemoth is either the elephant or the hippopotamus (40:15-24), and leviathan is no doubt the crocodile (ch. 41). The power of the latter creature is depicted with great fulness of detail. If Job cannot govern these animals, how can he assume the functions of the Creator and Moral Governor of the world?

The essential truth brought out by the speeches of the Lord in this part of the book is that God is always giving a sympathetic revelation of Himself in His own creation. He rejoices in the life and activity of His creatures, and in their own way they manifest His power and goodness. The Lord does not argue on His own behalf or justify Himself to Job. But Job's very afflictions make it possible for him to get such a revelation of God from these speeches as he never had before. It is when men are passing through the great trials of life that their hearts are especially sensitive. Then their minds are open to receive new revelations of God's character and to realize the deeper needs of their own lives.

JOB'S RESTORATION
(Ch. 42)

The speeches of the Lord have a profound effect on Job and make him feel his nothingness. The revelation of the greatness and goodness of God brings him to utter self-abasement. This prepares the way for new life and new blessing. God's final purpose in Job's trial is now reached. There are three steps in his restoration:

1. Self-Surrender (vs. 1-6). These verses form a dialogue. The first clause of v. 3 and all v. 4 are spoken by the Lord. Job has come to the end of himself. Instead of self-justification there is now humiliation and confession. "I had heard of thee by the hearing of the ear: but now mine eye seeth thee. Wherefore I abhor myself, and repent in dust and ashes". Thus the solution of Job's problem comes about, not through his intellectual discovery of new truth, but through the yielding of his heart and will.

2. Vindication (vs. 7-9). As soon as Job's self-surrender takes place and he ceases to vindicate himself, then the Lord vindicates him before his friends. They are reproved because they have been unjust to Job. They thought he was suffering because he was a sinner. They did not realize that God may call a man to suffer because he is a saint. The Lord uses the expression, "my servant Job", four times in these few verses. Job is the true serv-

ant of God. His three friends had been attempting to bring Job to God by their philosophy; Job now brings them to God by prayer and intercession.

3. Newness of Life (vs. 10-17). When Job prayed for his friends, that is, when he ceased from himself and entered into co-operation with God for the sake of others, then his affliction was removed and his prosperity was restored.

Job lived a new life from now on, a larger life than he had lived before. "Jehovah blessed the latter end of Job more than his beginning". His wealth was twice as much as it had been before. He enjoyed new fellowship with his kindred and his acquaintance. A new family grew up around him, and he lived a long and fruitful life. The material prosperity given to Job was the blessing of the Old Testament. It is representative and symbolical of that spiritual prosperity which is the highest blessing of the New Testament dispensation.

THE MESSAGE OF JOB

The story of Job illustrates the various uses of suffering in the moral government of God. It shows that Satan is the author of suffering and that God permits and overrules it for His own high ends. Each of the five parts of the book brings out a special purpose which suffering serves in the lives of the righteous. All these are to be found in the New Testament also, and they receive deeper significance in the light of the Cross. They may be stated as follows, in the order in which they occur in the story:

1. Suffering is a test of righteousness and faith. This was the reason why Satan was permitted to afflict Job. See Luke 22:31-32 and Jas 1:2-3.

2. Suffering is chastisement for actual wrongdoing. This was the theory of the friends. See Heb. 12:7-11.

3. Suffering is a means of restraining the believer from self-righteousness and possible sin. When properly borne it results in the suppression of self-will and the refining of character. This was the view of Elihu. See Rom. 6:11; Gal. 5:24; 6:14.

4. Suffering prepares one to realize a fuller knowledge of God and His ways and a deeper understanding of oneself and one's need. This was the experience of Job when the Lord spoke to him out of the storm. See Phil. 3:10; Heb. 2:10.

5. Suffering leads to the highest blessing and the richest life. This was the Lord's final purpose in the afflictions of Job. See Rom. 8:17-18.

THE BOOK OF PSALMS

THIS book is composed of hymns or sacred songs written by David and a number of other psalmists. It was Israel's book of praise and prayer. It contains the response of the heart of Israel to the revelation of God in the Law and in the nation's history. The historic background of the book stretches over a thousand years—from the time of Moses to the post-exilic period.

The Psalter is the very heart of the Bible. It occupies a unique place amid all the religious literature of the world. It has served as an instrument of worship not only for the Jews, but also for the Christian Church throughout the centuries. The mark of inspiration is more manifest here than in any other part of the Hebrew Scriptures. One fourth of all the quotations in the New Testament (40 out of 160) are taken from the Book of Psalms.

THE CHARACTER OF THE PSALMS

The hundred and fifty separate psalms which make up the book are marked by great variety. In general, they may be said to have a threefold character:

1. They are devotional. They are intended for worship. This is their primary purpose. They lead the worshipper directly into the Divine presence and express the thoughts and feelings of the devout soul before God. All the elements of true devotion are found in the book: adoration and praise, penitence and confession, submission and trust, love and gratitude. These are expressed in a great variety of forms. Here the Christian worshipper will find some expression for any attitude his soul may take in the presence of God.

2. They are experimental. All the varieties of the soul's experiences find expression in this book. There is no circumstance, and no combination of circumstances, into which any saint can come that is not represented in the Psalms. Here we find faithfully portrayed the believer's hopes and fears, his strength and weakness, his trials and triumphs. Here the inner life is laid bare and a mirror is held up in which the Christian may examine himself.

3. They are also prophetical. The Psalms are pervaded with the spirit of prophecy. It is not that they contain predictions in the same sense as the prophetic Scriptures, but that the experiences reflected in the Psalms are often foreshadowings of the experiences of our Lord. Expressions used by David and other psalmists describing their feelings under varied circumstances are applied in the New Testament to the Lord Jesus Christ. The words of these inspired poets were often so shaped by the Holy Spirit that they expressed by prophetic anticipation the mind of Christ in the days of His flesh.

THE THEMES OF THE PSALMS

While the purpose of the book is worship in its broadest sense, the separate psalms deal with many different themes. These may be grouped under the following general subjects:

1. The Law of the Lord (e.g., 1, 19, 119)
2. The Messianic King (e.g., 2, 45, 72, 110)
3. God's Glory in Creation (e.g., 8, 19, 29, 104)
4. God's Goodness in Providence (e.g., 34, 37, 91, 103, 107)
5. The Experience of the Saint, or God's Dealing with the Individual (e.g., 3, 4, 23, 27, 32, 51, 73)
6. The History of Israel, or God's Dealing with the Nation (e.g., 46, 68, 78, 81, 105, 106, 114, 135, 136, 137)
7. The Kingdom of God, or the Lord's Reign on Earth (e.g., 47, 93, 95-99, 145).

THE TITLES OF THE PSALMS

A large number of the psalms have headings or superscriptions prefixed to them. It is not known when these were given or how they originated. They do not belong to the inspired text, but they are very ancient and are not to be regarded as worthless. They embody the oldest tradition about the psalms and are not conjectures of a later age. They are varied in character and were intended to serve several purposes:

1. Authorship. One hundred psalms have titles referring to their reputed authors.
2. Historical occasion. Thirteen psalms have headings of this kind and in every case they relate to David.
3. Religious purpose. Headings of this kind are attached to Psalms 38, 70, 92, 100, 102, 120-134.
4. Literary character. The following terms occur: a song, a prayer, a praise, Maschil, Michtam, and Shiggaion. The meaning of the last three is obscure.
5. Musical directions. Fifty-four psalms are headed with the words, "For the Chief Musician". Probably they were given to him to be set to music for the Temple services. Twenty-seven of these have additional directions, the real meaning of which has been lost. They were lost very early, for the translators of the Septuagint in the second century B.C. did not understand them. They were doubtless technical terms belonging to the musical arrangements of the Temple in use before the Exile. The Temple services were suddenly terminated by the destruction of Jerusalem in 586 B.C. After that the meaning of these musical terms gradually faded from the minds of the Jews.

These musical directions always stand first in the headings where they occur. A comparison of these psalms with Hab. 3, which is a psalm with a title of authorship at the beginning and a musical direction at the end, has suggested the theory that, after their meaning was lost, the musical directions in the Book of Psalms dropped out of their proper place, which should be at the end of the preceding psalm in each case. This would remove the difficulty in the title of Psalm 88, which seems to attribute the psalm to two different authorships.

The "selah" which occurs in the body of many psalms seems to denote a musical interlude of some kind, perhaps a pause in the singing while the instruments continued to play. Another view regards it as a liturgical note marking an ascription of praise.

THE WRITERS OF THE PSALMS

The titles of authorship have not the authority of the sacred text, but that is not a sufficient reason for discarding them. They should not be rejected on subjective or hypothetical grounds, but should command our careful and respectful consideration as representing a venerable tradition that goes back into the age out of which the book has come.

The whole book is sometimes mentioned under the name of David (Heb. 4:7), in the sense that he was the originator of the collection and the outstanding author. Seventy-three of the hundred and fifty psalms bear his name. Fifty are anonymous. Some of these also may have been written by David. The Second Psalm is ascribed to him in Acts 4:25. The Ninth and Tenth are linked together by an acrostic structure in the original, which brings them both under David's name. The Thirty-third bears his name in the Septuagint.

Psalmody began long before David's day. Psalm 90 is ascribed to Moses, and the 91st also may be his, for the heading of one psalm sometimes extends to the one immediately following (e.g. 10, 43). Two other songs by the Lawgiver are contained in the Pentateuch (Exod. 15:1-18; Deut. 32:1-43). No psalm is attributed to any writer between Moses and David; yet the stream of sacred song had been flowing without intermission. We have Deborah's song in Jud. 5 and Hannah's song in 1 Sam. 2:1-10. In Samuel's time music was cultivated in the schools of the prophets (1 Sam. 10:5). Some of David's skill in psalmody may have been gained under Samuel and in association with these "sons of the prophets". Two psalms (72 and 127) are ascribed to Solomon.

The other writers named in the book belonged to the Temple singers. When David brought the Ark to Jerusalem he appointed three of the Levites to have charge of the service of song. They were Asaph, Heman, and Ethan who is also called Jeduthun (1 Chron. 15:16-19). These men, and their "sons" or descendants, conducted the music and song in the worship of the sanctuary from David's time onward (1 Chron. 25). Twelve psalms are attributed to Asaph (50, 73-83), some of which were probably composed by his descendants. Heman is named as the author of Psalm 88, and Ethan as the author of Psalm 89. The sons of Korah, to whom eleven psalms are ascribed (42-49, 84, 85, 87), probably composed Heman's choir. The genealogy of Heman recorded in 1 Chron. 6:33-38 shows that he was a descendant of Korah. The mercy of the Lord is manifested in taking up the descendants of the man who had been destroyed for his rebellion against Moses and Aaron (Num. 16) and giving them a place of honourable service in the Temple of Solomon.

David himself was the greatest of the psalmists; he was called "the sweet psalmist of Israel" (2 Sam. 23:1). He had by nature a rare poetic genius. The wide and varied experiences of his life gave him a thorough knowledge of the human soul. He was a man after God's own heart; he trusted God fully, and thus he came to know God and understand His ways. Above all this he was inspired by the Holy Spirit for the special purpose of praising God in psalm and song (2 Sam. 23:2).

Almost every part of David's life is reflected in the book. His early years in the open fields as a shepherd boy are seen in Psalms 8, 19, 23, 29; his persecution at the hands of Saul in Psalms 11-14. 27, 31, 34, 52-59; his reign in Zion in Psalms 15, 18, 24, 68, 101, 132; his wars in Psalms 20, 21, 60; his sin and repentance in Psalms 32, 38, 51; his flight from Absalom in Psalms 3-7, 41, 64; his last years in Psalms, 37, 61, 62, 65. When these psalms are read with the background of David's life in view, they receive a richer meaning for us and have a more direct application to our own spiritual experiences.

THE CURSES IN THE PSALMS

A few of the psalms contain curses upon enemies and seem to breathe the spirit of hatred and revenge. The most notable of these are Nos. 35, 58, 59, 69, and 109, which are known as the Psalms of Vengeance or Imprecation. A few isolated passages marked by a similar spirit occur in other psalms: e.g. Psa. 137:8-9. How are such psalms and such statements to be explained? Several considerations help us to understand them.

1. They belong to the Old Testament dispensation. They are to be judged from that point of view, and not as belonging to the dispensation of the Spirit where we now stand. The progressive character of Divine revelation is always to be kept in mind.

2. The above five psalms are all attributed to David. David was naturally generous, and his character was singularly free from malice and vindictiveness. Such psalms cannot be explained as the expression of his private feelings. The curses they contain were not pronounced merely upon personal enemies. The Messianic promise given to David made him a representative character. His enemies were God's enemies, and what he asks for is the vindication of God's cause and not his own.

3. The meek and lowly Jesus Himself used language about the punishment of the wicked as appalling as any that occurs in these psalms: e.g. Matt. 23:13-36; 13:41-42; Mark 9:42-48.

4. These psalms are quoted in the New Testament as prophetic of the Lord Jesus Christ. Psalm 69 is quoted five times in this way: John 2:17; 15:25; 19:28-30; Rom. 11:9; 15:3. Psalm 109 is applied in Acts 1:20 to Judas's betrayal of Jesus.

5. These curses, therefore, are to be regarded as revealing, in Old Testament language and from an Old Testament point of view, the mind of the Spirit regarding the enemies of God and His Kingdom. They express His righteous indignation and His zeal for the vindication of God's justice and righteousness. They emphasize the reality of Divine retribution and the majesty of Divine justice in the only way that this could be done under the old dispensation. The Old Testament punishes in this life: the New Testament transfers the final judgment to another world and another life. These Psalms remind us that there is such a thing as the vengeance of God (Deut. 32:35, Psa. 94:1, Nah. 1:2, Rom. 12:19), and the wrath of the Lamb (Rev. 6:16).

SOME GROUPS OF PSALMS

1. The Messianic Psalms. Many of the psalms seem to refer, by prophetic anticipation, to the life of the Lord Jesus Christ. David was a representative and type of the Messiah, and experiences which he records of his own life often reflect the experiences of Christ in His earthly life. The same thing is true in a lesser degree of other psalmists. The Spirit of Christ is subjectively present in the whole book, and circumstances which are primarily those of the writer often foreshadow the circumstances of our Lord's life. This is especially true of the sufferings of Christ.

There are a few psalms, however, which are so objectively Messianic that they can have no adequate explanation or fulfilment but in Christ alone, and are to be understood in the light of the New Testament. These are the following: No. 2, His resurrection and royal authority (Acts 4:25-26; 13:33).

No. 22, His sufferings on the cross (Matt. 27:46, Mark 15:34). No. 45, His union with the Church (Heb. 1:8-9). No. 72, His everlasting kingdom and universal reign (Rev. 11:15). No. 110, His ascension and heavenly priesthood (Matt. 22:44, Mark 12:36, Luke 20:42-43, Acts 2:34-35, Heb. 1:13).

2. The Penitential Psalms: Nos. 6, 32, 38, 51, 102, 130 and 143. Since the early days of the Church, these seven have been known by this name because their prevailing idea is penitence and confession of sin. They have been distinguished by the Church Fathers as marking seven steps in the ladder of repentance: fear of punishment (6:1), sorrow for sin (32:5), hope of pardon (38:15), prayer for cleansing (51:7), longing for heaven (102:16-17), distrust of self (130:5-6), and prayer against final doom (143:2).

3. The Pilgrim Psalms: Nos. 120-134. All these bear the same title: A Song of Ascents (A. V. Degrees), literally, "A Song of Goings up". The Israelites were to worship at the central sanctuary three times a year—at the feasts of the Passover, Pentecost, and Tabernacles (Deut. 16:16). This collection of fifteen psalms probably formed a separate song book for the pilgrims as they travelled up to the Temple. A musical people like the Jews would be sure to beguile the way with songs. There is a tender and graceful beauty about the whole group. With one exception (132), they are all short, the utterance of a single thought or feeling.

4. The Hallelujah Psalms. The word "Hallelujah", meaning "praise ye Jehovah", occurs first in the Bible in the last verse of Psa. 104. After that a number of the psalms either begin or end with the word. These are Nos. 104-106, Nos. 111-117 (see the note on Psalm 113), No. 135, Nos. 146-150. In this last group the Hallelujah occurs both at the beginning and at the end of each psalm. Psalms 113-118 formed a group, called "the Hallel", which was sung at the Passover. It was probably the "hymn" sung by the Lord and His disciples at the Last Supper (Matt. 26:30).

THE DIVISIONS OF THE BOOK

The Book of Psalms is composed of five parts, or five smaller books. These form separate collections, which are marked by doxologies at the end of Psalms 41, 72, 89, 106. Psalm 150 is itself a grand doxology closing the whole collection. These five divisions seem to indicate stages in the growth of the Psalter. This explains the note at the end of Psalm 72. It marked the end of a collection of David's psalms which was complete at the time. The whole Psalter was not complete till after the return from Babylon. Some of the psalms reflect the conditions of the Exile (e.g. 137), and some the period of the Restoration (e.g. 118). Each of the five books has a keynote of its own, which is usually found in the first psalm of the collection. According to the Rabbis, the five parts of the Hebrew Psalter correspond to the five books of the Law.

The two Divine names, Elohim (represented by our word God) and Jehovah (represented in the A.V. by Lord in capital letters), occur with great frequency in the Psalms. They are not used at random but with intelligent purpose. Elohim (sometimes El) is the common and more general name for God, and designates Him as the Creator and Providential Governor of the world. Jehovah is the special and peculiar name by which He revealed Himself to Israel, and designates Him as their Redeemer

and Covenant God. The use of this name gave a vivid personal touch to the religion of the devout Israelite.

Psalms in which the former name predominates have in view the power and holiness of God, and call out feelings of reverence and humiliation before Him. Psalms in which the latter name predominates have in view the mercy and faithfulness of God, and call out feelings of gratitude and love to Him. The proper name, Jehovah, is the prevailing one in the first division of the Psalter and in the last two divisions. The common name, Elohim, is the prevailing one in the second and third divisions. Psalms 14 and 53 illustrate the use of these names, for they are substantially the same, except that Jehovah is the Divine name in the one and Elohim in the other.

BOOK I PSALMS OF DAVID
(Nos. 1-41)

All the psalms in this group are attributed to David, except Nos. 1, 2, 10, and 33, which are anonymous. The keynote of the collection is holiness and happiness. The prevailing Divine name is Jehovah, which occurs 278 times. It is used in every psalm at least twice, and in one (29) as many as eighteen times. The word God occurs 48 times, and from thirteen psalms it is absent altogether.

Psalm 1 is an ideal description of the righteous man. It forms an appropriate introduction to the whole Psalter. Its complete realization is found in the Son of Man alone.

Psalm 2 introduces the Messianic King, and appropriately follows the ethical psalm. It is dramatic in character, and contains four scenes: The nations in rebellion on earth (vs. 1-3); Jehovah speaking from Heaven (vs. 4-6); Christ, the King, speaking from the throne (vs. 7-9); the psalmist speaking, announcing the call of the Gospel (vs. 10-12).

Psalms 3-5 are morning and evening prayers. No. 3 is a morning prayer of faith and courage (v. 5); No. 4 is an evening prayer of tranquil trust (v. 8); and No. 5 is a Sabbath morning prayer of worship (vs. 3, 7).

Psalm 6 is the first of the seven Penitential Psalms. It is the prayer of a soul in sore trouble under the chastening hand of God.

Psalm 7 is a slandered soul's appeal to God, the righteous Judge of all the earth. Cush, whose name occurs in the title, is not mentioned elsewhere. He is probably the same as Shimei, who is called "this Benjamite" in 2 Sam. 16:11.

Psalm 8 is the first of a number of psalms which celebrate the glory of God in the world of nature. It describes the impression produced in the heart of David as he gazed upon the heavens by night (v. 3). It has a prophetic import as foreshadowing the exaltation of Jesus as the Second Man. (Heb. 2:6-9).

Psalms 9 and 10 form a pair, being linked together by an alphabetic structure in the original. They are prayers for "times of trouble" (9:9; 10:1). One is marked by triumphant trust in God (9:10). The other is a plaintive appeal to God (10:12).

Psalms 11-15 are prayers of the righteous in the midst of "this present evil world" (Gal. 1:4). The psalmist was distressed because of the prevalence of wickedness around him, and he was driven to God in prayer about it. The prayer of the Old Testament saint for the coming of the promised

Redeemer is expressed in 14:7. This prayer suggests the description of the ideal citizen of Zion in Psalm 15, for that would be realized when the Messianic salvation had been accomplished.

Psalm 16 is prophetic of the resurrection of Christ (Acts 2:25-31; 13:35-37). Both Peter and Paul argue that, although the words quoted were spoken by David, they had a meaning that went beyond him. He spoke as the representative and type of Jesus Christ.

Psalm 17 also contains a foregleam of the resurrection (v. 15). The language of this psalm, like that of the preceding one, is inspired by the Spirit of Christ.

Psalm 18 is David's magnificent ode of thanksgiving for all the deliverances and victories which the Lord had given him. It is found, with a few variations, in 2 Sam. 22 also. In the metaphors he uses in vs. 1-2, David gathers together the results of a long experience of God's protecting care.

Psalm 19 contains David's daytime meditation on the glory of God as revealed in the heavens (vs. 1-6). Then it continues with his testimony as to what he found in the Law of the Lord (vs. 7-11), and closes with an appeal to the Lord as his Redeemer to keep him from sin (vs. 12-14).

Psalms 20 and 21 are closely connected. The first is a prayer of the people on behalf of the king as he goes forth to battle. The other is a thanksgiving when he returns from the battle with the victory won.

Psalm 22 is the first and greatest of the Passion Psalms. The others are Nos. 69 and 109. It is the psalm of the Cross; its opening words were used by Jesus in His cry out of the darkness (Matt. 27:46; Mark 15:34). It is in two parts: the lowly sufferings of the Saviour as He endured the Cross (vs. 1-21), and the joy that was set before Him as through the travail He saw the triumph (vs. 22-31).

Psalm 23 is the most beautiful of all the lyrics. It has a tenderness and sweetness all its own. There is no other psalm in which the absence of all doubt and fear is so remarkable. There are but two persons in view—Jehovah and David, the Lord and I. Every blessing mentioned in the psalm is personal.

Psalm 24 was probably composed for the bringing of the Ark up into Jerusalem (2 Sam. 6; I Chron. 15). The first part (vs. 1-6) would be sung at the foot of the hill as the procession approached. The second part (vs. 7-10) would be sung antiphonally before the gates as they were summoned to open for their true king. With this historic background the psalm can be taken as prophetic of Christ's triumphal ascension into Heaven.

The preceding three psalms form a trilogy in which Christ appears successively as Saviour, Shepherd, and Sovereign. In No. 22 the Good Shepherd is giving His life for the sheep (John 10:11). In No. 23 the Great Shepherd, brought again from the dead, is caring for the sheep (Heb. 13:20). In No. 24 the Chief Shepherd is entering into the glory from which He will come again for His sheep (I Pet. 5:4).

Psalms 25-28 are suitable for devout meditation. They combine various aspects of prayer and praise. No. 25 begins with prayer (vs. 1-7), passes on to meditation (vs. 8-14), and ends with prayer (vs. 15-22). No. 26 is a prayer of self-examination in preparation for worship in the house of the Lord. No. 27 is composed of praise (vs. 1-6) and prayer (vs. 7-14), and No. 28 of prayer (vs. 1-5) and praise (vs. 6-9).

Psalm 29 describes a thunder-storm coming down over the land from the mountains of Lebanon. It has been called the Psalm of the Seven Thunders because of the sevenfold occurrence of the phrase, "the voice of Jehovah." It begins with "glory in the highest" (vs. 1-2), and ends with "peace on earth" (v. 11).

Psalm 30 is a thanksgiving for recovery from some sickness which brought David to the verge of the grave, mingled with reflection on the lesson it was sent to teach him.

Psalm 31 shows how trust struggles through trial and finally triumphs over it. Here we may trace the four seasons of a soul in the experience of life: autumn (vs. 1-8), winter (vs. 9-13), spring (vs. 14-18), and summer (vs. 19-24).

Psalm 32 describes David's experience when restored to the Divine favour after his great sin. It is the second psalm to begin with the word "Blessed". In Psalm 1 we have the blessedness of innocence; here we have the blessedness of forgiveness.

Psalm 33 begins by repeating the call to rejoice in the Lord with which Psalm 32 ends. It is the first "new song" (v. 3) of the Psalter. This description always indicates that the theme is redemption in some of its manifestations (cf. 40:3, 98:1, 144:9, 149:1, Isa. 42:10, Rev. 5:9, 14:3).

Psalm 34 is full of a sense of the Lord's goodness. Its keynote is, "O taste and see that Jehovah is good" (v. 8). This psalm and the next alone mention "the angel of Jehovah". In the one he is the agent of Divine providence (34:7), and in the other the agent of Divine vengeance (35: 5-6). The Angel of the Lord in the Old Testament is always a foreshadowing of the Lord Jesus Christ as the Second Person of the Trinity (Isa. 63:9).

Psalm 35 is the first of the Psalms of Vengeance. It contains the suggestive and meaningful description of the saints as "quiet in the land" (v. 20), and it ends with a note of praise.

Psalm 36 begins and ends with references to the wicked, but the body of the psalm is a grand description of the character of God, in which His mercy or lovingkindness is especially emphasized (vs. 5, 7, 10).

Psalm 37 vindicates the righteousness of God in His government of the world. It is intended for those who are inclined to murmur because of the prosperity of the wicked. Its keynote is, "Fret not thyself" (vs. 1, 7, 8). It was written in David's old age (v. 25), and is the testimony of a lifetime of full and varied experience. His advice is, "Trust in Jehovah" (v. 3), "Delight thyself in Jehovah" (v. 4), "Commit thy way unto Jehovah" (v. 5), "Rest in Jehovah, and wait patiently for him", giving Him time to work out His purposes, (v. 7). Throughout the psalm runs a promise of inheriting the land, which is repeated again and again. To the Old Testament saint this "inheritance" is the sum of earthly blessing: to the New Testament saint it is the sum of spiritual blessing (Eph. 1:3).

Psalm 38 is the prayer of a soul under the chastening hand of God. It is used in the synagogue on the Day of Atonement when "there is a remembrance made of sins year by year" (Heb. 10:3).

Psalm 39 is a sequel to Psalm 38. It is the lament of a chastened soul, realizing that he is a stranger and pilgrim on the earth. It is an elegy on the vanity of life in the world.

Psalm 40 is applied in Heb. 10:5-10 to the Lord Jesus Christ, vs. 6-8 being quoted as expressing His attitude of mind in the Incarnation. The quotation is taken from the Septuagint, which interprets the figure used in the Hebrew. The original of the words, "mine ears hast thou opened" (v. 6) is literally, "mine ears hast thou bored through", and refers to the sign by which the life of a servant was entirely devoted to his master (Exod. 21:5-6).

Psalm 41 also, while recording the experience of David, is prophetic of the experience of the Lord (cf. v. 9 and John 13:18).

BOOK II PSALMS OF DAVID AND THE TEMPLE SINGERS
(Nos. 42-72)

In this collection of thirty-one psalms, eighteen are attributed to David, eight to the sons of Korah (42-69), and one to Asaph (50). One is under Solomon's name (72), and three are anonymous (66, 67, 71). The keynote of this book is trial and triumph. The prevailing Divine name is now God, being used 198 times. It occurs in every psalm at least twice, and in one (68) as many as 31 times. The name Jehovah occurs only 33 times, and from fifteen psalms it is absent altogether.

Psalms 42 and 43 form one song of three stanzas with a common refrain: "Hope thou in God". They are psalms for a soul cast down. The song begins with trust in God and ends with joy in God.

Psalm 44 expresses Israel's perplexity and appeal to God in a time of persecution. It is a prayer for saints who suffer for Christ's sake (v. 22, cf. Rom. 8:36).

Psalm 45 describes the marriage of a king after his victory in war. It is quoted in Heb. 1:8-9 as referring to the Son of God. Hence it has a Messianic significance. It foreshadows the union of Christ with His Church (Eph. 5:25-27) and is prophetic of the marriage of the Lamb (Rev. 19:6-8; 21:2).

Psalm 46 is a battle hymn. It was probably written to celebrate the deliverance of Jerusalem from the Assyrian army in the reign of Hezekiah (2 Kings 18-19; Isa. 36-37). It is in three stanzas, marked by Selah's, with a twice repeated refrain. The phrase, "Jehovah of hosts", occurs seven times in the Psalms, and the phrase, "the God of Jacob", thirteen times.

Psalm 47 may belong to the same period, as celebrating the God who wrought the deliverance. Its theme is the Great King. It is used by the Jews at the Feast of Trumpets on their New Year's Day. It is an appropriate psalm for Ascension Day.

Psalm 48 sings of the city of the Great King. It describes Jerusalem in the days of its deliverance from the Assyrian army. It is to be interpreted spiritually of the Zion mentioned in Heb. 12:22.

Psalm 49 seems to be connected with the last verse of the preceding psalm. It deals with the thought of death, and reaches the high-water mark of Old Testament faith in a future life. For this the psalmist's hope is in God Himself (v. 15). There is a foregleam of the resurrection of the saints in the words: "The upright shall have dominion over them in the morning" (v. 14).

Psalm 50 is the first of the psalms of Asaph. It has the marks of dignity and elevation which characterize all his psalms. It begins with a description of God coming in judgment (vs. 1-6). This is followed by God's address to His people (vs. 7-15), and to the wicked (vs. 16-21). Then the lesson of

the psalm is summed up in a closing appeal (vs. 22-23).

Psalm 51 is pre-eminently the penitential psalm. It is the prayer of a broken and contrite heart. Its burden is the thought that sin is so deep-rooted and so defiling that God alone can pardon it and cleanse the soul from it. It was the expression of David's penitence after Nathan had rebuked him for his sin (2 Sam. 12).

Psalms 52-59 form a group belonging to the period of David's life when he was a fugitive from Saul. They all describe some experience of trial or peril, and seek God's help in the midst of it.

Psalms 52 and 54 both contain the statement, "for it is good", in referring to the name of the Lord. This is David's testimony as to what he found in the character of God.

Psalm 53 is another version of Psalm 14, with God as the Divine name instead of Jehovah, and a slight variation in v. 5.

Psalm 55 foreshadows the persecution of Jesus by the Jews and His betrayal by Judas. While it describes primarily some experience of David's, it helps us to understand the nature of our Lord's sufferings.

Psalm 56 is a remedy for fear. Its keynote is, "What time I am afraid, I will trust in thee" (v. 3). And then the psalmist adds, "In God have I put my trust, I will not be afraid" (vs. 4, 11).

Psalm 57 has a similar message. Its keynote is trust in the midst of peril. It is divided into two stanzas by the refrain in vs. 5 and 11.

Psalm 58 may be set over against the 53rd. That psalm gave us a picture of the ungodly world, full of corruption and iniquity. This psalm gives us a vision of the God who judges in the earth. It is full of bold and striking images.

Psalm 59 is an appeal to God as the defence or "high tower" of the oppressed (vs. 9, 16, 17).

Psalms 60-67 form another group of David's psalms, all apparently relating to the time when he was king in Israel.

Psalm 60 shows how defeat was turned into victory by appealing to the promises of God.

Psalm 61 is the prayer of an exile seeking refuge in God: "Lead me to the rock that is higher than I".

Psalm 62 is an expression of faith's assurance. Its keynote is "God only". There is neither prayer nor petition in it, but just faith and trust in God alone.

Psalm 63 also has no petition. It is an expression of love for God, or the intense longing of a soul for communion with Him. This gives it special tenderness and beauty.

Psalm 64 is a prayer to be delivered from slanderers and secret foes. It ends with a triumphant assurance.

Psalm 65 is Israel's harvest hymn. It contains three scenes and presents God in three aspects: the congregation, or God in redemption (vs. 1-4); the nation, or God in history (vs. 5-8); and the harvest, or God in nature (vs. 9-13).

Psalms 66 and 67 have for their keynote, "Make his praise glorious" (66:2). They contain the praise of the congregation (66:1-12), the praise of the individual (66:13-20), and the praise of the nations (67:1-7).

Psalm 68 is a grand hymn about the entrance of God into His sanctuary in Zion. It was probably composed on the occasion of David's removal of the Ark (2 Sam. 6; 1 Chron. 15), as was Psalm 24.

This event prefigured the entrance of Christ into Heaven, and v. 18 is quoted in Eph. 4:8 as fulfilled in the Ascension. The psalm reviews what God did in redeeming His people and settling them in Canaan (v. 1-14). Then it refers to the choice of Mount Zion for His dwelling place, and goes on to describe the triumphal procession as the Ark is brought into the sanctuary (vs. 15-27). It closes with a forecast of the time when all nations shall submit themselves to God, and with a summons to all the kingdoms to praise Him (vs. 28-35).

Psalm 69, like the 22nd., contains prophetic anticipations of the Lord's passion. These two psalms are more frequently quoted and applied to Christ in the New Testament than any other except the 110th.

Psalms 70 and 71 may have been one originally. They are both made up largely of quotations from other psalms.

Psalm 72 fittingly closes this collection. Its theme is the reign of the righteous King. It is prophetic of the Messianic reign of righteousness and peace, the Kingdom of God on earth. This psalm and the 127th alone bear the name of Solomon.

BOOK III PSALMS OF THE TEMPLE SINGERS
(Nos. 73-89)

Of these seventeen psalms, eleven are ascribed to Asaph (73-83), three to the sons of Korah (84, 85, 87), and one each to David (86), Heman (88), and Ethan (89). The keynote is darkness and light. The name God still predominates, being used 60 times, occurring in one psalm (78) fifteen times, while Jehovah occurs 45 times.

Psalms 73-76 all refer to the sanctuary. No. 73 deals with the dark problem of the prosperity of the wicked, which oppressed the psalmist (vs. 2-3) until he went into the sanctuary and got light there (vs. 16-17). No. 74 bewails the desolation of the sanctuary by foreign foes (vs. 1-9), and appeals to God for help (vs. 10-23). No. 75 answers the cry of the preceding psalm with the assurance that God will come in judgment. No. 76 praises God for a judgment already wrought. Perhaps the reference is to the destruction of the Assyrian army of Sennacherib in Hezekiah's day.

Psalms 77-80 all refer to Israel as a flock under the care of God as their Shepherd (77:20, 78:52, 79:13, 80:1). No. 77 begins with a cry to God in which the psalmist broods over his own troubles (vs. 1-9). Then he acknowledges his infirmity and remembers God (v. 10), and in the rest of the psalm he sings of what God has done in redeeming His people and leading them through the wilderness like a flock (vs. 11-20).

Psalm 78 is the longest of the historical psalms. It reviews the history of Israel from the deliverance out of Egypt to the establishment of the kingdom under David. It magnifies the patient faithfulness of God over against the persistent failure of His people. The leading idea of the psalm is echoed in a kind of refrain: vs. 17-18, 40-41, and 56-57.

Psalm 79 is another lament over the ruin of the Temple similar to the 74th psalm.

Psalm 80 is a prayer for restoration from some national calamity. The appeal of its threefold refrain contains an ever enlarging conception of God (vs. 3, 7, 19).

Psalm 81 is full of the joy of the sacred seventh month and the consummation of the yearly feasts. "Blow the trumpet at the new moon, at the full moon, on our feast day" (v. 3). The month began

with the Feast of Trumpets at the new moon. The full moon came on the fifteenth day, and then the Feast of Tabernacles began as the crowning festival of the year. Between these two dates the Day of Atonement was observed (Lev. 23:24, 27, 34).

Psalm 82 is a solemn rebuke of unjust judges. It is quoted by our Lord in John 10:34.

Psalm 83 is an appeal to God for deliverance from an impending attack upon the people of God. It takes up the appeal with which the preceding psalm ends.

Psalm 84 is the song of a devout pilgrim on his way to worship the Lord in the Temple at one of the national feasts. Its three divisions may be regarded as three stages of the pilgrimage: The start, or longing for God (vs. 1-4). The journey, or seeking after God (vs. 5-8). The arrival, or dwelling with God (vs. 9-12).

Psalm 85 seems to have been written after the return from the Babylonian captivity. It is a song of "salvation": the word is used three times. (vs. 4, 7, 9).

Psalm 86 is the only one in this book ascribed to David. It expresses the personal devotion of a tried and faithful servant of the Lord. It appeals to Him on a great variety of pleas, the word "for" occurring again and again.

Psalm 87 celebrates the glory of Zion as the city of God, and foreshadows the glory and the joy of heavenly citizenship and spiritual fellowship (cf. Phil 3:20; Heb. 12:22-23).

Psalm 88 is the saddest in the whole Psalter. It is devoid of light, and its last word is "darkness". It may be taken as prophetically expressing the feelings of Jesus as He descended into death.

Psalm 89 is based on God's promise to David (2 Sam. 7:12-16; 1 Chron. 17:11-14) and may be called the psalm of "the covenant". The word is used four times (vs. 3, 28, 34, 39). Two attributes of God are named in v. 1 as the theme, and these are extolled throughout the psalm. His lovingkindness prompted Him to make the covenant, and His faithfulness prompts Him to keep it.

BOOK IV ANONYMOUS PSALMS
(Nos. 90-106)

Of these seventeen psalms, one is ascribed to Moses (90) and two to David (101, 103). All the rest are anonymous. The keynote of the collection is peril and deliverance. The name Jehovah now predominates, being used 116 times. In five of these psalms it occurs eleven times. The name God occurs only 18 times, and is absent altogether from five psalms.

Psalm 90 is entitled, "a Prayer of Moses the man of God". There is no reason to doubt this note of authorship. The psalm is a sublime composition on the eternity of God, and it bears the stamp of Moses' lonely and stately character.

Psalm 91 develops the theme of trust in the protecting care of God and rest in fellowship with Him (vs. 1-13), and closes with the Lord's response to His people's trust (vs. 14-16).

Psalm 92 is entitled "a Song for the sabbath day", and it indicates by its contents that the best and noblest use of the day is joyous thanksgiving to God and devout meditation on His works.

Psalms 93-99 form a group connected by the general idea of the Lord's righteous reign. Their keynote is, "Jehovah reigneth": with these words three of them begin. They look forward to the advent of the Lord and His righteous rule over all the earth. He is not only King (Psa. 93), but also Judge of the world as well (Psa. 94). He is to be praised for His greatness as God and King (Psa. 95-96). Special praise is given Him for His righteousness and justice (Psa. 97), for the salvation He has wrought (Psa. 98), and for His holiness (Psa. 99).

Psalm 100 is a grand doxology, closing the strain of the preceding group. It stands pre-eminent among the psalms for its simple grandeur as an expression of triumphant joy and praise.

Psalm 101 expresses David's resolution when he came to the throne to conduct himself and his kingdom aright—"in a perfect way" and "with a perfect heart" (v. 2).

Psalm 102 is the prayer of a soul in distress, who realizes that he is suffering on account of his sin. He begins by looking at his own affliction (vs. 1-11). Then he turns to God—"But thou, O Jehovah" (v. 12) ; and in the contemplation of the eternity of God he rests his hope for Zion in her affliction (vs. 13-22), and for himself (vs. 23-28).

Psalm 103 is the grandest song of pure praise in the book. It is a song of grace, and extols the God of redemption. It begins and ends with the same words: "Bless Jehovah, O my soul". It is progressive in the development of its theme. The "my" of personal experience in the beginning (vs. 1-5) passes into the "our" of social fellowship in the middle (vs. 6-18), and culminates in the "all" of universal blessing at the end (vs. 19-22).

Psalm 104 is a song of nature, and extols the God of creation. It begins and ends in the same way as the preceding psalm. In its main outline it follows the story of creation in the first chapter of Genesis. The Creator is represented as ever at work in His creation. He who made the earth renews the face of the ground continually.

Psalms 105 and 106 are companion historical psalms. They magnify the faithfulness of God in the history of Israel, and bring out two different aspects of His faithfulness. Each begins with a call to give thanks to the Lord and each ends with a "Hallelujah". Psalm 105 sings of the faithfulness and power of God from the time of the patriarchs until He established Israel in Canaan, and it closes with obedience as the condition of their possessing the land (vs. 44-45). Psalm 106 sings of the patience of God through all the backslidings and rebellions of Israel until they were scattered among the nations, and it closes with a prayer that suggests repentance as the condition of their restoration (v. 47). There is not a word or sentiment in these historical psalms that would tend to feed the national pride or vanity. All the glory of Israel's history is due to God alone.

BOOK V ANONYMOUS PSALMS AND PSALMS OF DAVID
(Nos. 107-150)

Of the forty-four psalms in this section, one is ascribed to Solomon (127), fifteen are ascribed to David, and twenty-eight are anonymous. The dominant name throughout is Jehovah, which occurs 268 times. The general name God is used only 28 times and is absent altogether from twenty-four psalms.

This closing book of the Psalter has for its keynote exultant praise and thanksgiving. It may be divided into seven subordinate groups as follows: Nos. 107-110 are songs of redemption. Nos. 111-118 are mainly Hallelujah psalms. No. 119 is the great psalm of the Law of the Lord. Nos. 120-134 are pilgrim songs. Nos. 135-137 are songs of Zion. Nos. 138-145 form the last group of David's psalms. Nos. 146-150 are all triumphant Hallelujah psalms.

Psalm 107 has for its keynote, "Let the redeemed of Jehovah say so" (v. 2). It gives four pictures of the perils that befall men in the world and of the goodness of God in delivering them ; and after each one comes the glad refrain: "Oh that men would praise Jehovah for his goodness, and for his wonderful works to the children of men" (vs. 8, 15, 21, 31).

Psalm 108 is a song of triumph, composed of the joyful and triumphal portions of Psalms 57 and 60.

Psalm 109 is the last of the Psalms of Vengeance. It contains curses upon one wicked man specially. Peter's application of v. 8 to Judas Iscariot in Acts 1:20 shows that it foreshadows the Lord's betrayal and passion.

Psalm 110 is a sequel to the preceding, its theme being the exaltation and triumph of the Messiah. There Christ is emptied of His glory; here He is given the highest place in Heaven. The psalm records the decree of God investing Him with the twofold dignity of kingship (vs. 1-2) and priesthood (v. 4). No other Old Testament passage is so frequently quoted in the New Testament as referring to Christ.

Psalms 111 and 112 are twin songs, closely connected. Both are acrostics in the original. The second begins where the first ends, with the reverential fear of the Lord. The first celebrates the works of the Lord, and the second the ways of the upright.

Psalm 113 begins the Hallel (Nos. 113-118) with a pure burst of praise. It begins and ends with a Hallelujah, but it is probable that the Hallelujah at the end should belong to Psalm 114. This is the way the Septuagint has it.

Psalm 114 sings of the presence and power of God as manifested in the miraculous events of the Exodus. It is the most graphic of all the psalms that deal with the early history of Israel.

Psalm 115 exalts the Lord as the supreme Ruler in contrast with the idols of the nations (vs. 1-8), and calls upon Israel to put their trust in Him (vs. 9-18). Its theme is the glory of His Name.

Psalm 116 is intensely individualistic. The first personal pronoun occurs in every verse but two. It is the utterance of one who has been near the gates of death and comes to pay his vows to the Lord.

Psalm 117 is the shortest in the book but by no means the least important. It is used in Rom. 15:11 to show that God intended His salvation for all nations.

Psalm 118, the last of the Hallel group, gives full utterance to the spirit of jubilant thanksgiving. It is a processional song and was evidently intended for use in the Temple worship. It may be analysed as follows: An introductory call to all Israel to join in praising the Lord (vs. 1-4). The procession on the way up to the Temple recounting the gracious acts of the Lord (vs. 5-18). The procession approaching the gates and entering into the Temple (vs. 19-24). Prayers and praises within the Temple (vs. 25-29). The psalm may have been composed for the dedication of the Second Temple (Ezra 6:15-18). Verse 22 is mentioned repeatedly in the New Testament as Messianic (Matt. 21:42; Acts 4:11; Eph. 2:20; 1 Pet. 2:7).

Psalm 119 has no title and its author is unknown.

That he was a young man may be inferred from vs. 9, 99, 100. Verse 141 in the Septuagint reads, "I was young and despised". The theme is the blessedness of walking in the Law of the Lord, or the will of God as the way of life. This is stated in the first three verses, which form the introduction. After that the whole psalm is a direct address to God. This gives it an eminently devotional character. There is a direct reference to the Law or the will of God in almost every verse.

The alphabetic structure of the psalm is indicated in our English Version. There are as many stanzas as there are letters in the Hebrew alphabet. Every verse in each stanza begins in the original with the letter named at the head of the stanza. Throughout the psalm eight different terms are used to designate the Law of the Lord, and each one occurs usually once in every stanza. In the eighth stanza (vs. 57-64) all these terms are found, one in every verse.

Psalms 120-134, the Pilgrim Psalms, form a manual of devotion for the pilgrimage of the soul in this world. Their separate themes may be suggested as follows: 120, the start; 121, the road; 122, the arrival; 123, supplication; 124, deliverance; 125, trust; 126, restoration; 127, labour; 128, the home; 129, the farm; 130, penitence; 131, humility; 132, the Ark of God, or the sanctuary; 133, brotherly love, or spiritual unity; 134, the farewell and the parting benediction.

Psalm 135 sings of the beginnings of Israel's national history, and calls upon all the people to praise the Lord for having chosen Israel for His own possession.

Psalm 136 has been called the national anthem of Israel. It was known among the Jews as "the great Hallel". It was probably sung antiphonally by the Levite choirs in the Temple, one choir taking the first clause of each verse, and another answering: "For his lovingkindness endureth for ever".

Psalm 137 is the song of the exiles, and is a plaintive memory of the Babylonian captivity.

Psalm 138 is a song of exalted praise and devotion. David magnifies God and declares: "Jehovah will perfect that which concerneth me" (v. 8, cf. Phil. 1:6).

Psalm 139 stands pre-eminent in the Psalter for its loftiness of thought about God and for its overwhelming sense of His omnipresence and omniscience. All this is expressed in language of great beauty and suggestiveness. It begins and ends with the thought of God as the searcher of hearts.

Psalms 140-143 deal with the need and helplessness of man. No. 140 is a prayer for defence against evil without. No. 141 is a prayer for grace to overcome evil within. No. 142 is the cry of a lonely heart. No. 143, the last of the Penitential Psalms, is the prayer of a soul in desolation and darkness.

Psalm 144 is a song of triumphant assurance. Here the sufficiency of God is seen encompassing the helplessness of man. The psalm is made up largely of passages from other psalms (vs. 1-11), and a concluding passage describing the happy condition of the people under God's protecting care (vs. 12-15).

Psalm 145 is the last psalm ascribed to David, and serves to introduce the last five psalms of the book, which constitute the final anthem of praise. It is characterized by a sense of majesty and universality which makes it stand apart.

Psalms 146-150, the last group of Hallelujah psalms, bring the whole Psalter to a magnificent and splendid close. All themes of praise are here pealed forth. No. 146 praises the Lord as the Helper of His people. No. 147 praises Him as the Ruler of His people. No. 148 is the praise of the whole creation. No. 149 is the praise of His redeemed people. No. 150 is a final burst of universal praise.

THE MESSAGE OF THE PSALMS

There is one distinctive message which belongs to the Book of Psalms as to no other book of the Bible. It may be expressed in the language of the Westminster divines in their Shorter Catechism: "Man's chief end is to glorify God and to enjoy him forever."

1. Glorifying God. The Psalms are full of God's praise and glory. His name is sounded out in every psalm, and in some psalms in almost every line. There is no praise of any man. If any one is mentioned, it is never to signalize the man but always to glorify God. Israel is not eulogized, nor are the doings of the nation celebrated. It is always "the mighty deeds" of God. The same is true of the nature songs. When the beauty and majesty of nature are described, it is because they reveal the glory and power of God.

2. Enjoying God. The Psalms are also full of the soul's experience of God. How often the possessive pronoun is used, "my God", "our God"! The soul finds its satisfaction in God in a great variety of ways. The Psalms are full of human longings and emotions and experiences which have their end in God. In this book all eyes are looking up to God, all hands are stretched out toward Him.

THE BOOK OF PROVERBS

THIS book contains instruction given in the form of proverbs. A proverb is a short sentence conveying some moral truth or practical lesson in a concise and pointed form. It is the wisdom of experience condensed into a brief and pithy saying.

The book is ascribed to Solomon in the sense that he was the originator of the collection (1:1). He wrote many proverbs himself and gathered many others (Eccl. 12:9-10). He was especially fitted to be the writer of proverbs because of his great wisdom, his varied gifts, and his wide knowledge (1 Kings 4:29-34). His wisdom was of the intuitive kind that penetrates at once to the heart of a matter. The collection of proverbs contained in the book was not completed till long after Solomon's time (25:1).

The purpose of the book is explained in the opening verses (1:1-6). The object is "to know wisdom", the wisdom needed for life and conduct. Wisdom in Proverbs has always a moral and practical end in view. The keynote is contained in v. 7: "The fear of Jehovah is the beginning of wisdom". All the instruction given in the book rests on a religious basis. It is the Law of the Lord applied to the daily life and conduct of His redeemed people. It is significant that the Divine name used throughout is the covenant name Jehovah. The proper use of the book is not to teach men how to live in order to be saved, but to teach men already saved how to live.

The book is arranged on a simple plan and is composed of four main parts:

I. The Praise of Wisdom—Chs. 1-9

II. The First Collection of Proverbs—Chs. 10-24

III. The Second Collection of Proverbs—
Chs. 25-29

IV. Supplementary Proverbs—Chs. 30-31.

There are many minor collections and independent passages. Besides the opening words which give a title to the book as a whole (1:1), the following headings of separate sections occur: "The proverbs of Solomon" (10:1); "Hear the words of the wise" (22:17); "These also are sayings of the wise" (24: 23); "These are the proverbs of Solomon, which the men of Hezekiah king of Judah copied out" (25:1); "The words of Agur the son of Jakeh" (30:1); and "The words of king Lemuel" (31:1).

THE PRAISE OF WISDOM
(Chs. 1-9)

This is a connected discourse on "wisdom" in the form of instructions from a father to a son or a teacher to a pupil. The hearer is usually addressed as "my son". Occasionally the plural, "my sons", is used.

1. Introduction (1:1-7). The purpose of the book is set forth in vs. 1-6, and its fundamental principle in v. 7. The beginning of wisdom is a right relation with God; self-will is folly.

2. The Appeal and Warning of Wisdom (1:8-33). Receive instruction and shun enticements to evil (vs. 8-19). Wisdom is personified, and warns men of the consequences of refusing her counsel (vs. 20-33). This passage foreshadows the call and warning of the Gospel.

3. The Search for Wisdom (Ch. 2). There must be willingness and eagerness in seeking wisdom (vs. 1-8). Then its value will be realized in the paths of life. It enables one to avoid the way of evil men and evil women, and to choose the way of good men (vs. 9-22).

4. The Cultivation of Wisdom (Ch. 3). Trust in the Lord and devotion to Him is the secret of prosperity (vs. 1-12). It also brings happiness and peace (vs. 13-26), and leads to an inheritance of glory (vs. 27-35).

5. On Getting and Keeping Wisdom (Ch. 4). A personal testimony from the experience of a father (vs. 1-9), followed by an appeal to walk in the way of wisdom (vs. 10-19), and to keep wisdom in the heart (vs. 20-27).

6. Practical Counsels and Warnings (Chs. 5-7). A series of parental exhortations against impurity (ch. 5), against indolence (6:1-19), and against the wiles of the evil woman (6:20—7:27).

7. The Call of Wisdom (Ch. 8). Wisdom is again personified, and gives another appeal to men to attend and receive her instruction (vs. 1-11). The benefits she gives are set forth (vs. 12-21). Then wisdom's eternal relation to God is unfolded (vs. 22-31). There is a striking parallel between this passage and John 1:1-4. The Wisdom of Proverbs is the eternal Word of John. The call then ends with a final appeal (vs. 32-36).

8. The Contrast of Wisdom and Folly (Ch. 9). Each is personified as a woman calling the simple to turn in to a feast in her house. Wisdom calls to the feast of life (vs. 1-12), and Folly to the feast of death (vs. 13-18).

THE FIRST COLLECTION OF PROVERBS
(Chs. 10-24)

We pass now from connected discourse to proverbs strictly so called. They have no common topic except that they refer to life and conduct. Those in this collection are expressed in couplet form, and their general character is antithetical. They present sharp contrasts between wisdom and folly in practical life.

1. The upright and the wicked, the wise and the foolish, the pious and the ungodly, contrasted (chs. 10-15).

2. General observations on life and conduct, and admonitions to walk in the fear of God (16:1—22:16).

3. Precepts and warnings from the words of the wise concerning righteousness in practical life and social relations (22:17—24:34).

THE SECOND COLLECTION OF PROVERBS
(Chs. 25-29)

An additional group of Solomon's proverbs gathered in the reign of Hezekiah (25:1), two hundred and fifty years after Solomon's time. They may have been handed down orally, or they may have been found scattered through other collections. Their general character is more picturesque than the first group. They abound in figures, pictures, and suggestive analogies. In a general way they may be summarized as follows:

Admonitions for kings and subjects (ch. 25). Warnings against dishonourable conduct (ch. 26). Warnings against self-praise, flattery, presumption, and contention (27:1-22). An admonition for the farmer (27:23-27). Warnings against unjust dealing, unscrupulous methods, and oppression of the poor (ch. 28). Warnings against stubbornness, lawlessness, and insubordination (ch. 29).

SUPPLEMENTARY PROVERBS
(Chs. 30-31)

The two closing chapters of the book form a kind of appendix. They contain the words of Agur (ch. 30) and the words of king Lemuel (ch. 31). Nothing is known of these men. There are some peculiar numerical proverbs in ch. 30 (vs. 18, 21, 24, 29). The last chapter contains the words which Lemuel's mother taught him (vs. 1-9), and a fine description of a worthy woman (vs. 10-31). The latter passage, which dwells upon the gracious features of a good wife's character, makes a beautiful ending for the book.

THE MESSAGE OF PROVERBS

The fundamental message of the Book of Proverbs is this: Morality is rooted in religion and in a right relationship with God. There is no wisdom without trust in God. There can be no real righteousness without devotion to God. This recognition of God is interwoven with all the moral teaching of the book. It appears again and again. It goes deeper than outward conduct and reaches the secrets of the heart (15:11; 20:27; 21:2).

Throughout the book there runs a continuous contrast between wisdom and folly. Wisdom is rooted in the fear of the Lord, and folly in self-will. All the virtues spring from wisdom and the fear of God; all the vices from folly and the self-will of man.

Wisdom is completely exemplified and embodied in the Lord Jesus Christ, "who was made unto us wisdom from God", and "in whom are all the treasures of wisdom and knowledge hidden" (1 Cor. 1:30; Col. 2:3). When personified in Proverbs, Wisdom is an adumbration of the living Word, who became flesh and dwelt among men (John 1:14).

THE BOOK OF ECCLESIASTES

THE title of this book means the Preacher. It is the Septuagint rendering of the Hebrew title, the significance of which is obscure. The book is a kind of sermon. The word "preacher" occurs seven times: three times at the beginning (1:1, 2, 12), once in the middle (7:27), and three times at the end (12:8, 9, 10). The Preacher is described as "the son of David, king in Jerusalem" (1:1). This can be none other than Solomon. Perhaps the thoughts contained in this book were proclaimed by him to those who crowded to his court from all parts to be instructed by his wisdom (1 Kings 4:34). While the book claims to contain the words of Solomon, it nowhere claims to have been written by him. The words of the Preacher seem to end at 12:8, and the closing passage indicates another hand as the compiler of the book.

The book is pervaded with a tone of sadness and melancholy. The predominant note is one of weariness and despair. The language is marked by several characteristic expressions:

1. The word "vanity" occurs thirty-seven times in the twelve chapters. The phrases "vanity of vanities", "all is vanity", and "a striving after wind" (A.V. "vexation of spirit"), occur again and again.

2. The phrase "under the sun" occurs twenty-nine times. The similar phrases, "under the heavens" and "upon the earth", are occasionally used. The point of view is this world alone. The writer never gets above the sun.

3. The only name of the Divine Being found in this book, except the title "Creator", is the common name for God, "Elohim", which is used forty times. The covenant name "Jehovah" is not found once. The covenant relationship of the redeemed to the Lord is not in the mind of the writer.

4. Another characteristic feature, which cannot be shown in the English Version, is the name most frequently used for man. It is the generic name "Adam", indicating mankind or man in general. It occurs forty-seven times. The name for man as an individual is used only seven times. It is the state of man by nature that is being considered by the writer.

It is evident from these features that Ecclesiastes is the book of the natural man. It is not the will of God, but the will of man, that is developed. The sentiments of the book are not inspired by the Holy Spirit, but the Spirit uses the book to show the workings of man's own wisdom and to reveal the vanity of man's life apart from God. It is a mirror in which man may see himself.

Taking the book as a sermon, we find in it the following general plan:

I. The Theme—Ch. 1:1-11
II. Proof from Experience—Chs. 1:12—2:26
III. Proof from Observation—Chs. 3:1—8:15
IV. The Application—Chs. 8:16—12:8
V. The Conclusion—Ch. 12:9-14.

I. The Preacher's Theme (1:1-11). This is stated in v. 2 as "vanity of vanities, all is vanity". It is then explained and illustrated. Even nature itself is found to be a reflex of man's endless toil (vs. 5-7). There is weariness and dissatisfaction with everything under the sun.

The word "vanity" means not so much that which is sinful as that which is unsubstantial and transitory. It is the emptiness and futility of man's life rather than its sinfulness that is the theme. The Preacher then goes on to prove his theme, first from his experience of life and next from his observation.

II. The Preacher's Experience (1:12—2:26). He proceeds to prove his theme that man's life is all vanity by first reviewing his own varied experiences of life.

1. The vanity of wisdom and knowledge (1:12-18). This was Solomon's experience of the first of the two great gifts bestowed upon him (1 Kings 3:12-13).

2. The vanity of pleasure and riches (2:1-11). This was his experience of the second of the two gifts. The three elements of the world as defined in 1 John 2:16 are noticeable in this experience: the lust of the flesh (vs. 1-3), the lust of the eyes (vs. 4-6), and the pride or vainglory of life (vs. 7-10).

3. The result of his experience (2:12-26). Death comes to all alike (vs. 12-17). Sorrow comes to all alike (vs. 18-23). The solution of these things is with God alone (vs. 24-26).

III. The Preacher's Observation (3:1—8:15). He goes on with the proof of his theme by reviewing his wide observations of life in the world.

1. The limitations of life (ch. 3). Its times and seasons only emphasize its monotony and ceaseless routine (vs. 1-8). Twenty-eight "times" are enumerated here, the world number "four" multiplied by the number of completeness. Man is unable to explain the meaning of these things or make out God's purpose in them (vs. 9-11). In v. 11 the Preacher makes one of his most profound utterances: "also he hath set eternity in their heart". He means that in God's beautifully arranged world-plan, in which everything has its appointed place, man is a creature limited by time, but in his innermost nature he is related to eternity.

As man cannot solve the problems of life, the best he can do is to enjoy life and get what he can out of it (vs. 12-15). After all, man seems no better than the beasts that perish, and he gets no more profit out of life (vs. 16-22).

2. The disappointments of life (ch. 4). Death seems better than life, for life is marked by tears (vs. 1-3), by envy (vs. 4-6), by loneliness (vs. 7-12), and by disappointed hopes (vs. 13-16).

3. The maxims of religion (5:1-9). It is still the natural man that is speaking. His observation of religious life brings no true satisfaction. There is no contempt for religion here, but the Preacher manifests no joy in it. His recognition of God is irksome.

4. The sorrows of the rich (5:10-6:12). Riches do not satisfy. On the contrary, they often bring pain and injury, and he that gets them cannot take them with him from the world (5:10-20). They provide no capacity for enjoyment, and life without enjoyment is worse than having no life at all (6:1-6). Present enjoyment is better than counting on enjoyment in the unknown future (6:7-12).

5. The results of the Preacher's observation (7:1-8:15). The section begins with a number of proverbs (7:1-14), in an apparent attempt to answer the question with which the preceding chapter ends: "Who knoweth what is good for man in his life?" Then the Preacher relapses into a gloomy indifference to all the facts of life (7:15-29), and goes on to

point out what he has seen of the inequalities of life (8:1-15).

IV. The Preacher's Application (8:16—12:8). He now proceeds to apply the results of his experience and observation. Here we have the worldly wisdom of the natural man. It may be summed up as follows:

1. Take life as it comes and make the best of life while it lasts (8:16-9:10).

2. Yet nothing is sure in this world: even wisdom does not get its reward (9:11-18).

3. Follow the advice of the wise (ch. 10). This chapter contains a series of brief sayings which are somewhat like proverbs. There is an element of truth in them all, but they are all inspired by self-interest. They are the essence of worldly wisdom. They are for men who have no sense of the spiritual.

4. Rejoice in the opportunities and activities of life (ch. 11). There is much good advice here, for worldly wisdom inculcates diligence and industry.

5. Remember the Creator when life is young (12: 1-8). Acquire the habit of gratitude to God before old age comes on. Old age is set forth here in the figure of a house falling into decay.

V. The Conclusion of the Book (12:9-14). The words of the Preacher end with the restatement of his theme in v. 8. The next verse may be rendered: "And the wiser the Preacher became, the more did he teach the people knowledge". The writer of the book then sums up his teaching. The final lesson to be drawn from his experience and observation is stated in v. 13: "Fear God, and keep His commandments; for this is the whole duty of man". This is the highest wisdom the natural man can reach, the best advice he can give. But it is not salvation, for judgment still awaits man (v. 14).

The Message of Ecclesiastes

Ecclesiastes illustrates the truth of our Lord's words in John 4:13: "Every one that drinketh of this water shall thirst again"; and of Paul's in 2 Cor. 4:18: "The things which are seen are temporal"; they belong to time, and time is always slipping away. This world cannot satisfy the heart of man. This is proved by the deepest experience and the widest observation of life in the world. All history and all biography since this book was written have only confirmed its truth. The greatest of the Church Fathers learned it from his own experience, and put it in these oft quoted words: "Thou hast made us for Thyself, and our hearts are restless till they rest in Thee".

THE SONG OF SOLOMON

This book is sometimes called Canticles (little songs). The title as given in the book itself is "The Song of Songs" (1:1). This means the best of all songs or the song of the highest excellence. Solomon, who is named as the author, was a writer of songs: "his songs were a thousand and five" (1 Kings 4:32). The poem reflects the time of Solomon and the surroundings of his court. The mind of the writer as revealed in the song agrees with all that we know about Solomon.

It is a song of love in oriental language and imagery. It is dramatic in character, the speaker and the scene changing frequently. The characters who speak are (1) the King, who is Solomon, (2) the Bride, who is called the Shulammite in 6:13 and was probably the Shunammite of 1 Kings 1:3, and (3) the Daughters of Jerusalem, who form the chorus and are the friends of both. The scenes are set in the country and in Jerusalem, in a garden and in the palace.

Under the symbol of human love, the poem sets forth the spiritual union between the Lord and His people. It is in accordance with the analogy of Scripture. The Old Testament represents the relation between the Lord and Israel as a marriage covenant (Psa. 45; Isa. 54:5; 62:5; Jer. 2:2). The New Testament represents the relation between Christ and the Church as that of the Bride and the Bridegroom (John 3:29; 2 Cor. 11:2; Eph. 5:25-27; Rev. 19:7; 21:9; 22:17). To interpret the book in this way is not to deny that there was a literal basis for the song; but only a spiritual significance can account for its inclusion in the sacred Canon.

It is practically impossible to make a strict analysis of the book. The scene changes continually. The speakers are not indicated, and their speeches can be distinguished from one another only by the sentiments expressed and the nature of the words used. The story which lies as a background behind the song seems to have two movements. These divide the book into two parts and may be stated as follows:

Part I. The Bride's Marriage with the King (Chs. 1-4). A humble country maiden in northern Palestine is chosen by Solomon for his bride, and is raised to a place of honour and bliss by marriage with him in Jerusalem.

Part II. The Bride as the King's Wife (Chs. 5-8). The once lowly Shulammite, now sharing the king's royal state, invites him to return with her and revisit her old home; and the book closes with the bride and the king among her former friends.

Each of these two movements can be divided into three scenes, and the six scenes of the book may be drawn out as follows:

I. The Bride in the King's Pavilion (1:2—2:7). The scene is laid in the north of Palestine, where Solomon for the time being is dwelling in tents near the country home of the bride.

1. A dialogue between the Bride and the Daughters of Jerusalem (1:2-8). The poem begins with two stanzas, spoken by the chorus in praise of the King, each ending with, "they love thee" (vs. 2-4). Then the Bride addresses the chorus (vs. 5-6), and invokes the absent King (v. 7), and the chorus replies (v. 8).

2. The entrance of the King (1:9-14). He commends the beauty of the Bride (vs. 9-10), and receives from her words of love and praise (vs. 12-14). The intervening words (v. 11) are spoken by the chorus.

3. A dialogue between the King and the Bride (1:15-2:7). The King addresses the Bride throughout the poem as "my love", and she addresses him as "my beloved". The reference in v. 17 is to the forest trees of Lebanon under which they are sitting. In 2:1 the Bride compares herself to a humble wild flower, and the King replies: "As a lily excels the thorny shrubs in beauty, so my love—".

II. Memories of the Wooing (2:8—3:5). Reminiscences related by the Bride to the Daughters of Jerusalem, taking us back to a former period and affording a glimpse of her previous relation to the King. She describes how the Beloved visited her one spring morning, and how she afterwards dreamed of him at night.

1. The visit of the Beloved (2:8-17). She describes how he came to her home in Lebanon (vs. 8-9), and tells of the invitation he addressed to her to come out into the happy spring time from the seclusion of her rock-girt home (vs. 10-14), and of her reply, dismissing him until the cool of the day (vs. 15-17).

2. The dream of the Bride (3:1-5). She relates an imaginary occurrence transacted in a dream, revealing her love for the King.

III. The Marriage Day (3:6—4:16). The scene now changes to Jerusalem. The Bride is brought into the city in royal state to be united in marriage to the King.

1. The bridal procession and royal entry (3:6-11). The chorus describes the magnificent appearance of the Bride, borne in a royal litter, and then that of the King, wearing a nuptial crown in the festive joy of the Bridegroom. "Like pillars of smoke" (v. 6): because of the frankincense and other perfumes burned in such abundance round the royal equipage as to give it this appearance. The "daughters of Zion" (v. 11) were the women of the city as distinguished from the Bride's companions.

2. The King's commendation of the Bride (4:1-6). In a lyric song he commends her beauty by images taken from scenes and objects in different parts of the kingdom. She replies in a few brief words (v. 6), modestly interrupting the flow of the King's commendation by saying she would fain withdraw to some quiet spot till eventide.

3. The King's invitation to the Bride (4:7-15). Expressing his love and admiration in the tenderest terms and figures, he calls her to forsake her mother's home and become entirely his henceforth. The similes no longer refer to graces of bodily form, but to those of adornment, speech, and gesture, as expressions of inward character. She is likened to a lovely garden, barred against intruders and watered with abundant streams.

The two verses, 4:16 and 5:1, form a kind of link between the two parts of the poem. The Bride accepts the King's invitation in a few words of entire devotion; and he expresses his supreme satisfaction, and invites the guests to the marriage supper. The last words in v. 1 should be taken as in the margin—"of love".

IV. Fellowship with the King (5:2—6:10). The scene is still in Jerusalem. The Bride relates another dream to the Daughters of Jerusalem, and they offer to aid her in seeking the Bridegroom, when suddenly he appears and addresses a noble commendation to his Bride.

1. The Bride's second dream (5:2-8). Some time has elapsed since the marriage. A transient cloud of doubt is passing over her soul and is expressed in this dream which she relates to her friends. She has lost the society of her Beloved but not his affection, and she seeks reunion with him.

2. The Bride's commendation of the King (5:9—6:3). The scene is introduced by a question of the chorus (v. 9). Then the Bride gives a glorious description of her Beloved as altogether lovely (vs. 10-16). This is her response to his praise of her on the bridal day. The chorus asks a further question about him (v. 1), and she replies with a further expression of her devotion to him (vs. 2-3).

3. The King's commendation of the Bride (6:4-10). He now appears and pours out an enraptured description of the beauty of the Bride. Tirzah and Jerusalem are named together as the two fairest cities in the land at the time. Vs. 5-7 are a repetition of 4:1-3, marking the continuance of the King's affection as unchanged. The Bride is the same to him still as on the day of their espousals. The scene ends with another description of the glorious beauty of the Bride from the chorus (v. 10).

V. Homeward Thoughts (6:11—8:4). The scene is the palace garden. The Bride tells the Daughters of Jerusalem how she first met the King, and they ask her to dance before them. The King himself appears and expresses his love and admiration of her. She responds by inviting him to return with her to visit her mother's home.

1. The Bride and the Daughters of Jerusalem (6:11-13). She recalls the occasion when she met the King in a garden of nuts in her own country (vs. 11-12). As she is about to withdraw, they call her back, desiring to look a little longer on her grace and beauty (v. 13). She wonders at their request: "Why will ye look upon the Shulammite?" They reply: "As upon the dance of Mahanaim", which was probably a sacred dance which took its name from the locality.

2. The King's admiration of his Bride (7:1-9). The Bride complies with the request of the Daughters of Jerusalem, and, as she glides before them in the dance, they sing in further commendation of her beauty of form and grace of movement, beginning with her sandalled feet and ending with her head and its wealth of nature's ornament (vs. 1-5). Their last words announce the King's approach, and he continues the commendation of the Bride (vs. 6-9).

3. The Bride's invitation to the King (7:10—8:4). She now desires to revisit with her Beloved the lowly scenes of pastoral life out of which his grace has raised her (vs. 10-13). She recalls the feelings that she had for him before the obstacles to their union were removed (vs. 1-4).

VI. The Return Home (8:5-14). The scene now returns to northern Palestine. There the Bride has arrived with the King, and her former companions see her sharing his honour as the object of his love. She commends them to his favour; and the song ends with a few final words of fellowship and love between the King and his Bride.

1. The arrival of the Bride and her Beloved (vs. 5-7). The scene begins with the wonder of the Bride's former companions when they see her com-

ing up from the open country toward her mother's home as the King's wife. Their words are similar to those in 3:6. But there the scene is all splendour and exaltation; here it is condescension and humility. The King calls the Bride's attention to a fruit tree as the trysting place of their earliest vows, and then they go on pouring out expressions of true love.

2. The Bride's intercession for her friends (vs. 8-12). The friends or brothers of the Bride show themselves mindful of a younger sister in the family and ask how they shall provide for her when she is asked in marriage (v. 8). The Bride replies by telling them how she "found peace" in the eyes of the peaceful one (vs. 9-10). Then she turns to the King and commends her brothers to him by a parable. Solomon had a vineyard which he rented out to keepers (v. 11). She, too, has a vineyard which her brothers kept (1:6), and which now belongs to Solomon. He is to have all the fruit of it, but the faithful keepers should have their due (v. 12).

3. The fellowship between the King and his Bride (vs. 13-14). The poem ends by compressing into two short verses all that has been related in it of the wooing and wedding of the King and the Bride.

The Message of the Song of Solomon

Following immediately after Ecclesiastes, the message of which may be summed up in the words of John 4:13, the Song of Solomon has for its message the truth of John 4:14: "Whosoever drinketh of the water that I shall give him shall never thirst".

The central feature in the union between Christ and His Church is the fellowship of love. The essential element in the spiritual life of the Christian is love for the Lord Jesus Christ. This is the meaning of the book in New Testament light.

The experiences of the Bride suggest stages of spiritual growth. Three steps can be traced in the development and refining of the Bride's love for the King:—"My beloved is mine, and I am his" (2:16). There is still self-interest in her love; her possession of him comes first in her thought. "I am my beloved's, and my beloved is mine" (6:3). Self-interest is dying away; his possession of her comes first in her thought. "I am my beloved's; and his desire is toward me" (7:10). Self-interest is now gone; there is no dwelling upon what she possesses, nor is she taken up with her fellowship with him for her own sake. She is absorbed in him and is thinking only of his desire.

THE BOOK OF LAMENTATIONS

The name "lamentation" means an elegy, or a song of grief and mourning. David's lamentation over Saul and Jonathan in 2 Sam. 1:17-27 is a good example. This book is a series of elegies over the fall and desolation of Jerusalem at the hands of Nebuchadnezzar king of Babylon. This event occurred in 586 B.C. and marked the beginning of the captivity and exile of Judah. It is recorded in 2 Kings 25 and Jer. 52.

Uniform Jewish tradition ascribes the book to Jeremiah. Its place in the Canon follows immediately after his prophecies. His name does not appear in the Hebrew text, but the Septuagint begins the book with the following preface: "And it came to pass after Israel was taken captive and Jerusalem was destroyed, Jeremiah sat down weeping and lamented with this lamentation over Jerusalem, and said—".

This agrees with what is known of Jeremiah. He composed a lamentation over king Josiah (2 Chron. 35:25). He felt keenly the disaster which he saw coming upon his people. He lived through the siege of Jerusalem and saw the desolation which the fall of the city brought. The Spirit of God used the broken heart of the prophet in the composition of the book. It reflects God's own sorrow in the judgment which He had to inflict upon His people. There is no sign of any exultation on Jeremiah's part over the fulfilment of his predictions.

The book is composed of five lamentations, each occupying a single chapter. It is constructed on an elaborate and systematic plan. Each chapter has twenty-two verses, except the third which has sixty-six, or three times twenty-two. All the chapters except the last are acrostics in the original, following the twenty-two letters of the Hebrew alphabet. The middle chapter is arranged alphabetically in twenty-two groups of three verses each, and each verse in the group begins with the same letter. The chapters all set forth different aspects of the main theme. The first verse in each chapter gives the keynote of the particular lamentation.

I. The Solitary City (Ch. 1). The book begins with a description of the desolation of Jerusalem, "the daughter of Zion". She is likened to a widow sitting in solitude and sorrow. Her people are gone into exile; her sanctuary is deserted; her glory is departed; her adversaries rejoice over her (vs. 1-11). Then Zion herself speaks. She bewails the calamity that has fallen upon her, and acknowledges that it is the righteous judgment of God (vs. 12-22). The sense of sin as the cause of the disaster pervades this part of the chapter.

II. The Anger of the Lord (Ch. 2). This is the essence of the calamity. The words "anger" and "wrath" occur frequently in the chapter. The prophet describes the judgment of the Lord's anger (vs. 1-10). He laments the miseries of Jerusalem, and calls upon her to cry to the Lord for comfort and help (vs. 11-19). Then comes the appeal which the city was commanded to make (vs. 20-22).

III. The Sorrow of the Prophet (Ch. 3). The prophet now identifies himself with his people, taking their affliction to heart and making their misery his own. This is the most elaborate and sublime of the poems that compose the book. Here sorrow passes into prayer. It is an ideal illustration of godly sorrow which "worketh repentance unto salvation" (2 Cor. 7:10).

The prophet first describes his grievous suffering (vs. 1-18). He recognizes that every stroke is from the hand of the Lord, thus acknowledging the connection of suffering with sin. Then he goes on to express his hope in the compassion and lovingkindness of the Lord (vs. 19-39). In the midst of this passage are some verses of rich comfort and consolation. Next he confesses the justice of God in sending the punishment, which has been intensified, however, by what their enemies have done to them (vs. 40-54). Lastly, he appeals to God for deliverance and for His righteous vengeance upon their enemies (vs. 55-66). A notable feature of this chapter is the nearness of God to the mind of the prophet: he does not think it necessary to mention the Divine name till he has got well on into the midst of the chapter.

IV. The Fall of Zion (Ch. 4). The prophet describes the misery of the siege of the city and the disaster that has fallen upon Zion (vs. 1-10). This has come upon her because of the sins of her prophets and priests (vs. 11-16), and because of the people's vain trust in the help of man (vs. 17-20). The chapter ends with a note of hope for Zion in the punishment of Edom, her bitterest foe (vs. 21-22).

V. An Appeal to the Lord (Ch. 5). Speaking on behalf of the nation, the prophet calls upon the Lord to consider what has come upon them. He describes the calamity again, telling how all classes of the people have suffered in it (vs. 1-18). The book closes with a prayer to the Lord to turn the people unto Himself and renew their days as of old (vs. 19-22).

THE MESSAGE OF LAMENTATIONS

Two characteristics of the Book of Lamentations should be kept in mind in drawing out its teaching: (1) It is marked by a keen sense of the righteousness of God's judgments. There is profound loyalty to God on the part of the prophet in describing His attitude toward sin. (2) It is marked also by a deep sorrow for the afflictions of the people. There is profound sympathy for Zion in the prophet's heart in describing the judgment that has fallen upon her. The mind of the Spirit, speaking through the prophet, reveals that anger against sin and sympathy for the sinner exist together in the heart of God.

The lamentations of the book should be compared with Christ's lament over Jerusalem (Matt. 23:37-39; Luke 19:41-44), and Paul's sorrow over Israel (Rom. 9:1-5). They foreshadow something of the inner nature of Christ's sufferings as including both sorrow over sin and sympathy for the sinner in the afflictions caused by sin.

The book also indicates something of the true nature of the believer's fellowship with Christ as involving love and sorrow combined, love for the world and sorrow for its sin. It manifests the spirit that should pervade the Church in her ministry of intercession for the world.

THE OLD TESTAMENT PROPHETICAL BOOKS

THE PROPHETICAL BOOKS

THE prophets are described in the Old Testament Scriptures, as to their character and function, by several different designations. They are called occasionally by such names as these: seer (1 Sam. 9:9; 2 Sam. 24:11), watchman (Isa. 21:11-12; Ezek. 3:17), man of God (1 Sam. 9:6; 1 Kings 13:1), servant of Jehovah (2 Kings 9:7; 14:25; Isa. 20:3), and messenger of Jehovah (Isa. 44:26; Hag. 1:13; Mal. 3:1). Their special designation, however, is a term which is used in all parts of the Old Testament and is always rendered by our word "prophet". The original Hebrew word means one who is the medium of a Divine revelation and speaks under Divine impulse.

The prophets, therefore, were God's spokesmen. The relation in which Aaron stood to Moses, as described in Exod. 4:15-16 and 7:1, was analogous to the relation in which the prophets stood to God. The prophets were also preachers, for the word they received from the Lord was delivered to the people in extended addresses. The messages of the prophets often had to do with the carrying out of God's purposes in the future, and so prediction came to form part of their function.

The prophetic office was not hereditary like the offices of priest and king. The prophets were called separately and individually. Every true prophet received a personal call to his office. Along with his call he also received a special communication from God which he delivered to the people under the inspiration of the Spirit of God.

The ministry of the prophets was directed first to their own time. They were raised up primarily as reformers and revivalists, to stir up the conscience of the people and turn them from sin and apostasy back to the Lord God of Israel. They stood up against the drift of the times, and they often had to endure suffering and persecution.

Their ministry was also related to God's purpose of redemption. While they dealt with conditions and events of their own day, the prophets saw these in the light of the coming Kingdom of God. In this connection the predictive element came more and more into prophecy. The great theme of prophecy was the coming of the Messianic King and the establishment of his Kingdom in Israel and the world.

Thus it is that the goal of prophecy is Jesus Christ. "The testimony of Jesus is the spirit of prophecy" (Rev. 19:10). The prophets were moved by the Divine urge at the heart of the Old Testament dispensation (2 Pet. 1:21). Though their preaching took its rise from the particular needs of the different periods to which they belonged and the different audiences which they addressed, yet it always pointed forward to one great Divine end. It anticipated the transcendent work of the grace of God in the redemption of the world (Rom. 16:25-26). The Spirit of Christ was in the prophets, though they did not always understand the full import of the messages they were inspired to deliver (1 Pet. 1:10-11). The prophets should be read with the background of their own times in view, but the essential significance of their various messages can be understood only when the light of the New Testament is brought to bear upon them.

Old Testament prophecy began with Moses, the first and greatest of the long line of the prophets of Israel. He was the true type of Christ, the perfect Prophet (Deut. 18:15; 34:10). From his time to the end of the Old Testament age the spirit of prophecy was never absent from Israel. It was shared at times by women; Miriam, Deborah, and Huldah were prophetesses (Exod. 15:20; Jud. 4:4; 2 Kings 22:14). Unnamed prophets appear during the time of the judges (Jud. 6:7-8; 1 Sam. 2:27). Samuel was the first prophet to be officially recognized by the nation (1 Sam. 3:19-21), and under him the prophetic order was founded and schools of the prophets were established (1 Sam. 10:10-11; 19:20). In the time of the monarchy from David onward, many prophets appear in the course of the historical narrative, the greatest of whom were Elijah and Elisha.

The age of written prophecy began with the rise of the great military empires that were used of God for the chastening and judgment of His own chosen people. It covered the last four hundred years of Old Testament history. It may be divided into three periods, corresponding with the three successive empires of the time:

1. The Assyrian Period (2 Kings 15-21; 2 Chron. 26-33). Assyria appeared upon the horizon of Israel about 800 B.C., when Jonah was sent on a mission to Nineveh its capital city. Not long after that time Assyrian kings began to threaten Northern Israel. In 721 they captured and destroyed Samaria, and the ten tribes were removed into exile. The power of the Assyrian empire began to decline about 630, and Nineveh finally fell before the rising power of Babylon in 612 B.C.

The prophets of this period were Jonah, Amos, and Hosea, who carried on their ministry in Northern Israel; and Joel, Isaiah, Micah, and Nahum, who belonged to Judah.

2, The Babylonian Period (2 Kings 22-25; 2 Chron. 34-36). The power of Babylon began to revive with the decline of Assyria. It became supreme with Nebuchadnezzar's defeat of Egypt at Carchemish in 605 B.C. (Jer. 46:2). In the same year began Judah's subjection to Babylon. Jerusalem was finally destroyed in 586, and the people of Judah were taken into captivity.

The prophets of this period were Jeremiah, Obadiah, Habakkuk, and Zephaniah, whose ministry was carried on in Jerusalem and Judah; and Ezekiel and Daniel, who belonged to the Captivity.

3. The Persian Period (Ezra, Nehemiah, and Esther). With the fall of Babylon before Cyrus in 538 B.C., the power of Persia became supreme and the period of Judah's captivity came to an end. Cyrus issued a decree allowing the Jews to return to Jerusalem and rebuild their Temple. A remnant of the nation did return; Judah and Jerusalem were restored by them, and the Covenant was renewed with them. The majority of the Jews, however, remained in the Dispersion.

The prophets of this period were Haggai, Zechariah, and Malachi, and their ministry was carried on in Judah among the Jews who had returned to the land. These were the last in the long line of the Hebrew prophets. Both Old Testament history and Old Testament prophecy came to an end in the time of Nehemiah.

The Prophetical Books, as they occur in the Old Testament, are arranged in two groups, the four Major Prophets and the twelve Minor Prophets. The terms major and minor have reference to the size of the books and not to the importance of the men. The Major Prophets—Isaiah, Jeremiah, Ezekiel, and Daniel—come in chronological order. Through them runs the general theme of the Messianic redemption in the main line of its development, which may be set forth as follows:

In Isaiah it appears as the Salvation of the Lord, in Jeremiah as the Judgment of the Lord, in Ezekiel as the Reconstruction of Israel, and in Daniel as the Advent of the Messiah.

The twelve Minor Prophets, which are counted as one book in the Hebrew Canon, are arranged in general, but not strict, chronological order. They cover a longer period of time than the Major Prophets, extending over the whole age of written prophecy from before 800 to about 400 B.C. Each of them illustrates and emphasizes some special aspect of the messages of the larger books.

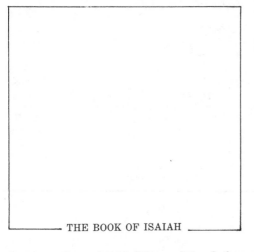

──────── THE BOOK OF ISAIAH ────────

ISAIAH was the greatest of all the prophets, whether we consider the character of his ministry or the scope of his message. He belonged to the kingdom of Judah and carried on his ministry in the city of Jerusalem. He was a kind of court preacher and lived on terms of intimacy with the king and the high priest. He was married and had two sons, who were given names that set forth certain aspects of his message: Shear-jashub, "a remnant shall return" (7:3), and Maher-shalal-hash-baz, "hasten to the spoil, hurry to the prey" (8:3). He gathered about himself a band of disciples, who received his messages into their hearts and preserved the prophecies which he committed to writing (8:16). They were the nucleus of the subsequent remnant (6:13).

Isaiah was called to the prophetic office in the closing year of Uzziah's reign (6:1), and continued in it throughout the next three reigns (1:1). Tradition says that he was sawn asunder in the idolatrous reaction at the beginning of Manasseh's reign. There may be an allusion to this in Heb. 11:37. His ministry extended over the latter half of the eighth century B.C. The history of the period is recorded in 2 Kings 15-20 and 2 Chron. 26-32.

Very little is known of Isaiah's personal history, but his character stands out clearly marked upon his prophecies. All the qualities that pertain to the prophetic office seem to be combined in him with perfect balance and harmony. This gives his book a majestic repose of style and a dramatic eloquence. His eyes had seen the King, the Lord of hosts (6:5),

and this vision dominated his whole life and gave a commanding character to all his preaching. A sense of the majesty and holiness of God, who sits upon the throne of the universe and rules over the affairs of men, pervades all Isaiah's prophecies.

The Book of Isaiah is composed of three parts—two prophetical sections with a short historical section between them. The first part (Chs. 1-35) contains prophecies of warning and judgment. The last part (Chs. 40-66) contains prophecies of comfort and salvation. In the first part the prophet speaks from the standpoint of his own life-time, when Assyria was invading the land of Israel and was the great foe to be feared. In the last part he speaks from a standpoint in the midst of the Babylonian exile and on the eve of the return, more than a hundred and fifty years beyond his own day.

The middle part of the book, the historical section (Chs. 36-39), forms a connecting link between the two separate prophetical sections. It contains the record of two events that occurred during Isaiah's ministry. One of these events delivered Judah from the peril of the Assyrian invasions and marked the close of the prophet's public ministry. The other event brought Babylon upon the scene and led to the prophet's prediction of the Babylonian exile and the private ministry of his later years. The one event looks backward to the first part of the book, and the other event looks forward to the last part. A single mind must have been behind this arrangement, for it gives the book of Isaiah a manifest and remarkable unity of structure. This is shown in the following general plan:

I. Prophecies of Warning and Judgment—
Chs. 1-35 (Historical background:—the Assyrian invasions)
1. Concerning Judah and Jerusalem (Chs. 1-12)
2. Concerning the Surrounding Nations (Chs. 13-27)
3. Concerning the World (Chs. 28-35)

II. Historical Link—Chs. 36-39
1. The End of the Assyrian Invasions (Chs. 36-37)
2. The Shadow of the Babylonian Captivity (Chs. 38-39)

III. Prophecies of Comfort and Salvation—
Chs. 40-66 (Historical background:—the Babylonian captivity)
1. The Preparation for Redemption (Chs. 40-48)
2. The Accomplishment of Redemption (Chs. 49-57)
3. The Realization of Redemption (Chs. 58-66).

PART I

The first of the three parts of Isaiah (Chs. 1-35) is composed of three sections of prophecy, all marked by warnings of coming judgment. Each section begins with local circumstances, branches out universally, and comes to a close with a description of Messianic blessedness. The three sections are progressive in their sweep. The circle of view expands, taking in first Judah and Jerusalem (Chs. 1-12), then the surrounding nations (Chs. 13-27), and finally the whole world (Chs. 28-35).

CONCERNING JUDAH AND JERUSALEM
(Chs. 1-12)

This section contains two groups of prophetic messages, one dealing with the sins that were corrupting the nation from within (chs. 1-6), and the other dealing with the perils that were threatening it from without (chs. 7-12).

I. National Sins (Chs. 1-6). These chapters contain the earliest messages of the prophet. They reflect the state of Judah during the reigns of Uzziah and Jotham. The prosperity of Uzziah's long reign had brought luxury and self-indulgence, and a general decay of religious and moral life had set in. The kingdom of Assyria, pressing westward from Nineveh, began to threaten Northern Israel when Jotham was reigning in Jerusalem (755-739 B.C.). The instrument of judgment was already being prepared for the chastening of both Israel and Judah.

1. An Impeachment of the Nation (Ch. 1). The heavens and the earth are called to hear the Lord's charge against His ungrateful and unfaithful people (vs. 2-4). "They have forsaken Jehovah, they have despised the Holy One of Israel". This is Isaiah's characteristic way of describing the Lord God. He uses the title almost thirty times; it occurs only five times elsewhere in the Old Testament. Two other titles used in this chapter also reveal the prophet's sublime conception of God: "Jehovah of hosts" and "the Mighty One of Israel" (vs. 9, 24).

The desolate state of their country is an evidence of the Lord's displeasure with His people (vs. 5-9). Their religious worship is formal and empty; their social and public life is corrupt (vs. 10-17). Then the prophet utters an earnest appeal for repentance (vs. 18-23), and a solemn warning of coming judgment which would purge the nation and purify Zion (vs. 24-31).

2. The Discipline of Judgment (Chs. 2-4). This prophecy is probably a series of connected addresses. It begins and ends with a description of the true glory God had in view for Zion. Between these two pictures lies the path of judgment by which this destiny was to be attained. Judgment was needed to chasten and purify Israel and to realize God's purpose with the nation.

(1) A vision of the latter days: Zion's place among the nations (2:2-4). The "latter days" mean the days of the Messiah, beginning with the first coming of Christ and extending to His second coming. Zion was to be the centre from which the word of the Lord should go forth and the will of the Lord should be done among the nations. The foundation of His Kingdom was to be "established on the top of the mountains" and "exalted above the hills". These phrases mean more than pre-eminence or supremacy in the earth. In the light of the New Testament, they indicate that the Kingdom would be founded in a heavenly order. They are the first intimations in the prophetic books that the Messianic Kingdom was to be, "not of this world" (John 18:36). The passage occurs in Micah 4:1-3 also. Both prophets were preaching at the same time, and one may have quoted from the other, or both from an earlier and unknown source.

(2) The course of judgment (2:5—4:1). The prophet makes an appeal to the nation to return to the Lord, and then he describes its condition as blinded and deluded by foreign fashions, by the display of wealth, and by the idolatry of self-trust and human pride (2:5-11). A day of the Lord was coming, which should bring judgment upon the pride of man and overthrow the objects of human confidence (2:12-22). The description combines features of an earthquake and a thunder-storm. It closes with an exhortation which forms a transition to ch. 3. The sense of awe in the whole passage is deepened by the threefold occurrence of the phrase: "From before the terror of Jehovah, and from the glory of his majesty" (vs. 10, 19, 21).

The nature of God's judgment upon Jerusalem and Judah is described as the weakening of the pillars of state and the dissolution of the social order. He would put the government in the hands of incompetent men, with consequent anarchy and ruin (3:1-12). The rulers and the women should be especially involved in the judgment for they were especially guilty—the rulers guilty of oppressing the poor, and the women guilty of pride and wantonness (3:13--4:1).

(3) The issues of judgment: a purified Zion (4:2-6). A remnant of Israel, purified by the judgment, should realize God's purpose in Zion, and His presence should be manifested in their midst. This was to be accomplished "by the spirit of justice (A.V. judgment), and by the spirit of burning". In these two phrases we have foregleams of the Cross (John 12:31), and of Pentecost (Matt. 3:11). The whole passage is a prophetic description of the spiritual order of the Christian dispensation.

3. The Parable of the Vineyard (Ch. 5). This is a further prophecy of the judgment announced in the preceding address. The vineyard was a symbol of the nation. The Lord expresses His disappointment with it and His purpose to bring judgment upon it.

After He had made complete provision for His people, they had made an ungrateful return in bringing forth "wild grapes" (vs. 1-7). Then follow six "woe's", descriptive of the nation's perverseness and wrong-doing. These were the "wild grapes" of Israel (vs. 8-25). Among the "woe's" are four "therefore's", explaining that judgment must follow such sin. The judgment is then described as coming in the form of an invasion of the land by foreign foes (vs. 26-30).

This passage describes the kind of sins that were bringing the judgment of God upon the nation. The six "woe's" denounce the greed of the wealthy landowners (v. 8), the self-indulgence and lust for pleasure of those who should have been leaders of God's people (v. 11), the defiant and mocking scepticism of the irreligious (v. 18), the confusion of moral distinctions among the people (v. 20), the self-satisfied astuteness of the politicians (v. 21), and the dissolute character and venal corruption of the judges (v. 22). All this gives us a dark picture of the moral condition of Israel at that time.

4. The Call of the Prophet (Ch. 6). This is Isaiah's account of an experience he had in the Temple at a time of special crisis in the nation, when he was quite a young man. It gave him a new revelation of God and called him to the ministry of his life. There were two features in it. (1) The vision of the Lord: "I saw" (vs. 1-7). This consisted of a revelation of His majesty and holiness (vs. 1-4), and a realization of His pardoning and purifying grace (vs. 5-7). All this was borne in upon the young prophet's soul by an overwhelming sense of heavenly realities. (2) The voice of the Lord: "I heard" (vs. 8-13). In response to the call of the Lord, Isaiah volunteered at once for service,

and was sent on a difficult and discouraging task (vs. 8-10). The terms of his commission meant that a series of desolating judgments were to fall upon the nation until only a holy remnant should be left (vs. 11-13). This remnant was to form the nucleus of a new Israel.

II. National Perils (Chs. 7-12). These chapters belong to the reign of Ahaz (739-723 B.C.), when the first great political crisis of Isaiah's time occurred. Pekah king of Israel and Rezin king of Syria formed a league to attack Jerusalem and set up another king over Judah. Ahaz, in a panic of fear and unbelief, sent to the king of Assyria for aid. This section of the book contains the messages delivered by Isaiah at this time. It was revealed to the prophet that Jerusalem should be delivered from this confederacy, but that a more severe judgment awaited her, which would come from Assyria. Trouble and anguish should continue to be the portion of Judah and Israel until the coming of the Messiah.

1. A Message for the King: the Sign of Immanuel (Ch. 7). The historical occasion is first described, and the fear which had seized the king and the people (vs. 1-2). The character of this invasion and its disastrous results for Judah are described in 2 Chron. 28. Isaiah was sent to Ahaz with his son, whose name was a reminder of the revelation about the remnant recorded at the close of the preceding chapter. The king was inspecting the water supply of Jerusalem at the time. The prophet delivered the Lord's appeal to him for courage and faith: "be quiet; fear not" (vs. 3-4). Such a plot by the two allied kingdoms should not stand, for it was an attack on David's line and throne; but the northern kingdom itself should be overthrown (vs. 5-9). Ahaz was offered any sign he might ask of the Lord as a pledge of His protection; but he refused on the pretext that it would be tempting God. The faith of Ahaz was found wanting; he was secretly trusting in the strength of Assyria instead of the Lord God of Israel (vs. 10-12).

The prophet then rebuked the king and announced the Lord's own sign, the coming birth of a virgin's son, whom she should name "Immanuel" (vs. 13-14). No interpretation of this remarkable prophecy can be adequate which does not find in it an explicit announcement of the coming of the Messianic King. The significance of the sign meant that God would raise up in the house of David, in place of the faithless Ahaz, one who should be in very truth "God with us". The ultimate fulfilment of the prophecy, as explained in Matt. 1:22-23, may not have been present to Isaiah's mind, and the birth of his own son (8:3-4) may have been the sign intended for Ahaz; but that he had the Messiah in view is shown by his use of the name "Immanuel" in 8:8, and his subsequent prophecies in 9:6-7 and 11:1-5, which followed directly from this one.

Following up this announcement, the prophet declared that the Child should grow up to the moral and spiritual stature of true manhood under conditions of scarcity and privation. And then he went on to predict that before sufficient time elapsed for that to take place the two nations leagued against Judah should be overthrown, and that a still more formidable attack upon Judah should come from the very nation to which Ahaz was secretly looking for help (vs. 15-17).

He then gave a graphic description of the desolating Assyrian invasions which would come upon the land "in that day". Judah was to become the theatre of war between Egypt and Assyria (vs. 18-20). The sparse population should be reduced to a poor pastoral existence, and the cultivated vineyards should be overrun with thorns and briers (vs. 21-25).

2. A Message for the People: the Comfort of Immanuel (8:1-15). Some time had passed since the prophet's message to Ahaz when this message was delivered. In the meantime, his second son was born and was given a name which was to be a sign to the people that the coming Assyrian invasion was near at hand; it meant "hasten to the spoil, hurry to the prey" (vs. 1-4). As the people had turned away from the quiet waters of Shiloah, a symbol of the spiritual rule of God in Judah, He would bring upon them the waters of the Euphrates, a symbol of the military might of Assyria. These waters should overflow Judah, Immanuel's own land, "even to the neck"; that is, they should reach Jerusalem but should not overwhelm it; the city itself would be saved (vs. 5-8).

The prophet then goes on to issue a challenge to the nations. No conspiracy of theirs against the Kingdom of Immanuel could ever succeed: "it shall not stand; for God is with us" (vs. 9-12). The Lord of hosts is the real defence of His people, the true source of comfort and assurance for those who trust Him, but a stumbling block and an offence to those who do not (vs. 13-15).

3. A Message for the Remnant: the Dawn of the New Day (8:16—9:7). At God's command the prophet deposited a written record of his testimony with his disciples, who formed an inner circle of religious fellowship while they waited on the Lord in faith. They were the beginning of the Lord's remnant (8:16-18). During the night of spiritual darkness and distress which was about to settle down upon the land, they were to tell the blinded and infatuated people not to resort to necromancy, but to go to the Word of the Lord their God for light (8:19-22).

The prophet describes the dawn of a new day breaking first over the north of Palestine, which was most exposed to the Assyrian invasions and suffered most from them (9:1-2). It was the beginning of the Messianic age. Matthew states that this prophecy was fulfilled in the Galilean ministry of Jesus (Matt. 4:12-16). Then there follows a prophetic description of the Messianic work: "Thou hast multiplied the nation, thou hast increased their joy." Their joy was to be like that of gathering a harvest, or dividing the spoils after a great victory (9:3-5). This figure sets forth fittingly the joy that marks the new spiritual life of the present Christian age, which began with the outpouring of the Spirit on the Day of Pentecost.

This was to come to pass when the Child announced in 7:14 should reign upon the throne of David (9:6-7). These two verses contain one of the grandest Messianic prophecies. We have here: (1) Messiah's two-fold nature, human and divine: "a child born" and "a son given". (2) His four-fold character. The eight words descriptive of Him are in four pairs when the first two are taken together as in the R.V. margin. (3) His everlasting kingdom of righteousness and peace, which He would administer from "the throne of David". In the light of Luke 1:32 and Acts 2:30-35, this prophecy began to be fulfilled in the resurrection and ascension of Jesus Christ. The prophet declared that all this would be accomplished by God Himself: "the zeal of Jehovah of hosts will perform this".

4. A Message for Israel: a Warning of Doom (9:8—10:4). The kingdom of Northern Israel now comes in for denunciation. This prophecy is in four strophes, each ending with the same awe-inspiring refrain: "For all this his anger is not turned away, but his hand is stretched out still" (vs. 12, 17, 21, 4). Divine discipline in Israel had failed; now only judgment remained. Each part of the prophecy describes a specific national sin and announces a specific judgment. The four judgments are progressive and cumulative: foreign invasion, anarchy, internal strife, and captivity.

5. A Message for Assyria: a Warning of Punishment (10:5-34). God was using Assyria as the instrument of judgment upon His own people (vs. 5-6). But the Assyrian went beyond the Divine intention in his arrogant and cruel ambition, and he, too, must be dealt with (vs. 7-11). When the Lord had first dealt with His own people, He would then punish Assyria (vs. 12-19).

The prophecy was intended for the comfort and assurance of the faithful remnant in Judah, that they might not fear during the Assyrian invasions (vs. 20-27). The last verses of the chapter are a graphic description of an invading army gradually approaching Jerusalem, and then meeting sudden destruction at the hand of the Lord (vs. 28-34). The passage foreshadows the event recorded in 37: 33-36.

6. A Message for Zion: the Messianic Salvation (Chs. 11-12). The glorious issues of judgment to be realized in the Messianic age are now described. The true King and his kingdom come into view in these chapters. He was to come of the family of David, at a time when the royal house should be broken down to the roots; and he was to be endowed with the complete fulness of the Spirit of the Lord (11:1-2).   Being thus equipped, he would administer his kingdom by methods very different from those of men: not "after the sight of his eyes", neither "after the hearing of his ears". His delight being "in the fear of Jehovah", he would follow the will of God. His weapons would be "the rod of his mouth" and "the breath of his lips". That is, he would proclaim the Word of the Lord and use the power of the Spirit of God. Righteousness would be the supreme quality of his work and the abiding result of his reign (11:3-5).

The results of his work are then described. They should comprise the peace and harmony of the creation (11:6-8), the universal knowledge of the Lord (11:9), the submission of the nations to the peaceful rule of the Son of David (11:10), and the return and restoration and reunion of scattered and broken Israel (11:11-16). Finally, a song of salvation is put into the lips of the inhabitants of the new Zion, expressing the joy of the ransomed people and declaring the praise of the Lord to the nations for the salvation that He has wrought (ch. 12).

Concerning the Nations
(Chs. 13-27)

I. National Judgments (Chs. 13-23). In these chapters a number of prophecies on the nations surrounding Judah, uttered at different times in Isaiah's ministry, are collected together.

1. The Doom of Babylon (13:1—14:27). In Isaiah's day Babylon was included in the Assyrian Empire. This prophecy stands first because Babylon was the world power ordained of God to complete the judgment upon His own people.   It was uttered more than a century and a half before the event it describes. It reveals the principle underlying all God's national judgments: nations are used one against another to serve His purposes.

The prophecy begins by announcing that the Lord has called His "consecrated ones" to execute His indignation and wrath against Babylon (13:2-5). They were "sanctified" (A.V.), not as made inwardly holy, but as designated for His holy purposes. Their invasion is likened to a terrible storm obscuring the sky (13:6-10). It would be a manifestation of the wrath of God upon the pride and wickedness of man (13:11-16). The Medes are named as God's agents in this judgment, and the result is described as the utter desolation of Babylon (13:17-22).

The purpose of God's judgment on Babylon was the deliverance of Israel (14:1-2). In anticipation of their day of restoration, a great song of triumph over the king of Babylon is put into the lips of the redeemed people (14:3-20). In the midst of it there is a reference to the fall of Satan, the real ruler of the kingdoms of this world, of whom the king of Babylon was a type (vs. 12-14). This is followed by a repetition of God's judgment against both Babylon and Assyria (14:21-27).

2. The Doom of Philistia (14:28-32). A warning to the Philistines is followed by a statement that the Lord's purpose in judgment was to establish His kingdom in Zion. The historical background of this prophecy is found in 2 Chron. 28:18.

3. The Doom of Moab (Chs. 15-16). The prophet describes the awful devastation that was to come suddenly upon Moab (15:1-4), and he is touched with pity at the plight of fugitives fleeing from Moab before an army coming down from the north (15:5-9). Moab is counselled to seek the help and protection of Zion in view of the coming Messianic reign of righteousness (16:1-5). But the pride of Moab was to be visited with a desolating judgment (16:6-8), and again the prophet gives vent to his sorrow at the prospect (16:9-12). This judgment was to fall within a very short time (16:13-14).

4. The Doom of Damascus (Ch. 17). The scope of this prophecy includes Northern Israel as well as Syria. It predicts the fate of the two nations that were allied against Judah. The impending overthrow of Damascus is announced (vs. 1-3); and this was to involve that of Israel, with the exception of a remnant who should turn from their idolatry to the Holy One of Israel (vs. 4-8). This judgment was to come upon Israel because the nation had forsaken the God of its salvation and the rock of its strength (vs. 9-11).   The chapter closes with a graphic description of invading armies and their sudden destruction (vs. 12-14).   These were the Assyrians, the oppressors of Israel and the instruments of judgment, who were themselves to be judged. The passage predicts the event recorded in 37:36.

5. Concerning Ethiopia (Ch. 18). The ambassadors from this land are bidden to return home and watch the Lord thwart Assyria's attempt to subjugate Judah (vs. 1-3). He will refrain from interfering with Assyria, and will let its power come to maturity. Then He will suddenly destroy it with an overwhelming overthrow (vs. 4-6). The vivid picture of God taking His rest in the summer heat

before the harvest indicates the calmness and deliberation of the workings of Divine judgment. As a result the Ethiopians should pay homage to the Lord on Mount Zion (v. 7).

6. The Doom of Egypt (Chs. 19-20). A time of anarchy and oppression was to come upon the Egyptians: their national industries should be ruined, and their princes and wise men should fail them (19:1-15). Yet the prophet sees hope for Egypt: judgment should result in part of the nation turning to the Lord (19:16-22). Egypt and Assyria, the two great powers then contending for the rule of the world, should be united with Israel in the worship of the Lord and become a blessing to the earth (19:23-25). This prophecy, which looks forward to the Gospel age, is followed by the warning of a judgment near at hand, the Assyrian conquest of Egypt (ch. 20).

7. A Group of Oracles (Ch. 21). The first is a vision of the fall of Babylon at the hands of the Medes (vs. 1-2). The phrase, "the wilderness of the sea", in the title of this prophecy refers to the plain of the Euphrates where Babylon was situated The vision produced fear and agitation in the heart of the prophet (vs. 3-4). It was that of a carousal within the walls, suddenly interrupted by a call to arms, and followed by an announcement of the fall of the city (vs. 5-9). It was intended for the comfort of the prophet's own people (v. 10).

Two other oracles, which are connected with the fall of Babylon, vividly picture the consequent anxiety of Edom (vs. 11-12), and the impending failure of the glory of Arabia (vs. 13-17).

8. Concerning Jerusalem (Ch. 22). The phrase, "the valley of vision", refers to the prophet's point of view in the valley between the two hills on which Jerusalem was built.   Probably his dwelling was there.   This prophecy is a denunciation of the inhabitants of the city. They were giving themselves up to revelry and self-indulgence when the enemy was at the gate and the Lord was calling for repentance (vs. 1-14). Shebna, the unfaithful steward, was to he replaced by Eliakim (vs. 15-21). The appointment of Eliakim is given a Messianic significance (vs. 22-25). The key of the house of David was to be placed in his keeping.   This symbolism is used in Matt. 16:19 and Rev. 3:7 of Christ and His Kingdom.

9. The Doom of Tyre (Ch. 23). Her commercial glory and her pride were to be humbled; and the dismay of the states affected by her fall is described (vs. 1-7). The purpose of the Lord was to bring down all earthly pride, and the overthrow of Tyre was in accordance with this principle of His government (vs. 8-12). It was to be brought about by the Chaldeans (vs. 13-14). After a period of seventy years, during which Tyre should be forgotten, she was to enjoy a revival of her commercial activity, but its profits were to be dedicated to the interest of the Lord's people (vs. 15-18).

II. World-Wide Judgment (Chs. 24-27). The series of separate judgments upon individual nations announced in the preceding chapters were to issue at last in a universal judgment, which Isaiah now describes. The judgment which began with God's own people was to involve the whole world finally. Out of this deluge of Divine justice there should come at last new life for the world.

1. The Desolation of the World (Ch. 24). The point of view in this prophecy is Isaiah's own day; but it looks forward through successive eras of judgment to complete fulfilment in the events attending the final Advent of the Lord. The prophet first announces the Lord's purpose to bring a universal judgment upon the earth which will level all classes of society (vs. 1-3). This judgment will come upon the earth because of the sin of men, their violation of God's everlasting moral order. "Therefore hath the curse devoured the earth" (vs. 4-6). This means that there is a mysterious sympathy between man and nature. Man infects the world he inhabits, and nature reacts against the sin of the human race. Then the prophet describes the desolation which the judgment will cause; the joy and gladness of life will vanish (vs. 7-12).

A remnant will be left in the earth rejoicing in the Lord in the midst of the judgment; and these redeemed are called to raise songs of praise, glorifying God throughout all the earth (vs. 13-16). But the prophet cannot share in these songs, and he returns to a further description of the judgment. It will be like a flood which none can escape, or like an earthquake overturning the structure of human society (vs. 16-20). It will extend to the hosts of wickedness in heaven (vs. 21-22), and will issue in the complete triumph of the Lord (v. 23).

2. Songs of Salvation (Chs. 25-27). The announcement of world-wide desolation is followed immediately by songs of praise to the glory of God as manifested in the judgment. They foreshadow the salvation that was to be accomplished through the work of the Messiah.

(1) The prophet's song of praise (ch. 25). The Lord is praised for His past judgments (vs. 1-5), and for His future salvation (vs. 6-8). This salvation is described in terms that are foregleams of the new spiritual and heavenly order created by the Lord Jesus Christ. He would "destroy the face of the covering that covereth all peoples"; that is, He would open up the unseen spiritual world from which man has been excluded since the Fall (2 Cor. 4:17-18). He would "swallow up death in victory" (1 Cor. 15:54), and "wipe away tears from off all faces" (Rev. 7:17; 21:4); that is, He would remove all the results of the Fall. Then the prophet puts into the lips of the redeemed in that day a song of praise to God for the humiliation of Moab, which was a symbol of the overthrow of all His foes (vs. 9-12).

(2) Judah's song of praise (ch. 26). The Lord is praised for the perfect peace He gives to those who trust Him and walk in the way of the just (vs. 1-7), for the righteousness He manifests through His judgments (vs. 8-10), for the deliverance He has wrought for the nation and the enlargement He has given it (vs. 11-15), and for the new life He gives His people out of death (vs. 16-19). Here we have the hope and promise of the resurrection. Then comes the Lord's call to His people to hide themselves in Him till the storm of judgment is past (vs. 20-21) and the great world powers are punished (27:1).

(3) The song of the vineyard (ch. 27). The figure of the vineyard here, under the care of the Lord (vs. 2-6), is in striking contrast with the picture in 5:1-7, where He passes sentence upon the vineyard. It sets forth the restoration of the nation as chastened, penitent, and forgiven (vs. 7-11). What we have here is the new Israel, "the Israel of God" of the New Testament dispensation (Gal. 6:

16). "In that day" the children of Israel "shall be gathered one by one" (v. 12), that is, by the individual Gospel call. "In that day" also "a great trumpet shall be blown" to summon the lost ones home to worship the Lord (v. 13). This, too, may refer to the call of the Gospel; but it may also be interpreted in the light of such passages as Matt. 24:31, 1 Cor. 15:51-52, and 1 Thess. 4:16-17.

CONCERNING THE WORLD
(Chs. 28-35)

Up to this point we have had the prophecies uttered during the earlier period of Isaiah's ministry. Now we pass on into the reign of Hezekiah (723-695 B.C.), when the prophet's prediction of Assyrian invasions came to pass. Early in that reign occurred the fall of the northern kingdom of Israel. The policy of Ahaz had been to make an alliance with Assyria. The policy to which Hezekiah was urged by his political advisers was to protect Judah against Assyria by an alliance with Egypt. The prophet denounced this worldly minded policy, and preached trust in the Lord God alone as the only way of salvation for Judah. This section of the book contains the prophecies dealing with this worldly alliance (chs. 28-33), and closes with a further announcement of world judgment (chs. 34-35).

I. World Alliance Denounced (Chs. 28-33). These chapters contain a series of woes pronounced upon the nations involved in these world movements, all heading up in denunciation of Judah's trust in a godless world power.

1. Woe to Samaria (Ch. 28). An announcement of the approaching downfall of Samaria, the proud and stately capital of the northern kingdom. The prophet uttered this prediction as a warning to Jerusalem. After denouncing the drunken revellers of the northern capital, which was situated in the territory of Ephraim (vs. 1-4), and giving a promise to the faithful remnant (vs. 5-6), he turns to the priests and prophets of his own city who are also guilty of drunken debauchery (vs. 7-8). They receive his words with mockery (vs. 9-10), and he replies with stern sarcasm. If they will not heed his warning now, the Lord will compel them to listen, some day, to the rough foreign speech of the invading Assyrian (vs. 11-13).

Then he denounces the rulers of Jerusalem for their Egyptian alliance, calling it "a covenant with death". Their trust should be in the sure foundation which the Lord is laying in Zion. "He that believeth shall not be in haste": he will not cast about frantically for earthly help, but will have the calm confidence of faith in the Messianic promise (vs. 14-16). The Lord's judgment in the coming Assyrian invasion is hastening on and will involve these scoffing rulers and their futile Egyptian policy in ruin (vs. 17-20). The Lord will interpose on behalf of His people and bring deliverance Himself, as He did in the case of David's victories over the Philistines, recorded in 1 Chron. 14:8-17 (vs. 21-22).

Then by a series of illustrations from the work of the farmer in producing food, the prophet shows that God's judgments are methodical and move forward with a definite end in view (vs. 23-29).

2. Woe to Jerusalem (Ch. 29). Isaiah now announces that the Lord will bring a judgment upon His own city. Jerusalem is addressed as Ariel, which means either "the lion of God", or "the hearth of God". Probably the latter meaning is intended,

as being the place where His altar-fire burns. He will bring her very low by a siege against her (vs. 1-4). But in the very hour of their triumph, her foes shall all be smitten with sudden discomfiture (vs. 5-8).

After uttering this prediction of the Assyrian army's attack on Jerusalem and its sudden destruction, the prophet rebukes the people for their unbelief. Spiritual blindness has come over them, and their leaders can see no vision (vs. 9-12). Because of their hypocrisy and formal worship, God will proceed to take startling measures with them (vs. 13-14). They foolishly think that by hiding their counsel from the Lord and working in the dark they will escape His notice (vs. 15-16). This is a reference to the Egyptian alliance.

At this point Isaiah turned toward the Messianic future and described the complete transformation and wonderful deliverance which should take place then (vs. 17-21). Both physical and spiritual features are combined in the description: it should be the renewal of both the land and the people. Israel would glorify their God when they saw what He was doing in their midst in regenerating the children of Abraham (vs. 22-24).

3. The Vanity of the Egyptian Alliance (Ch. 30). Isaiah now hurls a denunciation against the political party in the state who, without consulting the Lord, were making a league with Egypt. It consists of two "woe's", the first of which is contained in this chapter and the other in ch. 31. They had already sent an embassy on its way down to Egypt, but their trust in Egypt would be their confusion and shame (vs. 1-5). In the midst of his description of the journey of the embassy, the prophet utters an oracle about them (vs. 6-7).

Then the Lord bade the prophet write his protest and prophecy on a tablet as a perpetual memorial of Judah's rebellious disposition and refusal to listen to His word (vs. 8-14). The true policy was not alliance with Egypt but reliance on God: "In returning and rest shall ye be saved; in quietness and in confidence shall be your strength". Because they had refused this policy, they should be left solitary in the midst of a land devastated by war (vs. 15-17).

After this judgment the Lord would wait to be gracious and would bless those who waited for Him. His purpose for Zion should be accomplished, and His people should "weep no more" when they turned to Him in true repentance (vs. 18-22). Then their true prosperity should be realized and their real glory should be manifested (vs. 23-26). All this looks forward to the redemption which the Messiah was to accomplish and to the spiritual blessings of the Christian dispensation.

The chapter closes with an announcement of God's purpose to destroy the Assyrian by His own power, thus showing how unnecessary it was for Judah to make a league with Egypt Then, "ye shall have a song as in the night when a holy feast is kept; and gladness of heart, as when one goeth with a pipe to come into the mountain of Jehovah, to the Rock of Israel". Their joy should be that of the Feast of Tabernacles, the most joyful feast of the year (vs. 27-33).

4. The Folly of the Egyptian Alliance (Chs. 31-32). It meant trusting in chariots and horsemen instead of the Holy One of Israel, relying on the flesh and not the spirit, looking to the material world for help instead of the spiritual world (31:1-3). The Lord meant to protect Jerusalem Himself as a mother bird protects her nest. Therefore

let Israel trust in the Lord. He would destroy the Assyrian by His own intervention without the help of man (31:4-9).

Then there follows a striking description of the new age under the coming King. It would provide a refuge from wrong and evil. It would be marked by just and beneficent rule, by spiritual and moral transformation, and by the recognition of real worth and the exposure of folly and evil in character (32: 1-8).

Conscious of the great difference between the circumstances of his own time and those of the coming age, the prophet makes an appeal to the women to abandon their self-indulgent ease (32:9-12), for a time of desolation was to come upon the land until the ultimate outpouring of the Holy Spirit (32:13-15). Then the new age of righteousness should be ushered in, and peace should be the result. "The work of righteousness shall be peace; and the effect of righteousness, quietness and confidence for ever" (32:16-20).

5. Woe to the Assyrian (Ch. 33). The prophet's last "woe" is directed against the treacherous foe who had been plundering the cities of Judah and laying waste the land. The occasion of this prophecy was probably the event recorded in 2 Kings 18:13-16, when Sennacherib dealt treacherously with Hezekiah's "ambassadors of peace" (v. 7). After announcing his theme (v. 1), the prophet breaks into a prayer expressing faith in the Lord's salvation and assurance of coming glory for Zion (vs. 2-6). Then he laments what the Assyrians had done to the land, and declares that the Lord would be exalted in their sudden overthrow (vs. 7-12). This act of judgment on God's part would be a solemn warning to the sinners in Zion. The Lord God is a consuming fire to all but those who walk righteously (vs. 13-16).

Then comes a description of the time when the oppressor should be gone, and when the Lord Himself would reign in Zion, and His people should dwell in peace and security and fulness of life (vs. 17-24). This passage foreshadows the Messianic age and the Christian dispensation. The "king in his beauty" is primarily Hezekiah, no longer seen in sackcloth and ashes; but ultimately it means the Lord Jesus Christ in His glory. The "land that reacheth afar" is primarily the whole land of Israel, prosperous and peaceful when freed from the foe; but typically it represents the spiritual world of the new creation, the "better country" of Heb. 11:16, the "heavenly places" of Eph. 1:3, and also the Father's house of John 14:2.

II. World Judgment Announced (Chs. 34-35). The first part of the book, with its prophecies of warning and judgment, comes to a conclusion in these chapters. The sweep of Divine judgment, which began with Judah and Jerusalem and spread out to the nations around, takes in the whole world at last, and issues in a renewal of the world. These chapters deal with the same theme as chs. 24-27. They form a consummation to the prophecies of chs. 28-33 as those do to the prophecies of chs. 13-23.

1. The Desolation of the World (Ch. 34). As the heavens and the earth were called to bear witness to God's charge against Israel in the opening chapter of the book, so now all the peoples of the earth are summoned to hear His judgment upon the nations of the world (vs. 1-4). The universality of this judgment is marked by the frequent repetition of the word "all" in these verses. When warnings and signs hitherto local and national become universal in their scope, then the final day of the Lord is at hand. Edom is singled out for special notice in its hostility to God, because it was the one nation that bore perpetual hatred to God's chosen people (vs. 5-7).

The principle of the Lord's action in this judgment is stated in v. 8: "Jehovah hath a day of vengeance, a year of recompense for the cause of Zion". It is a part of His procedure of redemption. It vindicates His purpose concerning Zion, and clears the way in the world for the attainment of her true destiny, that destiny which has been foretold by the prophet already in 2:2-4 and 4:2-6. This is followed by a predictive description of the desolation of Edom, as a type and illustration of the desolation of the world when the Lord's vengeance falls upon it (vs. 9-15), and an assurance of the ultimate and complete fulfilment of every word of the Lord regarding the nations (vs. 16-17).

2. The Restoration of the World (Ch. 35). The world's renewal would be brought about by the coming of the Lord Himself: "Behold, your God will come; He will come and save you" (vs. 1-4). He came in the Incarnation, and with that transcendent event the new creation began. A beautiful description is given of the salvation that should be realized as the result of His coming (vs. 5-10). Two significant features mark its fundamental spiritual character: a new source of life, "streams in the desert", and a new way of life, "the way of holiness". The figure is that of a pleasant road made through desert regions on which a journey is made in safety.

The whole picture is symbolical of the new order of the present Christian age. The closing feature of the picture is that of the Lord's ransomed people coming home to Zion in the enjoyment of complete and perfect bliss. It was to this description of the Messianic age that Jesus referred John the Baptist in describing His own ministry (Matt. 11:2-6). The conditions to be realized in the redeemed and restored world of the new creation as described in this passage, may be drawn out more fully as follows: the removal of physical infirmity (vs. 5-6); the transformation of nature (vs. 6-7); holiness of life and freedom from defilement (v. 8); security of life and freedom from peril (v. 9); fulness of joy and freedom from sorrow (v. 10).

PART II

This historical section (Chs. 36-39) forms the connecting link between the two main divisions of Isaiah's prophetic ministry. These chapters are parallel with 2 Kings 18:13—20:19, and 2 Chron. 32:1-26. They contain the record of two events of great political importance. One of these events brought to an end the threat of an impending judgment from Assyria and closed the prophet's public ministry. The other event provided the occasion for his prediction of the more remote judgment from Babylon and led to the private ministry of his last days.

I. The End of the Assyrian Invasions (Chs. 36-37). This is the event toward which all the foregoing prophecies converge. A great Assyrian host, under the most cruel of the Assyrian kings, devastated the cities of Judah and came up against Jerusalem (701 B.C.). It was suddenly smitten by the hand of God, and Assyria never invaded Judah again. The story gathers around three men. The date mentioned in 36:1 belongs to the narrative of Hezekiah's sickness in ch. 38, which occurred before Sennacherib's invasion.

1. Rabshakeh the Assyrian (36:1-22). This was the title of the officer sent by Sennacherib to demand the surrender of Jerusalem. He represented the might and arrogance of Assyria. Met by Judah's officers of state (vs. 1-3), he taunted them with their weakness and defied their trust in the Lord (vs. 4-10). Alarmed at the effect his words might have on the people, the Jewish deputation urged him to speak in the Syrian tongue (vs. 11-12). Instead of complying with this request he immediately addressed the people on the wall in their own language, warning them against trust in Hezekiah, declaring that their God could not deliver them, and promising them plenty in another land (vs. 13-20). The people in obedience to the king remained silent, while his officers reported to him the Assyrian demand (vs. 21-22).

2. Hezekiah the King (37:1-20). Hezekiah immediately went into the Temple with marks of penitence and humiliation upon him, and sent messengers with the same marks upon them to Isaiah. The prophet bade them carry back to the king a message of encouragement (vs. 1-7). In the meantime the king of Assyria, when Rabshakeh returned to him, sent Hezekiah a letter of further defiance and arrogance (vs. 8-13). Hezekiah spread this letter before the Lord and appealed to Him for deliverance in a prayer of great simplicity and faith (vs. 14-20).

3. Isaiah the Prophet (37:21-38). Isaiah now sent a second and fuller message to Hezekiah, marked by sublime scorn and majestic faith. He sternly denounced Sennacherib for his blasphemy against the Holy One of Israel, declaring that his boasting was vain and his judgment imminent (vs. 21-29). He encouraged Hezekiah with the assurance that, beyond the brief period of hardship that would follow this invasion, there should be a new age of revival for the remnant of Judah, and declared that in the meantime the Lord Himself would defend Jerusalem (vs. 30-35). The chapter ends with an account of the destruction of the Assyrian army by the direct act of God, and the subsequent death of Sennacherib at the hands of his sons (vs. 36-38).

II. The Shadow of the Babylonian Captivity (Chs. 38-39). The first announcement of this judgment, which then lay in the remote future, was contained in a message which the prophet delivered to Hezekiah in connection with the visit of a deputation from the king of Babylon to congratulate him on his recovery from sickness.

1. Hezekiah's Sickness and Recovery (Ch. 38). In the course of the Assyrian invasions a serious illness fell upon Hezekiah, and Isaiah warned him to prepare for death. Hezekiah turned to the Lord in penitence and prayer, and Isaiah was sent to him with the promise that the Lord would prolong his life and deliver the city out of the hand of the king of Assyria (vs. 1-8). Then follows Hezekiah's psalm of thanksgiving and praise (vs. 9-20). It reveals the feelings of an Old Testament saint in the prospect of death, and breathes the new sense of solemn joy with which Hezekiah consecrated the remainder of his life to the Lord. The chapter closes by stating how he recovered (vs. 21-22).

2. Hezekiah's Folly and Warning (Ch. 39). An embassy came from Babylon to congratulate Heze-

kiah on his recovery. Flattered by their visit, he foolishly showed them the treasures of his kingdom (vs. 1-2). Isaiah rebuked him and foretold the ultimate issue. The days were coming when all that he had shown them should be carried to Babylon and the princes of Judah should be servants in the palace of the king of Babylon (vs. 3-7). Hezekiah received this message with meek submission (v. 8). Thus the way is prepared for the series of prophecies which begins with the next chapter.

PART III

The last part of the book (Chs. 40-66) consists of one unbroken series of prophecies, marked by the keynote of comfort and conveying an assurance of coming salvation. The theme of the whole is the redemption of Israel in one complete view. It includes the deliverance of the exiles from Babylon, the Messianic redemption from sin, and the final glory of the people of God, in one connected picture. The viewpoint of the prophet is in the Babylonian captivity on the eve of the return.

The fact that the historical background of this part of the book is so far beyond the life-time of our prophet has given rise to the theory of a "second Isaiah", which regards these chapters as the work of an unknown writer who lived during the Exile. While this theory seems to solve one problem, it also creates another one. If it were true it would mean that the greatest genius among the Hebrew prophets, the one who was endowed with the highest quality of prophetic inspiration and made the richest contribution to Messianic prophecy, has disappeared from history without leaving a trace of his personality behind. There is no other case in the literature of Old Testament prophecy where the name and identity of the prophet has not been preserved along with his writings.

That being the case, the most reasonable way to deal with the problem is to take the book as it has come to us from the Jews themselves and as we find it in the Bible. Jewish tradition is not to be discarded as worthless. There must be some explanation of the fact that Isaiah, the friend and adviser of Hezekiah, was regarded as the source of all the prophecies in this book. The New Testament knows of no other author. In John 12:38-40 a quotation from the last part of Isaiah (53:1) and a quotation from the first part (6:10) are both referred to one and the same man.

The chief difficulty felt by many consists in the actual naming of Cyrus, the future deliverer of Israel (44:28; 45:1). While this is peculiar and exceptional, it is not unprecedented. It had occurred before in the case of king Josiah (1 Kgs. 13:2). For those who believe that the prophetic gift is a supernatural power to enter into the mind of God, a prediction of this kind is not incredible. No one knows enough about the peculiar experiences of the Hebrew prophets under the Divine urge of prophetic inspiration to qualify him to pronounce Isaiah incapable of writing the last twenty-seven chapters of this book. Before the supreme miracle of the revelation of God in Jesus of Nazareth, every other miracle of any kind whatever loses its supernatural wonder and pales into insignificance.

This section of the book, then, may be regarded as the work of Isaiah's old age, several years after his more active ministry had closed. In anticipation of the Babylonian captivity, which he had already foretold, he wrote down his visions of the return from that captivity for the comfort of the exiles, and for the consolation and comfort of God's people in all ages. As he saw that return, he became a participant in its scenes, and passed in rapt contemplation to the still brighter and grander events which that deliverance typified.

There are three stages in the progressive development of redemption as we see it unfolded through this part of the book. Each stage occupies nine chapters. The first is a prophecy of the restoration from captivity in Babylon as the preparation for redemption (Chs. 40-48). The next is a prophecy of the redemption of Israel from sin by the suffering of the righteous Servant of the Lord (Chs. 49-57). And the last is a prophecy of the final glory of the redeemed people of God (Chs. 58-66). Each of the three divisions begins with a chapter which is a key to the whole and ends with a brief reference to the punishment of the wicked. Redemption is thus announced against a background of judgment.

THE PREPARATION FOR REDEMPTION
(Chs. 40-48)

The central idea in this section is assurance of deliverance for the exiles of Israel in the midst of their captivity and suffering. Their God would raise up a deliverer and call him to a career of conquest. His name is mentioned. He should accomplish the fall of Babylon and set the captives free. This was to be the first stage in the Lord's redemption of Israel.

I. The God of Redemption (Chs. 40-42). The Lord's purpose to deliver His people out of their affliction is first brought into view, and then the prophet goes on to show that He has the power and the sovereignty to carry out this purpose, and that He will raise up an agent to accomplish it.

1. His Purpose to Redeem (40:1-11). This passage forms an introduction to the rest of the book. It begins with the Lord's call to the prophets to convey a comforting assurance of pardon to His people (vs. 1-2). Then comes an imaginary description of the way His purpose of redemption is to be accomplished. The voice of a herald is heard announcing that His glory is to be revealed and calling for the preparation of a highway for Him through the wilderness (vs. 3-5). This "voice" was taken by John the Baptist as a prophecy of his own ministry in preparing the way for the Messiah (Matt. 3:3; Mark 1:3; Luke 3:4-6; John 1:23).

Another "voice" contrasts the frailty of man with the power of God as He moves forward on the highway of His purpose in fulfilment of His word (vs. 6-8). Then comes the announcement of His advent as the Ruler and Shepherd of His people (vs. 9-11). The call, "Behold, your God!" points forward to the advent of the Lord in the Incarnation. It has been foretold already in 35:4.

2. His Power to Deliver (40:12-31). The prophet now describes the majestic greatness of God, to show that He is able to fulfil His purpose of redemption. A survey of the created world reveals God's almighty power, unsearchable wisdom, and infinite greatness. Before Him the nations are as nothing (vs. 12-17). Can the gods which men manufacture be compared to Him who rules over the earth and the heavens and brings the rulers of the world to nothing (vs. 18-24)? This passage contains the first of several satirical descriptions which the prophet gives of an idol factory (41:5-7; 44:9-20; 46:6-7).

Then he goes on to declare that the Creator of the starry hosts, who marshals them all in their courses, will not fail His people or forget them. He is the everlasting God, the Creator of the ends of the earth, and He never wearies. Let His people only wait in faith for His salvation. He is the unfailing source of strength, and He renews the lives of those who put their trust in Him (vs. 25-31).

3. His Sovereignty in the World (Ch. 41). The Lord now summons the nations before Him and issues a challenge. He adduces the victorious career of one whom He has raised up from the east as a proof that He is the sovereign Ruler of the world (vs. 1-7). This is the first reference to Cyrus, God's instrument in the overthrow of Babylon and the deliverance of Israel. The passage describes his meteoric appearance on the eastern horizon of the world of the time (about the middle of the sixth century B.C.), and the alarm it caused among the states of western Asia who sought help against him from their idols.

This is followed by a comforting assurance of the Lord's help and deliverance to Israel, the chosen seed of Abraham (vs. 8-16). The message of this passage may be summed up in the following words: "I have chosen thee. Fear thou not. I will help thee. Thou shalt glory in the Holy One of Israel". Then the help which God would give to His poor and needy people is set forth under the figure of miraculous provision for travellers in the desert (vs. 17-20).

Next comes a challenge to the idols to prove their divinity by foretelling the future or explaining the past (vs. 21-24), and another reference to the raising up of Cyrus for the deliverance of Zion, which they were utterly unable to foresee or explain (vs. 25-29).

4. His Agent in Redemption (Ch. 42). The great Servant of the Lord is now introduced, who was to accomplish the work of redemption. His character and methods are first described (vs. 1-4). This passage foreshadows the lowly ministry of the Son of Man (Matt. 20:28). Then, in a solemn address to His Servant, the Lord God sets forth the task to which He has called him, and promises to uphold him in it. He was to bring salvation to the whole world, to the Gentiles as well as to Israel (vs. 5-9). Then the prophet breaks into praise for the redemption which God was going to accomplish (vs. 10-13).

This is followed by the Lord's own comment upon it. For a long time He had refrained from interposing on behalf of His people, but now He was proceeding to lead them out of their captivity and to overthrow their heathen foes (vs. 14-17). Israel had failed as the Lord's servant. Their blindness and disobedience to the Law, which He had made great and glorious for their sake, had brought them into captivity and destitution (vs. 18-22). This was His judgment upon them for their sin, and yet they had not laid it to heart (vs. 23-25).

II. The Manifesto of Redemption (Chs. 43-45). The Lord now announces Himself as the Redeemer of Israel and makes proclamation of His purpose and procedure. He does this in a series of messages to His redeemed people in which the name "Redeemer" is made prominent (43:14; 44:6, 24).

1. The Redeemer's Promise (43:1-13). This may be summed up as follows: "Fear not, for I have redeemed thee . . . . Fear not, for I am with thee". What God hath done for Israel in the past should

assure them of what He would do for them in the future (vs. 1-7). When His people were redeemed, they were to be His witnesses among the nations, bearing testimony to the fact that the Lord had saved them, and that He is the one true God (vs. 8-13).

2. The Redeemer's Work (43:14-44:5). The overthrow of Babylon is now explicitly announced as the beginning of the work of redemption. Thus the Lord, the King of Israel, would prepare the way for their deliverance, which should be like another exodus from Egypt (43:14-17). Then the Lord declares: "Behold, I will do a new thing". And this new thing should eclipse all "the former things" in Israel's history and thus set forth His praise (43: 18-21). It was not due to Israel's devotion to the worship of the Lord, for they had only burdened Him with their sins (43:22-24).

The passage goes on to indicate the nature of the "new thing"; it looks forward down the ages to the redemptive work of Jesus Christ. It was to deal with the sins of Israel and result in blotting them out. God would do this for His own sake (43:25-28). Then Israel should be brought into a new relation with Him, and He would pour out His Holy Spirit upon them (44:1-5). Here we have foregleams of the Cross and of Pentecost.

3. The Redeemer's Power (44:6-28). There is no God besides the King of Israel, Jehovah of hosts (vs. 6-8). In His light the utter folly of idolatry is exposed. The prophet pours scorn upon it as he describes the process of manufacturing idols (vs. 9-17). Idolaters are blind to the folly and futility of their own actions (vs. 18-20). The Lord now calls upon Israel to return to Him because He has undertaken to redeem them (vs. 21-23).

In support of His appeal as their Redeemer, He points to the tokens of His power as the God of creation and of prophecy. He is the Maker of all things, and He fulfils the words of His messengers. In this connection Cyrus is mentioned by name as the one whom He was to use for the restoration of Jerusalem and the Temple. This was to be the first step in His procedure of redemption (vs. 24-28).

4. The Redeemer's Procedure (Ch. 45). The figure of Cyrus is now brought upon the scene, and he is addressed directly. The Lord has raised him up as a great conqueror for Israel's sake and for His own glory among the nations of the world, though he has not known the Lord (vs. 1-7). God's ultimate purpose in this mission of Cyrus is to bring forth salvation for the whole world (v. 8).

In answer to those among the exiles who may object to this procedure of His in using a foreign agent as His servant, God declares His sovereignty over the world He has created, and announces that He has raised up Cyrus for His own righteous purpose (vs. 9-13). His primary purpose is the deliverance and salvation of Israel, so that the nations may acknowledge the presence and power of the God of Israel (vs. 14-17). His ultimate purpose is the salvation and blessing of the whole world, and He calls all the ends of the earth to look unto Him and be saved (vs. 18-25).

III. The Deliverance from Babylon (Chs. 46-48). The overthrow of Babylon by Cyrus in 538 B.C., which opened the way for Israel's deliverance from exile, was the first event in the prophet's view as he looked into the future and beheld the progressive unfolding of God's redemptive work. These chapters deal prophetically with that event.

1. The Overthrow of the Idols of Babylon (Ch. 46). Here the prophet pictures the ignominious flight of the gods of Babylon from the fallen city, and points the contrast between their helplessness and the sovereign might of the Lord God of Israel. The Lord undertakes to carry His people: they have to be carried out themselves on beasts of burden (vs. 1-7). Then comes a challenge to the transgressors in Israel who were lapsing into idolatry (vs. 8-13).

2. The Fall of the City of Babylon (Ch. 47). Her degradation is likened to that of a queen suddenly reduced to the shameful and humiliating condition of a slave. She was to lose her proud title of mistress of the nations, because she had shown no mercy to the Lord's people when He put them into her hands (vs. 1-7). In the midst of her careless security, sudden and complete desolation should come upon her because of her pride and wickedness, and her magicians and star-gazers should be unable to help her (vs. 8-15).

3. The Call of Israel out of Babylon (Ch. 48). The Lord describes the methods He has been using with His people because of their obstinacy. As to "the former things", they were predicted in advance, that Israel might not attribute them to false gods (vs. 1-5). From now on He will show them "new things", things they had not known nor heard of. He has tried them in the furnace of affliction; and now, for His own sake, He means to deliver them (vs. 6-11).

In accordance with His glory and power in the world, He has raised up one to perform His pleasure on Babylon (vs. 12-16). He expresses His disappointment over Israel's failure to obey Him in the past, when His purpose was to secure their peace and righteousness (vs. 17-19). Now He calls them to go forth out of Babylon with rejoicing and to declare the wonders of His salvation (vs. 20-21). Then the section closes with the declaration: "There is no peace, saith Jehovah, to the wicked". While His purpose is to bring peace to His people, they are solemnly warned that it cannot be realized if they continue in wickedness (v. 22).

After this there is no further reference to Cyrus or to Babylon in the book. The rest of the prophecy is concerned entirely with the Messianic Servant and His redemptive work.

The Accomplishment of Redemption
(Chs. 49-57)

The central idea in this section is Israel's deliverance from sin and restoration to God. This work was to be accomplished by the Servant of the Lord, whose figure is now presented with such fulness of prophetic detail that there is no mistaking the portrait. It is none other than Jesus Christ, the Messiah of Israel, the Saviour of the world. In the course of these chapters He appears in His three offices: as Prophet (49:1-52:12), as Priest (52:13-53:12), and as King (54:1-57:21).

I. The Call of the Servant (Chs. 49-50). The voice of the Servant of the Lord is heard in these chapters as he prepares to accomplish his task.

1. The Servant's Commission from the Lord (49: 1-13). In an address to the nations, the Servant declares his consciousness of being called by the Lord to a mission for Israel, and expresses his faith in it notwithstanding Israel's failure in the past (vs. 1-4). Then he describes the task given him to accomplish. It comprises not only the restoration of Israel unto the Lord, but also the salvation of the

whole world (vs. 5-7). Then the passage goes on to describe the Servant's mission in terms of the emancipation and return of the exiles (vs. 8-13).

2. The Lord's Message to Zion (49:14-50:3). The Lord answers Zion's complaint that He had forgotten her, by assuring her of His unchanging love (49:14-16), and foretelling the return of her children to her (49:17-18). Then comes a prediction of the enlargement of her land and the increase of her children (49:19-21). It is prophetic of the spiritual Israel of the Christian dispensation (Rom. 2:28-29; 4:13-16; Gal. 6:16).

The passage goes on to carry out this idea more fully and to foreshadow the triumphs of the Gospel. At a signal from the Lord, the nations would bring home the scattered children of Zion (49:22-23). No power could prevent the Lord from interposing and acting as the Saviour of His people (49:24-26). He had not forgotten His covenant with them; He had not put them away. It was because of their sins they were put away; and He had still power to deliver them (50:1-3).

3. The Servant's Consecration to His Task (50: 4-11). This is the Servant's response to the call of the Lord. He consecrates himself to a life of obedience and suffering, and acknowledges his reliance upon the help of the Lord. Here is foreshadowed the lowly character of Christ's earthly ministry. In v. 10 there is an anticipation of the experience of the Cross (Matt. 27:46; Luke 23:46), and in v. 11 a warning to all who would go after any human substitute for the divine Word.

II. The Suffering of the Servant (Chs. 51-53). Now we are to see the Servant accomplishing the work of salvation through suffering.

1. A Message of Encouragement (51:1-8). This passage contains a thrice repeated call, each time beginning with an appeal to listen. It is a message of encouragement to the faithful in Israel who are seeking the Lord. They are called to look backward to their origin in Abraham: when he was only one, God called him and made him many (vs. 1-3). They are called to look forward: God will establish His righteousness and His salvation for ever (vs. 4-6). They are called to look around: in the knowledge of this everlasting salvation they need not fear the reproach of men (vs. 7-8). Throughout the passage righteousness and salvation are linked together. The salvation of Israel was to be secured by the righteousness of God (Rom. 1:16-17).

2. An Assurance of Triumph (51:9-52:12). Here are three trumpet-calls heralding the salvation that is coming to Zion, each beginning with, "Awake, awake", and each followed by a message of comfort. First, the Lord is invoked to reveal the strength of His arm for the deliverance of His people as in former times (51:9-11). He replies in words of comfort and assurance for His captive people (51: 12-14), and for His Servant (51:15-16). Then Jerusalem is called to stand up out of the double calamity that has befallen her, the desolation of her land and the suffering of her people (51:17-20), for the Lord has taken the cup of His wrath out of her hand and will give it to her foes (51:21-23).

Finally, Zion is summoned to arise out of the dust, loose herself from her bonds, and put on her beautiful garments (52:1-2), for the Lord who delivered His people from former oppressions will Himself redeem them now (52:3-6). The passage goes on to picture the joy that breaks forth when heralds and watchmen announce the Lord's return to Zion to accomplish her salvation (52:7-10). In view of this the people are summoned to prepare for their departure from Babylon by cleansing themselves and putting themselves under the protecting care of God (52:11-12).

3. The Servant as the Saviour (52:13-53:12). This is the greatest passage in the Old Testament and the climax of Messianic prophecy. It takes us to the heart of redemption and to the foot of the Cross. It shows us the Servant being exalted through his suffering to become the Saviour of the world. Nearly all the New Testament writers identify the suffering Servant of this prophecy with the Lord Jesus Christ. The whole passage falls into five distinct sections of three verses each. Each section is occupied with a special aspect of the Saviour's ministry. They may be summarized as follows:

(1) His strange career and high destiny (52:13-15). This is a summary of his whole ministry. He was to pass through suffering to exaltation. "So shall he sprinkle many nations"—cleansing them, though himself counted unclean. "Kings shall shut their mouths at him"—in silent wonder at the great change from suffering to exaltation (Rom. 15:21).

(2) His rejected ministry (53:1-3). This depicts the impression he made upon his contemporaries and their attitude toward him. He was not recognized by the spiritually blind and was judged only by his outward appearance. Yet in him, "the arm of Jehovah was revealed"; the power of God was at work through him (John 12:38; Rom. 10:16).

(3) His vicarious sufferings (53:4-6). It was thus that he appeared to those whose eyes were opened and who realized the true significance of his sufferings. Note the use of the pronouns here. He was suffering as their substitute (Matt. 8:17; 1 Pet. 2:24-25).

(4) His voluntary death (53:7-9). Here is depicted the way of the Cross. In meek submission and self-surrender he went to his death in a sacrificial act. The essential nature of Christ's death—the fact that He consented to it—is more clearly foreshadowed in v. 7 than in any other Old Testament statement. "He was taken from prison and from judgment" (A.V.), or "By oppression and judgment he was taken away" (R.V.): both renderings describe the perversion of justice in the trial that preceded his death. The next words read thus: "As for his generation (his contemporaries), who among them considered that he was cut off out of the land of the living for the transgression of my people to whom the stroke was due." The fact was not considered that he was smitten, not for his own sins, but for theirs (Acts 8:32-33).

(5) His ultimate triumph (53:10-12). There was a Divine purpose in the Servant's sufferings, and they had a glorious issue. In him God provided a sin offering for the world, and then highly exalted him. "He shall see his seed"—the new seed of Israel, the redeemed people. "He shall prolong his days"—through the Resurrection and Ascension (Rev. 1:18). "The pleasure of Jehovah shall prosper in his hand"—through his mediatorial work (Heb. 9:24-28). "He shall see of the travail of his soul, and shall be satisfied"—in the enjoyment of his high-priestly ministry. "By his knowledge shall my righteous servant justify many" (A.V. and R.V. marg.)—either by their knowledge of him (John 17:3), or by his knowledge of God (John 17:25-26). "Therefore will I divide him a portion with the great"—by exalting him to the throne in Heaven

(Phil. 2:9-11; Matt. 28:18). Then the prophecy of the Servant closes with a further emphasis upon the voluntary nature of his humiliation (Mark 15:28; Luke 22:37).

III. The Triumph of the Servant (Chs. 54-57). These chapters bring into view the blessed results of the Servant's redeeming work.

1. The New Israel (Ch. 54). Zion is called to rejoice in the multitude of her children and to enlarge her tent so as to receive them (vs. 1-3). Paul finds this prophecy being fulfilled through the Gospel (Gal. 4:21-31). The barren one is the spiritual Israel of the New Covenant, while the married wife is Israel after the flesh. The shame and reproach of Zion are to be forgotten when she is reconciled to the Lord, for her Maker is her Husband (vs. 4-6). Her rejection was but a brief withdrawal of His favour: her restoration will be final and everlasting (vs. 7-10).

Then the glory of Zion's restoration appears in the new city which the Lord declares He will make of her. He describes her outward splendour (vs. 11-12), her inward peace (vs. 13-14), and her perfect security (vs. 15-17). The two figures used in this chapter to represent redeemed Zion appear again in the beatific vision of the glorified church in Revelation 21, where the holy city, new Jerusalem (v. 2), is also called the bride, the Lamb's wife (vs. 9-10).

2. Salvation Free for All (Ch. 55). An invitation is now given to all who realize their need to come and enjoy the spiritual blessings of salvation which are now offered freely (vs. 1-2). The Lord promises to extend to them the blessings of the covenant made with David. These blessings, it is implied, have been secured by the work of the Servant, and other nations are called to share them with Israel (vs. 3-5). The only requirement is that they turn from their wicked ways and seek the Lord, who will abundantly pardon (vs. 6-7). His way of accomplishing redemption transcends all the ideas of men (vs. 8-9). His promise of salvation is declared in His word, which has power to fulfil itself (vs. 10-11). The result will be a new life for men, the removal of the curse from the earth, and everlasting glory to God (vs. 12-13).

Throughout this chapter there is a combination of spiritual and material blessings. The work of the Servant creates a new spiritual order as a basis for a new material order. The new spiritual creation which Christ introduced by His first coming awaits the triumphant consummation of salvation at His second coming (Rom. 8:18-23). The whole passage is pervaded with a sense of joy and peace.

3. The Conditions of Blessing (Chs. 56-57). The prophet now applies to his own time the lessons of the preceding visions. There was a very great contrast between the state of Israel then and the new Israel of the future. In view of the salvation that was "near to come" and the righteousness that was "to be revealed" (56:1), the nation was called upon to fulfil certain conditions in the meantime.

(1) Its true religious attitude was to be manifested in the keeping of the Sabbath. Special blessing was promised to those who observed the Sabbath and thus showed their loyalty to the Covenant (56:1-8). The Sabbath was the distinctive sign to the world of Israel's special relation to God (Lev. 19:3, 30; 26:2). Profaning the Sabbath obscured Israel's witness to the nations, and was one of the reasons for the judgment of the Exile (2 Chron. 36:21; Ezek. 20:12-13, 19-20).

(2) Prophets who were blind to the signs of the times and gave no warning to the people, and rulers who indulged themselves and neglected their duty to the people, were to be visited with judgment and punishment (56:9-12). There were many false prophets in Israel and rulers who thought only of their own interests. Under such leaders the righteous were perishing and none were concerned about it (57:1-2).

(3) Apostates and idolaters were to be punished and removed from among the people. It was the evil of idolatry, shamelessly carried on, that led to the judgment of the captivity (57:3-10). Because of the fear of man, Judah had given up the fear of the Lord; and yet the Lord had refrained for a long time from inflicting the judgment (57:11-13).

(4) All stumbling blocks were to be removed out of the way of God's people. The Holy One Himself would come and dwell with the contrite and humble, and would give them new life (57:14-15). He would remove His judgment from them, and heal them and give them peace (57:16-19). Then the section is brought to a close with another solemn warning to the wicked (57:20-21).

THE REALIZATION OF REDEMPTION
(Chs. 58-66)

The preceding section, which brought into view the great Servant of the Lord, "testified beforehand the sufferings of Christ". The present section, which closes the book, describes "the glories that should follow them" (1 Pet. 1:11). It deals with the blessedness of the redeemed people in the Messianic kingdom, and brings into view the new heavens and the new earth in which redemption culminates.

I. The Divine Intervention (Chs. 58-59). These chapters continue to deal with the condition of Israel in the prophet's day. They show that nothing could save the nation but the intervention of the Lord Himself.

1. The Failure of Israel (58:1-59:15). God summons the prophet to declare unto His people their utter moral and spiritual failure, and to denounce their formality of worship and wickedness of life (58:1-5). True religion is showing compassion to the poor and needy and kindness to one's neighbour (58:6-12), and honouring God's holy day and giving Him due worship. If they do these things the Lord will reward them with spiritual blessing and earthly prosperity, the heritage of Jacob their father (58:13-14).

The prophet then takes up the message and declares that their sufferings had come upon them, not because the Lord could not help, but because of their moral corruption (59:1-8), which had separated them from Him and brought darkness and misery upon them (59:9-15). These last verses of the passage take the form of a confession of sin put into the mouth of the people, thus marking their repentance.

2. The Advent of the Lord (59:15-21). A new section begins in the middle of v. 15: "And Jehovah saw it"—the repentance of His people—, and it displeased Him that the penitents were still under oppression. When there was no one to help them, God undertook to save them Himself and to deliver them from their oppression (vs. 15-18). A Redeemer would come to Zion for those who should turn from their sin. He would make His covenant with them, and His Spirit should abide upon them for ever (vs. 19-21). This prophecy has been fulfilled by the

Lord Jesus Christ in the transactions of the Cross and Pentecost.

II. The Divine Kingdom (Chs. 60-61). These chapters contain a glorious picture of the ultimate realization of God's purpose in the redemption of Zion.

1. The New Jerusalem (Ch. 60). With the coming of the Redeemer to Zion (59:20), a new age dawns upon her and she is called to arise. The light of the glory of the Lord should shine upon her, and all the nations should be blessed thereby (vs. 1-3). Then there follows a description of her great enlargement and her manifold blessedness. Her sons and daughters should gather to her, bringing the wealth of the nations (vs. 4-9). Her walls should be built up by foreigners, and in through her open gates should come the treasure and the glory of the nations to beautify the sanctuary of God. The sons of her former foes should pay her homage, and recognize her to be "The city of Jehovah, The Zion of the Holy One of Israel" (vs. 10-14).

Instead of being shunned and hated, she should be abundantly provided with the wealth of the nations, and peace and righteousness should rule in her (vs. 15-18). The presence of the Lord in her midst should be her light and her glory for ever, and all her people should be righteous. The Lord Himself would bring this to pass in due time (vs. 19-21). This chapter is to be interpreted in the light of Heb. 12:22-24 and Rev. 21:9-27. It is the spiritual and heavenly city that is foreshadowed here. The description is given in terms of the old Zion, but it manifestly transcends everything earthly.

2. The New Blessedness (Ch. 61). Here the Servant speaks again. He begins by announcing his mission of salvation (vs. 1-3). Jesus took His text from this passage in the sermon at Nazareth, and declared that it was being fulfilled in His day (Luke 4:17-21). It foretold the Christian age of grace and salvation, which was then beginning. The Servant goes on to describe the new order resulting from his work in terms of the old order. The desolated land should be restored and become fruitful again, and the people should be recognized as priests of God among the nations. He would make an everlasting covenant with them, and they should exercise a ministry of blessing among the nations (vs. 4-9).

Then the Servant utters a song of joy and praise to the Lord because of the salvation which he has been enabled to accomplish. It would be like the renewal of nature in spring time—a new life of righteousness and praise for all the world (vs. 10-11). Here again, as in chap. 35, spiritual and material blessings are combined.

III. A Summary of Redemption (Chs. 62-66). These chapters review the Lord's redemptive work in a comprehensive survey. They show that redemption is accomplished in answer to the prayer of His people.

1. The Lord's Purpose (62:1-63:6). Here the Lord speaks, taking up the Servant's last statement in ch. 61. He begins by declaring that He will not rest till He has made the righteousness and salvation of Zion manifest to the world. Then addressing her directly, He promises to give her a new name, to restore her to Himself, and to rejoice over her (62:1-5). He has set prophets as watchmen upon her walls to keep reminding Him of His purpose till it is accomplished, and He gives her an assurance that He will no longer let her be despoiled by her foes (62:6-9). This encourages the prophet to renew the call uttered before (40:9-11), and to urge the exiles to depart from captivity and prepare the way for the coming salvation (62:10-12).

In order to accomplish the salvation of Zion, the Lord will bring vengeance upon her foes (63:1-6). The vision described here is a vivid and dramatic picture of a warrior in blood-stained garments returning victorious from a conflict with Edom, the inveterate foe of Israel. It should be interpreted in the light of such New Testament passages as John 12:31 and Col. 2:14-15. It is a pictorial representation of the Redeemer triumphing through the Cross over Satan and the principalities and powers of the spiritual world. It has had its fulfilment in the glorious ascension of the Lord Jesus Christ as seen from the heavenly side and as described in Rev. 5:6-14.

2. Israel's Prayer (63:7-64:12). The prophet now puts a prayer into the mouth of captive and exiled Israel, which includes thanksgiving for the Lord's mercy in redeeming them from Egypt and taking care of them in the wilderness (63:7-9), confession of their rebellion which turned the Lord against them so that they longed for the deliverances of the days of Moses (63:10-14), an earnest supplication to the Lord to "look down from heaven" upon His people in their present affliction (63:15-19), and a passionate cry that He would "rend the heavens and come down" for their deliverance from the pitiful and helpless condition which their iniquities have brought upon them (64:1-7). Then comes a humble, contrite, and plaintive appeal that the Lord would not withhold His mercy from them any longer (64:8-12).

3. The Lord's Answer (Ch. 65). In answer to the prayer of Israel, the Lord declares that those who have rejected His gracious invitation and provoked Him by persisting in their abominable idolatries are to be punished and destined to destruction (vs. 1-7). Those who have been faithful to Him— "my servants"—are to be saved. As the true seed of Jacob, the chosen remnant of Judah, they are to inherit the restored land of blessing (vs. 8-10). But those who have forsaken the Lord for false gods and do not respond to His call are to be given over to destruction (vs. 11-12). A final separation is to be made between the two classes, and their diverse fate is drawn out in five striking contrasts (vs. 13-16).

Then the Lord announces His creation of new heavens and a new earth, in which there will be a new Jerusalem for His people, where He and they will rejoice together and there shall be no sound of mourning (vs. 17-19). An idealized description is given of the conditions to be realized in the new Jerusalem—length of days and fulness of life (v. 20), enjoyment of the fruits of their own work (vs. 21-23), immediate answer to prayer, indicating complete agreement with the will of God (v. 24), and peace and harmony in the whole creation (v. 25).

The ideal here foretold appears in many forms in the New Testament—"the times of restoration of all things" (Acts 3:21), the deliverance of creation from its bondage at "the revealing of the sons of God" (Rom. 8:19-21), and the "new heavens and a new earth, wherein dwelleth righteousness" (2 Pet. 3:13). This prophecy is the Old Testament background of the vision the Apostle John describes in Rev. 21:1-7.

4. The Final Message (Ch. 66). The book closes with another description of the final issues of redemption. Addressing first those who thought of

building a temple to the Lord, He declares that He will be worshipped in spirit and in truth. It is not the formal act but the contrite spirit of the worshipper that is pleasing in His sight. Sacrifices without that are an abomination to Him, and He rejects them (vs. 1-4).

Then a word of comfort is addressed to the believing remnant in Israel—"ye that tremble at his word". Their brethren who had persecuted them should be put to shame and their enemies should be discomfited (vs. 5-6). Out of Zion's travail and sorrow the Lord would bring a new Israel into being (vs. 7-9). The prophet then calls upon all who love Jerusalem and sympathize with her in her present suffering to rejoice with her in her glorious future, because of the peace the Lord would give her in her inward life and the enlargement that should come to her from the nations of the world (vs. 10-14).

The judgment by which the Lord was to prepare the way for Zion's redemption is now more fully described (vs. 15-17). The course which Israel's history was to take is foreshadowed. The Lord would save a remnant from the judgment and send them out to declare His glory to the nations of the world that had not heard of Him, so that they might come and worship Him together with Israel in His holy mountain (vs. 18-21). Here we have a prophetic anticipation of Christ's commission to His apostles to evangelize the world, and of the breaking down of the middle wall of partition between the Jews and the Gentiles.

In the midst of the new heavens and the new earth which God was to create, the new Israel should occupy an eternal place as the centre of worship to be offered to the Lord continually (vs. 22-23). Then His warning to the wicked, which has been uttered twice before (48:22; 57:21), is given for the last time, with an added intensity, to end the prophecy and to emphasize the fact that the redemption which it foretells implies a background of eternal judgment for the impenitent transgressors (v. 24).

THE MESSAGE OF ISAIAH

The key-note of Isaiah's message is found in the account of his call (ch. 6). He was given then a majestic vision of the holiness of God, and this feature stands out in the book as the supreme attribute in the Divine character. To Isaiah, the Lord is "the Holy One of Israel". He uses the title thirty times, and it is spread equally over all parts of the book. It occurs three times in the Psalms (71:22; 78:41; 89:18) and twice in Jeremiah (50:29; 51:5), and nowhere else in all the Scriptures.

The Holy One is the "Redeemer" of His people. This name is applied to the Lord thirteen times (41:14; 43:14; 44:6, 24; 47:4; 48:17; 49:7, 26; 54:5, 8; 59:20; 60:16; 63:16), and the name "Saviour" seven times (43:3, 11; 45:15, 21; 49:26; 60:16; 63:8). Again and again the announcement is made to Israel that God will come and "save" them. This promise is given in the first part of the book (35:4), and it is more fully drawn out in the last part (40:9-10; 59:20). It has been literally fulfilled in the Incarnation and earthly ministry of the Lord Jesus Christ.

Isaiah has more to say about the person and work of the promised Redeemer than all the other prophets put together. In the first part of the book, there are Messianic passages in which divine and human features are blended together. The most notable of these is the picture of the King in 9:6-7, who was to be raised up and reign upon the throne of David. In the last part of the book, the figure of the Servant of the Lord appears. He is seen most fully in ch. 53, where the prophecies regarding him come to a head as he reaches his triumph through suffering. This is the special and peculiar contribution which Isaiah makes to the prophetic development of the plan of redemption.

The word "servant" occurs twenty times in chs. 40-53, and always in the singular number. After that it occurs eleven times, and always in the plural. When the word is used the first time, it means the whole nation of Israel (41:8-9). Afterwards, it is the chosen remnant of Israel, or Israel redeemed (44:1-5, 21-22). Finally, it becomes an individual who rises out of Israel and represents the redeemed people in his own person, and, by himself secures their salvation (52:13; 53:11).

Thus the idea of the Servant of the Lord in Isaiah is like a pyramid in three sections. In the light of the New Testament, it is seen to be as follows. The basis is the nation as a whole, or Israel after the flesh (Rom. 9:6-8). The middle section is the redeemed remnant of Israel, or spiritual Israel (Rom. 2:28-29; 4:11-12), "the Israel of God" (Gal. 6:16). The summit is the Person of the Redeemer Himself, "the Servant", who now proceeds to gather other "servants" around Him to form the new Israel. In this figure lies the principle on which the redemption described in Isaiah is wrought out, the identification of the Redeemer with the redeemed people. It foreshadows the fundamental spiritual principle of New Testament Christianity, the union of Christ with His Church.

THE BOOK OF JEREMIAH

JEREMIAH stands next to Isaiah as one of the two greatest prophets. He belonged to a priestly family in Anathoth, about three miles north east of Jerusalem. He was called to the prophetic office when quite young in the thirteenth year of Josiah's reign (626 B.C.). He carried on his ministry in Judah through the remaining eighteen years of that reign, and through the reigns of Jehoiakim (608-597) and Zedekiah (597-586), until the fall of Jerusalem and the captivity of the nation, a period of at least forty years (1:1-3).

These were the last decades of the Jewish monarchy. The history of the time is recorded in 2 Kings 22-25 and 2 Chron. 34-36. Josiah made an earnest attempt at reformation, but the corruption of the nation, due largely to the wicked reign of Manasseh (15:4) which had extended over more than half a century (695-640) had become so deep and widespread that the efforts of its last good king could not save it from destruction. The Babylonian conquest and captivity, foretold already by Isaiah, were fast hastening on.

Jeremiah was called to warn the nation of the impending judgment and to prepare the people for it. He saw it coming; he realized its nature; and he lived through it. He saw the city and the Temple destroyed and the nation taken away into exile. His lot was a lonely one, and his life was one of peculiar sorrow and suffering. Although a man of affectionate nature, he was forbidden to marry, and was charged to take no share in the social life of the community (16:2, 5, 8). He was to be a sign to the nation, and his mode of life was to reinforce his message. Though of a timid and shrinking spirit, he had unusual strength of character and power of endurance. He had to bear the reproaches of priests and prophets, and harsh treatment at the hands of the people, the princes, and the king. His sensitive and sympathetic nature felt keenly the sadness of the message he had to deliver.

Jeremiah lived a kind of Messianic life, and foreshadowed, in his own person, the suffering Servant of the Lord of whom Isaiah had spoken. After the fall of Jerusalem he was taken down to Egypt by the Jews who fled thither, and to them he delivered his last message. Tradition says that they stoned him to death.

The Book of Jeremiah, which is the longest of the prophetical books, contains considerable history, and the story of the prophet's experiences is also interwoven in it. Its main theme is the judgment of the Lord in the downfall of the kingdom of Judah. The central event upon which its prophecies converge is the capture and destruction of Jerusalem. It falls into three main divisions. The first division (Chs. 1-33) contains the bulk of Jeremiah's messages, which are prophecies of Judah's downfall. The second division (Chs. 34-45) is mainly autobiographic and historical, and contains the story of Judah's downfall. The third division (Chs. 46-52) deals with the nations of the world around. Thus we get the following outline of the book:

I. Prophecies of Judah's Downfall—Chs. 1-33
    1. Judah's Downfall Approaching (Chs. 1-6)
    2. Judah's Downfall Inevitable (Chs. 7-20)
    3. Judah's Downfall Imminent (Chs. 21-33)

II. The Story of Judah's Downfall—Chs. 34-45
    1. The Siege and Fall of the City (Chs. 34-39)
    2. After the Fall of the City (Chs. 40-45)

III. Prophecies Concerning the Nations—Chs. 46-52

PART I

The first division of the book (Chs. 1-33) contains the greater part of Jeremiah's prophecies and covers almost the whole of his ministry. It takes us from his call in the reign of Josiah, through the reign of Jehoiakim, and up to the eve of the fall of Jerusalem at the end of Zedekiah's reign. The prophet's messages during this period fall into three progressive groups, corresponding to these three reigns. The first group of prophecies (Chs. 1-6) belongs to the reign of Josiah, and contains appeals for Judah's repentance with warnings of her approaching downfall. The second group (Chs. 7-20) contains prophecies delivered in the reign of Jehoiakim, in which Jeremiah warned the nation that her persistent sin made her downfall inevitable. The third group (Chs. 21-33) belongs mainly to the reign of Zedekiah, and contains the prophecies delivered during the siege of the city, in which Jeremiah declared that Judah's downfall was imminent and that the only way of salvation now was to yield to Nebuchadnezzar.

JUDAH'S DOWNFALL APPROACHING
(Chs. 1-6)

These chapters contain a summary of the earliest messages of Jeremiah. They were delivered during the latter part of the reign of Josiah (639-608 B.C.)

when the prophet was probably assisting the king in his efforts at reform. His call came in the year after the reformation began (2 Chron. 34:3), and the discovery of the Book of the Law in the course of repairing the Temple would give special force to his preaching (2 Chron. 34:14; 2 Kings 22:8).

1. The Call of the Prophet (Ch. 1). After an introduction to the book as a whole (vs. 1-3), Jeremiah tells how he was called to the office of prophet and how he shrank from it at first because of his youth (vs. 4-6), and how the Lord encouraged him and empowered him for his task, which was to be concerned mainly with judgment and destruction—"to pluck up, and to break down, and to destroy, and to overthrow"—, and in a lesser degree with mercy and restoration—"to build and to plant" (vs. 7-10). Jeremiah's prophetic task was different from that of Isaiah. He was appointed "a prophet unto the nations". He lived in an age of crisis and transition in the Divine government of mankind, and he was called to expound its spiritual significance for the covenant people of God.

Two confirmatory signs were given him. One was a vision of mercy and grace. The almond-tree was the first to blossom out in the spring, and so it gave promise of the brighter days that lay beyond the winter of the nation's present state (vs. 11-12). The name of the tree provides a play on words in the original, which may be shown in this way: "I see the rod of a wake-tree". "Thou hast well seen: for I am awake over my word to perform it."

The other sign was a vision of judgment and punishment. The boiling caldron, tilted "from the north", not "toward the north" (A.V.), indicated that an invasion should come pouring down from the north over all the land and should attack Jerusalem and the cities of Judah for their wickedness in forsaking the Lord (vs. 13-16). Because of this, the Lord now commanded Jeremiah to arise and declare His message to them and not to be dismayed. Though all classes should oppose him—the kings, the princes, the priests, and the people—, yet the Lord would make him strong to withstand them and would be with him through his task (vs. 17-19).

The great truth impressed upon the young priest when he was thus called to become a prophet was the sovereignty of God in his life. Before his birth he had been fore-ordained and predestined for this office. For the fulfilment of his task he would be guided and directed, protected and empowered, by the Lord. The almighty power of the sovereign God, for whom Jeremiah himself declared at a later time in his life that there was nothing too hard (32:17), made out of this hesitating, trembling man "a fortified city, and an iron pillar, and brazen walls", among His rebellious people (1:18; 6:27; 15:20).

2. An Impeachment of Judah (2:1-3:5). The nation is charged with the sin of turning away from the redeeming love of God. Her early devotion to the Lord is contrasted with her subsequent ingratitude and unfaithfulness (2:1-8). The people have been doubly guilty: they have forsaken the Lord, the fountain of living water, and they have turned to other gods and hewed out for themselves broken cisterns that can hold no water (2:9-13). Punishment has already fallen upon them, for it is an evil and bitter thing that they have forsaken the Lord their God for an alliance with Egypt or Assyria (2:14-19). The prophet then enlarges upon the stubborn waywardness and the impenitent idolatries of the nation and her refusal to receive correction. Shame and confusion should follow her alliance with

Egypt as it followed her alliance with Assyria (2:20-37). Judah's guilt was like that of an unfaithful wife (3:1-5).

3. An Appeal to Return (3:6-4:2). Judah did not take warning from the punishment which God had meted out to the northern kingdom, "backsliding Israel". Judah is called Israel's "treacherous sister", because her reformation under Josiah was not sincere. She did not return unto the Lord "with her whole heart, but feignedly" (3:6-10). Israel had been in exile for a century since the overthrow of the northern kingdom by Assyria in 721 B.C.

And now the prophet was commanded to utter a tender appeal to the backsliding children of Northern Israel to return to the Lord, for He was merciful and would not keep anger for ever. He would take them, "one of a city, and two of a family", and bring them to Zion (3:11-15). This is Jeremiah's first reference to "the remnant", which has already appeared in Isaiah, and to the individualizing method by which the new Israel was to be gathered. Then comes a description of the blessings that should follow their return to the Lord (3:16-18). It foreshadows the spiritual worship of the Christian dispensation.

The Lord reverts again to Israel's ingratitude in turning away from Him, and makes another appeal to them to return (3:19-22). The prophet puts a prayer of confession upon their lips (3:22-25), and the Lord answers that if the conditions of true repentance are fulfilled by Israel, then the nations of the world shall own Him and be blessed by Him (4:1-2). The whole section containing the appeal to Israel to return is a revelation of the compassionate heart of God. He is wounded by the apostasy of His covenant people.

4. Announcement of Coming Judgment (4:3-6:23). The prophet was now compelled to announce that a judgment was fast coming upon the guilty and impenitent nation.

(1) The judgment determined (4:3-31). After a warning to Judah and Jerusalem to repent (vs. 3-4), a destructive invasion is announced which the Lord would bring from the north. A destroyer of nations was on his way to desolate the land, and all the leaders should be dismayed—the king, the princes, the priests, and the prophets (vs. 5-9). Jeremiah interposes with a sigh of protest to the Lord because He had allowed the people to be deceived by the false prophets (v. 10; cf. 14:13; 23:16-17). Then he goes on with a further description of the character of the coming evil, which the wickedness of Jerusalem was bringing upon herself (vs. 11-18). The passage is a prediction of the Babylonian invasions under Nebuchadnezzar.

A cry of anguish breaks out from the tender and compassionate heart of the prophet as he sees the calamity that was coming upon his people (vs. 19-22), and he goes on to liken the desolation it should cause to the chaos at the time of the creation of the world (vs. 23-26). This devastation of Judah had been purposed by the Lord, and it could not be averted by her intrigues with foreign allies (vs. 27-31). But the judgment would be tempered with mercy, for a remnant should be left: "yet will I not make a full end" (v. 27).

(2) The judgment justified (ch. 5). The moral condition of the people made it necessary. God would pardon if one good and true man could be found in Jerusalem. But the search failed, both among the common people (vs. 1-3) and among the great (vs. 4-6). The Lord could not pardon, for

there was universal moral corruption in the nation (vs. 7-9). A summons is given to the enemy to attack and destroy her for her treachery to the Lord. He would make His words in the prophet's mouth come to pass as a devouring judgment (vs. 10-18). When they should enquire the cause of this, they were to be told that their punishment corresponded with their sin (v. 19).

Their sin consisted in having no heart to worship the Lord. They had no consciousness of God, whose power set bounds to the mighty waves of the sea. They did not fear the Lord, who gave them the rains in their season (vs. 20-24). Among them were wicked men who practised iniquity and deceit; the result was the aggrandisement of the rich and the oppression of the poor. The Lord must be avenged on such a nation as this (vs. 25-29). All classes were equally guilty, and were running into a destructive judgment which they would have no power to avert (vs. 30-31). And still the note of mercy continues to be sounded in the midst of the announcement of judgment: "I will not make a full end with you" (v. 18).

(3 The judgment described (ch. 6). This chapter begins with a renewed description in vivid terms of the enemy's approach to Jerusalem and the siege of the city (vs. 1-6). And again her wickedness is declared to be the reason for the judgment that is to break over her (vs. 7-8). It should fall upon her people unsparingly, because they listened to no warning, but suffered themselves to be confirmed in their covetousness and shamelessness by false prophets and wicked priests who deceived them by saying, "Peace, peace;" when there was no peace (vs. 9-15).

The Lord's kindly appeal was disobeyed and His solemn warning disregarded (vs. 16-17). Therefore He would bring evil upon this people, and the formal offerings which they brought Him should not avert the judgment (vs. 18-21). It should be executed by a distant people coming from the north who were cruel and had no mercy. The prophet gives a vivid picture of the terror they should cause (vs. 22-26). The chapter closes with a statement of the object and the result of the prophet's discourses. The Lord had set him as "a trier" among the people —a tester of metals—to try their ways, and he had found them all to be dross (vs. 27-30).

JUDAH'S DOWNFALL INEVITABLE
(Chs. 7-20)

These chapters belong to the wicked reign of Jehoiakim, a selfish, godless, and perverse character (608-597 B.C.). Josiah had been defeated and slain by the Egyptians at the battle of Megiddo (2 Chron. 35:20-24), and his son Jehoahaz or Shallum, after reigning for three months, was taken to Egypt, where he died. Jehoiakim, another son, was then placed upon the throne, and under him the apostasy of the nation became deeper than ever. Judgment now came hurrying on. In the third year of his reign Nebuchadnezzar succeeded to the throne of Babylon after overthrowing Egypt at Carchemish, and made his first attack upon Jerusalem (Dan. 1:1). Jeremiah's messages during this period may be gathered around four themes: the Temple, the Covenant, the drought, and the potter.

I. False Trust in the Temple (Chs. 7-10). This seems to be one continuous address. It was delivered in the gate of the Temple, probably when the people of Judah and Jerusalem were flocking into it during the time of grave public anxiety that followed the tragic death of Josiah (cf. 7:1-2 and 26:1-2).

1. Sins of worship (7:1-20). The people were rebuked for putting their trust in the formal services of the Temple while they went on in ways of injustice, oppression, and wickedness. It was only by amending their ways that they could escape being cast out of the land (vs. 1-11). Let them remember what the Lord did to the tabernacle at Shiloh. He would do the same to the present house because they had refused to repent of their wickedness (vs. 12-15). The inward conflict in the prophet's soul is reflected in the prohibition which the Lord proceeds to lay upon him, in forbidding him to intercede for the people, for His wrath was to be poured out upon them (vs. 16-20; cf. 11:14, 14:11).

2. Apostasy and idolatry (7:21—8:3). The system of worship which the Lord gave Israel after redeeming them from Egypt was not intended to be an end in itself, but to set them apart as His people: the keeping of His commandments was the end in view (7:21-23). But they had gone on in their stubborn way and had ignored the words of the prophets whom He kept sending them, "rising up early and sending them" (7:24-26). This is Jeremiah's characteristic description of God's activity through the prophets. The expression is used only by him. It is another revelation of the deep concern in the heart of God for His wayward people. They had even brought their idolatrous abominations into His house and offered human sacrifices in Topheth in the valley of the son of Hinnom. Therefore it should be called "The valley of Slaughter" (7:27-34). Then the Lord would make the joys of life to cease and death should be chosen rather than life (8:1-3).

3. Backsliding perpetual (8:4-17). The prophet mourns the fact that the sin of the people was incurable and the judgment inevitable: they have "slidden back by a perpetual backsliding" (vs. 4-7). Their religious leaders, the prophets and the priests, had dealt falsely with them: "They have healed the hurt of the daughter of my people slightly, saying, Peace, peace; when there is no peace" (vs. 8-12). Then comes a further description of the coming judgment (vs. 13-17).

4. Judgment necessary (8:18-9:22). Jeremiah pours out his heart in lamentation for the desperate state of Zion and the sins that have made the judgment necessary (8:18-9:6). The Lord replies to his lament, declaring that He has no choice but to punish them, and expressing His own grief at the judgment He was bringing upon the land (9:7-11). There was a moral necessity for the judgment in the fact that the people had forsaken the Lord and followed Baalim (9:12-16). Then the Lord called for a lamentation on the part of the people in Zion (9:17-22).

5. The majesty of Jehovah (9:23-10:25). The prophecy of judgment having reached its climax, the prophet now sets forth the glory and majesty of the Lord. In Him the people should have put their trust, and in Him they would have found their salvation. He exercises lovingkindness and righteousness in the earth. He is impartial in judgment. He will visit the same punishment upon Israel as upon the uncircumcised nations, "for all the house of Israel are uncircumcised in heart" (9:23-26).

In the light of the greatness of the Lord, the God of Israel, the folly of idolatry is exposed (10:1-5). There is none like unto Him. He is the King of the nations. He is the true God, the living God (10:6-10). His almighty power is shown in that it was He who made the heavens and the earth, not the gods of the nations. The Creator of the universe is the God of Israel (10:11-16). Then Jeremiah bewails the inevitable desolation that the Lord is bringing on the land and the cities of Judah (10:17-22), and ends with a humble appeal to Him in behalf of the people to turn His wrath upon their foes (10:23-25).

II. The Broken Covenant (Chs. 11-13). The prophet was commissioned to proclaim throughout Judah the conditions of the Covenant. This would have special significance because of the discovery of the Book of the Law when the Temple was being repaired in the days of Josiah. The frequent use of the expression "this covenant" emphasizes the message (2 Kings 23:3; 2 Chron. 34:30).

1. Judah's faithlessness (11:1-17). The men of Judah were reminded of the curse attached to the covenant which the Lord made with their fathers when He redeemed them from Egypt (vs. 1-5). Their fathers had been false to this covenant, and now the people of Judah had broken it and gone back to the old idolatries (vs. 6-10). Therefore the Lord would bring evil upon them, and the gods whom they worshipped should not save them in the time of their trouble (vs. 11-13). At this point the prophet was again forbidden to pray for the people, for punishment must follow such wickedness (vs. 14-17).

2. A judgment on Anathoth (11:18-23). Jeremiah discovered that the men of his native town had laid a plot against his life. He appealed to the Lord about it, and a special judgment was pronounced upon the inhabitants of Anathoth. They should have no share in the remnant left after the judgment upon the nation.

3. The prophet's perplexity (ch. 12). Thinking of the treachery of his fellow-townsmen, Jeremiah made an earnest appeal to God in wonder at the prosperity of the wicked, and was told that greater trials still awaited him (vs. 1-6). The Lord went on to declare that He had forsaken His heritage and given it over to the destroyers (vs. 7-13). The neighbouring nations who had corrupted and despoiled Judah were to go into captivity and exile with her, and if they learned of the Lord from her, they should share with her the blessing of the restoration (vs. 14-17).

4. Symbols of judgment (ch. 13). The Lord now gave Jeremiah two signs. One was for himself, the emblem of the girdle, marred and destroyed by being buried at the Euphrates, illustrating the ruin and humiliation of the nation as God's covenant people (vs. 1-11). The other was for the people, the parable of the broken wine bottles, setting forth the confusion and dismay of the inhabitants of the land when the Lord's judgment should fall upon them (vs. 12-14). The prophet follows this with another appeal to Judah to repent of her pride (vs. 15-19). But her wickedness was inveterate and her humiliation was surely coming (vs. 20-27).

III. The Meaning of the Drought (Chs. 14-17). A drought had fallen upon the land of Judah at that time. According to the threatenings of the Mosaic Law, this was a Divine judgment upon apostasy (Deut. 28:23-24).

1. A controversy with the Lord (chs. 14-15). After a graphic description of the effects of the drought (14:1-6), there is recorded a remarkable controversy between the prophet and the Lord.

Jeremiah makes appeal after appeal to God not to cast off and destroy His people, and the Lord answers with a solemn and reiterated refusal.

The prophet first pleads that, though they have sinned, the Lord should not reject them because they are called by His name (14:7-9); and the Lord answers that, on account of their persistent apostasy, He cannot accept them (14:10-12). Then Jeremiah points out that the prophets had misled the people, and the Lord replies that the prophets had spoken lies in His name and should perish in the very calamities which they declared would never come (14:13-16), and goes on to put a lament into the mouth of Jeremiah, which seems like the germ of the Book of Lamentations (14:17-18).

Finally the prophet makes a contrite confession on behalf of the people and appeals to God on the ground of His own glory (14:19-22). The Lord answers that even Moses and Samuel could not turn Him from His purpose with His people. "I will cause them to be tossed to and fro among all the kingdoms of the earth." They had gone so far in sin that the judgment must be thorough. God was "weary with repenting" (15:1-9).

This controversy had a profound effect upon Jeremiah. He broke out in a personal lamentation of deep anguish, and the Lord reassured him that the trial and suffering through which he was going should be for his good (15:10-14). The prophet continued his complaint, and the Lord again assured him that He would protect him and deliver him from his foes (15:15-21).

2. A new charge to the prophet (ch. 16). Jeremiah was now called to a life of peculiar asceticism and special separation in view of the coming judgment. He was commanded not to marry, for children should die grievous deaths (vs. 1-4). He was to stand aloof from the lives of the people. He was forbidden to take part with them in mourning, for God had taken away His grace and mercy, and they should die, great and small alike, without lamentation. He was also to take no part in their mirth, for God would cause the voice of joy and gladness to cease (vs. 5-9).

When they should enquire why the Lord had pronounced all this evil upon them, he was to declare that they had sinned more than their fathers, and He would show them no favour (vs. 10-13). In days to come the Egyptian bondage would seem to be a light thing compared with that which they should suffer in "the land of the north", that is, in the Babylonian captivity, for in it God would "recompense their iniquity and their sin double" (vs. 14-18; cf. Isa. 40:2). In the midst of this passage is a gleam of hope in the promise, "I will bring them again into their land that I gave unto their fathers." At last the prophet expresses his confidence in the Lord in view of the judgment, and the Lord replies that it will result in His own glory (vs. 19-21).

3. The sin of Judah (17:1-18). The special sin that is denounced here is that of idolatry. It had become rooted deep in the heart of the nation and was indelible. Hence severe chastisement was necessary (vs. 1-4). Trust in man leads to desolation and destruction: trust in God leads to prosperity and security (vs. 5-8). "The heart is deceitful above all things; and it is exceedingly corrupt; who can know it?" But God searches the heart, and will punish all wicked devices (vs. 9-11). Then the prophet utters a prayer to God as the hope of Israel, affirming his faith, and appealing for the vindication of

his prophetic ministry and the destruction of those who oppose him (vs. 12-18).

4. A warning about the Sabbath (17:19-27). The prophet was commanded to stand in the gate of Jerusalem and utter God's warning about the Sabbath. Upon its observance depended the prosperity and continuance of the nation. It was a sign and witness of the Covenant (Deut. 5:15; Ezek. 20:12, 20).

IV. Lessons From the Potter (Chs. 18-20). These chapters contain incidents which illustrate one of the methods used by the prophets to enforce their messages, the use of symbolic actions.

1. The potter's clay (ch. 18). Jeremiah was sent down to the potter's house, and watched him working in the clay and remaking a vessel that had broken under his hands (vs. 1-4). Out of this incident came a message to Israel about the Lord's sovereignty among the nations. When a nation hinders God's purpose by resistance to His will, it may have another chance of being moulded by His hand if it repents (vs. 5-10). On this ground the prophet is bidden to make another appeal to the people of Judah and Jerusalem; but they reply with defiance, and the Lord renews His announcement of desolating judgment (vs. 11-17). The delivery of this message stirred up new opposition to the prophet, and he appealed to the Lord against his persecutors (vs. 18-23).

2. The potter's bottle (chs. 19-20). Jeremiah was commissioned to buy a potter's earthen bottle and take a deputation of the elders to the valley of the son of Hinnom, which was on the south of Jerusalem, and proclaim the judgment that God would bring upon them because they had been offering human sacrifices there—they had "filled this place with the blood of innocents". The day should come when the valley's name would be changed to "The valley of Slaughter" (19:1-9; cf. 7:31-34). Then the prophet was to break the bottle as a sign that the nation should be broken to pieces so that it could not be made whole again (19:10-13).

When Jeremiah returned to the city he repeated this prophecy of the coming judgment in the court of the Temple (19:14-15), and he was smitten and arrested by Pashur, the warden of the Temple, and put in the stocks (20:1-2). When released the next day, he uttered a special prediction of judgment upon Pashur and his house (20:3-6). Then he poured out his heart to God in an agonized lamentation, which passes from complaint about his lot (20:7-10) to confidence in God (20:11-13), and ends with an outburst of passionate grief (20:14-18). This prayer is a revelation of the conflict of feelings that went on continually in Jeremiah's heart.

JUDAH'S DOWNFALL IMMINENT
(Chs. 21-33)

This section belongs to the reign of Zedekiah (597-586 B.C.). Jehoiakim had lost his life in Nebuchadnezzar's second attack upon Jerusalem and was succeeded by his son Coniah or Jehoiachin, who after a reign of three months was taken to Babylon with ten thousand of the best classes of the people. He was succeeded by his uncle Zedekiah, the youngest son of Josiah, a weak, vacillating, and faithless ruler. He exhausted the patience of Nebuchadnezzar by joining Egypt in a coalition against Babylon, and brought the Chaldean monarch against Jerusalem for the third time. He came now in fierce wrath, and the judgment of the Babylonian captivity finally fell upon the guilty nation.

I. The Shadow of the Judgment (Chs. 21-24). There is a considerable gap at this point in the collection of Jeremiah's prophecies. These chapters contain announcements which the prophet uttered during the final siege of Jerusalem. They were occasioned by an enquiry which Zedekiah sent to Jeremiah when Nebuchadnezzar's attack began. His reply announced the nation's doom, and he followed it with denunciations of the wicked kings and false prophets whose evil-doing had brought it on. In the midst of these announcements comes a gleam of Messianic hope.

1. The coming disaster (ch. 21). When Nebuchadnezzar began the final siege of Jerusalem, Zedekiah sent a deputation asking Jeremiah to enquire of the Lord for them (vs. 1-2). He replied that the Lord Himself would fight against Jerusalem and deliver it into the hand of Nebuchadnezzar (vs. 3-7). The only hope of salvation was for the people to surrender to the Chaldeans (vs. 8-10), and for the king to execute justice (vs. 11-14).

2. The wicked kings (ch. 22). The prophet was commanded to go to the palace and pronounce God's judgment upon the royal house of Judah for forsaking the Covenant of the Lord (vs. 1-9). Then he declared the doom of the successors of Josiah, all of whom had done evil: Shallum (vs. 10-12), Jehoiakim (vs. 13-19), and Coniah (vs. 20-30).

3. The righteous King (23:1-8). After a denunciation of the false shepherds who had scattered the flock, meaning the rulers of the state as a whole (vs. 1-4), Jeremiah pronounced one of the few direct predictions of the Messiah to be found in the book (vs. 5-8). The Lord would raise up one of David's line who should be a righteous King, and under him the remnant of the flock should be gathered and Judah and Israel should be saved. His name, "Jehovah our righteousness", implies that through the agency of the Messiah the Lord Himself would bestow righteousness upon His people. It is significant that this prophecy was uttered during the reign of the faithless Zedekiah, whose name means, "the righteousness of Jehovah."

4. The false prophets (23:9-40). With a broken heart Jeremiah now denounced the prophets for their wicked practices (vs. 9-15) and their lying messages (vs. 16-22). They had deceived the people into a false security. They dreamed their own dreams and spoke out of their own heart instead of delivering the word of the Lord, and the Lord was now against them (vs. 23-32). As for those who mocked the Lord's prophet by asking Jeremiah derisively, "what is the burden (or oracle) of Jehovah?" they were to be told this burden: Jehovah would cast them off and bring everlasting shame upon them (vs. 33-40).

5. The fate of the people (ch. 24). Two baskets of figs were shown to Jeremiah as a symbol of the fate of the nation. One basket had good figs, and represented the exiles taken to Babylon with Jeconiah, whom the Lord would regard for good (vs. 1-7). The other had bad figs, and represented the people remaining in Judah with Zedekiah, whom the Lord would give up to judgment (vs. 8-10).

II. The Program of the Judgment (Chs. 25-26). These chapters go back into the reign of Jehoiakim. They take us to the first year of Nebuchadnezzar's reign, when Babylon reached the place of supremacy among the nations (604 B.C.). It was then that Jeremiah foretold the specific character of the judgment.

1. Seventy years' captivity (25:1-14). Ever since his call more than twenty years before, Jeremiah had been proclaiming the word of the Lord to the people of Judah, but they had not hearkened (vs. 1-3). They had treated all the prophets of the Lord in the same way; they had refused to hear their appeals to return from their evil ways, and had provoked Him to anger (vs. 4-7). Therefore the Lord would bring His servant Nebuchadnezzar upon them and upon all the nations round about, and they should be subjected to Babylon for seventy years (vs. 8-11). After that the Lord would punish Babylon and make it desolate for ever (vs. 12-14).

2. The judgment of the nations (25:15-38). Jeremiah was commanded to take the cup of the wrath of God, and compel all the nations to drink of it until they should become drunken, "because of the sword that I will send among them" (vs. 15-26). The frequent repetition of the word "all" in this striking passage makes it a picture of universal war. It culminates in a judgment on Sheshach, a name which occurs only here and in 51:41. It probably stands for Babylon in some cryptic sense, as Babylon stands for the godless world system. The prophet goes on to declare that, having begun with His own people, God must punish all the world (vs. 27-31). The judgment which was to begin with Jerusalem would become a great tempest sweeping from nation to nation (vs. 32-38).

3. The persecution of the prophet (ch. 26). On the occasion of Jeremiah's address in the Temple in the beginning of Jehoiakim's reign (vs. 1-7; cf. 7:1-2), his life was threatened (vs. 8-9). Accused by the priests and the prophets (vs. 10-15), he was acquitted by the princes and the people (vs. 16-19). The hostile attitude of the king is shown by the way he persecuted and murdered the prophet Uriah, whose message was the same as Jeremiah's (vs. 20-24).

III. Submission to the Judgment (Chs. 27-29). These chapters return to the reign of Zedekiah. The name "Jehoiakim" in 27:1 is obviously a mistake in copying for "Zedekiah", which occurs in the rest of the chapter (vs. 3, 12). It was now declared that the Lord had given the supremacy among the nations and over Judah to Babylon.

1. The yoke of Babylon (27:1-11). Jeremiah was commanded to make yokes as symbols of submission to Babylon. One of these he was to wear himself. The others he was to send to the neighbouring nations, informing them that the sovereign God had given the supremacy in the world for the present to the king of Babylon, and warning them to submit to him and not to listen to their diviners and sorcerers. Compare vs. 5-6 and Dan. 2:37-38, which are probably contemporaneous announcements.

2. A warning to Judah (27:12-22). The prophet followed up this warning to the adjoining nations with a warning to Judah. He first appealed to the king not to heed the false prophets, and declared that the only hope of saving Jerusalem from destruction was to submit to the king of Babylon (vs. 12-15). Then he went on to warn the priests and the people to the same effect, and uttered a prediction that the sacred vessels of the Temple should be carried to Babylon (vs. 16-22).

3. The fate of a false prophet (ch. 28). Hananiah having uttered a prediction contradicting Jeremiah's message (vs. 1-4), Jeremiah committed

the issue to the Lord (vs. 5-11), and foretold Hananiah's death within a year (vs. 12-16). And so it happened (v. 17). Nothing in Jeremiah's troubled life tried him more than the opposition of the false prophets.

4.   A message to the exiles (ch. 29). Jeremiah sent a letter to the exiles in Babylon, advising them not to listen to the false prophets that were among them but to settle down there in peace in the meantime (vs. 1-9), and promising that after seventy years God would visit them and hearken to their prayer and restore them to the land (vs. 10-14). He went on to tell them that the words of the false prophets in Babylon should be disproved by the disastrous fate of the people left in Jerusalem (vs. 15-20). Then he denounced certain false prophets, mentioning them by name, who had been deceiving the exiles, and foretold the judgment and punishment that should fall upon them (vs. 21-32).

IV. Restoration after the Judgment (Chs. 30-33). This section contains the positive and constructive message of the book. It records Jeremiah's prophecy of the Messianic age and of the redemption and restoration of Israel after the captivity.

1.   The promise of restoration (ch. 30). The Lord commanded Jeremiah to write all the words that He had spoken through him in a book, because He now promised to restore the nation to the land (vs. 1-3), to save them out of their time of trouble and fulfil the promise he gave to David (vs. 4-11), and to punish all the nations that had oppressed them (vs. 12-17). He would raise up a Ruler from among themselves who should have access to Himself, being Priest as well as King, and they should become His own people (vs. 18-22). In the meantime the tempest of judgment should sweep on till His purpose was accomplished (vs. 23-24). In v. 21 we have a foregleam of the Incarnation and the Ascension.

2.   The gathering of Israel (31:1-26). The Lord assures Israel of His everlasting love, and promises to gather the remnant of Israel from the uttermost parts of the earth, and turn their sorrow into joy. The reference is first to all the twelve tribes of Israel (v. 1). Then the restoration of Ephraim or the northern kingdom is dealt with (vs. 2-22), and afterwards the restoration of Judah or the southern kingdom (vs. 23-26).

The voice heard in Ramah of "Rachel weeping for her children" (v. 15) may refer to some atrocity inflicted upon that town by the Assyrians (Isa. 10: 29). Rachel, as the mother of Joseph and therefore of Ephraim, represents the northern kingdom in its suffering and sorrow. Matthew uses the passage as a forecast of the sorrow of the mothers of Bethlehem over their slaughtered babes because Rachel's tomb was in the neighbourhood (Matt. 2:17-18; Gen. 35: 16-20; 48:7).

3.   The new covenant (31:27-40). Israel and Judah are now taken together, and the conditions of the restoration are explained. It was to take place on the basis of a new covenant which the Lord promises to make with them. He would provide for a personal and individual relationship with Himself, so that they should no longer be condemned for their fathers' sins, but each for his own (vs. 27-30). The proverb recorded in v. 29 seems to have been in common use at this time, for it is quoted in Ezek. 18: 2 also.

The new covenant would be no longer outward and legal, but inward and spiritual, giving everyone access to the Lord and putting away sin and

iniquity once for all (vs. 31-34). It would be eternal in its duration and unfathomable in its reach (vs. 35-37). The New Testament interpretation of this promise is to be found in Heb. 8:6-12; 10:15-18. The idea of the New Covenant is carried on through the next two chapters as the ground and method of the restoration (32:37-41; 33:20-21). The present chapter closes by taking us back from the Gospel age into the state of Jerusalem in the prophet's own day (vs. 38-40).

4.   A sign of the restoration (ch. 32). During the siege of Jerusalem Jeremiah was imprisoned by Zedekiah for his declaration that the city should fall (vs. 1-5). At the Lord's command he purchased an ancestral field in his native town Anathoth, occupied at the time by the Chaldean army (vs. 6-15). Then he made an earnest appeal to the Lord to know the reason for this (vs. 16-25), and received the comforting assurance that it was a token of the coming restoration. Though the Lord was bringing all this evil upon the people because of their sin (vs. 26-35), yet He would also bring upon them all the good He had promised (vs. 36-44).

5.   A pledge of the restoration (ch. 33). While Jeremiah was still imprisoned, the word of the Lord came to him a second time, calling him to pray unto God and He would make known to him great and hidden things (vs. 1-3). Then the Lord went on with a renewed assurance of His purpose to restore Judah and Israel and cause peace and joy to return to Jerusalem (vs. 4-13). After that He explained how He would accomplish this.

He would cause a Branch of righteousness to grow up unto David, and under him Jerusalem should be called "Jehovah our righteousness" (vs. 14-16). Here we have a repetition of the Messianic prophecy of 23:5-6 with a remarkable difference. The name given to the Messiah in the earlier passage is given to the city itself in this passage, thus indicating that the righteousness bestowed upon his people by the Messiah is reflected in them and becomes their righteousness too. Following this comes a statement that David should never want a man to sit upon his throne, and the priests and Levites should never want a man to continue their priestly service (vs. 17-18). This means that the two offices of king and priest were to be united in the Messiah for ever. The first part of the prophecy is fulfilled in the exaltation of Christ to the right hand of God (Acts 2:30-33), and the second part in the heavenly priesthood of Christ (Heb. 6:17-20). This double promise is then confirmed by the Lord's solemn pledge that His covenant with David could no more be broken than His covenant of the day and of the night (vs. 19-26).

PART II

The second division of the book (Chs. 34-45) is mainly narrative. It contains a record of events that took place during the invasions of the land by the Babylonians, and tells of the final siege and fall of the city (Chs. 34-39). Then it goes on with a narrative of the fate of the people that were left in the land and went down to Egypt after the fall of the city (Chs. 40-45).

The Siege and Fall of the City
(Chs. 34-39)

1.   Messages During the Final Siege (Ch. 34). When Nebuchadnezzar and his huge army were carrying on the final siege of Jerusalem, Jeremiah was sent to Zedekiah with the announcement that

the Lord would give the city into his hand and he should burn it, and that the king himself should be taken captive to Babylon and die there in peace (vs. 1-7). Then he denounced the people for their breach of faith in not giving liberty to their Hebrew servants (vs. 8-11). This was a violation of the law of the Sabbatic year (Lev. 25:1-7), and a sin against the Covenant which the Lord had made with Israel when He redeemed the nation from Egypt (vs. 12-16), and they should be punished for it by being given into the hand of their enemies (vs. 17-22).

2. Incidents During the First Invasion (Chs. 35-36). Two incidents are recorded here which took place during the first invasion, in the fourth year of Jehoiakim's reign (604 B.C.).

(1) The devotion of the Rechabites (ch. 35). They had taken refuge in Jerusalem, but remained faithful to the instructions of their forefather in refusing wine when it was set before them (vs. 1-11). Jeremiah contrasted their continued loyalty to Jonadab with Judah's persistent disloyalty to the Lord (vs. 12-15). Therefore would Judah be punished, while a special promise was given to the Rechabites (vs. 16-19).

(2) The burning of Jeremiah's roll (ch. 36). At the command of the Lord, Jeremiah had his secretary Baruch write in a book all the prophecies which he had uttered up to that time and read them to the people in the Temple (vs. 1-10). The princes, hearing of it, had Baruch read the roll to them also. It had such an effect upon them that "they turned in fear one toward another", each man reading his own thoughts in his neighbour's face, and decided to inform the king (vs. 11-19). When they reported the matter to Jehoiakim, he sent for the roll, and while it was being read to him he cut it up and threw it into the fire burning in a brazier before him (vs. 20-26). Then Jeremiah was instructed of the Lord to rewrite what Jehoiakim had burned and to pronounce a special sentence of doom and humiliation upon him. Baruch then wrote in another roll all the words of the former book, "and there were added besides unto them many like words" (vs. 27-32).

3. Incidents During the Last Invasion (Chs. 37-38). When Nebuchadnezzar began his final siege of Jerusalem, Zedekiah sent a deputation to Jeremiah asking him to enquire of the Lord for them (21:1-2). Later in the siege an Egyptian army attempted to relieve the city, and the Chaldeans withdrew. Then Zedekiah sent another deputation to Jeremiah asking him to pray to the Lord for them (37:1-5). The prophet sent back a message of warning. The army of Pharaoh should return to Egypt, and the army of the Chaldeans should come back and capture the city and burn it (37:6-10).

During the interval when the Chaldean army was drawn away from the city, Jeremiah attempted to go out into the land of Benjamin on a matter of private business. He was arrested as a deserter and handed over to the princes, who imprisoned him in a dungeon (37:11-15). Zedekiah sent for him secretly and asked if he had any message from the Lord. The prophet protested against the treatment he had received, and the king had him removed to the court of the guard and provided with food (37:16-21).

By continuing to foretell the victory of the Chaldeans, Jeremiah aroused the anger of the princes, who moved the king against him and had him thrown into a pit with deep mire at the bottom (38:1-6). An Ethiopian eunuch in the palace heard of this evil deed and appealed to the king on behalf of the prophet. At the king's command, he rescued Jeremiah from the pit and restored him to the court of the guard (38:7-13).

Then the king sent for Jeremiah again and implored him to hide nothing from him, promising to spare his life and protect him from his foes (38:14-16). The prophet replied that submission to the king of Babylon was the only way to save the city (38:17-23). He was commanded by Zedekiah not to tell the princes of the advice he had given, and was kept in the court of the guard until the city fell (38:24-28).

4. The Final Catastrophe (Ch. 39). After a siege lasting a year and a half, the city was taken and destroyed. Zedekiah fled, but was captured and had his eyes put out. The people were carried away to Babylon, only the poorest being left in the land (vs. 1-10). Nebuchadnezzar charged his captain of the guard to afford protection to Jeremiah, and the prophet was released (vs. 11-14). The chapter closes with the promise which Jeremiah had been instructed to give to Ebed-melech the Ethiopian, who had delivered him from the miry pit. His life was to be saved because he had put his trust in the Lord God of Israel (vs. 15-18).

AFTER THE FALL OF JERUSALEM
(Chs. 40-45)

1. The Remnant Left in the Land (Chs. 40-41). Jeremiah was given his liberty and chose to remain with Gedaliah, whom Nebuchadnezzar had made governor of Judah (40:1-6). Gedaliah began a wise and beneficent rule with Mizpah as his capital (40:7-12). He showed his guileless character when he was warned of a plot against his life and refused to believe it (40:13-16). The plot was carried out, and Gedaliah was treacherously murdered at Mizpah, and all his associates with him, by Ishmael, one of the princes (41:1-3). Ishmael committed further massacres, and then fled to Ammon, taking captive the people of Mizpah (41:4-10). He was pursued by Johanan who had warned Gedaliah gainst him, and the captives were recovered. Then in fear of the Chaldeans they all prepared to go down to Egypt (41:11-18).

2. The Flight into Egypt (Chs. 42-43). In their distress the people asked Jeremiah to seek the guidance of the Lord for them, promising to obey whatever it might be (42:1-6). After ten days the prophet gave them his reply: If they remained in the land the mercy of the Lord would be upon them, but if they went down to Egypt the sword and famine and pestilence would destroy them (42:7-17). Knowing that they were set on going down to Egypt, for it was the refuge to which the worldly minded and unbelieving in Judah had always looked, Jeremiah went on to give them a solemn warning of what would happen to them there (42:18-22).

In the face of this warning, the leaders of the people charged Jeremiah with speaking under the influence of Baruch; and they all went down to Egypt, taking Jeremiah and Baruch with them (43:1-7). When they settled at Tahpanhes, Jeremiah announced, with an accompanying symbolic action, that Nebuchadnezzar would set up his royal pavilion in that very place and would smite the land of Egypt (42:8-13), thus showing them the folly of fleeing to Egypt to escape from Babylon.

3. Jeremiah's Last Message (Ch. 44). This was a warning delivered to a large gathering of the

Jews at Pathros (v. 15), probably some considerable time after their arrival in Egypt. The prophet denounced them for their wickedness in forgetting the Lord God of Israel and worshipping other gods in the land of Egypt (vs. 1-10), and declared that they should all be destroyed by the judgment of God (vs. 11-14). The women seem to have been especially addicted to the idolatrous practice of burning incense to the moon. Their husbands acquiesced in the practice and perversely attributed the evils that had fallen on their land to their formerly giving up idolatry there. Both the men and the women declared they would not hearken to Jeremiah (vs. 15-19).

The prophet renewed his .warning, reminding them of what had happened in the land of Judah (vs. 20-23), and declaring that the Lord would not have them profane His great name in the land of Egypt but would make an end of them (vs. 24-28). He added, as a sign of this coming judgment, that the reigning king of Egypt, who had been an ally of Judah against Nebuchadnezzar, should meet the same fate as Zedekiah king of Judah (vs. 29-30). This prophecy is the last recorded event in Jeremiah's life. The fall of Pharaoh Hophra took place in 570 B.C.

4. A Promise to Baruch (Ch. 45). In chronological order this chapter follows the story of Jeremiah's roll (ch. 36). The prophet's faithful secretary, who was depressed by the troubles of the time and the failure of his hopes, was warned against having any personal ambition when God was bringing judgments on the world. He was given a special promise that his life should be preserved through them all.

PART III

PROPHECIES CONCERNING THE NATIONS
(Chs. 46-52)

The last division of the book contains a collection of the prophecies uttered by Jeremiah regarding the Gentile nations at different times during his ministry (46:1). It is a prophetic survey of the world of his day, as he looked out upon it from Jerusalem. It begins with Egypt in the west, takes in the nations immediately around Judah, and passes on to Babylon on the east. In the course of this survey, the prophet reveals the principles of God's action when His judgments are in the earth. The last chapter is an appendix to the book, giving a fuller account of its central event, and forming a link with the Book of Lamentations.

1. Egypt (Ch. 46). The chapter contains two prophetic utterances about Egypt, foretelling two events that occurred in the struggle for supremacy between Egypt and Babylon.

(1) The defeat of Egypt at Carchemish (vs. 2-12). This is a graphic description of the army of Egypt in its preparation and its advance to the Euphrates, where it was defeated by Nebuchadnezzar (605 B.C.). In predicting this event the prophet declared that it would be the day of the Lord's vengeance upon Egypt (v. 10).

(2) Nebuchadnezzar's conquest of Egypt (vs. 13-28). A graphic description of the coming of Nebuchadnezzar into Egypt as the Lord's instrument for punishing that land (vs. 13-26), is followed by a message of comfort to Israel not to fear in the midst of these judgments which He was bringing upon the nations (vs. 27-28).

2. The Nations Around Judah (Chs. 47-49). Seven of the smaller states between Egypt and Babylon now came into view in the sweep of Divine judgment. In the midst of these judgments are promises of mercy (48:47; 49:6, 39).

(1) The Philistines (ch. 47). The sword of the Lord had been given a charge to destroy them.

(2) Moab (ch. 48). Moab was to be punished and laid waste because of his pride and haughtiness of spirit. He had "magnified himself against Jehovah" (v. 42).

(3) Ammon (49:1-6). The Lord would bring a fear upon Ammon and drive them out of their land.

(4) Edom (49:7-22). Edom should not go unpunished, for the Lord had decreed that it should become an astonishment, and all its cities perpetual wastes.

(5) Damascus and Syria (49:23-27). Damascus is named as the capital of Syria. That land was to be swept by the devouring fire of judgment.

(6) Kedar or Arabia (49:28-33). This nation "that dwelleth without care" was to be subjected to "fear that is on every side". Both Edom and Kedar were told to "dwell in the depths" (vs. 8, 30), that is, to retire as far as possible into the solitude of the desert in order to escape the invader.

(7) Elam (49:34-39). The Lord would scatter Elam to the four winds of heaven.

3. Babylon (Chs. 50-51). Throughout this book Babylon has been the instrument of God's judgment. But Babylon's time should come, for she, too, had provoked God's anger; and in this powerful prophecy Jeremiah utters the Divine judgment upon her. In these chapters her judgment is related to the deliverance of Israel.

(1) Babylon's fall as the means of Israel's deliverance (ch. 50). Babylon should fall and Israel return to the Lord (vs. 1-10). Babylon should be punished and Israel pardoned (vs. 11-20). Babylon should be destroyed and Israel liberated (vs. 21-28). Babylon's pride should be humbled by the Lord God of hosts (vs. 29-32). The Redeemer of Israel would call for judgment upon Babylon (vs. 33-40). A great nation from the north should execute His purpose against Babylon (vs. 41-46).

(2) Babylon doomed and Israel called to come out of her (ch. 51). The Lord would stir up a destroying wind against Babylon, and His people are called to come out of her because He had established their righteousness (vs. 1-10). The Medes are named as the agents whom He has stirred up to inflict His judgment upon Babylon (vs. 11-14). Then comes a repetition of 10:12-16 to set forth the majesty of the God of Israel, who decrees the destruction of Babylon (vs. 15-19). This is followed by a striking passage in which the Lord explains how He has used Babylon as His instrument of judgment upon the nations: "Thou art my battle-axe". Then the words, "With thee will I break in pieces", are repeated nine times with impressive effect, like the strokes of doom (vs. 20-23).

But now the Lord is against her, because of the evil she has done to Zion, and He summons the nations to set themselves against her (vs. 24-32). He will avenge the cause of Zion and execute judgment upon Babylon (vs. 33-44). He summons His people to come out of her, because her destruction is certain and she cannot escape it (vs. 45-58).

This prophecy against Babylon was to be taken by Seraiah, who was a brother of Baruch (32:12), when he went to Babylon in the service of Zedekiah, and was to be read there and then sunk in the

Euphrates as a sign that Babylon should rise no more (vs. 59-64).

4. The End of the Kingdom of Judah (Ch. 52). This chapter is a historical appendix to the book, and is almost identical with 2 Kings 24:18-25:30. It begins with a brief statement about the reign of Zedekiah, the last king of Judah, leading up to his rebellion against Babylon (vs. 1-3). Then it gives an account of the siege and capture of Jerusalem and the fate of the king (vs. 4-11), and of the destruction of the city and the exile of the people (vs. 12-16). Then comes a list of the treasures of the Temple that were taken to Babylon (vs. 17-23), and a record of the arrest and execution of the chief officers of the Temple and the city (vs. 24-27).

After giving a summary of the various deportations of people whom Nebuchadnezzar took to Babylon (vs. 28-30), the book closes with an account of the liberation of Jehoiachin from prison in Babylon and of the favour shown him by a later Babylonian king (vs. 31-34). This is the fourth account of the fall of Jerusalem in the Old Testament, the other three being in 2 Kings 25, 2 Chron. 36, and Jer. 39. To the Jews of that time it was as if their world had come to an end.

THE MESSAGE OF JEREMIAH

In this book God is longsuffering and patient with His sinful people, yearning over them to save them, and going to the utmost to draw them back to Himself. The characteristic expression that Jeremiah uses of God to describe this attitude of His is, "rising up early". This bold figure takes the highest form of activity by which human interest in anything is expressed and uses it to represent God's interest in man. It occurs eleven times in the book (7:13, 25; 11:7; 25:3, 4; 26:5; 29:19; 32:33; 35: 14, 15; 44:4).

Jeremiah makes few direct references to the coming Messiah; but in these he adds to the picture given by Isaiah. He declares that a righteous Branch would be raised up in the house of David, who should become the source of righteousness for His people (23:5-6; 33:15-16). The prophet himself was a type of Christ in his solitary suffering, and in his persecution by the religious leaders of the nation.

The special contribution which Jeremiah makes to the development of God's plan of redemption is his prophecy of the New Covenant (31:31-34). In contrast with the Old Covenant, which could not deal finally with sin and could only command obedience to the outward demands of the Law, the New Covenant would put away sin once for all and provide an impulse within the soul which would give power to fulfil the Law. The fulfilment of this great promise is recorded in Luke 22:14-20; and the significance of the New Covenant and its superiority to the Old are explained in the Epistle to the Hebrews (chs. 8-9).

THE BOOK OF EZEKIEL

LIKE Jeremiah, Ezekiel was born in a priestly family and was called to serve in the prophetic office. He was one of the captives taken to Babylon with king Jehoiachin in 597 B.C. (2 Kings 24:10-16). He lived among them on the river Chebar, one of the canals in Babylonia. His call came in the fifth year of his captivity and the thirtieth year of his age (1:1-3). This was the age when the Levites entered upon their duties (Num. 4:23). He was married and had a house of his own, where the elders among the exiles of Judah used to meet with him (8:1). His wife died in the ninth year of his exile, on the day when the final siege of Jerusalem began (24: 1-2, 18).

Jeremiah had been preaching in Judah and Jerusalem for more than thirty years when Ezekiel's ministry began among the exiles in Babylonia. Many of Ezekiel's prophecies are dated, though the dates do not all come in chronological order. Notes of time are found in 1:2, 8:1, 20:1, 24:1, 26:1, 29:1, 17, 30:20, 31:1, 32:1, 17, 33:21, 40:1. The latest date is in the twenty-seventh year of the prophet's captivity (29:17), so that he must have continued his ministry for at least twenty-two years. It was intended to comfort and strengthen the exiles of Israel amidst the idolatries and temptations with which they were surrounded while judgment was falling upon Judah and Jerusalem, and also to turn their eyes to the new Israel which was to arise upon the ruins of the old. The greatest of his prophecies, the vision of the new temple, is dated fourteen years after the fall of the old Temple (40:1).

The Book of Ezekiel abounds in visions, symbols, and allegories. Much of the imagery of the book is derived from the Temple and its services. This is due both to the fact that Ezekiel was a priest, and also to the fact that new spiritual realities were being revealed which had been already foreshadowed in the Temple ritual. These spiritual realities were clothed in forms with which Ezekiel and his countrymen were familiar. The material and earthly Temple with its symbolic ritual was only a type of the spiritual and heavenly order upon which the new Israel was to be based.

The Book of Ezekiel may be divided into two equal parts. The first part (Chs. 1-24) contains visions and prophecies of judgment and destruction; the second part (Chs. 25-48) contains prophecies and visions of reconstruction and restoration. The theme of the first part is the destruction of the old Israel; the theme of the second part is the reconstruction of the new Israel. On this basis we get the following analysis:

I. The Destruction of the Old Israel—Chs. 1-24
   1. The Prophet's Call (Chs. 1-3)
   2. The Impending Judgment (Chs. 4-7)
   3. The Lord's Withdrawal (Chs. 8-11)
   4. The Moral Necessity of Judgment
     (Chs. 12-19)
   5. The Divine Necessity of Judgment
     (Chs. 20-24)

II. The Reconstruction of the New Israel—
    Chs. 25-48
   1. The Doom of Hostile Nations
     (Chs. 25-32)

2. The New Nation of Israel (Chs. 33-39)

3. The New Temple of God (Chs. 40-48).

THE PROPHET'S CALL
(Chs. 1-3)

In the thirtieth year of his age, the age when as a priest he would have begun his service in the Temple at Jerusalem, Ezekiel received a vision of the glory of God among the captives in Chaldea, and was sent to them on a prophet's mission (1:1-3).

1. The Vision (Ch. 1). It was a symbolic and majestic vision of the throne of God. The whole appearance represented not only a throne on which the Lord sat but a chariot on which He rode. Its main features were as follows: four living creatures, with the faces of a man, a lion, an ox, and an eagle (vs. 4-14); beside them four wheels, with rims full of eyes (vs. 15-21); over their heads a firmament (vs. 22-25); and over the firmament a throne, and One sitting thereon (vs. 26-28). These features were all symbolic representations of the holiness and majesty and sovereignty of God.

This vision appears again and again throughout the book and seems to have been always present to the mind of the prophet. It was the background of all his prophecies. It is the most detailed and comprehensive of all the appearances of the Cherubim in Scripture (Gen. 3:24; Exod. 25:18-22; Isa. 6:2; Rev. 4:6-8). It is intended to appeal to the mind rather than to the eye, for it could not be transferred to canvas. The most significant feature about it is the presence of the Spirit in the midst of it (1:12, 20-21; 2:2; 3:12, 14, 24).

2. The Voice (Chs. 2-3). The prophet, who is always addressed as "son of man", was now given his commission. He was sent to the rebellious house of Israel as represented in the captivity (2:1-7). The word "rebellious" is used repeatedly, emphasizing the stubborn character of the people. Ezekiel was warned not to be rebellious, and was given a book to eat wherein were written "lamentations, and mourning, and woe". Thus was indicated the nature of the message he had to deliver. But it was sweet to his taste, because it was the word of God (2:8—3:3). He was commanded to speak to the house of Israel the words that God gave him, "whether they will hear, or whether they will forbear" (3:4-11).

Ezekiel was then carried by the Spirit to a community of the captives at Tel-abib, where he sat in silence seven days (3:12-15). There the Lord established him as a watchman to the house of Israel, to warn the wicked man from his wicked way (3:16-21). Here the individual relation of man to God is brought out, thus preparing for the building up of the new Israel on that principle. Ezekiel's office was to include the function of the pastor as well as that of the prophet. The glory of the Lord appeared to him again, and commanded him to shut himself in his house and speak only when the Lord opened his mouth and gave him a message (3:22-27).

The Divine name used by the prophet is not "Jehovah Elohim" (Lord God), but "the Lord Jehovah" (2:4; 3:11, 27). It occurs over two hundred times in the book, thus showing Ezekiel's conception of the sovereign majesty of the God of Israel, whose spokesman he is. In contrast with the glory of God, the prophet himself is only a "son of man". This title is used of him about ninety times.

THE IMPENDING JUDGMENT
(Chs. 4-7)

The prophet was now called upon to pronounce the judgment of the Lord against both the city of Jerusalem and the land of Israel.

1. Against the City of Jerusalem (Chs. 4-5). Four symbolic acts are described which the prophet was commanded to perform: portraying the siege of the city on a tile (4:1-3); lying on his side for two periods of time, thus symbolizing Israel and Judah bearing their iniquity (4:4-8); weighing his food and drink, thus suggesting scarcity and famine during the siege (4:9-17); using a sword as a razor upon his hair, denoting the slaughter of the inhabitants around the city on its capture and their dispersion over the world (5:1-4).

The lesson of these signs is then given (5:5-17). Jerusalem, set in the midst of the nations and favoured of God above them all, had even exceeded them in wickedness. She had defiled His sanctuary with her abominations. Therefore her chastisement would be unexampled in severity.

2. Against the Land of Israel (Chs. 6-7). The prophet was then commanded to set his face "toward the mountains of Israel", the seats of her idolatry, and declare that the Lord would bring the sword upon them with a desolating judgment of war, famine, and pestilence (6:1-7). After these awful descriptions of judgment comes a promise that there should be a remnant, scattered among the nations, who would turn to God in repentance and be saved (6:8-10). This is followed by a recapitulation of the preceding judgments (6:11-14).

The judgment of the nation would be complete and thoroughgoing: "the end is come" (7:1-13). Then a graphic description is given of the dissolution of the state and the paralyzing terror that should seize all classes (7:14-27). The Divine purpose in the judgment is indicated in a statement repeated again and again in these chapters: "They shall know that I am Jehovah" (6:7, 10, 13, 14; 7:4, 27). It occurs about fifty times in the book.

THE LORD'S WITHDRAWAL
(Chs. 8-11)

In this series of visions the prophet was transported in a trance from his place of exile in Chaldea to Jerusalem (8:1-4). There he was shown the abominations of idolatry that were practised in the very sanctuary itself, and the consequent withdrawal from it of the symbol of the Lord's presence.

1. The Pollution of the Temple (Ch. 8). Ezekiel was shown one after another the manifold and abominable idolatries carried on in the very house of God. Such abominations made it necessary for the Lord to withdraw—to "go far off from my sanctuary". His people having so defiled His house, He could no longer dwell there.

2. Judgment Beginning at the Temple (Ch. 9). The executioners of Divine judgment were now summoned. They were commissioned to smite the guilty in the city, the faithful being first set apart by a heavenly agent, a man "clothed in linen", who set a mark upon their foreheads. They were to begin in the Temple—"at my sanctuary" (vs. 1-7). The vision appalled the prophet, and he cried out in intercession. But the sin of Israel and Judah was so great that the judgment was irrevocable (vs. 8-11). This sublime and awful chapter depicts the discriminating and deliberate procedure of the wrath of God.

3. The Lord's Withdrawal from the Temple (Ch. 10). The vision of the Cherubim appears again. A command was given to "the man clothed in linen" to take fire from between the wheels and scatter it over the guilty city (vs. 1-8). The Cherubim then prepared to depart from the Temple, and the glory of the Lord moved from the inner court to the eastern gate of the outer court (vs. 9-22).

4. The Lord's Withdrawal from the City (Ch. 11). The prophet was taken to the east gate of the Temple, and he saw there a group of rulers plotting evil. Instructed by the Spirit, he uttered a prophecy against them (vs. 1-12). As he prophesied one of the princes died, and Ezekiel appealed to God for the remnant. The appeal was answered by a promise for the scattered exiles of Israel. The Lord would be a sanctuary for them in the countries where they should come (vs. 13-16). His spiritual presence would be with them instead of the symbolical presence that dwelt in the Temple. Here is the first hint of a spiritual temple.

The Lord goes on to say that He would restore them to their land, and give them a new heart and a new spirit to enable them to walk in His ways (vs. 17-21). Here we have the principles of the new Covenant, already announced by Jeremiah (Jer. 31: 31-34), coming into operation in the new order which Ezekiel is announcing. Then the prophet was shown a vision of the glory of the Lord finally departing from the city and standing over the Mount of Olives (vs. 22-25). The successive stages of withdrawal in this series of visions emphasize the great reluctance of the Lord in departing and leaving the guilty city to its doom.

The Moral Necessity of Judgment
(Chs. 12-19)

This section contains a series of prophetic announcements showing that the sin of the people made it necessary for the Lord to bring speedy judgment upon them.

1. The Exile of Judah Depicted (Ch. 12). The prophet was commanded to prepare "stuff for removing", and to dig through the wall of his house and carry it forth on his shoulders in the dusk of the evening (vs. 1-7). Next day he explained this action as a sign that the king and the people of Jerusalem would be removed into exile and captivity in Babylon (vs. 8-16). He was also charged to adopt another sign, that of eating and drinking with trembling and fearfulness, and so depict the nature of the desolations that were coming upon them (vs. 17-20).

Then the prophet was commanded to answer the current objections in Israel about prophecies of judgment, that such warnings had been uttered for a long time and had not come to pass, and that Ezekiel's present prophecies referred to a distant future. He was to tell them that the Lord would perform His word in their days and would delay these things no longer (vs. 21-28).

2. The False Prophets Denounced (Ch. 13). They speak out of their own heart, and say "Peace" when there is no peace, thus giving a sense of false security (vs. 1-16). The prophetesses also have been guilty of the same evil. They "hunt the souls" of God's people by their practices (vs. 17-23). False prophetesses are not mentioned elsewhere in the Old Testament.

3. The Secret Idolaters Denounced (Ch. 14). Some of the elders of Israel came to enquire of the prophet and yet had idols in their hearts. The Lord declared that these men were estranged from Him, and He would set His face against them (vs. 1-11). Then He goes on to declare that He would not spare the land for the sake of the righteous that might be therein: "though these three men, Noah, Daniel, and Job, were in it". He would send His "four sore judgments" upon it, the judgments described in Lev. 26: 21-26 (vs. 12-21). Yet a remnant should be left, to prove that what the Lord had done had not been in vain (vs. 22-23).

4. Judah's Ripeness for Judgment (Chs. 15-17). These chapters contain a number of symbolical and allegorical prophecies bringing out the fact that Judah was quite ready for judgment.

(1) The half-burned vine fit for nothing but the fire (ch. 15). Such is the nation that has failed to fulfil the purpose for which it was chosen.

(2) The foundling child who became a faithless wife (ch. 16). This allegory, which is wrought out at great length, sets forth the whole history of Israel in three parts, depicting her sin (vs. 1-34), her punishment (vs. 35-52), and her final restoration (vs. 53-63).

(3) The two eagles and the treacherous cedar (ch. 17). This chapter contains a "riddle" or "parable" about two eagles and a cedar plant (vs. 1-10), followed by its explanation (vs. 11-21). The eagles were Egypt and Babylon, and the treacherous plant was Zedekiah the king of Judah, who was put on the throne by Babylon but sought an alliance with Egypt. The chapter closes with the prophecy of "a goodly cedar", which was a type of the Messianic Kingdom (vs. 22-24). The "tender one" is the Messiah with reference to His lowliness. The "mountain of the height of Israel" is Mount Zion, and the prophecy corresponds with Isa. 2:2-4.

5. The Principle of the Divine Kingdom (Ch. 18). This chapter explains the principle that would operate in the new order announced at the end of the preceding chapter. The people should no longer be able to complain that they were punished for their fathers' sins (Jer. 31:29). The new Israel should be based upon the moral responsibility of the individual and his personal relationship with God. No one should have to answer for the sins of another, but only for his own (vs. 1-4).

Several examples of this principle are then given: the righteous man who follows the ways of the Lord (vs. 5-9), the wicked son of a righteous man (vs. 10-13), the righteous son of a wicked man (vs. 14-20), and a moral change on the part of an individual one way or the other (vs. 21-24). Still the people complained that the Lord's ways were unjust, and He replied with another statement of the fundamental principle of His moral government: their ways were unjust and He judged them according to their ways (vs. 25-30). Then He made a tender appeal to them to return to Him, so that their iniquity should not be their ruin and that they might get a new heart and a new spirit: "for why will ye die, O house of Israel?" (vs. 30-32).

6. A Lamentation for the Princes of Judah (Ch. 19). The prophet was commanded to utter this dirge over the fall of the royal family in the closing years of the kingdom. The figure of the lioness represents the monarchy as a whole. Her two whelps, captured in pits, represent Jehoahaz who was taken to Egypt (vs. 1-4), and Jehoiachin who was taken to Babylon (vs. 5-9). The figure of a

vine transplanted to a barren land represents the fate of Zedekiah (vs. 10-14).

Josiah, the last good king of Judah, fell at Megiddo in 608 B.C. Jehoahaz his son succeeded him and reigned three months. Jehoiakim, another son of Josiah, reigned till 597, when he perished in Nebuchadnezzar's second attack on the city. He is not included in this lamentation. Jehoiachin his son followed him on the throne and reigned three months. Zedekiah, the youngest son of Josiah, was the last of the kings of Judah.

THE DIVINE NECESSITY OF JUDGMENT
(Chs. 20-24)

This section contains a series of prophecies showing that Jehovah's regard for His own honour made it necessary for Him to bring judgment on Israel.

1. The Motive of the Lord's Action (20:1-44). Certain elders of Israel having come to Ezekiel to enquire of the Lord (vs. 1-4), the prophet was commanded to declare unto them that the Lord's regard for His own name had saved Israel from destruction in the past (vs. 5-26), and that the same principle required Israel's punishment now. The result would be the ultimate restoration of Israel and the sanctification of the Lord in them in the sight of the nations (vs. 27-44).

Several significant declarations occur again and again in this chapter: "I am Jehovah your God" (vs. 5, 7, 19); "I wrought for my name's sake" (vs. 9, 14, 22); "that they might (or, that ye may) know that I am Jehovah" (vs. 12, 20, 26); "and ye shall know that I am Jehovah" (vs. 38, 42, 44).

2. The Drawn Sword of the Lord (20:45—21:32). The prophet was told to set his face against the land of Judah (20:45-49), and against the land of Israel (21:1-7). The sword of the Lord was sharpened and furbished against His own people (21:8-17). This was further explained as the sword of the king of Babylon, who is represented as at the parting of the ways between Ammon and Jerusalem consulting the oracle and drawing his lot for Jerusalem (21:18-23).

Sentence was pronounced against the royal office in Israel (21:24-27). It should be overthrown and not restored, "until he come whose right it is"; that is, until the Messiah Himself should come, the reference being to the prophecy in Gen. 49:10, which may be read, "till he come whose it is" (R.V. marg.). The Ammonites also were to be destroyed for the sword was drawn against them too (21:28-32).

3. The Indictment of Jerusalem (Ch. 22). The prophet was commanded to act as judge of "the bloody city", and cause her to know her abominations (vs. 1-2). Sins of bloodshed, oppression, impurity, and greed did abound in her (vs. 3-12). Therefore she should be scattered among the nations (vs. 13-16). Israel had become dross unto the Lord. Therefore they must be purified as in a furnace (vs. 17-22). All classes were involved in her guilt, prophets and priests, princes and people (vs. 23-31).

4. The Allegory of the Two Sisters (Ch. 23). Under the figure of the sins of two women, Oholah and Oholibah, there is set forth here the unfaithfulness of Samaria and Jerusalem. The infidelities of Oholah represent the intrigues of Samaria with Assyria and Egypt (vs. 1-10). The infidelities of Oholibah represent the intrigues of Jerusalem with Assyria, Babylon, and Egypt (vs. 11-35). Then there follows an announcement of their punishment (vs. 36-49).

5. The Final Signs of the Judgment (Ch. 24). This prophecy is dated on the day when the siege of Jerusalem began (vs. 1-2). It announced the inevitable issue by the parable of the rusty caldron set on the fire to have its rust consumed (vs. 3-14). On the same day in the evening the death of the prophet's wife took place suddenly, and he was commanded to abstain from mourning, as a sign of the stupefaction which the news of the city's fall should occasion (vs. 15-24). He was to remain dumb and speak no more to the people until a fugitive from Jerusalem should bring news of the city's fall (vs. 25-27).

THE DOOM OF HOSTILE NATIONS
(Chs. 25-32)

The ground is first cleared for the account of Israel's reconstruction by the announcement of judgments on the nations that have been hostile to her. With their disappearance one of the great obstacles to her restoration would be removed. The section contains a series of judgments on seven nations.

1. The Doom of Neighbouring Nations (Ch. 25). Four of the nations around Judah are mentioned, and judgment is pronounced upon each of them: Ammon (vs. 1-7) and Moab (vs. 8-11) on the east; Edom (vs. 12-14) on the south; and Philistia (vs. 15-17) on the west. The reason given in each case is the enmity the nation had shown to Israel. The result in each case is declared to be the vindication and glory of God: "They shall know that I am Jehovah".

2. The Doom of Tyre and Sidon (Chs. 26-28). These states to the north of Judah now come in for judgment.

(1) The destruction of the city of Tyre (ch. 26). This prophecy is dated in the year of the fall of Jerusalem, and Tyre is doomed because of her malicious exultation over that event (vs. 1-6). Her conquest by Nebuchadnezzar is foretold (vs. 7-14), and its effect upon all other sea-faring nations is described (vs. 15-18). Then is announced the Lord's purpose to make her utterly desolate (vs. 19-21).

(2) A lamentation over the fall of Tyre (ch. 27). She is likened to a gallant ship trafficking among the nations (vs. 1-25), and ultimately wrecked, to the consternation of them all (vs. 26-36).

(3) A denunciation of the prince of Tyre (28: 1-19). Because of the pride of his heart and his vanity he should be brought down and die a shameful death (vs. 1-10). A lamentation over him follows in which the sin and fall of Satan, whose instrument he was, seem to be depicted (vs. 11-19).

(4) A prophecy against Sidon (28:20-26). Sidon should be involved in the overthrow of Tyre (vs. 20-24). As this prophecy closes the circle of nations that had exulted in the fall of Jerusalem, it is appropriately followed by a promise of restoration to Israel when these judgments upon her enemies have been executed: "And they shall know that I am Jehovah their God" (vs. 25-26).

3. The Doom of Egypt (Chs. 29-32). These chapters contain a series of seven separate prophecies against Egypt uttered at different times. The people of Judah looked upon Egypt as the great power opposed to the Chaldeans and hoped for aid from this source. Hence the teaching of these prophecies was very necessary for them. The Lord's people were not to rely on any earthly aid. Throughout these chapters runs the refrain, "they shall know that I am Jehovah."

(1)   The might of Pharaoh king of Egypt should be brought down, and Egypt should be laid waste by the sword and become the basest of kingdoms (29:1-16).

(2)   Egypt should be given into the hand of Nebuchadnezzar king of Babylon as his wages for the service he rendered against Tyre (29:17-21).

(3)   The Lord would bring a day of judgment upon Egypt and the nations around her. He would humble the pride of Egypt at the hands of Nebuchadnezzar (30:1-19).

(4)   The Lord would break the power of the king of Egypt by the power of the king of Babylon (30:20-26).

(5)   Pharaoh is warned by the fate of Assyria, which is likened to a lordly cedar of Lebanon brought low (ch. 31).

(6)   A lamentation for Pharaoh king of Egypt, whose fall, likened to the taking of a sea monster in a net, should amaze the world (32:1-16).

(7)   A wail for the multitudes of Egypt, who should go down into the grave with the multitudes of the nations, "slain by the sword" (32:17-32).

THE NEW NATION OF ISRAEL
(Chs. 33-39)

The prophet's mouth had been closed regarding Israel from the time the siege of Jerusalem began until word was brought to him by one of the fugitives that the city had fallen (24:25-27; 33:21-22). Now that the judgment had actually come and the kingdom was in ruins and the Temple destroyed, the prophet began the consoling and constructive part of his ministry. A great restoration was to take place. Out of the ruins of the old nation the Lord would build a new nation. These chapters contain a prophetic description of the new Israel to which Jesus referred when He told the rulers of the Jews that the Kingdom of God should be taken away from them and given to "a nation bringing forth the fruits thereof" (Matt. 21:43).

1. The True Prophet (Ch. 33). His function was to be that of a watchman; the pastoral aspect of his ministry is now in view. He was responsible for warning the wicked man to turn from his wicked way (vs. 1-9). Here we have a hint of the way the new Israel was to be built up—by the Gospel call to the individual. Past sin would be pardoned when the sinner turned to the Lord (vs. 10-20).

When the news of the fall of Jerusalem came, Ezekiel declared that a desolating judgment should overtake those that remained in the land, because they continued in the sins for which the city fell (vs. 21-29). The confirmation of the prophet's past predictions by the news of the city's fall awakened the interest of his fellow exiles in his words, but they were moved by curiosity rather than by genuine seriousness (vs. 30-33).

2. The Good Shepherd (Ch. 34). The Lord was against the unfaithful shepherds who fed themselves and not the sheep (vs. 1-10). He Himself would be the Shepherd of His people (vs. 11-16). This passage is the basis of our Lord's words about "the good shepherd" in John 10:11-16. The gathering of the sheep here is not merely the gathering of scattered Israel, but also of the other sheep, "which are not of this fold". He would judge between the sheep, too, and "set up one shepherd over them, even my servant David" (vs. 17-24). He would also make "a covenant of peace" with them

and make their land fruitful with "showers of blessing", and none should make them afraid (vs. 25-31). All this is a prophetic description of the redemption of the Lord Jesus Christ, and the blessings of the Christian dispensation.

3. The Fruitful Land (35:1-36:15). This section begins with the Lord's judgment on Edom: "Behold, I am against thee, O mount Seir." She was to be made a perpetual desolation because of her perpetual enmity to Israel (ch. 35). The prophecy continues with the Lord's announcement to Israel of His judgment upon the foe who had made the land desolate (36:1-7).

Over against this desolation of Edom is set the promise of abundant blessing for "the mountains of Israel". "Behold I am for you", declared the Lord. The land was to become luxuriantly fruitful; men were to be multiplied in it; the cities were to be built, and waste places restored (36:8-15). As Canaan was a type of the "rest" of Heb. 4:8-11, the spiritual life of the Christian dispensation, so this picture of its abundant fruitfulness is symbolical of those "spiritual blessings in the heavenly places" that Christ has provided for His people (Eph. 1:3).

4. The Purified People (36:16-38). The Lord now declared that the reason for His restoration of Israel was regard for His holy name, which they had profaned among the nations (vs. 16-23). His method of redeeming and restoring His people is also declared. It should be that of inward cleansing and spiritual renewal. He would cleanse and purify them, give them a new heart, and put His Spirit within them (vs. 24-31), and this not for their sakes but for His own glory (vs. 32-36). Here is a further enlargement of Jeremiah's prophecy of the New Covenant (Jer. 31:31-34). Then the Lord goes on to declare the condition of this restoration; it should depend upon their own turning to Him in faith. "For this will I be inquired of by the house of Israel to do it for them" (vs. 37-38).

5. The Renewed Nation (Ch. 37). There was now given to Ezekiel the vision of a valley filled with dry bones, which came to life when he prophesied over them (vs. 1-10). The vision was explained to mean that the Lord would restore His people Israel and bring them to life again by putting His own Spirit into them (vs. 11-14). The prophet was then commanded to take two sticks and join them into one stick, as a sign that the Lord would reunite Judah and Israel and make them one people (vs. 15-23).

Thus the method of redemption by the gift of God's Spirit announced in ch. 36 is shown to be the secret of life and the principle of union in the new Israel. Then the promise was repeated that they should all have one Shepherd, "my servant David", who should be their Prince, and the Lord Himself would dwell among them for evermore (vs. 24-28).

6. The Vanquished Foe (Chs. 38-39). These chapters foretell a great invasion of Israel by Gog and his hosts, and their overthrow and destruction by the intervention of the Lord. This attack is described as coming from the outer limits of the world and occurring in the distant future, at a time when Israel would be dwelling in peace and security in the land.

The whole passage is marked by great vividness and force. Some of its features indicate that it is to be taken in a symbolical and not in a literal sense: the seven years for burning the weapons (39:9), and the seven months for burying the corpses (39:11-12). The prophecy should be interpreted in the light of Rev. 20:7-10. It sets forth the final attempt of Satan and his hosts to destroy the Kingdom of God in the world, and their final overthrow and destruction at His hand, an event which lies in the far off future.

THE NEW TEMPLE OF GOD
(Chs. 40-48)

This section is the record of one continuous vision. It occurred in the fourteenth year after the fall of the city. It was the crowning experience of the prophet's life. His ministry began with a vision of the glory of God, and then proceeded to show how the Lord was obliged to depart from the midst of His people and give them up to judgment. It now culminates in a vision of the Lord returning to dwell in the midst of His people and imparting to them the blessings and glories resulting from His redemption of them.

1. The Vision of the Temple (Chs. 40-42). Ezekiel was brought in a trance into the land of Israel, and set down upon a lofty mountain on which the frame of a city was spread out. There he was commanded to behold with his eyes and declare to Israel all that he saw (40:1-4). He was shown a temple already built, with all its courts and chambers. An angel took him from point to point and gave him the measurements of its various parts: the walls and gates (40:5-16), the outer court (40:17-27), the inner court (40:28-49), the temple house (ch. 41), and the chambers surrounding the house (42:1-14). Finally the outside measurements of the whole temple were given, 500 reeds on each side (42:15-20). As the measuring reed was "six cubits long, of a cubit and a handbreadth each," which would be about ten feet, (40:5), the temple of the prophet's vision covered nearly a square mile, and so would give the impression of great spaciousness.

No command is given anywhere in the course of the vision that the Israelites were to build this temple; nor did they ever understand it so. When they returned from the Exile, they did not attempt to rebuild the Temple on this plan. This is a temple not made with hands, for God is its architect and builder. It is exhibited to the mental eye of the prophet in an idealized form. All the objects seen by him "in the visions of God" were of this nature (1:1; 8:3; 40:2). It represents the Lord's provision for dwelling in the midst of His people in the new age, according to His promise already given in the closing verses of ch. 37. As the old Temple was an embodied representation of God's relation to Israel under the old dispensation, so the temple of this vision is a symbolic representation of His relation to the new Israel when redeemed and restored (Eph. 2:19-22; Heb. 8:1-2).

The old Temple had been defiled by the sin and idolatry of Israel. The measurements of this spacious temple were intended to set forth the complete and abundant provision that God was going to make for the separation of His people from defilement and for their fellowship with Him in holiness and righteousness.

2. The Lord's Return to the Temple (43:1-12). Ezekiel had told before of seeing the glory of the Lord departing from the old Temple (ch. 11). Here he sees the same Divine symbol returning to the new temple, and coming by the way that He had gone (vs. 1-5). Then the voice of the Lord is heard from within the house, saying that He has come to dwell in the midst of His people for ever (vs. 6-9).

Ezekiel is now commanded to show Israel the form and fashion of the house (vs. 10-12).

In the preceding description of the temple no mention is made of the Ark of the Covenant, which was the very heart and centre of the old system. The interior of the sanctuary stood empty, waiting for the entrance of the Lord Himself, that He might come and fill it with His glory. He comes now in His own Person. This vision has had its fulfilment in the descent of the Holy Spirit on the Day of Pentecost, when the Lord Himself came to dwell in the midst of His disciples and make of them His spiritual temple (Acts 2:1-4; 1 Cor. 3:16; Eph. 2:22).

3. The Altar of Burnt Offering (43:13-27). The measurements of the altar are given (vs. 13-17), and the sacrifices by which it was to be consecrated, "in the day when they shall make it", that is, when the vision should be realized (vs. 18-27). These instructions do not mean that the old ritualistic sacrifices are to be restored, for this altar, like the temple, is not erected by man. These sacrifices are symbolic of the atoning sacrifice by which the spiritual temple of Ezekiel's vision was opened to Israel, and they were fulfilled on Calvary. The seven days through which these sin offerings were to be made mark the completeness and sufficiency of the sin offering that was offered there.

4. The Ordinances of the Temple (Chs. 44-46). These chapters contain regulations for preserving the holiness of the house. Israel is warned to keep it free from defilement (44:1-8). The duties of the priests are then set forth (44:9-27). They were to "teach my people the difference between the unclean and the clean". There is no mention of the high priest, for Christ Himself was to be the High Priest of this temple. The priests were to have no property, for the Lord was to be their inheritance (44:28-31).

The section also describes the setting apart of what was to be "a holy portion of the land". It was to be occupied by the priests and the Levites and the prince, and in the midst of it was to be the sanctuary (45:1-8). Then follow the duties of the prince, and the offerings to be given him for the support of the sacrifices (45:9-17), the offerings for the monthly cleansing of the sanctuary (45:18-20) and for the Passover and the Feast of Tabernacles (45:21-25), the offerings of the prince on the various feasts (46:1-15), and his rights and obligations regarding gifts (46:16-18). Finally Ezekiel was shown the boiling houses where the servants of the sanctuary prepared the sacrifices of which the people were to partake (46:19-24).

Here again there is no reference to literal sacrifices. All this is still part of the prophet's vision. These offerings and sacrifices were intended to set forth the spiritual conditions under which the people of the new Israel should maintain their fellowship with God in the new age. There was no other way of representing these conditions to an Old Testament saint. To take these chapters literally would do violence to other Scriptures. The restoration of the Levitical sacrifices, even as a memorial of the sacrifice of Christ, would be out of keeping with the new age.

The prophet Isaiah had already foreseen that a time would come when a material temple and actual sacrifices would not be required for the worship of God (66:1-3), and the Epistle to the Hebrews shows that it would be dishonouring the sacrifice of Christ to return to them (6:6). In Ezekiel there is no reference to the Day of Atonement or the Feast of Weeks, for these were typical events that were to happen once for all. They were fulfilled in the Cross of Christ and the Day of Pentecost. But the redeemed people must be kept continually under the efficacy of the Cross and in the fellowship of the Spirit, and that is the significance of the sacrifices of Ezekiel's vision.

5. The River Flowing from the Temple (47:1-12). The prophet was now shown a stream of living water issuing from within the temple and flowing down toward the Dead Sea. This symbol of spiritual life and blessing is no new thing in the Old Testament. It is found in Psa. 46 and Isa. 35. Its fulfillment takes us into the New Testament age and the Christian dispensation, as is revealed by such passages as John 4:14; 7:37-39; and Rev. 22:1-2.

Here the vision shows that the river of living water was to spring from the new spiritual order which Ezekiel's temple symbolized. Its source was within the temple house, where the Lord Himself dwelt (vs. 1-2). In its course it kept deepening all the way (vs. 3-5). Its effect was healing, fertilizing, and life-giving wherever it went (vs. 6-12). It was symbolical of the spiritual blessings that began to flow with the outpouring of the Holy Spirit at Pentecost, and have been flowing ever since from the ascended Lord in the midst of the Throne.

6. The Inheritance of the Land (47:13—48:7). The inheritance of Israel is next set forth. The people were to inherit the land equally, "one as well as another", all that the Lord had promised to give them (47:13-20). They were also to share it with the strangers who became members of the new Israel (47:21-23). Here we have a symbol of "the inheritance of the saints" (Col. 1:12; Eph. 1:14). The tribes were to be arranged in parallel strips of equal width running east and west: seven north of the city (48:1-7), and five south of the city (48:23-29).

7. The Sanctuary and the City (48:8-35). Besides the portions allotted to the various tribes, a special section of the land was to be set apart with the sanctuary in the midst of it, which is described as "the oblation that ye shall offer to Jehovah" (vs. 8-9). Portions of this were for the priests and the Levites, and none of it was to be sold, for it was most holy (vs. 10-14). Another portion was assigned to the city, including its "suburbs", which meant land for cultivation by the inhabitants of the city (vs. 15-19).

The remaining portion was to constitute the inheritance of the prince. This was in two parts, comprising territory on each side of the oblation, and the sanctuary was in the middle (vs. 21-22). This sacred portion of the land, which was to be offered as "a holy oblation," extended around the city and the sanctuary. It occupied a great square of 25,000 reeds on each side (v. 20). As the mea-

suring reed was about ten feet long (40:5), this would mean that it was about fifty miles square. It would give the impression of great enlargement over the area occupied by the old city of Jerusalem.

Ezekiel began his account of the vision of the new temple of God by referring to "the frame of a city" which he saw on the south (40:2). Now he brings his account to a close by telling us about its gates (vs. 30-35). It was an exact square; and it had twelve gates, three on each side, named after the twelve tribes of Israel, giving every tribe an entrance into the city. The circuit of the city was 18,000 reeds, which would be nearly thirty-five miles.

Then the prophet closes his vision and his book with the name of the city: "Jehovah is there". This gives us the key to the whole vision. It is a symbolic and ideal representation of the Lord's presence in the midst of His people in the new age. Its New Testament counterpart is "the holy city, new Jerusalem," which John saw "coming down out of heaven from God", when a voice from the throne declared: "Behold, the tabernacle of God is with men, and he shall dwell with them, and they shall be his peoples, and God himself shall be with them, and be their God" (Rev. 21:2-3).

THE MESSAGE OF EZEKIEL

This book magnifies the majesty and glory of God. The usual title given Him is, "the Lord Jehovah", and the motive of His action, both in judgment and in mercy, is his own glory: "They shall know that I am Jehovah".

Ezekiel makes very few personal references to the coming Redeemer, but he adds one important feature to the portrait which the preceding prophets have drawn. The Messiah, whom the Lord calls "my servant David", was to be the Shepherd of His people (34:23-24; 37:24-25). The promise is fulfilled in the One who called Himself "the good shepherd" (John 10:11), whom Peter calls "the chief shepherd" (1 Pet. 5:4), and the writer to the Hebrews calls "the great shepherd" (Heb. 13:20).

The special contribution which Ezekiel makes to the developing plan of Divine redemption is the idea of a spiritual world. This is not stated in so many words, but the very symbolism of the book suggests it, and the light of the New Testament brings it out. Isaiah had told of the coming redemption, and had shown that it would be accomplished by the righteous Servant of the Lord, suffering for His people and making atonement for their sin. Jeremiah had declared that it would be secured by a New Covenant, through which God's law should be written on the hearts of His people and they should be given power to fulfil it. Ezekiel now reveals the fact that all this would result in the establishment of a new Israel and a new order of things. Salvation would be realized in a new spiritual system, of which the old Mosaic system was but a shadow and type.

THE BOOK OF DANIEL

DANIEL was one of a group of high born youths among the captives of Judah taken to Babylon by Nebuchadnezzar in 604 B.C. (1:1-4). He and his three companions were given Babylonian names, and were instructed in the language and learning of the Chaldeans and afterwards employed in the king's service. Among them Daniel became pre-eminent. He rose to a place of the highest honour and dignity among all the wise men of Babylon (2:48-49). He remained in office throughout the seventy years of the captivity (1:21).

Daniel was one of the greatest men in all Scripture history. He seems to stand apart from other men in the solitary nobility and refinement of his character. All through his career he was distinguished by two supreme qualities, piety and wisdom. The impression he made upon his own time is shown by the way Ezekiel, a contemporary prophet, linked him with Noah and Job, whose characters were already dignified by antiquity (Ezek. 14:14, 20; 28:3). What Heaven thought about him is revealed in the way the angelic messenger repeatedly addressed him as a man "greatly beloved" (9:23; 10: 11, 19). The secret of his character was his profound sense of the reality and sovereignty of the Lord God, and his steadfast loyalty to Him.

Although Daniel is called a prophet in the New Testament (Matt. 24:15), he did not occupy the prophetic office in Israel. He was a seer rather than a prophet in the ordinary sense. He was also a statesman occupying a high position in the government of a great Gentile power. There he bore faithful and continuous witness to the Lord God of Israel. By the strength of his personality and by his devotion to God, he exerted a powerful influence upon such rulers as Nebuchadnezzar and Darius. And yet, great as Daniel was in himself, the deepest impression produced by his story in this book is not the greatness of the man, but the greatness of his God.

The Book of Daniel was not included among "the Prophets" in the Hebrew Canon. It differs from the prophetic books in not being composed of prophetic utterances. It is made up of two distinct parts, a narrative of certain events in Daniel's life (Chs. 1-6), and a record of certain visions given him toward the close of his life (Chs. 7-12).

Because of its peculiar character, the book stands without a parallel in the Old Testament. It has been attacked as not genuine and as not belonging to Daniel's time. The credibility of the narrative in the first part has been denied on the ground of the historical difficulties and the stories of miracles which it contains. The visions in the second part contain such particular and detailed descriptions of the time of Antiochus Epiphanes and the Maccabees in the second century B.C. that the book is regarded by many as a product of that age.

This view rests mainly upon a disbelief in miracles and in predictive prophecy. It takes the book simply as one of the Jewish apocalypses that began to spring up in the age between the Testaments. But the apocalyptic literature of the Jews was largely due to a misunderstanding of Messianic prophecy. It ignored the ethical and spiritual elements in the canonical Prophets, and looked for heavenly aid only for national and secular purposes. The Book of Daniel, on the other hand, has a distinct Messianic element and a genuine spiritual quality. The march of archæological research tends to support its historicity, and its miracles present no obstacles to reverent faith. It occupies a unique place in the Canon, and serves two important purposes in the unfolding of God's redemptive plan.

1. It vindicates the honour and glory of the Lord God of Israel among the nations of the world. When Jerusalem fell before Nebuchadnezzar and Judah was in captivity, it appeared to the world of that time that the God of Israel had been discredited and that the gods of the nations had triumphed. The fidelity of Daniel and his three companions in the midst of the proud pagan Babylonian empire proved that the Lord God of Israel was God alone, the God of all the earth.

The miracles recorded in the book are an essential part of its message. Miracles occur in the Old Testament only at long intervals, and on occasions of crisis in the development of God's purpose. The time of Daniel was such a crisis. The issue was between the Lord God of Israel and the false gods of the world. The miracles by which the Lord delivered His servants in Babylon proved that He was the living and true God, and that He was the Most High, ruling in heaven and on earth.

2. The book also gives the background of world history from the fall of Jerusalem to the coming of the Messiah and the establishment of the Kingdom of God. Although the Lord had put His own chosen nation aside for the time being, His purpose of redemption was still moving on. The point of view, however, has now been changed from Judah and Jerusalem to the Gentile kingdoms of the world. The times of the Gentiles have begun (Luke 21:24). From his high position in the government of a great world empire, Daniel looked out upon a world in which his own people were exiles. He was given a series of visions which revealed the general course and character of world history from his time onward.

Thus Daniel is the seer of the times of the Gentiles. His message was intended to comfort the faithful remnant among the Jews in the midst of the sufferings through which they were to pass while waiting for the Messiah, and to assure them that God was carrying on His purpose still and that His promised Kingdom was sure to come.

The book may be analysed under its two main divisions as follows:

I. The History of Daniel—Chs. 1-6.
    1. Daniel and His Three Friends (Ch. 1)
    2. Nebuchadnezzar's Dream (Ch. 2)
    3. Daniel's Friends in the Fire (Ch. 3)
    4. Nebuchadnezzar's Madness (Ch. 4)
    5. Daniel and Belshazzar (Ch. 5)
    6. Daniel and Darius (Ch. 6)

II. The Visions of Daniel—Chs. 7-12
    1. The Four Beasts from the Sea (Ch. 7)
    2. The Ram and the He-Goat (Ch. 8)
    3. The Prophecy of the Seventy Weeks (Ch. 9)
    4. The Prophecy of a Great Warfare (Chs. 10-12)

THE HISTORY OF DANIEL
(Chs. 1-6)

It is not a connected story these chapters record, but a number of isolated events from Daniel's career. These events reveal the nature of the world in which the Jews were exiles, its proud and cruel character, and its deep hostility to God and His people. They also bring out the high qualities of Daniel's character.

1. Daniel and His Three Friends (Ch. 1). The book opens with the event which marked the beginning of the seventy years of the Babylonian captivity (vs. 1-2). Nebuchadnezzar is called the king of Babylon by anticipation. He set out for Jerusalem in his campaign against Egypt in the third year of Jehoiakim, and fought the battle of Carchemish early in the next year (Jer. 46:2). Soon after that in the same year, he succeeded his father on the throne of Babylon (Jer. 25:1). On this occasion he took captive a number of the choicest young men among the princes and nobles of Judah, that he might train them up for service in his court. Among them were Daniel and his three companions, all of whom were given Babylonian names (vs. 3-7).

These young men remained loyal to God in the midst of heathen Babylon by refusing to take food that was forbidden by the Law. The incident recorded here shows the strength of Daniel's character, his wisdom and prudence, and his high courtesy toward those in authority over him (vs. 8-13). The result of the test that he proposed vindicated him. He and his friends were allowed to proceed with their training without being ceremonially defiled. When their training was finished and they were examined by the king, these four men were found to be far ahead of all the wise men of his kingdom (vs. 14-21).

2. Interpreting Nebuchadnezzar's Dream (Ch. 2). In the second year of his reign, Nebuchadnezzar was troubled by a dream which he could not recall. He called upon his magicians to make known to him the dream and its interpretation, and when they failed he commanded that all the wise men of Babylon should be destroyed (vs. 1-13). While the king's decree was that of a despot, yet he had the insight to see that if the claims of these men were true they ought to be able to discover the dream as well as interpret it.

Daniel and his companions were among those condemned to death. He showed his qualities of leadership and faith by obtaining an interview with the king at once, and promised to interpret the dream if time were given him (vs. 14-16). Then all four young men waited upon God in prayer, and the secret was revealed to Daniel in a night vision. He gave thanks to God in a prayer of adoring praise, and then requested to be brought before the king (vs. 17-24).

In the presence of the king, Daniel first ascribed to God all the glory for the revelation of the dream and its interpretation, disclaiming any credit for his own wisdom. Then he described the imposing image which Nebuchadnezzar had seen, and its overthrow and destruction by a stone "cut out without hands", which smote the image upon its feet and then "became a great mountain and filled the whole earth" (vs. 25-35).

Next he proceeded to interpret the dream (vs. 36-45). The great image represented the course of world power in its unity and historical sequence up to the time when God would set up His kingdom. The times of the Gentiles are here summed up. The head of gold represented Nebuchadnezzar himself and his kingdom (the Babylonian Empire, beginning with the defeat of Egypt in 605 B.C.). Then there should follow an inferior kingdom represented by the breast and arms of silver (the Medo-Persian Empire, beginning with the fall of Babylon in 538 B.C.), and a third kingdom represented by the belly and thighs of brass (the Grecian Empire, beginning with the overthrow of Persia in 331 B.C.). Finally, there should arise a fourth kingdom represented by the legs of iron (the Roman Empire, beginning with the battle of Actium in 31 B.C.).

This kingdom would crush all others by its mighty and destructive power; and it would deteriorate into a condition of mingled strength and weakness represented by the feet, which were part of iron and part of clay. When this last condition should be reached in the course of world history, then God would set up a kingdom of supernatural and heavenly origin, represented by the stone which, Nebuchadnezzar saw, "was cut out of the mountain without hands" and "brake in pieces" the whole image. This kingdom, which should never be destroyed, would overthrow the kingdoms of the world and take their place.

The effect of this interpretation upon Nebuchadnezzar was overpowering. It carried conviction to his mind. He acknowledged Daniel's God to be the supreme God, "the God of gods and the Lord of kings", and advanced Daniel to the head of the government of Babylon and of all the wise men (vs. 46-49).

3. Daniel's Friends in the Fire (Ch. 3). Nebuchadnezzar set up an image of gold of great height, which he commanded all those who held any office in his kingdom to worship, or they would be cast into a furnace of fire (vs. 1-7). Here we have an example of the state assuming control of religious worship. This act, which was prompted by the king's pride, probably had some connection in his mind with the head of gold in the image of his dream.

Daniel's three friends, who had been appointed at his request to official positions in the province of Babylon (2:49), were reported to the king as not worshipping the image. They were summoned before him, and in reply to his threat they declared that their God was able to deliver them out of his hand, and that they would not worship his gods (vs. 8-18).

In a furious rage, Nebuchadnezzar commanded the furnace to be heated seven times hotter. The men who cast in the three Jews were slain by the heat of it (vs. 19-23). Then these three men were seen walking unharmed in the midst of the fire, and another with them of divine aspect. Nebuchadnezzar in his astonishment had them brought forth, and all his officers of state saw that the fire had not even touched their bodies or their garments. Then the king issued a decree acknowledging that the God of Shadrach, Meshach, and Abed-nego had "delivered his servants that trusted in him", and forbidding any one to speak against Him, "because there is no other god that can deliver after this sort". Then he promoted the three Jews to higher office (vs. 24-30).

4. Nebuchadnezzar's Madness (Ch. 4). This chapter contains a proclamation published by Nebuchadnezzar himself. He begins with an ascription of praise to the Most High God (vs. 1-3). Then he goes on to tell of a dream that troubled him. When the magicians could not interpret the dream for him, he told it to Daniel (vs. 4-9). He saw a tree, towering to heaven, giving shelter to the beasts and the birds. Then an angel from heaven gave a command to cut it down, leaving only the stump in the

earth, till seven times should pass over it (vs. 10-18).

The effect upon Daniel when the meaning of the dream flashed upon him was profound, and shows his high regard for Nebuchadnezzar. The king, who had become so great, was to be driven from men and live with the beasts of the field for seven years, till he should acknowledge that "the Most High ruleth in the kingdom of men, and giveth it to whomsoever he will". Daniel followed up this interpretation with an earnest appeal to Nebuchadnezzar to turn from his sins (vs. 19-27).

All this came upon Nebuchadnezzar a year later. While he was walking in his royal palace, proudly boasting of the city he had built, a voice from heaven declared that the kingdom was departed from him. He was stricken with madness, and driven from among men to live among the beasts of the field (vs. 28-33). At the end of the time he lifted his heart to God, and his reason returned to him. He was restored to his throne and established in his kingdom again. In gratitude for his recovery he issued this edict, in which he praises and extols the Most High God, who rules in heaven and earth, and can abase those that walk in pride (vs. 34-37).

This statement about the power and character of God is a further advance on the two earlier confessions which Nebuchadnezzar had made (2:47; 3:28-29). It marks the final result of Daniel's influence upon him. It is not improbable that the great Babylonian monarch was led at last out of his heathen superstition into the knowledge of God.

5. Daniel and Belshazzar (Ch. 5). Belshazzar, whom recent archæology has identified as the son of Nabonidus the last king of Babylon, and as co-regent with his father, now comes upon the scene. During a great feast that he made to a thousand of his lords, he defied the Lord God of Israel by having the sacred vessels of the Temple brought in for a carousal in which to praise the gods of Babylon (vs. 1-4). Then follows a graphic picture—the fingers of a man's hand seen writing upon the wall where the light was brightest, the consternation of the king, his frantic call for an interpreter, and the dismay of his court when the magicians failed (vs. 5-9).

At this juncture the queen-mother—possibly Nebuchadnezzar's widow, but more probably the wife of Nabonidus—came into the banquet hall and told the king of Daniel whom "the king Nebuchadnezzar thy father, the king, I say, thy father, made master of the magicians". The wife of Nabonidus was probably the daughter of Nebuchadnezzar, and the queen-mother could speak of him as the father (grandfather) of Belshazzar. Then Daniel was brought in, and Belshazzar offered him high rewards if he would interpret the writing (vs. 10-16). Daniel spurned the king's gifts, reminded him that the pride of Nebuchadnezzar had been humbled, and charged him with lifting up himself against the Most High God. The writing on the wall announced his doom and that of his kingdom (vs. 17-28).

That same night the judgment fell, and Belshazzar was slain (vs. 29-31). This story agrees with that of the Greek historian Xenophon, who tells us that Babylon fell during a night of "high festivity", and that its "king" was overpowered and slain. Darius the Mede who "received the kingdom" is otherwise unknown to history, but it is possible to identify him with Gobryas, who commanded the army of Cyrus at the capture of Babylon and was made governor afterwards.

6. Daniel and Darius (Ch. 6). When the kingdom was organized under the rule of the Medes and Persians, Daniel was given a high position, and his pre-eminent ability was recognized by Darius (vs. 1-3). This aroused the jealousy of the other officers of state, and they planned the downfall of Daniel. Knowing that they could find no occasion against him except through his piety, they got the king to sign a decree that for thirty days no petition should be asked of God or man except of the king (vs. 4-9).

This request of theirs, which was intended to flatter the king, shows that Daniel's habit of prayer was well known. His loyalty to God never wavered. He continued his acts of prayer and praise three times a day as before, with his windows open toward Jerusalem, and the fact was reported to the king. Darius was greatly disturbed, and showed his esteem and affection for Daniel by the prolonged effort he made to deliver him. But according to the law of the Medes and Persians he could not change his own decree (vs. 10-15).

The king gave the command, and his loyal servant, the aged Daniel, who must have been nearly ninety by this time, was cast into the den of lions. Darius committed him to his God, and spent the night in fasting and mourning. Early in the morning he hurried to the den, and found to his great joy that Daniel was unharmed. In the midst of the lions he was unhurt, "because he had trusted in his God" (vs. 16-23). Then the king consigned Daniel's accusers and their families to the doom they had intended for him, and issued a decree that all people under his dominion should honour the God of Daniel, "for he is the living God, and steadfast for ever, and his dominion shall be even unto the end" (vs. 24-28). Thus Daniel's steadfast piety brought Darius into the light of the knowledge of "the living God".

THE VISION OF THE FOUR BEASTS
(Ch. 7)

The second part of the book (Chs. 7-12) contains four visions seen by Daniel in the closing years of his life. They all belong to the period stretching between Daniel's day and the consummation of God's purpose with Israel. They were intended to give light and comfort to the devout and faithful Jews during the long dark age between the cessation of prophecy and the coming of the Messiah. The vision of the four beasts in ch. 7 is parallel with Nebuchadnezzar's dream of the great image in ch. 2.

1. The Vision (vs. 1-14). In the first year of Belshazzar this vision came to Daniel in a dream one night. The winds of heaven stirred up a storm upon the great sea (the Mediterranean), and out of the sea came four great beasts one after another: a lion with eagle's wings, a bear with three ribs in its mouth, a leopard with four wings on its back and four heads, and a monster of mighty power and dreadful aspect with great iron teeth. This fourth beast, which was different from all the others and more destructive, had ten horns, and among them a little horn arose having eyes of a man and a mouth full of proud words (vs. 1-8).

As Daniel beheld, he saw the Ancient of days sitting upon a throne of fire in the midst of the heavenly court of judgment with the angelic hosts before Him. Because of the proud words of the little horn, the beast was slain and its body destroyed (vs. 9-12). Then out of the clouds appeared one in human form, who was brought near before the Ancient of days. To him was given universal dominion and a kingdom that should not be destroyed (vs. 13-14). These verses recall pictures drawn in Psalms 2 and 110. In New Testament light they set forth the exaltation of the Lord Jesus Christ to the throne in Heaven, and His reign there (1 Cor. 15:25; Mark 16:19; Acts 1:9; Rev. 5:6). This event, in one sense, was a day of judgment for the nations.

2. The Interpretation (vs. 15-28). Daniel was troubled by the vision and asked one of the angels that stood by what it meant, and he was given the interpretation. The four beasts were four world powers that should arise in the course of history. But the saints of God should be given the kingdom and possess it for ever (vs. 15-18). As a whole, the four beasts correspond with the four parts of the great image of Nebuchadnezzar's dream. There, however, world power is seen as a colossal human figure, resplendent and imposing. That is world power as man sees it. Here it is represented in the form of savage and ravenous beasts. This is world power as God sees it, in its essential character of brutalized self-interest.

Daniel wished to know more about the fourth beast, so different from the rest in its terrible destructiveness, and about the ten horns, and about the other horn before which three of them fell, "whose look was more stout than its fellows", the horn that made war with the people of God and prevailed until the Ancient of days gave the judgment to them and they possessed the kingdom (vs. 19-22). The heavenly interpreter then went on to tell more about this fourth beast, and especially about the horn that came up last. It represented a different kind of power from the other horns. It would "speak words" against the Most High, and wear out His saints until the time of judgment arrived; and then the kingdom should be given to them (vs. 23-28).

As all these beasts are symbolical, so also are all the details in the description of them. The fourth beast represents the Roman Empire. The ten horns —a symbolical number—represent the nations that came into being from the break-up of the Empire. The little horn, which came up after them but was different from them, represents another kind of power, a religious power, which arose out of the Roman Empire in the midst of these civil powers, usurping the rule of the Most High, persecuting the people of God, and using the civil powers for its purpose.

Here the Roman Papacy is depicted. The Papal system grew to be the most subtle and powerful of all the institutions that developed out of ancient Rome. No other power in human history has "spoken words against the Most High" as the Papacy has done, by usurping the place of the Spirit of God in the Church of God. No other power has "worn out the saints of the Most High" as the Papacy has done, by its remorseless and unceasing persecution of evangelical Christianity.

In the light of Christian history, the fourth beast, taken as a whole with its ten horns and its other little horn, represents the world order of national governments, with the Papacy in the midst of them making its arrogant claims and exerting its malignant influence. This is the legacy that pagan Rome bequeathed to the world. It all developed out of the old Roman Empire.

According to the vision, this condition of things would continue in the world "until a time and times and half a time" (v. 25), a phrase which occurs again in 12:7, where its significance is indicated. In due season "the great words which the horn spake" (v. 11) would bring down Divine judgment and destruction upon the beast. The national world order would be overthrown because civil governments allowed themselves to be used and perverted by the little horn. The vision points forward to a supernatural intervention of the Lord in human history, and to the establishment of His universal and everlasting Kingdom (v. 27; Rev. 11:15).

THE VISION OF THE RAM AND THE GOAT
(Ch. 8)

1. The Vision (vs. 1-14). Two years later another vision appeared to Daniel, supplementary to the first. He seemed in the vision to be in Shushan, which at a later period became the capital of the Persian Empire. There he saw a ram with two horns pushing west, north, and south, which overthrew every beast in its way and became very powerful (vs. 1-4). Then a he-goat with a conspicuous horn came rushing from the west in the fury of its power, and overthrew the ram. When the he-goat was at the height of its power, the great horn was broken, and four other horns came up in its place toward the four points of the compass (vs. 5-8).

Out of one of these horns there came a little horn, which grew very powerful toward Palestine, "the glorious land." It made war against the host of Heaven (the people of the Lord), and even against the Prince of the host (the Lord Himself). It took away the daily burnt offering and broke down His sanctuary. This desolation of the sanctuary was permitted because of the transgression of the Law, and it was announced that it should continue for 2,300 days, and then the sanctuary should be cleansed (vs. 9-14).

2. The Interpretation (vs. 15-27). As Daniel sought to understand the vision, the angel Gabriel appeared to him, and was commissioned to give him the interpretation. Daniel was at first overpowered by the majestic appearance of the angel, who began by telling him that the vision would be fulfilled at "the time of the end". This phrase means the time between the end of the Old Testament dispensation and the appearance of the Messiah, during which God's redemptive purpose with Israel would be coming to a head (vs. 15-18). The ram with the two horns was the double kingdom of Medo-Persia, the second beast of the preceding vision. The rough he-goat was the Grecian empire, the third beast of the preceding vision. The great horn was its founder, Alexander the Great; and the other four horns were the four parts into which his empire broke up after his death (vs. 19-22).

The angel then went on to explain the career of the little horn. It represented a king of fierce and crafty power, who should arise when the apostate Jews had filled up the measure of their guilt. He would exercise his power and craft against the Lord's people, and "also stand up against the Prince of princes"; but he should be overthrown by an act of God (vs. 23-25). This prediction was fulfilled in the person of Antiochus Epiphanes king of Syria, who attempted to destroy the Jewish race and blot out their religion. His terrible persecution of the Jews began about 171 B.C., and was brought to an end by the deliverance of Jerusalem and the restoration of the Temple services under the Maccabees in 165 B.C.

It was the most subtle, malicious, and persistent attack on the chosen people of God in all the ages before Christ. Behind it was a Satanic attempt to prevent the coming of the Messiah. The vision was intended to comfort the faithful Jews in the days of their persecution, and assure them that their sufferings should last only for a limited time. The revelation was to be shut up and kept safe, for the time of its fulfilment was yet far off. The effect upon Daniel when he heard the angel's message was overpowering (vs. 26-27).

THE PROPHECY OF THE SEVENTY WEEKS
(Ch. 9)

1. The Prophet's Prayer (vs. 1-19). In the first year of Darius, Daniel learned from the prophecies of Jeremiah (Jer. 25:11-12; 29:10) that seventy years were the allotted measure of Jerusalem's desolation at the hands of Babylon (vs. 1-2). As this period was drawing to a close, Daniel set himself to wait upon God with prayer and fasting. Making himself one with his people, he confessed their sin and rebellion against God in disregarding the words of the prophets (vs. 3-8), and acknowledged the righteousness and justice of God in all the evil that He had brought upon Israel (vs. 9-14). Then he appealed to God, whose redemption of His people from Egypt had gotten Him a great name, to turn away His wrath from them now because they had become a reproach among the nations (vs. 15-16). Daniel closed his prayer with an earnest and fervent appeal that the Lord would accomplish His redeeming work for His people (vs. 17-19).

2. The Angel's Message (vs. 20-27). While Daniel was still praying, the angel Gabriel appeared to him for the second time, being sent in answer to his prayer to instruct him and give him a further revelation (vs. 20-23). The revelation was communicated in the prophecy regarding the seventy weeks (vs. 24-27). It is a prediction of the time when Christ's advent should take place, of the work of redemption which He should accomplish, and of the further desolation that should fall on Israel because of their rejection of Him.

The message was delivered with great solemnity. Gabriel speaks in the strain of one who moves within the clear light of the purpose and plan of God. He knows what has been "decreed". He views the whole period from the Divine standpoint. The "going forth of the commandment" is its promulgation in Heaven. It is not the development of human forces that he is tracing, but the working out of the Divine purpose in the details of human history. The passage contains one of the greatest of the Messianic prophecies. Its significance is so important that it will be well to give an extended exposition of it. It is best analyzed verse by verse.

Verse 24. A general statement of the whole period still remaining for the accomplishment of God's purpose with His people. Not seventy years, but seventy weeks of years were still to pass before God's redemptive purpose should be accomplished. Six objects are stated which were to be achieved in the work of redemption. These may be grouped into three pairs. The first pair relate to the sins of Israel which Daniel had been confessing. It was God's purpose, by an act of redeeming grace, "to finish transgression, and to make an end of sins".

This He did when Jesus Christ put away sin by the sacrifice of Himself (Heb. 9:26).

The second pair indicate the means by which this should be accomplished: "to make reconciliation for iniquity, and to bring in everlasting righteousness". Here we have the atonement of Christ on the Cross, and the righteousness of God which He wrought out, now revealed and offered in the Gospel (Rom. 1:17; 3:21).

The third pair refer to the results which should follow: "to seal up vision and prophecy, and to anoint the most holy." Here we have the consummation of the Old Testament dispensation and the establishment of the Christian Church. The death and resurrection of Jesus Christ sealed up "vision and prophecy", by fulfilling and accomplishing their one great theme (Heb. 1:1-2; Rom. 1:1-4). The outpouring of the Holy Spirit on the Day of Pentecost anointed "the most holy", by bringing into being the new spiritual temple of the Church (Acts 1:4-5; 1 Cor. 3:16; 12:12-13; Heb. 10:19-20).

Verse 25. A specific prediction of the time of Christ's appearance in Israel and the intervening period. "From the going forth of the commandment to restore and to build Jerusalem unto the anointed one", should be a period of sixty-nine weeks or 483 years. There are three possible dates from which this period of time may be reckoned, for there are three decrees recorded in Ezra and Nehemiah by which "the going forth of the commandment" from Heaven was progressively fulfilled on earth. They are 537 (Ezra 1:1-4), 457 (Ezra 7:11-28), and 444 (Neh. 2:1-8). By trying each of these in turn, we find that from the second date to the appearance of Jesus at the Jordan in A.D. 26, when He was anointed by the Holy Spirit and publicly introduced to Israel by John the Baptist (Matt. 3:16-17; John 1:29-34), was exactly the period mentioned.

The sixty-nine weeks are divided into two periods of "seven weeks, and threescore and two weeks." During the seven weeks (49 years) Jerusalem was to be rebuilt, and these should be times of trouble. This takes us to the close of the Old Testament age, leaving the sixty-two weeks (434 years) for the long gap between the cessation of Divine prophecy and its restoration in the person of John the Baptist at the beginning of the New Testament age.

Verse 26. A specific prediction of Christ's rejection by Israel, and of the consequent destruction of the city and the Temple by the Romans. After the sixty-two weeks—how long after is not stated— "shall the anointed one be cut off, and shall have nothing". He should appear to have achieved nothing and gained no following, and His life should seem to have ended in failure. This prediction was fulfilled in the Jews' rejection and crucifixion of Christ in A.D. 30.

"And the people of the prince that shall come"— the Prince of the preceding verse, the Messiah Himself, the only "prince" in the prophecy—"shall destroy the city and the sanctuary", and leave desolation behind. This prediction was fulfilled in the capture and destruction of Jerusalem and the Temple by the Romans in A.D. 70. The Romans are called "the people of the prince", because they were His agents of judgment, in the same sense as Babylon was God's "battle-axe" (Jer. 51:20) and Nebuchadnezzar was His "servant" (Jer. 43: 10), and the Medes were His "consecrated ones" (Isa. 13:3). Jesus speaks of them in Matt. 22:7 as "his armies".

Verse 27. A specific prediction of the seventieth week and the Messianic work that was wrought in it.

This verse now takes up the final week, in which God's purpose was to be accomplished in Israel. "He shall make a firm covenant with many": the subject is still the Messiah, for the one consistent theme of the whole passage is Christ and His work of redemption. The reference is to the New Covenant already foretold by Jeremiah (Jer. 31:31-34). The Messiah should confirm the covenant "with many", that is, with the believing remnant in Israel.

The very words of this verse were used in Christ's institution of the Supper in the upper room, when He spoke of His blood of the covenant being poured out "for many" (Mark 14:24). The completion of redemption, represented by the confirming of this covenant, was the work accomplished in the seventieth week. The words rendered "for one week" also mean "in one week", for there is no preposition in the original, and they could be so rendered here. They do not indicate a limited time during which the covenant was to last, but the period within which the covenant was to be confirmed with the remnant of Israel.

The seventieth week began with the baptism of Jesus. By His death "in the midst of the week", three and a half years afterwards, when His "hour" had come (John 17:1), Christ caused "the sacrifice and the oblation to cease". The Levitical system of sacrifices and offerings came to an end in the sacrifice of the Cross (Matt. 27:50-51). The rest of the verse describes the age-long desolation which came in with the Roman invasion, and followed the destruction of the Jewish ceremonial system, which had now lost its true character in God's sight.

Nothing is said in the prophecy about the last half of the week. The three and a half years after the death of Christ extended to the martyrdom of Stephen, when Jewish unbelief finally hardened (Acts 7). The same group of rulers who had condemned Jesus for His Messianic claims condemned Stephen for his testimony to Jesus. After that, the Gospel was given to the Gentiles; the "seventy weeks" allotted to the Jews had come to an end.

THE REVELATION OF A GREAT WARFARE
(Chs. 10-12)

1. The Vision (10:1-11:1). In the third year of Cyrus, two years after the exiles had returned to Judah, Daniel received his last vision. He had been giving himself to fasting and prayer for three whole weeks, when an angel of glorious aspect appeared to him (vs. 1-9). This angel told Daniel that he had been sent in answer to his prayer on the first day, but had been delayed by a conflict with the prince of Persia throughout the twenty-one days.

Here we have a glimpse of the spiritual background of world history. Behind the conflicts of the nations there is a conflict of unseen powers. The prince of Persia was one of "the world-rulers of this darkness" and belonged to "the spiritual hosts of wickedness in the heavenly places" (Eph. 6:12). It is with this invisible world that the prayers of the saints have to do. The angel was now come to tell Daniel what should befall his people "in the latter days", that is, during the time when God's purpose with them would be coming to a head (vs. 10-17). Daniel, who had been overpowered by the vision of the angel, was now strengthened and prepared for the revelation that he was about to receive (vs. 18-19).

Then the angel went on to tell Daniel that he would continue to fight against the prince of Persia, and after that he would meet the hostile approach of the prince of Greece. This was preparing the prophet for the troublous times which, he was to be informed, his people should pass through under the coming Grecian Empire. But the angel encouraged Daniel by assuring him that Michael would stand with him in the conflict as the champion of Israel (vs. 20-21), as he had done at the beginning of the Persian Empire when Babylon fell (11:1).

2. The Revelation (11:2—12:4). This is a prophetic view of world history in its relation to Israel from Daniel's day to the consummation of God's redeeming purpose. It tells of the warfare of the nations through which Israel was to pass. Divine revelation was about to cease, and Gentile powers were to trample Israel under foot for a long time to come.

This prophecy was given to Daniel in order that the faithful Jews might derive comfort and strength from it, by having light on their way as they passed through their time of trial. This accounts for its studied minuteness of detail. It sets forth the nature of world history as a tangled web of earthly politics, full of intrigue, ambition, selfishness, and violence. But it shows how God overrules the schemes of men for His own purposes, and how they work out the will of God in the end.

The historic fulfilment of the prophecy may be drawn out as follows: The course of kingly rule in Persia and Greece up to the death of Alexander the Great ("a mighty king") in 323 B.C., and the subsequent division of his empire (11:2-4). The rival kingdoms of Egypt ("the king of the south") and Syria ("the king of the north") contending for Palestine (11:5-19). The career of Antiochus Epiphanes ("a contemptible person") and his war with Egypt (11:20-27). His persecution of the Jews and his attempt to destroy their religion ("the holy covenant"), and the exploits of the Maccabees ("the people that know their God") and their restoration of the Temple services in 165 B.C. (11:28-35). The career of Herod the Great ("the king"), his godless reign over the Jews, his opposition to the purposes of God and his hostility to the infant Messiah ("the desire of women"), and his ambitious intrigues with the rising power of Rome (11:36-39). The conflicts in and around Palestine during his reign in the early years of the Roman Empire, his policy of favouring both the Romans and the Jews, and his terrible end in 4 B.C. (11:40-45).

At this point a Divine intervention is announced: "At that time shall Michael stand up, the great prince who standeth for the children of thy people". This brings the course of the prophecy to the time of Jesus Christ—the appearance of the Messiah in Israel. But here the detailed prediction stops. The next words foretell the great tribulation which came upon the Jews because of their rejection of Christ (12:1; cf. Matt. 24:21), and proceed with a general description of the Christian age and its final issue (12:2-3; cf. John 5:25-29). This brought the revelation to a close, and Daniel was told to have the book in which it was recorded made safe and secure, "even to the time of the end". Many would then anxiously search for the truth it contained, and the book would give them the knowledge of God's ways (12:4).

3. A Final Message to Daniel (12:5-13). After the revelation had been given, Daniel saw two other heavenly beings standing by the river Tigris where he saw the vision (10:4). One of them asked the angel who had given Daniel the revelation how long

all this should continue. The reply was uttered with great solemnity: "for a time, times, and a half; and when they have made an end of breaking in pieces the power of the holy people all these things shall be finished" (vs. 5-7). When this answer is compared with the statement of Jesus in Luke 21:24, "Jerusalem shall be trodden down of the Gentiles, until the times of the Gentiles be fulfilled", it appears that this symbolic period, "a time, times, and a half". represents that portion of the times of the Gentiles that coincides with the Christian age.

Three times and a half is the same as half a week, and the expression is probably based on the second half of the seventieth week of the preceding vision (9:27). Jesus Christ accomplished His Messianic work in the first half of that week. The second half marks the period in which the New Covenant was finally established with the "many" in Israel, thus bringing to an end the Jewish dispensation, and bringing into being the Christian Church. It then takes on a symbolic significance as meaning the rest of the Messianic age, or the whole Christian dispensation. It has been used already in describing the career of the little horn (7:25); and it appears again in the Book of Revelation (11:2-3), where the same age is described symbolically as 42 months and as 1260 days. Both these periods are three years and a half, and correspond with "a time, times, and a half".

Daniel did not understand the answer of the angel, but the matter was not explained any further. He was told to be at peace, and was given a comforting assurance that the wise should understand when the time for the fulfilment arrived (vs. 8-10). Then the angel added another prediction for Daniel's comfort, which is somewhat obscure (vs. 11-12). Its probable meaning is, that when the sacrificial system of worship would be swept away by the desolating armies of pagan Rome, the time of that tribulation should be limited, and a blessing should await those who patiently endured throughout the period and beyond it.

Our Lord refers to this passage in His prophecy of the destruction of Jerusalem (Matt. 24:15-22). The mention of "the abomination that maketh desolate" being set up (cf. 9:27; 11:31) means that pagan worship would take the place of the worship of God in the Holy Land. Since the Roman destruction of the Temple in A.D. 70, Palestine has been under this "abomination" in one form or another ever since. The prophecy closes with a promise to Daniel that at the end he should receive his allotted portion of the inheritance given to the people of God (v. 13). Here we have a foreshadowing of "the inheritance of the saints" (Col. 1:12; Heb. 9:15; 1 Pet. 1:4), and with this promise the Book of Daniel comes to an end.

The Message of Daniel

This book magnifies the sovereignty of God. The great truth stands out upon it that there is a God in Heaven who rules over the affairs of men. The statement that occurs three times in the fourth chapter may be taken as its key-note: "The Most High ruleth in the kingdom of men and giveth it to whomsoever he will" (vs. 17, 25, 32). Daniel looked down the ages of human history and saw the kingdoms of the world come and go. Behind them he saw another Kingdom arise of a heavenly order which should not pass away.

Through all these successive ages God was working out His purposes of redemption for His people, and would accomplish it when the fulness of the time should come. The Messianic Prince, promised by previous prophets, would come and establish the New Covenant and bring in the New Kingdom. In the meantime, God was watching over His servants and caring for His own in the midst of the tribulation through which they had to pass while waiting for the coming of the Redeemer.

Daniel is thus the prophet of the Advent. The significant feature of his visions and predictions consists in the fact that they indicated the point of time in the course of Israel's history when the Saviour would appear on the stage of world affairs.

THE BOOK OF HOSEA

HOSEA belonged to Northern Israel, and his message was directed to that kingdom. He addressed it under various names—as Israel, Ephraim (37 times), Samaria, and Jacob. He had the southern kingdom also in view, for Judah comes in for an occasional warning. Hosea was an early contemporary of Isaiah (1:1; Isa. 1:1). His ministry began in the reign of Jeroboam II and continued for a long time after the death of that king. Jeroboam died before his contemporary Uzziah, and Hosea continued to prophesy until Hezekiah was reigning in the southern kingdom. His ministry probably extended over the last fifty years of Northern Israel.

This was the darkest period in the life of that kingdom. The story is told in 2 Kings 15-17. The reign of Jeroboam II had been one of expansion and prosperity, but it was followed by anarchy and misrule. Kings came to the throne by the murder of their predecessors. Four of the six kings who followed Jeroboam died by violence.

Through all this period the national character and conduct was very corrupt. The prosperity of Jeroboam's reign had only given increased opportunity for self-indulgence and sin. The calf-worship set up by Jeroboam I had never been stopped. Worse forms of idolatry also were practised. Northern Israel was fast hurrying on to its ruin. The nation sought to strengthen itself against the growing power of Assyria by foreign alliances, but these only brought further trouble. Assyrian invasions occurred more than once (2 Kings 15:19, 29). At last the

Assyrians laid siege to Samaria, the proud capital of the kingdom, which they finally captured and destroyed in 721 B.C. Most of the inhabitants of the land were removed into exile, and thus the northern kingdom came to a disastrous end.

During this period of rapid decline between Jeroboam II and the fall of the kingdom, the prophet Hosea was preaching the messages contained in this book. He had a sad domestic history. His wife proved unfaithful. But the very nature of her sin was the means of helping the prophet to realize the true nature of Israel's sin against God and the great strength and tenderness of God's love for Israel.

The book falls into two clearly marked but unequal parts. The first part (Chs. 1-3) deals with the training of the prophet, and shows how the Lord used the tragic history of Hosea's home to prepare him for his special mission to Israel. The second part (Chs. 4-13) contains the messages which Hosea delivered to Israel after being thus prepared and trained. Through him the Lord carried on a controversy with His people.

THE LORD'S TRAINING OF THE PROPHET
(Chs. 1-3)

Through a sorrowful domestic experience, Hosea was prepared for his special mission, and was brought to understand God's feeling toward His unfaithful people Israel.

1. The Prophet's Family (1:1—2:1). Looking back upon his life, Hosea saw that the impulse that resulted in his marrying Gomer and in bringing such sorrow upon him was part of the Divine method of preparing him for his subsequent ministry to Israel (vs. 2-3).

His family was a symbol of the nation. The names given to the children foreshadowed God's punishment and rejection of Israel (vs. 3-9). The name Jezreel, which means "God will scatter", also implied a reference to the fact that the chief crimes of the kings of Israel since Ahab's time had been committed at the city, or in the valley, of Jezreel. Lo-ruhamah ("not pitied") meant that Israel had forfeited the mercy of God. Lo-ammi ("not my people") meant that Israel was now rejected.

Immediately after this announcement of God's judgment, there comes a promise of the ultimate restoration of Israel. Judah and Israel should be reunited under one head with their numbers greatly increased (vs. 10-11). The nation should yet be recognized as God's people and should yet obtain His mercy. This is indicated by the change in the names (2:1). This verse is closely connected with the latter part of v. 11: "Great shall be the day of Jezreel". The name of the first son does not need to be changed, but is used in another sense: "God will sow".

2. The Unfaithful Wife (2:2-23). The shameful sin of the mother of the family was a revelation of the sin of Israel as God saw it. Israel's apostasy from God was like Gomer's unfaithfulness to her husband. God would visit it with judgment by removing the blessings of the land and bringing desolation upon it, and putting the nation to shame in the eyes of the world (vs. 2-13).

Out of the wilderness of her discipline and suffering the Lord would draw her back to Himself. There should be a national conversion and restoration of Israel, and she should return to the Lord as her Husband (vs. 14-20). He would renew the blessings of the land and take her back into fellowship with Himself (vs. 21-23).

3. The Faithful Husband (Ch. 3). In obedience to an impulse from the Lord, the prophet bought back his erring wife for the price of a slave (vs. 1-2). For a time after that he kept her in seclusion and suspended fellowship (v. 3). This action on the part of Hosea was symbolic of the unfailing love of God in the redemption of Israel, and of His tender patience in chastening His wayward people. The isolation of Gomer foreshadowed a condition into which Israel should be brought when they should be neither in fellowship with God nor worshipping idols (v. 4).

This prophecy had a primary fulfilment in the Assyrian and Babylonian exiles, but has been fulfilled completely in Israel's long history since their rejection of Christ and the subsequent destruction of Jerusalem and the Temple. They are "without king, and without prince"; that is, they have no civil government, neither one central head nor lower officers of state. They are "without sacrifice, and without pillar"; that is, they have neither their old sacrificial system of religious worship nor any idolatrous system. They are "without ephod or teraphim"; that is, they have neither their old means of receiving divine communications nor any false means.

The ultimate issue of this discipline, the prophet declared, would be the national repentance and conversion of Israel. They "shall return and seek Jehovah their God, and David their king"—not the David of the past, but the promised son of David, the Messiah himself (v. 5). This is the prophetic event to which Paul refers in Rom. 11:25-26.

THE LORD'S CONTROVERSY WITH ISRAEL
(Chs. 4-14)

These chapters contain the substance of the messages that the prophet delivered to Israel throughout his long ministry, after being trained and equipped by the experiences through which he had passed. In them are set forth the shameful nature of Israel's sin and the infinite tenderness of God's love. The first verse of ch. 4 contains the key-note of the whole: "Jehovah hath a controversy with the inhabitants of the land".

1. The Essence of Sin (Chs. 4-5). Hosea sees the heart of sin as unfaithfulness to love, and brands the sin and apostasy of Israel in terms taken from the sin of Gomer.

In ch. 4 the address is directed to the people as a whole: "Ye children of Israel". There is first a denunciation of the nation because of the breakdown of all morality, in which both priests and prophets were involved (vs. 1-5). The cause of their sin is declared to be the failure of the priests to teach the people the Law and their rejection of the knowledge of God (vs. 6-10). Then comes an account of the terrible apostasy of the people (vs. 11-14), followed by a warning to Judah to shun the sin of Israel (vs. 15-19). The prophet contemptuously calls Bethel ("house of God"), which was the centre of the calf-worship, Beth-aven ("house of vanity," cf. 10:5, 8). For this idolatry there was no cure but the storm-wind of judgment.

In ch. 5 Hosea addresses the priests and the rulers. They are responsible for the corrupt state of the nation, for the people have followed their lead (vs. 1-7). The prophet then summons the trumpet to be blown in the central places of the land, for God's judgment is coming upon Israel (vs. 8-11). His processes of judgment are depicted in three forms: moth and rottenness, as emblems of slow destruction; a young lion, as a symbol of devouring judgment; and finally, the withdrawal of God from the midst of His people till they seek His face (vs. 12-15).

2. The Need of Repentance (Chs. 6-7). The prophet now associates himself with the people and utters a plaintive appeal for repentance (6:1-3). Whatever local application these words may have had, there is an evident Messianic reference in them, for they have their ultimate fulfilment in the resurrection and ascension of Christ and in the subsequent outpouring of the Holy Spirit.

But there was no evidence of repentance in Israel in those days, and the Lord's disappointment over them is declared in the next verses (6:4-11). In the statement, "I desire goodness and not sacrifice", there is no repudiation of the sacrificial system, but an indication of God's purpose in it all.   Jesus quoted this passage on two occasions against the hypocrisy and religious formalism of the Pharisees (Matt. 9:13; 12:7). The Lord desired to produce in Israel the character of goodness and trust in Himself. But instead of this there had been persistent and treacherous transgression of their covenant with Him. "But they like Adam have transgressed the covenant" (v. 7 cf. Job 31:33). The sin of Israel was like that of the first man, a transgression of the known will of God in the face of His great goodness.   Let Judah also take warning: "There is a harvest appointed for thee" (v. 11).

The prophet then goes on to declare that the Lord's desire to heal Israel is being frustrated by the widespread corruption of the people. They are all alike involved in it—the kings, the princes, and the judges (7:1-7). The folly of the nation is shown in its sinful alliances and idolatrous intercourse with other nations, and in its utter ignorance of the decay and ruin coming upon it (7:8-12). There is no sign of repentance, no return to Him when He chastens them, but only a hypocritical pretence of religious zeal (7:13-16).

3.   The Nature of Judgment (Chs. 8-10). The prophet begins his pronouncement of judgment with the statement, "Set the trumpet to thy mouth", and follows it with the announcement of an eagle coming against the house of the Lord. This is a reference to the threatening Assyrian invasion. Judgment is the necessary and inevitable sequel of sin. Having sown the wind, Israel should reap the whirlwind (8:1-7). Because of their alliances with the nations, they should be scattered among the nations; and because of the multiplied idolatries of their cities, their cities should be destroyed (8:8-14).

The character of the judgment is set forth in ch. 9. Israel is bidden to rejoice not, for the elements of joy should fail her. The people should be removed from the land and from the fellowship of the Lord, and prophecy should cease to give them any divine light (vs. 1-9). Israel should become abominable and degenerate, and should be cast away by God to wander among the nations (vs. 10-17).

The case against Israel is summed up in ch. 10. The passage is full of difficulties, but its general sense may be drawn out as follows: The land of Northern Israel was luxuriantly fruitful, and the people were using its very fruitfulness to minister to their idolatry. They were multiplying altars, but God would find them guilty and destroy their altars.

They had no king worthy of the name; and because they had no reverence for the Lord, the king they did have could do nothing for them. Their false swearing in making covenants should yield a bitter harvest of judgment (vs. 1-4).

The citizens of Samaria should be in abject fear for the safety of their gods—the calves of their empty idol worship. The golden calf of Bethel was helpless to save them and should be carried off itself as a present to the fighting king of Assyria. Their own king should be cut off as worthless, like foam upon the water. The high places where their vain idolatrous worship was carried on should be grown over with thorns and thistles to cover the sin and shame of Israel (vs. 5-8). The language Hosea uses throughout is strongly sarcastic. He even scoffs at the military might of the Assyrian monarch by applying a nickname to him—"king Jareb"—which may be rendered, "king Combat," (cf. 5:13).

The sin of Israel went far back: they had sinned since the affair at Gibeah (Jud. 19-20). Therefore the Lord would chastise them and bring the nations against them, now that "they are bound to their two transgressions" (vs. 9-10). The reference here is either to the two golden calves (1 Kgs. 12:28-29), or to the double apostasy of the ten tribes—from the worship of the Lord and from the royal house of David. The nation should have a yoke put upon her fair neck and be compelled to toil for another (v. 11).

The prophet goes on to make an earnest appeal to Israel to break up their fallow ground and seek the Lord "till he come and rain righteousness" upon them (v. 12). In these words there is a foregleam of Christ as the righteousness of God sent down from Heaven. But in the meantime, the wickedness of Israel was to be punished by an overwhelming judgment which should ruin the nation (vs. 13-15). Here we have the prophet's forecast of the final Assyrian invasion.

4.   The Triumph of Love (Chs. 11-14). The last section of the book reveals the very heart of God and expresses the deep tenderness of His love for Israel.

(1)   The Lord's unfailing love for Israel (11:1-11). He reminds the people of His tender love for them when He brought them out of Egypt and trained them in the early days of their national history (vs. 1-4). He is obliged to punish them now and deliver them over to the power of Assyria, because they are bent on backsliding (vs. 5-7).

Then He makes a tender appeal, revealing the yearning compassion of His heart over His wayward people. He would not destroy them completely as He destroyed the cities of the Plain (Deut. 29:23): "for I am God, and not man: the Holy One in the midst of thee". In Him justice and mercy were blended. His purpose was that they should ultimately return unto Him in humble repentance from all quarters of the world (vs. 8-11). At this point the prophecy foreshadows the gathering of spiritual Israel by means of the Gospel.

(2)   Israel's base return for the Lord's love (11:12—12:14). After a reference to Judah's faithfulness (11:12), the prophecy goes on to contrast the faithlessness of Israel, in making alliances with Assyria and Egypt, with the example of their forefather Jacob and his devotion to the Lord (12:1-6). Israel's deceitful and iniquitous method of getting rich is contrasted with Jacob's long and patient service for his wife (12:7-12). Having redeemed

Israel out of Egypt, the Lord must bring home to them their guilt (12:13-14).

(3) Israel's deep fall and ruin (ch. 13). This chapter contains the prophet's final review of Israel's sins and announces their consequences in the fall of the nation. The sin that brought destruction upon them was their turning to the worship of Baal (vs. 1-3). They had forgotten the Lord their God who had redeemed them from Egypt. Therefore He would destroy them in His wrath like a wild beast (vs. 4-8). Their kings were unable to save them, but only proved a curse and brought the doom of death (vs. 9-14). Israel's national existence was to be utterly dried up and Samaria was doomed to a terrible overthrow (vs. 15-16).

(4) A final appeal and promise (ch. 14). The chapter opens with the prophet's last appeal to Israel to return to the Lord their God, and he puts a humble prayer of penitence into the mouth of the people (vs. 1-3). Then comes the Lord's promise of final restoration, in words that are full of love and grace (vs. 4-8). The book closes with a solemn proclamation calling attention to the message which it contains (v. 9). The ways of the Lord are right, and the destiny of men is determined by their relation thereto.

THE MESSAGE OF HOSEA

The lovingkindness of God is revealed more clearly in this book than in any other book in the Old Testament. It brings out the tenderness of His love towards His sinning people. This is His sovereign attribute. The word for lovingkindness or mercy is used sixteen times; its New Testament equivalent is "grace". Herein consists the real and fundamental difference between God and man. It is not a difference between His greatness and our littleness, but between His love and our lovelessness.

Hosea points out that the essence of true religion consists in knowing God: "Let us follow on to know Jehovah". He uses the expression frequently (2: 20; 4:1, 6; 6:3, 6; 8:2; 13:4; 14:9). The New Testament aspect of this truth was stated by Jesus in His last prayer: "This is life eternal, that they should know thee the only true God, and him whom thou didst send, even Jesus Christ" (John 17:3).

THE BOOK OF JOEL

NOTHING is known of this prophet but his father's name (1:1). His own name was borne by many others in the Old Testament. He seems to have belonged to the southern kingdom, for his prophecy has Judah and Jerusalem in view and he makes no allusion to Northern Israel. As there is no reference in the book to Assyria or Babylon, it may be inferred that it dates from before the time when those military powers began to threaten Israel. This inference is supported by the mention of other foes who fit the earlier period of the kingdom (3:4, 19). The place which the book occupies among the Minor Prophets also points to an early date. There is some evidence that the prophecy was uttered before that of Amos. See the note on Amos 1:1-2. This would place it as early as 800 B.C. and make Joel the first of the prophets of Judah.

The occasion of Joel's prophecy was a severe plague of locusts which had devastated the land. This calamity was used by him as a type and warning of a more awful judgment that was to come. It was a sign of "the day of Jehovah". This phrase occurs five times in the book (1:15; 2:1, 11, 31; 3: 14). Any time when God's judgments are in the earth is "a day of the Lord". In its full sense, however, and in the light of the New Testament, it looks forward to the judgments attending the coming of Christ, when the Lord will intervene to punish the wicked and deliver the righteous (2 Thess. 1: 6-10).

The Book of Joel is in two parts, which are separated by the statement in 2:18. In the first part (1:1—2:17) the prophet speaks and utters a summons to repentance. In the second part (2:18—3:21) the Lord speaks and promises deliverance to His people.

A SUMMONS TO REPENTANCE
(1:1—2:17)

The prophet himself speaks throughout this section and utters three separate calls, each more urgent than the one before.

1. A Call for Humiliation and Repentance (Ch. 1). In view of a destructive plague of locusts which has fallen on the land, the prophet calls upon the people to cry to God in prayer and penitence. He first describes the effects of the plague. These appear as he addresses the different classes affected by it: the old men, whose memory goes back farthest (vs. 2-4); the drunkards, who use the fruits of the land for their own self-indulgence (vs. 5-7); the worshippers and the priests, who use the produce of the earth in the offerings of the Temple (vs. 8-10); the husbandmen and the vinedressers, who have lost their harvests (vs. 11-12).

The four different names in v. 4 represent successive swarms of locusts, and so mark the cumulative nature of the destruction they caused. In v. 8 Judah is likened to a young wife who has lost her husband, because the locusts have destroyed her means of offering worship to the Lord.

Then comes the prophet's appeal. The priests are summoned to appoint a solemn fast and gather all the people to the Temple (vs. 13-14). The destruction caused by the plague foreshadows the judgment of the day of the Lord (vs. 15-18), and Joel utters a prayer voicing the cry of the people (vs. 19-20).

2. A Second Call for Humiliation and Repentance (2:1-14). In view of a greater disaster impending, of which the locust-plague was a symbol and warning, the prophet calls upon the people again to turn to God. The call begins with a trumpet-blast, and the judgment is announced as the coming of the day of the Lord (v. 1). It is then described, in terms taken from the locust-plague, as the invasion of a great army.

A plague of locusts was a dreadful and appalling disaster. They came in huge clouds, darkening the sky and making a great noise with their wings. They stripped every green thing from the land as they passed over it. They entered the houses in the villages on their way, for nothing could stop them. They caused a vague feeling of terror and utter helplessness. Their first appearance is described as thy roll up from the horizon (vs. 2-3), then their nearer approach (vs. 4-6), and finally their actual onset (vs. 7-9). The plague was a significant sign of the day of the Lord, and the description now passes from the type to the antitype (vs. 10-11).

Yet the threatened judgment may be averted if the people show real contrition. And so Joel appeals to them to turn to the Lord their God in true humiliation, rending their hearts and not their garments, "for he is gracious and merciful, slow to anger, abundant in lovingkindness". It may be that He will turn from His purpose of judgment and leave a blessing behind Him (vs. 12-14).

3. A Third Call for Humiliation and Repentance (2:15-17). The two preceding calls are now gathered up in a universal summons, introduced with another trumpet-blast. The prophet calls all the people, from the oldest to the youngest, to be gathered for a solemn assembly and fast. Let the priests lead them in a lamentation and in a humble prayer for deliverance.

A PROMISE OF BLESSING
(2:18—3:21)

Verse 18 is rendered correctly in the R.V.: "Then was Jehovah jealous for his land, and had pity on his people." It implies that the summons to repentance uttered by the prophet had been heeded.. The fast day had been held. The people had turned to the Lord, and He had heard their cry. The rest of the book contains His reply to them: "And Jehovah answered and said unto his people" (v. 19). Then the passage goes on to describe the blessings that were to follow their repentance.

1. Earthly Blessing to be Restored (2:19-27). The Lord promises to remove the effects of the locust-plague and to restore the grain and the fruits of the land. He will drive out the locusts into the desert and into the seas—"the eastern sea" means the Dead Sea, and "the western sea" the Mediterranean, (vs. 19-20). The locusts are called "the northern army", probably as a prophetic allusion to the Assyrians, who always invaded the land from the north, and whose subsequent attack on Israel constituted the impending judgment of which the locust-plague was a type and warning.

Then Joel takes up the Lord's promise and calls upon the land and the people to rejoice. The rains shall be given again in their season, and fertility and prosperity shall be restored (vs. 21-25). The people shall come to know that the Lord their God is in their midst and has dealt wondrously with them (vs. 26-27). This part of the promise was doubtless fulfilled in the prophet's own day, in the restor-

ation of the blessings of the earth after the ravages of the locusts.

2. Spiritual Blessing to be Bestowed (2:28-32). The prophet now passes from the nearer blessing to the more remote, from that which is outward and earthly to that which is inward and spiritual. The one was the symbol of the other: compare, "he causeth to come down for you the rain" (v. 23), and, "I will pour out my Spirit" (v. 28). This part of the promise is a prophecy of the age of the Holy Spirit, and its fulfilment began at Pentecost. So Peter interprets it in Acts 2:16-21. Looking down the future from the judgment of his own day, which was a warning of the day of the Lord, the prophet saw the nature of the period that was to intervene before the final day of the Lord should come. It was to be an age of grace, giving men an opportunity of salvation. Paul quotes v. 32 in Rom. 10:13 as referring to the present dispensation of the Gospel.

3. The Nations to be Judged (3:1-13). In the day when the Lord restores Israel, He will execute His judgment upon the nations for the wrongs they have done to His people. The Phoenicians of Tyre and Sidon and the Philistines were singled out for special retribution, because they had sold the children of Judah and Jerusalem into slavery among the Greeks (vs. 1-8). The reference is probably to the pillaging of Judah and Jerusalem by the Philistines and Arabians in the time of Jehoram (2 Chron. 21:16-17).

The judgment is represented as taking place in "the valley of Jehoshaphat". The name means "the judgment of Jehovah", and the play on words indicates the symbolical nature of the prophecy. It was probably based on the event recorded in 2 Chron. 20, which occurred in the reign of king Jehoshaphat. Judah was then threatened by an imposing confederacy of hostile nations. A call is addressed to all the nations round about to equip themselves for battle and march into the valley of Jehoshaphat, to war against the people of God, but in reality to be judged by the Lord through His "mighty ones", whom He sends down for the purpose (vs. 9-11). The judgment is represented under the double figure of reaping the fields and. treading out the grapes (vs. 12-13). The passage should be interpreted in the light of Matt. 25:31-33 and Rev. 14:14-20. It is a prophecy of the final judgment of the world.

4. Zion to be Renewed (3:14-21). The prophecy goes on to picture the great multitudes gathered "in the valley of decision", and to describe the issues of the judgment of the day of the Lord. It would shake the heavens and the earth, but in the midst of it the Lord would be a refuge for His people (vs. 14-17). The activity of the Lord in judgment is represented as going forth from Zion and Jerusalem. Zion, the earthly dwelling place of the Lord in the Old Testament dispensation, was but a type of His heavenly dwelling place. It stands for the seat and centre of power in the spiritual world (Heb. 12:22-23).

The prophecy closes with a beautiful description of the land, once desolated by the locust-plague, abounding with fertility and blessing, and enriched by streams from the house of the Lord (vs. 18-21). The descriptive terms used here signify a combination of material and spiritual blessing. Judah and Jerusalem should abide in perpetual peace and purity. The closing sentence, "Jehovah dwelleth in Zion", is to be compared with the closing words of Ezekiel, "Jehovah is there". God's final purpose in

His plan of redemption for the world is to make a dwelling place for Himself in the midst of men (Rev. 21:3).

THE MESSAGE OF JOEL

Although the theme of this book is the coming of the day of the Lord, yet its central message is one of grace. It is the announcement of the day of salvation, which was to precede the day of judgment. There was to be an age of grace, and it would be ushered in by the outpouring of the Holy Spirit. The promise is fulfilled in the present Christian dispensation.

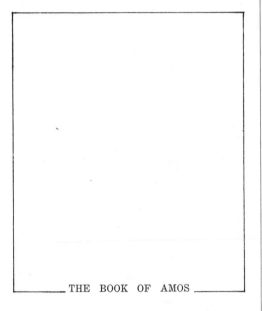

_____ THE BOOK OF AMOS _____

AMOS was originally a herdsman and a dresser of sycamore trees at Tekoa, about six miles south of Bethlehem (1:1). He had no training in the schools of the prophets, but was called directly from his work in the fields to carry God's message to Israel (7:14-15). Although a man of Judah, his ministry was exercised in the northern kingdom.

He dates his prophecy "two years before the earthquake", in the days when Uzziah was reigning in Judah and Jeroboam II in Israel (1:1). This would be shortly after 800 B.C. The memory of this earthquake lingered long in the mind of the nation. It is mentioned by Zechariah more than two centuries afterwards (Zech. 14:5). Amos seems to have foretold this earthquake, for there are two predictions of such an event in the course of the book (8:8; 9:5).

The period of the prophet's ministry was marked by the greatest material prosperity in Northern Israel. But the calf-worship established by Jeroboam I was still going on, and ungodliness and wickedness were increasing. Amos appeared at Bethel, one of the centres of that worship, and spoke against the sins of the king and the upper classes especially with great boldness and freedom. He was charged by Amaziah, the priest of Bethel, with conspiracy against the king and was warned to flee (7:10-13). Amos persisted in his ministry and predicted the fall and captivity of Israel. The burden of his message is national accountability and Divine judgment.

The book falls naturally into three parts. The first part (Chs. 1-2) contains judgments upon the nations, heading up in judgment upon Israel. The second part (Chs. 3-6) contains discourses concerning Israel, and the third part (Chs. 7-9) visions concerning Israel.

JUDGMENTS UPON THE NATIONS
(Chs. 1-2)

These chapters contain a series of predictions of Divine judgment upon the nations, beginning with the heathen nations round about, then taking in Judah, and finally Israel.

1. Introduction and Theme (1:1-2). "Jehovah will roar from Zion"; that is, He will declare Himself in judgment. The words occur in Joel 3:16, and Amos probably took his text from that prophet.

2. Judgments on the Heathen Nations (1:3—2:3). Each judgment is introduced with the statement, "Thus saith Jehovah". Amos is sure of the Divine origin and authority of his message. The expression occurs more than thirty times in the book. The sweep of judgment includes Syria and Damascus (1: 3-5), Gaza and the Philistines (1:6-8), Tyre (1:9-10), Edom (1:11-12), Ammon (1:13-15), and Moab (2:1-3).

The judgment is announced in each case with the same expression: "For three transgressions, yea for four, I will not turn away the punishment thereof". This implies both the cumulative guilt of the nation and the long-suffering patience of God, as though He had hitherto been interposing in His mercy to keep judgment back. The sins denounced in every case are national and social sins, such as slavery, cruelty in war, perversion of justice, violation of covenants and national dishonesty. The judgment in each case is described as a fire that "shall devour the palaces". The palace was the mark of human pride and self-indulgence. The word occurs eleven times in the book.

3. Judgment upon Judah (2:4-5). The sin denounced in Judah's case is rejection of the Law of the Lord. The nation is held accountable for the light it has. Judgment will be according to privilege and opportunity.

4. Judgment upon Israel (2:6-16). This is the real theme to which the rest of the book is devoted, and the prophet has tactfully approached it. All the foregoing has prepared for this. The sins of Israel's national life are described (vs. 6-8). There are four counts in the indictment: maladministration of justice, oppression of the poor, immorality, and inordinate self-indulgence practised in the name of religion. Their guilt has been aggravated by the privileges which God has bestowed upon them as His own redeemed people (vs. 9-12). The "I's" in this paragraph are emphatic. Their judgment will be an oppression from which there will be no escape (vs. 13-16).

DISCOURSES CONCERNING ISRAEL
(Chs. 3-6)

These chapters contain three addresses, each beginning with "Hear this word", and each drawing to its conclusion with a "Therefore".

1. The Guilt of Israel (Ch. 3). "Hear this word" (v. 1)—"Therefore" (v. 11)—. The Lord's verdict is first pronounced against the people whom He redeemed from Egypt. He has chosen them as His own, and therefore He will visit their sin with

special punishment (vs. 1-2). Then by a series of picturesque figures in the form of questions, Amos establishes his right to prophesy. His utterances originate with the Lord Jehovah, who "will do nothing, except he reveal his secret unto his servants the prophets" (vs. 3-8).

The heathen are called to witness the wickedness of the nation and the justice of its doom (vs. 9-10). An adversary shall overrun the land and reduce the city of Samaria to ruins, where the people now sit in careless and luxurious ease (vs. 11-12). In that day a judgment of destruction shall descend upon the false religious system at Bethel and upon the grand houses of the rich and the great (vs. 13-15).

2. The Impenitence of Israel (Ch. 4). "Hear this word" (v. 1)—"Therefore" (v. 12)—". The address begins with a denunciation of the self-indulgent women of Samaria—"ye kine of Bashan" (vs. 1-3). The last clause of v. 3 is very obscure. The R.V. rendering—"ye shall cast yourselves into Harmon"—is a conjecture, which treats the doubtful word rendered "palace" in the A.V. as a proper name, probably meaning Armenia. Whatever interpretation is adopted, the drift of the prophet's words is plain. The nobles of the capital should be cast out of it with dishonour, to minister to the luxury of their conqueror in his palace (cf. 2 Kings 20:18), or to spend their days as exiles in some remote region. Amos then goes on to pour ridicule upon the false religious zeal of their idolatrous worship, which was only adding to their sin (vs. 4-5).

All chastisement hitherto has been in vain. The prophet describes five warning judgments which God has already sent upon the land, and follows each with the solemn statement: "Yet have ye not returned unto me, saith Jehovah" (vs. 6-11). These chastening judgments were famine, drought, blight, pestilence, and earthquake. Finally comes the startling and arresting summons: "Therefore—prepare to meet thy God, O Israel" (vs. 12-13).

3. The Overthrow of Israel (Chs. 5-6). "Hear this word" (5:1)—"Therefore" (5:16)—". This is a lamentation for Israel, a kind of funeral dirge. It announces the approaching fall of Israel in a decimating judgment of war ((5:1-3). The people of Israel have not heeded the Lord's repeated appeals and warnings to seek Him and not to go enquiring at pagan shrines (5:4-6). All the places mentioned had evidently become centres of idolatrous worship. They have been called to turn from their injustice and unrighteousness and seek the Lord their God, whose power is omnipotent in the universe both for blessing and for judgment (5:7-9). It is He who "turneth the shadow of death into the morning", and also "bringeth sudden destruction upon the strong".

They hate the prophet who rebukes them, and go on in their manifold transgressions. And so the prudent man will be compelled to keep silence and leave them to their doom (5:10-13). At this point Amos utters a word for the remnant of Israel, those that will be left after the judgment, and points out the way of deliverance for them (5:14-15). Then comes the "therefore" of doom pronounced by the Lord (5:16-17), and this introduces two "woes," each of which has its own "therefore".

(1) Woe to the hypocrites (5:18-27). These were they "that desire the day of Jehovah", and deceive themselves with false hopes. While hoping to avoid one calamity, they will only fall into a worse (vs. 18-20). The Lord despises their worship, rejects their offerings, and refuses to hear their songs.

It is justice and righteousness that He requires (vs. 21-24). He declares that His people have been addicted to idolatry ever since they practised it in the wilderness. The pagan rites He mentions were of Egyptian origin (vs. 25-26). "Therefore" He will drive them into captivity "beyond Damascus" (v. 27). Here the Assyrian overthrow and captivity is foreshadowed.

(2) Woe to the indifferent (ch. 6). These were they "that are at ease in Zion" and put off the evil day. Let them take warning from the heathen states around them that have fallen, for the same fate awaits Israel (vs. 1-3). They abandon themselves to luxurious living and inordinate self-indulgence, with no thought for the future (vs. 4-6). "Therefore" they shall be the first captives when the Lord delivers up the city to its besiegers (vs. 7-8). Then the prophet describes a scene in the besieged city, when deaths occur by famine and pestilence, and the judgment of God falls on rich and poor alike (vs. 9-11). Their foolish and boastful trust in their own power will by no means avert the judgment, for the Lord God of hosts is raising up a nation against them, which shall overrun the whole land (vs. 12-14). The questions in v. 12 represent what is absurd and futile. The nation referred to in v. 14 is Assyria, but Amos nowhere mentions it by name.

VISIONS CONCERNING ISRAEL
(Chs. 7-9)

These chapters record a series of visions enforcing the discourses. In the midst of them occurred an attempt on the part of the priest of Bethel to stop the prophet's preaching. The visions are progressive, indicating the approach, the imminence, and finally the execution of the judgment. The last vision closes with a prediction of Israel's restoration.

1. The Approach of Judgment (7:1-9). A vision of locusts (vs. 1-3), and a vision of devouring fire (vs. 4-6). In these two visions the judgment is averted at the prayer of the prophet. A third vision follows, that of a plumbline testing a wall (vs. 7-9). This time the prophet makes no intercession, for he sees what the plumbline has revealed. The judgment must now fall.

These three visions may have been designed to represent the three Assyrian invasions of the land recorded in the history of Israel; the invasions of Pul (2 Kings 15:19), Tiglath-pileser (2 Kings 16:7-9), and Shalmaneser (2 Kings 17:3-6). The last of these ended in the fall of the kingdom.

2. The Prophet and the Priest (7:10-17). This incident arose out of the last vision, which contained a warning against the house of Jeroboam. Amaziah, the high priest of the calf-worship at Bethel, denounced the prophet to the king, and then bade him go back to his own land and earn his living there—"there eat bread, and prophesy there" (vs. 10-13). Amos calmly refuted Amaziah's insinuations by declaring that he was not a prophet by profession, but was simply obeying a call that God gave him. Then he foretold the shame and doom of the house of Amaziah (vs. 14-17).

3. The Imminence of Judgment (Ch. 8). The next vision was a basket of summer fruit, that is, fruit over-ripe and ready to spoil (vs. 1-3). There is a play on words here which cannot be reproduced in English. The words for "summer" and "end" sound alike in Hebrew, and this gives point to the

Lord's verdict upon His people. The tragic end of Israel is pictured in a few strong touches.

The prophet followed up this vision with an impassioned address to the money-makers, denouncing their lust for gain and their dishonest practices in business (vs. 4-7). He declared that the land should "tremble for this", and went on to foretell the earthquake and describe its phenomena and the tragic nature of the catastrophe (vs. 8-10). The final issue of judgment would be a famine of hearing the words of the Lord. They that had rejected the word of God should fail to find it when they sought for it. They that had gone after other gods and refused the water of life should perish with an unsatisfied thirst (vs. 11-14).

4. The Execution of Judgment (Ch. 9). This is a graphic vision of the Lord smiting the sanctuary of the calf-worship at Bethel and slaying the worshippers there. The judgment is described as overwhelming and irresistible: all attempts to escape from it would be futile (vs. 1-4). Then the prophet enforces his warning with another reference to the earthquake, which he had predicted, as a manifestation of the omnipotent power of God (vs. 5-6). Israel's election will not save the nation. The fact that God brought them out of Egypt avails no more than His bringing the Philistines and the Assyrians from their former dwelling places (v. 7). Though God will destroy the sinful nation, yet the judgment will result in the sifting of Israel, and no grain of wheat, no true Israelite, will be lost (vs. 8-10). Here · we have an indication of the method of calling out the new Israel by means of the individual call of the Gospel.

The book closes with the final issues of the judgment, and the prophecy now brings us into the Christian age. God promises to restore the house of David, that all nations may gather round it (vs. 11-12). This promise was quoted by James at the council in Jerusalem (Acts 15: 13-18). He saw its fulfilment in the earthly ministry of Jesus Christ as the Son of David and used it as a prophecy of the preaching of the Gospel to the Gentiles. James quoted the passage freely from the Septuagint, which reads "the rest of men" instead of "the remnant of Edom". The final promise is that of the renewal and great enrichment of the land which God had given His people to dwell in (vs. 13-15). This prophecy has its spiritual fulfilment in "the heavenly places" (Eph. 1:3), of which the land of Canaan was a type; but it also foreshadows the restoration of the whole material creation (Rom. 8:19-21).

The Message of Amos

A passion for righteousness pervades this book. Amos represents the Lord as a God of absolute justice. He is the impartial Judge of the nations of the earth, and they are all accountable to Him. He judges them according to the light and privileges they have enjoyed, and according to the use they have made of their gifts and opportunities. This is the prophet's one theme, and only at the end of the book does he point out that, although God's judgment is certain and unescapable, yet its purpose is to prepare for a new order of spiritual and material blessing.

THE BOOK OF OBADIAH

NOTHING is known of this prophet but his name. It was a common name among the Jews and meant "servant of Jehovah". In this case the servant is hidden behind his message.

Obadiah's prophecy is directed against Edom. It was occasioned by Edom's exultation over Judah in a day of calamity, when Jerusalem fell into the hands of a foreign foe (vs. 10-12). There is no reference to the time when this occurred, and the date cannot be fixed with certainty. Several calamities of this kind happened during the history of Judah.

The earliest occurred in the reign of Rehoboam about 950 B.C., when Shishak king of Egypt plundered the Temple (1 Kings 14:25-26; 2 Chron. 12:9). Another took place in the reign of Jehoram about 860 B.C., when the Philistines and the Arabians broke into Jerusalem (2 Chron. 21:16-17). In the reign of Amaziah about 820 B.C., Joash king of Israel broke down the wall of Jerusalem and plundered the Temple and the palace (2 Kings 14:8-14; 2 Chron. 25:17-24). This cannot be the event referred to, for the Israelites could not be called "strangers and foreigners". The last event of the kind was the fall of Jerusalem at the hands of Nebuchadnezzar in 586 B.C., when the city and the Temple were completely destroyed (2 Kings 25:8-10; 2 Chron. 36:17-19). The place which the book occupies among the Minor Prophets would suggest one of the earlier dates, but the description of Jerusalem's calamity in vs. 12-14 best fits the last event. Edom's conduct toward Judah at that time is reflected in such passages as Psa. 137:7, Lam. 4:21-22, and Ezek. 25:12.

The Book of Obadiah is an amplification of the judgment pronounced upon Edom in Amos 1:11-12, and that may account for its being placed where it is. The Edomites, who were descended from Esau, the twin brother of Jacob, were the most bitter and implacable foes of Israel. Edom represents in principle the world in its enmity and antagonism to the Kingdom of God. The utter desolation that reigns among the rocks where Edom once felt so secure bears ample witness to the fulfilment of Obadiah's prophecy. The prophecy may be divided into three parts.

1. The Doom of Edom Announced (vs. 1-9). The nations are summoned by the Lord to make war upon her (v. 1). Her proud and haughty spirit should be humbled (vs. 2-4). Her secret places should be ransacked and plundered (vs. 5-6). Her allies should deceive her, and her own wisdom and might should fail (vs. 7-9).

2. The Guilt of Edom Declared (vs. 10-16). This consisted in violence done to her brother nation Jacob (v. 10). The incidents mentioned in these verses imply that Edom had taken part with foreign foes in an invasion of Judah, entering the cities, casting lots for the spoil in Jerusalem itself, betraying those who sought to escape, and doing all this with a malicious delight (vs. 11-14). But the day of the Lord that was coming upon all nations should bring retribution upon Edom. What she had done should return upon her own head (vs. 15-16).

3. The Future of Zion Foretold (vs. 17-21). In the midst of the judgment which would fall upon

the nations, Mount Zion should be a refuge for the remnant of Israel, and they should be restored to their possessions (v. 17). The restored children of Israel should also have their possessions enlarged, and these should include the territory of Edom and of all the nations around (vs. 18-20).

All this means that the Kingdom of God, which was to begin with Zion, would ultimately extend to all the nations of the world. The book closes with a statement that the rule of God should be exercised from Mount Zion, and His Kingdom should be established in the world (v. 21). The word "saviours" in this verse is an allusion to the times of the judges, who were in a sense types and foreshadowings of the Messianic King.

THE MESSAGE OF OBADIAH

This is the shortest book in the Old Testament, but it has an important message. It foretells the ultimate triumph of Zion over Edom, of Christ over Antichrist, of the Kingdom of God over the kingdoms of the world. The prophecy is a warning of the Spirit of God to taunting and arrogant unbelief. The opposition of Edom to Israel culminated in the attempt of the Edomite Herod to destroy the infant Child in Bethlehem.

The book also states the principle of Divine retribution. Nations will have their own sins visited upon themselves (v. 15). National pride will be humbled by the judgment of God. Edom disappeared from history soon after the Christian era began.

THE BOOK OF JONAH

THIS book differs from the rest of the Minor Prophets in being a narrative about Jonah and not a collection of his prophecies. It is a prophetic story rather than a prophetic message, and it should be read with an imagination that is sympathetic and spiritually quickened. The interest centres in the prophet himself and not in his preaching. Jonah was a native of Gath-hepher in the northern kingdom. He is mentioned in 2 Kings 14:25 as having foretold the restoration of the land of Israel to its original boundaries under Jeroboam II. This would make his date somewhere about 800 B.C., or even earlier.

The Book of Jonah is not an allegory. Jonah himself was a historical person, and the whole story gives the impression of having been written as historical fact. The author would have condemned a guiltless prophet to lasting ignominy if there had been no historical foundation for his story. Our Lord used incidents related in the book (Matt. 12: 39-41 and Luke 11:29-32), and His words would have had no force if He were referring only to imaginary events. Solemn and serious conclusions are not based upon fictitious premises.

The only reasons urged against the historicity of the book are based upon the unusual nature of the narrative and the miraculous incidents it contains. But subjective considerations alone cannot prove these incidents untrue without other evidence. There is no positive evidence of any kind that would go to show that the narrative is imaginary or was written for an allegorical purpose.

The story is consistent and harmonious. It deals with a commission which the Lord gave to Jonah to go and preach to Nineveh, and tells how the prophet first renounced it and finally fulfilled it.

JONAH'S COMMISSION RENOUNCED
(Chs. 1-2)

1. His Disobedience (1:1-3). The charge to deliver a message to Nineveh was repellent to Jonah, and he refused it. His motive was not fear, but uncharitableness. He was unwilling to extend the Lord's mercy outside Israel. This is his own explanation of his action (4:2). He proceeded to renounce his commission and his prophetic function, and to flee from the land of Israel and from the presence of the Lord.

2. His Punishment (1:4-17). Jonah did not escape from the Divine government by his flight. The Lord sent out a great wind upon the sea, presided over the casting of the lots so that they fell upon Jonah, and had a great fish ready to receive him when he was cast out of the ship. The incidents that occurred during the storm are described with great vividness, and bring out the character of the heathen sailors. A significant feature is their kindly and compassionate attempt to save the life of Jonah.

3. His Prayer (2:1-9). Jonah's prayer is made up mainly of quotations from the Psalms, and expresses mingled penitence and confidence in God. It is not said that the prayer was arranged in this orderly form in the belly of the fish. It was composed afterwards, and expresses the penitent appeal he made in the belly of the fish, and his thanksgiving for the deliverance that followed. It ends with a renewal of his consecration to the Lord: "I will sacrifice unto thee—I will pay that which I have vowed".

4. His Deliverance (2:10). "Jehovah spake unto the fish", that is, He impelled it to do His will. The dry land was probably the coast of Palestine, from which the ship had started.

JONAH'S COMMISSION FULFILLED
(Chs. 3-4)

1. The Prophet's Preaching (3:1-4). The patient grace of God is manifested in His renewal of the command to Jonah to go to Nineveh. This time it is accompanied with a suggestion of Divine authority which the prophet would now appreciate: "the preaching that I bid thee". Nineveh was a city of vast extent—"of three days' journey", that is, it would take three days to walk around it. Beyond the city proper were suburbs with a circumference of sixty miles. "Jonah began to enter into the city a day's journey", not in a direct line, but moving about in the more frequented places.

2. Nineveh's Repentance (3:5-10). Before Jonah could finish one day's journey, the impression made by his words and his appearance was so great that he had no need to go farther. The people of Nineveh were profoundly moved, proclaimed a fast, and put on signs of humiliation. This penitential movement spread till it "reached the king". He manifested his own penitential sorrow, and issued a proclamation to make it universal. The repentance on the part of Nineveh was met by the repentance of God, and the threatened doom of the city was averted.

This astonishing result is to be accounted for by the explanation provided by Jesus Himself, who said that Jonah was "a sign unto the Ninevites" (Luke 11:30). News of the prophet's experience would have preceded or accompanied his arrival in Nineveh, and his very appearance doubtless bore marks which confirmed the report. He preached as one who was believed to have come back from the dead.

3. The Prophet's Displeasure (4:1-5). Jonah resented the sparing of Nineveh after he had pronounced judgment upon it, and his uncharitable spirit was manifested in the sullen complaint he made to the Lord, and in his waiting to see what would happen to the city. In this he represented the ancient people of God in their wrong attitude toward the nations around them.

4. The Lord's Rebuke (4.6-11). Again the overruling providence of God appears in His use of the gourd and the worm and the sultry east wind, in order to reveal Jonah's wrong spirit. The book closes abruptly with the picture of the uncharitable prophet, angry because the gourd was destroyed and because Nineveh was spared, set over against the character of God, full of pity and compassion for the great wicked heathen city with its innocent children and harmless beasts, and willing to spare it when it turned in penitence to Him. Thus the book shows how ancient Israel, as represented in the prophet Jonah, missed the deepest thing in the character of their God, and failed in their witness to the nations of the world.

THE MESSAGE OF JONAH

While the chief purpose of the story of Jonah is to reveal the tender compassion of God's nature and the universal sweep of His mercy, it also illustrates the conditional character of prophecy. When the Lord sent warnings and threatenings through His prophets, and the nation repented to whom they were sent, then He did not carry out His threatened judgment (Jer. 18:7-8). On the other hand, also, the promises of blessing which He gave to His people would be fulfilled only when they asked for them (Ezek. 36:37). The prophecies of Israel's national restoration are conditioned on Israel's national return to the Lord.

Our Lord gave the story of Jonah a typical significance by applying it to Himself on two occasions (Matt. 12:38-40; 16:1-4). He spoke of "the sign of Jonah the prophet", and regarded Jonah's experience in the belly of the great fish as a symbolical prophecy of His own death and resurrection.

THE BOOK OF MICAH

MICAH belonged to the village of Morasheth, about twenty miles south-west of Jerusalem, near the Philistine border. He was a younger contemporary of Isaiah, carrying on his ministry in the reigns of Jotham, Ahaz, and Hezekiah (1:1; Isa. 1:1). While Isaiah was preaching in the capital and among the ruling classes in Jerusalem, Micah was preaching in the country districts and among the villages of Judah. Although he was a man of Judah, his prophecies concerned the northern as well as the southern kingdom. He is referred to in Jer. 26: 17-19 as having predicted the overthrow of Jerusalem.

The book consists of three parts, each containing an address beginning with "Hear ye". The first part (Chs. 1-2) is addressed to the Gentile nations, and concerns the sin and judgment of Israel. The second part (Chs. 3-5) is addressed to the rulers, and concerns the coming Ruler. The third part (Chs. 6-7) is addressed to the people, and concerns the way of salvation. Each address threatens judgment and ends with a promise.

THE JUDGMENT OF ISRAEL
(Chs. 1-2)

1. The Coming Judgment Announced (Ch. 1). The prophet begins with an appeal to all the nations to observe the coming of the Lord in judgment (vs. 2-4). The reason for this judgment is declared to be the apostasy of the whole nation as manifested in the sins of the two capitals, Samaria and Jerusalem (v. 5). Then comes the Divine announcement of the doom and destruction of Samaria (vs. 6-7). This is followed by the prophet's lamentation as he sees the invading army reach Judah and threaten Jerusalem (vs. 8-9).

The lament continues with a wailing description of the judgment as it rolls over the towns and villages of Judah (vs. 10-16). It takes up the strain of David's lamentation over Saul and Jonathan, "Tell it not in Gath" (2 Sam. 2:20), and goes on to mention ten places, indicating the completeness of the overthrow. It is a graphic description of the results of Sennacherib's invasion as they were felt in one city after another. Micah's own city was one of them. The fulfilment of this prophecy is not to be restricted to the time of Sennacherib, but extends over all the judgments that fell upon Judah from the Assyrian invasion in 701 B.C. to the Roman catastrophe in A.D. 70.

2. The Cause of the Judgment Declared (Ch. 2). The sins denounced are those of injustice and oppression in the national life. A woe is uttered upon those who "devise iniquity" (forming their plans) upon their beds, and "practise it" (executing their plans) when the morning comes (vs. 1-2). Therefore, the Lord declares, He will "devise an evil" against them, punishing oppression by oppression. They shall receive no further part in the inheritance of the Lord (vs. 3-5).

This prophesying on Micah's part meets with violent contradiction from those guilty of oppression and from the false prophets, who base their protests upon the goodness of God (vs. 6-7). Micah replies by showing that the people have been abusing the goodness and mercy of God by oppressing the poor (vs. 8-9). Then he bids them depart from the land for it would be no resting place for them because they have polluted it, and utters an ironical description of the kind of man they choose as their prophet (vs. 10-11).

Then comes a promise for the remnant. Led by "the breaker" (the coming Messiah), they should break through their bondage and pass on out into life and liberty (vs. 12-13). The verbs used here in the original describe in a pictorial way progress that cannot be stopped by any human power. They look forward to the triumph of the Lord Jesus over death and the grave.

THE COMING RULER
(Chs. 3-5)

1. The Failure of the Rulers (Ch. 3). Addressing himself to the rulers of the people, the prophet denounces the unjust conduct of the princes, whose cruel outrages he likens to cannibal feasting (vs. 1-4). Then he turns to the prophets, who preach peace to those who pay them well, and proclaim war against those who pay them nothing. They should lose all power of vision and be brought to shame and contempt (vs. 5-7). In contrast with them, Micah declares that his own prophetic ministry is animated by the Spirit of the Lord (v. 8). Then he sums up the sins of all the ruling classes together —princes, priests, and prophets. All alike pursue worldly gain and yet profess to worship the Lord and trust in Him. For their sake Jerusalem and the Temple should be destroyed and the kingdom come to an end (vs. 9-12).

2. The New Kingdom (4:1—5:1). The promise of another kingdom is now introduced immediately after the destruction described at the end of ch. 3. The old earthly Zion should give place to a new spiritual Zion, which would be established "in the latter days"—the time of the Messiah. It should be a centre of righteousness, justice, and peace for all nations (4:1-3). This passage is almost identical with Isa. 2:2-4. One prophet may have been quoting the other, or both may have quoted from an older oracle. The prophecy is to be interpreted in the light of Heb. 12:22. There should be plenty and security for all in the new kingdom, and they should walk in fellowship with the Lord for ever. He would gather into it the scattered and afflicted remnant of Israel, and the throne of David should be restored (4:4-8). The phrase, "tower of the flock", is probably an allusion to the fact that David was a shepherd.

In the meantime Zion should pass through a time of trial and suffering before the promised restoration took place. She should lose her king and her government and wander to Babylon in captivity. But the Lord would deliver her out of the hand of her enemies (4:9-10). After that another period of trouble for Zion looms up in the prophet's view of the future. The nations should come against her, but the Lord would give her strength to win a great victory over them (4:11—5:1). This strength was manifested in the exploits of the Maccabees in the second century B.C., but the prophecy has a still wider and deeper application.

3. The New King (5:2-15). The lowly origin of the coming ruler is now announced. It was given to Micah, the village prophet, to foretell that the Messiah should come out of the village of Bethlehem. With this humble earthly origin is contrasted his eternal heavenly pre-existence: "whose goings forth are from of old, from everlasting." (v. 2). In the meantime Israel should be given up to the power of the nations until the time that his virgin mother gave him birth, and then the remnant of Israel should return (v. 3). In this verse Micah refers to two prophecies of his contemporary Isaiah and gives an interpretation of them (7:14 and 11:12).

The results of the new king's rule are then described (vs. 4-6). He would combine the strong tender care of a shepherd with the dignity and majesty of a king, and his rule should extend to the ends of the earth. Under him his people should enjoy peace, and be given victory over all their foes. The numbers in the expression, "seven shepherds and eight principal men", are used proverbially, to indicate the sufficiency of the leaders that should be raised up in his cause. In him also Israel's mission to the world should be fulfilled, for he himself would be "the remnant of Jacob" (vs. 7-9). He would be "as dew from Jehovah", bringing grace and blessing, and "as a lion", executing judgment. In accordance with this prophecy Christ is represented as both "the Lamb of God" (John 1:29, 36) and "the Lion of the tribe of Judah" (Rev. 5:5).

Micah then goes on to announce the Lord's final purification of Israel in the days of the new king. The process is described as that of destroying all instruments of war and everything that pertains to idolatry (vs. 10-14). Then He would visit His wrath upon all nations that resist His will, so that nothing should be able to disturb the peace of His people again (v. 15).

THE WAY OF SALVATION
(Chs. 6-7)

1. The Lord's Controversy with His People (Ch. 6). Israel is now summoned to a lawsuit in the presence of the mountains to hear the Lord's controversy with His people (vs. 1-2). The Lord opens the controversy with His complaint—"O my people". He reminds them of what He has done for them in redeeming them from Egypt (vs. 3-5). The phrase, "from Shittim unto Gilgal", stands by itself. The sense is, "remember what happened between Shittim and Gilgal". Shittim was the last camping place of the Israelites on the other side of the Jordan, Gilgal the first in the land of Canaan.

Then the anxious enquiry of the people is heard, asking how they can come before the Lord (vs. 6-7). The prophet replies by telling them that what He required of them was righteous conduct, a kind heart, and a humble walk with God (v. 8). The controversy continues with the voice of the Lord crying to the city of Jerusalem, describing its sins (vs. 9-12) and telling it why His judgments were visited upon it (vs. 13-16).

2. Israel's Prayer of Repentance (Ch. 7). The prophet, in the name of his people, now confesses and laments the sins of the nation (vs. 1-6). Then he turns to God, representing the true attitude of the believer in Israel, looking to the Lord for salvation and waiting upon Him, confident that in His own good time God will interpose for his deliverance (vs. 7-10). Then he addresses Israel, assuring her of the ultimate restoration of Zion and the great extension of her borders (vs. 11-12). The meaning of "the decree" in v. 11 is obscure. Most probably it refers to the Divine law of Israel's separation from the nations. This makes the prophecy foreshadow the breaking down of "the middle wall of partition" between Jews and Gentiles (Eph. 2: 14-15), and leads naturally to the next verse. The

prophet reminds Israel, however, that before their restoration takes place the land is to be desolate (v. 13).

Next comes the prophet's prayer for the accomplishment of salvation (vs. 14-17), and finally his description of the character of God as a God of mercy (vs. 18-20). The sin of the people is met and overcome by the Lord Himself, who would find a way of pardoning their iniquity, and would fulfil His promise to their fathers. This is the prophet's epilogue, ending the controversy and closing the book with one of the finest accounts of the redeeming grace of God in the Old Testament.

THE MESSAGE OF MICAH

Micah gives the best Old Testament definition of true religion in 6:8, which may be compared with the New Testament definition in Jas. 1:27. The three elements in this definition—justice, kindness, and humility—are closely related to one another. A man can do justly only as he loves kindness; and he will love kindness only as he walks humbly with God.

Micah foretold the birth of Christ in Bethlehem (5:2; Matt. 2:4-6). The significance of this prophecy lay in the fact that the Messiah was to come, not from among the ruling classes in Jerusalem, but from among the humblest classes in the land.

Micah has also something to say about the character of the coming Saviour. He would be "the breaker" (2:13), breaking the way open before His people: the New Testament parallel is "the captain of their salvation" (Heb. 2:10 A.V.). He would combine the majesty of a king with the tenderness of a shepherd (5:4), and He would secure peace for them (5:5; John 14:27; 16:33).

The supreme contribution which this book makes to the Old Testament message of redemption is this, that the ground of redemption lies in the character of God Himself. "Who is a God like unto thee?" (7:18). The Lord is gracious: man's part is to look unto Him, to wait for Him, and to trust Him as the God of his salvation.

THE BOOK OF NAHUM

NOTHING is known of this prophet beyond what is told in the first verse. The epithet, "the Elkoshite", probably means "an inhabitant of Elkosh", but the location of the place is not known. There are several traditions, but none of them helps.

The prophecy is entitled "the burden of Nineveh" (1:1), and it foretells the overthrow of that great city. Nahum refers to the fall of No-amon, the capital of Egypt, as having occurred recently (3: 8-10). This city, the ancient Thebes of the hundred gates, was captured by the Assyrians in 663 B.C. Nineveh was captured by the Medes and Babylonians in 612 B.C. The prophecy therefore falls between these two dates, probably about the middle of the century.

At that time the power of Nineveh was at its height. The Assyrian empire, of which it was the capital, stretched from the Persian Gulf to the Nile, and included Western Asia and Egypt. Nineveh's armies had destroyed the kingdom of Israel, and had frequently overrun the territory of Judah. The Assyrians were a sensual and arrogant race. Their wars were conducted with brutal ferocity. Nahum announces God's vengeance upon them. When Nineveh repented at the preaching of Jonah, God showed mercy to her. When she returned to her sin and cruelty, He must punish her.

The key-note of the book lies in the statement, twice repeated, "Behold I am against thee, saith Jehovah of hosts" (2:13; 3:5). While the main theme is God's vengeance upon violence and wrongdoing, the book also conveys a message of comfort to His people. The prophet's name is in keeping with this, for it means "consolation" or "consoler". The Lord is a refuge for those that trust Him, and because He is the God of vengeance He will surely avenge His elect. Each chapter may be taken separately, and the book analysed as follows:

NINEVEH'S DOOM DECREED: THE LORD GOD AVENGES
(Ch. 1)

1. The Lord as a God of Vengeance (vs. 2-8). The doom of Nineveh is based upon the very character of God. He exercises a moral government over the world, and He avenges (Deut. 32:35; Rom. 12: 19). Although He is slow to anger, yet He will not clear the guilty (vs. 2-3). Under the figure of a great storm, the prophet describes the overwhelming majesty of the wrath of God (vs. 3-6). In the midst of the storm He is a refuge for those that trust Him (vs. 7-8).

2. The Lord's Purpose in Vengeance (vs. 9-15). Addressing himself to Nineveh, the prophet asks, "What do ye devise against Jehovah?" Then he passes on to describe the irresistible nature of the judgment that was to fall upon her. Her kings have devised mischief against the Lord and against His people, and the Lord has determined the destruction of Nineveh and the deliverance of His people. The reference in v. 11 may be to Sennacherib, who through his representative had defied and blasphemed the Lord God (Isa. 36:13-20). Vs. 12, 13, and 15 are comforting messages addressed to Judah.

NINEVEH'S DOOM DESCRIBED: HOW THE
LORD AVENGES
(Ch. 2)

1. The Assault and Capture of the City (vs. 1-7). A very graphic picture of the attack on the city—the steady and deliberate approach of the besieging army without, and the wild terror and disorder of the defending host within. "The gates of the rivers are opened" (v.6). Nineveh was situated on the Tigris, and the ancient story of the siege states that the river became an enemy to the city and was swollen by violent rains, and that a great inundation took place, breaking down part of the massive walls.

The meaning of v. 7 is obscure because of a peculiar expression in the original. The A.V. takes it as a proper name—"Huzzab". Then it would be either a reference to the queen or a symbolical name for the city itself. The R.V. attempts to interpret it—"it is decreed". Then it would refer to the certainty of Nineveh's fall and emphasize it.

2. The Sack and Desolation of the City (vs. 8-13). The complete collapse of her people's resistance is described, and the utter dismay that has taken possession of them (vs. 8-10). The description in v. 10 consists of a series of vivid exclamations. The words rendered, "she is empty, and void, and waste", are marked by alliteration, a figure of speech which the prophets were fond of using. They might be put this way: "Sack, sacking, and ransacking", or, "A wild and weary waste".

Then the prophet breaks out into exultation over the doomed city. The Lord is against her, and when His judgment falls upon her, the den of lions will be gone, and the cruelty of Nineveh will have come to an end (vs. 11-13). Lions appear frequently on Assyrian monuments, and it is evident that the people compared themselves to this powerful animal. This fact gives special point to the prophet's sarcasm.

NINEVEH'S DOOM JUSTIFIED: WHY THE
LORD AVENGES
(Ch. 3)

1. Her Cruelty and Crimes (vs. 1-7). The Assyrians were characterized by barbarous cruelty in their wars and by gross sensuality in their religion. The prophet declares this to be the reason for the destruction of "the bloody city". She should be brought down in humiliation and shame, and be exposed as a gazing-stock to the nations.

2. The Certainty of Her Fall (vs. 8-19). No-amon was not so corrupt and was as strongly defended as Nineveh, yet she fell and her nobles were taken captive (vs. 8-10). Nineveh, too, should fall (vs. 11-13). All precautions taken for the siege would be of no avail (vs. 14-15). Her merchants would leave her and her warriors would fail her (vs. 16-17). The reference is to the fact that Nineveh was a great commercial centre as well as a great military power. Her rulers would slumber in death, her inhabitants would be scattered, her wound would be incurable, and all people would rejoice over her fall (vs. 18-19).

Throughout the prophecy Nahum had addressed the city of Nineveh, and at the end he turned to the king. As Nineveh was the image of the godless world in its brutal power and wickedness, so its king was the image of the prince of this world. So fully was Nahum's prophecy fulfilled, and so utterly was Nineveh destroyed, that the very site of the city remained for centuries unknown.

THE MESSAGE OF NAHUM

There is a stern but majestic sublimity about this book. It is aflame with the moral indignation of the sovereign God. The prophet has but one theme, and he treats it with tremendous force. God's face is set against the brutal power of the godless world. There is such a thing as the vengeance of God: "Vengeance belongeth unto me; I will recompense, saith the Lord" (Rom. 12:19). This truth runs right through the Bible (Deut. 32:35, 41, 43; Psa. 94:1; Isa. 34:8; 35:4; 61:2; 63:4; Luke 18: 7-8; Heb. 10:30; Rev. 6:9-10).

THE BOOK OF HABAKKUK

NOTHING is known about this prophet but his name. From the liturgical terms used at the beginning and end of ch. 3, it may be inferred that Habakkuk was a member of the Levite choir. His designation, "the prophet" (1:1, 3:1), implies a public ministry in that capacity. It is not used elsewhere in the superscriptions of the Prophetical Books except of Haggai and Zechariah (Hag. 1:1; Zech. 1:1).

The prophecy of Habakkuk foretold God's judgment upon the Chaldeans, and was intended to comfort the righteous in Judah during a time of injustice and violence in the kingdom. It probably dates from the early years of Jehoiakim's reign, which began in 608 B.C. This king is charged with the commission of such crimes as those denounced in the opening verses of the book (Jer. 22: 13-19). At that time the Chaldeans were appearing on the scene as the rising world power and the coming enemies of Judah. They had obtained the throne of Babylon under Nebopolassar in 625 B.C. After the fall of Nineveh in 612, they began to push their conquests westward. They brought Judah under their power when Nebuchadnezzar became king, and they destroyed Jerusalem and took the Jews into captivity in 586 B.C.

The book deals with the problem which faith has to face in view of the perplexing fact that wickedness seems to triumph over righteousness in the world. It may be taken in three parts according to the three chapters.

THE PROPHET'S COMPLAINT: THE PROBLEM OF FAITH
(Ch. 1)

The book opens with a dramatic dialogue between the prophet and the Lord about the apparent triumph of wrong and violence to which the Lord seems to pay no heed.

1. The First Complaint (vs. 2-4). Habakkuk gives utterance to his problem: "O Jehovah, how long shall I cry?" Why does God not hear? Why is evil allowed to go unchecked in the land? Why is the Law of the Lord ignored?

2. The First Answer (vs. 5-11). "Behold—I am working a work in your days". The Lord points to the Chaldeans, "that bitter and hasty nation", whom He is raising up to execute judgment on the wicked, and describes the irresistible power of their armies and the sweep of their conquests (vs. 5-10). The Chaldean was the instrument of God's judgment, but he would transgress God's purpose and offend and become guilty, because he made his might his god (v. 11).

3. The Second Complaint (vs. 12-17). In the light of God's holiness, the prophet's problem has now become deeper still. How can He who is "of purer eyes than to behold evil" use such a treacherous and rapacious people? Are not the Chaldeans more wicked than those upon whom they execute the Lord's judgment? Are they to go unchecked?

THE LORD'S REPLY: THE ANSWER OF FAITH
(Ch. 2)

1. The Prophet on the Watch Tower (vs. 1-4). He now takes the place of a watchman upon his tower of observation, looking out for the answer to his complaint. This figure indicates the spiritual seclusion of the prophet in a place of private meditation, and on a height from which he may look out over the far distance and hear the voice of God. The Lord's answer comes, and the prophet is commanded to write it so plainly that the reader may run his eye quickly through it and get its import at once. The vision was to be committed to writing, because its realization lay at a point of time in the future determined by God. It would be sure to come in its own time, and it would not disappoint those that waited for it (vs. 1-3).

Then the answer is stated in v. 4: "Behold, his soul is puffed up, it is not upright in him; but the righteous shall live by his faith". The two great principles of the Lord's government of men in the world are set forth in this verse. They are pride or self-dependence, and faith or dependence on the Lord. Pride is the principle by which the wicked are destroyed. Faith is the principle by which the righteous are saved. Thus the destiny of the two classes of men is determined, not by an arbitrary act or judgment of God, but by the inward and distinguishing attitude of their own lives. The last clause is quoted three times in the New Testament in connection with the Gospel (Rom. 1:17; Gal. 3: 11; Heb. 10:38). The meaning of "faith" here is not faithfulness as a quality of character, but trust as an attitude of the heart toward God.

2. Woes Against the Chaldeans (vs. 5-20). The prophet goes on to tell of "a parable and a taunting proverb" taken up by the nations against the Chaldeans (vs. 5-6). This takes the form of five woes, each denouncing some characteristic sin of theirs as the cause of their doom. These are, their rapacity and lust of conquest (vs. 6-8), their greed and covetousness (vs. 9-11), their violence and cruel ambition (vs. 12-14), their insolence and base treatment of other people (vs. 15-17), and their gross idolatry (vs. 18-19). In contrast with the idolatry of the Chaldeans, the prophet states the fundamental truth of the reality of the Lord, and calls all the earth to worship Him (v. 20; cf. Zeph. 1:7; Zech. 2:13).

THE PROPHET'S VISION: THE ASSURANCE OF FAITH
(Ch. 3)

This chapter takes the form of a psalm, which has three parts. The word "Shigionoth" in its title occurs only once elsewhere (Psa. 7). It probably signifies an irregular poem expressing intense feeling.

1. A Prayer (v. 2). The prophet beseeches the Lord to carry out the work that He has just revealed to him, a work in which both wrath and mercy should be manifested.

2. The Vision (vs. 3-15). This is the account of a great tempest in the heavens, coming up from the south, the region of Sinai and the Law. In the midst of it God is present, advancing in terrifying splendour. It is a symbolic prediction of the coming of God in power and majesty to judge the nations and redeem His people. The descriptions are drawn from events in the days of Moses and Joshua. The approach of the Lord is first described (vs. 2-7), and then His operations in judgment as related to nature (vs. 8-11), and to the nations (vs. 12-15). All this activity of His had the salvation of His people in view.

3. Its Effect (vs. 16-19). The prophet now describes the feeling aroused in him by this manifestation of God. There was first fear and trembling, because of the desolation that was coming (vs. 16-17), and yet joyful trust in the Lord God, because He was working out the salvation of His people (vs. 18-19). The last words of the poem are reminiscent of Psalm 18:33, and are prophetic of the heights of salvation to which God was to bring His people.

THE MESSAGE OF HABAKKUK

This book opens with perplexity and doubt, and closes with certainty and joy. The perplexity and doubt were caused by the apparent triumph of wickedness and God's apparent indifference to it all. The assurance and joy sprang from the revelation that was given the prophet. God is at work in the world in the midst of wrong and violence. He is acting in wisdom and righteousness notwithstanding all appearances to the contrary. He has an end in view, and ultimately "the earth shall be filled with the knowledge of the glory of Jehovah, as the waters cover the sea" (2:14).

In the meantime the righteous find their place in God's plan through faith. Trust in God is the true principle of life in a world in which God is at work. Those who are centred in Him and rely upon Him will be upheld by Him. "The righteous shall live by his faith" (2:4); he shall be carried through life triumphantly.

THE BOOK OF ZEPHANIAH

THIS prophet was one of the princes of Judah: his descent is traced from King Hezekiah (1:1). The words "this place", used of Jerusalem in 1:4, indicate that he lived in the capital. His ministry was carried on in the reign of Josiah (638-608 B.C.), but it is not associated with any historic event.

During the early years of Josiah's reign hordes of Scythians from the region of the Caspian Sea poured down over Western Asia, but there is no evidence that they came as far as Judah. Rumours of this invasion, however, may have reached Jerusalem and given Zephaniah the occasion for his prophecy. In the light of that "scourge of God" he foretold "the day of Jehovah's wrath". This phrase, or the idea it expresses, occurs several times in the course of the book (1:7, 14-15, 18; 2:2-3; 3:8).

The book is not composed of a series of addresses, but contains one continuous prophecy. This is arranged in three sections by a kind of refrain. The thought expressed in 1:18, "the whole land shall be devoured by the fire of his jealousy", is repeated in 3:8, "all the earth shall be devoured by the fire of my jealousy". This gives the book a threefold division.

THE NATURE OF THE DAY OF WRATH
(Ch. 1)

Its coming is first announced in general terms and then described more particularly. After that the prophet goes on to set forth its dreadful and appalling aspect. It will be universal in its scope, and complete and final in its character.

1. A Universal Judgment (vs. 2-13). It will fall upon all creatures in the whole world, but especially upon man as the object of the Divine anger (vs. 2-3). It is to begin with the idolaters and apostates in Judah and Jerusalem (vs. 4-6). Several forms of false worship are mentioned. The Chemarim, who were the black robed priests of Baal, are linked together with the Levitical priests in the judgment. Those "that swear to Jehovah and swear by Malcam", which means "their king", divided their worship between the true God and some false god.

Then with a call for silence at the presence of the Lord because of the imminence of the judgment (v. 7), the prophet goes on to describe it more particularly and to show that it will involve all classes of men. He pictures the different classes in Jerusalem as being overtaken by the wrath of God: the princes and governing classes, who assumed foreign fashions and perverted justice for purposes of gain (vs. 8-9); the merchants, who made themselves rich by avarice and fraud (vs. 10-11); and the people of Jerusalem generally, who were sunk in apathy, religious indifference, and self-indulgence (vs. 12-13).

2. A Final Judgment (vs. 14-18). It will be a sudden, swift, and terrible act of God. A graphic description is given of the helplessness of man when God proceeds to judge and punish human sin. There will be a completeness and finality about it: "He will make an end, yea a terrible end" (v. 18).

A WARNING IN VIEW OF ITS COMING
(2:1—3:8)

The prophet now summons the nation to repent, and enforces the call by describing the sweep of the judgment as it falls upon the nations around Judah and upon Jerusalem itself.

1. A Call to Repentance (2:1-3). These verses contain an appeal to God's own people to seek the Lord and escape from the coming wrath. The nation as a whole had lost all sense of shame; but if the meek would seek the Lord they should be hid in the day of His anger.

2. The Punishment of the Wicked (2:4-15). This section depicts the crash of the surrounding nations. It is a picture of world-wide judgment. Representative nations from the world immediately around Judah are mentioned. Looking out from his own viewpoint in Jerusalem, the prophet sees the wrath of God falling first upon the nations on the west (vs. 4-7), then upon those on the east (vs. 8-11), next upon the south (v. 12), and finally upon the north (vs. 13-15). The desolation of Nineveh is described here in language similar to that of Nahum, who prophesied shortly before Zephaniah. There are references through this chapter to the remnant, who were to be saved in that day (vs. 3, 7, 9).

3. A Denunciation of Jerusalem (3:1-8). Zephaniah now turns with startling suddenness to Jerusalem without even mentioning her name, and describes again the sins that were rampant within her, especially the sins of her ruling classes—princes, judges, prophets, and priests (vs. 1-4). Then he denounces her for not receiving correction and not taking warning from God's judgments upon the nations around her (vs. 5-7). Finally he calls upon the "meek of the earth", whom he had addressed in 2:3, to wait until God accomplishes His purpose through judgment: "until the day that I rise up to the prey" (v. 8).

A PROMISE CONCERNING ITS ISSUES
(3:9-20)

The prophet now deals with the issues of the judgment. The manifestation of God's wrath would lead to the conversion of the nations to Him, the redemption and purification of the remnant of Israel, and the renewal of Jerusalem to be His dwelling place among His people.

1. The Conversion of the Nations (vs. 9-10). This follows from the statement in v. 8, and the warning there given to the nations. Through His judgments upon them, God would obtain from the nations those that should confess His name and thus fall to Him as "the prey". Then He would turn to them "a pure language"; that is, He would work such a change in them that their sinful lives should be purified for the worship and service of the Lord.

2. The Cleansing of the Remnant (vs. 11-13). The remnant of Israel would repent of their transgression, and be redeemed and purified. God would remove from among them the proud who trusted in themselves, and would leave in their midst "an afflicted and poor people", who should trust in the Lord. They should be redeemed from all iniquity, and delivered from all fear. They should live in security and peace. Here we have a prophetic description of the inner character of the Christian dispensation.

3. The Blessedness of Jerusalem (vs. 14-20). Zion is now bidden to sing and rejoice in prospect of her future glory and bliss. She will be delivered from all her foes, and the Lord will dwell in her midst. He will gather His people into her and make her a name and a praise among all the nations. He will rejoice over her Himself. The book closes with this

exquisite picture of God resting in His love, and singing for very joy over His redeemed people.

The Message of Zephaniah

This book looks forward from the standpoint of Judah and Jerusalem to the consummation of world history. All local and temporary manifestations of judgment are but preparatory signs of the coming day of the wrath of the Lord. God's righteousness and justice require Him to deal with the accumulated sin of the world. There is a "day" in which this will be done. The New Testament refers to it again and again (Acts 17:31; Rom. 2:5; Jas. 5:9; 1 Pet. 4:7; 2 Pet. 3:10-12; Rev. 6:17).

The motive of God's wrath is love; it is the attitude of His own nature toward sin. He could not manifest His love to the world, in which sin exists, without revealing His wrath also. Love without wrath would be indifference. Zephaniah shows that God's purpose in wrath is the final deliverance and purification of His redeemed people so that He may dwell among them.

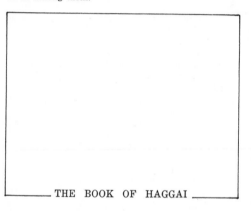

THE BOOK OF HAGGAI

HAGGAI is the first of the prophets of the Restoration, or the post-exilic period. The history of the Restoration is contained in the Books of Ezra and Nehemiah. Babylon had passed off the scene, and Persia was the great world empire under which the Jews were living. Cyrus, the conqueror of Babylon, had issued a decree giving them permission to return to Judah and rebuild the Temple in Jerusalem. Only a small part of the nation responded, about 50,000 in all. But this was "the remnant", gathered back from exile and restored to the Holy Land, through whom God was to carry on His purpose, and from whom He was to bring the Redeemer of the world (Isa. 6:11-13).

Nothing is known of Haggai's personal history. His prophecy is dated in the second year of Darius king of Persia (520 B.C.). Before this, Hebrew prophecies have been dated in the reigns of Hebrew kings, marking the independence of the nation; but now Israel was under Gentile power. The prophet's ministry was carried on among the Jews who had returned to the land, and was intended to encourage them in the rebuilding of the Temple. It may be inferred from 2:3 that Haggai had seen the Temple of Solomon. If so, he must have been a comparatively old man, for that Temple was destroyed sixty-six years before.

The return of the Jews under Zerubbabel had taken place in 537 B.C., and the foundation of the new Temple had been laid in the next year. But opposition arose from the Samaritans, who suc-

ceeded in getting the work stopped, and nothing more was done for sixteen years. In 520 the two prophets Haggai and Zechariah appeared upon the scene and summoned the people to arise and proceed with the work. As a result of their preaching, the building of the Temple was resumed, and four years afterwards it was completed and dedicated (Ezra 1-6).

The Book of Haggai is composed of four addresses, each dated by the day of the month, and all delivered within a period of less than four months, corresponding with the last four months of our year.

I. A Message of Rebuke (Ch. 1). The first address was delivered on the first day of the sixth month of the Jewish year, which was in the late summer or early fall. It was directed to the two leaders of the people, Zerubbabel the governor and Joshua the high priest (v. 1).

1. The Burden of the Message (vs. 2-11). Haggai reproached the people for their indifference in leaving the Lord's house lying waste while they built comfortable houses for themselves to dwell in (vs. 2-4). Let them consider their ways. They had been getting poor harvests. They had a small return for their toil, and they did not enjoy what they did have (vs. 5-6). Then he summoned them to consider the work they had left unfinished. Let them resume the building of the Temple. Then the Lord would take pleasure in His house and He would be glorified (vs. 7-8). It was because of their neglect of His house that the Lord had withheld the blessing of the harvest and had brought a drought upon the land (vs. 9-11).

2. The Result of the Message (vs. 12-15). A new spirit now took possession of the leaders and the people. They "obeyed the voice of Jehovah their God", and they "did fear before Jehovah". Then Haggai encouraged them with the assurance that the Lord was with them. The spirit of Zerubbabel and Joshua was stirred up, and the work of rebuilding the Temple was resumed in the twenty-fourth day of the same month. The intervening time was probably spent in preparation.

II. A Message of Encouragement (2:1-9). This address was delivered on the twenty-first day of the seventh month, which was the last day of the Feast of Tabernacles (vs. 1-2). Some of the old men who remembered the former Temple lamented the comparative inferiority of this one. This tended to discourage the people, and the prophet now appealed to them to be strong and to work, for the Lord would be with them. He would fulfil the covenant He made with them when they came out of Egypt (vs. 3-5). As He shook the world at Sinai, so He would shake all nations, and He would fill this house with glory (vs. 6-8). In the light of Heb. 12:26-28, this prophecy refers to the introduction of the Christian dispensation. The shaking of the nations began with the coming of Christ in the flesh and will continue till His coming in glory.

The middle clause of v. 7 is ambiguous in the original. Literally it reads thus: "the desire of all nations, they shall come." The subject is in the singular and the verb in the plural. The A.V. takes the subject to mean the central longing of all nations, the One whom they desire. The R.V. takes it, in the light of the next verse, to mean the desirable things of all nations, their precious treasures (cf. Rev. 21:26). Then comes the promise that the latter glory of this house should be greater than the former, and there God would "give peace" (v. 9). This prophecy was fulfilled by the Lord Jesus Christ, who came to that Temple in His earthly ministry, and there accomplished His redeeming work of making peace between God and man (John 14:27; 16:33).

III. A Message of Instruction (2:10-19). This address was delivered about two months later, on the twenty-fourth day of the ninth month. By putting two questions to the priests, Haggai drew out the principles of the Mosaic ritual regarding holiness and uncleanness (vs. 10-13). Flesh that had been offered in sacrifice hallowed only what it touched: it did not communicate its holiness any further (Lev. 6:27). That is, holiness is not communicated by holy things. On the other hand, what was unclean defiled what it touched (Num. 19:22). That is, defilement is communicated by unclean things. Then the prophet made the application to the people (v. 14). Their disobedience defiled all their sacrificial service. The altar which they had raised on their return (Ezra 3:2-3), so far from hallowing them, was itself defiled by them.

Haggai went on to draw out the application more particularly. Let them take a backward view (vs. 15-17). Before the work of building the Temple was resumed (three months ago), there was no blessing on the harvests: they were smitten with a curse. Then let them take another backward view —from today to the time when they began to build the Temple (vs. 18-19). Although at present there is nothing to indicate a harvest, yet God promises blessing because the people have set themselves earnestly to the work. The prophet regards the resumption of the building operations as really laying the foundation, and he so describes it—"the day that the foundation of Jehovah's temple was laid".

IV. A Message of Hope (2:20-23). This is a special message to Zerubbabel the governor, delivered on the same day as the last address. The heavens and the earth should be shaken, and the kingdoms of the world should be overthrown by the nations fighting one another. On the background of this universal shaking of the nations, the book closes with a Messianic promise to Zerubbabel: "In that day I will make thee as a signet; for I have chosen thee, saith Jehovah of hosts". Thus the promise to establish David's throne in the world is handed on through David's heir Zerubbabel to David's greater Son.

THE MESSAGE OF HAGGAI

Haggai's prophecy was the first message of God to the Jews who had returned from the Exile. It was a call to a work of faith in the face of adversity. They were a very small remnant compared with the rest of the nation, who were prospering in the Dispersion, and they had been discouraged since they returned. But it was through them alone that God's redemptive purpose was being carried forward; therefore they were to be strong and work. Their work was to be directed towards the building of the Temple; and though its former earthly glory had passed away, yet a greater glory was coming to it, the glory of the spiritual.

THE BOOK OF ZECHARIAH

ZECHARIAH was a priest as well as a prophet. His grandfather Iddo was one of the priests who returned with Zerubbabel in 537 B.C. (Neh. 12:4, 16). Zechariah, therefore, must have been comparatively young when his prophetic ministry began. This inference is confirmed by the way he is referred to in 2:4 as "this young man".

Zechariah began to prophesy in the same year as Haggai (520 B.C.), in connection with the building of the Temple, and he continued his ministry for some time after its completion. His message was intended to encourage the little colony of Jews by the glorious prospect of the future of Israel and Zion, and to give them hope in the midst of discouragement.

The Book of Zechariah is in two parts. The first part (Chs. 1-8) contains addresses delivered during the building of the Temple, and is composed mainly of visions concerning the future of Israel. The second part (Chs. 9-14) contains addresses delivered after the completion of the Temple, and is composed mainly of prophecies concerning the advent of the Messiah.

CONCERNING THE FUTURE OF ISRAEL
(Chs. 1-8)

These prophecies are dated like Haggai's, and belong to the time when the rebuilding of the Temple was going on.

1. A Call to Repentance (1:1-6). This is an introductory message, opening the prophet's ministry and giving the key-note of the whole book. Zechariah began his prophetic ministry in the month after Haggai had delivered his second message. He enforced the Lord's call to repentance, by a warning from the experience of the fathers, and by an emphatic repetition of the Divine name, "Jehovah of hosts". This title of God occurs with great frequency throughout the book, nearly forty times.

2. The Visions of the Night (1:7—6:8). This prophecy is dated on the twenty-fourth day of the eleventh month, two months after Haggai's last message, and five months after the building of the Temple had been resumed. In the space of one night this whole series of eight symbolic visions passed before the prophet's inner eye. They were intended to strengthen the Jews and to encourage them with hope in regard to their future. That future, as foreshadowed in these visions, is realized in the new Israel—"the Israel of God" (Gal. 6:16)—of the Christian dispensation.

The prophet first describes what he saw in each vision, and then a heavenly being—"the angel that talked with me"—gives an explanation or interpretation in each case. The nature and significance of the several visions may be set forth as follows:

(1) The horsemen among the myrtle-trees (1:7-17). These were the Lord's scouts, who had come back from patrolling the earth bringing their reports. The myrtle-trees probably represented Israel in her lowly and depressed condition. Though as yet there might be little sign that God was overthrowing the kingdoms of the nations as Haggai had foretold (2:22), yet He was watching over Jerusalem and Zion, and He was preparing to fulfil His word and bring in the Messianic age.

(2) The four horns and the four smiths (1:

18-21). Each of the four horns, which represented Israel's foes, had a smith (not a carpenter as in the A.V.) to break it down. Every hostile power should meet its judgment. The nations that had scattered Israel were finally to be overthrown and destroyed.

(3) The man with a measuring line (ch. 2). Jerusalem was to be greatly enlarged and become very populous. The Lord would be unto her a wall of fire round about her, and "the glory in the midst of her" (vs. 1-6). Then the prophet uttered a call to all the children of Zion who had not yet come out of the exile in Babylon to hasten to return to her, for the Lord was about to display His glory in the judgment of the nations that had plundered her (vs. 7-9). Let Zion sing and rejoice, for the Lord would come and dwell in the midst of her, and many of the Gentiles should join themselves to Him and become His people in that day (vs. 10-13). This vision has its fulfilment in "the heavenly Jerusalem" of Heb. 12:22.

(4) The reclothing of Joshua (ch. 3). Joshua the high priest, clad in filthy garments, is accused by Satan before the angel of the Lord. But the Divine judge rebukes the adversary and has Joshua reclothed in rich and clean priestly garments (vs. 1-5). Joshua here represents the nation, which had been "plucked out of the fire" of the Babylonian captivity; and the vision means that she was to be cleansed from her iniquity and restored to her priestly function.

A solemn declaration is now made to Joshua, promising him, if he will be faithful, "a place of access among them that stand by", that is, fellowship with God's immediate servants in the courts of Heaven (vs. 6-7). Then Joshua and his fellow-priests are given a special Messianic promise: "Behold, I will bring forth my servant the Branch" (v. 8). Here two Messianic titles taken from earlier prophets are combined (Isa. 42:1; 49:6; Jer. 23:5; 33:15). The promise goes on to describe the priestly work that should be accomplished by the Messiah and its blessed results (vs. 9-10). "I will remove the inquity of that land in one day"—the day of the Cross, the day to which all the yearly Days of Atonement pointed forward.

(5) The candlestick and the two olive-trees (ch. 4). The prophet saw a golden candlestick, with seven lamps which were fed by seven pipes from a bowl or reservoir of oil above it, and two olive-trees standing beside the ·candlestick, one on each side, which supplied oil to the reservoir (vs. 1-3). He asked the meaning of the vision, and was told that it was a Divine message for Zerubbabel: "Not by might, nor by power, but by my Spirit, saith Jehovah of hosts". All obstacles were to be removed from before him; he should bring forth the top stone of the Temple in triumph, and the grace of God should rest upon it for ever (vs. 4-7). The work which Zerubbabel had begun by laying the foundation of the Temple should be carried to completion, not by earthly means or by human power, but by the power of the Spirit of God running to and fro throughout the whole earth (vs. 8-10).

All this meant that the material temple, which the Jews were building then, was but a shadow and type of the real temple. The material would ultimately pass, like a dissolving view, into the spiritual: the type would give place to the antitype. Here is foreshadowed the truth contained in such New Testament passages as John 2:19 and Eph. 2:21-22. The prophet then asked about the two olive-trees, and was told that they were "the two anointed ones"

—the kingly and priestly offices represented by Zerubbabel and Joshua—through whom the Lord would cause His Spirit to be given to His people (vs. 11-14). These two types are combined and fulfilled in Christ, who, as the heavenly Priest and King, communicates the Holy Spirit to His Church.

(6) The flying roll (5:1-4). The character of the visions now changes. Those that preceded were encouraging and comforting: those in this chapter are concerned with wickedness. This one was a scroll floating in the air and represented the curse of the Law going out against evil doers, searching them out and cutting them off. The dimensions of the roll were the same as those of the Holy-place, and were probably intended to indicate that the standard of conduct for judging sin was that set by the Lord Himself (Lev. 11:44). The two sins mentioned—perjury and theft—represent the two tables of the Law.

(7) The woman in the ephah (5:5-11). The ephah held about one bushel and was the standard dry measure among the Jews. The prophet saw "the ephah that goeth forth", that is, coming into the realm of the visible in the vision. The angel added the comment, referring to the individual sinners of the preceding vision: "This is their appearance in all the land". Then lifting up the disk of lead which covered the ephah, he disclosed a woman sitting in the midst of it, and said, "This is Wickedness", and closed it again (vs. 5-8).

As the former vision represented judgment upon the sin of individuals, this vision represented judgment upon corporate sin—the sin of the nation or of any organized system. The prophet then saw the ephah, with the woman in it, being lifted up and removed to "her own place" in the land of Shinar (vs. 9-11). The significance of this lies in the fact that the first manifestation of corporate sin, the first organized rebellion against God, took place in the land of Shinar (Gen. 11:2).

(8) The four chariots (6:1-8). These were the agents that God used for His administration of justice and judgment in the world going forth from His heavenly presence—"from between two mountains; and the mountains were mountains of brass," symbols of impregnable strength. The adjective "strong", describing the horses of the last chariot, properly belongs to the horses of all the chariots, for in the Hebrew it comes at the end of the sentence, summarizing them all (vs. 1-3).

The prophet was told that they represented "the four winds of heaven", which themselves were symbols of the invisible but mighty agencies of God (Psa. 104:3; 148:8; Dan. 7:2). They were commanded to "walk to and fro through the earth", thus counteracting Satan's "going to and fro in the earth, and walking up and down in it" (Job 1:7). Then the angel announced that those that went toward the north country—the region of the Babylonian exile—"have quieted my spirit in the north country". They had caused God's anger toward that region to rest. In Zechariah's time Babylon alone of the four great world powers had been finally punished (vs. 4-8).

3. The Crowning of Joshua (6:9-15). A deputation from the Jews remaining in Babylon had arrived in Jerusalem with gifts, which were probably intended as a contribution toward the building of the Temple. Zechariah was commanded to take from these gifts enough silver and gold to make a composite crown, which he was to place upon the head of Joshua the high priest, and thus set him

forth as a type of "the man whose name is the Branch". Then he was to announce: "even he shall build the temple of Jehovah; and he shall bear the glory, and shall sit and rule upon his throne; and he shall be a priest upon his throne; and the counsel of peace shall be between them both."

This coronation scene is the most composite and complete type of Christ and His mediatorial work in the Old Testament. It is a symbolic prophecy, foreshadowing the exaltation of the Saviour to the throne in Heaven after accomplishing His priestly work on earth. It is fulfilled in the Melchizedek priesthood of Jesus as explained in the Epistle to the Hebrews. There the inspired writer brings his explanation to a head in these words: "Now in the things which we are saying the chief point is this: We have such a high priest, who sat down on the right hand of the throne of the Majesty in the heavens" (8:1). From His position there He is going on with the building of the spiritual temple during the present Christian age, as foretold in this passage of Zechariah.

4. Messages Concerning the Fasts (Chs. 7-8). Two years after Zechariah had begun his ministry, a deputation from Bethel came enquiring as to whether they should keep the fast of the fifth month (7:1-3). Since the fall of Jerusalem in 586, the Jews had been accustomed to fast on the anniversaries of the four outstanding events connected with their captivity, namely, when Jerusalem was taken in the fourth month (Jer. 52:6), when the Temple was destroyed in the fifth month (Jer. 52:12), when Gedaliah the governor was murdered in the seventh month (Jer. 41:1-2), and when the siege of Jerusalem was begun in the tenth month (2 Kings 25:1). The four messages which follow, each introduced with the phrase, "the word of Jehovah of hosts", contain the prophet's reply to this deputation.

(1) The first message (7:4-7). God disowns self-appointed fasts and feasts. Rather should the people give heed to the word of the Lord. It is a spiritual service that He demands, the worship of the heart.

(2) The second message (7:8-14). It is the execution of justice and the manifestation of mercy that the Lord requires. Disobedience to the words of His prophets was the cause of their former misery.

(3) The third message (8:1-17). The prophet emphasized this message by a sevenfold repetition of the statement, "Thus saith Jehovah of hosts". The Lord declares His affection for Zion and His purpose to restore His favour to her and dwell in her midst, and promises her people a future of great peace and happiness (vs. 1-5). This may seem incredible to them at the time, but it is not marvellous to the Lord. He will gather His people from all countries to dwell in the midst of Jerusalem (vs. 6-8). He bids them be strong and work with good courage in view of the future, for instead of being a curse among the nations, as in the past, they shall be a blessing (vs. 9-13). As the Lord's threatenings of judgment upon them in the past did not fail, so now He purposes to do them good. Let them obey Him and turn from the things that He hates (vs. 14-17).

(4) The fourth message (8:18-23). Here there is a threefold repetition of the expression, "Thus saith Jehovah of hosts". Fasts shall be turned into cheerful feasts (vs. 18-19). People and nations shall come seeking the favour of the Lord in Jerusalem (vs. 20-22). "In those days"—the days of the new dispensation—men of all the languages of the world shall become followers "of him that is a Jew", Jesus of Nazareth, when they find God revealed in Him (v. 23).

CONCERNING THE ADVENT OF THE MESSIAH
(Chs. 9-14)

These prophecies bear no date. They belong apparently to the period of the prophet's ministry that followed the completion and dedication of the Temple. They are in two groups with similar headings (9:1; 12:1). "The burden of the word of Jehovah" means a Divine utterance involving judgment. The two groups together deal with the establishment of the Messianic Kingdom, and show how it was to be accomplished notwithstanding the rejection of the Messiah Himself. The whole section contains a symbolic account of the Messianic transactions that were to be accomplished at Jerusalem and of the salvation they were to secure for all the nations.

I. Th Coming King Rejected (Chs. 9-11). These chapters contain a prophetic view of the history of Palestine, with special reference to the city of Jerusalem, looking down from the prophet's day toward the time of Christ. The word "Hadrach" (9:1), which occurs nowhere else in the Old Testament, was the name of a district north of Palestine near Damascus. Three great events stand out in the prophecy like mountain peaks. Each event is merged into, or connected with, the Messianic hope. They are all related in the prophet's view with the city of Jerusalem and the Messianic King, and they head up in His rejection. These events are as follows: The invasion of Alexander the Great and the protection of the city in 332 B.C. compared with the coming of Zion's true King (9:1-10), the Maccabean wars and the deliverance of the city in 165 B.C. compared with the Messianic deliverance (9:11—10:12), the Roman invasion and the destruction of the city in A.D. 70 following His rejected ministry (Ch. 11).

1. The King's Coming (9:1-10). Here we have the first movement, the preparation for His coming in the judgment upon the nations (vs. 1-7), and the protection of the city of Jerusalem at that time (v. 8). This is followed by a description of the manner in which Zion's true King would come, and of the character of His reign (vs. 9-10). Matthew declares this prophecy to have been fulfilled in the way Christ made His final entry into Jerusalem (Matt. 21:4-5).

2. The King's Program (9:11—10:12). This passage begins with the wars of the Maccabees and the deliverance wrought by them in the time of the Greek supremacy (9:11-17), and leads on to the spiritual deliverance wrought by Christ Himself, which is described in terms of the overthrow of idolatry and the punishment of false leaders (10:1-7), and the final redemption of the people of God, which is described in terms of the gathering home of the exiles of Israel (10:8-12). In the midst of the passage is a prediction that the Messianic King should come out of Judah (10:4). "From him shall come forth the corner-stone, from him the nail". This is an allusion to two prophecies of Isaiah (28:16 and 22:23).

3. The King's Rejection (Ch. 11). This chapter begins with the desolating judgment of the Roman invasion (vs. 1-3). The cause of this judgment is

then set forth symbolically in the rest of the chapter. The Lord commanded the prophet to assume the office of shepherd over His people, called "the flock of slaughter" because doomed to slaughter (vs. 4-6). In this the prophet represented the Messiah, and his two staves, Beauty and Bands, represented blessings which his ministry would bring to the people. He cut off the three false shepherds by whom Israel was ruled, probably representing the three official classes, princes, priests, and prophets. But his own ministry was rejected (vs. 7-8).

Then the flock were left to the fatal consequences of their rejection of the shepherd (vs. 9-11). He asked for his hire and was given thirty pieces of silver, the price of a slave. As a token of the rejection of these wages the Lord bade him, "Cast it unto the potter", which was probably a proverbial expression for throwing it in the scrap-heap. The breaking of the staves, Beauty and Bands, represented the loss of what they stood for (vs. 12-14). All this foreshadowed the rejection of Christ by the Jews (Matt. 27:11-26).

Then the prophet was commanded to enact another symbolical prophecy, and take "the instruments of a foolish shepherd". Having rejected the Good Shepherd, Israel was to be given over to the rule of a shepherd who would destroy the sheep— a foreshadowing of the tragic history of the Jews ever since that time (vs. 15-17).

II.   The Rejected King Enthroned (Chs. 12-14). This section has to do with the Messianic hope of Israel, and with the establishment of the Kingdom of God upon the earth. It contains a prophetic view of events as the prophet looked down from his own day toward that consummation. These events are described in two movements. In the first movement they are viewed from the standpoint of Israel, as she is purified and restored through her repentance and conversion. In the second movement they are viewed from the standpoint of the King, who has been rejected, but now comes in triumphant power to reign.

The whole section looks forward to the consummation of the work of Christ. It describes in Old Testament terms, and from the standpoint of Judah and Jerusalem, the accomplishment of that Messianic work of which the building of the Temple was but a type. The book closes with a picture of the nations of the world coming up to Jerusalem to worship the King in the true house of the Lord.

To interpret these chapters aright, we need to keep in mind the special characteristic which has already appeared in Zechariah's prophecies. They occupy the border land, as it were, between the material and the spiritual, between the visible and the invisible world. Through the symbolism of the material we have been given intimations of the reality of the spiritual. The one merged into the other. Political happenings that belong to this world are linked with Messianic transactions that affect the other world. In the light of the New Testament, Zechariah's prophecies are seen to teach that, while the work of the Messiah would be accomplished in this present visible and material world, its result would be the opening of another world, a spiritual and heavenly order of things.

1.   The Final Triumph of Jerusalem, or the City of the Great King (12:1—13:6).

(1)   Its siege and deliverance (12:1-9). The city of Jerusalem stands here for the whole nation. Its siege is described in such a way as to indicate the kind of treatment Israel would receive among the nations of the world after the rejection of the King. They would be perpetually hostile to Israel, and yet Israel would be a perpetual cause of trouble to them —"a cup of reeling" and "a burdensome stone". God would not allow the nation to be destroyed, but would deliver it Himself and exalt it, and would punish and destroy its foes.

(2)   Its repentance and conversion (12:10-14). This passage shows how Israel's deliverance would come. It is the prediction of a great revival to take place in the nation. They would come to realize that they had rejected and crucified their Messiah. This would produce a deep and wide-spread penitential sorrow. Their repentance would be individual and personal, spreading through the whole nation, every one repenting and mourning for himself. The reference in v. 11 is to the national mourning over the death of Josiah (2 Chron. 35:22-25).

(3)   Its purification and cleansing (13:1-6). The penitent people would find that God had overruled their rejection of the Messiah to provide a way for their forgiveness and cleansing from sin. By means of the Cross He had opened a fountain for the spiritual blessing and renewal of Israel (v. 1). The process of cleansing the nation is described in figures taken from the purification of the land from idolatry and false prophecy after a time of apostasy (v. 2).

So thorough would be the purification that if one of the false prophets should arise again, his own parents would put him to death (v. 3). These pretenders would all be so ashamed of their former claims that every one of them would strip off the outward tokens of his profession and say that he was a farm labourer (vs. 4-5). And if one were still suspected and were questioned about the scars on his breast, which were marks of idol worship, he would reply that they were the result of chastisement received in the house of his relatives (v. 6).

2.   The Final Triumph of the Lord, or the Glory of the Great King (13:7—14:21).

(1)   The smiting of the shepherd (13:7-9). From the wounds of the false prophet in the preceding passage, we pass now to the smiting of the true Shepherd. Christ found in this passage a reference to His own rejection (Matt. 26:31). The scattering of the disciples was a partial fulfilment, the scattering of the nation a fuller one. "I will turn my hand upon the little ones"; that is, He would interpose in their favour. The "little ones" were the humble and despised followers of Christ from among the Jewish people (Matt. 10:42).

The passage goes on to say that two-thirds of the nation should perish, and one-third should survive to be brought through a trial that would refine them. Out of this they should call upon the Lord and be restored to His fellowship and favour. This prophecy foreshadows what was to befall the Jews after their rejection of the Messiah, and indicates that a minority would return to the Lord through the Gospel.

(2)   The interposition of the Lord (14:1-8). In this prophecy there is a remarkable mingling of the material and the spiritual. It begins with a battle of all nations against Jerusalem, which gives an idealized picture of the world's wicked treatment of God's people. Then there comes a sudden intervention of the Lord for their deliverance (vs. 1-3). The next verses describe the nature of that intervention (vs. 4-5). "His feet shall stand in that day upon the mount of Olives". This event happened at the ascension of Christ, and we are not justified in looking for any future fulfilment of the prophecy.

From the Mount of Olives in the earthly world He passed into the presence of God in the heavenly world, and thus He opened a way into that world for His people. This is the significance of the way of escape which the Lord's intervention provided: "Ye shall flee by the valley of my mountains." (cf. 6:1)

The next verses describe the character of the age that was to be introduced by the Lord's intervention (vs. 6-8). "It shall be one day"—a unique day— "which is known unto Jehovah", that is, in its true nature known only to Him. It was to be the age of His own Holy Spirit. "At evening time there shall be light": toward the close of the twilight time of distress—the present age of tribulation—full and everlasting light should spring up. This looks forward to the final Advent of the Lord. "Living waters shall go out from Jerusalem": streams of spiritual blessing should flow from the throne of God poured out by the Holy Spirit. All this is a prophetic description of the unique character of the present Christian dispensation as seen through the windows of the old Jewish dispensation.

(3) The reign of the King (14:9-21). It is first announced that the Lord Himself is to be the King of all the earth. He is to be worshipped as God without a rival—"in that day shall Jehovah be one, and his name one" (v. 9). Jerusalem is to be elevated above all the land and become a safe dwelling place, freed from the curse (vs. 10-11). Thus is prefigured the spiritual exaltation of the new Jerusalem (Rev. 21:2-4; 22:3-4).

The reign of the Lord is described in language that is unmistakably figurative. It sets forth the process of destroying all the foes of Jerusalem and putting away all the wickedness of the land, till at last only that which is holy remains (vs. 12-15). It corresponds with Paul's statement in 1 Cor. 15:24-25 about the risen and ascended Christ, who "must reign, till he hath put all his enemies under his feet".

This is followed by an account of all the nations that are left of those that fought against Jerusalem coming up to worship the King and keep the Feast of Tabernacles (vs. 16-19). This feast was the consummation of the yearly system of Jewish times and seasons. It was the supreme Levitical type of the blessings of redemption. The prophet is here describing, in Old Testament language, the gathering of the nations into the Kingdom of God. Then the book comes to a close with a description of the holiness of Jerusalem, when the distinction between the sacred and the secular shall have passed away (vs. 20-21). Every common thing shall be dedicated to the Lord, and no godless or profane person shall be found among His people. All who worship in the new Temple shall be righteous and holy.

The Message of Zechariah

This book is the consummation of Messianic prophecy. It gathers up lines of hope and promise which were separate in previous prophets. It stands, as it were, on the border line between the old dispensation and the new, between the material order and the spiritual. From the viewpoint of the one it foreshadows the other. The prophet is not only looking into the future for the Messianic age; he is looking also into another order of things, the world of spiritual realities.

In the light of the New Testament, the outlook of this book upon the subsequent course of Israel's history and upon the development of God's redeeming purpose in the world is as follows:

1. The Messiah would combine in Himself the two offices of king and priest, and would raise up the true temple of the Lord by the power of the Holy Spirit (chs. 1-6; John 2:19; Eph. 2:19-22).

2. Jerusalem would be rebuilt and expanded into a heavenly city. It would become the city of the living God, and the habitation of all His redeemed people (chs. 7-8; Heb. 12:18-24).

3. The Messiah would come to Jerusalem as a Prince of peace, but would be rejected by Israel. As a result the Jews would be subjected to oppression at the hands of the nations of the world (chs. 9-11; Luke 21:24).

4. Whenever Israel should repent and turn in true contrition to the Messiah whom they had rejected, then He would come in heavenly power for their salvation and deliverance, and for the final establishment of His Kingdom (chs. 12-14; Acts 3:19-21; Rom. 11:13-16, 25-29).

THE BOOK OF MALACHI

Nothing is known of this prophet but his name (1:1). It means "my messenger". It is not the name of any other person in the Old Testament, and this has led some to think that the word is not a proper name at all, but has been taken from 3:1 as a title for the book in the absence of information about the author. However, "Malachi" has been regarded as the prophet's own name since the early Christian age, and it is convenient so to use it still. The most probable date for Malachi's prophecy is the time of Nehemiah, about eighty years after Haggai and Zechariah. He seems to have occupied the same relation to Nehemiah that they did to Zerubbabel.

Reaction had followed the restoration of Israel and the rebuilding and dedication of the Temple. The people had become indifferent to the sacredness of the Temple services and the significance of their covenant with the Lord. Malachi's efforts were directed against this moral and religious decline and against the formalism and hypocrisy that marked the period. He foretold the coming of the Messiah in a purifying judgment, and also the dawning of the new age of salvation. The book may be analysed in four parts.

1. A Message to the Nation about Religious Indifference (1:1-5). The prophet begins by setting the Lord's declared love for Israel over against Israel's scepticism about it: "I have loved you— Wherein hast thou loved us?" This question indi-

cates the nation's religious indifference. Proof of the Lord's love for them is given in the contrast between their lot and that of Edom. The prophet refers to Jacob and Esau, not as individuals, but as representatives of the nations descended from them.

2. A Message to the Priests about Spiritual Insensibility (1:6—2:9).

(1) Their sin declared (1:6-14). They were dishonouring God with polluted worship, by offering blemished and inferior animals in the sacrifices. This showed how insensible they were of the majesty of God (vs. 6-9). It were better to close the Temple altogether, for the Lord had no pleasure in such sacrifices as these. The time was coming when pure worship should be offered to the Lord throughout the whole Gentile world (cf. John 4:21-24). But the priests were profaning His name and treating the service of His sanctuary with contempt by the cheap offerings they brought (vs. 10-14).

(2) Their punishment announced (2:1-9). Their blessings should be turned into curses, and they should be made contemptible in the eyes of the people (vs. 1-4). A contrast is drawn between their conduct and the Lord's ideal of the priesthood when He established the office with Levi (vs. 5-9).

3. A Message to the People about Moral Insensibility (2:10—3:15).

(1) Their sin declared (2:10-17). They were marrying idolators and divorcing their Jewish wives. They were dealing treacherously with their brethren and hypocritically with their God. The nature of their sin is declared as "profaning the covenant of our fathers" (v. 10), that is, the special covenant which God made with their fathers (Exod. 19:5-6). The peculiar significance of Israel's sin in this case is indicated in v. 15. He made the Israelites one people and separated them from the other nations, not because He had no "residue of the Spirit", no Divine blessing left for them, but because "He sought a godly seed". Marriage with foreign women before the Messiah came would subvert this Divine purpose.

(2) Their punishment announced (3:1-6). It would be brought on by the coming of the Lord Himself. He would come to His Temple at a time when they did not expect Him, with a purifying judgment that should begin with the priests and extend to the people. This prophecy is based on the one in Isa. 40:3-5. The long line of the prophets should end in a special messenger who would introduce the Lord Himself. Malachi's own name makes him such a messenger. The Angel of the Covenant is identified here with the Lord Himself, which marks the identity of this Angel throughout the Old Testament with the Second Person of the Trinity. The phrases, "Whom ye seek" and "Whom ye desire", refer back with some irony to the people's demand in 2:17.

(3) An appeal to return to God (3:7-15). They have been robbing God in tithes and offerings. Let them bring in the whole tithe and He will pour out a blessing upon them (vs. 7-12). The practice of giving the tenth to God goes back to primitive times (Gen. 14:20; 28:22). It was embodied in the Mosaic Law (Lev. 27:30-32) as a means of supporting the priests in their service (Num. 18:26-31). They have also been complaining that their observance of the forms of religion brought them no profit, and that it was the wicked who prospered (vs. 13-15).

4. A Message to the Remnant about Coming Judgment (3:16—4:6).

(1) A promise to the faithful (3:16—4:3). These are contrasted with those addressed in v. 13, and are described as "they that feared Jehovah and thought upon his name." They should be spared in the day of His judgment (3:16-17). The figure in the phrase, "a book of remembrance", is taken from the Persian practice of keeping a record of those who had rendered service that they might be rewarded in due time (cf. Est. 6:1-3). "In the day when I make up my jewels" (A.V.); preferably, "in the day when I do this" (R.V. marg.); that is, at the time when God acts and carries out His purpose of judgment. Then they should perceive the difference between the righteous and the wicked (3:18). That day should be one of burning and destruction for the wicked but of healing and deliverance for the righteous (4:1-3).

(2) A warning to all (4:4-6). Let them remember the Law of Moses and how God gave it to him for all Israel. The Lord promises to send them Elijah the prophet before His day of judgment comes, that he may prepare the nation by turning their hearts back to God. According to the teaching of Jesus, this promise was fulfilled in the person of John the Baptist (Matt. 11:10, 14; 17:12; Mark 9:13; Luke 7:27). Thus the last voice of the Old Testament introduces the first voice of the New Testament.

THE MESSAGE OF MALACHI

This book contains the last message of God to Israel for four hundred years. It was a warning of judgment, as the heading of the prophecy indicates. The Exile had cured the Jews of idolatry, but now, when they were back in their own land, they were giving way to another form of sin. That self-righteousness which produced the Pharisees in the age between the Testaments, and which resulted at last in Israel's rejection of their Messiah, had already begun to appear. It was against this that Malachi's prophecy was directed. Its roots lay in moral and spiritual insensibility, and this attitude on the part of the people is reflected in their question, seven times repeated in the book, "Wherein"? (1:2, 6, 7; 2:14, 17; 3:7-8).

Although Malachi announces the coming of the Lord in a purifying judgment, yet he also gives us the beautiful Messianic image of the sun of righteousness rising with healing in its beams (4:2), which has its New Testament parallel in "the dayspring from on high" (Luke 1:78).

THE NEW TESTAMENT

INTRODUCTORY

THE GOSPELS

ACTS

THE purpose of this work was stated in the Preface to the first section. It will be well to explain that purpose again. It is implied in the title given to the whole series: "Thinking Through the Bible". By the term "the Bible" is meant the Book through which God speaks, not the "documents" or the "sources" from which the writers may have drawn their material. The spiritual world in the Bible, the world from which God speaks, is not discovered by a critical search for the sources behind the Scriptures, but by patient and reverent meditation upon the contents of the Bible itself.

The Old and New Testament Scriptures, in the form in which they have come down through the ages and have made their impact upon the world, have always been recognized by the Church of Christ as the Word of the living God. The most significant thing about the Bible lies in this fact, and the most important thing in the study of the Bible is the search for the mind of God in that Word. Even if the original sources behind the Scriptures could be discovered, the mind of God would not be found in them.

There is a legitimate critical approach to the Bible which prepares the way for this study. Its work is to lead the student through the outer courts of the temple and introduce him to the inner sanctuary where real Bible study begins. What is known as the "modern" critical approach seeks to do something quite different. It comes with a philosophic

theory and a linguistic hypothesis, and attempts to reconstruct the temple upon what it assumes to be its original lines. In doing this it pays the Bible a unique and significant tribute. No other ancient book, no other religious canon, has ever received the same kind of attention from critical scholarship.

But after nearly a century of learned labour, this attempt to reconstruct the Scriptures has proved inconclusive and unconvincing. The scholars themselves do not agree. The Christian Church as a whole, with a sound instinct, declines to use the Bible on the new lines. The Word of God still lies on the pulpits of Christendom in its old form. It still goes marching abroad throughout the world on its own feet. Subjective criticism fails to explain the mind of God. The "problems" with which it deals only touch the fringe of the objective revelation which the Scriptures contain. The thing that lives in the Bible eludes scientific search. Other methods of approach and other attitudes of mind are required to find it.

One result, however, has been left—a tendency to drop the historical perspective out of the Bible and to regard it merely as a source-book for Christian doctrines. This introduces an element of weakness into the whole Christian system. Christianity begins with the New Testament; but when the historical perspective is lost and the New Testament is divorced from the Old, then Christianity is deprived of the momentum that gave it purpose and direction.

INTRODUCTORY

THE AGE BETWEEN THE TESTAMENTS

THE New Testament is separated from the Old Testament by a great historic gap. Four hundred years lie between Malachi and Matthew. During that long period many changes took place among the Jews in Palestine, and the whole background of Biblical history was altered. When we enter the New Testament we are in an altogether different world.

For two centuries after the return from Babylon in 537 B.C. the Jews were under the dominion of Persia. The story of that return and of the establishment of the little Hebrew colony in Jerusalem, is told in the books of Ezra and Nehemiah. The Temple was rebuilt and dedicated, and the Covenant of the Law was restored. Then Old Testament history comes to an end, but a hundred years of Persian supremacy still remained.

It was then that the power of the high priests began to rise, for the Persians left the ruling authority in Judah and Jerusalem for the most part in their hands. Under them the Sanhedrin came into existence as the Jewish national council, and over it the high priest of the time presided. The synagogue, which probably originated in the Exile, now became an important religious institution. Its main purpose was to provide for the reading of the Law

in every Jewish community and for giving instruction in the Law to all classes of the people. The new zeal for the Law and the increased attention devoted to it, gave a new importance to the Scribes as the teachers of the Law; and they rose to a place of prominence in the nation above that of the priests. As their power grew and as more authority was given to them, they loaded the Law with tradition, and thus legalism entered into the religion which Moses had established in Israel.

After the fall of Persia in 331 B.C. the Jews were under Greek rulers for more than a century and a half. For a considerable part of that period they were exposed to the devastating effects of war, as the rival kingdoms of Egypt and Syria contended for the possession of Palestine. It is these two powers that are meant by "the king of the south" and "the king of the north" in the prophecy of Dan. 11, which describes the age of trouble through which the Jews were to pass before the Messiah should come.

When the war ended with the supremacy of Syria, the Jews were subjected to the cruel and malicious persecution of King Antiochus Epiphanes, who sought to blot out the Hebrew religion. During his time many Jews apostatized, some under the pressure of the persecution, but more under the subtle and alluring influence of the cultured Greek paganism that was spreading over Palestine. Then came the revolt of the Maccabees and their heroic exploits, which resulted in 165 B.C. in the triumphant deliverance of Jerusalem and the cleansing and rededication of the Temple.

For a hundred years after that event, the Jews enjoyed comparative independence under a line of rulers sprung from the Maccabean family, who held the office of the high priest. This was the flourishing period of Jewish history in the age between the Testaments. The territory occupied by them was extended northward till it comprised the three political divisions of the land existing in the time of Christ—Judea, Samaria, and Galilee.

The two chief Jewish sects of the New Testament age, the Pharisees and the Sadducees, who appear in the Gospel story as the most bitter foes of our Lord, arose during this period. The Pharisees were the party of the Scribes. The two names are often linked together in the Gospel narratives. Their aim was the complete and exact fulfilment of the Law as interpreted and built up by the Scribes. They did not represent any special religious tendency, but simply stood for a strict and mechanical legalism, for the letter of the Law without any thought of its spirit.

While the Pharisees were the popular party, the Sadducees were the party of the aristocracy. They were not numerous, but they were influential. They usually held the highest offices, and especially that of the high priest. Their spirit was not religious but distinctly secular, and their interests were political. They were materialists, men of this present world alone; and they gave themselves to the enjoyment of the general culture of the age without any belief in an after-life.

Jewish independence came to an end with the Roman conquest of Palestine in 63 B.C. This took place in a time of internal intrigue and revolution, which continued for some years afterwards. Out of the strife and confusion of the period the Edomite Herod, wrongly called the Great, finally succeeded in gaining the throne with the favour and help of Rome. During his long reign, which continued from 37 to 4 B.C., he sought to please the Romans and also to win the favour of the Jews. He adorned the land with magnificent buildings and new cities built on the Roman model. His crowning achievement in behalf of the Jews was the rebuilding and beautifying of the Temple. This work was begun in the year 20 B.C. and was still going on during the Lord's public ministry (John 2:20). With all this, Herod was a jealous and cruel tyrant, and the slaughter of the babes of Bethlehem was but one of his characteristic crimes.

At his death his kingdom was divided among three of his sons. After a reign of nine years, Archelaus (Matt. 2:22) was deposed for misgovernment, and a Roman governor was appointed over Idumea, Judea, and Samaria. Herod Antipas ruled over Galilee and the district beyond Jordan called Perea, and Philip over the district to the north and east of the Sea of Galilee. It was thus the land was governed during the public ministry of Jesus (Luke 3:1).

Although the Messianic transactions which brought the Old Testament stage of Divine revelation to its fulfilment were accomplished among the Jews in Palestine, it was the Jews of the Dispersion who laid the ground for the universal character of the New Testament age and for the entrance of the Gospel into the Gentile world. The centre of gravity in that world had moved, during the age between the Testaments, from Babylon in the east to Rome in the west. The Persian Empire had given way to the Grecian, and the Grecian in turn to the Roman. The background of the New Testament is the Roman Empire and the Mediterranean world. Throughout the whole of that world outside Palestine, the Jews of the Dispersion were scattered. They were more numerous and more prosperous than the Jews of the home-land. They were to be found in every city of any size, and even the smallest Jewish community had its own synagogue for the reading of the Law and the Prophets.

The Greek language, which had become universal and was now the common medium of intercourse among the nations, was spoken by the Jews in the Gentile world. They used the Greek version of the Old Testament in their synagogues. This translation of the Hebrew Scriptures, commonly known as the Septuagint, had been made at Alexandria during the third and second centuries B.C. Although intended specially for the Jews of the Dispersion, it was used largely by the Jews in Palestine as well. The writers of the New Testament quote from it more frequently than from the original Hebrew. The widespread use of this version of the Old Testament providentially helped to prepare the way for the New Testament Scriptures, which were given to the world in Greek.

THE MAKING OF THE NEW TESTAMENT

THE books which make up the New Testament were written during the last half of the first century. The need for a collection of apostolic writings was not felt during the earliest years of the Church. The Scriptures of the Old Testament were in the hands of the Christians, and these, together with the oral teaching of the Apostles, supplied their spiritual wants.

As the Gospel spread into distant regions and Christian communities multiplied, the need for written records soon became evident. The churches could not all have a personal visit from one of the Apostles of the Lord. The Apostles themselves were passing away. It was then that there began to be circulated among the churches, and added to the sacred books of the Old Covenant, the writings of the Apostles of the New Covenant.

The first desire would naturally be to have an authentic record of the Gospel story. Numerous narratives of the ministry of Christ were drawn up (Luke 1:1-4). But only those that had been written by the hand, or under the sanction, of members of the apostolic band were accepted by the Church as authoritative. No other Gospel records have come down to us from the age of the Apostles. We have no information about Jesus Christ from any source besides that which has been preserved in our four canonical Gospels. It would also be felt that there should be a record of the fulfilment of the Lord's last commission to the Apostles. Hence an authentic account has been preserved of the origin and growth of the Christian Church. The Book of Acts, too, is the only record of its kind that has been handed down from the apostolic age.

It would be necessary also to preserve the teaching which the Apostles gave to the Church as it grew. It was recognized that they had been endowed with Divine inspiration and that their teaching had Divine authority. The Lord had promised that the Holy Spirit should teach them all things, bring His own teaching to their remembrance, and guide them into all the truth (John 14:26; 16:13).

The Apostles employed letters as a means of instructing the various churches that came into existence as the Gospel spread from place to place. The Apostle Peter, writing toward the end of his life, refers to Paul's epistles as already well known, and classes them with the writings of the Old Testament Canon under the title of Scriptures (2 Pet. 3:16). By so doing he acknowledges them to have the same inspired authority. As time went on the Christian communities began to collect the letters left by the Apostles and use them in their church services along with the Old Testament Scriptures.

The collection of the New Testament books was not made all at once. The number of canonical books in the possession of different churches would necessarily vary for some considerable time. Churches situated near the place where a particular book was first published would obtain copies earlier than churches more remote. Efforts would be made to secure copies of the Gospels and the larger and more important Epistles, while there would not be so strong a desire to obtain copies of the smaller Epistles. These would not be spoken about so much and would not be so generally known. And thus it happened that, although the New Testament was all written before the end of the first century, yet nearly two more centuries passed before all the churches everywhere came to recognize the full canonical authority of all the twenty-seven books.

This unanimity of the Church at large regarding the New Testament was not due to the decision of any Church council. No human authority was used in the settlement of the Canon. It was due entirely to the providence of God, who presided by His Spirit over the recording and the preservation of His Word.

The several books carried full authority from the time they were published, before they were collected into a single volume. Their authority rested solely upon their apostolic source or their apostolic character. It was this alone that gave them a right to a place in the sacred Canon. This was understood throughout the Church from the beginning. It was the spiritual instinct of the Christian communities in general that fixed the New Testament Canon. They recognized the unique quality of inspiration in these writings. The Spirit in the heart of the Church bore witness to the voice of the Spirit in the books that make up the New Testament.

THE NEW TESTAMENT

THE GOSPELS

THE FOUR GOSPELS

THESE four books are properly not four different gospels, but four accounts of the one Gospel. In the New Testament the word "gospel" always means the message of "good news" that Jesus and the Apostles proclaimed. After the apostolic age the name came to be applied to the written records of the story of Jesus.

The purpose of the Gospels is not to give a complete account of His life, for the largest part of it is passed over in silence in each of them. They are not biographies in the modern sense. They are concerned only with Christ's redemptive work. They record just so much of His works and words as is necessary to set Him forth as the Saviour of the world.

While this purpose is manifested in all the Gospels, there is a marked difference between the first three and the fourth in the way it is carried out. The first three give the same general account of the ministry of Jesus; they describe it from the same point of view. For this reason they are known as "the Synoptic Gospels", from a Greek word meaning "seeing together". The fourth takes a different point of view and gives an entirely different account.

The difference is seen in two respects. The first three Gospels confine their narrative almost entirely to Jesus' ministry in Galilee, while the fourth Gospel confines its narrative mainly to His ministry in Judea and Jerusalem. The first three Gospels deal chiefly with the outward aspect of the Lord's ministry. They record its events and incidents, and contain accounts of His miracles, parables, and discourses. The fourth Gospel, on the other hand, is occupied almost altogether with the inward aspect of His ministry. It sets forth the heavenly glory of His person and the spiritual nature of His work. One of the early Church Fathers (Clement of Alexandria) characterized it as "a spiritual Gospel", saying that John wrote it to supplement the others, in which "the body of the Gospel", as he called it, had been sufficiently set forth.

The four books were written by the men whose names they bear. This has been the belief of the Church throughout all the centuries. Matthew and John were Apostles of the Lord. The other two Evangelists were associated with Apostles. Mark was the companion of Peter, and probably his convert—his "son" in the faith (1 Pet. 5:13). Luke was Paul's fellow-labourer and close companion to the end of his life (2 Tim. 4:11). All the four Gospels, therefore, come from the apostolic circle and thus bear apostolic sanction.

The first three Gospels are so much alike and have so much in common that they seem to be dependent either upon one another or all upon some common source. This has given rise to what is known as "the Synoptic Problem". As a solution for it, nearly every conceivable way in which these books could be related to one another has been proposed. Various attempts have also been made to find some original source for them all. According to the latest theory, the primitive tradition lies behind Mark's Gospel, which preserves it in the earliest form, and the other two Gospels, while making use of Mark, show the influence of other forms of the tradition. But no theory based on subjective grounds alone, although supported by learning and philosophy, has ever lasted long or aroused more than academic interest in the Church. The piety, common sense, and spiritual instinct of Christians in general have always had their part to play in a just and true appreciation of these early Christian records. The universal Church continues to accept all the Gospels at their face value.

The first "Gospel" was the preaching of the Apostles. It was an oral message, not a written record. The Apostles were all witnesses of the whole ministry of the Lord Jesus Christ (Acts 1:21-22). The oral Gospel, as proclaimed by the different Apostles, would follow the same general plan. It would cover the main facts of the ministry, and would come to a head in the crowning facts of the Cross and the Resurrection. It would tend to take a fixed and settled form, and this is no doubt represented in the general form of the Synoptic Gospels. The step from that oral Gospel to the written Gospels was easy and natural. The specific forms which these Gospels take are easily explained by the individual character and purpose of the writers, and by the different classes of readers for whom they were originally intended.

When each of these four books is examined as a whole, it is found to be characterized by one leading theme. All the four themes are related to the Old Testament preparation for the Redeemer. The prophecies that pointed forward to Him represented Him in diverse aspects and bestowed upon Him diverse titles. He was to come both as a King and as a Servant; He was to be both human and divine.

The four Gospels correspond with these four prophetic portraits of the Messiah. In Matthew Jesus appears as the King, come to introduce the Kingdom of Heaven and to reign. In Mark He is the Servant of the Lord, fulfilling man's neglected duty and accomplishing the will of God. In Luke we see Him as the Son of Man, incorporated with the human race and living a true and perfect human life. In John we behold Him as the Son of God, none other than Jehovah Himself, come to visit and redeem His people and bring them into fellowship with Himself. In this respect, the messages of the four Gospels may be summed up in the following words from four Old Testament passages: "Behold, thy King" (Zech. 9:9); "Behold, my Servant" (Isa. 42:1); "Behold, the Man" (Zech. 6:12); and "Behold, your God" (Isa. 40:9). In each case the reference pointed to the Redeemer who was to come.

This does not mean that the four writers deliberately chose to picture these four aspects of the Redeemer when they set out each upon his own task. We are not to suppose that they were conscious of distinct and separate purposes. They had all one common purpose, although writing spontaneously and independently. Their purpose was to tell the story of Jesus under the urge of the Divine Spirit, as each one knew it, with the material each had at his disposal. But each of them was peculiarly fitted to bring out that particular aspect of the person and work of Christ which his own Gospel sets forth.

The Apostle who had been called from an official position in an earthly kingdom (Matt. 9:9) thought in terms of the Kingdom of Heaven and presents Jesus in His kingly relations. The man who had been a servant of Apostles (Acts 13:5) presents Jesus as the Servant of God. It was "the beloved physician" (Col. 4:14), whose calling gave him a sympathetic understanding of the nature and needs of men, who portrays the Son of Man. And it was "the disciple whom Jesus loved" (John 13:23; 21:20), the one member of the Twelve that truly understood the inner nature of the Master, who has left us a portrait of the Son of God.

The particular class of readers for whom each Evangelist wrote also had its bearing upon the special character of his book. The traditions of the early Church have something to say about the readers as well as about the writers, and in every case there is a correspondence with the particular characteristic of the writer's Gospel.

Matthew's Gospel was originally written in Aramaic, the Hebrew spoken in Palestine, and was evidently intended for the Jews. Mark wrote his Gospel at the request of the church in Rome for circulation in Italy. It was peculiarly adapted for the energetic and practical Romans. Luke addresses his Gospel to a man of culture with a Greek name (1:3). He obviously wrote it for the Greeks of the Gentile world, who were characterized by wide human interests. Last of all, John wrote his Gospel at the urgent request of the Christians of Asia, who were troubled by spreading heresies regarding the person of the Lord. These four classes of readers—Jews, Romans, Greeks, and Christians—are representative of the whole human race.

All this goes to show how the Spirit of God, in presiding over the development of the Christian Church and the progress of Divine truth, so ordered it that in these four independent apostolic records we are given a complete portrait of the Saviour of the world, and we are also shown that He is able to meet the needs of all classes of men. This could not have been done in any single book; and thus we see the reason why there are four Gospels in the New Testament.

It is not known, and it cannot be determined, at what exact dates the various Gospels were written. They would not be written before the need of permanent and authentic records began to be felt, which would probably be about the middle of the century. The Synoptic Gospels belong to the period before the fall of Jerusalem and the destruction of the Temple (A.D. 70), for their three accounts of the Lord's Olivet prophecy (Matt. 24, Mark 13, Luke 21) bear evidence that the event had not yet taken place. Their dates probably lie between the years 55 and 65. The fourth Gospel was written many years later, probably between 80 and 90, for it manifestly presupposes an acquaintance with the other Gospels on the part of its readers.

THE GOSPEL ACCORDING TO MATTHEW

THE first Gospel has never been ascribed to anyone but the Apostle whose name it bears. The earliest testimony about it says that Matthew composed it first in the vernacular Hebrew, evidently intending it for the Jewish Christians in Palestine. The earliest writers who refer to it also regard the present Greek text as an authentic translation or a true representative of the original Hebrew Gospel, but they are silent as to how it was made, whether by Matthew himself or by another writer of apostolic authority.

Matthew was a publican, a collector of taxes, when he received his call to follow Jesus (Matt. 9:9). Mark and Luke call him Levi (Mark 2:14; Luke 5:27-28). He may have had the two names before, or he may have assumed the new name, which means "gift of God", to mark his change of life. His prompt response to his call marks him as a man of decision. He showed his courage, too, by inviting the companions of his former life to a feast, that they might see and hear his Master (Matt. 9: 10-13; Mark 2:15-17; Luke 5:29-32). He was chosen by Jesus from among His disciples as one of the twelve Apostles (Matt. 10:3; Mark 3:18; Luke 6:15). Mark and Luke place his name before that of his companion Thomas. Matthew shows his humility by reversing the order and adding to his own name the opprobrious title that marked his former life.

The key-note of the Gospel is struck in the opening verse. Its theme is the promised Messiah, and so it properly stands at the beginning of the New Testament Canon. Jesus Christ is presented as "the son of David, the son of Abraham", fulfilling the two great covenant promises of the Old Testament that had a Messianic import. One of these was the promise to David that in his seed an everlasting kingdom should be established (2 Sam. 7:13). The other was the promise to Abraham that in his seed all the nations of the earth should be blessed (Gen. 22:18). The promise regarding the son of David had in view the Kingdom of God. The promise regarding the son of Abraham had in view the redemption of the world. Matthew shows that both of these promises have their fulfilment in Jesus Christ. He is the true son of David and King of Israel, and the true son of Abraham and Saviour of the world.

This theme is manifest in the structure of the book. After an introductory section dealing with the Messiah's preparation (1:1-4:16), the rest of the Gospel is composed of two sections dealing with His ministry, each beginning with the same expression: "From that time began Jesus . . . " (4:17; 16:21). These words introduce a new note into the narrative in each case, a note which characterizes the section that follows. In the one case Jesus began to proclaim the message of the Kingdom of Heaven; in the other case He began to announce His approaching death and resurrection. On the basis of this threefold division we get the following working analysis of the book:

I. The Preparation of the Messiah—Chs. 1-4
   (Jesus Christ, Son of David and Son of Abraham, being manifested to Israel and prepared for His ministry)
   1. His Coming into the World (Chs. 1-2)
   2. His Equipment for His Task (3:1-4:11)
   3. His Entrance upon His Work (4:12-25)

II. The Ministry of the Kingdom—Chs. 5-16
   (Jesus Christ, Son of David, making proclamation of the Kingdom of Heaven to Israel)
   1. The Principles of the Kingdom (Chs. 5-7)
   2. The Works of the Kingdom (Chs. 8-9)
   3. The Messengers of the Kingdom (Ch. 10)
   4. The Opposition to the Kingdom (Chs. 11-12)
   5. The Mysteries of the Kingdom (Ch. 13)
   6. The Rejection of the Kingdom (Chs. 14-16)

III. The Ministry of the Cross—Chs. 17-28
   (Jesus Christ, Son of Abraham, making propitiation for the sin of the world)
   1. The Preparation for the Cross (Chs. 17-18)
   2. The Approach to the Cross (Chs. 19-20)
   3. The Final Testimony to Israel (Chs. 21-23)
   4. The Final Prophecy to the Disciples (Chs. 24-25)
   5. The Suffering of the Cross (Chs. 26-27)
   6. The Victory of the Crucified (Ch. 28)

Behind this progressive plan Matthew followed a topical method in arranging his material. The teachings of Christ are grouped in five extended addresses, which are marked by similar expressions such as, "When Jesus had finished these words" (7:28; 11:1; 13:53; 19:1; 26:1). In each case the address seems to be composed of teachings given by the Lord on the same topic at different times in His ministry. The whole narrative of the Gospel might be built around these five addresses. They are as follows: the sermon on the mount (chs. 5-7), the charge to the Twelve (ch. 10), the parables of the Kingdom (ch. 13), instructions for discipleship (ch. 18), and the Olivet prophecy (chs. 24-25).

THE COMING OF THE MESSIAH
(Chs. 1-2)

The Gospel begins with an account of the way Jesus Christ came into the world. This account links Him with the Old Testament dispensation, and shows how Messianic prophecy began to be fulfilled in Him. The opening words recall the statement with which the fifth chapter of Genesis begins: "This is the book of the generations of Adam". They are probably the heading of the genealogy, but they might be taken as a title for the whole Gospel. These two expressions are unique in Scripture: they occur nowhere else in the same form. The one begins the story of man fallen, after an introductory account of his creation and fall; and that is continued throughout the whole Old Testament. The other introduces the story of man redeemed; and that is the theme of the whole New Testament.

1. The Genealogy (1:1-17). It is arranged in three stages, marking three great epochs in the preparation of Israel for the promised Messiah. Several generations are omitted in the list of names,

and the thrice repeated "fourteen generations" (v. 17), summing up the whole period, is probably used as a symbolical number, intended to show that Christ appeared "when the fulness of the time came" (Gal. 4:4).

The genealogy is traced through Solomon and the kings of Judah, and thus gives the royal line of David. It leads to "Joseph the husband of Mary, of whom was born Jesus, who is called Christ" (v. 16). Four women are named in the list besides Mary, two of whom were Gentiles and three were women of ill fame, thus marking the identification of Jesus with sinful humanity, both Jew and Gentile. The line becomes poorer and more obscure as it approaches the time of Christ. The Redeemer came "as a root out of a dry ground" (Isa. 53:2).

2. The Birth (1:18-25). This passage is significant as showing both the divine and the human origin of Jesus—begotten by the Holy Spirit, and born of the Virgin Mary. It shows also that Jesus came as David's heir; for Joseph, who would be regarded as His father in the eyes of the law, was a son of David. The two names given to the coming Messiah—Jesus (Saviour) and Immanuel (God with us)—indicate the fundamental purpose of His mission in the world (Luke 19:10), and the essential nature of His presence among men (2 Cor. 5:19).

3. The Infancy (Ch. 2). Two events recorded in this chapter show how diversely the Saviour's arrival was received by different classes. Thus was foreshadowed the world's subsequent treatment of Christianity.

(1) The homage of the wise men (vs. 1-12). They came from lands east of Palestine, and represented the seeking souls of the Gentile world. The religious leaders of the Jews, who were able to answer Herod's question from their own Scriptures, were so indifferent that they made no attempt to follow up the enquiry of the wise men.

(2) The enmity of Herod (vs. 13-23). He represented the hatred and hostility of the godless world. Through him Satan attempted to frustrate the purpose of God in sending the Redeemer (Rev. 12:1-5). His slaughter of the babes of Bethlehem revealed his jealous and cruel character, and was an ominous sign of the persecution Christianity was to receive in the world.

Matthew finds two features in the infancy of Jesus to be of Messianic significance. The fact that the young child was taken down to Egypt identified Him with the people of God who were redeemed out of Egypt: "Out of Egypt did I call my son" (v. 15; Hos. 11:1). The fact that He was brought up in Nazareth fulfilled the prophetic descriptions of the Messiah as being despised among men: Matthew sums these up in the expression, "He should be called a Nazarene" (v. 23; cf. John 1:46; 7:52).

One of the principal features of this Gospel is prominent in these first two chapters. Matthew calls attention again and again to the fulfilment of prophecy in the life of Jesus. Compare 1:23 and Isa. 7:14; 2:6 and Micah 5:2; 2:15 and Hosea 11:1; 2:18 and Jer. 31:15. This linking of events in the life of Christ with the Old Testament preparation for the Messiah continues throughout the Gospel. The expressions, "it is written" and "that it might be fulfilled", occur very often. It has fifty-three quotations from the Old Testament, almost as many as all the other Gospels combined. They cover the whole of the Lord's life, and refer to a great variety of incidents.

Between chs. 2 and 3 lies a gap of thirty years. The preaching of John the Baptist was the signal for the manifestation of the Messiah and His appearance to Israel (John 1:31). Leaving the obscurity of Nazareth, Jesus went down to John at the Jordan, and was baptised of him and anointed by the Spirit for His Messianic task. Then followed His temptation and conflict with Satan. On the imprisonment of John, Jesus went back into Galilee and began His public ministry there, with Capernaum as His headquarters.

1. The Herald (3:1-12). John's preaching had two notes. It was intended to turn the hearts of the people back to God ("repent ye"), and to prepare them for the new order that was coming ("the kingdom of heaven is at hand"). He was the herald who, according to the prophet Isaiah, was to prepare the way for the Messiah (Isa. 40:3). John introduced the rite of baptism for those who repented, as a preparation for and a sign of the baptism of the Holy Spirit, which, he declared, would be the result of the Messiah's work (v. 11).

All the Gospels note this relation of John's baptism with water to the subsequent baptism of the Holy Spirit (Mark 1:8; Luke 3:16; John 1:33). It was based upon promises in the Prophets (Isa. 44:3; Ezek. 36:25-27), and looked forward to the pouring out of the Spirit at Pentecost (Acts 1:5). John required proofs of repentance from those who came to him for baptism, and refused to baptize the Pharisees and Sadducees, whom he denounced instead as the "offspring of vipers".

2. The Baptism (3:13-17). This was Jesus' formal entrance upon His Messianic office. In this rite, He (1) dedicated Himself to the task of accomplishing redemption by identifying Himself with those whom He came to redeem, and also (2) yielded Himself to God to receive the anointing of the Holy Spirit to equip Him for His task. This is the significance of His reply when John expressed reluctance to baptize Him: "Thus it becometh us to fulfil all righteousness". The emphasis falls on the word "thus" because of its position in the sentence. It refers to the anointing of the Spirit, which was the reality behind the symbolical rite to which Jesus was submitting Himself.

Jesus meant that He was undertaking to accomplish man's neglected duty—"to fulfil all righteousness"—by the power of the Holy Spirit which He was now to receive, and not by the power of His own divine nature. By doing so He became the true representative of His people. His baptism was followed at once by the descent of the Holy Spirit upon Him from the opened heavens, and by the voice of the Father approving and accepting the self-dedication of the Son.

3. The Temptation (4:1-11). The knowledge of this mysterious experience must have been derived from Jesus Himself, for He was alone in the wilderness. It took place immediately after he had received the anointing of the Holy Spirit, and was the first outcome of that experience. It was an attack on the attitude of complete surrender to the will of

God which He had taken at His baptism. It was a subtle attempt on the part of the devil to introduce the element of self-will into the work of the Messiah. The shadow of that supernatural personality who is the fountain of evil, and who brought the human race under the bondage of sin, now falls across the life of our Lord. His suggestions were temptations, not to have Jesus abandon the Messianic task, but to have Him do it in the wrong way —to approach it from the standpoint of His own will, not the will of God.

The tempter's attacks on the Lord were made on three sides: (1) On the ground of His humanity— a suggestion to satisfy the natural instinct of hunger in a supernatural way. (2) On the ground of His deity—a suggestion to prove His relationship to God by acting on His own impulse. (3) On the ground of His Messiahship—an offer to surrender the kingdoms of the world to Christ on Satan's own terms. In every case Jesus refused to have the question referred to Himself, and fell back on the revealed will of God. On all three occasions He quoted from the Mosaic book of Deuteronomy (8:3; 6:16; 6:13). He overcame the tempter, not by His own divine power, but by taking the word of God for His guide as the true representative of man.

It does not follow, because the temptations are described separately, that they took place separately. They may have been presented to the mind of Jesus simultaneously. Luke gives them in a different order (4:1-12). The picturesque form in which they are described was chosen by the Lord as the best means of conveying to the minds of His disciples the essential facts of an experience that was utterly beyond the reach of human understanding.

HIS ENTRANCE UPON HIS WORK
(4:12-25)

After His baptism and temptation, Jesus began His official work by presenting Himself as the Messiah in Jerusalem, the religious capital of the nation and the headquarters of the religious authorities; and He carried on a ministry for some time in the province of Judea. John's Gospel records this part of the Lord's life, but all the Synoptics pass it over. He received no recognition from the leaders of the nation. On the imprisonment of John the Baptist, He changed the place and the mode of His work. He withdrew into Galilee, and made Capernaum His headquarters for a ministry among the common people in that province (vs. 12-13).

Matthew finds in this another fulfilment of prophecy (vs. 14-16; Isa. 9:1-2). That region was the first to suffer from the foreign invasions of Isaiah's day, which came into Palestine from the north. It was also to be the first to see the "great light" of the Messianic day. This prophecy was now being fulfilled in the ministry that Jesus was carrying on in Galilee and in the Gospel that He was preaching to the poor and suffering people there.

In the statement, "from that time began Jesus to preach" (v. 17), the Apostle marks the beginning of the Galilean ministry of the Messiah and indicates its nature. Jesus took up the same message that John had been preaching, and began to announce that the Kingdom of Heaven was at hand. This Kingdom was the new spiritual and heavenly order which He was to bring into being by His redemptive work. It had been foretold by the Old Testament prophets. It was now "at hand": it was only a few short years away.

Jesus had first to lay the foundation of the Kingdom by accomplishing His Messianic task. When He returned to Heaven, the Kingdom would then be opened to men by the descent of the Holy Spirit at Pentecost. It was called "the kingdom of heaven" because it was to be administered from the heavenly side: it would be the rule of Heaven on earth. It is the essential spiritual reality behind the whole Christian system. Jesus Christ came to establish an order of things in which the will of God would be done on earth by the power of the Spirit sent down from Heaven.

The narrative goes on to record the call of the first disciples—two pairs of brothers—from their fishing nets to become fishers of men (vs. 18-22). Then it describes the general character of the Galilean ministry (vs. 23-25). Jesus carried it on by touring the country, teaching in the synagogues, preaching the good news of the Kingdom, and healing all kinds of sickness. His fame spread far and wide. His miracles of healing caused great popular excitement. His fame spread beyond the limits of Palestine, and throngs gathered to Him from all quarters.

THE PRINCIPLES OF THE KINGDOM
(Chs. 5-7)

In carrying on His official work as the Messiah, Jesus not only made public proclamations of the nearness of the Kingdom He had come to establish; He went on to make a formal statement of its nature, explaining its laws and principles. This He did in an address to the disciples in the presence of the multitudes, which is usually called the Sermon on the Mount because of the place where it was delivered (5:1-2). Jesus no doubt repeated the teaching of this sermon again and again, and it is probable that Matthew has gathered into these three chapters the substance of addresses given at different times on the same theme.

1. The Members of the Kingdom Described (5:3-16). These verses describe the kind of life that was to be lived by the citizens of the Kingdom when it should come into being (Phil. 3:20). It is the ideal life of the Christian dispensation, which Christ has made possible for His disciples by His redemptive work (Rom. 8:3-4).

(1) Their blessed character (vs. 3-9). These seven beatitudes describe the blessed life. They are not given as a code of laws to be obeyed, but as a group of qualities which make the perfect moral character. They describe the character of Jesus Himself, wrought out first in His own earthly life, and then transmitted to His disciples by the Holy Spirit. They correspond with the fruit of the Spirit described in Gal. 5:22-23. The peculiar quality of this character is self-effacement, as indicated by the first beatitude—the elimination of the element introduced into human nature by the fall of Adam. The kingdoms of the world are founded on self-will and maintained by self-assertion. The Kingdom of Heaven is founded on the will of God, and it belongs to those who follow the way of self-denial.

The first four beatitudes represent the disciples of Jesus as conscious of their need of salvation; the last three represent them as having found salvation and realizing it. The blessedness promised in each case is not so much an arbitrary reward as the necessary and essential result of the state of heart described.

(2) Their experience in the world (vs. 10-12). This is a double beatitude based on the fact that the righteousness which Jesus was to introduce by His Messianic work would be alien to the spirit of the world. The citizens of the Kingdom would meet with hatred and hostility, but there should be great blessedness in that experience, and they should have a great reward in Heaven.

(3) Their influence in the world (vs. 13-16). This is described as two-fold. It would be like salt, arresting the progress of corruption and decay; and for this reason they must not lose their savour. It would be like light, diffusing the knowledge of the Light of the world (John 8:12). For this reason they must live among men in such a way as to show by the light of their lives what true life is (Phil. 2:14-16).

2. The New Kingdom and the Old Order (5:17-48). Jesus now goes on to explain how the new order which He was to introduce was related to the Old Testament dispensation. He came not to abrogate the Law and destroy its authority, but "to magnify the law, and make it honourable" (Isa. 42:21).

(1) The Old Testament Law confirmed (vs. 17-20). Jesus fulfilled the Law in two ways: (a) by living a life in which all its requirements were perfectly and completely obeyed, and (b) by bringing out and revealing the inner spiritual meaning of the Law. He required a righteousness that was not merely outward and mechanical like that of the Scribes and Pharisees, but was inward and spiritual.

(2) The Old Testament Law deepened and expanded (vs. 21-32). Jesus now applies the principle stated in v. 20 to two of the ten commandments of the Law, the sixth and the seventh. He demands a fulfilment of the Law in the thoughts and intents of the heart. When He declared, "Ye have heard . . . but I say unto you", He was not placing His own authority above the Law, but claiming the right to explain its true meaning, which the traditionalists had misunderstood.

In dealing with the sixth commandment, Jesus adds a sort of parenthesis on the duty of hastening to remove any uncharitable relation in which we may stand to others (vs. 21-26). In dealing with the seventh commandment, He urges those necessary steps of self-discipline which will enable men to avoid sin. Then He goes on to deal with the law of divorce, and proclaims the indissolubility of marriage (vs. 27-32). His legislation on this subject is repeated in 19:3-9, where He declares that in the Mosaic Law divorce was permitted because Israel was not yet ready for the moral standard of the Creator.

(3) New laws given in advance of the old (vs. 33-48). The principle stated in v. 20 is now applied in a new way, showing that it goes far beyond the express commands of the Law. This is illustrated in reference to three of the special regulations of the Old Testament: the law of oaths, which was an application of the third commandment (vs. 33-37); the law of retaliation, which allowed revenge up to a certain point (vs. 38-42); and the

law of love, which had a limitation put upon it (vs. 43-48).

In the first case Jesus points out that God is everywhere, and all words are uttered in His presence; therefore truthfulness is of universal obligation. He would not prohibit oaths in a court of justice, for He Himself consented to be sworn by the high priest at His trial (26:63-64). In the second case, where the law of the Old Covenant put a limitation upon the human instinct of revenge, Jesus eliminates it altogether. He takes away from us the right to administer justice in our own case, and requires us as individuals to follow self-effacement as the law of His Kingdom. We are not to resist legal injustice or resent public claims upon us.

To the law of love in Lev. 19:18 the Scribes had added "and hate thine enemy", as if the one were a legitimate inference from the other. In a sense it seemed to express the attitude of the law. Jesus now teaches the duty of loving one's enemies and desiring their good. It is to be expected of members of Christ's Kingdom that they should be unlike others in doing more than others. "Be ye therefore perfect" (v. 48), perfect in love; the reference is to the preceding verses. To love as God loves is moral perfection. This perfection Christ required of His disciples; and He was to make it possible for them by His Spirit.

3. The Righteousness of the Kingdom (6:1-18). The general principle is stated in v. 1: "Take heed that you do not your righteousness before men". This looks back to the "righteousness" of the Scribes and Pharisees mentioned in 5:20, and refers to acts of a religious character. These should be real and sincere, and not done for display. The new "righteousness" looks toward God and not toward men.

The principle is then applied to three branches of conduct that were regarded as the chief elements in religion, and might be called exercises of righteousness. It is this aspect of righteousness that Jesus has in mind, and in each case He deals with the motive. Self in all its forms is to be left out of view. Christian righteousness looks for the praise of God, never for the praise of men.

(1) Almsgiving (vs. 2-4)—religious exercise in relation to our fellow men. Jesus is teaching by metaphors. He forbids ostentation in doing good. "They have received their reward": they sought the applause of men, and this is all they have got.

(2) Prayer (vs. 5-15)—religious exercise in relation to God. The characteristics of true prayer are reality (vs. 5-6) and simplicity (vs. 7-8). Then comes a parenthesis in which Jesus gives a model of true prayer, usually called the Lord's Prayer. It consists of an introductory approach to God as Father and three petitions regarding Him (vs. 9-10), followed by four petitions regarding ourselves and a closing doxology (vs. 11-13). He follows it up by reverting to the petition for forgiveness, and stating that a forgiving spirit is an essential element in our experience of the forgiveness of God (vs. 14-15).

(3) Fasting (vs. 16-18) — religious exercise in relation to ourselves. Fasting is the typical example of abstinence from whatever hinders growth in the divine life. The principle stated here applies to all acts of self-denial done for spiritual profit. They have to do with the soul and with God alone.

4. The Members of the Kingdom and the Present World (6:19-34). This section deals with questions that relate to the wealth of this world and the necessities of life. They are not discussed in detail, but Jesus explains the attitude His disciples should take toward them. The general principle is summed up in vs. 33-34: "Seek ye first the kingdom of God, and his righteousness; and all these things shall be added unto you". The true attitude is heavenly mindedness regarding wealth and filial trust regarding necessities. The qualities involved are described in the verses that precede:

(1) Unworldliness (vs. 19-21). To lay up treasure in Heaven is to do things that promote the interests of God's Kingdom. The Lord forbids hoarding wealth for its own sake, for the sake of possessing it. To set one's heart on earthly treasure is to risk losing all.

(2) Singleness of purpose (vs. 22-24). This is what gives clearness and force to life. One cannot put God first and also set the heart on the wealth of the world.

(3) Freedom from anxiety (vs. 25-32). God cares for His creatures, how much more for His children. The heavenly Father knows His children's needs.

5. The Members of the Kingdom and their Fellow Men (7:1-12). This section deals with the attitude that disciples should take toward those who are still outside the Kingdom. The general principle is stated in v. 12; it is equivalent to, "love your neighbour as yourself". In the preceding verses this principle is applied in three ways. Jesus emphasizes:

(1) Charity and kindness (vs. 1-5). Avoid fault-finding and censoriousness. These are marks of self-righteousness and hypocrisy.

(2) Discrimination and caution (v. 6). Do not go to the other extreme, which makes no distinction between the good and the bad.

(3) Prayer for others (vs. 7-11). In a former passage (5:5-15) prayer was regarded as a religious duty: here it is enjoined as a means of helping others (Luke 11:5-13).

6. A Call to Enter the Kingdom (7:13-27). Having shown the true nature of the Kingdom of Heaven, Jesus now gives some closing appeals and warnings about the way to find and enter it.

(1) Enter by the narrow gate (vs. 13-14). This is the gate of a new birth, the birth from above (John 3:3). The narrow way is the way of the Cross (Matt. 16:24; Luke 14:27; Gal. 6:14).

(2) Beware of false teaching (vs. 15-20). This peril is all the greater because it wears a cloak of goodness. False teaching is to be detected by its results, either in the character of the teachers or in the lives of those who follow them.

(3) Beware of false profession (vs. 21-23). Jesus assumes the tone of the judge at this point. He is not only the founder of the Kingdom, but He also judges evil in it and purges evil from it.

(4) Be doers as well as hearers (vs. 24-27). Jesus enforces the message of the Sermon with two very graphic illustrations, which must have left a deep impression on His hearers, for they would well understand them—the house built upon the rock and the house built upon the sand.

The astonishment which His teaching produced upon the people, and the sense of authority which it carried, are noted by Matthew in the next verses (vs. 28-29). It was all so different from the teaching of the Scribes. They could only pass on their learned traditions about the Law. His teaching illumined the Law with a sense of reality. The divine authority behind the Old Testament Scriptures lived again on the lips of Jesus.

THE WORKS OF THE KINGDOM
(Chs. 8-9)

The principles of the Kingdom of Heaven having been explained, the Gospel goes on to reveal something of its nature and to show that Jesus had power to establish it, by giving an account of some typical miracles. Ten of the twenty miracles recorded by Matthew are grouped in these chapters. They are as follows: Cleansing the leper (8:1-4), healing the centurion's servant (8:5-13), healing Peter's wife's mother and the sick in Capernaum (8:14-17), stilling the storm on the sea (8:23-27), casting out demons from the two Gadarenes (8:28-34), healing the palsied man (9:1-8), healing the woman that touched His garment and raising the ruler's daughter (9:18-26), healing two blind men and a dumb demoniac (9.27-34).

In the midst of this list of miracles occur two incidents. In one case, Jesus warns His followers of the cost of discipleship and reveals His own sense of homelessness in the world (8:18-22). In the other case, Matthew is called and obeys at once (9:9). The feast that follows was given by Matthew himself to his former companions (Luke 5:29). Jesus was present, and that raised questions on the part of the Pharisees, who criticized the Lord's conduct in associating with sinners, and also on the part of John's disciples, who were puzzled by His neglect of fasting (9:10-17).

The miracles in these chapters were all Messianic signs, or works of salvation, showing that Jesus had power and authority to save men. They manifested His power in all the four realms to which human life is related. The stilling of the storm revealed Him as Lord of the natural world. The cure of the demoniacs showed that His authority reached into the spiritual world. The raising of the dead girl showed that His power extended beyond the grave. The other miracles were all works of healing, and were performed in a variety of ways, showing how thoroughly the Lord knew our physical nature and could meet its needs.

Some of these miracles were performed in such a way as to show that they were inseparably related to His own Person. His touch is mentioned several times (8:3, 15; 9:21, 25, 29). As His words showed that He came from the centre of ultimate truth, so His works showed that He was at the centre and source of ultimate power. They were all complete and thoroughgoing; in no case did the result leave anything unfinished. In some cases they were performed in response to faith (8:10, 13; 9:2, 22, 29). In one case of healing Jesus performed the cure to prove that He had authority to forgive sins (9:6).

THE MESSENGERS OF THE KINGDOM
(Ch. 10)

Jesus now took measures for the wider proclamation of the message of the Kingdom. The occasion for this new step was the spiritual destitution which He saw among the people as He went about the cities and villages of Galilee (9:35-38). His compassion went out to them, because they were like weary and helpless flocks of sheep that had no shepherd.

The twelve disciples who were chosen as Apostles were given authority to perform the signs and works of the Kingdom. Their names occur in pairs (vs. 1-4), probably indicating how they were sent out "by two and two" (Mark 6:7). There are three other lists of their names (Mark 3:16-19; Luke 6: 14-16; and Acts 1:13). When the four lists are compared, it appears that the Twelve were composed of three groups of four each. The order of their names is always different, but each group is always composed of the same names. Simon Peter always stands at the head of the list and Judas at the foot. Philip always heads the second group, and James, the son of Alphæus, the third group. The three groups probably indicate degrees of intimacy with the Lord, the first four enjoying His closest confidence (Mark 13:3).

Their instructions, as recorded in this chapter, fall into three divisions, each closing with an emphatic statement beginning, "Verily I say unto you". These seem to be summaries of instructions given at different times during the ministry of Jesus. Like all the discourses in Matthew's Gospel, this address is marked by dignity, order, and progress.

1. Instruction for their Present Mission (vs. 5-15). During the Lord's earthly ministry the mission of the Apostles was limited to Israel. They were to proclaim the same message as He was preaching, and perform the same works as He was doing. They were the messengers of Israel's Messiah to the nation, and so they were worthy of the people's support. These instructions, therefore, did not apply to their mission in the Gentile world afterwards. The ultimate judgment of the cities of Israel would be determined by their treatment of the Messiah's messengers.

2. Instruction for their Future Mission (vs. 16-23). This passage applies to the period between the Ascension of Christ in A.D. 30 and the destruction of Jerusalem in A.D. 70; that is, to the generation between the rejection of the Messiah and the judgment upon Israel. The circumstances of the Apostles' ministry are described as very different now. They should be "as sheep in the midst of wolves", hated and persecuted everywhere and by all men. But they should have the support of the Holy Spirit in their witness to their foes. They should not have finished their mission to Israel "till the Son of man be come"; that is, till He should come in judgment on the guilty nation. The conditions described in this passage are all illustrated in the Acts of the Apostles.

3. Instruction for Discipleship in General (vs. 24-42). This deals with Christian life and service in the world during the present age. The general principle means that the disciple should be as his Master, the Christian should be identified with Christ (vs. 24-25). This is stated first, and then its implications are drawn out as follows: freedom from fear, because of the Father's care (vs. 26-31); confessing Christ before men and giving Him supreme affection (vs. 32-37); following Christ by

carrying one's cross (vs. 38-39). This is our Lord's first mention of the Cross, and it implied a prophetic reference to His death, for a cross was carried to die on. Taking one's cross and following after Christ means leading a life of dying to self as He did. The charge to the Twelve then closes with words of encouragement for them in view of the mission on which they were sent (vs. 40-42).

THE OPPOSITION TO THE KINGDOM
(Chs. 11-12)

Christ had explained the nature of His Kingdom, shown His power to establish it, and taken measures to propagate its message. Matthew now goes on to show how this was being received by the nation. In ch. 11 we see how the message about the Kingdom was received by different classes among the people. In ch. 12 we see the bitter and malignant opposition to the King Himself which was growing among their religious leaders.

1. The Varying Reception of the Message (Ch. 11). Four kinds of hearers are represented in this chapter.

(1) John the Baptist represents those who believed Jesus to be the Messiah but were impatient because the Kingdom did not at once appear. John had testified of One coming with a fan in his hand to make a thorough separation between the wheat and the chaff in Israel (3:12). Jesus was not doing this, but was following a very different course. John sent his disciples to ask Him if the promised Messiah was still to come, and Jesus sent them back to tell John what they had seen and heard Jesus doing. The ministry of Jesus was fulfilling the prophetic account of the Messianic days as described in Isa. 35; and John, the last of the prophets, would understand the significance of this reply (vs. 1-6).

When John's messengers were gone, Jesus spoke to the people about him. He vindicated His sturdy herald from the imputation that his enquiry was due to fickleness of character or to the hardship of his imprisonment (vs. 7-8). Then He pronounced the highest praise upon him. John was more than a prophet: he was the messenger sent of God to prepare the way before the Lord Himself (Mal. 3:1). Thus he was the greatest among mankind up to that time; but the least member of the Kingdom of Heaven is greater than John (vs. 9-11).

In this statement Jesus reveals His standard of greatness: it is nearness of relationship to Himself. John was greater than all the prophets before him, for he not only told of the coming of Christ but actually introduced Him to Israel. But John lived before the Kingdom was inaugurated at Pentecost, and he did not enjoy the close relationship with Christ of those who are born of the Spirit. Jesus went on to say that one of the reactions of John's preaching was such a violent desire for the Kingdom that men of violence sought to establish it by force. The Law and the Prophets were brought to a head in John, and in him was fulfilled the prophecy that Elijah should come (vs. 12-15; Mal. 4: 5-6).

(2) "This generation" was the nation as a whole, especially as represented by its religious leaders. They found fault both with Jesus and with John, because neither conformed to their preconceived ideas (vs. 16-19).

(3) Then Jesus went on to upbraid another class, the impenitent cities of Galilee (vs. 20-24). They were condemned, not for gross wickedness, but for the self-satisfied indifference of their inhabitants to the miracles and teachings of Jesus in their midst. The doom He announced upon them implied His divine authority in judgment.

(4) At this point in the narrative Matthew records the Lord's thanksgiving to God for the faith of His own disciples—the "babes"—who had received with childlike simplicity and understanding the message He had brought from His Father (vs. 25-27). Then follows a gracious invitation from the very heart of the Saviour to all such as belong to this class and feel their need (vs. 28-30).

2. The Bitter Antagonism to the King (Ch. 12). This is manifest in the various accusations that were made against Him. The first had to do with His relation to the Sabbath. The Pharisees charged Him with sanctioning a breach of the Sabbath law on the part of His disciples (vs. 1-8). He defended them by citing examples from the Old Testament to show that ceremonial laws yielded to the higher claims of necessity and mercy (1 Sam. 21:6; Num. 28:9-10; Hosea 6:6). Then He declared, "the Son of man is lord of the sabbath". He was not claiming authority to abolish the Sabbath, but asserting His right as the representative Man to determine how the principle of the Sabbath should be carried out for man's benefit.

A synagogue scene follows in which a man with a withered hand was present (vs. 9-13). On this occasion another collision occurred with the Pharisees over the Sabbath. Jesus first exposed the heartless nature of their formalism, and then healed the man. This marks the time when they began to plot for His destruction (v. 14).

Jesus withdrew from there to carry on His healing ministry quietly, fulfilling another prophetic description of the Messiah (vs. 15-21; Isa. 42:1-3). When He healed a blind and dumb demoniac who had been brought to Him, the people in amazement wondered if He could be the Messiah. But the Pharisees explained the miracle by accusing Him of being in league with the prince of the demons (vs. 22-24). This led to a prolonged discourse, in which Jesus refuted the charge by an appeal to common sense, and then gave the true explanation of His cures. Satan would not fight against Satan, as even their own exorcists well knew (vs. 25-27). The power He used was that of the Spirit of God, which showed that the Kingdom of God came near to them. As the Head of that Kingdom, He had shown Himself stronger than Satan by freeing demoniacs from his power (vs. 28-29).

Jesus went on to point out that there was no place for neutrality in the conflict which He was carrying on with Satan, and to add a solemn warning (vs. 30-32). There is forgiveness for all kinds of sin, even sin against the Son of Man, but not for sin against the Holy Spirit. To attribute the work of the Holy Spirit to demonic power is to put oneself on the side of Satan and out of reach of God's forgiveness for ever. Jesus closed his discourse by appealing to the general experience of mankind, in order to show that His own character was to be known from His conduct and their character from their conduct (vs. 33-37). The distinction between good men and bad men is made by the kind of words and acts they produce.

The Scribes and Pharisees answered Christ's warning with a request that He should show them a sign, thus ignoring the Messianic character of His whole ministry. He called those who made such a demand "an evil and adulterous generation", because of their unfaithfulness to the marriage covenant that bound the nation to Jehovah; and the only sign that would be given to it was that of the prophet Jonah, which was a sign of His resurrection (vs. 38-40). The impenitence of the unbelieving Jews of that generation, who rejected the teaching of Christ, would be condemned in the coming judgment by the men of Nineveh, who repented at the preaching of Jonah, and by the Queen of Sheba, who came to hear the wisdom of Solomon (vs. 41-42).

Then Jesus likened that generation of Jews to a demoniac who had been cured, but afterwards allowed himself to be possessed by more evil demons. The idolatry of the old days had been given up, but such a spirit of formalism had now taken its place as to make the last state of the nation worse than the first (vs. 43-45).

Just then, Jesus was told that His mother and brethren were outside seeking to speak to Him. His reply is not a censure upon them, nor a denial of family ties. He uses their appeal to point out that there are far stronger and closer ties than these. Relationship in the Kingdom is based on the doing of the will of God, and not on any natural kinship (vs. 46-50).

THE MYSTERIES OF THE KINGDOM
(Ch. 13)

The growing opposition to the message of the Kingdom led Jesus to adopt a new method in proclaiming it. He began to speak in parables (vs. 1-3). The disciples asked Him why He was doing this, and he explained His reason (vs. 10-17). By using parables He would conceal the truth from those unwilling to receive it, and yet reveal it more fully to those who were ready to believe it. He quoted Isaiah (6:9-10) to show that a judicial blindness came upon those that refused to see, and a judicial hardening of heart upon those that would not hear.

The parables put His teaching in a form which attracted attention at the time and was easily remembered afterwards. They were stories or illustrations in which an analogy or similitude was drawn between the natural and the spiritual world. Our Lord did not use fables, nor did He ever invent a story from imaginary material. His parables were always based on the facts of the natural world and the experiences of every-day life. They were used to set forth the facts of the spiritual world and the nature of spiritual life. Earth is full of analogies of Heaven; earthly things are often shadows of heavenly realities. Parabolic teaching was therefore especially fitted to explain the Kingdom of Heaven. It could feed and instruct the Lord's genuine disciples, and sift out those who sought only temporal power and earthly glory and had no sense of the spiritual.

The seven parables in this chapter describe what Jesus called "the mysteries of the kingdom of heaven" (v. 11). This meant those aspects of it which could be understood only in the light of Divine revelation. These parables are descriptive of the present Christian order introduced by the coming of the Spirit at Pentecost. They set forth the condition of the Kingdom during the New Testament dispensation. The seven parables fall into two groups, spoken under different circumstances.

Four parables were spoken to the people from a boat at the sea-side (v. 2). They contain a view of the Kingdom as seen on its earthward side. They describe Christianity as a visible movement in the world of human affairs.

1. The Sower and the Four Kinds of Soil (vs. 3-9). Jesus explained this parable to the disciples after He told them why He spoke in parables (vs. 18-23). It describes the method by which the Gospel—"the word of the kingdom"—is propagated in the world. Its growth and progress depend upon the kind of reception it gets in the hearts of those who hear it. Four kinds of hearers are depicted in the parable, and then described in the Lord's interpretation of it.

2. The Wheat and the Tares (vs. 24-30). The tares were bearded darnel, a kind of mock wheat, very much like wheat in the earlier stages of its growth, but producing a poisonous fruit. Jesus explained this parable also when asked by the disciples about it (vs. 36-43). It describes the presence of evil in the Kingdom during the present age, and the source from which it comes. The good and the evil, the true and the false, "the children of the kingdom" and "the children of the wicked one", will develop and mature together until a crisis comes which is represented by the harvest. Their separation is not to be attempted by man, but will be made by the Son of Man through His angelic agents at the end of the age. Angels are everywhere represented as accompanying the Lord at His return (Matt. 16:27; 24:31; 2 Thess. 1:7; Rev. 19:14). Then the wicked will be consigned to their doom, and the righteous will appear in their true glory.

3. The Mustard Seed (vs. 31-32). This parable represents the growth of the Kingdom in its outward aspect as a visible, organized system in the world. It sets forth the contrast between the small and insignificant beginning of Christianity and its vast extent as it spreads and organizes itself throughout the world. It describes the nature and appearance of the visible Church. This parable and the next form a pair, dealing with the progress of the Gospel in human society.

4. The Leaven (v. 33). The significance of leaven when used as a symbol lies in its hidden, penetrating force. It usually represents an evil influence. Here it represents the influence of the Kingdom as a pervading energy working under the surface of human society. Our Lord did not mean to teach by this parable that the world would be converted to Christianity, but that the Gospel would introduce a kind of ferment into the world, which would continue to act and spread till it affected the whole human race. The parable describes the nature of the impact which Christianity makes in its contact with human society.

Having finished these four parables, Jesus left the people and entered the house (vs. 34-36). The remaining three parables were spoken to the disciples alone. They contain a view of the Kingdom on its Godward side, and deal with the spiritual reality that is the heart of Christianity.

5. The Hid Treasure (v. 44). This represents the new life in the Kingdom of Heaven, or salvation itself, as the greatest wealth or the highest good. A man comes upon it unexpectedly, without searching for it; and in order to secure it he joyfully sacrifices all that he has.

6. The Pearl of Great Price (vs. 45-46). This represents the new life as that which satisfies the deepest desires of the heart and fulfils the highest ideal of-the pure and the beautiful. A man finds it after long search; and for it he sacrifices everything he has. These two parables also form a pair; they deal with the effect of the Gospel upon personal and individual life. The idea is not that we purchase salvation, but that we secure it on the surrender of all earthly treasure.

7. The Drag-net (vs. 47-50). The last parable in the list describes the separation of the good from the bad, the true from the false, in the Kingdom. This is to take place at the end of the present age, when the preaching of the Gospel has been accomplished; and it is to be carried out by the angels. It is represented as a deliberate and final act of judgment.

Having finished the seven parables, Jesus addressed a final word to His disciples about this method of teaching. It had instructed them, and they were to use it for the instruction of others. They were to do for the Gospel of the Kingdom what the Scribes were doing for the Law (vs. 51-52).

Then Jesus departed from the Sea of Galilee and visited His own home-city of Nazareth. He came in His public capacity and taught in their synagogue. His townsfolk were astonished at His wisdom and at the report of His mighty acts. But they were offended at all this, because He belonged to one of their own families, and they resented His being different from themselves. Their unbelief prevented the continuation of His ministry among them (vs. 53-58).

THE REJECTION OF THE KINGDOM
(Chs. 14-16)

The death of John the Baptist took place at this time, and it brought about a change in the ministry of Jesus, for the death of John was a fore-warning of His own death. After this He withdrew from time to time from the crowded parts of central Galilee, and took the disciples with Him into outlying districts for greater privacy. His purpose was to instruct them more and more about Himself, and to prepare them for His approaching death. The miracles He performed after this were manifestations of what He was in His own Person rather than evidences of what He was able to do. Formerly He had been revealing His power; now He began to reveal His heavenly character and His real relation to God.

1. The Death of John (14:1-12). John was the herald of Jesus in more than one sense. Events in his life seem to have marked turning points in the life and ministry of Jesus. The first appearance of John led Jesus to leave the privacy of Nazareth and enter on His public ministry to Israel. The im-

prisonment of John led Jesus to leave Judea, where He had been presenting Himself to the leaders of the nation, and enter upon a ministry among the common people in Galilee. And now the death of John was followed by a series of withdrawals from His headquarters in Galilee to more distant parts of the country. In the present passage Matthew narrates the story of John's death at the hands of Herod.

2. The First Withdrawal (14:13-15:20). When Jesus heard of the death of John, He withdrew in a boat to an uninhabited district on the north-eastern side of the Sea of Galilee. The people followed Him in crowds around the shore. Moved with compassion for them, He healed their sick, and then performed one of His most significant miracles. He fed the multitude—five thousand men besides women and children—with five loaves and two fishes (14:13-21). This miracle was an acted parable, setting forth Christ's spiritual relation to Israel. When He saw a movement among them to make Him a king by earthly means (John 6:15), He hurried the disciples back in the boat while He sent the people away, and then went up into the mountain alone to pray (14:22-23).

When the night was far spent He came walking upon the water to the disciples, who were labouring against an adverse wind on their way to the other side. Peter's impulsive attempt to walk out toward Him showed his devotion to Jesus, but exposed his lack of faith (14:24-33). When Jesus came back to the land of Gennesaret, the people came gathering from all around bringing their sick to be healed (14:34-36).

Some Pharisees and Scribes who had come up from Jerusalem asked Him why His disciples did not observe Jewish ceremonial tradition. He replied by pointing out that by adding their tradition to the Law they made void the Word of God (15:1-9). Then He went on to denounce their hypocrisy to the crowd that had gathered, and explained that defilement came from the heart. The Pharisees were blind guides, blind to the spiritual realities (15:10-14). Even the disciples were without spiritual understanding, as Peter's question showed, and Jesus had to give them further instruction about the things that defile men (15: 15-20).

The mass of the Jews, and especially their religious leaders, completely misunderstood the purpose of the ceremonial regulations of the Mosaic Law. These were given as a means of separating Israel from other nations to be a spiritual people prepared for the Messiah. The Jews made the means the end. Even the Apostles shared this misunderstanding, and the serious trouble which arose in the early Church over it shows how firmly it had taken possession of the Jewish mind.

3. The Second Withdrawal (15:21 — 16:12). Jesus now withdrew to the western side of Galilee in the district of Tyre and Sidon. There a Canaanitish woman appealed to Him as "thou son of David" for her demon-possessed daughter. Being a Gentile she had no claim upon Him on that ground; but when she persisted in her appeal without basing it on any claim, willing only to take the crumbs, He answered her request and commended her faith (15:21-28). On his way back toward the Sea of Galilee, he passed through a district where crowds gathered about Him with their sick folk for healing, who seem to have been mainly Gentiles. This is indicated by the unusual statement that "they glorified the God of Israel" (vs. 29-31). In this place He performed another miracle of feeding the multitude, and thus set forth His spiritual relation to the Gentile world (15:32-39).

When He arrived at the Sea of Galilee again, the Pharisees and Sadducees came asking for a sign from heaven. He condemned them for not knowing the signs of the times, and repeated what He had told them before, that no sign would be given them but the sign of Jonah (16:1-4; cf. 12:38-39). He subsequently warned the disciples to beware of the evil influence of the teaching of the Pharisees and Sadducees, and He had to rebuke them for their spiritual dullness in misunderstanding His warning (16:5-12).

4. The Third Withdrawal (16:13-20). This time Jesus withdrew into the most northern district of Galilee, the parts of Cæsarea Philippi. Here took place Peter's great confession of Christ, His own first announcement of the Cross, and the Transfiguration. Only the first of these events is included in the present passage. It contains two great truths now revealed for the first time:

(1) The nature and office of the Christ (vs. 13-17). The first question which Jesus put to the disciples brought out the fact that popular opinion regarded Him as one of the greatest of men, but fell far short of recognizing His true nature or seeing in Him the Messiah. The second question was intended to bring out what they themselves, who knew Him most intimately, had come to see in Him. Peter, always the spokesman of the Apostles, replied immediately: "Thou art the Christ, the Son of the living God". The significance of this confession, which brought great joy to the heart of Jesus as His commendation of Peter shows, lies in not only recognizing in Him the promised Messiah, but also recognizing in the Messiah the Divine nature. Jesus Christ was more than the best and greatest of men; He was God come down among men, God manifest in the flesh.

(2) The nature and office of the Church (vs. 18-20). Jesus followed up His commendation of Peter with a statement based on his confession: "Thou art Peter (a piece of rock) and upon this rock (Himself) will I build my church". Because of Israel's refusal to accept Him as the Messiah, Jesus now undertook to establish a new Israel—"my church"—built upon Himself as the "rock". This title is never used of men in the Old Testament, but always of the Lord God (Deut. 32:4; 2 Sam. 22:32; Isa. 26:4; 44:8; Psa. 62:2; 95:1). The main theme of the whole conversation, introduced by the Lord Himself, is the nature of His own Person: and it breaks the thread of His argument to refer "this rock" to Peter. Jesus would probably accompany His play on words by a gesture, pointing to Peter first and then to Himself.

The "church" is the same as the "congregation" of the Old Testament (Deut. 31:30; 1 Chron. 29:1). The congregation was Israel in its collective capacity gathered around the Temple. The Church was to be the new Israel gathered around Jesus Christ. By "the gates of Hades" Jesus meant the power of death and the grave (Isa. 38:10; Psa. 9:13). The old Israel was confined to this world. The Church of Christ would reach out into the world beyond death. Its members could not be held within the grave.

To the Church in the person of Peter, Jesus entrusted the keys of the Kingdom of Heaven, that is, the right and privilege of opening the Kingdom to men by the preaching of the Gospel. Peter was the first to use the keys when He preached the Gospel at Pentecost. "Binding" and "loosing" were Rabbinical terms for forbidding and allowing, and they implied the right of spiritual discipline. The Lord conferred this upon Peter as the representative of the Church. It was given afterwards to all the disciples (Matt. 18:18; John 20:23).

5. The Announcement of the Cross (16:21-28). The phrase, "from that time", marks a new stage in the ministry of Jesus (cf. 4:17). He now began to tell His disciples of His approaching suffering and death and resurrection. Israel's rejection of the Kingdom would culminate in the Cross. It was by this road the King was to attain His Kingdom, for the Cross carried with it the Resurrection (v. 21). He repeated the prediction of His death several times after this, and on each occasion He foretold His resurrection as well. This announcement was made first only after Peter's confession had shown that the disciples were coming to understand the secret of His own Person, for only in the light of that could they understand the significance of His death. Even yet they did not understand, and Peter's protest was met at once by the Lord's sharp rebuke (vs. 22-23). He saw in it another attempt of Satan to divert Him from His path by the offer that he had made to Him in the wilderness (4:8-10).

In immediate connection with this first announcement of His own sufferings, Jesus pointed out the path for His disciples to take in following Him, and then went on to foretell His own coming in glory (vs. 24-28). The members of the Church, those who would follow Him henceforth during the days of His rejection, must do so by the way of the Cross; and the way of the Cross is the way to glory.

THE PREPARATION FOR THE CROSS
(Chs. 17-18)

The Transfiguration marked the highest point in the life of Jesus. It was the culmination of His sinless and perfect humanity. He might have entered Heaven by that way at this point in His life, for upon Him death had no claim. It also foreshadowed the glory of His coming Kingdom (2 Pet. 1:16-18). But Jesus deliberately turned back from the open door of Heaven through which He might have left the world, and set His face toward the Cross, in order to accomplish the redemption of the world by giving Himself to death for the sin of the world.

1. The Transfiguration and its Issues (Ch. 17). This event brings us to the crowning act of self-renunciation in Jesus' life of surrender to the Father's will. It is followed in the narrative by incidents illustrating phases of self-denial.

(1) The scene on the mount (vs. 1-8). The Transfiguration of Jesus was not a manifestation of His Divine nature shining through His human nature. It was the manifestation of His human nature, now perfected, in its true glory. Moses and Elijah were present, not as immaterial spirits, but in bodily form as Jesus was. They were men who had got beyond the reach of death, Elijah by translation and Moses by resurrection, and were now in glory. (It is implied in Jude 9 that Moses was raised from the dead). They represented the Law and the Prophets; and their presence with Jesus on the mount marked the essential connection of the Saviour with the Old Testament dispensation.

The three men stood there, as it were, in the midst of the heavenly world. Peter's impulsive wish expressed the sense of bliss which the sight gave to the three disciples whom Jesus had taken with Him to see His glory. The voice that came out of the cloud which finally overshadowed the vision expressed the Father's approval of the Son's self-surrender in turning back to the Cross. It had been heard before, when Jesus dedicated Himself at His baptism to fulfil the Father's will as the Messiah (3:17).

(2) The descent from the mount (vs. 9-21). On the way down Jesus again referred to His death and resurrection. In answer to the disciples' enquiry why the Scribes said that Elijah must first come, He explained that the prophecy regarding the coming of Elijah (Mal. 4:5-6) had been fulfilled already in the person of John the Baptist (vs. 9-13). The failure of the other disciples to heal the demoniac boy when Jesus was absent from them, He attributed to the weakness of faith when not supported by prayer and self-denial. Faith is victorious only when accompanied by communion with God and victory over self (vs. 14-21).

(3) The final stay in Galilee (vs. 22-27). During this period He uttered another prediction of His death and resurrection (vs. 22-23). On His return to Capernaum the Temple tax was being collected (Exod. 30:11-16). As the Son, Jesus claimed to be exempt; but in order to give no offence to others, He provided the tax for Himself and Peter by a coin found in the mouth of a fish that Peter caught by following His instructions (vs. 24-27). It was another example of self-denial: He had declined to assert a right that was His as the Messiah.

2. Further Instructions for Discipleship (Ch. 18). The occasion of this address to the disciples was their question: "Who is the greatest in the kingdom of heaven?" (v. 1). This very question came from a wrong attitude: they had forgotten His warning about the Cross. Jesus now gave them instructions from the new point of view. He explained the peculiar qualities that should characterize those who take up their cross and follow Him. These may be summed up under three heads.

(1) The spirit of humility and trustfulness (vs. 2-14). Jesus put a child in the midst, and then said to the disciples, "Except ye turn, and become as little children"; that is, except you give up this spirit of self-seeking and ambition, and become humble and trustful like little children. He is the greatest in the Kingdom who thinks least of greatness (vs. 1-4).

Having answered the question asked of Him, Jesus takes up the thought of what the child represents in its trustfulness and simplicity, and identifies Himself with childlike believers, whom He speaks of as "these little ones". To receive such an one in His name, that is, for His sake, is to receive Himself. Then He adds a solemn and awful warning against putting "offences" — temptations or stumbling blocks — in their way (vs. 5-7), and points out the great peril of having any stumbling blocks in one's own life (vs. 8-9). He goes on to emphasize His warning against despising "one of these little ones", and declares that they are under the special care of heavenly guardians who have access to the Father (Heb. 1:14), and it is not His will that any one of them should go astray like a lost sheep (vs. 10-14).

(2) The spirit of unity and unanimity (vs. 15-20). The principle of spiritual unity is stated in v. 20: Christ Himself is the centre. It is His presence that gives spiritual unity to a company of believers. This principle has different manifestations. Three of them are dealt with in these verses: spiritual discipline (vs. 15-17), spiritual authority (v. 18), and spiritual power (vs. 19-20). Jesus confirmed the right of discipline given to His Church in 16:19. The mind of God is expressed in the judgment of a company of believers who are united to Christ in a spiritual unity, and the prayers of such a company have divine power, for Christ Himself is in their midst.

(3) The spirit of love and forgiveness (vs. 21-35). Forgiveness toward an offending brother should have no limit (vs. 21-22). This was the meaning of Jesus' reply to Peter's question; and He went on to illustrate it by the parable of the unmerciful servant (vs. 23-34). Our sin against God is beyond comparison with the sin of our fellow-men against us. Since God has forgiven us the greater debt, we ought to forgive our brother the lesser debt (Eph. 4:32; Col. 3:13). Those who do not show the spirit of forgiveness have not the faith that receives the forgiveness of God (v. 35). He who follows Christ in the way of the Cross will have the spirit of forgiveness in his heart.

THE APPROACH TO THE CROSS
(Chs. 19-20)

Jesus now left Galilee for the last time, and made His way slowly toward Jerusalem through the district on the eastern side of the Jordan, teaching and healing as He went. The progress of His journey is marked at several points in the course of the narrative (19:1-2; 20:17, 29; 21:1). A number of incidents are recorded in these chapters as belonging to this period.

On one occasion the Pharisees came trying Him with a question regarding the Mosaic law of divorce, and He repeated the teaching He had given in the Sermon on the Mount (19:3-9). The fact that the Creator made man both male and female meant that the marriage bond should be inviolable. The Mosaic regulation was a concession to moral weakness in Israel's primitive state. The strictness of this moral standard brought a question from the disciples, and to them Jesus gave a further word of instruction and advice (19:10-12).

At one place Jesus received and blessed little children who were brought to Him, commanding the disciples not to turn them away, but let them come to Him, "for of such is the kingdom of heaven" (19:13-15). Childlikeness, the spirit of humble trust, is the characteristic quality of the members of the Kingdom.

A rich young man came asking Him what good thing He should do to have eternal life, and went away downcast when Jesus put to him the final test of self-denial, which he would not meet. The principle implied in the self-sacrifice that the Lord demanded of him was the duty of the rich to regard their riches as a trust with which to minister to others (19:16-22). This led Jesus to tell the disciples how hard it is for a rich man, a man who has the roots of his life in this world, to meet the test of self-denial required for entrance into the Kingdom of Heaven, where life belongs to another world (19:23-26).

Then Peter reminded Him that they had met the test, having left all to follow Him, and asked what they should have. Jesus commended their devotion and gave them a promise of abundant reward in His Kingdom (19:27-30). He followed this with the parable of the labourers in the vineyard, in order to warn them against the bargaining spirit (20:1-16). The parable hangs on the closing words of ch. 19, and ends with a similar statement. Rewards will not be of works, but of grace: not according to the length of service or the amount of toil, but according to His own will; and His will is always good and kind and considerate. Therefore the true motive in serving the Master is not that of the hireling, fulfilling a contract, but that which is inspired by grateful, loving trust.

As He was getting nearer Jerusalem, Jesus told His disciples for the third time, and more fully than before, of what was to happen there—His betrayal, His condemnation to death by the Jews, His crucifixion by the Gentiles, and His resurrection on the third day afterwards (20:17-19). Then the wife of Zebedee came with an ambitious request on behalf of her two sons, James and John, for the highest places in His Kingdom (20:20-23). The consequent indignation of the other disciples against the two brothers led Jesus to call them all together, and warn them against the worldly desire to rule and exercise authority. Greatness among them would be reached by the way of service. He Himself came among men not to be served, but to serve, and even "to give His life a ransom for many" (20:24-28).

As they were leaving Jericho on the final stage of the journey, followed by a great company of pilgrims going up to the Passover, Jesus healed two blind men who were sitting by the wayside. When they heard that He was passing, they appealed to Him as "thou son of David", thus implying a belief that He was the Messiah (20:29-34). The whole incident reveals a rising tide of interest on the part of the people in the Messianic claims of Jesus as He kept going on toward Jerusalem.

THE FINAL TESTIMONY TO ISRAEL
(Chs. 21-23)

The time had now come for Jesus to make the final presentation of Himself to the Jewish nation. He made a public entry into Jerusalem in a way that was a manifest claim to be the Messiah. This was followed by several days of teaching in the Temple and controversy with the Jewish leaders. But there was no recognition of His claim on their part. Then came His final denunciation of them.

1. Final Messianic Acts (21:1-22). Three acts are recorded in this passage, in each of which He manifested His Messianic character and claimed Messianic authority.

(1) The royal entrance into Jerusalem (vs. 1-11). Jesus deliberately entered the city in the manner that prophecy had foretold the King should come

(Zech. 9:9). As He did so, He accepted the acclamations of the people who hailed Him as the Messiah.

(2) The cleansing of the Temple (vs. 12-17). He swept away the unholy traffic which was carried on in the outer court for the convenience of the people and the profit of the priests. He followed this up by healing the blind and the lame who came to Him. He welcomed the praises of the children in its courts, and spurned the indignant and jealous protest of the chief priests and scribes.

(3) The curse upon the fruitless fig-tree (vs. 18-22). He pronounced this curse on His way into the city next morning, as a symbolic act of judgment on Israel. The reply which Jesus gave to the question of the disciples implied that He wrought this miracle by faith in answer to prayer.

2. Final Messianic Teaching (21:23—22:14). The religious leaders came to Jesus as He was teaching in the Temple, and demanded to know what authority He had for doing these things. He replied with another question, whether the baptism of John was from Heaven or of men. Their answer exposed their hypocrisy and showed their unfitness to be religious leaders (21:23-27). Jesus then went on to speak three parables against them.

(1) The two sons (21:28-32). This parable brought out the real nature of their sin as disobedience to God, and set their religious profession and spiritual indifference over against the repentance of those who had made no profession before.

(2) The wicked husbandmen (21:33-46). In this story Jesus drew a picture of the persistent disobedience to God of the religious leaders of Israel throughout the history of the nation, leading up to their rejection of the Messiah Himself. He told the story in such a graphic and impressive way that He drew out from them their own condemnation (v. 41). Then He went on to declare that the Kingdom of God should be taken from them and given to a new Israel, a nation no longer disobedient, but "bringing forth the fruits thereof". This roused their anger, and they would have arrested Him then, but feared the people.

(3) The marriage feast (22:1-14). In this parable Jesus carried His survey of the national disobedience still further. It depicts the rejection of Israel from the privileges of the Kingdom, and the subsequent calling of the Gentiles. In the incident of the man who was discovered without a wedding garment, there is a foreshadowing of the essential nature of salvation as a free gift accepted from God. The garments for the feast were provided by the host for the invited guests. The whole parable is a prophetic picture of the present Christian age.

3. Final Controversy with the Jewish Leaders (22:15-46). The Pharisees now plotted with the other religious parties among the Jews to ensnare Jesus in His teaching, and three questions were put to Him by three different groups. Having answered them all, He put His own question to them, and they could not reply. All His foes were silenced; they had been completely baffled.

(1) A political question about the taxes (vs. 15-22). The Herodians, whom the Pharisees got to put this craftily designed question, seem to have been a small political party who supported the dynasty of Herod and favoured the rule of Rome. The wisdom of Christ's answer made them marvel. It is a perfect summary of the duty of a citizen.

(2) A doctrinal question about the resurrection (vs. 23-33). This was raised by the Sadducees, who disbelieved in another world and accepted only the books of Moses. Christ's answer exposed their ignorance even of those Scriptures that they professed to believe. By quoting Exod. 3:6, where God calls Himself the God of Abraham, Isaac, and Jacob, after they had all died, Jesus showed that the books of Moses teach a future life.

(3) A moral question about the Law (vs. 34-40). One of the Scribes belonging to the orthodox party of the Pharisees, who magnified the letter and ignored the spirit of the Law, asked Jesus which was the greatest of the commandments of the Law. By quoting Deut. 6:5 and Lev. 19:18, Jesus summed up all the Law and the Prophets in the duty of love to God and love to man.

(4) A Scriptural question about the Messiah (vs. 41-46). It was now the Lord's turn, and the question He put to the Pharisees, "What think ye of the Christ?" brought out the fact that their idea of the promised Messiah was quite inadequate and was due to their ignorance of the Scriptures. They believed that the Messiah was David's son, but they could not explain why David in Psa. 110:1 showed such reverence for him as to speak of him as "my Lord". They were looking only for an earthly monarch, an heir to occupy David's throne and restore his earthly kingdom. They failed to see that the long-promised Messiah of the prophetic Scriptures was of a far higher nature.

In this argument Jesus not only assumed the Messianic character of Psalm 110, but also declared that David wrote it and did so by inspiration. Subjective literary criticism denies the Davidic authorship, but attempts to justify Jesus on the ground that His reasoning was based on what the Pharisees thought of the psalm. If this were the case, our Lord's words would have no weight for us now, whatever weight they might have had for the Pharisees then.

4. Final Denunciation of the Scribes and Pharisees (Ch. 23). It was useless for Jesus to try any longer to make the leaders of the Jews see His true character. He now uttered a solemn and deliberate address about them to the Jewish people and His own disciples. He recognized their position as religious authorities, but denounced their bad example, and warned His disciples against them (vs. 1-12). Then He pronounced His judgment upon them in a series of seven "woe's" of terrific condemnation (vs. 13-31). Their sin completed the iniquity of their fathers, and the long-withheld judgment of God would now fall upon the guilty nation (vs. 32-36). With a sorrowing cry over the city that had refused to receive Him, He finally left it to its doom (vs. 37-39).

THE FINAL PROPHECY TO THE DISCIPLES
(Chs. 24-25)

As Jesus was leaving the Temple with His disciples for the last time, they drew His attention to the massive structure of its buildings, doubtless with national Jewish pride in their hearts. He then startled them with the declaration that the whole place was to be completely destroyed. When they arrived on the Mount of Olives they asked Him, "When shall these things be?" and added another question: "What shall be the sign of thy coming, and of the end of the world?" (24:1-3). The disciples no doubt thought that such a catastrophe as the destruction of the Temple would mark the end of the world, when His second coming would take place.

His reply is contained in these two chapters, and is of greater length than any other recorded answer to a question addressed to Him. In the course of it He keeps the two events in view. The destruction of the Temple, marking the end of the Jewish age, is in the immediate foreground. His own second coming, marking the end of the Christian era, is in the distant background. Taken as a whole, the address is not so much a program of historic events as a statement of historic principles. The destiny of a nation, like that of the individual, is determined by its relation to Jesus Christ. So also will be the destiny of the world.

1. General Warnings regarding the Christian Age (24:4-14). This passage applies primarily to the period ending with the fall of Jerusalem, but also to the whole age ending with the coming of Christ. It contains warnings about things that might be mistaken for signs of His coming, rather than descriptions of true signs. Jesus begins by telling the disciples not to be led astray by false religious teachers, nor to be troubled when they hear of wars among the nations and calamities in the natural world. These things will mark the age, but will not be signs of the end (vs. 4-8).

The followers of Christ will meet with persecution and trial and hatred in the world (vs. 9-10). False prophets will arise, and there will be a decay of devotion to Christ in the midst of the iniquity of the world. Only those that endure will be saved (vs. 11-13). When the Gospel shall have been preached throughout the world for a witness to all the nations, then the end will come (v. 14). It is probable that this condition was fulfilled in the world of the Roman Empire before the fall of Jerusalem. It awaits fulfilment in the whole world before the end of the Christian age.

2. Special Warnings regarding the Fall of Jerusalem (24:15-28). This passage contains a prophetic warning of the Roman invasion of Palestine, which began in A.D. 66, and resulted four years later in the capture of Jerusalem and the destruction of the Temple. The phrase, "the abomination of desolation" (v. 15), is a reference to Dan. 9:27. The prophecy was fulfilled when the pagan Roman army invaded the holy land, bringing the desolation of divine judgment upon it. The parenthetic words, "let him that readeth understand", were inserted by the author of the Gospel as a warning to his readers. This shows that the book was written before the event took place.

The Lord goes on to warn His followers to flee from Judea and Jerusalem speedily when they see the Roman army approaching the city (vs. 16-20). This warning was heeded. The Christians escaped from the city before it was completely surrounded, and established themselves at Pella across the Jordan.

A great tribulation would then set in such as had never happened before and would never happen again (vs. 21-22). This unparalleled affliction is described in Jer. 30:7 as "the time of Jacob's trouble", and in Dan. 12:1 as "a time of trouble, such as never was since there was a nation". It is the long-foretold judgment that was to fall upon Israel for the national rejection of their Messiah. The tribulation of the Jews is unprecedented, both in the severity of its fall upon the nation at that time, and also in its age-long continuance ever since. It is also unparalleled: it is of such a nature as no other nation has ever suffered. "Except those days had been shortened", the days of the siege of Jerusalem, "no flesh would have been saved": no part of the Jewish nation would have survived. "But for the elect's sake", for the sake of the believing Jews in the nation, "those days shall be shortened". The slaughter of life was tremendous and appalling, but the siege was not prolonged.

Then Jesus uttered a warning against those who give false teaching and raise false hopes about Christ's coming (vs. 23-26). The coming of the Son of Man will not be a secret event; it will be seen and recognized simultaneously everywhere, like a flash of lightning (v. 27). Then comes a final word of doom (v. 28). By "the carcase" in this proverbial expression, Jesus referred to the Judaism of His day. It had lost all spiritual life, and was only a dead body, attracting upon itself the agents of destruction—the false Christs, the false prophets, and the pagan armies of Rome.

3. Special Warnings regarding the Coming of Christ (24:29-51). The prophecy now passes to the end of the Christian age and the coming of the Son of Man. This is described as happening "immediately after the tribulation of those days": that is, when the tribulation of Israel, which began with the fall of Jerusalem, should be drawing to an end (v. 29). Then a period of trouble for all the world should set in, which Jesus describes in terms taken from the Old Testament predictions of national judgments (Isa. 13:10; 24:23). When this collapse of the present world order takes place, then shall the Son of Man appear in power and glory, gathering His chosen people to Himself (vs. 30-31). He is represented as "coming in the clouds of heaven", that is, from behind the veil of the heavenly world (Acts 1:11). This brings us to the resurrection and the rapture of the saints, which Paul describes as taking place at the second coming of Christ (1 Cor. 15:51-52; 1 Thess. 4:16-17).

The fulfilment of the prophecy was to begin in that very generation. As the budding of the fig-tree indicates the sure approach of summer, so the events of that time would be a sure indication of the coming of the Son of Man (vs. 32-33). "This generation shall not pass away, till all these things be accomplished", or come to be; that is, till their accomplishment should begin (vs. 34-35). The actual time of His coming, however, is known only to God; no visible sign of it is given. It will be sudden and unexpected, like the judgment of the flood in the days of Noah. Human life will be going on in its usual way, and men will be engaged in their ordinary occupations, when the final separation among men is made (vs. 36-41).

Hence the need of watchfulness. This is the attitude the disciples are to take during the whole age (v. 42). The warning is enforced by two illustrations: the householder and the thief (vs. 43-44), and the servant and his master (vs. 45-51).

4. Preparation for the Coming of Christ (25: 1-30). The idea of watching is now taken up and explained in two parables. These illustrate the kind of preparation that is meant by "watching".

(1) The virgins waiting for the bridegroom (vs. 1-13). This parable teaches the lesson of vigilance and patient waiting, and the need of inward preparation. This consists in the possession and cultivation of spiritual life. The ten virgins were all alike in outward profession: they all carried lamps. The two groups differed in the matter of oil, which is the symbol of the Holy Spirit. The wise virgins, who took oil to supply their lamps, represent those whose lives are fed by the inward presence of the Spirit (Rom. 8:9). The lamps of the others went out when the crisis came.

(2) The talents and their use (vs. 14-30). This parable teaches the lesson of diligence and faithful work, and the need of outward preparation. This consists in active service for Christ. The talents are intended to represent spiritual gifts and opportunities for spiritual service. These usually have a special relation to natural endowments (1 Cor. 12: 4-11). The lord of the servants in the parable gave them "his goods", to every one "according to his several ability". They were not given as a personal possession, but as a trust to be used in his interest.

5. The Throne of the Son of Man (25:31-46). This sublime scene is a symbolic representation of the power and glory of the Lord when He comes as the representative Head of the human race. It is not intended to give the program of judgment, but rather to set forth the nature and principles of judgment. During the present age Jesus is manifested as Saviour: then He will be manifested as King and Judge.

He is represented as sitting on the judgment-seat of the world, attended by hosts of angels, the whole human race before Him awaiting His verdict (vs. 31-33). These tremendous words were uttered by Jesus within three days of the Cross. He went on to explain and illustrate His method of judgment (vs. 34-45). He will act as the representative Man, and proceed on the principle manifested in redemption. Only two classes of men will be recognized. They will be distinguished by one test alone—their attitude toward Himself. In putting this test, He identifies Himself with His disciples. The attitude of men to Him is judged by the way they treat His followers. The separation He makes among men by this test will be final and unalterable—eternal punishment for the one class and eternal life for the other (v. 46).

THE SUFFERING OF THE CROSS
(Chs. 26-27)

We come now to the heart of the Gospel, the climax of revelation, the central act in the work of redemption. The importance of the event is marked by the fulness of detail with which the story is told. The death of Christ was no after-thought on God's part (Act 2:23). The time and the circumstances were ordered by Him without interfering with the free action of Christ's foes or lessening their guilt. This is strikingly illustrated by the fact that the crucifixion took place at the Passover, contrary to the intention of the Jews (26:5). The great Paschal Lamb was slain at the hour and in the manner appointed, as set forth in the type.

1. The Preparations (26:1-16). All the lines of the narrative now begin to converge toward the Cross. Jesus Himself sought to prepare His disciples for the event, which He had foretold so often and which was now so near (vs. 1-2). The Jewish council of religious rulers plotted in the house of the high priest to capture and kill Him (vs. 3-5). At a supper in the house of Simon the leper in Bethany, Mary (John 12:3), whose name is not given by Matthew, probably because she was still living, poured a flask of precious ointment on His head. He saw in the act, which the disciples thought was a great waste, a preparation for His burial, and gave her His highest commendation (vs. 6-13). Judas Iscariot, one of His own Twelve, went out after this and bargained with the chief priests to betray Him (vs. 14-16).

2. The Last Supper (26:17-35). The disciples prepared the Passover, according to the directions Jesus gave them, in the house of an unnamed follower (vs. 17-19). When He sat down with them, He announced that one of them should betray Him; and in answering the troubled enquiries which this caused, He gave a direct warning to Judas (vs. 20-25). The Passover feast having fulfilled its purpose, Jesus now instituted a new feast for His disciples, embodying the fundamental truth of Christianity as the Passover had embodied that of Judaism (vs. 26-29).

The Lord's Supper was to be a memorial of His death and a sign of the New Covenant foretold in the Old Testament (Jer. 31:31; Dan. 9:27), which He was now about to seal with His blood, thus securing the final remission of sins. The hymn which they sang at the end of the Supper, before going out to the Mount of Olives (v. 30), was probably part of the Hallel (Psalms 113-118), which the Jews sang in the course of the Passover feast. Then Jesus disclosed the increasing loneliness of His spirit by announcing that they should all desert Him that night, but that He would meet them after His resurrection in Galilee (vs. 31-32). This evoked a boastful profession of loyalty on Peter's part, to which the Lord replied by foretelling that disciple's three-fold denial of his Master (vs. 33-35).

3. Gethsemane (26:36-56). Here took place both the agony and the betrayal. The agony was the final stage of the conflict with Satan which had begun with the temptation in the wilderness. He took the chosen three with Him when He went into the garden to pray, that He might have them near by to watch with Him. He came back again and again, only to find them asleep. They failed Him in His hour of awful loneliness, and He had to tread the winepress alone (vs. 36-44). Jesus prayed first: "If it be possible, let this cup pass away from me"; and then: "If this cannot pass away, except I drink it, thy will be done". It was not the fear of physical pain or the dread of impending death that made Him pray thus, "with strong crying and tears" (Heb. 5:7). It was the mysterious nature of the agony which He could not escape if He would redeem the world. He who knew no sin was being made sin (2 Cor. 5:21). He was now coming to know the cost of giving His life as a ransom (20:28).

The answer to His prayer was not the removal of the cup, but a view of the triumph that lay beyond it (Heb. 12:2). He came out of that hour with the sublime calmness of complete and final surrender to the Father's will (vs. 45-46). This was manifest during the shameful scene that followed, when He was betrayed by Judas into the hands of His foes, and deserted by the rest of His disciples (vs. 47-56). Throughout the whole scene He was master of the situation, and declared that He could call twelve legions of angels to His aid; but He yielded Himself to their will.

4. **The Jewish Trial** (26:57-75). Jesus was taken to the house of Caiaphas the high priest, where the Jewish Council was gathered. They sought for some ground on which to condemn Him to death by means of false witnesses, but failed (vs. 57-62). At length the high priest challenged Him on oath to declare whether He was the Messiah, the Son of God. He admitted the claim, and added a calm and majestic "Nevertheless I say unto you". In contrast with His present appearance as a prisoner before them, they should see Him some day enthroned in heavenly power and glory. At that they condemned Him at once as worthy of death for blasphemy, and vented their hatred upon Him by insult and buffetting and ridicule (vs. 63-68).

While the trial was going on, Peter, who had followed afar off and slipped into the courtyard of the high priest's house with the crowd (v. 58), was subjected to the taunts of those who stood by, and three times denied his Master, the last time with a storm of oaths and curses. Then he heard the cock crow, and his repentance when he went out took as vehement a form as his denial (vs. 69-75).

5. **The Roman Trial** (27:1-31). Having been condemned by the Jewish Council, Jesus was sent early in the morning to the Roman governor for the death sentence, for the Romans reserved that legal right for themselves (vs. 1-2). At this point there is a break in the narrative. Matthew tells of the remorse and suicide of Judas, the sequel of his bargain with the chief priests (vs. 3-5). They used the money he returned to them to buy a burying place for strangers, and Matthew found in this another fulfilment of prophecy (vs. 6-10). The quotation which the text attributes to Jeremiah is taken freely from Zech. 11:12-13. It is arbitrary to attribute this error to a lapse of memory on Matthew's part. It is just as likely to have crept into the first published edition of the Gospel as a copyist's error, and to have persisted in the subsequent editions.

Matthew resumes his narrative of the trial by noting Pilate's surprise when Jesus stood before him. There is an emphasis on "thou" in the governor's question: "Art thou the King of the Jews?" Jesus replied in the affirmative, but gave no answer to the accusations of the Jewish hierarchy (vs. 11-14). The shrewd Roman judge saw through their motive in delivering up Jesus, and knew that He was innocent, but he made a cowardly attempt to escape from his own responsibility. He tried to have the people ask for His release by offering them a choice between Barabbas and Christ (vs. 15-18).

At this point Pilate received a warning message from his wife, who must have heard of Jesus before, while the religious leaders incited the people to ask for the release of Barabbas (vs. 19-21). When Pilate then asked what he should do with Jesus, they cried out at once for His crucifixion, and became more vehement when Pilate protested that He had done no evil (vs. 22-23). The Roman governor had been deeply impressed by the bearing of Jesus, and was convinced that he should release Him; but fearing to increase the tumult that was rising in the crowd, he made a spectacular display of washing his hands "of the blood of this righteous man", and delivered Him to their will. They accepted the responsibility: "His blood be on us, and on our children". Thus they sealed the national character of the crime (vs. 24-26). Then comes another scene of shame—the mocking insults heaped upon Jesus by the heathen soldiers of the Roman governor (vs. 27-31).

6. **The Crucifixion** (27:32-44). On the way out to Golgotha, a non-Palestinian Jew was found and pressed into the service of carrying the cross. Matthew notes the fact that Jesus refused to drink the drugged cup, which was usually given to dull the senses of those that were crucified (vs. 32-33). He then describes the scene round the cross: the soldiers casting lots for the garments of Jesus as they sat and watched Him, the special significance of what was written over His head, the robbers crucified on each side, the raillery of the passers-by, and the mockery of the Jewish religious leaders standing near (vs. 34-44). The chief point at which the railing and mocking was directed was His claim to be the Son of God.

7. **The Death of Christ** (27:45-56). The crucifixion took place at nine o'clock in the morning (Mark 15:25), and at noon a darkness came over the whole land which lasted till three o'clock. Just about that time Jesus uttered a loud cry of desolation, which came from the profoundest depths of agony and loneliness (vs. 45-46). It is the only utterance from the cross recorded by Matthew and Mark; and both of them give the words in the language that Jesus used before putting them in the language in which they wrote (Mark 15:34). This indicates the unforgettable impression which the cry made upon the memory of the Apostles, while it was strangely misunderstood by others standing by (vs. 47-49). It expresses, in the opening words of Psalm 22, the innermost secret of the Cross, and the real significance of His death.

With another loud cry Jesus "yielded up his spirit" (v. 50). The words describe the voluntary nature of His death. In the midst of that darkness, when He was utterly alone and could not find the face of God, He deliberately gave His life away by an act of His own will. Thus He "put away sin by the sacrifice of himself" (Heb. 9:26). He was obedient to His Father's will, "even unto death, yea, the death of the cross" (Phil. 2:8). It was the death for the world's sin, and differed from every other death.

The extraordinary events which accompanied the actual death of Christ marked its unique and supernatural character (vs. 51-53). The rending of the veil that hid the Holy-of-holies in the Temple, which would be observed by the priests, many of whom afterwards became believers (Act 6:7), symbolically announced that the sacrificial services of the Mosaic ritual were no longer needed, for redemption had now been accomplished (Heb. 10:19-22). The earthquake which rent the rocks and opened the tombs marked Nature's sympathy with her suffering Lord.

Another portent occurred which Matthew alone records, the resurrection of some of the saints. Who they were is not stated; but Matthew's language gives the impression that they were disciples who had died before the crucifixion of Jesus, and accompanied Him when He rose again. By appearing to many afterwards they bore witness to the fact that Christ had conquered death and the grave for His people. The centurion in command of the soldiers, who must have witnessed many a crucifixion, was overawed by what happened at the crucifixion of Jesus (v. 54). The women who had followed Jesus from Galilee and ministered unto Him, among whom were Mary Magdalene and two mothers who had sons among the Apostles, stood watching afar off when He died (vs. 55-56).

8. His Burial (27:57-66). Joseph of Arimathea, one of the few rich men among His disciples, asked Pilate for the body of Jesus, and placed it in his own tomb, while Mary Magdalene and another Mary sat near by, reverently watching (vs. 57-61). Next day the Jewish leaders got Pilate's permission, and took special measures to close the tomb and seal it against a possible attempt they thought the disciples might make to steal the body away and declare that He had risen from the dead (vs. 62-66).

THE VICTORY OF THE CRUCIFIED
(Ch. 28)

The Resurrection is not described in any of the Gospels. No one saw Jesus rise from the dead. The evidence that He had risen was first discovered in the empty tomb. This was accompanied by an angelic announcement of the wondrous fact. Then there followed His own appearances, beginning on the day of the Resurrection and continuing from time to time till the Ascension forty days afterwards (Acts 1:3). The impressions produced upon the disciples, as the news spread and the evidence accumulated, are reflected in the various accounts of the four Evangelists. They are all distinct and independent narratives, differing so much in substance and detail as to show that the writers could not have used one another's accounts. Matthew tells of the visit of the women to the tomb on the Resurrection morning, the bribery of the Roman guard by the Jews, and the Lord's missionary commission to the Apostles.

1. The Women at the Tomb (vs. 1-10). The two women who had watched the burial of Jesus on the evening of the crucifixion waited over the Sabbath, and came back to the sepulchre at dawn on the first day of the week. There they saw something extraordinary. An earthquake occurred, and an angel of glorious aspect rolled away the stone to show the empty tomb, and announced that Jesus had risen. The very words of his message quiver with the joy that thrilled the angelic world over the great event: "Come, see the place where the Lord lay. And go quickly, and tell his disciples" (vs. 1-7). As they ran to tell the news, Jesus revealed Himself to them, and gave them a message for His disciples—"my brethren"—to meet Him in Galilee (vs. 8-10).

2. The Bribery of the Guard (vs. 11-15). In the meantime some of the Roman soldiers set to guard the tomb reported to the chief priests what had happened. After consulting together, the Jewish authorities gave a large bribe to the soldiers to circulate the story that the disciples stole the body while they were asleep, and promised to secure them against the danger of getting into trouble with Pilate over the matter. This was the Jewish explanation of the empty tomb. The incident is recorded by Matthew alone.

3. The Apostolic Commission (vs. 16-20). Jesus met His eleven Apostles in Galilee at the place where He had appointed them, and gave them a command to evangelize the world. They were to gather disciples from all nations, and teach them to observe all that He had commanded them. The sign and seal of discipleship was to be baptism into the name of the Trinity. Two great new facts were revealed to them, which were the results of His redemptive work: all authority had been given Him in Heaven and on earth; and His unseen presence would be with them always, even to the end of the Christian age. With these two transcendent truths our Lord buttressed His last command.

* * * *

THE KINGDOM OF HEAVEN IN MATTHEW

The most prominent idea in the Gospel of Matthew is "the kingdom of heaven". The expression is used thirty-three times; the word "kingdom" itself over fifty times. Matthew alone describes the Kingdom in this way. In the other Gospels the expression is always "the kingdom of God", which Matthew uses only four times.

The whole public ministry of Jesus, as shown in Matthew's narrative, was marked by the preaching of the Kingdom of Heaven. He began with the message of John the Baptist that the Kingdom of Heaven was "at hand" (4:17). When He sent the Twelve forth on their mission, it was to proclaim the same message (10:7). The Kingdom of Heaven was the key-note of the Sermon on the Mount (5:3), and the theme of most of the parables. All but four of the fourteen parables in this Gospel are introduced by the Lord as illustrations of what "the kingdom of heaven is like". The whole of His teaching is summed up under the comprehensive term, "the gospel of the kingdom" (4:23). At the end of His ministry He told the disciples that the work to be accomplished after He had gone was to preach "this gospel of the kingdom" throughout the whole world (24:14).

The Kingdom of Heaven was no new theme. It came out of the Old Testament. Daniel had declared that "the God of heaven" would set up a kingdom which should never be destroyed (Dan. 2:44). The idea goes back to the time of David. God had promised to establish his kingdom forever (2 Sam. 7:13; 1 Chron. 17:14). This promise was developed by prophets and psalmists into the promise of the Messianic Kingdom. They described its glories and privileges, and they represented its blessings as intended not for Israel alone but for the Gentiles as well. All this Old Testament background lay behind the teaching and preaching of Jesus.

The Messianic Kingdom was the true Old Testament hope. But the Jews took it in an earthly and carnal sense, and ignored the spiritual element that was in it. They thought only in terms of this world, and they failed to see that a spiritual order was foreshadowed by the symbolism of their own system of worship, and that the heart of Messianic prophecy was the redeeming purpose of God. The apocalyptic literature which sprang up in the age between the Testaments suppressed the redemptive element entirely, and turned the national hope into another channel.

Thus it had come to pass that, along with the eager expectation existing among the people in the days of John and Jesus, there was also a complete misunderstanding of the nature of the coming Kingdom. It was conceived as an exalted kingdom of this world and as intended for Israel alone. A "son of David" was to restore David's earthly kingdom, sit on his royal seat in Jerusalem, and exercise dominion over the Gentiles from there.

It was necessary, therefore, that much of the teaching and preaching of Jesus should be directed toward removing this carnal conception from the minds of the people and creating in the minds of the disciples a true idea of the promised Kingdom. The Messianic Kingdom was to be established upon a spiritual basis, not upon a material or earthly basis. The principle of David's throne, which was the doing of the will of God (1 Sam. 15:23; Acts 13:22), was to be made fundamental and eternal. The purpose of the Messiah's coming into the world was to create an order of things in which men would do the will of God spontaneously and habitually.

It was a system of this kind that Jesus had in view in the prayer He taught His disciples: "Thy kingdom come. Thy will be done, as in heaven, so on earth" (6:10). These words indicate the nature of the new order as it lay in the mind of the Lord. When the Kingdom should come into being, the will of God would be done among men as the angels do it in Heaven—not by the compulsion of law and force, but by the glad and free constraint of willing and selfless obedience. In order to make this possible, He had to recreate the nature of man by taking it through the experience of the Cross and the Resurrection in His own Person.

In His teaching and preaching of the Kingdom, Jesus never gave the disciples the idea that He expected them to establish it. It was a supernatural and transcendent order, the founding of which was His work alone. During His earthly ministry it was only "at hand". It was being made ready for men by the Messianic transactions which He had come into the world to accomplish. Men were called to enter the Kingdom; and entering into it would not be an easy thing. It would require a complete revolution of life and the renunciation of this present world (18:3; 19:23-24). The new order was essentially a kingdom "of heaven". Its powers and principles were to have their seat in the heavenly world, and were to operate upon the lives of men in this world from the Godward side of the veil.

The keys of the Kingdom of Heaven were given to Peter (16:19), and he used them at Pentecost. His was the high honour of opening the Kingdom to men by being the first to proclaim the Christian Gospel. The descent of the Spirit from the risen and ascended Lord on that day was the final step in the preparation of the Kingdom of Heaven. Then it was ready for men to enter. Up to that time it had been "at hand". Since that time it has been open to all the world through the Gospel. The Kingdom is the essential reality at the heart of the Christian system. It is the unseen order behind the visible Church, and the ground for its existence in the world. It is the spiritual basis for the new world that is to be ushered in by the Second Coming of Christ.

THE GOSPEL ACCORDING TO MARK

THE Second Gospel has always been ascribed to the writer whose full name was John Mark. He was the son of a certain Mary whose house in Jerusalem was the meeting place of the early Christians (Acts 12:12). His conversion seems to have been due to Peter, who speaks of him as "Mark my son" (1 Peter 5:13). He was related to Barnabas (Col. 4:10), and was chosen by Barnabas and Paul to accompany them as their assistant on their first missionary journey (Acts 12:25; 13:5). Although he lost the favour of Paul by turning back during that journey (Acts 13:13; 15:37-40), yet at a later period in the Apostle's life Mark is named among his friends and fellow-labourers (Philemon 24; 2 Tim. 4:11).

According to the early Church Fathers, Mark wrote the Gospel in Rome. This tradition agrees with the character of the book. It was addressed specially to the Latin element in the world of the time, and its story of the mighty Servant of God was peculiarly fitted to appeal to the energetic and practical Roman temperament.

Ancient testimony declares that Peter's preaching was the basis of Mark's narrative. It seems to have been Peter's intention, when the time of his death drew near, to leave behind him some account of the Gospel history (2 Pet. 1:14-15). This book of Mark's fulfils that purpose, so that it might be called the Gospel according to Peter. Mark gives no hint of his own authorship, but it is not improbable that in recording the incident of the unnamed young man in 14:51-52 he was referring to himself, for to others it would have appeared insignificant.

This testimony as to the origin of the Second Gospel is supported by the internal evidence of the book. The narrative bears the marks of Peter's recollection of events (1:36; 11:21; 14:72; 16:7). Peter is not put forward as prominently as in the other Gospels (cf. Mark 1:29 with Matt. 8:14 and Luke 4:38; Mark 7:17 with Matt. 15:15; Mark 8:29-30 with Matt. 16:17-19). His failures are sometimes made more conspicuous than those of the other disciples (cf. Mark 14:37 and Matt. 26:40).

The special theme of the Gospel is Jesus Christ as the Servant of God. This is indicated in the way the book opens. It starts with a heading: "The beginning of the gospel of Jesus Christ, the Son of God". And then without any reference to the way He came into the world, the narrative plunges at once into the public ministry of Jesus. It portrays Him in His actual daily life, working among men in the fulness of his energy and self-sacrifice, accomplishing the will of God. The title "Son of God" is used of Jesus Christ in this heading with special reference to the Divine power He manifested in His ministry, rather than the Divine qualities He showed in His character. The Son of God is in view as the Servant of Jehovah, whose figure was foreshadowed in Isaiah (42:1-4; 49:1-6; 52:13-15).

Peter's words to Cornelius in Acts 10:36-38 describing the earthly ministry of Jesus are an epitome of Mark's Gospel. The Lord's own words recorded by Mark in 10:45 also sum up the Gospel: "The Son of man came not to be ministered unto, but to minister, and to give his life a ransom for many". On the basis of the two ideas in this statement, the book may be divided into two parts and outlined as follows:

I. Jesus Christ as the Servant Working—
   Chs. 1-9. (An account of the Lord's Ministry in Galilee)
   1. The Beginnings of His Ministry (Ch. 1)
   2. The Beginnings of Opposition (Chs. 2-3)
   3. Parables and Mighty Works (Chs. 4-5)
   4. Increasing Opposition (6:1—7:23)
   5. Retirements in Northern Galilee (7:24—9:50)

II. Jesus Christ as the Servant Suffering—
   Chs. 10-16. (An account of the Lord's Passion in Jerusalem)
   1. His Last Journey to Jerusalem (Ch. 10)
   2. His Last Ministry in Jerusalem (Chs. 11-12)
   3. His Last Prophecy to the Disciples (Ch. 13)
   4. His Suffering and Death (Chs. 14-15)
   5. His Resurrection and Ascension (Ch. 16)

Mark seems to have arranged his material in chronological order in narrating the events of the Lord's life. When the three Synoptic Gospels are compared, it is found that Matthew and Luke differ less from Mark than they differ from each other in the order of their narrative. The inference is that Mark's narrative follows most closely the actual sequence of events. When he comes to the last week in Jerusalem, he gives notes of time distinguishing the successive days.

THE BEGINNINGS OF THE MINISTRY
(Ch. 1)

Without any mention of the birth and childhood of Jesus and with only a brief reference to the ministry of John the Baptist, this opening chapter of the Gospel relates some typical acts and events in the early part of the Lord's Galilean ministry.

1. The Preparatory Ministry of John (vs. 1-8). After the opening headline of the Gospel, Mark begins by quoting two passages from the Prophets (Mal. 3:1 and Isa. 40:3), and then goes on to explain how they were fulfilled in the work of John the Baptist. John called the people to repentance in preparing the way of the Lord. He baptized with water, and preached the coming of One mightier than himself who should baptize with the Holy Spirit.

2. The Servant's Preparation (vs. 9-13). This consisted in receiving the Holy Spirit when He was baptized by John (vs. 9-11), and being tempted forty days by Satan in the wilderness (vs. 12-13). Mark records these events very briefly, but he adds graphic touches not found in Matthew. Jesus "saw the heavens rent asunder" when He was baptized. The Spirit "driveth him forth" into the wilderness; and there He was "with the wild beasts" during His temptation.

3. The Call of the First Disciples (vs. 14-20). Mark gives a brief statement of the fact that after John was put in prison Jesus came into Galilee, proclaiming that the Kingdom of God was at hand, and calling for repentance because the time for its coming was fulfilled. Then he describes the way that Jesus called the fishermen disciples from their nets —two pairs of brothers, Peter and Andrew, James and John. They were to follow Him, and He would make them fishers of men.

4. A Sabbath in Capernaum (vs. 21-34). This is the most complete account of a Sabbath day's work in the life of Jesus in all the Gospels. There are three scenes in it. The first is a morning scene in the synagogue, when He addressed the congregation and cured a demoniac who had disturbed the service by crying out against Him. Mark's description of the startling effect upon the people conveys the impression of an eye-witness. They were amazed both at the new tone of authority in Jesus' teaching and at His commanding power over evil spirits (vs. 21-28).

This miracle is typical of our Lord's method of dealing with those that were possessed with demons. The demonism of the Gospels is not to be dismissed as only a form of insanity. It was a real manifestation of evil of a supernatural origin. It has always existed in the heathen world, and it lurks in a deceptive and alluring form behind present-day spiritualism. The demons belonged to the kingdom of Satan, which was especially active when Christ was among men. They recognized in Jesus the Son of God, who had come to break their power and destroy them. He always cast them out at once, addressing the evil spirit as distinct from the man possessed.

The next scene occurred at midday in the home of Simon and Andrew. There Jesus cured Simon's wife's mother of fever when they told Him of her, taking her by the hand and raising her up. The fever left her so completely, and her strength was restored so fully, that she began to minister to them when she rose (vs. 29-31). The third is an evening scene in the street when the sun was set and the Sabbath was past. Then they brought all the sick folk of the city to Jesus for healing. There was such a throng that Mark says, "All the city was gathered together at the door" (vs. 32-34).

5. A Tour in Galilee (vs. 35-46). In the early morning before daylight, Jesus went out to spend time in prayer in a place of solitude. The disciples followed Him till they found Him. When they told Him how all were seeking Him, He replied that He must fulfil His mission by preaching in other towns also. Accordingly, He took them with Him and visited the synagogues throughout Galilee. Mark adds, "casting out demons", as if that was the most significant feature of his healing ministry and made the deepest impression (vs. 35-39).

In the course of the tour a leper came appealing to Him to be made clean. Jesus cleansed him by His touch and His word: "I will; be thou made clean". This would indicate that Jesus performed His miraculous cures by an act of His will through power that went forth from His own person (cf. 5:30). Although warned to say nothing to anyone about his cure but to go through the necessary ceremony with the priest to have his cleansing certified (Lev. 14:2-7), the man spread the story widely, and such crowds came from every quarter that Jesus had to avoid the cities and keep in the open country where they would have easy access to Him (vs. 40-45).

Two striking features of the ministry of the Servant are brought out in this chapter. (1) His energy and ceaseless activity as He went about His work. This is marked by the frequent use of the word "straightway", which occurs ten times in the chapter and forty-two times in the book. The A.V. varies the rendering and uses several terms for the same original Greek word. (2) The great popular enthusiasm which His teaching and His miracles evoked. Mark refers to this not only in this chapter (vs. 27-28, 45), but many times afterwards (2:1-2, 12, 13; 3:7-9, 20). There was great excitement wherever Jesus went.

THE BEGINNINGS OF OPPOSITION
(Chs. 2-3)

The thronging multitudes around Jesus are now constantly in view. In the midst of all the excitement and wonder among the people there is beginning to arise a movement of unbelief and antagonism among their religious leaders. This opposition was due to several causes. These are brought out in a number of the incidents recorded in these chapters.

1. His Claim to Forgive Sins (2:1-12). He healed a palsied man in Capernaum, whose friends let him down through the roof in the crowded house, after first announcing that his sins were forgiven. He did this in order to prove that He had this authority, when He perceived that some Scribes sitting there were criticizing Him in their hearts and charging Him with blasphemy. All the others there were amazed at what they saw, and gave God the glory: "We never saw it on this fashion".

2. His Companionship with Sinners (2:13-17). The Pharisees complained about this to His disciples when they saw the company that He sat with at a meal in the house of Levi, whom He had just called to discipleship from his office as a tax collector. Jesus replied that He came "not to call the righteous, but sinners". It is they that are sick, and not they that are whole, who need the physician.

3. His Neglect of Fasting (2:18-22). On one occasion when John's disciples and the Pharisees were observing a fast, Jesus was asked why His disciples did not fast. He replied by using the figure of "the bridegroom", under which John the Baptist had formerly spoken of Him (John 3:29), and pointing out that in His fellowship there was no need to fast. He spoke of a time when that fellowship would be broken by His removal, and then there would be a reason for such spiritual discipline as fasting signified (vs. 18-20). He added two parabolic sayings, vividly illustrating the fact that He was not adding any new rites or rules to the old system of Judaism, but was introducing something entirely new (vs. 21-22).

4. His Attitude to the Sabbath (2:23-3:6). This had to do specially with the traditional laws that had been added to the Sabbath law. The Pharisees criticized Him for allowing His disciples to pluck and eat ears of wheat as they passed through the grain fields on the Sabbath (2:23-28). He replied by pointing out from the example of David (1 Sam. 21:1-6) that the ceremonial law was subordinate to human needs. Then He added, "The sabbath was made for man, and not man for the sabbath; so that the Son of man is lord even of the sabbath". He meant that as the representative Man He had the right to determine how the Sabbath should be used for man's good.

On another Sabbath day, while in the synagogue, they watched Him to see if He would heal a man who was there with a withered hand, intending to accuse Him. This aroused His indignation and grief. He put a question to them which exposed their hypocrisy and hardness of heart; and then He healed the man as he stood before them all. From that day the Pharisees and the Herodians, two mutually hostile parties among the Jews, began to plot together to accomplish His destruction (vs. 1-6).

5. The Choice of the Twelve (3:7-19). The more the religious leaders opposed our Lord, the more the common people flocked to Him. They came from all parts of the land, and even from more distant places, drawn mainly by His fame as a healer. He withdrew to the sea-side and had a little boat wait upon Him there that He might the more easily minister to the crowds of people (vs. 7-12).

At this time He chose the twelve Apostles from among the larger number of His followers, and their names are now given. They are the same as in Matthew's list (10:2-4), but Mark notes that Jesus surnamed James and John Boanerges, "Sons of thunder". Mark's brief account emphasizes the deliberate nature of the Lord's choice — "whom he himself would"—and the twofold purpose of their appointment—(1) for training: "that they might be with him"; and (2) for service: "that he might send them forth to preach" (vs. 13-19).

6. The Anxiety of His Kinsfolk (3:19-21, 31-35). While He was in a house in Capernaum, His mother and brethren came seeking to withdraw Him from

His work, for His zeal made them think He was beside Himself. When He was told about it, Jesus looked round upon His disciples sitting in the crowd about Him, and indicated them as His true kinsfolk. He did not mean by this to break the ties of family relationship, but to show that there was a closer bond than that—the doing of the will of God.

7. The Accusation of His Foes (3:22-30). Some Scribes who had come down from Jerusalem, representing the religious authorities there, charged Him with casting out demons by Satanic power. In replying to this accusation Jesus pointed out the folly of such a charge: it would mean that Satan had risen up against Himself. Then He uttered a solemn warning about the great sin of blaspheming against the Holy Spirit: it can never be forgiven. The Lord's statement about this is more fully given in Matt. 12:25-32. It is explained in the exposition of that passage.

PARABLES AND MIGHTY WORKS
(Chs. 4-5)

These chapters tell of a day of teaching by the sea-side when Jesus began to use parables, and describe four great miracles which He wrought in succession soon afterwards.

1. Teaching in Parables (4:1-34). This passage is parallel with Matt. 13, but contains only two of the parables recorded there, those of the sower and the mustard seed. The Evangelist begins with a renewed description of the scene at the sea-side in the last chapter (3:7-9; 4:1). Then he goes on to record the parable of the sower as spoken to the multitude (vs. 1-9), and its interpretation as given privately to the disciples (vs. 10-20). The passage that follows (vs. 21-25) contains a group of our Lord's sayings which occur in Matthew scattered in different places. They were probably seed thoughts which He would drop repeatedly.

Then comes the parable of the seed growing secretly, which Mark alone records (vs. 26-29). It is an appendix to the parable of the sower, giving the history of the seed that falls into good soil. It is followed by the parable of the mustard seed (vs. 30-32). There is only one other parable in this Gospel, that of the wicked husbandmen (12:1-9), while it contains eighteen miracles. Mark is concerned with the works of Jesus more than with His words.

2. Four Mighty Works (4:35—5:43). In this section we have an account of four typical miracles wrought one after the other, apparently within the space of a few days. They are described in greater detail and with more graphic touches than in Matthew, where they also occur in the same order. They represent the four classes of mighty works wrought by the Servant of God.

(1) Stilling the storm on the sea (4:35-41). This manifested Christ's power and authority over the forces of nature. Mark connects this miracle with the teaching in parables by telling us that at the end of the same day Jesus said to the disciples, "Let us go over unto the other side". They took Him, "even as He was, in the boat", without making any preparation for the voyage. They were accompanied by other boats, which probably had to put back because of the storm. It must have been unusually severe when the disciples, some of them

fishermen accustomed to the lake, were afraid of perishing.

Jesus had fallen asleep, tired out after the long day's teaching; and He continued to sleep through the storm because of His complete trust in His Father. This is implied in what He said to the disciples when the storm was stilled. His rebuke of the wind showed that He traced all the evils in the natural world, as well as those in the spiritual world, to their source in the will of Satan. The result of His command to the sea was "a great calm". In the hour of her uproar Nature knew the voice of her rightful Lord and returned to her allegiance to Him. Here Jesus appears as the representative Man, to whom was given dominion over the creation (Heb. 2:5-8). The effect upon the disciples was profound. There was something mysterious in their Master, which they had not realized before.

(2) Casting out a host of demons (5:1-20). This miracle manifested His power and authority over the spirit world. It is one of the most circumstantial of all Mark's stories. He tells of only one demoniac, while Matthew spoke of two. This man was no doubt the more conspicuous case. The description of his condition illustrates the utter confusion and misery of man's life under Satan's power, and brings out the double personality of one possessed by an evil spirit. In this case a host of demons had taken possession of one man, and he had become fierce and untamable.

Jesus always treated a demoniac as the victim and thrall of an alien and hostile spirit, whom He addressed as distinct from the man himself and at once commanded to depart from him. Evil spirits recognized and confessed the Divine nature and origin of Jesus, but He always silenced them, refusing to receive any testimony from such a source. The request of the demons in this case to be allowed to enter the swine only led to their utter discomfiture. The effect upon the ignorant people of the district was one of superstitious terror. They were moved by the loss of the swine rather than by the change in the man, but they did not accuse Jesus of responsibility for their loss. The Lord departed from among them, for no good purpose would have been served by remaining. He left the man behind to be His witness there.

(3). Healing the woman who touched His garment (5:21-34). This showed His power in the realm of our physical nature. Mark tells how the poor woman's trouble had only been aggravated and all her means had been exhausted by attempts to have physicians cure her. Then he describes the kind and considerate way in which Jesus led her, fearful and trembling as she was, to come forward and make a voluntary confession when she found herself healed by her touch of His garment in the crowd, and then tenderly sent her away with a word of peace.

(4) Raising the daughter of Jairus (5:35-43). Here we see the Lord's power over death. Mark gives a vivid account of the whole event: the tumult in the house made by the professional mourners, and His rebuke and expulsion of them; the scene within the room where the child lay, when He went in with only her parents and His three chosen disciples; His taking her by the hand; and His word of command, so impressive that it is quoted in the very language Jesus used; the amazement when she rose

up and walked, so great that He had to remind them that she needed something to eat.

INCREASING OPPOSITION
(6:1—7:23)

Two events at this time marked the growing antagonism to Jesus, and foreshadowed His ultimate rejection by the nation—the unbelief He met with in Nazareth and the death of John the Baptist at the hands of Herod. After that a change began to appear in the character of His ministry. He withdrew again and again from the crowded centres to more remote parts.

1. Jesus' Rejection at Nazareth (6:1-6). In the course of one of His tours He visited His own city. The attitude of the people when He taught in the synagogue there was a combination of astonishment and prejudice. They wondered—"Whence hath this man these things?" But they were offended at Him—"Is not this the carpenter?" This attitude of unbelief limited His power to bless: "He could there do no mighty work". Mark adds to what Matthew records in the parallel passage of the First Gospel (13:54-58) that, "he marvelled because of their unbelief".

2. The Mission of the Twelve (6:6-13). They had been chosen already (3:14), and now Jesus for the first time sent them out, while He was Himself engaged in a tour of the villages of Galilee. Mark alone tells us that they were sent forth "by two and two". The instructions he records here are more fully given in Matt. 10:5-15.

3. The Death of John the Baptist (6:14-29). The fame of Jesus reached Herod and troubled his guilty conscience for his beheading of John the Baptist (vs. 14-16). The story of Herod's crime is told here (vs. 17-29), with more fulness of picturesque detail than in the parallel account in Matthew (14:1-12).

4. The Return of the Twelve and the Feeding of the Multitude (6:30-44). When the Apostles returned from their mission and reported what they had done and what they had taught, Jesus invited them to come "apart into a desert place and rest a while". There were streams of people constantly coming and going, leaving no intervals for refreshment—"no leisure so much as to eat". He took them in a boat across the sea away from the thronging crowds. But the people followed them on foot around the shore, "and outwent them".

When the boat arrived and Jesus saw the great crowd of people awaiting Him, His compassion went out at once toward them, for He saw them as sheep not having a shepherd, and He taught them till the day was far spent (vs. 30-34). Then there followed the feeding of the five thousand (vs. 35-44). Mark adds some picturesque details to Matthew's account (14:13-21). He tells us of the Lord's orderly method of arranging the crowd for the easier distribution of the food. He had them sit down "by companies upon the green grass"; and they sat down "in ranks, by hundreds, and by fifties". The original word for "ranks" means literally "flower-beds". Peter remembered the colourful scene that the crowd made as they spread over the grass.

5. Walking on the Water and the Arrival in Gennesaret (6:45-56). That night Jesus spent in prayer on the hill after sending the disciples away in the boat. In the early morning, while they were struggling against a contrary wind, He came to them walking on the sea. Mark does not tell of Peter's attempt to walk on the water, which Matthew records, but he quotes the words of cheer that Jesus addressed to them all, and tells of their amazement when He entered the boat and the wind ceased. Then He remarks upon their spiritual insensibility in failing to understand the significance of the miracle of the loaves (vs. 45-52).

When they arrived in the land of Gennesaret on the north-west side of the lake and Jesus was recognized, there was great excitement. The people throughout the whole region brought their sick folk into the market-places of the villages He visited, pleading to be allowed to touch only the border of His garment. "And as many as touched him were made whole" (vs. 53-56).

6. Denouncing Ceremonial Tradition (7:1-23). This passage is parallel with Matt. 15:1-20. Mark, however, introduces the question of the Pharisees and Scribes by explaining for his Roman readers the Jewish custom of ceremonial washings (vs. 1-4). The term he uses in the expression, "except they bathe themselves" (A.V. "wash"), is literally "baptize themselves", which implies a ceremonial or religious act, and does not refer to washing for the purpose of cleansing. Some manuscripts read, "except they sprinkle themselves". The rest of the passage (vs. 5-23) is substantially the same as Matthew's.

RETIREMENTS IN NORTHERN GALILEE
(7:24—9:50)

The remainder of Jesus' stay in Galilee was largely spent in journeys into northern regions for the purpose of retirement. His desire was to get away from the crowded places where He was known, that He might have more private fellowship with His disciples (7:24; 8:27; 9:30). These journeys took Him into districts where the people were mainly Gentile.

1. The First Northern Journey (7:24—8:26). The course of this journey took Him toward the coast into the borders of Tyre and Sidon (7:24), and back by a roundabout route to the region of Decapolis east of the Sea of Galilee (7:31); then across the sea to Dalmanutha, the site of which is unknown (8:10), and afterwards to the northern side of the Sea at Bethsaida (8:13, 22).

The passage is parallel with Matt. 15:21—16:12. Mark tells of the cure of the daughter of the Syrophœnician woman who was a Greek (7:24-30), the feeding of the four thousand (8:1-10), the Pharisees' demand for a sign and the Lord's warning the disciples of the leaven of the Pharisees (8:11-21), all of which is contained in Matthew's account.

Two other miracles occurred during this period which Mark alone records—the healing of a deaf man who had an impediment in his speech (7:31-37), and the giving of sight to a blind man (8:22-26). In each case Jesus took the man apart and dealt with him privately, encouraging his faith by touching the afflicted parts of his body and connecting the cure with His own person. In the second case the cure was gradual. The way He performed these cures seems to indicate that the growing opposition of the religious leaders and the popular attitude of mingled curiosity and unbelief were weighing heavily upon His spirit, and making His work as the Servant more and more difficult.

2. The Second Northern Journey (8:27—9:32). The course of this journey lay through the villages of Cæsarea Philippi, where Peter made his great confession (8:27-30) and Jesus gave the first announcement of His approaching death and resurrection (8:31-38); then into the mountain where the Transfiguration took place and the second reference to His passion (9:1-13), followed by the healing of a demoniac boy at the foot of the mountain (9:14-29); and finally back through Galilee, where He repeated the prediction of His passion (9:30-32).

In the account of Peter's confession, Mark omits Jesus' reply commending Peter and announcing the founding of His Church. In the account of the Transfiguration, after Peter's impulsive request this significant explanation is added: "For he knew not what to answer, for they became sore afraid". In the account of the scene at the foot of the mountain, which is more graphic and detailed than Matthew's, Mark says that "all the multitude, when they saw him, were greatly amazed, and running to him, saluted him". Perhaps traces of the Transfiguration still lingered on His face.

3. The Final Sojourn in Galilee (9:33-50). Jesus returned to Capernaum after His last journey to the north, and these verses record two incidents there which revealed some things in the lives of the disciples inconsistent with His own spirit. In the one case they had been disputing among themselves who was the greatest, and Jesus set a little child in their midst and taught them a lesson in humility (vs. 33-37). In the other case John announced that they had seen one casting out demons in Christ's name and had forbidden him, because he was not of their group, and Jesus gave them a lesson about intolerance and stumbling blocks (vs. 38-50).

THE LAST JOURNEY TO JERUSALEM
(Ch. 10)

The story of this journey occupies two chapters in Matthew (chs. 19-20), and nearly ten in Luke (9:51—19:28). Although Mark's account is quite brief, it contains some graphic scenes.

Leaving Galilee for the last time, Jesus came into the region beyond Jordan and took up His public ministry again, which was now devoted mainly to teaching (v. 1). Not many miracles are recorded after the Transfiguration. The hostility of the Pharisees followed Him, and they came asking a question about divorce, which He answered by declaring that the Creator intended the marriage bond to be indissoluble by man (vs. 2-12). In relating the incident of the children that were brought to Jesus, Mark tells us that He was indignant with the disciples for rebuking those who brought them, and that He took them in His arms when He blessed them (vs. 13-16).

When the rich young man, who came running to Jesus with the question about eternal life, addressed Him as "Good Teacher", Jesus replied, "Why callest thou me good? None is good save one, even God". He meant that all human goodness is derived from God, which is no less true in the character of the perfect man, Christ Jesus, than in that of others. When the young man could not stand the test that Jesus lovingly gave him, because "he was one that had great possessions", Jesus "looked round about"

and said to His disciples, "How hardly shall they that have riches enter into the kingdom of God". When they showed their amazement, He repeated, more tenderly, "Children, how hard is it for them that trust in riches to enter into the kingdom of God!" (vs. 17-25).

Jesus meant that those who have riches are naturally inclined to trust in riches, and riches belong to the life of this world, and so they are naturally disinclined to seek or appreciate the life of the world to which the Kingdom belongs. When the disciples expressed their great astonishment and asked, "Who then can be saved?" Jesus, "looking upon them", went on to say, "With men it is impossible, but not with God". The repeated reference to the way Jesus looked upon the young man and the disciples during the whole incident reflects the deep impression it had made upon Peter's memory (vs. 26-31).

As Jesus drew nearer to Jerusalem the intensity of His spirit deepened, and the disciples were moved with fear and awe as they followed Him on the road. It was then that He gave them the most circumstantial and detailed prediction of His approaching passion (vs. 32-34). He answered the ambitious request of James and John by telling them that they knew not what they asked (vs. 35-40), and by telling the other ten, who were indignant with their two brethren, that it was not by exercising authority over others but by serving others that greatness among the members of His Kingdom would be reached (vs. 41-44). Then He referred to His own example and uttered one of His great declarations about the significance of His mission in the world (v. 45).

The last incident on the way to Jerusalem was the healing of blind Bartimæus at Jericho (vs. 46-52). Matthew told of two blind beggars being healed. Mark mentions only one and gives his name, probably because he had become a believer in Jesus and was known to the Christian community. Mark's account of the miracle bears evidence of an eye-witness:—the crowd rebuking the man first for crying out, and, when they saw Jesus stop and take an interest in him, calling to him: "Be of good cheer; rise, he calleth thee"; then the sudden action of the man, casting away his garment, springing up, and coming to Jesus.

THE LAST MINISTRY IN JERUSALEM
(Chs. 11-12)

These chapters run parallel with Matt. 21-23 and record the same series of events. Mark's account of the passion week contains notes of time by which the various days can be distinguished (11:11-12, 19-20; 14:1).

1. A Day of Triumph (11:1-11). In describing the royal entry of Jesus into Jerusalem, Mark gives the most circumstantial account of the finding of the colt (vs. 1-7). After telling of the acclamation of the people, who recognized the Messianic character of the event, he sums up the remainder of the day, when the Lord was present in the Temple, in these significant words: "And when he had looked round about upon all things, it being now eventide, he went out unto Bethany with the twelve". The claim, which Jesus had made so publicly and plainly, received no recognition from the religious leaders (vs. 8-11).

2. A Day of Warning (11:12-19). The cursing of the barren fig-tree on the way into the city next morning was an ominous warning of the judgment upon faithless Israel. Mark puts in the explanatory statement: "For it was not the season of figs". The season of figs was about a month later, and the fruit of the fig-tree came along with the leaves and not afterwards. This tree, by its display of leaves, professed to have fruit; and, by bearing leaves so early, boasted that it was ahead of others. Thus it was a fit symbol of both the pride and the barrenness of Israel (vs. 12-14). The cleansing of the Temple of its unholy traffic was another act of Messianic warning, which only made the religious heads still more determined to destroy Him. Mark notes the fact that "every evening he went forth out of the city". Probably He stayed at Bethany during the passion week (vs. 15-19).

3. A Day of Controversy (11:20—12:44). On the way into the city next morning, Peter pointed out the fig-tree already withered away, and Jesus gave the disciples a lesson on praying in faith. Evidently the withering of the fig-tree had followed His curse upon it in answer to a prayer of faith on His own part (11:20-26). When they arrived in the Temple again the religious leaders came asking Jesus by what authority He was doing these things, and He exposed their hypocrisy when they would not answer His question about the authority of John the Baptist (11:27-33). Then He went on to reveal the real nature of their sin and forecast their judgment, by telling the story of the vineyard and the wicked husbandmen. They saw that the parable was directed against themselves, and they would have seized Him then, but dared not for fear of the people (12:1-12).

After that they made several attempts to ensnare Him with captious questions. The Pharisees and the Herodians, who held opposing views about paying tribute to Rome, tried to get Him to commit Himself to one side or the other, and His answer only roused their wonder: "They marvelled greatly at him" (12: 13-17). The Sadducees, who did not believe in a resurrection and accepted only the books of Moses, tried to entangle Him with that doctrine, and He exposed their ignorance of their own Scriptures (12:18-27). One of the Scribes, the teachers of the Law, who was present and heard the Lord answering the others, asked Him what was the first commandment of all. Jesus answered him by summing up all the commandments under love to God and love to one's neighbour. Mark adds that his answer won the praise and commendation of the Scribes (12:28-34).

Jesus followed these questions of His foes with a question of His own, which showed the Scribes' inadequate teaching about the promised Messiah. Mark does not tell of their failure to answer Jesus, but he remarks that "the common people heard him gladly" (12:35-37). Then He pronounced His denunciation upon the Scribes, of which Mark gives only a brief summary (12:38-40). The account of the public ministry of Jesus in this Gospel ends with His commendation of the poor widow whom He saw cast her two mites into the treasury in the Temple (12:41-44).

THE LAST PROPHECY TO THE DISCIPLES
(Ch. 13)

This chapter contains Mark's account of the Olivet prophecy, which is more fully given in Matt. 24. In describing the occasion which called it forth, he tells us that it was the first four disciples— Peter and James and John and Andrew—who asked Jesus the question (vs. 1-4). The Lord's reply as recorded here is substantially the same as that given in Matthew, and it may be analysed in the same way.

1. General Warnings regarding the Christian Age (vs. 5-13). After forecasting its general character, Jesus declared that before it comes to an end, "the gospel must first be preached among all the nations" (v. 10). In describing the persecutions which the disciples would meet with while preaching the Gospel, Mark adds the Lord's promise of the aid they should receive from the Holy Spirit, which Matthew embodied in an earlier address (10:19-22).

2. Special Warnings regarding the Fall of Jerusalem (vs. 14-23). Mark put in the same parenthetical warning for his readers as Matthew did when reporting the Lord's prophecy of the invasion of the land by the pagan Roman armies (v. 14), showing that he too was writing before the event. His account also emphasizes the urgent need for a hasty flight from the city on the part of the Christians (vs. 15-18). He mentions the greatness of the affliction that would fall upon the nation at that time, and adds the warning against those who gave false announcements of the coming of Christ (vs. 19-23).

3. Special Warnings regarding the Coming of Christ (vs. 24-37). This part of the prophecy is somewhat briefer than the corresponding part in Matthew. It describes the coming of the Son of Man as taking place "after that tribulation", and in the midst of such commotions as indicate the collapse of the whole world system (vs. 24-27). It emphasizes the certainty of the event and the uncertainty of the time (vs. 28-32), and dwells upon the warning to watch (vs. 33-37). Mark does not record the rest of the Lord's address, in which He enforced the warning to watch by the parables of the virgins and the talents, but he closes the prophecy with a repetition of the Lord's warning: "And what I say unto you I say unto all, Watch".

THE SUFFERING AND DEATH
(Chs. 14-15)

Mark's account of the last night and the last day of Jesus' earthly life is substantially identical with Matthew's (chs. 26-27). The course of events may be drawn out as follows:

1. The Preparations (14:1-11). These include the plotting of the Jewish leaders (vs. 1-2), the anointing of Jesus at the supper in Bethany (vs. 3-9), and the bargain of Judas Iscariot with the chief priests (vs. 10-11). Although both Matthew and Mark place the supper in Bethany at this point in their narrative, John's Gospel shows (12: 1-2) that it took place before the triumphal entry.

2. The Last Supper (14:12-31). Mark gives a more circumstantial account than Matthew of the Lord's instructions for the preparation of the Passover. He sent two disciples into the city where they would meet a certain man carrying a pitcher of

water, whom they were to follow and ask for the guest-chamber for the Master and His disciples. He would show them a large upper room furnished and ready, and there they were to make ready the Passover (vs. 12-16). This unnamed man was probably one of the unknown friends of Jesus, who do not appear personally in the Gospel story. The account of what took place there in the evening when Jesus came with the Twelve is the same as in Matthew. It includes the announcement of His betrayal (vs. 17-21), the institution of the Supper (vs. 22-26), and the announcement of His desertion by all of them and His denial by Peter (vs. 27-31).

3. In Gethsemane (14:32-52). Here again the story of the agony in the garden (vs. 32-42) and the betrayal by Judas (vs. 43-50) is substantially the same as Matthew's. The incident related in vs. 51-52 is peculiar to this Gospel, and the young man referred to was probably Mark himself.

4. The Jewish Trial (14:53-72). This account follows the same order as Matthew's. It includes the examination of Jesus before the Council, His silence in answer to the false witnesses, His affirmative answer to the high priest's question asking if He was the Messiah, the Son of God, His condemnation on the ground of that claim, and their shameful treatment of Him afterwards (vs. 53-65). During the course of this trial Peter's denial took place, and the narrative here is marked by Peter's vivid recollection of the event and his feelings at the time (vs. 66-72). Mark gives no account of the suicide of Judas.

5. The Roman Trial (15:1-20). Here we have Jesus brought before Pilate, and the governor's examination of Jesus and his awed wonder at the prisoner's bearing (vs. 1-5). He saw that Jesus was innocent and had been brought before him because of the envy of the chief priests, and he offered to release Him when the Jewish mob came with their usual request at the Passover time. But the Jews demanded Barabbas instead, and cried out for the crucifixion of Jesus (vs. 6-14). Pilate then made his weak and cowardly submission to the Jews. He had Jesus scourged and delivered over to the mockery of the soldiers before being crucified (vs. 15-20).

6. The Crucifixion (15:21-41). Mark alone tells us that Simon of Cyrene, who was impressed to carry the cross, was "the father of Alexander and Rufus" (v. 21). These two persons must have been well known to his readers, and were probably members of the Roman Church (Rom. 16:13). In describing the scene at Golgotha Mark includes all the incidents related by Matthew:—Jesus' crucifixion between two robbers (vs. 22-28), the railing of the passers by and the mocking of the chief priests and Scribes (vs. 29-32), the three hours' darkness and the cry from the cross, which Mark, like Matthew, gives first in the very words Jesus used (vs. 33-37), the rending of the veil in the Temple, the impression produced upon the Roman centurion by the manner of Jesus' death, and the women from Galilee beholding the scene from afar (vs. 38-41).

7. The Burial (15:42-47). Mark says that Joseph of Arimathea "boldly went in unto Pilate" to ask for the body of Jesus, and that Pilate "marvelled if he were already dead", and sent for the centurion to certify the fact.

THE RESURRECTION AND ASCENSION
(Ch. 16)

Matthew's Gospel closed with the Resurrection and the great commission. Mark's Gospel closes with the Ascension and the carrying out of the great commission. At the end of Matthew we see the risen Lord: at the end of Mark, the ascended Lord.

We are told of the discovery made by the women in the morning that the tomb was empty, and of the message given them by the angel whom they saw sitting inside. Mark reports the angel's message in almost the same words as Matthew, but makes a significant addition. The women were to tell the disciples, "and Peter". Peter would always bear witness to the fact that the Master, whom he had so basely denied, sought him out specially on the very morning of the Resurrection (vs. 1-8).

Then comes a summary of the appearances of the risen Lord on the same day: to Mary Magdalene, to the two on their way to Emmaus, and to the eleven as they sat at meat in the evening (vs. 9-14). The Gospel then records the missionary commission given to the Apostles and the promise of supernatural aid in carrying it out (vs. 15-18), and closes with a brief reference to the Ascension and the subsequent fulfilment of the commission (vs. 19-20).

The last twelve verses (9-20) are separated from the rest of the book in the R.V., because they are not found in the two oldest known Greek manuscripts, and four other manuscripts have a shorter ending. The longer ending, however, is found in the vast majority of Greek manuscripts and in the ancient versions, and appears as the recognized ending in the earliest Christian writings which show the influence of this Gospel. These verses have been generally accepted as the work of Mark since the second century, and they have come down through the ages as the genuine ending of the Second Gospel. Though their compressed style makes them differ somewhat from the rest of the book, yet they are quite consistent with its general theme. The two closing verses present the most fitting consummation for the Gospel of the Servant of God.

* * * *

THE PERSONAL WAYS OF JESUS

Although Mark's is the shortest of the Gospels, yet it contains more picturesque details than any of the others. Its narrative is the most realistic account we have of the ministry of Jesus. The scenes and incidents it describes are lit up with many vivid and graphic touches. It shows us the living personal ways of the Lord. The story of Jesus in this Gospel is told in such a way that it enables us to see Him and hear Him as if we were present at the time.

We see Him using His hands and touching people when He healed them. He took Peter's wife's mother "by the hand, and raised her up" (1:31). He "stretched forth his hand, and touched" the leper (1:41). Mark shows us every movement in the way Jesus went about opening the ears and loosing the tongue of the deaf and dumb man in Decapolis (7:33-35), and giving sight to the blind man at Bethsaida (8:23-25). He tells us how tenderly Jesus received the little children that were brought to Him, and how He "took them up in his arms, and blessed them, laying his hands upon them" (9:36; 10:16).

Mark also depicts the play of feeling on the face of Jesus and tells us how He looked at people. It was the Lord's habit to look round about upon the crowds when He was in the midst of them. We see the indignation and grief with which He "looked round about" on those in the synagogue who did not want the man with his hand withered to be healed on the Sabbath day (3:5). We see the deep affection with which He "looked round about" on His own disciples as they sat in the midst of a crowded house when His mother and His brethren came seeking for Him (3:34). We see the tender and sympathetic interest in His face as He "looked round about" to see the woman who had touched His garment (5:32).

This play of feeling in the "looks" of Jesus is especially manifest in the way Mark tells the story of His interview with the rich young ruler who came seeking eternal life. We see first the earnest, wooing love in His face while "looking" upon the young man, and next the disappointment there when the young man went away and Jesus "looked round about" on His disciples and told them how hard it was for rich men to enter the Kingdom, and then the changed expression on His face when, "looking upon them" again, He told them that all things were possible with God (10:21, 23, 27).

Perhaps the most significant "look" of all was the action which Mark describes as taking place in the Temple after the triumphal entry into Jerusalem: "When he had looked round about upon all things, and now the eventide was come, he went out unto Bethany with the twelve" (11:11). The Messiah had come to His own, and His own had received Him not (John 1:11).

There was something also in the quality of the Lord's voice which Mark helps us to hear. When he gives us the actual words that Jesus used in calling the dead girl back to life (5:41) and in opening the deaf ears (7:34), before he translates them for his readers, Mark implies that there was something in their very tones that could not be translated. To understand it we should have to hear his voice. Jesus was asserting His authority in the face of an unseen foe, and that gave a peculiar emphasis to the very sounds that came from His lips. Sometimes His words were uttered in tones of disappointment, accompanied with sighs (7:34; 8:12); and that shows how keenly He felt the atmosphere of unbelief in which He had to carry on His ministry.

It is through the voice of Jesus that we get nearest to the innermost secret of the Cross. This lies in the cry that came out of the darkness; "My God, my God, why hast thou forsaken me?" It is recorded both in Matthew (27:46) and in Mark (15:34); and each Evangelist gives it first in the actual words that Jesus uttered before rendering them into the language in which he wrote. There must be some reason for this. It was a loud cry, and it penetrated the air. It carried on its very accents and in its every syllable something untranslatable, notes of a mysterious agony and an uttermost loneliness. This could not be separated in the memory of the Apostles from the sounds themselves that fell upon the ear; and when they told the story afterwards, they first passed on with solemn awe the very words they heard before they dared to put them

in any other tongue. Behind that cry was something far beyond physical pain or mental anguish. In its profound depths lay the mystery of the atonement. Thus the voice of Jesus carried out upon the stricken air the suffering heart of the Servant of God and the Saviour of the world, as He "put away sin by the sacrifice of himself" (Heb. 9:26).

THE GOSPEL ACCORDING TO LUKE

THE author of the Third Gospel was Luke, the companion and fellow-labourer of Paul. His name is mentioned only three times in the New Testament (Col. 4:14; Philemon 24; 2 Tim. 4:11), but these passages throw considerable light upon him. He is called a physician, and that implies that he was a man of culture and education. His literary culture appears in the classical preface to the Gospel (1:1-4), in which he follows the manner of Greek historians. Traces of his medical knowledge occur throughout the book (4:23, 38; 5:12; 8:42-43, cf. Mark 5:26; 13:11; 22:43-44). He was probably a Gentile, for Paul does not include him among those "who are of the circumcision" (Col. 4:10-11). He does not include himself among the eye-witnesses when stating his purpose to write a story of the Gospel.

Luke was the author of the Acts as well (Acts 1:1-2), and his companionship with Paul may be traced in the record of the Apostle's missionary labours contained in that book. The preaching of Paul would naturally provide the basis of the Gospel written by Luke. The prominence which Luke gives to the relations of Jesus with all kinds and classes of men, and with people outside Judaism, is closely connected with the universality of the Gospel as preached by the Apostle.

Luke gathered his material both from written

records and from the evidence of eye-witnesses. He claims to have investigated the whole Gospel story, to have "traced the course of all things accurately from the first". He would have abundant opportunity for doing this during his travels with the Apostle, and especially during the two years spent in Palestine when Paul was a prisoner in Cæsarea (Acts 24:27). He may have written the Gospel before the end of that period.

The Gospel is addressed to a Christian named Theophilus, who must have been a man of some prominence, but is otherwise unknown (1:1-4). It is the only personal introduction to any historical book in the Bible except the Acts. Luke aims to set forth the historical foundations of the faith in which Theophilus believes. He writes as a historian, and presents the Saviour in His complete human relations. His book is the Gospel of the Son of Man. Under this general theme it may be divided as follows:

I. The Advent of the Son of Man—Chs. 1-2
II. The Manifestation of the Son of Man—
    Chs. 3:1—4:13
III. The Ministry in Galilee—
    Chs. 4:14—9:50
IV. The Journey to Jerusalem—
    Chs. 9:51—19:28
V. The Ministry in Jerusalem—
    Chs. 19:29—21:38
VI. The Departure of the Son of Man—
    Chs. 22-24

This Gospel is set in the frame of contemporary history. It begins "in the days of Herod, king of Judea" (1:5). It mentions the imperial decree that brought Joseph and Mary up from Galilee, so that Jesus was born in Bethlehem, the city of David (2:1). In the course of the story Luke pays careful attention to dates and marks of the time (1:26; 2:21, 42). When he begins the narrative of the public ministry he notes the year of the reigning Cæsar and the age of Jesus, and takes a survey of the civil and religious rulers who were specially concerned with Palestine (3:1-2, 23).

THE ADVENT OF THE SON OF MAN
(Chs. 1-2)

Luke begins his Gospel with a simple and modest preface, which tells of the care he took to secure fulness and accuracy for his narrative (1:1-4). The book combines research with inspiration. These two chapters contain the most complete account we have of the facts connected with the Incarnation. Heaven and earth unite to give peculiar beauty to the opening scenes of the Gospel story. Here are visions of angels, hymns of praise, and simple domestic incidents.

1. The Announcement of John (1:5-25). The first scene takes place in the Temple. The centre of the Old Testament worship becomes the cradle of the New Testament order. The course of Abijah to which Zacharias belonged, was one of the twenty-four courses into which the priests were divided in David's time (1 Chron. 24:10). Each course was on duty in the Temple for a week every six months, and incense was offered every morning and evening. The narrative tells us first of the righteous character of Zacharias and Elisabeth (vs. 5-7), and then of the angel's appearance to the priest as he minis-

tered at the altar of incense in the sanctuary (vs. 8-12).

The first words of the angel's message, the words that open the New Testament age, were "Fear not". Then he told Zacharias of the answer to his prayer and the coming birth of a son, whom he should name John, and who should grow up as a Nazirite from his birth and go before the Lord in the spirit and power of Elijah, to prepare a people for Him (vs. 13-17). The angel's words recall the closing prophecy of Malachi (3:1; 4:5-6), and thus the New Testament begins where the Old Testament ends.

When Zacharias received the message with doubt because of the advanced age of himself and his wife, the angel disclosed his own name and high position, and pronounced a judgment upon the priest for his unbelief. He should be dumb until the angel's word came to pass (vs. 18-20). The narrative then goes on to tell of the fulfilment of both the judgment (vs. 21-22) and the promise (vs. 23-25).

Gabriel and Michael are the only angels given names in Scripture, and these are no doubt intended to symbolize their character and function. Gabriel, "the mighty one of God", is the angel of mercy, announcing and promoting God's redemptive purpose among men. He was sent on two former occasions to Daniel, whose prophetic messages were concerned with the advent of the Messiah (Dan. 8:16; 9:21). Michael, "who is like God", is the angel of judgment, contending with Satan and overthrowing all who dare to oppose God (Dan. 10:13, 21; 12:1; Jude 9; Rev. 12:7).

2. The Announcement of Jesus (1:26-38). From the Temple in Jerusalem the narrative takes us to the home of a humble Jewish maiden in a Galilean village. The same angel who announced the birth of John was sent to the Virgin Mary to announce a more transcendent birth. He greeted her with such a new kind of salutation that Mary wondered what it meant (vs. 26-29). She should have a son, whom she should name Jesus ("Saviour", Matt. 1:21), and who should be also "the Son of the Most High". He should be given "the throne of his father David", and of his kingdom there should be no end (vs. 30-33). Thus in him would be fulfilled the promise given to David on which the Messianic hope was based (2 Sam. 7:12-13).

Mary's question of the angel does not imply doubt, but simply asks for an explanation. The angel's reply reveals the combined feelings of joyful exaltation and adoring wonder with which he conveyed the explanation to Mary. God was to be the Father of her son (vs. 34-35). Thus the birth of Christ was a new creation of man. The angel went on to encourage Mary by telling her about Elisabeth; and Mary's final words express the humble submission with which she put herself at God's disposal. It was a sublime act of faith and self-sacrifice (vs. 36-38).

3. Mary's Visit to Elisabeth (1:39-56). Elisabeth was Mary's kinswoman (v. 36), but how the two were related is not known. Mary went up to Judea with lively eagerness, and Elisabeth met her with an inspired salutation of intense feeling (vs. 39-45). Mary's song breathes a calm, deep, inward repose, and a sense of profound exaltation (vs. 46-55). It is modelled on Hannah's song (1 Sam. 2:1-10), and contains several sentences from the Psalms. It shows how familiar she was with the Old Testa-

ment Scriptures. Mary remained with Elisabeth probably until the birth of John (v. 56).

4. The Birth of John (1:57-80). The circumstances attending the birth and naming of the child made a profound impression on the people round about (vs. 57-66). The song of Zacharias is modelled on the prophecies, and is full of the idea of redemption. It shows that the spiritual significance of the Messianic age, which was now being ushered in, was well understood by the devout souls in Israel. He gives thanks for the coming of the Messiah, which implies that he knew of the Incarnation, and for the deliverance which His presence is about to procure for Israel (vs. 67-75). Then he expresses his joy at the part assigned to his own son in this work, and the song overflows with a closing thanksgiving for the Messianic salvation (vs. 76-79). The historical conclusion of the narrative, telling of the growth of John (v. 80), corresponds with the statement in v. 66 that "the hand of the Lord was with him".

5. The Birth of Jesus (2:1-20). The story begins with a historical note (vs. 1-3). The decree of the Roman Emperor brought Joseph and Mary from Nazareth to Bethlehem, their ancestral city; and there, in the most humble and obscure circumstances, the Son of Man was born (vs. 4-7). Heaven's interest in the event was marked by the "good tidings of great joy" which the angel brought to the shepherds in the field, and by the praise of the heavenly host (vs. 8-14). Shepherds from the same pastures where David watched his flock visited the new-born babe, and then spread abroad the angel's message about the child (vs. 15-17). Thus the Gospel news began among the poor and lowly. Various impressions were produced by what had taken place. Luke implies that there was a great contrast between the momentary and superficial wonder of the people and the profound thoughts and feelings of Mary (vs. 18-20).

6. The Infancy of Jesus (2:21-39). Jesus was circumcised, because it was as a Jew and under the Mosaic covenant that He was to realize the ideal of human life (v. 21; Gal. 4:4). His parents fulfilled all the requirements of the Law (vs. 22-24). The offerings which they brought when presenting the child in the Temple were those that were prescribed only for the very poorest (Lev. 12:8).

The song of Simeon (vs. 25-32) is marked by suppressed rapture and vivid spiritual insight. He represents himself as a watchman now released from duty because the Messianic hope for which he was commanded to wait has appeared. His address to Mary (vs. 33-35) shows that he had some insight into the meaning of the prophecies which foreshadowed the sufferings of the Messiah. Anna the aged prophetess, who was in some respects a contrast to Simeon, confirmed his testimony regarding the child (vs. 36-38). The narrative closes by telling of the return to Nazareth after every prescription of the Law had been fulfilled (v. 39).

These aged saints, Simeon and Anna, represent the devout people in Israel who were not blinded by the false hopes of the carnally minded Jews, but were enlightened by the spiritual significance that lies in Old Testament prophecy. There seems to have been an expectation among them at that time that the advent of the Messiah was approaching.

7. The Boyhood of Jesus (2:40-52). This is the only passage in all the Gospels that tells anything of the life of Jesus in Nazareth. His growth was that of complete and fully rounded human nature. He grew in body, mind, and spirit — developing through boyhood (v. 40) into manhood (v. 52). When twelve years old, the age at which a young Jew became "a son of the Law" and a member of the congregation of Israel, Jesus was taken up to the Passover in Jerusalem for the first time. The incident related on this occasion reveals the unique and sinless nature of the growing boy (vs. 41-51).

His first recorded words, which were spoken to His parents when they found Him in the Temple after an anxious search, throw a revealing light back over His earliest years, and contain the keynote of His subsequent life (v. 49). There was something about him which He was surprised His parents did not know—"Knew ye not?" It matters little whether the phrase He used is rendered "about my Father's business" (A.V.) or "in my Father's house" (R.V.). Its real significance lies in the indefinite character of the original words, "the things of my Father" (R.V. marg.). He had always been occupied with His Father's affairs and had no interests of His own to engage Him. This is what His parents might have known.

Here is revealed the inner life of a child who had no self-will. The boy Jesus was conscious of never having been anything but right with God and occupied with doing His will. Here was a young human life free from the bias transmitted to mankind by the Fall. His words do not imply consciousness of a Divine nature, but rather consciousness of an unfallen human nature. During the eighteen silent years from this point down to His manifestation to Israel, He continued to live this kind of life within the narrow limits of the crowded home in Nazareth. There were at least six other children in the family (Mark 6:3). In Jesus, the nature of man was being made "perfect", by being subjected to all the conditions of man's life in the world (Heb. 2:10).

THE MANIFESTATION OF THE SON OF MAN
(3:1—4:13)

Luke begins his account of the events that led to the public appearance of Jesus with a historical reference to the rulers of the time (3:1-2). He also states that Jesus was "about thirty years of age" when He began His ministry (3:23). As Jesus was born before Herod's death in 4 B.C., this would make A.D. 26 the year of His manifestation to Israel.

1. The Preaching of John the Baptist (3:3-20). Luke points out that John's preaching of repentance was the fulfilment of Isa. 40:3-5, and dwells upon his warning to the crowds who thronged to be baptized of him to bring forth fruits worthy of repentance (vs. 3-9). He corrected their mistaken notions of salvation, and gave practical directions to each class of hearers to forsake their besetting sin and do the duty required by their particular position in the social order (vs. 10-14).

In the midst of the general excitement awakened by his preaching, which made people wonder whether he were the Messiah, John announced the coming of the Messiah after him. He himself could only baptize with water; but the Messiah should baptize them with the Holy Spirit (vs. 15-18). He himself could only use a symbol; the Messiah would bring in the reality. Luke completes his narrative of the Baptist at this point by telling how his ministry was abruptly terminated by his imprisonment at the hands of Herod (vs. 10-20).

2. The Baptism of Jesus (3:21-22). Luke adds one feature to the scene which is more fully described by Matthew (3:13-17). Jesus was praying at the time, and the Spirit came down upon Him as the answer to His prayer. He was baptized as the Son of Man, surrendering Himself to God as the representative Man, that He might do the will of God in dependence upon the power of the Holy Spirit.

3. The Lineage of Jesus (3:23-38). This differs from the genealogy in Matthew (1:1-17) because it gives the line of Mary instead of the line of Joseph. Luke traces the human ancestry of Jesus back through David and Abraham to Adam, thus showing His connection, not only with Israel, as Matthew does, but with all mankind as well. The two lines differ between David and Joseph. Matthew traces the royal line of David from Solomon down to Joseph, showing Jesus to be the heir of David. Luke traces Mary's ancestry back to Nathan, another son of David (v. 31), showing that Jesus was "of the seed of David according to the flesh" (Rom. 1:3; Rev. 22:16). Mary's name is not mentioned, but Joseph is called the son of Heli (v. 23) as being his son-in-law. Luke ends his genealogy by calling Adam "the son of God". In him humanity had its first beginning as the result of a creative act of God. In Jesus Christ humanity had a new beginning by another creative act (1:35).

The names of Shealtiel and Zerubbabel occur in both lists, with Neri as the father of Shealtiel in Luke (v. 27) instead of Jechoniah as in Matthew (v. 12). The explanation seems to be that Jechoniah died childless, leaving no heir of the royal line from Solomon (Jer. 22:30), and that Shealtiel, the son of Neri of the line of Nathan, took his place in the line of inheritance. It is significant that after the Exile the house of Nathan is mentioned for the first time as invested with special pre-eminence (Zech. 12:12).

4. The Temptation of Jesus (4:1-13). The order in which the three special temptations occur here differs from the order in Matthew's account. Luke's order makes the three temptations correspond with the three elements of the world as described in 1 John 2:16—"The lust of the flesh, the lust of the eyes, and the vain-glory of life". They are also parallel with the three steps by which Eve yielded to the temptation in Eden: "When the woman saw that the tree was good for food, and that it was a delight to the eyes, and that the tree was to be desired to make one wise" (Gen. 3:6).

Thus Luke's account of the temptation of Jesus presents it in the form of Satan's attack on the Second Man. The Head of the new humanity met the tempter on the same ground on which the first man fell, and foiled him at every point by holding to the Word and the will of God. Luke closes his account by telling us that "when the devil had com-pleted every temptation"—that is, every temptation to which the Lord's human nature was open (Heb. 4:15)—"he departed from him for a season." This is probably an allusion to the final assault in Gethsemane.

THE MINISTRY IN GALILEE
(4:14—9:50)

This Gospel, like the other Synoptics, omits the early ministry of Jesus in Judea, and links the beginning of the Galilean ministry with His baptism and temptation. Luke's account of the Lord's ministry in Galilee begins with Nazareth, His home-town, and ends with the Transfiguration, the consummation of His human life. The whole period is marked by an abundance of miracles. There are fourteen miracles and only two parables in this section of the Gospel. It may be divided into four parts, marked by steps in the calling and training of the disciples.

I. Up to the Call of the First Disciples (4:14-44). Luke brings out the fact that Jesus came from His baptism "full of the Holy Spirit", and proceeded to carry on His work "in the power of the Spirit" (4:1, 14). Special prominence has already been given to the Holy Spirit in the earlier chapters of the Gospel (1:15, 35, 41, 67; 2:25-27).

1. A Visit to Nazareth (vs. 14-30). After a general reference to the fame which resulted from His work in Galilee (vs. 14-15), Luke tells how Jesus was rejected in His own home-town when He visited it. The phrase, "as his custom was", refers to His habit of attending the synagogue during the previous years of His life. He read from Isa. 61:1-2 and applied the prophecy to Himself and to the Gospel that He was preaching. The people bore witness to the gracious message that came from His lips, but when He referred to Old Testament cases of God's grace being shown to the Gentiles, He aroused their rage. It was this foreshadowing of the universality of the Gospel that led them to reject Him.

2. A Sabbath in Capernaum (vs. 31-44). This passage is parallel with Mark 1:21-39. It includes the casting out of an unclean spirit in the synagogue, the restoration of Peter's wife's mother in his home, the healing of the sick people of the city at sunset, and the departure for a tour in Galilee. Mark tells the story with more fulness and vividness, but Luke adds some touches which reveal the physician. The sickness of Simon's wife's mother was "a great fever". Jesus "stood over" her and "rebuked the fever". In healing the sick who were brought to Him in the evening, Jesus "laid his hands on every one of them".

II. From the Call of the First Disciples to the Choice of the Twelve (5:1—6:11). Up to this time Jesus had been winning adherents by His preaching, but had not formed a band of personal followers. Now He began to attach to Himself regular disciples. During this period His work began to arouse opposition from the religious leaders of Israel.

1. The Call of Simon Peter (5:1-11). This incident is probably the same as that narrated in abridged form in Matt. 4:18-22 and Mark 1:16-20. Luke alone tells of Jesus teaching the people from Simon's boat (vs. 1-3), of the great catch of fishes which resulted from obeying the Lord's command

to put out into the deep and let down their nets (vs. 4-7). This miracle made a profound impression upon Simon Peter, for he had been doubtful of any result after they had fished all night and caught nothing, and he now saw that Jesus was thus rewarding him for the use of the boat. It brought home to him in a new way the contrast between his own sinful self-confidence and the thoughtful kindness of the Lord. He alone was addressed, but all four fishing partners obeyed the call (vs. 8-11).

2. The Ministry of Healing (5:12-26). The cure of the leper occurred during a tour among the cities of Galilee (vs. 12-16). It is recorded more briefly by Matthew (8:1-4), and more fully by Mark (1:40-45); but Luke the physician alone describes the man as "full of leprosy". The healing of the paralytic (vs. 17-26) is also recorded in the other Synoptic Gospels (Matt. 9:2-8; Mark 2:1-12). There were Pharisees and Scribes present on this occasion from all over the land, attracted by the fame of Jesus, and Luke mentions them here for the first time. This miracle marks the point in the Galilean ministry when Jesus began to come into conflict with the religious leaders.

This passage brings out three features that characterized the whole ministry of Jesus Christ. (1) His habit of retiring from the crowds to some quiet spot for prayer in the midst of His busy work: "He withdrew himself in the deserts, and prayed" (v. 16). Luke means that He did this habitually. (2) His dependence upon the power of God: "The power of the Lord was with him to heal" (v. 17). The phrase means that the power of Jehovah was present for Jesus to use in His miracles of healing. (3) His use of the phrase "Son of man" in speaking of Himself (v. 24). It implies that He regarded Himself as the representative Man. It is Christ's own phrase. None of the Evangelists use it of Him, and no one ever addressed Him by this title. It occurs about eighty times in the four Gospels.

3. Matthew's Discipleship (5:27-39). Levi, better known as Matthew, was called from his toll-booth, and responded immediately (vs. 27-28). The feast which he made in his own house brought his fellow-publicans and Jesus together. The publicans, as tax collectors for a Gentile power, were despised and counted as sinners. In accepting Levi's hospitality Jesus gave another occasion to the religious leaders to find fault with Him. He answered them by explaining the real purpose of His mission in the world (vs. 29-32).

The conversation continued with a question why His disciples did not fast like the disciples of John and the Pharisees. In His reply Jesus gave the first hint about His death and departure (vs. 33-35), and followed it with two parabolic statements illustrating the fact that He was not patching up the old Mosaic order but was introducing an entirely new order (vs. 36-39). The whole passage is parallel with Matt. 9:9-17 and Mark 2:14-22.

4. The Question of the Sabbath (6:1-11). Two incidents brought Jesus into conflict with the religious authorities on the observance of the Sabbath law. He defended His disciples when they were criticized by the Pharisees for rubbing ears of grain to eat as they passed through the fields on the Sabbath (vs. 1-5). He healed a man with a withered hand in the synagogue on the Sabbath, after challenging the Scribes and Pharisees, who were there watching for

an occasion to accuse him, to declare whether it was lawful to do good or to do harm on the Sabbath day (vs. 6-11). This passage is parallel with Matt. 12:1-14 and Mark 2:23—3:6.

III. From the Choice of the Twelve to their First Mission (6:12—8:56). In this section of the Gospel the work of Jesus in Galilee reaches the height of its power and popularity. It begins with the appointment of the Apostles, contains the most important of His Galilean discourses, and records a series of remarkable miracles.

1. The Appointment of the Apostles (6:12-19). Before choosing the Twelve, Jesus went up into the mountain that slopes back from the shore near Capernaum, "and continued all night in prayer to God" (v. 12). When they were appointed next day He named them "Apostles", to distinguish them from the rest of the disciples and to indicate His purpose for them (vs. 13-16). The names are the same as in the lists of Matthew (10:2-4) and Mark (3:16-19), except that "Judas the son of James" is called Thaddæus in the other lists. Then Jesus came down with them to "a level place" on the mountain side, not "the plain" (A.V.). A large group of His disciples and a mixed throng of people from Judea and the sea-coast gathered about Him, and there He performed many miracles among them (vs. 17-19).

2. The Sermon to the Disciples (6:20-49). In the midst of that scene Jesus "lifted up his eyes on his disciples" and delivered the discourse usually called the Sermon on the Mount. It is fully recorded in Matt. 5-7. Parts of it were probably repeated on different occasions. Luke's account begins with the qualities that characterize members of the Kingdom of God, and the contrast between the happiness of those who possess them and the misery of those who do not (vs. 20-26).

The main part of the discourse deals with the duties of members of the Kingdom (vs. 27-45). Luke omits most of what Matthew reports regarding Christ's relation to the Mosaic Law, which would have little meaning for his Gentile readers. The point he emphasizes is that love is the principle of the Kingdom and the distinguishing quality of its members. Several illustrations are given of the way it is to be manifested. The Sermon closes with a warning of the judgments that await the professed disciples of the Lord (vs. 46-49). A contrast is drawn between the result of following and the consequences of not following His words.

3. Two Works of Power (7:1-17). The healing of the centurion's servant took place when Jesus returned to Capernaum. Luke's story of the miracle is much fuller than the condensed account in Matthew (8:5-13), which represents the centurion as doing himself what Luke says he did through a deputation of Jewish elders (vs. 1-8). This centurion was probably a Roman soldier in the service of Herod. He had been attracted by the worship of the Jews and had built them their synagogue in Capernaum. He had heard of the fame of Jesus, and his experience of the authority possessed by a military commander helped him to believe that the authority Jesus possessed would similarly extend beyond His immediate presence.

The faith of this Gentile surpassed any faith the Jews had shown and made Jesus marvel (vs. 9-10). He marvelled on another occasion, but it was at the unbelief of the people in His own home-town (Mark 6:6). Luke's account of this miracle is in harmony with his universal outlook. It is also characteristic of him to tell us that the centurion's servant "was dear unto him". All the centurions of the New Testament are mentioned with honour (Matt. 27:54; Acts 10:1; 22:26; 27:43).

The raising of the widow's son at Nain, which is recorded only in Luke, reveals the tender and compassionate quality of Jesus' character and the majestic reach of His authority (vs. 11-17). Nain was about twenty-five miles from Capernaum out on the plain in the southern part of Galilee. The young man was "the only son of his mother, and she was a widow". Her utterly desolate state touched the compassion of Jesus. He stopped the funeral procession, called the young man back to life, and "gave him to his mother".

There was a profound and essential difference between the way that Christ raised the dead and the way that others did—Elijah (1Kings 17:19-22), Elisha (2 Kings 4:32-35), and Peter (Acts 9:39-41). They struggled and sought after a power that was beyond them: He acted with a calmness and majesty all His own, and awoke the dead as easily as one awakens a sleeper. This miracle produced a deep sense of awe, and spread the fame of Jesus still more widely.

4.   A Message from John the Baptist (7:18-35). This passage is substantially identical with Matt. 11:1-19. Luke says that it was John's disciples who brought him news of Jesus while in prison, and that John sent two of them to Jesus with his question. Luke reports the answer that Jesus sent back to John (vs. 18-23), and the address that He gave concerning John to the people afterwards (vs. 24-35). He omits what Matthew says about the Kingdom of Heaven suffering violence, and inserts instead a statement about the different treatment John received from the common people and from the religious leaders.

5.   In the House of Simon the Pharisee (7:36-50). This incident belongs to Luke alone. The anointing of Jesus by the sinful woman here is to be distinguished from the anointing by Mary at Bethany. The name of the host in each case is the same (Matt. 26:6; Mark 14:3), but the women are entirely different (vs. 36-38). Jesus answered the unspoken thought of the proud and supercilious Pharisee by telling the story of two debtors and then applying it to his case. His indifference toward his guest and his failure as a host were in sharp contrast with the emotion and the behaviour of the woman (vs. 39-46). The final word which Jesus spoke to her indicates that the love she had shown Him sprang from her faith in Him, and her faith in Him implied that her sins were forgiven (vs. 47-50). The incident shows that Christ looks for love from those who are forgiven.

6.   Another Tour in Galilee (8:1-21). Luke describes a feature in our Lord's ministry at this period that is not mentioned elsewhere (vs. 1-3). He and the Twelve formed one travelling company, going from city to city and from village to village with the message of the Kingdom of God; and another company, composed of women of means, arranged for His reception and provided for His support as He went from place to place. This group of women is mentioned again. They followed Him even to the Cross (23:49).

Luke continues this section with the parable of the sower and its interpretation (vs. 4-18), which is recorded more fully in Matt. 13 and Mark 4. Then comes a brief account of the incident that occurred when Jesus' mother and brethren came seeking Him and could not reach Him for the crowd (vs. 19-21), which is recorded also in Matt. 12:46-50 and Mark 3:31-35.

7.   A Series of Typical Miracles (8:22-56). All the Synoptic Gospels record these four miracles, and give them in the same order: the stilling of the storm on the sea, the casting out of a legion of demons from the Gadarene, the cure of the woman who touched His garment, and the raising of the daughter of Jairus. Matthew's account is the briefest and most compact (8:23-24; 9:18-26), and Mark's the longest and most detailed (4:35—5:43). Luke's account, though not quite as long as Mark's, is substantially the same. In telling of the raising of the dead girl, Luke adds a characteristic touch: she was "an only daughter, about twelve years of age". These four miracles belong to the four realms in which our Lord wrought His mighty works: the natural world, the spirit world, disease, and death.

IV.   From the Mission of the Twelve to the Departure from Galilee (9:1-50). This section brings the Galilean ministry to its consummation. It includes Peter's great confession and the Lord's transfiguration.

1.   The Mission of the Twelve (vs. 1-9). The instructions given to the Apostles (vs. 1-5) are recorded more fully in Matt. 10. It was probably the stir caused by the mission of the Twelve throughout Galilee that brought the fame of Jesus to Herod's ears (vs. 6-9). Luke alone tells us that Herod sought an interview with Him.

2.   The Feeding of the Multitude (vs. 10-17). This miracle was wrought after the return of the Apostles. It is the only miracle in the whole ministry of Jesus that is common to the four Gospels. It is found in Matt. 14, Mark 6, and John 6. They all record the special detail of the Lord blessing the five loaves and the two fishes, seeing in this the secret of the power displayed. It marked the climax of the Lord's Galilean ministry. Henceforth attention was diverted more and more to His approaching death, which was to bring His work to a close.

3.   Peter's Confession of Christ (vs. 18-27). Luke does not mention the place where this occurred, but he tells us that Jesus was praying in private at the time and that His disciples were with Him. The passage is parallel with Matt. 16:13-28 and Mark 8:27-38. Peter's confession is told as briefly as in Mark, and is followed by the Lord's first prediction of His rejection and death at the hands of the Jewish leaders and His subsequent resurrection (vs. 18-22). Then comes the first reference to His coming in glory, which is connected with a warning to the disciples about taking up their cross and following Him, and not being ashamed of Him (vs. 23-27).

4.   The Transfiguration (vs. 28-36). Luke's account of this scene throws further light upon the record in Matt. 17:1-7 and Mark 9:2-8. It was while Jesus was praying that His transfiguration took place. The theme of the conversation with Moses and Elijah was "his decease which He was about to accomplish at Jerusalem". This does not mean His death alone, but His "departure" (marg.)—His way

of going out of the world, including His resurrection and ascension as well as His death. He might have crowned His earthly life as the Son of Man by departing by the way of the Mount of Transfiguration; but He turned back to accomplish the redemption of men by departing by the way of the Cross and the Mount of Olives. This theme would be of peculiar interest to both Moses and Elijah, one of whom had departed by death and resurrection and the other by translation.

5. The Close of the Galilean Ministry (vs. 37-50). Jesus' cure of the demoniac boy at the foot of the mountain next day (vs. 37-43) is contrasted in all three Gospels with the failure of the disciples to cast out the evil spirit. Luke marks the pathos of the scene by including in the father's appeal for the boy his statement, "he is mine only child". He also adds the tender touch that when Jesus healed him, He "gave him back to the father". His account of the Galilean ministry then comes to a close with a few further incidents: another prediction of the Cross (vs. 43-45), an object lesson in humility and a warning against intolerance (vs. 46-50).

THE JOURNEY TO JERUSALEM
(9:51—19:28)

The narrative contained in this section is almost wholly peculiar to the Third Gospel. In Matthew the record is compressed into two chapters (chs. 19-20) and in Mark into one (ch. 10). It is the story of a slow journey lasting many months, during which Jesus was moving steadily on toward Jerusalem for the consummation of His ministry. It is characterized by an abundance of parables. There are sixteen parables and only five miracles in this part of Luke's Gospel. It may be considered in three divisions, corresponding with three stages of the journey as indicated in the course of the narrative (9:51; 13:22; 17:11; 19:28).

It is possible to regard these stages as separated by different visits to Jerusalem, for John's Gospel shows that Jesus was in the city on two occasions during this period before His final arrival there just before the last Passover. These occasions were the Feast of Tabernacles in the fall (John 7:2, 10, 37) and the Feast of the Dedication in the winter (John 10:22-23).

I. The First Stage of the Journey (9:51—13:21). Luke does not tell us what direction Jesus followed in leaving Galilee, but it may be gathered from the first incident he relates.

1. Rejected in Samaria (9:51-62). Jesus sent messengers into Samaria in advance to prepare for His arrival. One of the villages refused Him hospitality because He was on the way to Jerusalem; and James and John drew a rebuke from the Lord for desiring to call down fire from heaven upon it (vs. 51-56). Turned aside from Samaria, Jesus would cross over to the eastern side of the Jordan and make His way down through Perea. As He went on He showed His knowledge of the hearts of men in dealing with three doubtful disciples (vs. 57-62).

2. The Mission of the Seventy (10:1-24). As Jesus had sent the Twelve into the northern parts of the province, because the labourers were so few and the harvest was so great, so for the same reason He now sends a much larger number of His followers into the southern parts (vs. 1-2). The charge He gave them was similar to that given to the Twelve (vs. 3-12). It closes with a denunciation of the impenitent cities in Galilee (vs. 13-16). The number seventy is significant. It probably had some reference to the seventy nations of Gen. 10, which were regarded as making up the whole human race. If Christ's choice of the Twelve was based on the number of the tribes and was particularly related to His mission to Israel, the mission of the seventy was probably intended to foreshadow His relation to the Gentiles.

The joy which these disciples manifested on their return evoked such exultation on His part as is unique in the life of the Saviour (vs. 17-20). His statement, "I beheld Satan fallen as lightning from heaven", meant that Jesus saw in the success of the disciples a symbol and earnest of the complete overthrow of Satan. Then He went on to express His joy that the truths of His new order were being revealed to the simple, and to congratulate His disciples that they had seen them . While doing this, He made one of those sublime assertions of Divine power and authority which flash out again and again from His teaching (vs. 21-24).

3. The Good Samaritan (10:25-42). The occasion of this parable was a practical question put to Jesus by a lawyer which betrayed a false view of eternal life, for it implied that eternal life could be secured by the performance of some one act. Jesus referred him back to the Law, which a lawyer ought to know. The lawyer showed that he rightly understood the Law by quoting the heart of it as summed up in love to God and love to one's neighbour (Deut. 6:5; Lev. 19:18). Jesus approved the answer, and added, "This do, and thou shalt live", implying by this that life consists in the continuous performance of acts of love. This touched the lawyer's conscience and put him on the defensive, and he asked another question: "And who is my neighbour?" (vs. 25-29).

In reply, Jesus told the story of the good Samaritan, which was probably taken from real life, as He would hardly represent a priest and a Levite as so callous and indifferent if there had been no actual incident to justify Him in doing so. The parable illustrates the true operation of the law of love. Jesus shifted the lawyer's ground from the selfish attitude implied in his question, which sought to limit the meaning of "neighbour", to the attitude of love, by asking, when He had finished the story, "Which of these three proved neighbour?" If a Samaritan could prove himself a true neighbour to a Jew by showing mercy to him, then all men are neighbours (vs. 30-37).

The exquisite picture of Jesus in the home of Martha and Mary, which is preserved by Luke alone, may have been inserted here (vs. 38-42) to supplement the answer that Jesus gave to the lawyer's question about eternal life in the preceding incident. Practical benevolence, such as that of the Samaritan, is not enough. It must be combined with communion with the Lord. This was "the good part" which Mary had chosen.

4. A Lesson on Prayer (11:1-13). On one of the occasions when Jesus had been praying, a request was put to Him by one of the disciples: "Lord, teach us to pray". He gave them as a model what is usually called the Lord's Prayer (vs. 1-4). Matthew reports it in the Sermon on the Mount (6:9-13). Then He proceeded to give them an encouragement

to pray in the parable of the importunate friend (vs. 5-8).

Three persons are to be carefully distinguished: the host—"which of you"—with nothing to supply his guest, his near-by friend who has abundance, and his guest who has come to him, at midnight, needy and hungry. The parable teaches its lesson by contrasting the reluctance of the selfish friend, who has to be roused by continued and importunate asking, with the willingness of the loving and bountiful God. Jesus then adds an exhortation that they should persevere in prayer, and supports it by their own human experience of a father's nature (vs. 9-13). "How much more" will the heavenly Father give the Holy Spirit to them that ask Him. This gift implies all other good gifts.

5. The Blasphemy of the Pharisees (11:14-36). On one occasion when Jesus had cured a dumb demoniac, He was accused of complicity with Beelzebub, and was challenged to perform a sign to clear Himself of the charge (vs. 14-16). He first refuted the charge by an appeal to common sense. Satan would not fight against himself, as even their own exorcists would say (vs. 17-19). Then He gave the true explanation of His cures: the power of God was present with Him, and the Kingdom of God was come among them (vs. 20-23). In contrast with His own cures, He drew a picture of the result when their exorcists cast out an unclean spirit (vs. 24-26). At this point an incident occurred which shows the deep impression produced upon the people by the Lord's words (vs. 27-28).

This was followed by a further discourse, in which Jesus denounced that generation of Israel as "an evil generation" for seeking after a sign, and would give it no sign but the sign that Jonah was to the people of Nineveh. It should be condemned in the final judgment by the queen who came from afar to hear the wisdom of Solomon, and by the Ninevites who repented at Jonah's preaching (vs. 29-32). It is significant that Jesus took these two instances from among the Gentiles. They should condemn by their example the Jews of that day who had a greater than Solomon and Jonah in their midst. Then He went on to show that those whose spiritual vision had not been darkened by impenitence and indifference had no need of a sign from heaven. Their whole soul was full of the light that was shining all around them. This light was shed by Christ Himself (vs. 33-36).

6. At Dinner in a Pharisee's House (11:37-54). A Pharisee had asked Jesus to dine with him, and was surprised that He did not perform the usual act of ceremonial washing before dinner (vs. 37-38). This led Jesus to pronounce a series of rebukes upon the Pharisees for the hypocrisy and externalism of their religious practices and for their vainglorious spirit (vs. 39-44). A remark interposed by one of the lawyers present led Jesus to include them too in the series of "woe's", and to announce the approaching doom that should fall upon that generation of Jews (vs. 45-52).

The blood of all the prophets, "from the blood of Abel unto the blood of Zechariah", should be required of that generation. The murder of Zechariah is recorded in 2 Chron. 24:20-21, and as this book comes last in the Hebrew Canon, these two murders are the first and the last in the Bible of the Jews. When the Lord left the Pharisee's house a scene of violence occurred (vs. 53-54). This marks the culminating point of the conflict between Jesus and the Pharisees so far as the Galilean ministry is concerned.

7. A Series of Discourses (12:1—13:9). The commotion drew together an immense crowd, whose sympathies were probably divided. Jesus addressed His next words to His disciples rather than to the multitude. He warned them against hypocrisy, the characteristic spirit and secret sin of the Pharisees, which should ultimately be exposed (12:1-3), and encouraged them with the assurance of God's loving care over them in this world (12:4-7), and with the promise of a recompense of glory with Himself in Heaven, which should be denied to those who denied Him and blasphemed the Holy Spirit (12:8-10). They were not to be anxious before persecuting tribunals, for the Holy Spirit would aid them in their testimony (12:11-12).

A covetous request from a man in the crowd was the occasion of the parable of the rich fool. Jesus declined to interfere in the affairs of civil life, and uttered a warning against coveting this world's goods (12:13-15). He went on to tell the story of the foolish rich man, whose ground was blessed of God, but who left God out of his account and lived for himself alone. He was making provision for the flesh to fulfil the lust thereof when God called him to his account (12:16-20). A man is made rich, not by the possession of this world's wealth, but by the possession of that spiritual wealth that counts with God (12:21).

The address to the people being ended, Jesus once more turned to the disciples. They were not to be anxious, but were to trust in their Father's loving care (12:22-30). They were to seek His Kingdom, for it was their Father's good pleasure to give them the Kingdom, and they were to have their treasure in Heaven (12:31-34). They were to be always ready, with their loins girded and their lamps burning, like servants watching for their master's return, "for in an hour that ye think not the Son of man cometh" (12:35-40).

At this point, in answer to a question by Peter, Jesus addressed the Apostles in particular, and reminded them of their special responsibility to be faithful and wise stewards during their Master's absence, and warned them against being unprepared for His return (12:41-48). Then He gave voice to the emotion that filled His heart in view of the moral revolution and the family divisions which He was about to cause on the earth (12:49-53).

He addressed the multitude once more, and denounced them for not recognizing the signs of the times. They did not see the significance of what was happening in the world (12:54-59). Then came three warnings of judgment and exhortations to repentance that are found only in Luke. Two of them were based on recent incidents (13:1-5). The third was the parable of the barren fig-tree, in which Jesus pictured the failure of Israel to respond to the patient dealing of God with the nation, and foreshadowed the coming judgment (13:6-9).

8. A Synagogue Scene (13:10-21). This incident is peculiar to Luke and is the last recorded visit of Jesus to a synagogue. The ruler of the synagogue, angry because Jesus had healed the infirm woman on the Sabbath, attacked Him indirectly by turning to the people and charging them not to come for healing on the Sabbath day. Jesus rebuked him for his hypocrisy, and put His adversaries to shame

before the people (vs. 10-17). Seeing how the people rejoiced at the miracles He was working, Jesus repeated the parables of the mustard seed and the leaven describing the effect of the Kingdom of God in the world (vs. 18-21). These two parables occur in the sermon of parables recorded in Matt. 13.

II. The Second Stages of the Journey (13:22—17:10). Jesus continued His journey, proceeding slowly through the country, stopping to teach at every city and village as He went on toward Jerusalem (v. 22).

1. Warnings on the Way (13:23-35). One of these arose out of a question as to the number of the saved. Jesus replied by repeating sayings found in Matt. 7:13 and 8:11-12 and making further statements foreshadowing the calling of the Gentiles (vs. 22-30). Another came out of an attempt by some Pharisees to frighten Jesus with a threat from Herod through whose dominion He was travelling. It failed to disturb Him. The cunning of "that fox" could not turn Him aside from the work given Him to do, and He would go on fulfilling it day by day till He had finished it in Jerusalem (vs. 31-33). This thought drew out a lamentation over the city which had so often refused to receive His ministry. She had rejected the salvation that He offered; and now He could only leave her people to the desolation that was coming. They should not see Him till, in response to the national repentance of Israel, He would come again (vs. 34-35).

2. A Sabbath Meal in a Pharisee's House (14:1-24). Here we are allowed to see something of Jesus' in-door life and familiar table-talk. The scene is peculiar to Luke and is amply described. It was the Sabbath day, and they had a man with the dropsy there and were watching Jesus to see if He would heal or not. The refusal of the lawyers and Pharisees to answer His question about healing on the Sabbath betrayed their bad faith. After healing the man and sending him away, He exposed their hypocrisy with another question which they could not answer (vs. 1-6).

As the guests sat down, Jesus marked how they took the chief seats for themselves, and He gave them a lesson on humility, clothing it in the form of a recommendation to intelligent self-interest (vs. 7-11). When He observed how the guests belonged to the richer classes, He gave His host a lesson on charity toward the poor and needy, promising him a reward in the resurrection of the just (vs. 12-14).

This reference to the resurrection drew from one of the guests a remark about the blessedness of sharing in the heavenly feast of the Kingdom of God, and Jesus spoke the parable of the great supper to show how little this privilege was appreciated. The man who made the supper bade many, but when he sent his servant to tell them that all things were now ready, "they all with one consent began to make excuse" (vs. 15-24). The parable depicts the indifference of the Jews to spiritual things, their rejection of the Gospel, their exclusion from the Kingdom, and the ultimate calling of the Gentiles.

3. The Conditions of Discipleship (14:25-35). As Jesus resumed His journey great crowds followed Him. They were disposed to believe that He was the Messiah, but they misunderstood the nature of the Kingdom and the conditions of discipleship. These Jesus now pointed out. The disciple of Jesus

must bear the cross after Him (vs. 25-27). He must count the cost of following Him to the end (vs. 28-32). He must renounce all that he has for Christ's sake and maintain the spirit of self-sacrifice, so that the salt in his life may not lose its savour or its influence upon others (vs. 33-35).

4. Three Parables of Grace (Ch. 15). These three stories form a connected series, and were spoken in answer to the Pharisees and Scribes who were criticising Jesus for associating with publicans and sinners (vs. 1-2). Their purpose was to show that it was just such as these—the lost and the outcast—that Jesus came to save. Luke alone has preserved them, and they are especially characteristic of his Gospel. They all illustrate aspects of redemption, and they suggest the work of the three Persons of the Godhead in the salvation of the lost.

The parables of the lost sheep (vs. 3-7) and the lost coin (vs. 8-10) set forth the seeking love of God, depicting the aspect of grace shown in the work of the Son and the work of the Spirit. The parable of the lost son sets forth the pardoning love of God, and depicts the aspect of grace as manifested by the Father. It is in two parts. The first part, which tells the story of the prodigal son (vs. 11-24), reveals the attitude of God's heart toward the world of sinners. The second part, which tells of the elder brother (vs. 25-32), was intended to depict the spirit of the Pharisees and Scribes in their murmuring against Jesus, and to reveal the attitude of God's heart toward them.

The whole chapter is full of singular beauty. The note of joy rings through it. Each of the first two parables ends with a refrain which reflects the joy of Heaven over the salvation of the sinner. The third parable, which occupies two-thirds of the chapter, seems to rise into poetry as the story approaches its close. Each of its two parts ends with a refrain, which expresses the father's joy over the finding of his lost son, and reflects the Father-heart of God.

5. Two Parables of Warning (Ch. 16). These two parables also are peculiar to Luke. They have to do with the use of the wealth of this world. One was spoken to the disciples and the other to the Pharisees.

In the parable of the prudent steward (vs. 1-8), Jesus drew a lesson for the disciples from the man's prudence and foresight in providing for his future. The steward was not acting dishonestly in cutting down the debts that were owed to his master, for in each case it is implied that he would make up the amount himself. He is called "the unrighteous steward" with reference to the primary charge of wasting his master's goods, not with reference to his dealing with his master's debtors. His lord could not have commended him for a transaction which would have made free with his income. The steward was commended "because he had done wisely": when put out of his former position he used his present wealth to make provision for the future. Jesus was not using a dishonest transaction as an illustration of wisdom. He was describing the kind of wisdom the people of this world show in providing for their earthly future, in order to point a lesson for "the children of light" in providing for their eternal future.

Jesus added some comments to enforce the lesson of the parable (vs. 9-13). He bade the disciples make to themselves friends "by means of the mammon of unrighteousness; that, when it shall fail, they may receive you into the eternal tabernacles". They were to use earthly wealth, called "the mammon of unrighteousness" because it tends to promote unrighteousness, in helping the poor and needy and serving the Kingdom of God. By so doing they should win friendships that would outlast the wealth of this world and endure into the eternal world. If they were not faithful in the use of earthly riches, they would not be trusted with heavenly riches. "That which is another's", is earthly wealth, which we have only in trust and cannot keep. "That which is your own", is spiritual wealth, which we possess forever.

The Pharisees scoffed at this teaching, and Jesus reminded them that God knew their hearts, and their pride was an abomination in His sight. The old dispensation was being superseded by the Kingdom of God, and the Law on which they trusted was being fulfilled completely in a new spiritual order where moral principles prevail (vs. 14-18). Jesus went on to illustrate these principles by the story of the rich man and Lazarus, in which He pictured the disastrous and eternal consequences that follow the wrong use of earthly riches.

The parable contains two scenes, one on earth and the other in another world, which are set exactly over against each other. In the scene on earth (vs. 19-22), a striking contrast is drawn between the rich man and the beggar, first in life and then in death. Every detail in this picture has its significance in bringing out the selfish neglect of the rich man, who used his wealth for himself alone and got a burial in this world, over against the utter helplessness and misery of the poor man, who had nothing in this world but his faith—his name means "God is my help"—and got a welcome in Heaven.

The other scene is in Hades—not "hell" (A.V.), but the world where all the departed go to await the final judgment, including a place of punishment and a place of bliss. Here the contrast is completely reversed, and between the two men there is a great gulf fixed. Of the two interviews composing the scene, one relates to the rich man's lot after death (vs. 23-26), and the other to that of his five brethren on earth (vs. 27-31). His own lot is fixed unalterably, and he is suffering from the torture of lustful desires which his life on earth has inflamed and which he cannot satisfy now. His brethren, who refused to hear Moses and the Prophets, would not repent if one rose from the dead. By this conclusion of the parable Jesus once more rebuked the demand of the Pharisees for a sign.

6. Further Teaching for the Disciples (17:1-10). This passage contains four brief sayings addressed to the disciples, which appear to have no connection with the preceding discourses. They deal with the greatness of the sin of causing others to sin (vs. 1-2), the duty of forgiving a sinning brother when he repents (vs. 3-4), the power of even the smallest faith (vs. 5-6), and the fact that obedience and good works imply no merit on our part and give us no claim on God (vs. 7-10). The last saying is based on the system of slavery, and seems to represent the Lord as a slave-master. The illustration, however, was not intended to depict the Lord's attitude to the disciples, but only to show how they were to regard their service for Him. The other side of their relation to the Lord and His service is brought out in 12:35-37.

III. The Third Stage of the Journey (17:11—19:28). For the third time Luke tells us that Jesus was moving on toward Jerusalem. This last portion of the journey brings Him to Bethany just before the triumphal entry into Jerusalem.

1. The Ten Lepers (17:11-19). These men, standing off by themselves as Jesus was entering a village, cried out to Him for mercy, and He bade them go to the priests. This implied a promise of cleansing. Their faith was shown in their obedience to His command, and as they went they were cleansed. Christ's miracles of healing were so common that nine of them took their cure as a matter of course without returning to thank Him. The gratitude of the Samaritan won an additional blessing from the Lord. This is another illustration of the universal human outlook of this Gospel.

2. The Coming of the Kingdom (17:20-37). Asked by the Pharisees when the Kingdom of God would come, Jesus replied that it was not coming with any visible demonstration or outward sign that men could observe; "for behold", He went on to say, "the kingdom of God is in the midst of you" (vs. 20-21, marg.). The phrase in the text, "within you", is correct enough as a translation, but does not suit the context, for the Kingdom of God was not in the hearts of the Pharisees. Jesus was referring to Himself and to His own presence in their midst. The powers and principles of the Kingdom were already in action in the kind of life that He was living among them.

Christ then turned to the disciples, and, continuing the subject which the Pharisees had introduced, He told them of the future coming of the Kingdom. The days would come when they should not have His presence in their midst and should long for His return (v. 22). His Second Coming would not take place secretly, nor locally; it would be like a flash of lightning, seen suddenly and simultaneously everywhere (vs. 23-24). Before that, however, He must suffer and be rejected by the present generation (v. 25).

Men will be living their ordinary lives and giving themselves up to worldly enjoyment, and the revelation of the Son of Man will come upon them suddenly (v. 26-30). Only those will be ready for Him who have not identified their lives with the interests of this world (vs. 31-33). Then the closest relations of this life will be broken, for separations will be made according as one belongs to the Kingdom and another does not (vs. 34-36). The question that the disciples asked at the end assumed what He had just denied, that the revelation of the Son of Man would be local (v. 37). He replied with what was probably a proverb, meaning that when the conditions are fulfilled, then the agents of judgment come.

3. Parables about Prayer (18:1-14). Luke alone records these two parables. The parable of the unrighteous judge and the importunate widow (vs. 1-8), following the preceding discourse on the Lord's Second Coming, teaches the necessity of persevering prayer in view of that event. The alternative is either praying continually or fainting. The argument is this: If an unrighteous judge will give a righteous judgment in the case of a helpless widow in whom he has no interest because of her ceaseless petition, how much more will the righteous and holy God answer the unwearied cry for justice of His chosen people whom He loves. If He does not inter-

pose immediately to deliver them, it is because He is long-suffering to their oppressors. Jesus closed the parable with a warning: "Nevertheless, when the Son of man cometh, shall he find the faith on the earth?" (marg.), that is, the faith of the widow, the faith that persists in prayer.

The parable of the Pharisee and the publican (vs. 9-14) was addressed to some members of the company that was following Jesus who manifested a haughty spirit of self-righteousness. Both men were alike in going up into the Temple to pray, but were quite different in the spirit and purpose of their prayers. The Pharisee, standing proudly in a conspicuous spot, thanked God that he was not like the rest of men, and told Him of his meritorious works. The publican, standing away off by himself, pleaded with humility and contrition for mercy as a sinner. He was the one that went home "justified" (Luke uses Paul's word), with his prayer for pardon answered, and not the self-righteous Pharisee.

4. Incidents in Perea (18:15-34). At this point Luke's narrative joins those of Matthew (19:13) and Mark (10:13). The incidents recorded are: the blessing of the babes brought to Jesus (vs. 15-17), the interview of Jesus with the rich ruler on the question of eternal life (vs. 18-23) and His conversation with the disciples about it afterwards (vs. 24-30), and a final prediction of what was to happen to Him at Jerusalem (vs. 31-34).

5. Jesus at Jericho (18:35—19:28). This was His last stopping place before reaching Bethany. When Luke's account of the miracle at Jericho (18:35-43) is compared with the accounts in Matthew (20:29-34) and Mark (10:46-52), it appears that there were two blind men healed. One of them, probably Bartimæus, heard the travelling company entering Jericho as he sat by the wayside, and was told that Jesus was in it; and both of them appealed to Jesus and received their sight as He was leaving Jericho next day. Jesus spent the intervening night at the house of Zacchæus the publican. The story of this man's conversion, which is contained only in Luke, is full of human interest (19:1-10). It tells of the device he adopted as a small man because of his eagerness to see Jesus in the crowd, the call that Jesus addressed to him, and his complete surrender to the conditions of discipleship.

The parable of the pounds was apparently spoken when Jesus was still in Jericho (19:11-28). It is to be distinguished from the parable of the talents, which was addressed to the disciples privately on a different occasion (Matt. 25:14-30). Two reasons are given to explain why Jesus spoke the parable at this time—"because he was nigh to Jerusalem", the city that was to reject Him and whose guilt is depicted in the parable, and because those who accompanied Him "supposed that the kingdom of God was immediately to appear". There was evidently increasing excitement among these pilgrims as they drew nearer Jerusalem. They were expecting that Jesus would set up the Messianic Kingdom there at once. The parable depicts the Lord's departure from the world as necessary in order that His Kingdom should be established, and it goes on to indicate how His disciples were to be occupied in working and waiting for His return.

The phrase used of the nobleman, "to receive for himself a kingdom", was a prophetic announcement of the Lord's enthronement in Heaven in prepar-

ation for the establishment of His Kingdom on earth. It can hardly be an allusion to the mission of Archelaus to Rome after the death of his father Herod (Matt. 2:22), for that took place more than thirty years before. Each of the ten servants was given the same sum. The pound, therefore, must represent what all believers have in common, either the grace of salvation or the Gospel as a trust (1 Thess. 2:4; 1 Tim. 1:11). The parable describes the attitude of the Jews toward their Messianic King—"We will not that this man reign over us" (v. 14). It closes by depicting the punishment that was to come upon them for rejecting Him.

THE MINISTRY IN JERUSALEM
(19:29—21:38)

We have now reached the end of the journey which has brought Jesus step by step nearer Jerusalem. He was accompanied by a multitude of pilgrims who were going up to the Passover. He was about to enter Jerusalem for His final ministry there. At this point Luke rejoins the other Gospels in describing the closing week of the Lord's life. The present section is parallel with Matt. 21—25 and Mark 11—13. Luke omits the supper at Bethany where Mary anointed Jesus, and connects the events that he records immediately with the Temple. His narrative may be taken under three main themes.

1. Entering into the Temple (19:29-48). Jesus now deliberately presented Himself as the Messiah in the nation's capital and in the Temple. He accepted the Messianic salutations of the multitude, and claimed Messianic authority in His Father's house. All the details of the story emphasize the solemnity which He attached to the event. The sending of the two disciples indicates a deliberate plan on His part. The remark, "whereon no man ever yet sat", is in keeping with the kingly use that was to be made of the animal (vs. 29-36). From the moment Jesus seated Himself upon the colt He became the centre of the homage and enthusiasm of the crowd (vs. 37-40).

His lament over the city (vs. 41-44) is not to be confounded with the lament recorded in 13:34-35. It was uttered on the spot where the road from Bethany, rounding the Mount of Olives, brings the city into view. The incident is related by Luke alone. Jesus entered the Temple as a sovereign, discharged the functions of a judge, and established Himself there as a teacher (vs. 45-48). Luke adds the graphic statement, "the people all hung upon him, listening".

2. Teaching in the Temple (20:1—21:4). As soon as Jesus began teaching in the Temple, the leaders of the nation sought some way to destroy Him. Fear of the people kept them from proceeding against Him openly, and so they first tried to discredit Him in the eyes of the people. As religious authorities they came demanding to know what authority He had, and He met them with a question which exposed their failure as religious leaders (20:1-8). He followed this with the parable of the wicked husbandmen, in which He depicted their sin and forecast the judgment that was coming upon them (20:9-19). Luke, along with Mark, omits both the parable of the two sons, which precedes this one in Matthew, and that of the marriage feast, which follows it.

Then came the questions put to Jesus by the different Jewish sects. Luke says that spies were sent with the question about giving tribute to Cæsar, in an attempt to ensnare Him and hand Him over to the Roman governor. He saw through their purpose, and His answer silenced them before the people and made them marvel (20:20-26). The Sadducees came next with their question about the resurrection. Jesus answered it with an exposition of a verse from Moses in the passage about "the bush" (Exod. 3:6), which won the approval of the Scribes (20:27-40). Then He brought his public teaching to an end, and silenced His adversaries among the Jews, by quoting a passage about the Messiah from the Psalms (110:1) which they could not explain (20:41-44). Finally he denounced the Scribes in the hearing of the people (20:45-47), and commended the poor widow who cast her two mites into the treasury (21:1-4).

3. Foretelling the Destruction of the Temple (21:5-38). Matthew (ch. 24) and Mark (ch. 13) tell us that this prophecy was delivered on the Mount of Olives after Jesus had pronounced His final denunciation of the Jewish leaders and left the Temple for the last time. Luke gives no indication of the time and place, but only tells of the question that called it forth (vs. 5-7). His report of the address has the destruction of Jerusalem chiefly in view. The Second Coming of Christ is treated very briefly, for it had been given fuller treatment in an earlier address called forth by a question of the Pharisees (17:20-37). The question of the disciples, as Luke records it, refers simply to the sign that should announce the coming destruction of the Temple, which took place in A.D. 70. The Lord's answer may be analysed as follows:

(1) The troubles that would follow the departure of Christ and must not be mistaken for true signs (vs. 8-19). False Christs would come; wars would arise among the nations; and the disciples of Christ would be persecuted—hated of all men for His name's sake.

(2) The destruction of Jerusalem and the true sign that would announce it (vs. 20-24). The disciples were to flee when they saw it, for the long-foretold judgment upon Israel was about to fall, and Jerusalem's age-long desolation at the hands of the Gentiles was about to begin. The words, "these are days of vengeance", correspond with the statement about "great tribulation" in Matthew.

(3) The coming of the Son of Man in power and glory, which would bring their redemption to its consummation (vs. 25-28). This would take place when the "times of the Gentiles" should be fulfilled; that is, when the preaching of the Gospel in the Gentile world should be completed. The sign of this would be distress among the nations and alarming commotions, indicating the collapse of the whole system of human society.

(4) The illustration of the fig-tree and its lesson (vs. 29-36). The destruction of the Temple would take place before that generation passed away. The day of the Son of Man would come upon the world suddenly. Hence the need of increasing watchfulness on the part of Christ's followers.

The chapter closes with a statement of the way that Jesus spent the last days and nights of His public ministry—every day teaching the people in the Temple, and every night lodging in the Mount of Olives (vs. 37-38).

THE DEPARTURE OF THE SON OF MAN
(Chs. 22-24)

These chapters tell us how Jesus accomplished His departure from the world by the way of the Cross, the Resurrection, and the Ascension. This was the theme of His conversation with Moses and Elijah on the Mount of Transfiguration (9:31 marg.). These chapters are parallel with Matt. 26—28 and Mark 15—16. Luke gives many details not found in the other Gospels.

1. The Preparations (22:1-13). As the Feast of the Passover drew near the Jewish leaders were plotting how to put Jesus to death without causing a tumult among the people, when Judas Iscariot came to their aid. Yielding to Satanic influence, he offered to betray his Master, made a bargain with them, and then sought to carry it out without the people knowing (vs. 1-6). In the meantime, Jesus sent Peter and John into the city to prepare the Passover when the day came. Luke alone tells us that they were the two disciples chosen for this purpose. They should meet a man carrying a pitcher of water, who would let them have his guest-chamber to prepare the Passover in (vs. 7-13).

2. The Last Supper (22:14-38). At the proper time Jesus sat down with the Apostles, telling them that He had eagerly looked forward to this occasion, and that it was the last time He would eat the Passover with them and drink of the fruit of the vine till the Kingdom of God should come (vs. 14-18). He was referring symbolically to the consummation of salvation in the future. Then He instituted the service that was to commemorate the sealing of the New Covenant by His death (vs. 19-20). In the course of the supper He announced the presence of the traitor at the table and pronounced his doom (vs. 21-23).

A dispute took place among the disciples as to which of them should be accounted the greatest, and Jesus rebuked them by pointing out that the conditions of greatness in human society did not hold in the society that He was founding. He Himself was among them "as he that serveth". Because of their loyalty to Him in His trials, He would give them high places in His coming Kingdom (vs. 24-30). He warned Simon specially of the peril in which he stood at Satan's hands. He added an encouraging word, but foretold that disciple's threefold denial of his Master (vs. 31-34).

Then Jesus went on to instruct all the disciples to make provision for the new conditions which they were now going to meet in the world. He did not mean that they were to use force, but they took His figurative reference to a sword literally and told Him that they had two swords ready. Saddened by their obtuseness and lack of spiritual insight, He dismissed the subject with a brief and final word: "It is enough". Luke alone mentions this incident (vs. 35-38).

3. In Gethsemane (22:39-53). Luke does not mention the fact that Jesus took the three disciples with Him when He went into the garden to pray. In the story of the agony (vs. 39-46), he alone tells us that an angel from Heaven appeared unto Jesus,

strengthening Him, and that His sweat was like great drops of blood. In the story of the betrayal and arrest (vs. 47-53), Luke alone tells us that Jesus healed the ear of the high priest's servant. The Lord's command, "Suffer ye thus far", was a flash of inherent power and dignity, compelling them to pause till He performed this act of mercy before yielding Himself up to them.

4. The Religious Trial (22:54-71). Jesus was taken first to the high priest's house, where He was mocked and reviled (vs. 54-65). In the course of this scene Peter sat in the midst of a group in the light of a fire in the court, where he was repeatedly challenged and every time denied his Master. Luke tells us that when the cock crew, "the Lord turned, and looked upon Peter". At daylight the meeting of the Jewish Council was held (vs. 66-71). Jesus confessed before them that He was the Christ, and went on to declare that they should yet see Him as the Son of Man seated at the right hand of power. Then He confessed that He was the Son of God, and for this claim He was condemned.

5. The Civil Trial (23:1-25). Bringing Jesus before Pilate, the Jews laid a political charge against Him: they accused Him of stirring up sedition and claiming to be a king. In answer to Pilate's question, He confessed Himself to be the King of the Jews. But Pilate told His accusers that he could find no count on which to condemn Him. Then learning that Jesus was from Galilee, he sent Him to Herod who was in Jerusalem at that time (vs. 1-7).

Luke alone tells us of this particular incident in the trial (vs. 8-12). Herod was delighted, because his desire to see Jesus was now fulfilled. But Jesus answered none of his questions nor the accusations of the chief priests and Scribes who followed Him there. This silence was the Lord's way of showing that He was not on trial before Herod. Then Herod subjected Him to mockery at the hands of his soldiers, and sent Him back to Pilate.

When Jesus appeared before Pilate again (vs. 13-25), the governor called the Jewish authorities and informed them that neither he nor Herod found anything worthy of death in Jesus, and proposed to chastise Him and let Him go. But they demanded the release of Barabbas instead, a rebel and a murderer, and in the face of Pilate's repeated protest they clamoured for the crucifixion of Jesus. At last he yielded to their will, released the murderer, and delivered Jesus over to be crucified.

6. The Crucifixion (23:26-49). On the road to Calvary, besides the impressing of Simon the Cyrenian, an incident occurred which Luke alone records, that of the women following and lamenting Him, whom He warned to weep for themselves and not for Him, because of the days of judgment that were coming (vs. 26-31).

Luke's account of the scene at Calvary contains the following incidents not found in the other Gospels:—The prayer of Jesus when they were nailing Him to the cross: "Father, forgive them; for they know not what they do" (vs. 32-38). His word to the penitent thief who appealed to Jesus to remember him when He came into His kingdom: "To-day shalt thou be with me in Paradise" (vs. 39-43). His loud cry at the moment of His death after the three hours of darkness: "Father, into thy hands I commend my spirit" (vs. 44-46). The consternation and remorse manifested by the crowd that were drawn by curiosity to the sight: "They returned smiting their breasts" (vs. 47-49).

7. The Burial (23:50-56). In telling how Joseph of Arimathea obtained the body of Jesus from Pilate and laid it in a new tomb, Luke informs us that though he was a member of the Jewish Council, he had not voted for the condemnation and crucifixion of Jesus: "he had not consented to their counsel and deed".

8. The Resurrection Morning (24:1-12). In telling how the fact of the Resurrection was discovered, Luke gives substantially the same story as the other Gospels. The women from Galilee came with their spices at early dawn on the first day of the week, and found the stone rolled away and the tomb empty. In the midst of their perplexity, two angels appeared and told them that Christ was risen, and reminded them of His prediction that He should be crucified and rise again the third day (vs. 1-7). The women returned and told the Apostles, who at first would not believe. Peter, however, ran to the tomb to see for himself, and went home wondering at what had happened (vs. 8-12).

9. The Risen Lord (24:13-43). The beautiful story of the manifestation at Emmaus, which was noticed briefly by Mark (16:12-13), is narrated at length by Luke. It occurred in the afternoon of the Resurrection day. Nothing is known of Cleopas. Luke gives his name probably because he got the story directly from him. What the two disciples said to Jesus, when He drew near to them, reflects the perplexity and wonder that had taken possession of all the disciples because of what was told them by the women (vs. 13-24). As they walked together toward Emmaus, Jesus gave them a talk on the central theme of the Old Testament: "Beginning at Moses and all the prophets, he expounded unto them in all the scriptures the things concerning himself" (vs. 25-27).

The meal He partook with them when they arrived at the village was not the Lord's Supper; but something in His manner of breaking the bread and blessing it opened their eyes to recognize Him. Then He disappeared from their sight without seeming to move—such was the mysterious nature of His risen body—, and they recalled the glow of their hearts while He talked to them on the road. They hurried back at once to Jerusalem to tell the Apostles and other disciples what had happened to them. They found them gathered together and full of joy, reporting that the Lord was risen indeed and had already appeared to Simon Peter (vs. 28-35).

Immediately after the two disciples from Emmaus had related their experience, Jesus Himself stood in the midst of the group and greeted them with a salutation of peace. To calm their fears and prove His identity, He showed them His wounded hands and feet, and then, to put them at their ease, He asked for something to eat (vs. 36-43).

10. The Ascension (24:44-53). Luke follows his narrative of these appearances to the disciples on the day of the Resurrection with a summary of the instructions that Christ gave to the Apostles during the forty days between the Resurrection and the Ascension (vs. 44-49). It contains their missionary commission, and closes with a command to wait

in Jerusalem until they were "clothed with power from on high". Then there comes a brief account of the Ascension, and the Gospel closes with the great joy which that transcendent event produced among them. While waiting for the Holy Spirit, the disciples "were continually in the temple, blessing God" (vs. 50-53).

This passage and Luke's further account in Acts 1:6-12 are the only narratives that describe the Ascension. By the Incarnation, Jesus Christ took our human nature unto Himself. By His righteous life, He perfected it. By the Cross, He sacrificed His perfected humanity that He might share it with us sinners. By the Resurrection, He glorified it that we might share it with Him. By the Ascension, He was seated at the centre of ultimate power, that He might administer the redemption which He had accomplished for us.

*   *   *   *

THE HUMAN LIFE THAT JESUS LIVED

The full-orbed manhood of Jesus stands out upon the story of Luke's Gospel. Here we see Him pass through all the stages of a normal human life. He lies as a babe in the manger, and is presented as an infant in the Temple (2:16, 27). He grows up as a child in the home, and sits as a boy among the teachers (2:40, 46). He develops as a youth in mind and body (2:52), and arrives at mature manhood before entering upon the special work of His life (3:23).

He touched human life on all sides. He entered the domestic life of the people, and moved among all classes of society. We find Him visiting in the home of Martha and Mary (10:38-39), staying over night with Zacchæus the publican (19:5), and dining in the houses of Pharisees (7:36; 11:37; 14:1). The parables of this Gospel reflect the interest that Jesus took in all aspects of human life. Of the nineteen parables in Luke, all but four begin with, "A certain man", or "What Man?" or a similar expression.

Luke makes it clear that the sympathy of Jesus went out especially to the poor, who comprise the vast majority of mankind. The announcement of His mission in His own home-town was made by quoting Isa. 61:1 in these words: "The Spirit of the Lord is upon me, because he anointed me to preach good tidings to the poor" (4:18). Luke's version of the Sermon on the Mount, which was addressed to His disciples, begins: "Blessed are ye poor" (6:20). The Lord meant that poverty was a blessing for them, because it helped to preserve their dependence on God and so qualify them for His Kingdom. At the same time His sympathy went out to the rich in another sense, because their wealth ministered to self-dependence and so made it difficult for them to enter His Kingdom (18:24).

Luke's Gospel not only depicts the outward aspect of the Lord's life, but also gives us a glimpse of its inner springs. It was lived in complete dependence upon His Father. His first recorded words (2:49) have been explained in the exposition of the passage as giving the key-note of His whole life on earth. It was set in the frame of the will of God. He was always "in His Father's things". He had no other interests to serve, no self-will to seek. In this attitude of mind lies the secret of His way of life. When all the Gospel narratives are examined in the light of it, we find four main elements in the kind of life that Jesus lived,

1. He made the will of God the purpose of His life. "I am come down from heaven," He declared, "not to do mine own will, but the will of him that sent me" (John 6:38). This cannot mean, what it would mean in the case of any other man, that the will of Jesus differed from His Father's will, and that he put aside the one and chose to carry out the other. It is the action of His will and not its content that is in view. He willed to have no self-will and no self-interest. He came down from Heaven, He meant, to live a human life, under human conditions and within human limitations, which would be free from the bias of self-will in all other human lives. And at the end of it He was able to say, "I glorified thee on the earth, having accomplished the work which thou hast given me to do" (John 17:4). All through His life His mind moved, with complete freedom of choice and with all the fullness of its human powers, in accordance with the mind of God.

2. He found the will of God in the Scriptures, and not in His own consciousness. He made the Word of God His constant guide. He ordered His life in accordance with a Divine revelation already given to men. He subjected Himself, as man, to all the limitations set by the Creator around human life and conduct. He consented to live under the strict and narrow limits of the Law as it was given to Israel. There is abundant evidence of this in all the Gospel records.

We never find Jesus vindicating Himself on subjective grounds, or defending His conduct by falling back on reasons which He might use but other men could not. He always pointed to the objective revelation of the will of God which was in the hands of the Jews. When He purged the Temple of its unholy traffic, He did not justify the act on the ground of His Messianic claims, but by a reference to the Word of God (Matt. 21:13). When His disciples were charged with violating the Sabbath law, He defended them on the ground of a principle which He found in the Scriptures (Matt. 12:3). When a practical question of life and conduct was referred to Him, He directed the enquirer to the Word of God—"What is written in the law? How readest thou?" (Luke 10:26). When His enemies came upon Him to entangle Him with a doctrinal question, He put them to silence by exposing their ignorance of the Word of God—"Ye do err, not knowing the scriptures" (Matt. 22:29).

It is obvious, therefore, that Jesus meditated much upon the Old Testament Scriptures. They filled His thoughts, and He found in them the mind and will of His Father. He brought His own mind and will under their authority; and, as He followed their light, the plan of His life unfolded before Him. He rested His soul upon them in the great crises of His life. It was upon the written Word of God He took His stand in meeting the assaults of Satan in the wilderness. And in the awful darkness of the Cross, He sank His soul in the Father's will with a final prayer in the words of Scripture: "Father, into thy hands I commend my spirit" (Luke 23:46; Psa. 31:5).

3. In carrying out the will of God He depended upon the power of God. He surrendered Himself completely to the Spirit of God. All the Gospels tell us how the Holy Spirit came upon Him at His baptism; but Luke's narrative is especially enlightening in showing us how this experience in-

fluenced His life. He left the Jordan full of the Holy Spirit, "and was led in the Spirit in the wilderness" (4:1). He came back triumphant from the Temptation, and "returned in the power of the Spirit into Galilee" (4:14). Speaking in the synagogue of Nazareth, He explained the change that had taken place in His life by reading the passage in Isaiah which begins, "The Spirit of the Lord is upon me" (4:18).

After that, with one doubtful exception (10:21), Luke makes no further reference to the Holy Spirit in the life of Jesus. The reason for this silence is not far to seek. After it had been shown how Jesus was filled with the Spirit and entered upon His ministry under the power of the Spirit, and how He was led by the Spirit and was working and teaching in the fulness of the Spirit's power, it was quite unnecessary to dwell any more upon the fact. There was no need of mentioning the Holy Spirit in any particular case when nothing Jesus said or did was of Himself alone.

This feature of the narrative also goes to show that Jesus lived in quite a natural way, and in full accord with the principles of human nature. There was nothing abnormal in His life. He always manifested the presence and power of the Spirit of God according to the laws and within the limits of the nature of man. His life was the natural expression of His own Spirit-filled personality.

4. His dependence on God was maintained by prayer. This was one of the most remarkable features of His ministry. It was the background of all He said and did. It pervades the Gospel narratives like an atmosphere. All the Evangelists refer to the prayer-life of Jesus, but Luke gives it special emphasis. There are nine instances of prayer in the Lord's life mentioned by him alone (3:21; 5:16; 6:12; 9:18; 11:1; 22:31-32; 22:44; 23:34; 23:46).

The prayer-life of Jesus was different from anything ever seen before. It was not merely an expression of religious life, as in the case of the Old Testament saints. There was a great consciousness of God in the life of Jesus. He hung upon God in prayer, and the power to carry on His ministry as He went along came out of His life of prayer. It made a deep impression on His disciples and on all who came under His influence. They would often see Him withdraw and go away into the wilderness or up on the mountain side to spend time alone in communion with His Father.

He had an access to God which even His disciples did not have. Sometimes He took them with Him when He withdrew for prayer, but even in these cases there are indications in the narrative that His praying was apart from theirs. We are nowhere told that He prayed with them; but instead of that we have such a statement as this: "And it came to pass, as he was praying apart, the disciples were with him" (Luke 9:18). They might be in His presence when He was praying; but He was in the presence of the Father, and they were not.

This, then, was the kind of life that Jesus lived on earth. While it was thoroughly human, it was different from any other life ever seen among men. It was a life on earth ruled from Heaven. Here was human nature with all its springs in God, and with all its activity responding to the will of God. Here we see the will of God functioning perfectly in the nature of man. By living this kind of life Jesus created human nature anew, unbiased by self-will, and inclined to do the will of God.

THE GOSPEL ACCORDING TO JOHN

THE authorship of the Fourth Gospel has been hotly contested since the beginning of the last century. Up to that time its apostolic origin was never seriously questioned. The modern attack on the supernatural character of Christianity has persistently concentrated upon this book in an attempt to bring it down to a date long after John's day, and thus break the force of the special witness it bears to the deity of Christ. The most recent theory of subjective criticism attributes the authorship to the writer who calls himself "the elder" in the Second and Third Epistles of John, but regards him as a different person from John the Apostle.

The Gospel was accepted as the Apostle's by the general body of Christians in the last quarter of the second century. The external evidence for an earlier date was weaker than in the case of the Synoptic Gospels until quite recently. A manuscript fragment of the Gospel has come to light which tends to show that the book was in existence before the end of the first century. The internal evidence for its apostolic authorship is very strong, and has always appeared convincing to devout scholarship, which recognizes the spiritual as well as the linguistic qualities of style. It may be summed up as follows:

The narrative is marked by innumerable touches which could come only from an eye-witness of the events recorded. Some of these can be seen, for example, in such passages as 1:35-42, 7:37-44, and 11:30-44. It also contains minute descriptions of scenes at which only Apostles were present, and shows an intimate acquaintance with the thoughts and feelings of the Apostles (4:27, 33; 16:17; 18:2; 20:19). The author called himself "the disciple whom Jesus loved" (21:20, 24). This could only be one of the inner group of the chosen three—Peter, James, or John. In the context he is distinguished from Peter, and James was put to death before the Gospel was written (Acts 12:2). The author is very careful in mentioning names to make clear whom he means (1:40, 44; 11:16; 14:22; 21:2); but in speaking of the forerunner of Christ, he alone among the Evangelists never uses the epithet, "the Baptist". The writer of this Gospel sees only one John, because he himself is the other.

After the Ascension of the Lord, John was associated with Peter in the leadership of the Church during its early days (Acts 3:1; 4:13, 19; 8:14). His name is not mentioned in New Testament history after the council in Jerusalem, which is to be dated about the middle of the century (Gal. 2:9). According to a unanimous tradition, the Apostle's later life was spent in Ephesus, which became the chief centre of Christianity after the fall of Jerusalem; and he lived there to a great age, dying at the very end of the century.

It is the consistent testimony of early Christian writers that John wrote the Gospel at Ephesus toward the close of his life, when the other Gospels were already well known, at the request of the churches of Asia. They desired to have an authentic record of the oral teaching of the last of the Apostles, because erroneous views of the Person of the Lord were infecting the Church and heretics were attacking His deity. This agrees with the author's own statement of his purpose (20:31). He intended his readers to get a two-fold blessing from his book —a deeper faith in Christ ("that ye may believe that Jesus is the Christ, the Son of God"), and a deeper spiritual life ("that believing ye may have life in his name").

John was especially well qualified for this task. He had a strong and ardent nature (Mark 3:17), and a deep and intense devotion to Christ (Mark 9: 38; Luke 9:54), all of which was now mellowed and softened by age. His supreme quality was profound spiritual insight, joined to a heart of great tenderness and affection. During his long life he had pondered over the companionship with Jesus which he and his fellow-disciples had enjoyed, and he had come to see more and more clearly the Divine nature of his Master shining out through that earthly ministry. "We beheld his glory", he declares, "the glory as of the only begotten from the Father" (1:14). The lapse of time only deepened the wonder he felt at what he had seen manifested in the life of Jesus. This is the impression he gives us by the way he begins his First Epistle (1:1-2). And so it was that the aged Apostle John wrote what was called in the early Church "a spiritual Gospel".

Its date cannot be fixed exactly, but it must be very close to A.D. 85 on one side or the other. Its special theme is Jesus Christ as the Son of God, and it may be analysed as follows:—

I. The Manifestation of the Son of God—
 Chs. 1—4
 1. The Incarnation of the Son (1:1-18)
 2. The Witness to the Son (1:19—2:12)
 3. The Work of the Son (2:13—4:54)
II. His Conflict with the Unbelief of the Jews—
 Chs. 5—12
 1. The Outbreak of Unbelief (Chs. 5—6)
 2. The Development of Unbelief
 (Chs. 7—10)
 3. The Culmination of Unbelief
 (Chs. 11-12)
III. His Revelation to the Faith of the Disciples
 —Chs. 13—17
 1. His Last Acts of Love (Ch. 13)
 2. His Farewell Messages (Chs. 14—16)
 3. His High-Priestly Prayer (Ch. 17)
IV. The Victory of the Son of God—Chs. 18—21
 1. The Final Work of Unbelief
 (Chs. 18—19)
 2. The Final Reward of Faith (Chs. 20—21)

The Fourth Gospel assumes that its readers are familiar with the Synoptic Gospels. These dealt with the Galilean ministry alone. John passes over nearly all the events of the Galilean ministry, and draws his material mainly from the Judean ministry, and especially from the Lord's visits to Jerusalem. From the Synoptic Gospels it might be inferred that the whole public ministry of Jesus covered little more than one year. John's Gospel refers to three Passovers before the last one (2:13; 5:1; 6:4), and thus shows us that the ministry of the Lord stretched over three full years. The narrative of the Gospel is set in the frame of these four Passovers.

THE INCARNATION OF THE SON
(1:1-18)

This passage is usually called the Prologue. It forms an introduction to the Gospel, and indicates the special theme and the general plan of the book. But it is an integral part of the narrative also, for it is John's account of the Incarnation. As each Evangelist begins his book in a manner suited to his narrative, so John goes back into eternity. Matthew and Luke describe the coming of Christ from the human side: John describes it from the Divine side. He traces the course of the pre-existence of the Son from the glory He had with the Father "before the world was" (17:5) down into time and the field of human history. With a stately simplicity he introduces the Lord Jesus Christ out of the eternal past.

1. Christ in Eternity (vs. 1-2). The opening phrase carries us back to the first words of Genesis and looks out into the eternity beyond the Creation. Christ was in existence "in the beginning", before time began. He was "with God", in active personal communion with Him. He "was God", sharing in the glory of the very Godhead. The Apostle may have taken his term, "the Word", from the philosophical theory of the Logos which was current in his time, but he got the meaning that he put into it from a far richer and truer philosophy. His background was the Old Testament revelation, and it was there that he found "the Word". With profound spiritual insight John's illumined mind summarizes, in these opening verses of his Gospel, the whole self-revelation of God down through the ages. The agent of that revelation was the pre-incarnate Son.

2. Christ in Creation (vs. 3-5). These verses describe the relation of the Son of God to the world and the human race before the Incarnation. He was the active agent in the creation of the world (v. 3). It was He that was at work behind the oft-repeated words, "and God said", in the story of Creation. He was the source from which men derived life and light after that (v. 4). It is His voice we hear when Wisdom speaks in the Book of Proverbs: "Jehovah possessed me in the beginning of his way, before his works of old. When he established the heavens I was there. Then I was by him as a master workman; I was daily his delight, rejoicing always before him, rejoicing in his habitable earth; and my delight was with the sons of men" (Prov. 8:22, 27, 30-31). In the moral darkness that followed the fall of man, He continued to exercise this function, but the darkness caused by sin prevented men seeing the light (v. 5).

3. Christ in History (vs. 6-13). In these verses we are brought to the historic appearance of the Son of God in the Incarnation. They tell of the mission of John the Baptist, who was sent of God to bear witness of the Light that was coming into the world, and to prepare men to believe in Christ as the perfect light for every man (vs. 6-9). Yet Christ met with unbelief when He came; even His own people Israel rejected Him (vs. 10-11). But those who did receive Him were given something entirely new. They became children of God: they received a Divine life by virtue of their faith in Him as the Son of God (vs. 12-13).

Three Christian writers of the second and third centuries, who antedate the earliest existing manuscripts of the Gospel by more than a hundred years, quote the last verse of this passage in the singular, showing that they had a text which read thus: "the name of him who was born (begotten), not of blood, nor of the will of the flesh, nor of the will of man, but of God". This implies the Virgin Birth of Jesus, and leads naturally to the next verse, which gives a specific statement of the Incarnation. It is probable that this represents the original text, and that the plural crept into the manuscript copies afterwards.

4. Christ in the Heart (vs. 14-18). The Apostle now goes on to describe the effect which Christ's presence in the world produced upon the disciples. He explains the result of the Incarnation in their personal experience. They saw in Him the glory of the Father, and the essential features of the character of God (v. 14). From His inexhaustible fulness they all received increasing supplies of grace (v. 16). The testimony of John is introduced again as the final word of prophecy (v. 15), and the Law of Moses is mentioned as the symbolical system that foreshadowed the grace and truth now completely embodied in Jesus Christ (v. 17).

Then the Apostle sums up in one final statement the full significance of the Incarnation (v. 18). God is never seen or heard Himself. Whenever He reveals Himself, or whenever He speaks, it is always the Word that men see or hear. And the Word has become incarnate in Jesus Christ. In describing Him as "the only begotten Son", John was not thinking of eternal generation but of the Virgin Birth. He was referring back to his former expression, "the only begotten from the Father" (v. 14), which means that the Lord Jesus Christ was the only Being who came into the world by a birth divinely and supernaturally caused, and not by an ordinary natural birth.

The plan of the whole Gospel is epitomized in this introductory section. Christ is presented as the Son of God in those manifestations of His life and work that revealed unbelief or drew out faith. Here we have the manifestation of the Word (vs. 1-4), the unbelief of the Jews (vs. 5-11), and the faith of the disciples (vs. 12-18). These three fundamental ideas are developed together in the course of the Gospel, until they finally culminate in the Cross and the Resurrection, and result in the new life of the Son of God.

THE WITNESS TO THE SON
(1:19—2:12)

This section is the record of a single week—four successive days at the Jordan, and the third day afterwards at Cana. It is the first week in the story of our Lord's earthly ministry, and so is a kind of counterpart of the last week. It contains the witness of John the Baptist, the witness of the first disciples, and the witness of the first miracle, all going to show that Jesus Christ was the Son of God (1:34, 49; 2:11).

1. The Witness of John the Baptist (1:19-34). This was given on two successive days at the place beyond the Jordan where he was baptizing at the time (v. 28).

(1) The first day (vs. 19-28). John gave his first witness in a reply to an official deputation sent by "the Jews" from Jerusalem to interview him. The Apostle uses this term for the religious leaders of the nation, whose headquarters were in Judea, to distinguish them from "the multitude" or the common people, who belonged mainly to Galilee. They had their own pre-conceived Messianic program, and they did not see how John fitted into it. John told them that he was not the Messiah, but was the voice that Isaiah had foretold (40:3) was to prepare the way for the Messiah.

When he was asked what authority he had for baptizing, John did not reply directly. He admitted that he did baptize with water, but went on to say that One who was greater than himself was already in their midst. John implied that his baptizing with water was a preliminary rite in preparation for this other One. But the deputies went away without enquiring who this Person was. Here begins the national unbelief which is seen developing in the rest of the book.

(2) The second day (vs. 29-34). On the next day, as John saw Jesus coming toward him, probably returning from the Temptation, he pointed Him out as the promised Redeemer of the world, and went on to explain how he came to know Him. He had seen the Holy Spirit come down from heaven and abide upon Jesus. He had been informed of God, who had sent him to baptize with water, that this would be the sign by which he should know the Coming One, whom he was to introduce to Israel, and who would baptize with the Holy Spirit.

Three times does the Baptist insist that his baptism was only "with water" (vs. 26, 31, 33). It was the symbol of a baptism "with the Holy Spirit" which he could not administer. Twice John says, "I knew him not" (vs. 31, 33). Even he did not know that Jesus was the Messiah till the promised sign was given. After that he bore witness to the two distinctive truths about Him that were to be embodied in Christianity: Jesus Christ is the world's Sin-bearer (v. 29), and the Son of God (v. 34).

2. The Witness of the First Disciples (1:35-51). Two more days follow; and now the beginnings of faith appear in the spiritual insight of the first disciples.

(1) The first group (vs. 35-42). In the presence of two of his disciples, John pointed Jesus out again as "the lamb of God". They would understand the significance of this term quite well. What the Passover lamb only symbolized, that Jesus was in reality. The two disciples "followed Jesus", thus taking the first step of faith; and then they had a day's communion with Him. By "the tenth hour" the Apostle probably meant ten o'clock in the morning, not four o'clock in the afternoon; for an early hour suits best the fulness of the day's events. The official Roman method of reckoning the day started from midnight. The Jewish method, which is used in the Synoptic Gospels, started from sunset. John seems to have followed the practice of noting the hours that was used in the province of Asia in which he was living (4:6; 4:52; 19:14).

That day of fellowship with Jesus convinced the two men that He was indeed the Messiah. This is reflected in the enthusiastic exclamation of Andrew in fetching Simon Peter. The unnamed disciple was no doubt John himself, who always remains anonymous in this Gospel. The special language that he uses here of Andrew—"He first findeth his own brother Simon"—implies that John himself went off next and found his own brother James. This made four disciples gathered to Jesus that day. He met Simon with a look of special penetration, and gave him a special promise, which received its fulfilment when Peter made his great confession of Jesus Christ as the Son of God (Matt. 16:18).

(2) The second group (vs. 43-51). On the next day Jesus prepared to return to Galilee, and He "findeth Philip" and called him to accompany Him. The first group of disciples had followed Jesus as the crowning of John's work. The finding of Philip was the beginning of His own work. Philip "finding Nathanael", who is to be identified with Bartholomew, whose name is always coupled with Philip's in the Synoptic lists of the Apostles (Matt. 10:3; Mark 3:18; Luke 6:14). In spite of his prejudice against such an obscure village as Nazareth being the home of the Messiah, Nathanael's first interview with Jesus made such an impression upon him that he acknowledged both the Divinity and the Messiahship of the Lord in a transport of homage and adoration. In His reply Jesus for the first time used the expression, "verily, verily", which occurs twenty-five times in this Gospel, and always on the lips of Jesus Himself. He thus expresses some truth in the most emphatic way. Nathanael was to see the communion between earth and Heaven realized in the ministry of "the Son of man".

This phrase is the Lord's own title for Himself. It completes the revelation of His Person which has been unfolded step by step throughout this chapter. He has been acknowledged as the Lamb of God (vs. 29, 36), as the Son of God (vs. 34, 49), as the Messiah (vs. 41, 45), and as the King of Israel (v. 49). He chooses for Himself the title that sets forth His relation to humanity as a whole and describes Him as the true representative of the race.

Jesus had now six disciples, all of whom had begun to follow Him before He wrought any miracle, primarily because of the testimony of John the Baptist, and finally because of their own personal knowledge of Him. This was the beginning of that individual faith in Him which is developed throughout the Gospel, and which finally created the Christian Church. These disciples went back to their homes and their daily occupations in Galilee. Later on they received their call to a closer relationship with Jesus and to an official position as Apostles. This is the call recorded in the Synoptic Gospels.

3. The Witness of the First Miracle (2:1-12). This domestic scene took place on the third day after Jesus and His disciples left John to return to Galilee. They probably arrived in the midst of the marriage festivities, which were frequently continued for several days. The conversation between Jesus and His mother, and her subsequent words to the servants, do not mean that Mary was looking for a miracle. They rather indicate that she had leaned upon her eldest son for advice and help during all the previous years in the home in Nazareth, and had never found Him to fail. Jesus' reply to Mary did not imply a rebuke, for she did not take it in that way. It was a gentle announcement that the domestic relation was henceforth to be subordinated to the Messianic mission on which He was entering, even though that mission still awaited the hour of its public manifestation and had not yet moved out of the sphere of family life.

The manner of working the miracle is described with singular reserve. There is nothing in the text to indicate that all the water was turned into wine in the waterpots. The significance of the miracle comes out with greater force if the change was wrought in the water as it was borne in faith to minister to the special need of the moment. John calls it the beginning of "signs" (v. 11), which is always his term for the miracles of Jesus. Its result was to bear witness to the essential character of Christ as the Lord of the old creation and the Author of a new creation. It manifested forth the glory of His nature, and it deepened the faith of the disciples in Him. The statement in v. 12 forms a transition in the narrative. It falls in with what is said in the Synoptics (Matt. 4:13; Luke 4:31) of the Lord's removal from Nazareth to Capernaum at the beginning of the Galilean ministry.

THE WORK OF THE SON
(2:13—4:54)

Having privately gathered a small group of disciples inspired by true faith in Himself, the Lord began His public ministry by manifesting Himself to Israel as the Messiah. He chose the time of the Passover to make His first public appearance in Jerusalem. This feast, which was held in the spring, commemorated the birth of the nation and was attended by great numbers from all Israel. Receiving no recognition from the religious authorities in the capital, Jesus spent some time after that in Judea. Finding little response there, He travelled north through Samaria, and returned to Galilee. Thus He was manifested in all the main districts of Palestine. The present section describes the various ways in which He revealed Himself, and tells of the different kinds of reception which He met with.

1. In the Temple at Jerusalem (2:13-22). Christ's first public act after John had introduced Him to Israel was a significant sign, which faith should have recognized as a fulfilment of Malachi's prophecy: "The Lord, whom ye seek, will suddenly come to his temple" (3:1). He made a manifest claim to Messianic authority when He cleansed the Temple court of its unholy traffic, which was vitiating the whole atmosphere of His Father's house, but was carried on under the sanction of the religious authorities (vs. 13-16). The Lord's action had a double effect: it deepened the faith of the disciples (vs. 17, 22), but the Jews only found in it an occasion to demand further proof of His authority (vs. 18-21). His reply to them contains the first intimation of His death at their hands and His subsequent resurrection. It implies that the Temple was a symbol of His own Person, as John goes on to point out: "He spake of the temple of his body". The statement of the Jews that the Temple was forty-six years in building refers to its reconstruction, which was begun by Herod in 20 B.C.

The Synoptic Gospels record a similar act of Messianic authority at the close of the ministry (Matt. 21:12-13; Mark 11:15-17; Luke 19:45-46).

But the character of the two acts is distinct, and there is a significant difference in the words that Jesus used in the two cases to justify them. John records the act by which Jesus revealed Himself as the Messiah at the beginning of His ministry, by entering as the Son into the Temple, which He called "my Father's house". The other Gospels record the act by which He came at the close of His ministry, acclaimed as the Messiah by the people, and asserted His royal authority in the Temple, which He declared was intended to be "a house of prayer for all the nations" (Mark 11:17; Isa. 56:7).

2. During the Passover in Jerusalem (2:23-25). The act by which Jesus purified the Temple probably took place on the eve of the Passover, when the Jews removed all leaven from their houses (Exod. 12:15). Having been rejected by the authorities in the Temple, Jesus wrought miracles among the people in the city during the Feast of Unleavened Bread, which was kept for seven days after the actual Passover. But the faith they showed was superficial; it was based upon the miracles alone and lacked personal devotion. The Apostle contrasts the false faith of the people with the perfect insight of Christ, who was never deceived as to inward character and would not commit Himself to them. He then goes on to record an instance of the Lord's dealing with one of their religious leaders, a Pharisee and a member of the Jewish Council, to whom He revealed some of His deepest secrets.

3. The Conversation with Nicodemus (3:1-21). This occupies the same place in John's Gospel as the Sermon on the Mount in Matthew's Gospel. It has an inaugural character, and gives the key-note to the teaching of Jesus in the rest of the book. Nicodemus had been impressed by Jesus, but as yet regarded Him as only "a teacher come from God". It may have been some timidity that led Nicodemus to come by night, but Jesus treated him as a representative teacher of Israel, who had come as an earnest inquirer for a serious interview which he could not have had by day (vs. 1-2). He appears later in the Gospel as friendly to Jesus and probably a secret disciple (7:50-51; 19:39).

The Kingdom of God was evidently the theme of Jesus' teaching at the time, for He began His reply to Nicodemus with a statement about it (v. 3). This is the only passage in John's Gospel where the Kingdom of God is mentioned. Jesus said that no one could even understand the Kingdom without such a change in his nature as meant being born anew. When Nicodemus expressed his doubt about the possibility of such a thing (v. 4), Jesus described the change as being "born of water and of the Spirit" (v. 5). By these phrases He referred both to the water baptism of John and the spiritual baptism which would be His own work. The one marked the negative side of the change required for entrance into the Kingdom, which was the renunciation of the old life. The other referred to the source of the new life, and marked the positive side of the change described as being born anew.

Then Jesus went on to explain that there are two different spheres of life, two different orders of being—the earthly sphere of the present world order, into which one enters by being born of the flesh, and the spiritual sphere of the Kingdom of God, into which one enters by being born of the Spirit (vs. 6-7). The Divine Spirit is not subject to earthly laws, but is free to operate as He will (v. 8): "So is every one that is born of the Spirit". Jesus meant that the manifestations of spiritual life in the Kingdom of God are free: "Where the Spirit of the Lord is, there is liberty" (2 Cor. 3:17).

Nicodemus wondered how this could be, and Jesus expressed surprise that a teacher of Israel did not understand these things (vs. 9-10). The Old Testament Scriptures should have prepared Nicodemus for the idea of a new birth and a spiritual order of life (Psa. 51:10; Isa. 35:6-7; Jer. 31:33; Ezek. 36:25-27). If the Jews rejected Jesus' teaching when He spoke of things that belong to human experience, how could they receive His teaching when He spoke of things that belong to Heaven, which He alone knew (vs. 11-12). Then He proceeded to state the two great transcendent facts about Himself on which the Kingdom of God was to be based, namely, the Incarnation and the Cross. By the way of the Incarnation the Son of Man descended from Heaven, and by the way of the Cross He would ascend back to Heaven. Those who put their faith in Him would be born into the new order: they would have eternal life (vs. 13-15).

The rest of the passage (vs. 16-21) is the Apostle's comment on the conversation which he has reported. He explains the redemptive nature of the mission of Jesus in the world. Its origin was due to the love of God for the world. It was accomplished by the sacrifice of His only begotten Son. It was designed for the purpose of giving eternal life to all who should believe in the Son, and saving them from the judgment resting upon the world. The whole passage contains a comprehensive statement of the Gospel.

4. In the Country of Judea (3:22-36). As His Messianic claims received no recognition in Jerusalem, Jesus went out into the country districts of Judea and carried on with His disciples the same kind of ministry as John the Baptist, thus making preparation for a further manifestation of Himself as the Messiah (vs. 22-24). The Apostle's statement that "John was not yet cast into prison" implies that his readers were familiar with the Synoptic Gospels, which alone tell of the imprisonment of John. It also indicates that the Lord's Galilean ministry had not yet begun (Matt. 4:12; Mark 1:14).

In the eyes of some, Jesus now appeared to be a rival of the Baptist, and this gave John an occasion for further testimony to Jesus as the Christ (vs. 25-30). In the statement, "He that hath the bride is the bridegroom", John referred to the figure constantly used in the Old Testament to describe the relation between Jehovah and Israel. "The bride" was the Messianic community, the spiritual remnant of Israel, whom John as "the friend of the bridegroom" had been calling out and getting ready for the Messiah. The same figure is used in the New Testament to describe the relation between Christ and the Church (Eph. 5:25-27; Rev. 19:7; 21:9). The ministry of John the Baptist in preparing the Bride was nearly ended, and his joy was now fulfilled in seeing Christ gathering around Him disciples, who were the beginnings of a new Israel and would form His Church. John's last words, "He must increase but I must decrease", mark his true greatness, the greatness of humility, and fitly close his active ministry.

The rest of the passage (vs. 31-36) contains the reflections of the apostolic writer on the testimony of the Baptist to the superiority of Jesus, as he looks back over the intervening years. Having come from Heaven, the Son is above all other teachers, who have only an earthly origin. He speaks of heavenly things with the authority of an eye-witness, and yet His testimony is rejected. He alone has the complete and absolute revelation of God, for God has given Him the Spirit without measure and has put all power and authority into His hand. The ground of all this is the Father's love for the Son. On their relation to the Son hangs the eternal destiny of men.

5. In the District of Samaria (4:1-42). The growing popularity of Jesus in Judea aroused the jealousy of the Pharisees; and He decided to withdraw into Galilee, where His popularity would excite less hostility on their part. He took the direct road which passed through Samaria (vs. 1-4). The passage goes on to record His conversation with a sinful Samaritan woman at Jacob's well. He had stopped there to rest in the evening, after a long day's journey, while the disciples were gone to the village to buy food (vs. 5-6).

Beginning with a simple and natural request for a drink of water, Jesus led the woman step by step to ask for the water of eternal life (vs. 7-15). "Living water" means water issuing from a spring or fountain, in contrast with water standing in a well or cistern. It was therefore an appropriate figure for Jesus to use in setting forth the spiritual blessing which He was able to give. But the woman was not ready for that gift yet—not until her conscience was probed and her sin confessed (vs. 16-18).

At this point she diverted the conversation to the standing controversy between Jews and Samaritans about worship. Jesus declared that the knowledge of God and the way of salvation came through the Jews, and then went on to reveal to her the sublime truth of the reality of God as Spirit, and the spiritual nature of true worship (vs. 19-24). When He said "the hour cometh, and now is", He was referring to the purpose of His own mission in the world; and this led Him to answer the woman's expression of faith and hope in the coming of the Messiah by revealing Himself: "I that speak unto thee am he" (vs. 25-26).

During the conversation the woman became more and more respectful toward the Jewish stranger, showing how Jesus was impressing her. She addressed Him first with a curt question, but after that she began with "Sir" (vs. 11, 15, 19). She came to recognize Him as a prophet, and finally learned that He was the Messiah.

The conversation had immediate results. When the disciples came back, they wondered at finding their Master talking with a woman, but reverently refrained from speaking to Him about it. The woman in her joy and excitement, forgetting all about her waterpot, ran off to tell the people in the village of the profound impression made upon her by "a man who told me all things that ever I did", raising the question that it might be the Christ. They came out at once to see Him (vs. 27-30). In the meantime Jesus told the disciples, who were puzzled because they had left Him tired and hungry and now found Him refreshed, that in their absence

He had been engaged in His Father's work, and that had revived Him. Then He pointed to the crowd of approaching Samaritans as the harvest now ready for them (vs. 31-38).

Jesus remained two more days among the Samaritans at their request, and the impression made by the woman's testimony was confirmed by their personal intercourse with Him (vs. 39-42). It resulted in a strong expression of faith in Him as "indeed the Saviour of the world", although He had performed no miracle among them.

6. In Galilee Again (4:43-54). When Jesus was welcomed by the Galileans, He pointed out that the apparent failure of His ministry in Judea, where the Messiah should have been received, illustrated the common proverb that a prophet has no honour in his own country (vs. 43-45). But the faith of the Galileans was mixed with carnal elements. They believed because of the miracles which they had seen Him do in Jerusalem at the feast.

This attitude is illustrated by the story of the healing of the nobleman's son at Capernaum when Jesus was at Cana about twenty miles away (vs. 46-54). The father had come to fetch Jesus down before his child should die. But Jesus, to test his faith without showing him a miracle, sent him back with the word alone: "Go thy way; thy son liveth". On the way home his servants met him with the news that his son was restored; and he learned that the fever had left the boy at the very hour Jesus had spoken. As a result, the faith of the nobleman was confirmed, and his whole household believed.

THE OUTBREAK OF UNBELIEF
(Chs. 5-6)

Up to this point Jesus had been manifesting Himself to representative sections of the Jewish nation in different parts of the land—in Jerusalem, in Judea, in Samaria, and in Galilee. True faith had been found in a few cases, but the general attitude was one of unbelief and indifference, or of merely outward admiration. The situation now took a more definite character. Unbelief began to show itself in open hostility, and the conflict began which resulted at last in His death. These two chapters contain the story of two miracles and their immediate consequences, showing how unbelief broke out first in Jerusalem (ch. 5) and afterwards in Galilee (ch. 6). Each miracle was followed by a prolonged discussion in which Jesus explained its spiritual significance. In Jerusalem He revealed His relation to God, and in Galilee His relation to men.

I. Unbelief in Jerusalem (Ch. 5). The feast which Jesus went up to attend (v. 1) was probably the Passover, which was the first important feast to be held after He returned to Galilee. Jesus had passed through Samaria in January (4:35), and the Passover was held in April. It was the feast most largely attended by the Jews in Palestine.

1. The Miracle at the Pool (vs. 2-9). The healing of the man at the pool of Bethesda, who had been impotent for thirty-eight years, was wrought by Jesus spontaneously, after asking him if he would like to be healed, and it occurred on the Sabbath day. The statement in v. 4 was added by some copyist to explain the popular belief about the inter-

mittent character of the spring. It does not belong to the original text of the Gospel, and is omitted by the R.V.

2. The Accusation of the Jews (vs. 10-18). When the Jews found the man carrying his bed on the Sabbath day and learned that Jesus had healed him, they took an attitude of settled hostility toward Him, because His acts of mercy were offences against their traditional interpretation of the Law (vs. 10-16). Jesus met the charge of breaking the Sabbath with a statement which meant that He was carrying on His Father's work, and His Father was working "even until now". He meant that God was working during the present Sabbath of rest since the Creation. The Jews rightly saw in these words that Jesus claimed equality with God, and that made them still more determined on His death (vs. 17-18).

3. The Defence of Jesus (vs. 19-29). Jesus answered the charge of the Jews by explaining His essential relation to the Father in a profound and closely reasoned discourse. Three times He repeated the phrase, "Verily, verily, I say unto you" (vs. 19, 24, 25), thus showing the solemn importance of the declaration He was making, and marking three stages in the progress of His thought.

(1) In vs. 19-23 He declared that, as the Son, He was one with the Father in everything. In no case did He act of Himself, but only for the Father (v. 19). Because of His love for the Son, the Father took Him into all His counsels for the world, and would give Him greater works to do than these miracles of healing (v. 20), even the resurrection and the judgment of mankind (vs. 21-22), that through honour given to the Son men might honour the Father (v. 23).

(2) These "greater works" of giving life and executing judgment are now taken up and defined more exactly, and it is shown how they are carried out by the Son. In v. 24 Jesus explains that it is by faith in Him that men receive life and escape judgment. When they accept His message and believe that He came from God, they pass out of death into life at once, and will not come into judgment.

(3) In vs. 25-27 the "greater works" are described as they apply to the present age, the hour that "now is". Through the preaching of the Gospel of Christ, spiritual resurrection and moral judgment take place. In vs. 28-29 the future age is in view, the hour that "cometh". At His Second Advent these "greater works" will issue in the physical resurrection and the universal judgment of mankind.

4. The Witness of Jesus (vs. 30-40). He would not bear witness of Himself, but appealed to the witness of God alone. John the Baptist bore witness to Him, and He might appeal to that, because of the interest they showed in his ministry (vs. 30-35). But Jesus had greater witness than that of John, a witness which was threefold:

(1) His miracles, which the Father had given Him to do (v. 36). These proved that the Father had sent Him.

(2) The voice of the Father, uttered at His baptism (v. 37). This proclaimed Him to be the Son of God.

(3) The Word of God (vs. 38-40). The Jews searched the Scriptures in the outward letter, think-ing to get eternal life in that way. They failed to find the inward spiritual witness which the Scriptures bore regarding Him, and so they refused to come to Him that they might have life. This passage shows that Jesus saw Himself reflected in the mirror of the Old Testament Scriptures.

5. The Rejection of the Witness (vs. 41-47). The Lord went on to show that the Jews' want of faith in Him was due to their want of love for God. They had no welcome for Him who came in His Father's name and sought no glory from men, because they sought glory from one another and not the glory that comes from God. They would prefer a Messiah who came in his own name and sought self-glory. It was not He but Moses that would accuse them, for they had misunderstood Moses when Moses wrote of Him. Having rejected the teaching of Moses, they could not accept His teaching.

II. Unbelief in Galilee (Ch. 6). After narrating the incidents that brought out the unbelief of the Jews in Jerusalem, John goes on to tell how unbelief broke out in Galilee also. The crisis of the Galilean ministry took place in connection with the feeding of the five thousand. In the discourse at Jerusalem Jesus declared Himself to be the Giver of life because of His special relation to God. In the discourse that followed the miracle in Galilee, He declared Himself to be the Support of life because of His special relation to men.

1. The Feeding of the Multitude (vs. 1-13). Nearly a year of the Galilean ministry lies between chs. 5 and 6, for when this miracle took place another Passover was approaching (vs. 1-4). It is the only miracle recorded in all four Gospels. It appears from John's account that a conversation took place early in the day, when Jesus saw the great crowd gathering (vs. 5-9). He had already decided what to do, but He suggested to Philip the problem of feeding the multitude as a test for the disciples. Philip made a rough calculation of what it would cost at the least, and Andrew discovered a lad with five barley loaves and two fishes, which was all the food he could find among the people. The rest of John's narrative (vs. 10-13) goes on with the story where the Synoptic accounts begin, and tells of what Jesus did at the end of the day, when the disciples came to Him with their problem still unsolved and could only suggest that He send the multitude away to buy themselves food (Matt. 14:13-21; Mark 6:30-44; Luke 9:10-17).

2. The Effect upon the People (vs. 14-21). The carnal element in the faith of the Galileans was manifested in the movement which the miracle started among them, to make Jesus to be a king by force. He withdrew into the mountain to be alone, while the disciples set out across the sea in the boat. During the night He joined them by walking over the water. The full story of the night's events is contained in Matthew's account (14:22-33).

3. The Discourse on the Bread of Life (vs. 22-59). Next morning the people who had been fed with the loaves and fishes and had remained all night on the other side of the sea, not finding Jesus there, came across to Capernaum seeking for Him (vs. 22-24). In order to correct their mistaken expectation of an earthly kingdom and to remove the carnal element in their attitude toward Him, Jesus gave a

long discourse in the synagogue (v. 59) explaining the spiritual significance of the miracle wrought among them. It is composed of three parts, each introduced by some question or expression of feeling on the part of the people (vs. 25, 41, 52).

(1) The first part contains answers to four successive questions or requests which they put to Him. Instead of seeking from Him material food for the body that perishes, they should be working for the food that nourishes eternal life, and He would give them that (vs. 25-27). The way to work for it, the work that God requires of them, is to believe in Him whom God has sent (vs. 28-29). The manna which was given to their fathers in the wilderness was only a type of the true Bread of God. This Bread comes down out of Heaven and gives life to the world (vs. 30-33).

Then at their request, "Lord, evermore give us this bread", Jesus presented Himself plainly as that Bread: "I am the bread of life". He satisfies the hunger and thirst of all who come to Him and believe in Him. He receives all who come to Him, and will not cast them out (vs. 34-37). Their rejection of Him does not alter the Divine purpose: all that the Father has given Him shall come to Him and believe in Him, and every one who believes in Him shall attain to eternal life, and He will raise him up at the last day (vs. 38-40).

(2) The second part of the discourse follows the murmuring among the Jews at the claim of Jesus to have come from Heaven, when they knew who his parents were (vs. 41-42). Jesus replied that a spiritual influence coming from God was needed to understand His true nature and His special relation to the Father, and this had been promised in the Prophets (vs. 43-46; Isa. 54:13). Again He declared Himself to be the Bread of life, the living Bread which came down from Heaven, and the source of eternal life for men. The Bread which He would give for the life of the world was His own flesh, by which He meant His whole human nature (vs. 47-51).

(3) The third part follows the question, "How can this man give us his flesh to eat?" (v. 52). In using that form of expression Jesus was alluding to the Passover feast. Now He goes on to enlarge upon its symbolism in order to show how to appropriate what He gives: "Except ye eat the flesh of the Son of man and drink his blood, ye have not life in yourselves". His "flesh" means His human nature as living for us. His "blood" means His human nature as dying for us. To eat His flesh and drink His blood is to accept for oneself the virtue of His life and His death. "He that eateth my flesh and drinketh my blood abideth in me, and I in him". This means that the believer's life is rooted in, and nourished by, the life of Christ (vs. 53-56).

It is thus, Jesus points out, that the believer shares the life of God Himself. The Divine life is put within our reach by being incarnate in the Son of Man. The Father gives Himself to the Son, and the Son gives Himself to us. By feeding on Christ we live through the very life of God, as Jesus did (vs. 57-58). Here we have the secret of eternal life and the mystery of salvation. Three times in the course of these discourses does Jesus say, "I will raise him up at the last day" (vs. 40, 44, 54), showing that spiritual feeding on Christ as the Bread of life carries with it ultimately the resurrection of

the body and the full restoration of the whole personality.

4. The Sifting of the Disciples (vs. 60-71). The result of the whole discourse was to test the faith of the disciples. Some of them were offended because Jesus spoke of His sacrifice and death, and so He gave them a hint of the Ascension. They should then understand that the life-giving principle is the Spirit and not the flesh (vs. 60-63). It was by means of the Spirit given at Pentecost that the promises of these discourses were to be realized. But Jesus knew that many of them did not believe Him, and He gave them a warning about it (vs. 64-65). Many disciples at this point turned back and ceased to follow Him. The Twelve remained, and Peter uttered a warm and earnest expression of faith on their behalf. Jesus then warned them of the traitor in their midst. Perhaps the defection of Judas began at this time (vs. 66-71).

THE DEVELOPMENT OF UNBELIEF
(Chs. 7-10)

These chapters contain the account of a long controversy with the Jews at Jerusalem, in which the national unbelief was more fully revealed. It took place during visits which Jesus made to the city at two of the annual feasts in the last year of His ministry. These were the Feast of Tabernacles in the early fall and the Feast of the Dedication in the winter.

I. At the Feast of Tabernacles (Chs. 7-8). This feast lasted for seven days, and commemorated the life of the Israelites in the wilderness. Between chs. 6 and 7 is a gap of about six months, occupied by the closing part of the Galilean ministry referred to in 7:1.

1. Before the Feast (7:1-13). These verses give a lively picture of the situation in which Jesus stood at the time. His brethren, who were not yet convinced by His Messianic claims, urged Him to make some decisive manifestation of His power publicly in Jerusalem. He replied that His hour had not yet come, meaning the hour of His final public manifestation as the Messiah. He remained in Galilee for a few days after they went up, and then He went up privately (vs. 1-10). He had by this time become an object of national interest, and His absence from the feast at the beginning gave rise to speculation about Him. The people who gathered at Jerusalem were divided between faith and unbelief. But the enmity of the religious leaders toward Him suppressed all open discussion of His claims (vs. 11-13).

2. During the Feast (7:14-36). In the midst of the feast Jesus appeared publicly in the Temple and began to teach. He defended His teaching as coming from God who sent Him, and declared that anyone willing to do God's will would know whether His teaching came from God or from Himself. Thus He laid down the principle that the test of truth is moral, not intellectual (vs. 14-18). He also defended His conduct in healing on the Sabbath day as consistent with the Law. The accusation of breaking the Sabbath had been hanging over Him ever since His former visit to Jerusalem (ch. 5). He was not indifferent to it, and He wished to deprive unbelief of all excuse in this respect. They

should "judge not according to appearance, but judge righteous judgment", that is, according to the spirit of the Law (vs. 19-24).

As the discussion about Him went on among the people, He made an explicit declaration of His Divine origin publicly in the Temple (vs. 25-29). The effect of this was to confirm the Jewish leaders in their hostile purpose and to increase the faith of many of the people. Fearing a movement among them in favour of Jesus, the chief priests and Pharisees sent police officers to arrest Him (vs. 30-32). Then He announced that He would be with them only a little while longer before going back to Him that sent Him. He implied that they should make haste to believe in Him, for after that they would seek Him in the time of their distress and would not be able to find Him. They treated the Lord's warning with contempt: "What does this man mean? After being rejected by us, the Jews, will He go and teach the heathen Gentiles?" (vs. 33-36).

3. On the Last Day of the Feast (7:37-52). This was the eighth day, which was kept as a Sabbath after the special ceremonies of the feast were over (Lev. 23:36; Num. 29:35; Neh. 8:18). One of these ceremonies commemorated the miraculous stream of water that issued from the smitten rock in the wilderness (Exod. 17:5-6). Each day, at the time of the morning sacrifice, a priest brought water from the pool of Siloam in a golden pitcher and poured it out beside the altar amid great rejoicing on the part of the people, while the Levites sang, "With joy shall we draw water from the wells of salvation" (Isa. 12:3).

On the last day, instead of this ceremony, there seems to have been a solemn pause in the usual place. At that moment Jesus stood forth and cried out: "If any man thirst, let him come unto me, and drink". This was a manifest claim to be the true fountain of life, of which that rite was but a type and symbol (vs. 37-38). The phrase, "as the scripture hath said", combines the gist of many prophecies (Isa. 58:11; Jer. 31:12; Ezek. 47:1-12; Joel 3:18; Zech. 14:8). John adds his own comment to explain that this promise was to be fulfilled through the Holy Spirit, who would come only after Jesus Christ was glorified (v. 39).

The impression made upon the hearers is then described. The twofold development of faith and unbelief went on. Some were favourably disposed and inclined to believe that Jesus was the Messiah. Others were skeptical, and some were even so hostile that they would have seized Him if they dared (vs. 40-44). The officers sent to arrest Him came back to the chief priests and the Pharisees, and reported that they could not take Him, because they were overawed by His words: "Never man so spake". The answer they got discloses the self-complacent pride of the Pharisees and their contemptuous scorn of the common people. They evaded the point raised by Nicodemus, who played an honourable part on this occasion, and flew off into personalities (vs. 45-52).

4. An Episode (8:1-11). This passage, including v. 53 of the preceding chapter, is enclosed in brackets in the R.V., because it does not belong to John's Gospel. It breaks the course of the narrative by separating two closely connected sayings of

Christ (7:37 and 8:12). It has no place in the earliest manuscripts, or the earliest versions. It seems to embody, however, a genuine portion of the Gospel history, narrating an incident that occurred during one of the Lord's visits to Jerusalem, but its origin is unknown. Its special importance lies in recording the only occasion in which Jesus dealt with a specific sin. He did so by referring to the inward spring of sinful action, and by bringing the case before a more searching tribunal than that of the Law. He admitted the legality of the procedure required by the Mosaic code, but made its application a moral question for those who administered the law.

5. After the Feast (8:12-59). The controversy continued after the feast had closed, and Jesus went on making further revelations of His Messianic character. The discourses in this section bring out several special truths about Him.

(1) Christ is the light of the world (vs. 12-20). During the Feast of Tabernacles two great golden lamps, erected beforehand in the Temple, were lit every evening amid dancing and rejoicing. This was to commemorate the fiery pillar which led the Israelites in the wilderness and gave them light by night. These lights were in the women's court, which contained the treasury (v. 20), and it was there, where the absence of the lights would be most marked, that Jesus claimed to be the fulfilment of that type also, probably at the very time when the lamps were being removed: "I am the light of the world: he that followeth me shall not walk in darkness, but shall have the light of life". The Pharisees challenged His witness of Himself, and showed themselves spiritually incapable of recognizing His heavenly origin. Christ's clear consciousness of His essential oneness with God is very manifest in this passage. It is in virtue of this that He is the light of the world.

(2) Christ is the object of faith (vs. 21-30). Asserting again His heavenly origin, Jesus gave the Jews a solemn warning of the consequences of not believing in Him. Only faith in Him could bridge the gulf between the world above, to which He belonged, and this world beneath, to which they belonged. He stated the content of faith in the pregnant phrase, "I am he" (vs. 24, 28; cf. 13:19), which implies His Deity (Deut. 32:39; Isa. 41:4; 43:10). When He spoke of His unbroken communion with the Father and His constant obedience to Him, some of the Jews were inclined to believe in His claims.

(3) Christ is the source of truth (vs. 31-47). This conversation was carried on with those that were disposed to believe in Him, but retained their own mistaken views, and did not see that the Messiah was the fulfilment of the Jewish dispensation. Their Messianic hope was deliverance from the Roman yoke, but He offered a spiritual freedom, deliverance from sin. They boasted of freedom as children of Abraham, but He affirmed that true freedom consisted in salvation from the bondage of sin. If the Jews were children of God they would recognize the Son of God. They had no love for God, and therefore no understanding of the teaching of Jesus. If they were true children of Abraham they would show it in their conduct, whereas their hostility to Him, who is the truth, showed them to be spiritually children of the devil, in whom there is no truth.

(4) Christ is the giver of life (vs. 48-59). A new turn is given to the argument here as the Jews proceeded to heap insults upon Jesus. He met these with a simple denial. They were of but little importance to Him, for He left the care of His own honour with God. Then He made a solemn declaration, promising that if any man kept His word he should never see death (v. 51). The Jews saw that this involved a claim to be the conqueror of death, and to be greater than their father Abraham and the prophets, all of whom were dead. In answer to their angry resentment, Jesus declared that Abraham had looked forward with joy to the day of Christ (he had caught a glimpse of it through his faith in offering up Isaac), and that before Abraham was born He Himself was in existence. Here again He used the pregnant words, "I am". On hearing this the Jews attempted to stone Him, and He slipped out of their sight and left the Temple.

II. At the Feast of the Dedication (Chs. 9—10). The occasion of the incidents and discourses in these chapters is stated in 10:22. This feast commemorated the purification of the Temple in the time of the Maccabees, after it had been profaned by Antiochus Epiphanes. It was held in the middle of December, about three months after Tabernacles. It was known also as the Feast of the Lights, because of the brilliant illumination with which it was celebrated.

1. The Cure of the Man Born Blind (9:1-12). Of the six miracles of giving sight to the blind recorded in the Gospels, this is the only case described as blindness from birth. When they saw the sufferer, the disciples raised the old question of the connection between sin and suffering. Jesus replied that this was not an occasion for speculation, but an opportunity for doing the work of God while time for doing it was given (vs. 1-4). The Lord's statement in v. 5 may have been an allusion to the kindling of the lights at the feast, or a suggestion of the nature of the miracle He was about to perform.

By putting clay on the man's eyes and sending him to wash in the pool of Siloam, Jesus meant to connect the cure with Himself, and to declare Himself the reality of which the waters of Siloam were a type (Isa. 8:6). This is confirmed by the Evangelist's explanation of the word. Jesus often referred to Himself as "sent" of God (vs. 6-7). The rest of the narrative is a vivid description of the surprise among the neighbours when they saw the change in the man's face made by the new light in his eyes (vs. 8-12). It bears witness to the reality of the miracle, and then to the way it was wrought by the "man that is called Jesus".

2. The Investigation of the Case (9:13-41). The genuine nature of the miracle was questioned by the Pharisees because it was wrought on the Sabbath. The narrative here presents a typical example of the simultaneous growth of faith and unbelief. On the one side the Pharisees grew more determined and violent. On the other side the man grew more confident, gained an ever enlarging conception of Jesus, and finally confessed Him to be the Son of God (v. 38). John traces the investigation step by step.

(1) The first examination of the man (vs. 13-17). The Pharisees were divided, some of them holding to their preconceived opinion, others recognizing the significance of the miracle. The man affirmed his belief that Jesus was a prophet.

(2) The examination of the parents (vs. 18-23). This established the fact that their son was born blind. But they shrank from incurring the displeasure of the rulers by confessing that Christ had healed him. The cowardice of the parents was a prelude to that of the whole people.

(3) The second examination of the man (vs. 24-34). This brought the case to a decisive issue. Over against their subjective theory, he placed the objective fact: "One thing I know, that, whereas I was blind, now I see". And then he met their inability to explain that with the irony of his common sense. They covered their confusion by reviling him, and in their pride of office they expelled him from their presence and excommunicated him.

(4) The moral issues (vs. 35-41). These were twofold: In the case of the man, who acknowledged his ignorance—Jesus gave him a further revelation of Himself as the Son of God, and received his sincere worship. In the case of the Pharisees, who deluded themselves with the idea that they had the light — their religious pride increased their blindness and deepened their sin.

3. The Call of the True Shepherd (10:1-21). The Pharisees had shown themselves to be false shepherds by the way they dealt with the man born blind whom Jesus had cured. Contrasting Himself with them, Jesus now claimed to be the true Shepherd and explained how He dealt with the sheep. He was preparing to call out His own sheep from the nation, which was rejecting Him, and form of them a new Israel, a new society of the redeemed.

(1) The figure of the sheepfold (vs. 1-6). A sheepfold was an enclosure in which several flocks of sheep were gathered for safe-keeping during the night under the care of a porter. In the morning the porter opened the door of the sheepfold for each shepherd as he came to call out his own sheep. The sheepfold represented the nation itself, which contained the flock of the Lord, the true Shepherd of Israel (Psa. 79:13; Ezek. 34). The door stood for the Messianic office, the divinely appointed way of entering, the way by which the Shepherd was to come for His sheep. The porter was John the Baptist, who introduced the Messianic Shepherd into the fold. The thief and the robber were the Pharisees, who had usurped the religious leadership in Israel and were false shepherds. By this "parable" (v. 6) Jesus described the way He was going to call out the true flock of the Lord and begin the formation of His Church.

There is a remarkable analogy between the situation in which Jesus uttered these words and the picture of the Messianic shepherd drawn in Zech. 11. Having vainly endeavoured to gather Israel, He renounced the hope of saving the nation, and left to the Pharisees the flock as a whole, which was being led by them to the slaughter (Luke 19:41-44). He confined Himself to leading out from this flock the few poor sheep who, like the blind man, believed in Him. It is in such spiritual analogies as this that the organic unity of the Old and New Testaments is brought out in this Gospel.

(2) The door of the sheep (vs. 7-10). In this figure Jesus described the true nature of the Messianic office which he had come to fulfil. Its purpose was to provide salvation in all the fulness of

its meaning. The three main elements of Christian life—safety, liberty, and sustenance—are described in the experience of the man who enters by the door: "He shall be saved, and shall go in and out, and find pasture". This is explained as having life, and having it abundantly.

(3) The shepherd of the sheep (vs. 11-21). Jesus drew out the contrast between the Pharisees and Himself in describing the difference between the hireling shepherd and the Good Shepherd. The hireling cares not for the sheep and thinks only of his own interest (vs. 11-13). As the Good Shepherd, Jesus knows His own sheep thoroughly. There is the same mutual tenderness of love and trust between Him and them as between Himself and the Father. He will lay down His life for them. The mention of His sacrificial death carries His thought to the "other sheep" of the Gentile fold, who will hear His voice in the Gospel call and be gathered into one flock with the sheep from the fold of Israel (vs. 14-16).

Returning to the thought of His sacrificial death, Jesus explains its essential nature. It was to be voluntary in the absolute sense of the term. Being without sin, Jesus was not obliged to die; He consented to die and to rise again. By an act of His own will He would lay down His life. By an act of His own will He would take it again, that He might continue to be the Shepherd of the sheep (vs. 17-18). These words perplexed the Jews, and caused further discussion and division among them (vs. 19-21).

4. Christ's Oneness with the Father (10:22-42). The Feast of the Dedication was the last national festival that Jesus attended before the final Passover. It lasted for eight days, and in the course of it He made an explicit declaration of His Deity. This came in the reply that He gave to the rulers when they challenged Him to tell them plainly if He was the Messiah (vs. 22-24). He had given proof of His Messiahship in the works that He was doing. These works revealed His special relation to the Father, but they had not the faith to recognize this. He was not the kind of Messiah they desired, and they were not of His sheep (vs. 25-26). His work as Messiah was to call out the sheep that His Father had given Him and give them eternal life. They were eternally secure, and no one could snatch them out of His hand. He was carrying on God's work of redemption, and in this there was essential oneness between Himself and the Father (vs. 27-30).

At this point, notwithstanding the many good works that He had shown them from the Father, they threatened to stone Him for blasphemy, for making Himself God (vs. 31-33). Jesus defended Himself by pointing out that in the Old Testament Scriptures the rulers of Israel are called "gods" (Psa. 82:6), as being the representatives of the Most High in an office of Divine appointment. Therefore they ought not to charge Him with blasphemy for calling Himself the Son of God when He was set apart to the Messianic office and sent into the world on the mission of redemption (vs. 34-36). And again He appealed to His works as the final proof of the inner fellowship between Himself and the Father (vs. 37-38). The Lord's argument in this passage implies that the revelation of God in the Old Testament dispensation was ever moving forward to the final revelation in the Incarnation.

The Jews made another attempt to arrest Him, as they had done several times before (7:30, 32, 44). But He passed from their midst, and retired from Jerusalem to the district beyond Jordan where John had been baptizing. There the testimony of His own works, combined with the testimony of the Baptist, although not accepted in Judea, led many to believe in Him (vs. 39-42).

THE CULMINATION OF UNBELIEF
(Chs. 11—12)

The unbelief of the Jews came to a head immediately after the raising of Lazarus. It was when they learned of this miracle that the Jewish high court deliberately resolved to put Jesus to death.

1. The Raising of Lazarus (Ch. 11). This was the last and greatest of the seven miracles of Christ which John relates. Taken as a whole they form a significant series of "signs". The other six are: turning water into wine (2:1-11), healing the nobleman's son (4:46-52), healing the impotent man (5:1-9), feeding the multitude (6:1-13), walking on the sea (6:15-21), and giving sight to the man born blind (9:1-7). The story of the raising of Lazarus is told with the evident feeling of one who not only was present at the time, but also had personal knowledge of all the circumstances.

(1) The prelude to the miracle (vs. 1-16). Mary and Martha are introduced as already well known to the readers of the Gospel (vs. 1-2). The episode Luke related about them (10:38-42) had made their names familiar to the Christian communities. The message which the sisters sent to Jesus is marked by delicacy and fine feeling. They urged no plea, but simply sent the word, "he whom thou lovest is sick". Here is revealed one of the unrecorded friendships of Jesus. He received the news of the sickness of Lazarus as an occasion for promoting the glory of God (vs. 3-4). This was always His supreme aim. His delay in waiting two days was due to His love for the family. He would bring a great blessing to them all by what He intended to do after Lazarus died (vs. 5-6).

The conversation that took place between Jesus and the disciples when He proposed to go into Judea again brings out vividly the imminent danger there. The disciples were well aware of the settled purpose of the Jews to kill Him (vs. 7-8). But Jesus knew that His "day" was not yet over; and as long as that lasted there was no need for fear or undue haste (vs. 9-10). The Lord's saying here is the counterpart of the one in 9:4, that work could not be done in the night. There is also a mystical meaning behind the words of Jesus. Literally they mean that so long as a man walks in the light of day he is safe, but the night is the time of danger. Mystically they mean that he who walks in the light that Jesus gives does not walk in spiritual darkness or spiritual danger.

Then Jesus told them that Lazarus was dead, using the metaphor of sleep at first, which He had to explain to them afterwards. He was going in order to awake him out of sleep, and He called them to go with Him, that their faith might be strengthened by seeing the evidence of His power over death (vs. 11-15). The final remark of Thomas, who usually saw the worst side of things, brings out the peril again, but also reveals the devotion of the disciples to their Master (v. 16).

(2) The scene in the village (vs. 17-35). The situation in Bethany when Jesus arrived is described (vs. 17-19). Lazarus had been in the tomb four days, and many sympathizing friends from Jerusalem were there with the sisters. Martha went out in her restless grief and met Jesus with an expression of mingled complaint and confidence. He replied by bringing her thoughts back to Himself as the source of all life: "I am the resurrection and the life"; and He evoked a confession of faith on her part (vs. 20-27). Mary waited in her submissive sorrow till she was called, and then fell at His feet in worship. Jesus did not address her, for she did not need His teaching; but He manifested the feelings that were in His heart (vs. 28-35). "He groaned in the spirit"—showing indignation in the presence of Satan's temporary triumph. And "Jesus wept"—showing sympathy in the presence of the sorrow of His friends.

(3) The scene at the tomb (vs. 36-44). The strong emotions of Jesus were manifest again as He approached the tomb, which was outside the village. Martha's sisterly feeling shrank from the thought of exposing her brother's decaying body, and Jesus reminded her that she was to see the power of God triumphant over death and corruption (vs. 36-40). The prayer of Jesus reveals the complete understanding that existed between Himself and the Father, and shows that the miracle was to be wrought in answer to an unrecorded prayer (vs. 41-42). Then was heard the commanding call of Jesus spoken into the mouth of the opened cave: "Lazarus, come forth". When he did come forth, "bound hand and foot with grave-clothes", Jesus had to tell the awe-struck crowd to "loose him, and let him go" (vs. 43-44).

(4) The issues of the miracle (vs. 45-57). This miracle was a final and decisive test of faith and unbelief for those who witnessed it (vs. 45-46). The Jews on the one hand and the Lord on the other prepare themselves for the end. The Council, acting now under the influence of the Sadducean hierarchy, decide that Jesus must be put to death. John notes that the words of Caiaphas, the representative head of the nation at that time, were an unconscious prophecy, and had a deeper significance than he intended (vs. 47-53). The Lord then withdrew from "among the Jews", and waited "with the disciples" in a place of retirement for the approaching Passover (v. 54). Then the Evangelist gives a vivid picture of groups of people, who came up from the country to prepare themselves beforehand for the Passover, discussing the question of Jesus as they stood about in the Temple courts (vs. 55-57). All this serves to emphasize the tenseness of the situation in Jerusalem.

2.   The Supper at Bethany (12:1-11). Jesus had joined the caravan of pilgrims from Galilee which had come up through Perea. He stopped at Bethany, and there the people gave Him a banquet in grateful recognition of the great miracle that he had wrought in their midst. Matthew and Mark say that it was held in the house of Simon the leper. In their Gospels the event is recorded, without any mark of time, in connection with the treachery of Judas (Matt. 26:6-16; Mark 14:3-11). John singles out the traitor as the one who instigated the criticism of Mary's act, and tells us of his secret sin while acting as treasurer of the apostolic band. It is only in this Gospel that Mary is named as the woman who anointed Jesus. By the time it was written the mention of the names would no longer embarrass the members of the family. John's account brings out the profound adoration that inspired Mary's self-sacrificing action. She not only anointed the head of Jesus, as the Synoptic accounts say, but His feet as well. John also adds a feature that lingered in his memory: "The house was filled with the odour of the ointment" (vs. 1-8).

The news of Jesus' arrival at Bethany soon spread to Jerusalem, and many of the people went out to the village to see Him and Lazarus. The priestly party, in their jealousy of Jesus and in their antipathy to the idea of a resurrection (Acts 5:17; 23:8), considered putting Lazarus to death as well as Jesus (vs. 9-11).

3.   The Entry into Jerusalem (12:12-19). John gives more explicit details of this event than the Synoptists. The whole scene was one of tumultuous excitement. Jesus yielded to the enthusiasm of the people, who seem to have been animated by a feeling of heavenly joy. The disciples did not understand the significance of the event till the Ascension had shown them the spiritual nature of the Lord's sovereignty. In connection with the enthusiasm of the people, John mentions the chagrin of the Pharisees, who felt as if their power was slipping from their grasp.

4.   The Request of the Greeks (12:20-36). These Greeks represented the Gentile world outside Judaism. They were probably "proselytes of the gate", the term applied to those who worshipped with the Jews but did not become followers of Judaism. They sought a personal interview with Jesus (vs. 20-22). The incident doubtless took place in the precincts of the Temple. They had probably been present when Jesus cleansed the court of the Gentiles, and had heard Him say, "My house shall be called a house of prayer for all the nations" (Mark 11:17). This approach of theirs at the close of His ministry, like the homage of the wise men at His birth, was an earnest of the allegiance He was to get in the Gentile world. His reply was addressed to the two disciples who brought their request, but we are not told that the Greeks were present.

Jesus first told them that the hour was come when He was to be glorified as the Son of man (cf. 7:30; 8:20). Then He stated the great law of His Kingdom, the principle of the Cross, by which He was to attain His glory, and by which His followers were to share it with Him (vs. 23-26). This contemplation of the path of suffering which lay before Him brought the old temptation of the wilderness upon His soul again, offering the sovereignty of the world by another road.

His next words may be read as follows: "Now is my soul troubled; and what shall I say? (Shall I say) Father, save me from this hour?" His answer came at once: "But for this cause came I unto this hour"; and, with a renewed consecration of Himself to the will of God, He prayed, "Father, glorify thy name". Then the voice of the Father came from heaven for the third time, expressing approval of His Son: "I have both glorified it"— in the Lord's ministry to Israel, now drawing to a close—, "and will glorify it again"—in the coming ministry of the Holy Spirit in the Gentile world (vs. 27-28).

The people around heard only a sound, but some of them recognized its supernatural origin. Jesus declared that it came on their account, to impress them with the solemn importance of the judgment that was now coming upon the world. In the Cross the moral condition of the human race was to be exposed. By the Cross the power of Satan over the world was to be broken: "Now shall the prince of this world be cast out". These words should be read in the light of Col. 2:14-15 and Rev. 12:7-12. Through the Cross He would ascend to the Throne and from there His power would be extended by the Holy Spirit over all mankind (vs. 29-33).

The people were perplexed, because their idea of the Messiah as a permanent king on the earth did not agree with His idea of the Son of Man being lifted up into another world. Jesus did not reply directly to their question, but uttered a final warning that they should walk in the light of His teaching while He was yet with them lest darkness should overtake them (vs. 34-36).

5. The Jews' Rejection of Jesus (12:37-50). In this passage the Evangelist first comments upon the rejection of Jesus by the Jews and explains its cause (vs. 37-43). It was due to the judicial blindness and hardness of heart, foretold by Isaiah (53: 1; 6:10), which their own unbelief had brought upon them. In the statement of v. 41 John identifies the vision of Jehovah which Isaiah saw in the Temple (6:1) with the glory of the Lord Jesus Christ, and implies that in rejecting Him the Jews had rejected Jehovah. Among some of the rulers there had been an intellectual conviction, but fear of losing their position and their prestige kept them from making a public confession. Then John gives a general summary of the teaching of Jesus in the Lord's own words, to explain the truth which the Jews had rejected (vs. 44-50).

THE LORD'S LAST ACTS OF LOVE
(Ch. 13)

From the dark picture of Jewish unbelief, we turn to the Lord's last ministry of love to the disciples. His public ministry to Israel was ended, and His "hour" had come. He now poured forth His love to them: "Having loved his own that were in the world, he loved them unto the end" (v. 1). This verse introduces the whole section (chs. 13-17), which contains the revelation that Jesus gave to the faith of the disciples before going back to the Father. As He loved His disciples and had shown them His love before, so now when He was about to pass through His suffering, He carried His love to the last. Under the shadow of His own death, His whole thought was fixed upon them alone.

1. Washing their Feet (vs. 2-20). This was an acted parable. It was probably occasioned by the dispute which Luke records (22:24-27). Jesus wished to root out of their hearts the last remnants of the pride and ambition that still corrupted the faith of His Apostles. He was also aware of the treachery of one of them. And so He gave them this example of true greatness in His Kingdom. Because of the glory into which He was going, He humbled Himself to perform the office of the lowest. John describes the scene with the vividness of

personal reminiscence, as if he were beholding it at the moment (vs. 2-5). Peter's impulsive remonstrance when Jesus came to him was characteristic. But Jesus corrected His disciple's false humility by explaining that what He was doing had a spiritual significance, which he should understand hereafter (vs. 6-11). When Jesus had finished and sat down again, He told them what He meant by His action. He had given them an example of the spirit in which they should act toward one another. It was a symbol of the humble service of mutual helpfulness which their Master required of them (vs. 12-17). Then He gave them the first hint that one of them had turned against Him (vs. 18-20).

2. Dismissing Judas (vs. 21-30). Jesus was "troubled in the spirit": His feelings were under restraint while Judas was present. John describes this act of Jesus in greater detail and with more feeling than any of the other Evangelists. The giving of the sop, which was a mark of honour to a guest, was the Lord's last attempt to turn Judas from his treachery; but it only confirmed the traitor in his purpose. Judas must have concealed his methods and plans with great skill, for even at this last moment none of his fellow-disciples had any suspicion of his design. John adds significantly that when Judas went out, "it was night".

3. Warning Peter (vs. 31-38). Jesus' feeling of relief is manifest in the first words He spoke after the traitor's departure. He began to pour out the fulness of His heart and prepare the disciples for the separation that was coming: "Now is the Son of man glorified". The deed that Judas went out to do meant for Him the Cross; but beyond the Cross was His glorification as the Son of Man (vs. 31-32). This involved His separation from them, and He now tenderly prepared them for that, and gave them a commandment to love one another with the love that He had for them. Thus they should show the world that they were His disciples (vs. 33-35). Peter would not accept the thought of separation from the Master, and protested his own willingness to die for Him. Jesus checked this boastful and self-confident enthusiasm by warning Peter that he would utter a three-fold denial of his Master that night (vs. 36-38).

THE LORD'S FAREWELL MESSAGES
(Chs. 14—16)

These chapters contain the last discourses of Jesus. They are farewell messages to His disciples. They follow naturally the announcement of His departure at the close of the preceding chapter. They may be taken in four parts: comfort in view of His departure (ch. 14), their new life after His departure (ch. 15), the mission of the Holy Spirit in His place (16:1-15), and His last farewell (16: 16-33).

1. Comfort in View of His Departure (Ch. 14). This chapter is made up largely of answers to questions asked by individual disciples. It begins by carrying on the reply to Peter's question (13:36), "Lord, whither goest thou?" and continues by replying to the questions of Thomas (v. 5), Philip (v. 8), and the other Judas (v.22). The main thought throughout is, "Let not your heart be troubled" (vs. 1, 27). In the course of the chapter He gives them seven grounds for comfort.

(1) He was going to prepare a place for them (vs. 1-4). By His Father's house He meant the unseen spiritual world of Heaven. This was the antitype of the Temple, to which He had formerly applied the name (2:16). There was room enough there for them all, but it would not be ready for them until He went back with His redeeming work on earth accomplished.

(2) He Himself is the way to the Father (vs. 5-7). It was characteristic of Thomas to see difficulties and to want his doubts removed before taking the step of faith. Jesus tells him that one finds access to the Father's house by coming to the Father, and that one comes to the Father only by coming to Jesus Himself: "I am the way, and the truth, and the life". He is the only "way" by which one can pass into the heavenly world of the Father's presence, because He is the revelation of ultimate "truth", and the source of eternal "life". That the disciples did not know what Jesus meant by going to the Father, was because they had not yet learned to know the Son.

(3) He Himself is the revelation of the Father (vs. 8-11). Philip's request surprised and disappointed Jesus. It seemed to imply a failure on the Master's part to make Himself known to the disciples. There is a pathetic note in His personal appeal to Philip. He points out to him the signs by which he should have recognized the presence of God in the Person of his Master—His words and His works. These were the proofs of His union with the Father. That union had a two-fold aspect: "I am in the Father"—His words showed that He was in the closest communion with the Father; "and the Father in me"—His works showed how the Father wrought in Him.

(4) The disciples were to continue His work (vs. 12-14). "The works that I do shall he do also"— the physical miracles which the Apostles wrought in the early days of the Church. "Greater works than these shall he do" — the spiritual miracles which are wrought by the Church through the preaching of the Gospel. The phrase, "in my name", occurs here for the first time, and is used again and again in these chapters (14:26; 15:16; 16:23-26). It means "as my representative", and implies the spiritual union of believers with Christ.

(5) He would send the Holy Spirit to take His place (vs. 15-21). The word rendered "Comforter" means one called to the side of another to help him. The Holy Spirit was to come and continue Jesus' work for the disciples. He is called "the Spirit of truth", because He would make the truth that Jesus taught a reality for them. The world could not receive Him, for it had no vision or knowledge of spiritual things. But the disciples would recognize Him, because He would remain with them and dwell in their hearts (vs. 15-17). As a result, they should not be left alone, for Christ Himself would be present with them and become a living reality to them. "In that day"—the age beginning with Pentecost—they should realize the fact of the Lord's union with the Father and their own union with the Lord (vs. 18-20). Then Jesus put in other words the stages of the experience that He had been describing (v. 21).

(6) The Holy Spirit would explain and complete His teaching (vs. 22-26). The question of Judas shows that the disciples expected a public manifestation of the Lord's Messianic glory. Jesus did not answer the question directly, but repeated what He had just said about an inward and spiritual manifestation (vs. 22-24), and then went on to tell them that the Comforter would complete the teaching He had given them and explain all things to them. The Father would send Him as Christ's representative — "in my name". As the purpose of Christ's mission was to reveal the Father, so the purpose of the mission of the Holy Spirit is to reveal Christ (vs. 25-26).

(7) He leaves the disciples His legacy of peace (vs. 27-31). His peace means the peace that He had during His earthly life through His fellowship with the Father, peace that had its springs in the world to which He was going and not in this world. He would have them rejoice, too, in His departure, because He was going to the Father in order to share His power and glory, and so be able to complete His work for them.

Here the discourse is broken by the thought of the conflict at hand, and Jesus goes on to say, "The prince of the world cometh: and he hath nothing in me". This means that there was no sin in Him, and therefore Satan could not inflict death upon Him. But Jesus proceeds to offer Himself willingly, that He might carry out the Father's commandment and fulfil the mission of redemption on which He was sent into the world. The last verse may be read as follows: "But, that the world may know that I love the Father, and that, as the Father gave me commandment, even so I do, arise, let us go hence". Thus He summons the Apostles to rise from the table and go out with Him, as He proceeds towards the Cross.

It is not at all likely that chs. 15 and 16 were spoken on the streets of the city, or even on the road down to Gethsemane outside the walls. It is more probable that on the way to Gethsemane they entered the courts of the Temple. That was the most suitable place for the rest of the discourse and for the last prayer.

2. The New Life of the Disciples (Ch. 15). The Lord went on to give instructions regarding the new life the disciples would live after He was gone. The new situation in which they would be placed is described from three points of view: their relation to Christ (vs. 1-11), their relation to one another (vs. 12-17), and their relation to the world (vs. 18-27).

(1) Union with Christ (vs. 1-11). This is set forth under the similitude of the vine. It may have been suggested by the great golden vine which, Josephus tells us, adorned the gates of the Temple. The vine is one of the symbols of Israel in the Old Testament, and appears there in various relations. (Psa. 80:8; Isa. 5:1; Jer. 2:21). The use of the metaphor here to illustrate the spiritual union between Christ and His believing followers signifies the formation of a new people of God in place of the old Israel. The vine comprises both trunk and branches in one living organism, and manifests its life in the fruit borne by the branches (vs. 1-2). So Christ and His disciples form one body of life.

The one purpose of the vine is to bear fruit. The word is repeated again and again. By fruit Jesus meant spiritual life, the manifestation of His life in the lives of the disciples, what Paul calls the fruit of the Spirit (Gal. 5:22-23). The law of life for the branches, and the one condition of fruitfulness, is to abide in the vine (vs. 3-4). The disciple must set his life in Christ, and let Christ live in him. The word "abide" occurs ten times in this passage. This is the way to maintain union with Christ. The results of union, and the consequences of loss of union, are set forth in a sharp contrast (vs. 5-6). The blessings of union are power in prayer (v. 7), abundant fruit (v. 8), continual experience of the love of Christ (vs. 9-10), and fulness of joy (v. 11).

(2) Love for one another (vs. 12-17). This passage begins and ends with the Lord's commandment that His disciples should love one another. Their love should be after the pattern of His love for them. The greatness of His love is shown in laying down His life for them (v. 13). Because of it He exalted them from being servants to be His friends, and had chosen them to be His representatives in the world.

(3) Hatred from the world (vs. 18-27). In contrast with the love which the disciples were to have for one another, the Lord now tells them of the hatred they would receive from men in general (vs. 18-19). By their union with Christ, they belonged to a different kind of world, the unseen and eternal realm of the Spirit. They were to expect persecution from the world because of the world's hatred of Christ (vs. 20-25). But when the Holy Spirit should come from the Father to be His supreme witness, then they too were to bear witness to the fellowship that they had with Him from the first (vs. 26-27).

3. The Mission of the Holy Spirit (16:1-15). Having referred to the coming of the Holy Spirit, whom He was to send from the Father, Jesus now goes on to explain more fully the nature of the Spirit's work. It was necessary for Him to depart from the world, that His work might be carried to completion by the Holy Spirit. There was something for the Spirit to do for the disciples which Jesus could not do by Himself.

(1) The coming of the Spirit (vs. 1-7). Jesus had said these things to prepare the disciples for the persecution that awaited them after His departure (vs. 1-3). He had not told them of these things before, but reserved them for the eve of His departure (vs. 4-6). It was better for them that He should depart and go to the Father, for the Spirit could not come until He had gone (7:39). After that He would send Him to them.

(2) The Spirit's relation to the world (vs. 8-11). His work would be to convict the world in respect of sin and of righteousness and of judgment. This would be the result of the preaching of the Gospel. "Of sin, because they believe not in me"; that is, the sin of rejecting the Saviour. The result of Peter's preaching at Pentecost is the best illustration of this (Acts 2:37). "Of righteousness, because I go to the Father, and ye behold me no more"; that is, the righteousness wrought out by Jesus Christ on earth and confirmed by His ascension into Heaven. This is the "righteousness of God" now revealed in the Gospel (Rom. 1:17). "Of judgment, because the prince of this world hath been judged"; that is, the judgment executed upon the Cross. In that transaction Satan's case against the children of God was met and settled by Christ

Jesus in taking upon Himself the Divine judgment for human sin (John 5:24; 12:31; Rom. 8:33-34; Col. 2:14-15; 1 John 2:1-2).

(3) The Spirit's relation to the disciples (vs. 12-15). As the Spirit of truth, He would carry forward the work which Christ had begun for the disciples, by guiding them into the truth which they could not understand until after His redemptive work had been fully accomplished. The Holy Spirit would glorify Christ by making Him known in the fulness of His revelation of the Father.

4. The Last Farewell (16:16-33). Jesus now returns to the thought with which He began—His approaching departure. "A little while, and ye behold me no more"—the interval between the present moment and His death. "And again a little while, and ye shall see me"—the interval between the Cross and Pentecost. After that they should have a spiritual vision of His glory with the Father (v. 16). Some of the disciples were perplexed by these words, and Jesus proceeded to explain what He meant (vs. 17-19).

After the first "little while" they should be overwhelmed with great sorrow, but after the second "little while" their sorrow should be turned into the greatest joy. This joy could not be taken from them, because it would be the realization of His spiritual presence with them (vs. 20-22). This fulness of joy would be due to the new illumination which the Holy Spirit would give them, and to the new relationship which they should have with the Father, giving them the privilege of praying to Him in Christ's name (vs. 23-24).

In this teaching of His, Jesus had to use figures and parables, because He could not yet speak plainly. After Pentecost the Spirit would give them direct knowledge of the Father and His love (vs. 25-27). In v. 28 Jesus summed up His whole redemptive work in four steps: "I came out from the Father (emptying Himself according to Phil. 2:6-7), and am come into the world (the Incarnation): again, I leave the world (the Cross), and go unto the Father (the Ascension)". This drew out from the disciples a confession of their faith in Him (vs. 29-30), to which He replied with a warning of what was to happen that night (vs: 31-32). Then He gave them a final word of assurance and triumph: "Be of good cheer; I have overcome the world." In the world they should have tribulation, but in Him they should have peace (v. 33).

THE LORD'S HIGH-PRIESTLY PRAYER
(Ch. 17)

This is properly "the Lord's prayer", the prayer that He used Himself, as distinguished from the prayer that He taught His disciples to use. It was probably uttered while they were still in the Temple. Nowhere could our High Priest more fitly offer Himself and His followers to the Father than in the place in which God had chosen to set His name. Having received from them an emphatic expression of their faith (16:30), Jesus saw that His work in training and instructing them was finished. Nothing was left now but the supreme act of sacrifice for which He had come into the world. His "hour" had come, and He committed Himself and His disciples to the Father's love and care. The main thought of the prayer is the glory of the Father as revealed in the work of the Son. This is developed in three parts:

1. Prayer for Himself (vs. 1-5). Jesus prays that He may be glorified; that is, that His real nature may be fully manifested. And this in two respects. (1) "Glorify thy Son" (v. 1). This refers to His humanity. It is a petition for the manifestation of His incarnate glory in victory over death through His resurrection and ascension. (2) "Glorify thou me with thine own self" (v. 5). This refers to His Deity. It is a petition for the restoration of the former glory of equality and fellowship with God which He had before the Incarnation (Phil. 2:6; 1 John 1:1-2). Christ's motive in seeking His own glory was that He might glorify the Father by giving eternal life to men, and so make the Father more fully known (vs. 2-3). The ground of His petition was His having glorified the Father by His earthly life of perfect obedience (v. 4).

2. Prayer for His Disciples (vs. 6-19). Jesus now prays for the Apostles, whom He is about to leave, and who are to continue His work in the world. The relation in which they stand both to Himself and to the world pervades this part of the prayer, and is the ground upon which its special petitions are based. The disciples were given to Him out of the world (vs. 6-10). They have been kept by Him from the world (vs. 11-15). They are sent by Him into the world (vs. 16-19). By "the world" Jesus means mankind in general as separated from God and alien to Him.

The Lord makes two special petitions for the disciples. (1) That they should be kept: "Holy Father, keep them in thy name which thou hast given me". "I pray . . . . that thou shouldst keep them from the evil one" (vs. 11, 15). Jesus asks that their preservation in the world and their deliverance from the evil in it may be maintained through the revelation of the Father which He has given them. The Scripture to which He refers as fulfilled (v. 12) is probably Isa. 43:13 rather than Psa. 41:9. (2) That they should be sanctified: "Sanctify them through thy truth: thy word is truth" (v. 17). He asks that they may be consecrated and set apart for their mission in the world by the whole system of spiritual truth into which they have been introduced. As He has represented the Father in the world, so they are to remain in the world and represent Christ.

3. Prayer for all Believers (vs. 20-26). Jesus next goes on to pray for the whole Church, for all who should believe in Him through the Gospel proclaimed by the Apostles. This part of the prayer contains two main petitions.

(1) For the unity of the Church (vs. 20-23). This is put in different ways: "that they may all be one"; "that they also may be in us"; "that they may be perfected into one". It is a prayer that the spiritual unity which has its ground in the unity of the Father and the Son may be realized in the Church. The Father lives in the Son and the Son lives in the Father and thus they are one in will and purpose. Jesus prays that this oneness of fellowship and love may be manifested in the life of the Church. This spiritual unity would exhibit such a quality, and would be so different from any earthly unity, that it should convince the world that He from whom it proceeds came from God. Jesus looked forward to this unity as the crowning evidence of His Divine mission.

(2) For the glorification of the Church (vs. 24-26). The final glory of the Christian consists in being with Christ and beholding His glory. His supreme glory, according to His own explanation, consists in the Father's love for Him. The phrase, "before the foundation of the world", gives us a glimpse of the profound depths of His own eternal pre-existence, and of the love that existed in the heart of the Godhead then. The emotion of Jesus seems to deepen as He comes to the end of His prayer, and as He thinks of His mission being consummated in having that same love shared by His disciples.

THE FINAL WORK OF UNBELIEF
(Chs. 18-19)

Jewish unbelief reached its final form and showed its true nature in the condemnation and crucifixion of the Son of God. This Gospel does not contain a complete story of the sufferings of Jesus. The Evangelist had the earlier Gospels constantly in mind, and evidently endeavoured simply to fill up the vacancies left in their narratives, so as to present the facts, which were now well known, in their true light. Three ideas are prominent in John's narrative: the voluntary nature of Christ's sufferings (18:4, 8, 11, 36; 19:28-30), the fulfilment of a divine plan in them (18:4, 9, 11; 19:11, 24, 28), and the majesty of the Son of God shining through them (18:6, 20-23, 36-37; 19:11, 26-27).

1. The Betrayal and Arrest of Jesus (18:1-11). John omits the agony in the garden, but gives vivid details of the rest of the scene when Judas and his band arrived. He tells us that "Jesus oft-times resorted thither" (vs. 1-2). Jesus "went forth" to meet them, probably going out to the gate of the garden to deliver Himself up and provide for the safety of the disciples. The moral majesty of His bearing had a startling effect upon the soldiers (vs. 3-9). The incident of Peter and Malchus is recorded by all the Evangelists, but John alone mentions their names, for he was writing so long after the event that there was no longer any need for reticence (vs. 10-11). The rebuke that Jesus addressed to Peter, which is more fully given in Matthew (26:52-54), shows how completely He was master of the situation, and also how completely He was surrendered to His Father's will. The cup had not been taken away and was now willingly accepted. The answer to His prayer in the agony is revealed in His calm self-composure through the rest of the scene in the garden, as well as through the scenes that now follow.

2. The Jewish Trial (18:12-27). John alone tells of the preliminary examination before Annas, the aged high priest (vs. 12-14). In the course of it Jesus declared that He had spoken publicly to the world and His teaching contained no secret mystery. There is no account of the trial which took place afterwards before the Council under Caiaphas (vs. 19-24). The story of Peter's threefold denial, which is recorded in all the Gospels, is told by John in a more circumstantial way than by any of the other Evangelists (vs. 15-18, 24-27). His account has the unmistakable marks of an eye-witness. John was evidently present throughout all the trial, both before the Jewish court and before Pilate. He is doubtless "the other disciple" mentioned in v. 16.

3. The Roman Trial (18:28—19:16). This part of the trial of Jesus is most fully recorded by John. He begins by telling us that the Jews would not enter the Roman judgment-hall, for that would mean ceremonial defilement and prevent their eating the Passover; and so Pilate went out to them. They began by asking him to confirm their sentence of death against Jesus without examination, and this Pilate refused to do (18:28-32). Then they brought a political accusation against Jesus—He made Himself a king. Taking Jesus into his judgment-hall, Pilate asked, "Art thou the King of the Jews?" Before answering, Jesus asked in what sense he put the question, whether in a political sense or otherwise; and then He took the opportunity of testifying to His kingship before Pilate, but showed how different His Kingdom was from the kingdoms of this world. Its sway depended not upon military power, but on the revelation of the truth (18:33-37). Pilate treated this reference to truth with supercilious disdain. Then he went out to the Jews and told them that he found Jesus innocent and made an attempt to have them approve of His release. But they chose Barabbas instead of Jesus (18:38-40).

Pilate made a further attempt to release Jesus by appealing to the pity of the crowd. He had Him scourged and brought before them with the crown of thorns and the purple robe which the soldiers had put upon Him, and again declared Him innocent, exclaiming, with a mixture of respect and sarcasm, "Behold, the man!" But the chief priests and officers of the Jews anticipated any possible expression of pity by loud cries for His crucifixion. Pilate, for the third time, declared Him innocent, and ironically referred the whole case back to them (19:1-6).

Then the Jews advanced a new charge—"He made himself the Son of God". At this Pilate became alarmed, for he had already recognized something mysterious in the strange prisoner before him. He entered the judgment-hall again and questioned Jesus. Although his haughty Roman pride was offended by the Lord's silence at the first question, he was awed by the majesty of His answer to the second question (19:7-11). When Pilate made another attempt to release Jesus, the Jews threatened to charge him with disloyalty to Cæsar; and this brought him at last to a cowardly submission to their demand. At the same time he treated them with savage irony. He brought Jesus forth to them, saying, "Behold, your King!" They responded, not only by the rejection of their Messiah, but also by the repudiation of their Messianic hope: "Away with him, away with him, crucify him!... We have no king but Cæsar" (19:12-16).

4. The Crucifixion (19:17-30). John does not give a full account of the crucifixion of Jesus, but he adds some details to those recorded by the Synoptists so as to supplement and complete their narratives. He tells us that Pilate refused the request of the chief priests to change the superscription which he had put over the cross (vs. 17-22), that the soldiers cast lots for the seamless coat among the garments of Jesus (vs. 23-24), that Jesus' mother was among the women standing by the cross and that Jesus committed her to John's own care (vs. 25-27).

John makes no reference either to the darkness or to the cry of anguish which Matthew and Mark record. He adds, however, two of the Lord's words from the cross which were uttered after that cry (vs. 28-30). Jesus expressed His sense of physical suffering in exclaiming, "I thirst". This word was spoken only when He knew that His task was finished and prophecy was fulfilled. The word, "It is finished", was a cry of triumph, corresponding with the last word that He had spoken to the disciples in His farewell message (16:33). The actual death is described as the voluntary surrender of His life— "He bowed his head, and gave up his spirit". Thus John marks the unique manner of the Lord's death.

5. The Burial (19:31-52). John alone records the incident of the soldier's spear-thrust, and the peculiar phenomenon that resulted from it: "there came out blood and water". He evidently regarded it as significant of something, and therefore bore his witness to it. It has been held to mean that the physical cause of the Christ's death was a rupture of the heart. It is more probable that in John's thought it was connected somehow with the Resurrection. It marked the exceptional nature of a body which had never been tainted by sin, and was not subject to corruption, and which, from the moment of death, underwent the beginnings of that change that issued in the Resurrection (vs. 31-37).

All the Gospels record the request of Joseph for the body of Jesus. John alone tells of the part that Nicodemus had in the burial, who brought a hundred pounds of spices to put in the grave-clothes. These two members of the Jewish aristocracy had been secret disciples of Jesus. His death evoked a courage in them which had been latent during His lifetime. John notes the fact that the tomb where Jesus was laid was in a garden close to the spot where the cross stood (vs. 38-42).

THE FINAL REWARD OF FAITH
(Chs. 20—21)

These closing chapters of the Gospel explain the triumphant fact of the Resurrection, and reveal the new life of the Son of God as the source of eternal life for all who believe on Him. John writes from his own experience, and narrates those incidents that led the faith of the disciples to triumph over sorrow and fear and doubt. His record is a revelation of spiritual truth through outward fact.

1. The Empty Tomb (20:1-10). We are first told how he attained to faith in the Resurrection. He came to realize its transcendent nature by seeing how the grave-clothes were left lying in the empty tomb. The part of Mary Magdalene is only that of the messenger who brought the news that the body was gone and called the two disciples to the sepulchre (vs. 1-2). When Peter and John arrived at the tomb and entered it, they saw something that struck them with amazement. It was not merely the disappearance of the body; it was the way the grave-clothes were left. The linen cloths were lying exactly as they had been wrapped around the body, and the head cloth lay a short distance away, just where the head had rested.

Nothing had been disturbed, and yet the body was gone. It had passed through those grave-clothes without moving them. John records what he observed, and then adds simply, but with great significance, "he saw, and believed" (vs. 3-8). The true nature of the event had broken in upon him. He now began to understand what the Lord meant by saying that He must rise again from the dead. All that was Jesus of Nazareth had passed into another plane of being. His body had been spiritualized, and it now transcended the physical world. Peter and John then "went away again unto their own home", to think of the wonder of it, and to recall to their remembrance what the Lord had said about His rising again from the dead (vs. 9-10).

2. **The Appearance to Mary Magdalene (20:11-18).** After being the messenger to the two chief Apostles, Mary Magdalene was to become the herald of the risen Lord. He made His first appearance to the humble disciple whose personal love for Him kept her lingering at the tomb (vs. 11-15). When He uttered her name, she knew Him by the tone of His voice, and she wheeled about with an exclamation of surprise and rapture. The Lord's warning, "Touch me not", implies that Mary was about to express her devotion by clasping His feet on the ground of the old human relation and with a desire to retain His presence.

Jesus proceeded to explain that the time to enjoy full communion with Him would not come till He had ascended to the Father, and bade her go and tell the disciples that He was on His way to that Ascension (vs. 16-18). The Lord's use of the expression, "my brethren", would emphasize the unity that was to exist between Him and them in their new life; while the expressions, "my Father and your Father", and "my God and your God", would remind them of the essential difference between His own unique relation to God as the Son and their relation to God as believers in the Son.

3. **The First Appearance to the Apostles (20:19-23).** This is the same appearance as that recorded in Luke 24:36-49, which took place on the evening of the Resurrection day. Two other manifestations of the risen Lord had already taken place that day, the appearances to Peter and to the two disciples at Emmaus; but this was the first appearance to the apostolic group. The Lord greeted them with a salutation of peace, and then showed them His wounds in order to assure them that it was Himself. John reflects the feelings of one who was present, when he adds, "the disciples therefore were glad when they saw the Lord" (v. 19-20).

With another benediction of peace, Jesus announced that He was sending them to continue the mission on which the Father had sent Him—to bring to the world salvation from sin. By the symbolic action of breathing on them when He said, "Receive ye the Holy Spirit", He indicated that the promised Spirit would come to them as the gift of life from His own glorified Person. There may be an allusion here also to the origin of life at the creation of Adam, when the Lord God "breathed into his nostrils the breath of life" (Gen. 2:7). The risen Jesus now stands forth as the Creator of a new humanity, the Author of the new spiritual creation.

4. **The Second Appearance to the Apostles (20:24-31).** Thomas was not present at the first appearance, and he would not believe that his fellow-disciples had seen the Lord without tangible evidence (vs. 24-25). The Apostles spent the whole Passover week in Jerusalem, and on the first day of the following week they were gathered again in the same place and under the same circumstances; and this time Thomas was present. Again the Lord stood in their midst and greeted them with the same salutation (v. 26). Then He spoke to Thomas directly, and offered him the tangible evidence he had demanded. Thomas did not need it. He recognized the real nature of his Master at once, and broke out in a sublime and rapturous confession of faith: "My Lord and my God" (vs. 27-28). The record of this confession forms the appropriate close of John's narrative. The words which the Lord addressed to Thomas after it show that He accepted the declaration of His Deity as the true confession of faith (v. 29). This accounts for the two closing verses of the chapter, in which John states the purpose of the narrative that he has written (vs. 30-31).

5. **The New Work of the Apostles (21:1-14).** This chapter forms an appendix to the Gospel, which was added after it had been brought to a formal close but before it was put into public circulation. It contains the story of another appearance of the risen Lord, in which He deals first with the Apostles as a group and then with two of them individually

The Apostles seem to have returned to their ordinary work in Galilee while waiting for further instructions about their future. Seven of them are here engaged in fishing (vs. 1-3). There are several significant differences between the miraculous catch of fishes recorded here and that which took place when they were called to discipleship at the beginning of the Galilean ministry (Luke 5:1-11). On the earlier occasion Jesus was in the boat with the disciples, and the miracle was symbolical of their work during His earthly ministry when He was still in their midst. On the present occasion He directed them from the shore, and the miracle symbolized their work after His departure into Heaven (vs. 4-8). It depicts the work of the Church during the present Christian age. When their fishing was done and they had gathered in all the fish, He invited them to a meal which He had prepared on the shore and served them Himself. But the human intimacy and simple familiarity of their former intercourse was gone. There was a mysterious change in Him which inspired a reverential awe and claimed their silent adoration (vs. 9-14).

In the course of the story the characteristic qualities of Peter and John stand out again. John, keen of insight, is the first to see that the stranger on the shore is the Lord. Peter, prompt of action, is the first to make his way toward Him. The rest of the chapter deals with the Lord's relation to these two individual Apostles, who have now come to be the leading members of the group.

6. **The Special Work of Peter and John (21:15-25).** This passage first tells how Peter was restored to his place in the Apostolic band and to leadership among them (vs. 15-19). The three questions which the Lord put to him could not but recall his threefold denial, and were doubtless intended to give him a full opportunity to withdraw it. Peter had been forgiven when the Lord appeared to him privately on the day of the Resurrection (Luke 24:34; 1 Cor. 15:5). That interview was too sacred to be narrated, but its result required to be manifested to the other disciples. The words, "more than these", in the Lord's first question referred to Peter's claim to possess greater devotion than the rest of the disciples (13:37; Matt. 26:33). In asking, "Lovest

thou me?" Jesus laid the basis of Christian life and service in personal devotion to Himself, not in intellectual belief.

In his answers, Peter used a different word for "love" from that which Jesus used. He would not lay claim to the higher love which the Lord's word implied, but only to the personal affection and devotion of which he was sure. In His third question Jesus took up Peter's own word; and Peter was grieved because the Lord seemed thereby to call in question even that personal attachment which His disciple had claimed. Peter was then thoroughly humbled, and threw himself entirely upon the Lord's complete and perfect knowledge of his heart. Having restored to Peter his apostleship in a threefold charge, the Lord went on to tell him what the end of his ministry would be. His love and devotion would be proved and sealed by martyrdom. Then the bold declaration of His devoted Apostle (13:37) would receive a literal fulfilment.

The incident that follows, when Peter asked what John should do, reveals the special attachment that existed between these two Apostles (vs. 20-23). The fact that John was following when Jesus and Peter turned aside showed that he too sought to know the Lord's will about his future. The answer Jesus gave implied that John should not die by martyrdom like Peter, but that he should live on far beyond the rest of the Apostles. It had other implications also, which John himself does not claim to understand; but it did not mean that he should not die at all, as some in the Church had inferred. Jesus had simply said, "If I will that he tarry till I come, what is that to thee?" John leaves the Lord's meaning to be explained in the course of Christian history. Its supreme significance lies in Jesus making His own Second Coming the final hope of the Church and the final end of its work on earth.

*   *   *   *

THE DIVINE GLORY OF THE LORD JESUS

While the Synoptic Gospels answer the question, "What are the facts on which faith rests?" the Fourth Gospel answers the question, "What is the meaning of those facts?" Its key-words are "witness", which occurs in one form or another about forty times, and "believe", which occurs nearly one hundred times. It bears "witness" to the fact that Jesus is the Christ, the Son of God, so that men may "believe" in Him and have eternal life. The Divine glory of His Person, which appears occasionally in the Synoptic Gospels, shines all through John's Gospel. It is manifested in several special ways.

1. Jesus Christ is represented as the reality of which the Mosaic system was only the shadow. This is what ohn means when he declares that "the law was given through Moses; grace and truth came through Jesus Christ" (1:17). He carries out this idea in his narrative by setting the whole life and ministry of the Lord upon the background of the Old Testament dispensation. There are numerous allusions and references to Old Testament types and symbols. In many cases Jesus claimed to be the fulfilment of these Himself. In the course of the Gospel He is seen to be foreshadowed by the symbolism of the following types: the tabernacle (1:14, literally, "tabernacled among us"), the Passover lamb (1:29, 36), the ladder of Jacob's dream (1:51), the Temple (2:19-21), the brazen serpent (3:

14-15), the manna (6:22), the water from the rock (7:37), the pillar of fire (8:12), and the waters of Siloam (9:7).

2. A tone of sublime self-assertion marks the discourses of Jesus in this Gospel. This is revealed especially in the way He used the expression, "I am". Our translators have supplied the word "he" after it in several cases, but it is not in the original: "except ye believe that I am" (8:24); "then shall ye know that I am" (8:28); "that ye may believe that I am" (13:19). The word "Messiah" might be supplied as a predicate; but, standing alone as they do, the words mean that Christ was speaking out of the very being of God (Exod. 3:13-14). This is more clearly seen in the statement, "Before Abraham was, I am" (8:58).

On seven occasions Christ Himself added a predicate to the words; and when these are taken as a whole they reveal the wealth provided for human need in His own Divine Person: "I am the bread of life" (6:35); "I am the light of the world" (8:12); "I am the door" (10:9); "I am the good Shepherd" (10:14); "I am the resurrection and the life" (11:25); "I am the way, and the truth, and the life" (14:6); and "I am the true vine" (15:1).

3. Jesus was conscious of an eternal pre-existence. The memory of a pre-incarnate state pervades the language of the Lord in this Gospel. This is manifested in His repeated statement that He came from Heaven on a mission from the Father (6:38; 8:29, 42). The word "sent" was often on His lips. Again and again He declared that the Father had sent Him (5:36-37; 7:28-29; 8:18; 10:36; 16:27-28; 17:25). He spoke of the heavenly world with the confidence of one who was familiar with it. "I know whence I came", He declared, "and whither I go" (8:14). "Ye are from beneath; I am from above; ye are of this world; I am not of this world" (8:23). His knowledge of heavenly things was such as to give Him ample authority to tell men about them (3:12).

This consciousness of an eternal pre-existence comes out most clearly at the end of the Lord's ministry, when He was facing the Cross. It is the ground of His assurance to the disciples in the upper room: "In my Father's house are many mansions; if it were not so, I would have told you" (14:2). It is manifested most fully in the opening sentences of His high-priestly prayer (17:1-5). He began with a petition that He might be glorified: "Father, the hour is come; glorify thy Son, that the Son may glorify thee". This was a request that He might be carried through the supreme sacrifice of His humiliation into the triumph of the Resurrection and the Ascension. He went on to sum up His life-work, the mission on which He had been sent, in these words: "I glorified thee on the earth, having accomplished the work which thou hast given me to do". And then He repeated His petition in this form: "And now, Father, glorify thou me with thine own self, with the glory which I had with thee before the world was". There was a glory lying behind Him in the eternal past, as well as the glory into which He was going in the eternal future.

4. Christ's superhuman claims reveal the transcendent nature of His Person. No sin could be found in His life (8:46; 14:30). He possessed a unique oneness with God (10:30; 14:9). He had power to give eternal life (10:28; 17:3), and authority to judge the world (5:22, 27). The most significant

of all His supernatural claims, in view of His re- demptive mission in the world, was the assertion He made about the absolute control He had over His own life: "No one taketh it away from me, but I lay it down of myself. I have power to lay it down, and I have power to take it again" (10:18).

This is the only explanation that can account for the mystery of the Cross. When the four Gospel records of the event are read with attentive care, when the unbroken objective calmness of all the narratives is considered, when every circumstance in the story is given its due place in the scene which the mind contemplates, then there comes in upon the soul an irresistible impression of mystery un- fathomable. Something happened there that was wholly new and strange.

The death of Jesus was the only death of its kind that the human race has ever seen. It was a voluntary sacrifice in the absolute sense of the term. He was not overcome of death. He gave His life, by a deliberate act of His own free will, "a ransom for many" (Matt. 20:28; Mark 10:45). By con- senting to share the death of men, although under no obligation to die, He bore the sin of men, al- though Himself without sin. In the mysterious depths of that voluntary sacrifice of His there is something which, while it perpetually baffles the human intellect, brings a strange and ineffable peace to the human heart. By the grace of God Christ tasted death for every man, and "through the eter- nal Spirit offered himself without blemish unto God" (Heb. 2:9; 9:14).

THE NEW TESTAMENT

THE ACTS

THE APOSTOLIC AGE

THE Acts of the Apostles is the one historical book in the New Testament. It covers only thirty years of the apostolic age (A.D. 30-60), but in that time the Church had been established in the world and Christianity had entered the field of human his- tory as the universal religion of redemption.

The age of the Apostles extended to the end of the century, when John, the last remaining member of the Twelve, passed away. Its culminating point, however, was reached in the year 70, when the fall of Jerusalem and the destruction of the Temple at the hands of the Romans brought the Mosaic sys- tem to an end and set Christianity completely free from Judaism. That event marked the final separa- tion of the Old Testament dispensation of the Law from the New Testament dispensation of the Gospel. After that Christianity went on its way in the world as a new religious movement, and the Church took its own place among men as a new spiritual fellow- ship.

In the light of the Book of Acts, several stages can be distinguished in the historical progress of Christianity and the growth of the Church through the Apostolic Age.

The first stage takes us from the birth of Chris- tianity at Pentecost to the martyrdom of Stephen in the year 33 or 34 (Acts 1-7). This was the period of Christian beginnings and of the primitive Church. Christianity did not begin as a new religion. The first Christians were Jews, and they continued to attend the Temple services and perform the rites and duties of Judaism. They differed from the rest of the Jews only in believing in Jesus as Messiah and Saviour, and in maintaining a special fellow- ship of their own. They were not conscious of hav- ing changed their own religion for another, but they were profoundly conscious of a new experi- ence. They "were being saved" (2:47, marg.). They had entered into "the life"; they had found "the way" (5:20; 9:2; 22:4).

These early Christians had no thought of break- ing with Judaism, but Judaism cast them out. The condemnation and stoning of Stephen by the Jewish Council confirmed and sealed the national rejection of Christ, which had taken place three or four years before. This event marked the end of the "seventy weeks" which Daniel had been told still remained for his people until the Messianic redemption should be accomplished and God's purpose with Israel should be finished (Dan. 9:24-27). As Christ had come to be the fulfilment of the Law, so Christianity arose as the fulfilment of Judaism. But Judaism re- fused to recognize it as such. Having repudiated the redeemed remnant in its midst and cast it out, noth- ing remained for the nation now but the judgment foretold by the Lord, which fell a generation later.

The next stage in the progress of Christianity takes us about another ten years farther on, when another attack on the Church took place (Acts 8-12). The persecution that began with the stoning of Stephen drove many of the members of the Church from Jerusalem, and so scattered the seeds of Christianity abroad. Christian churches sprang up in many parts of Palestine, and even beyond its borders. God-fearing Gentiles as well as Jews were being converted. When the Gospel reached Antioch and was preached there, many pagan Greeks accepted the message of salvation through Christ. This resulted in a church being established in that great Gentile city, which was so manifestly "Christian" in its character, as distinct from Jewish, that the name came to be identified with the followers of the new faith.

In the meantime Saul of Tarsus had been converted, and the Jewish churches in Palestine were enjoying a respite from persecution, and were growing steadily. The Apostles had not yet left Jerusalem. They seem to have remained there for some years after Pentecost, in order to maintain oversight over the Church as a whole. By this time James, the Lord's brother, had become the pastor of the mother-church in the city. He continued to preside over it long after the Apostles departed. He was held in high esteem by the Jews, and was called by them "the just". His Epistle is the earliest book of the New Testament, and was probably written about the middle of the century.

During this period changes took place in the government of the land. Pilate was removed from Judea in A.D. 36, and Herod Antipas from Galilee in the following year. In the year 41 the former dominions of Herod the Great were united under the rule of his grandson, Herod Agrippa I, who was given the title of king. This meant the restoration of the Jewish kingdom under the Herodian dynasty. As his grandfather had struck at the infant Christ, so this Herod struck at the Apostles of Christ. At the time of the Passover in the year 44, he had James the son of Zebedee beheaded. His attempt on Peter's life was frustrated by the Apostle's miraculous deliverance from prison. Herod's sudden death, which occurred soon afterwards and was regarded by the Church as a judgment of God, brought to an end the short-lived attempt to restore the Jewish kingdom in Palestine. After that the land was put under the direct rule of Roman governors, whose headquarters were in Cæsarea.

In the next stage of the Church's progress an important forward step was taken—the extension of Christianity into the Gentile world and the admission of Gentiles into the fellowship of the Church on the same terms as Jews. This period takes us to the first Christian council, which was held in Jerusalem in A.D. 50 (Acts 13-15). Paul and Barnabas had been sent out from Antioch on the first evangelizing mission into the heathen world, and they had founded a number of churches in the southern districts of the province of Galatia in Asia Minor. It was to these churches that Paul wrote, not many years afterwards, what is known as the Epistle to the Galatians.

On the return of the missionaries to Antioch, they were challenged by some Jewish Christians from the parent Church for preaching the Gospel freely to uncircumcised Gentiles; and the question was raised whether men could be saved without coming through the gateway of the Mosaic Law. The matter was referred to the Apostles and elders in Jerusalem. The decision, which was reached unanimously and was regarded as the mind of the Holy Spirit, vindicated Paul and Barnabas. The ceremonial law was to have no place in the Christian Church. The Gospel was to be equally free to Jews and Gentiles.

This important decision opened the way for the next stage in the progress of the Gospel—the planting of Christianity in the great cities of the Roman Empire. This was mainly the work of Paul, and it occupied most of the next ten years of his life. He travelled about among Greeks and Romans as one familiar with their world, for he had known the pagan mind and heart from his earliest days. This period saw those churches founded with which his Epistles have made us familiar. It takes us to the Apostle's arrival as a prisoner in Rome in A.D. 60 (Acts 16-28).

In the early years of this decade Paul carried the Gospel into Europe, and planted Christianity in the provinces of Greece. He founded the churches in Philippi and Thessalonica, preached in Athens, and spent a considerable time in Corinth, establishing the church in that great commercial city. While there he wrote the two Epistles to the Thessalonians. His next evangelizing mission was devoted mainly to Ephesus, where he spent another prolonged period. Christianity was firmly established in that great centre of pagan worship, and from there the Gospel spread far and wide. It was then that "the seven churches of Asia" (Rev. 1:11), and also the church at Colossæ, had their beginning.

After leaving Ephesus Paul visited Greece again, and spent three months at Corinth in the winter of 56-57. There he wrote the Epistle to the Romans. He had written the two Epistles to the Corinthians shortly before that, the First from Ephesus, and the Second while travelling through Macedonia towards Corinth. Then he journeyed back through Macedonia and went on to Jerusalem, bringing a contribution which he had collected from the churches of the Gentiles as a thank-offering for what they owed to the parent church in Judea. The Apostle intended this to be a means of binding the Jews and the Gentiles in the Church more closely together. We are not told how this gift was received. Paul's purpose was frustrated by what happened when he arrived in Jerusalem.

There were many in the church there at that time who were zealous for the Law and did not accept the liberty of the Gospel for which Paul stood. Taking the advice of James and the elders, he attempted to conciliate this group by undertaking the cost of ceremonially purifying four Jews who were under a vow. But his presence in the Temple led to a riot on the part of the fanatical Jewish mob. As a result Paul was arrested by the commander of the Roman garrison and sent down to the governor at Cæsarea.

The fact that the Apostle was kept a prisoner there for two years without having his case settled, and finally had to exercise his right as a Roman citizen and appeal to Cæsar, is evidence of the laxity and corruption of the Roman rule in Palestine at that time. This appeal led to Paul's being sent to Rome, where he remained in captivity for another two years (A.D. 60-62). During that time he wrote the Epistles to the Ephesians, the Philippians, the Colossians, and Philemon.

New Testament history ends at this point, and for the rest of the apostolic age we have to depend on tradition. It was the general belief of the early Church that Paul was released from Rome in the year 62 and resumed his evangelizing work in the Mediterranean world. In the course of the next few years he visited the churches in the east, and then went as far west as Spain. To this period belong two of the Pastoral Epistles—First Timothy and Titus. In the meantime the first Roman persecution of Christianity, the most terrible the Church had yet suffered anywhere, broke out in the imperial capital under Nero. Before it was ended Paul was arrested and brought to Rome a second time. From his prison there he wrote his Second Epistle to Timothy, and soon afterwards suffered martyrdom, probably in A.D. 66 or 67.

During the same period the Christians in Palestine were also passing through severe trial. The early years of the decade before the fall of Jerusalem were full of unrest and disorder. During one of the tumults in the Temple, James was stoned to death for bearing witness to Jesus as the Christ. In the year 66 the Jews rebelled against Rome, and the war began which resulted four years afterwards in the destruction of the Temple and the dissolution of the Jewish national order. Just before the final siege of the city, the Christians fled to Pella beyond the Jordan; and there the Jewish church maintained its headquarters for several years. Some time during this decade the Epistle to the Hebrews was written, and also the Epistles of Peter and Jude.

Peter had been entrusted with the work of evangelizing the Jews outside Palestine. We have no account of the way he fulfilled this mission. There is reason to believe that he made an evangelizing tour through Asia Minor (1 Pet. 1:1). Some suppose that he went as far east as Babylon (1 Pet. 5:13), but the reference in this verse may be to the capital of the Empire. There is no historical evidence that he was ever Bishop of Rome or had anything directly to do with the church there. It is not unlikely, however, that the tradition is true which says that he, as well as Paul, was put to death there during the Neronian persecution.

The Apostle John probably remained in Jerusalem, or in Judea, as long as Mary the mother of Jesus was living, fulfilling the charge that the Lord had committed to him. After the fall of the city he seems to have settled in Ephesus, which then became the main centre of the Christian Church. There he wrote the Gospel and his three Epistles. There is a tradition that he was banished to the island of Patmos during the persecution of Domitian's reign in the last decade of the century, and that out of that exile came the Book of Revelation.

There is no authentic information about the labours of the rest of the Apostles. Oral traditions about them floated among the later Christian communities, but none of these is trustworthy. The silence of Scripture regarding their work is significant. One fact is clear, that the movement of Christianity was westward, following the track of the Apostle Paul, and that all the vital interests of the Church centred in the work of that one man. Rome was the point of departure for the subsequent spread of the Gospel. So far as New Testament history is concerned, the apostolic age properly ends with Paul in Rome.

THE ACTS OF THE APOSTLES

THE Book of Acts was evidently intended to be a companion to the Third Gospel. Written by the same author and addressed to the same person (Luke 1:1-3; Acts 1:1-2), it continues the same story. The Gospel is described as a narrative of what Jesus "began both to do and to teach" up to the time of His ascension. The Acts is a narrative of what He continued to do and to teach after His ascension, through the Holy Spirit who was sent to take His place in fulfilment of His promise (John 14:16-18).

The book closes with Paul's two years' imprisonment in Rome. Probably it was written at that time or soon afterwards, and there was no more to tell. In the meantime the author's purpose had been accomplished, which was to write an account of the spread of the Gospel and the establishment of the Church in the world. The Apostle of the Gentiles had arrived at last at the world's capital, and was teaching the new faith there (28:30-31). The narrative covers a period of about thirty years.

The Book of Acts occupies an important place in the New Testament. It provides the link between the Gospels and the Epistles. It rests on the facts of the Gospel history, especially the death and resurrection of Jesus Christ, and it assumes that these facts are well known. It tells how the promises recorded in the Gospels, which the Lord gave to the disciples regarding their future work, were fulfilled. These promises pointed forward to the founding of the Church (Matt. 16:18-19), the coming of the Holy Spirit (Luke 24:49; John 16:7), and the participation of the Gentiles in the blessings of the Gospel (Matt. 28:19-20; Luke 24:46-47). This book narrates the events which brought all these results about.

The Acts also prepares us for the Epistles. It introduces the Apostle Paul, who wrote most of the Epistles, and whom the Gospels never mention. This book relates what we need to know about his conversion and his missionary labours. It also gives an account of the origin of most of the churches to which Epistles are addressed. These Epistles reveal a condition of things in which the separation between Jews and Gentiles, which prevailed throughout the Old Testament and was continued through the Gospels, has disappeared altogether. The Acts shows how this change came about.

The title of the book occurs in various forms in the earliest manuscripts. It was probably added by a later hand than the writer's. Luke himself may have issued it without a title, as a natural sequel to his "former treatise". The word "Acts" was used in the first and second centuries for what we now call "memoirs" or "biographies"; and that simple title seems to have been the first one prefixed to Luke's second book. Afterwards it was enlarged in one way and another until the present title, "Acts of the Apostles", became fixed. This title does not accurately describe the contents; for the book does not record the acts of all the Apostles, and it contains extended notices of men, like Stephen and Philip, who were not Apostles. Taken in a limited sense, however, it may be understood as referring to the particular Apostles by whom the Church was established in the world. The chief agents in this work were Peter and Paul, and the narrative is occupied mostly with the acts of these two Apostles.

The book falls accordingly into two main parts. The first part (Chs. 1—12) deals with the establishment of the Church among the Jews in Palestine, which was largely the work of Peter. The second part (Chs. 13—28) deals with the establishment of the Church among the Gentiles beyond Palestine, which was almost entirely the work of Paul. Thus we get the following working outline of the Book of Acts:

I. The Church Among the Jews—Chs. 1-12

  1. The Founding of the Church (Chs. 1-2)

  2. The Growth of the Church (Chs. 3-5)

  3. The Beginning of Church Organization (Chs. 6-7)

  4. The Spread of the Gospel in Palestine (Chs. 8-9)

  5. The Extension of the Gospel to the Gentiles (Chs. 10-12)

II. The Church Among the Gentiles—Chs. 13-28

  1. The First Gentile Mission (Chs. 13-14)

  2. The First Christian Council (Ch. 15)

  3. Paul's European Mission (Chs. 16-18)

  4. Paul's Ephesian Mission (Chs. 19-20)

  5. His Arrest in Jerusalem (Chs. 21-23)

  6. His Imprisonment in Cæsarea (Chs. 24-26)

  7. His Journey to Rome (Chs. 27-28)

THE FOUNDING OF THE CHURCH
(Chs. 1—2)

The story of Acts begins with the two great supernatural events which gave birth to Christianity and brought the Church into being — the ascension of Jesus Christ into Heaven and the outpouring of the Holy Spirit from Heaven. By His ascension the risen Lord took His place in the heavenly world as the Head of the Church (Eph. 1:20-23), and by the descent of the Spirit upon them the disciples were united with Him into one spiritual body (1 Cor. 12:13). A new corporate community was thus created, based upon a new spiritual order and manifesting a new kind of fellowship. This new community was the Church of Jesus Christ.

1. The Ascent of the Lord (Ch. 1). During the forty days between the Resurrection and the Ascension, Jesus gave His disciples convincing evidence of His own new life: "He showed himself alive". He also instructed them regarding the nature of the new spiritual order into which they were about to enter through the baptism of the Holy Spirit — "the things concerning the kingdom of God" (vs. 1-5).

In answer to a question about the future of the Kingdom, He warned them to leave that in the Father's hands. They should be equipped by the Holy Spirit with power for their own special work, which was to be His witnesses and spread His Gospel from Jerusalem throughout the whole world (vs. 6-8). The question asked by the disciples never comes up again in the New Testament. Pentecost gave them new light about the Kingdom and a new

point of view. It removed from their minds the last lingering elements of their former carnal conceptions.

Jesus was taken up and disappeared from their sight behind the veil of a cloud. As they stood gazing upward, "two men stood by them in white apparel" and told them that He had been received from earth into Heaven, and that He should return in the same manner as they had seen Him go (vs. 9-11). That is, as He had disappeared into the unseen so He would reappear out of the unseen. It is not said that these men were angels. They may have been Moses and Elijah, who had been with Jesus on the Mount of the Transfiguration.

What the Apostles beheld on the Mount of Olives was the earthly side of a transcendent event. On the heavenly side of the cloud there took place the exaltation and enthronement of the Saviour of the world. This is mentioned several times in the Epistles. God "raised him from the dead, and made him to sit at his right hand in the heavenly places" (Eph. 1:20). "God highly exalted him, and gave unto him the name which is above every name" (Phil. 2:9). "When he had made purification of sins, he sat down on the right hand of the Majesty on high" (Heb. 1:3).

It is described most fully in the sublime symbolism of the Book of Revelation. In the midst of the Throne in Heaven John saw "a Lamb standing as though it had been slain" (Rev. 5:6). It was the Saviour of men, just come from His sacrifice on the cross, taking His place at the centre of power in the unseen world, there to exercise all authority in Heaven and on earth (Matt. 28:18), and there to reign, till He has put all His enemies under His feet (1 Cor. 15:25).

After the Ascension the Apostles and disciples in Jerusalem, numbering about a hundred and twenty, among whom were Mary the mother of Jesus and His brethren, waited in prayer for the coming of the Holy Spirit (vs. 12-14). This is the last mention of the mother of Jesus in the New Testament. His brethren had evidently come to believe in Him after the Resurrection. One of the Lord's appearances was made to His brother James (1 Cor. 15:7). During this time, under Peter's direction, they chose one of themselves to take the place of Judas in the apostolic band as a witness of the resurrection of the Lord, which was the primary function of an Apostle (1 Cor. 9:1). The Apostles used their own judgment as far as they could in first selecting two; and then they prayerfully left the final decision to God by means of the lot (vs. 15-20). This is the last use of the lot in Scripture history. Matthias is not mentioned again in the New Testament.

2. The Descent of the Spirit (Ch. 2). This event took place on the morning of the Day of Pentecost, ten days after the Ascension, so called because it was the "fiftieth" day after the offering of the first fruits during the Passover season (Lev. 23:15-16). In the Old Testament it was called the Feast of Weeks (2 Chron. 8:13). Of the three great feasts of the Jewish year, it was that which attracted the largest number of pilgrims from distant lands. The disciples "were all together in one place" (v. 1). This must have been in one of the courts of the Temple, for there all devout Jews would be gathered for the special services of the day. There, too,

the disciples had been meeting for praise and prayer every day since the Ascension (Luke 24: 52-53). It was the time of the morning sacrifice, "the third hour of the day" (v. 15).

Thus the Temple became the birthplace of the Church. The building of the spiritual House began on the site of the material house, which was its type and symbol. All that pertained to the old dispensation centred in the Temple; and it was fitting that the new dispensation should start there and spread out from there into all the world. This was the significance of Ezekiel's symbolic vision of the river flowing out from within the temple (47:1-5), and the fulfilment of Joel's prophecy of the fountain coming forth from the house of the Lord (3:18).

The signs accompanying the event gave some indication of its transcendent nature (vs. 2-3). The sound of wind and the appearance of fire meant that the power and presence of God were there. The fact that "it sat upon each of them" marked the fulfilment of the Lord's promise about the Spirit: "He shall be in you" (John 14:17).

The "other tongues" with which the disciples spoke were not other languages than their own, but new powers of utterance due to the new experience of the Spirit coming into their hearts (v. 4). He had put a new song in their mouths (Psa. 40:3). It was the ecstatic utterance of rapturous devotion, which could be translated spontaneously into the various languages of mankind, thus overcoming the old confusion of tongues. Amazement took possession of the Jewish worshippers, who had come from all parts of the Roman world to attend the feast and were thronging the Temple courts (vs. 5-12). Some of them began to mock, and this gave Peter the occasion for addressing them (vs. 13-14).

He began with a brief defence of the disciples, explaining the sudden change that had come over them and the nature of the event that had happened. It was the fulfilment of the prophecy of Joel, that a time should come when God would pour out His Spirit upon mankind, and bring in a new age in which whosoever should call upon the name of the Lord should be saved (vs. 15-21; Joel 2:28-32). Peter then went on to preach the Gospel to the Jews, telling them that salvation had been secured by the death and resurrection of Jesus Christ.

His argument was as follows: Jesus of Nazareth was proved to be the Messiah by His miraculous ministry (v. 22), by His resurrection from the dead after they had crucified Him (vs. 23-24), by David's prophetic anticipation of the resurrection of Christ as the fulfilment of God's promise to him regarding his throne (vs. 25-31; Psa. 16:8-11), by the Apostles' personal witness (v. 32), and by the pouring out of the Holy Spirit from His exalted place at the right hand of God in Heaven, the signs of which they themselves now see and hear, an event which David also foretold (vs. 33-35; Psa. 110:1). Peter then stated the conclusion from all this evidence: "God hath made him both Lord and Christ, this Jesus whom ye crucified" (v. 36).

This produced conviction among his hearers, who began to enquire what they should do. Peter urged them to repent and be baptized for the remission of sins and they should receive new life through the Holy Spirit. As a result, about three thousand were added to the company of the disciples that day (vs. 37-41). Thus the first Christian church was formed.

The new converts continued under the instruction of the Apostles. They manifested a new kind of corporate life, a fellowship that was marked by a spirit of unity and love, and an atmosphere of joy and gladness and praise (vs. 42-47). "Fear came upon every soul": there was a sense of awe, because of the presence of the supernatural. The believers "had all things common", because their hearts were flooded with a new love for one another, the love of Christ Himself. Christ was present again in their midst, and His Spirit pervaded their lives. It was the fulfilment of His own farewell promise (John 14:18; 16:16, 22).

THE GROWTH OF THE CHURCH
(Chs. 3—5)

These chapters tell how the new community developed, how it met opposition from without, and how sin within was dealt with. The Church grew steadily in numbers (2:41; 4:4; 5:14; 6:7), and in spiritual power (4:31, 33; 5:12-13).

1. Apostolic Witness in the Temple (Ch. 3). One afternoon, as Peter and John were going up into the Temple at the hour of prayer, they healed a lame man lying at the gate which led into its courts, Peter invoking over him "the name of Jesus Christ of Nazareth" (vs. 1-10). The scene is described with great vividness—the manner of the cure, the change in the man, and the effect upon the people. They came running together in the colonnade called Solomon's porch, greatly amazed at the manifest miracle. Peter then began to address them, and declared that the man had been healed by faith in the name of Jesus Christ, the Prince of life, whom they had killed and God had raised from the dead (vs. 11-16).

He went on to say that they and their rulers had done this in ignorance, and that God had thereby fulfilled the prophecies about the sufferings of the Messiah. He appealed to them to repent, that their sins might be blotted out and seasons of spiritual refreshing come, and that God might send their Messiah, "whom the heaven must receive until the times of restoration of all things" (vs. 17-21). Here we have an indication of the Apostolic outlook upon the future. The return of Christ in power and glory awaited the repentance and conversion of His own people Israel. Peter went on to show that Moses and all the prophets had spoken of these days, and that the blessing promised through the seed of Abraham to all the nations of the earth was being fulfilled in this Saviour from sin whom God had sent first to them (vs. 22-26).

2. Apostolic Witness in the Council (4:1-22). As Peter and John were speaking to the people, the Temple authorities, who belonged to the Sadducean party, had them arrested and put in prison over night (vs. 1-4). When they appeared next morning before the Council, which was the same group of rulers that had condemned Jesus, Peter told them what he had told the Jewish people in the Temple. The impotent man had been healed "in the name of Jesus Christ of Nazareth, whom ye crucified, whom God raised from the dead". Then he went on to declare that there was no salvation in any other name (vs. 5-12).

The unaffected but confident bearing of the two unlearned men, who reflected the spirit of their

Master, impressed the rulers with wonder. They were unable to deny the notable and manifest miracle, yet they sought how to stop the spread of the new teaching (vs. 13-17). They warned the two Apostles "not to speak at all nor teach in the name of Jesus", that is, not to make the name of Jesus the basis of their teaching or to refer to it as the source of their power. But Peter and John replied: "We cannot but speak the things which we saw and heard". The Council then threatened them and let them go, for they dared go no farther in their opposition at this time because of the feeling among the people, who were praising God for the miracle of healing wrought on a man lame from his birth and more than forty years old (vs. 18-22).

3. The Fellowship of the Church (4:23-37). When the Apostles returned to the company of the disciples and reported what had happened in the Council, there was a united expression of praise and prayer, and a fresh manifestation of the presence and power of the Holy Spirit in their midst (vs. 23-31). The new spirit created at Pentecost was deepened. The Apostles continued their witness of the Resurrection with great power. Great grace was upon the whole body of believers. There was no self-interest among them. They had all things common, sharing their own possessions with others who were in need, because of the love that prevailed among them (vs. 32-35). A notable example of this spirit of self-sacrifice was shown by Barnabas, a Levite of Cyprus (vs. 36-37).

4. The First Sin in the Church (5:1-16). The sin of Ananias and Sapphira was due to spiritual pride. They were envious of the reputation of Barnabas for self-sacrifice. But their own spirit was that of self-interest, and it led them to an act of deception which the two of them deliberately planned. This was the first case of sin in the Church, and it was punished by a signal act of God's displeasure, which followed Peter's exposure of the deceit as lying unto God. This produced a sense of awe, for it manifested the peculiarly sacred character of the new community: the Lord was in its midst (vs. 1-11).

After this the spirit of unity and power was manifestly deepened. The Church had its public meeting-place in Solomon's porch, and the number of believers greatly increased. Signs and wonders were wrought among the people by the Apostles. Peter became the centre of an extended ministry of healing, sick people being brought in from round about Jerusalem (vs. 12-16).

5. The Persecution of the Apostles (5:17-42). The high priest, and the party of the Sadducees to which he belonged, who were troubled by the preaching of the Resurrection and had formerly caused the arrest of Peter and John, now took similar action against all the Apostles (vs. 17-18). It was the first occasion of an official persecution, and God interposed with a miraculous sign confirming the teaching of the Apostles. They were brought out of prison by an angel during the night, and sent to speak to the people in the Temple "all the words of this Life" (vs. 19-21).

The frequency of angelic activity in the early days of the Church is remarkable. The word "angel" occurs twenty times in Acts, and six distinct works of angels are recorded (5:19; 8:26; 10:3; 12:7, 23;

27:23). When the rulers met in the morning to try the prisoners, they were perplexed when they heard of their strange disappearance. But they made no attempt to enquire into it, thus ignoring the divine sign that had been given them (vs. 21-24). When the Apostles were found teaching in the Temple, and were brought before the Council and charged with disobedience for teaching in the name of Jesus, Peter replied for them all: "We must obey God rather than men" (vs. 25-29).

This principle was followed by all the leaders of Christianity in the New Testament. But while refusing to obey any command of men contrary to the will of God, they submitted quietly and without murmuring to any penalty the law of the land might lay upon them. Peter continued his address to the Council by giving the same witness about the essential facts of the Gospel as he had given on the former occasion. "And we are his witnesses of these things", he declared, "and so is the Holy Spirit, whom God hath given to them that obey him" (vs. 30-32). Peter meant that the Holy Spirit, as the secret of the new life and power of believers in Christ, thus bore witness to His resurrection and His exaltation into Heaven.

Their foes in the Council were enraged; but they were sobered by the warning and the wise advice spoken by the eminent Pharisee Gamaliel, the teacher of Paul (Acts 22:3), and the most famous Jewish scholar of the time. Let them refrain from these men, he said, and leave them alone; for if their work was of men it would be overthrown of itself, and if of God they could not overthrow it. He spoke of two leaders of insurgent bands, each of whom had pretended to be the Messiah, and both of whom had perished (vs. 33-39). The Council agreed with his advice; but before letting the Apostles go, they beat them and charged them not to speak "in the name of Jesus". The Apostles departed with the joyful assurance of the Lord's favour, and continued to preach Jesus as the Messiah, both publicly in the Temple and privately in the homes of believers (vs. 40-42).

THE BEGINNING OF CHURCH ORGANIZATION
(Chs. 6—7)

These chapters tell how the first office-bearers came to be appointed, and how one of them carried on an evangelizing ministry among the foreign-born Jews in Jerusalem and became the first Christian martyr.

1. The Appointment of the Seven (6:1-7). The Church had proved itself able to meet and overcome opposition that came from without. Now it showed itself able to meet difficulty that sprang up within. Some trouble had arisen because of its growing numbers. The Grecians (Greek-speaking Jews who had been born outside Palestine) complained that the poor families among them were being neglected by the Hebrews (Hebrew-speaking Jews who had been born in Palestine) in the daily ministration of help. The very nature of the trouble is evidence of the poverty of the early Christians, and it raised the question of the temporal side of the Church's work. In order to deal with it, the Apostles had new officers chosen from among its members. They are not called "deacons", although the subsequent office of deacon had similar func-

tions, and are only once referred to afterwards (21:8).

The plan adopted was based on the organization of the synagogue. The new officers were to "serve tables", that is, preside over the distribution of alms and care for the physical needs of the congregation. The Apostles themselves would continue to carry on the spiritual functions of prayer and the ministry of the Word (vs. 1-4). The Seven were chosen by the members of the Church, and were solemnly ordained by the Apostles. They seem to have been taken from among the Grecian Jews, for all the names are Greek (vs. 5-6). Only Stephen and Philip are mentioned again, but what is said of them shows that these men did more than merely "serve tables".

In the meantime the Church went on growing rapidly in numbers. Many of the priests became believers. Their special familiarity with the sacrificial system of worship in the Temple would enable devout men among them to recognize the spiritual fulfilment of the Law in the new faith (v. 7).

2. The Ministry of Stephen (6:8-15). The narrative now takes up the story of Stephen, who was conspicuous among the Seven for his personal qualities and spiritual gifts, and for the miraculous signs that attended his work among the people. He is the first case of one not an Apostle working miracles. He carried on a witness in the synagogues of the Grecian Jews with great wisdom and spiritual power (vs. 8-10). There are probably three synagogues referred to here: that of the Libertines or "Freedmen", most of whom were descended from Jewish slaves taken to Rome by Pompey a hundred years before; that of the Cyrenians and Alexandrians, Jews from North Africa; that of them of Cilicia and Asia, two Roman provinces in Asia Minor. Saul of Tarsus no doubt belonged to the last of these synagogues.

Stephen's opponents were unable to withstand his reasoning. They stirred up opposition to him on a false charge of disloyalty to the Law of Moses. They had him arrested and brought before the Council, setting up false witnesses against him. Something of Stephen's message is reflected in the charge laid against him. He was teaching that the Mosaic system of symbolical worship was now fulfilled in Jesus Christ. He seems to have understood clearly the spiritual nature of the new dispensation, and this gave occasion to his foes to charge him with saying that Jesus would destroy the Temple and change the customs of Moses (vs. 11-15).

3. Stephen's Martyrdom (Ch. 7). Stephen's address before the Council is given at length, because it marked a crisis in the history of Israel. The rulers who had rejected Jesus were now given another opportunity to consider the evidence for His Messiahship. But they rejected Him again. This event brought to an end the "seventy weeks" of the Messianic prophecy in Daniel 9:24-27, and sealed the nation's doom. It ultimately led to the extension of the Gospel to the Gentiles.

Saul the Pharisee was present at the trial of Stephen, and "was consenting unto his death" (8:1). He approved of it, though he did not take part in the stoning. But he had seen Stephen's face (6:15) and his steadfast upward gaze (7:55); and he heard his prayer for his murderers as he died (7:60). He would be impressed with the argument of Stephen's address, and doubts would arise in his heart and mind about his own position. He kept kicking against these pricks of conscience until the Lord finally arrested him on the Damascus road (26:14).

In his address Stephen reviewed the history of God's dealings with Israel from Abraham down through the patriarchal age (vs. 1-16) and the Mosaic period (vs. 17-43), and on to the time of Solomon (vs. 44-50). His purpose was to show that the Mosaic system of the Law was only preparatory for something higher that was to come. The tabernacle in the wilderness and the temple of Solomon were but types of a spiritual and heavenly order. At this point, probably because of the deepening hostility he saw in the Council, Stephen denounced his hearers for resisting the Holy Spirit as their fathers did. Their fathers killed the prophets; they themselves had slain the Righteous One. They had failed to keep the Law (vs. 51-53).

His words roused his hearers to fury. Gazing upward with steadfast face, he declared that He saw Heaven opened and the Son of Man standing on the right hand of God. Refusing to listen, they rushed upon him, cast him out of the city and stoned him, while Saul kept the garments of the official witnesses (Deut. 17:7). In his death Stephen showed the very spirit of his Master. His prayers under the stoning echo two of the Lord's prayers on the cross: "Lord Jesus, receive my spirit", and "Lord, lay not this sin to their charge". The whole passage bears the marks of Paul's vivid memory of the scene (vs. 54-60).

THE SPREAD OF THE GOSPEL IN PALESTINE
(Chs. 8—9)

The narrative now goes on to tell how the persecution which began with Stephen's death was the means of scattering the Church from Jerusalem and spreading the Gospel into Samaria and throughout Palestine.

1. The Church Established in Samaria (8:1-25). With the stoning of Stephen a bitter persecution broke out against the church in Jerusalem, which scattered its members throughout Judea and Samaria. In this Saul was the most active agent. Wherever the disciples went they preached the Gospel (vs. 1-4). Philip, one of the Seven, proclaimed it in the city of Samaria, and carried on a ministry of healing among the people there which brought joy to the city. Among those that were baptized was Simon the sorcerer (vs. 5-13).

When the Apostles in Jerusalem heard that the Samaritans had received the Gospel, they sent Peter and John to visit them. When these Apostles prayed for them and laid their hands upon them, some of the outward manifestations of Pentecost were repeated. Thus the faith of the Samaritans was confirmed and the Church was established among them (vs. 14-17). Peter, however, had to expose and rebuke the false and carnal faith of Simon before he and John returned to Jerusalem (vs. 18-25).

2. The Further Work of Philip (8:26-40). Another illustration of the way the Gospel was spreading is contained in the beautiful story of Philip's interview with the Ethiopian eunuch on the desert road to Gaza. Philip had been sent down there by

an angel of the Lord, and he met a high official of the queen of Ethiopia, who had been worshipping in Jerusalem and was on his way back toward Egypt. The incident shows how the early believers saw Christ in the Old Testament Scriptures. Philip continued to evangelize the coast district of Palestine from there up to Cæsarea, where he seems to have settled afterwards (21:8).

3. The Conversion of Saul of Tarsus (9:1-30). In the midst of his persecution of the disciples of Christ, the chief persecutor himself was converted to Christianity by a supernatural intervention of the Lord Himself. The importance of this event is shown by its being recorded three times in the book—not only here in the course of the author's narrative, but also in two of Paul's speeches (chs. 22 and 26).

Saul secured a commission from the high priest to go to Damascus and arrest any that were of "the Way" (vs. 1-2). This was the primitive description of the Christian faith (19:9, 23; 22:4; 24:14, 22). As he was nearing the city he was smitten to the earth by a heavenly light which blinded him, and he heard the voice of Jesus speaking directly to him : "Saul, Saul, why persecutest thou me?" "Who art thou, Lord?" he asked; and the reply came: "I am Jesus whom thou persecutest". He was led into the city and remained for three days without sight under the overpowering effect of the vision, neither eating nor drinking (vs. 3-9). Then a disciple of Damascus, named Ananias but otherwise unknown, was used of the Lord to lead him into the light and receive him into the Church (vs. 10-19).

Saul began at once to preach in the synagogues of Damascus, to the amazement of all who heard him, proclaiming Jesus to be the 'Son of God and proving Him to be the Messiah. A plot of the Jews against his life was discovered, and the disciples helped him to escape from the city (vs. 20-25; 2 Cor. 11:32-33). When he came to Jerusalem the disciples there were afraid of him at first; but Barnabas introduced him to the Apostles, and told them of the manner of his conversion, which had taken place three years before (Gal. 1:18). He carried on his testimony among the Grecian Jews of the city till his life was in danger again. Then the brethren took him down to Cæsarea and sent him on to Tarsus (vs. 26-30).

4. Peter's Work in Judea (9:31-43). In the meantime the persecution of the Christians seems to have subsided when no longer led by Saul, and the Church throughout Palestine was enjoying a time of peace and growth (v. 31). Peter made a tour of visitation among the believers in the maritime district of Judea. In the course of it he healed Aeneas of the palsy at Lydda (vs. 32-35), and raised Dorcas to life at Joppa (vs. 36-43). These miracles resulted in many turning to the Lord throughout the region. The story of Dorcas, with its vivid details, illustrates the place and influence of women in the early Church. It also reveals Luke's sympathy for womanhood, and especially for widows. This is manifested both in his Gospel and in the Acts.

THE EXTENSION OF THE GOSPEL TO THE GENTILES
(Chs. 10—12)

While Peter was at Joppa, another important step was taken in the development of the Church, which resulted in the reception of the first Gentile convert. The story shows how the Divine initiative prepared for it on both sides—in the heart of the devout Gentile and in the mind of the Jewish Apostle. The brethren in Jerusalem approved of Peter's action when he reported the matter to them, and the narrative goes on to tell of the way that the Gospel was preached in Antioch to Gentiles outside the limits of Judaism, and how a Christian church was established in that great Greek city.

1. The Conversion of Cornelius (Ch. 10). Cornelius was an army officer in the Roman headquarters at Cæsarea, who had learned to believe in God and worship Him. He was a representative of those God-fearing Gentiles who were attracted by the worship of the Jewish synagogue, but did not become proselytes and submit to the ceremonial law. He received an angelic message which commended his devout life and instructed him to send to Joppa for Simon Peter (vs. 1-8). In the meantime Peter was being prepared on his part by a vision that he saw in a trance while at prayer on the house-top, which showed him that the ceremonial distinction between the clean and the unclean was now abolished (vs. 9-16). While he was wondering what the vision might mean, the messengers of Cornelius arrived. Peter received them, and next day went with them (vs. 17-23).

When Peter arrived in Cæsarea, he found Cornelius waiting for him, with a company of his relatives and friends whom he had gathered in his house. Peter told them why he had come, and Cornelius told him why he had sent for him (vs. 24-33). Peter then began to address them. He saw now that "God is no respecter of persons"; that is, He has no longer a chosen people whom He favours more than others: "but in every nation he that feareth him, and worketh righteousness, is acceptable to him" (vs. 34-35). Peter did not mean that such a man was thereby saved, but that he was in an acceptable state for receiving the Gospel. Hitherto it was thought that the Gospel of Christ was only for the Jews; now Peter had come to see that it was for devout and God-fearing Gentiles as well. This is not the whole truth, of course, but Peter was dealing only with the case before him.

He then went on to proclaim the story of Jesus Christ, dwelling on His miraculous ministry, His crucifixion, and His resurrection. He closed by declaring that He "is ordained of God to be the Judge of the living and the dead", and that "everyone that believeth in him shall receive remission of sins" (vs. 36-43). While Peter was yet speaking the Holy Spirit fell upon the assembled company, with manifestations similar to those of Pentecost. Peter and the Jewish disciples whom he had brought with him from Joppa saw that God had poured out the gift of the Holy Spirit on Gentile believers just as He had done on Jewish believers; and at Peter's suggestion they were baptized, and thus received into the Christian Church (vs. 44-48).

2. Peter's Report of the Case (11:1-18). When Peter returned to Jerusalem he was challenged by believing Jews of the legalist type for his fellow-

ship with "men uncircumcised" (vs. 1-3). He then proceeded to give a full report of the matter to the Apostles and the members of the church (vs. 4-14). After relating all the circumstances that led him to the house of Cornelius, he said that when he began to speak "the Holy Spirit fell on them, even as on us at the beginning"; and he went on to declare that since God had given the same gift to Gentiles as to Jews when they believed in the Lord Jesus Christ, who was he, that he could withstand God? His hearers were silenced, and praised God for granting salvation to the Gentiles (vs. 15-18).

3. The Church Established in Antioch (11:19-30). This passage takes up the story of the spread of the Gospel begun in 8:4, and carries it beyond Palestine. The disciples who had been scattered into countries outside Palestine during the persecution proclaimed the Gospel wherever they went, but only to Jews. But some of those who came to Antioch preached to pagan Greeks as well, with the result that great numbers of them believed and turned to the Lord (vs. 19-21).

When the church in Jerusalem heard of it they sent Barnabas, a man of wide sympathies, on a tour of visitation as far as Antioch. When he came and found a genuine work of grace going on he was glad, and encouraged the new believers in their devotion to the Lord. He fetched Saul from Tarsus to help in the work; and the two men remained with the church in Antioch for a year. It was there that the name "Christians" was first used to distinguish the disciples. Given as a nick-name to begin with, it was gradually adopted as a title of honour (vs. 22-26).

During a famine in the reign of Claudius, which occurred in A.D. 45-46, and of which they had been warned beforehand by prophets from Jerusalem, the disciples in Antioch sent help of their own accord to their afflicted brethren in Judea, and thus proved that the Gentile church in Antioch possessed the same spirit of unselfish love that was first manifested in the Jewish church in Jerusalem. This help was taken to the elders in Judea by Barnabas and Saul (vs. 27-30).

4. The Persecution of the Church in Jerusalem (Ch. 12). Hitherto persecution had come from the religious leaders of Israel. The persecution by Herod Agrippa I, who was king of all Palestine from A.D. 41 to 44, was the first that came from the civil authorities. It was directed against the Christian leaders, and occurred at the time of the Passover. The Apostle James was put to death, the first of the Twelve to be martyred. When Herod found it pleased the Jews, he proceeded against Peter also (vs. 1-4).

In answer to the earnest prayers of the church, Peter was delivered from prison during the night by an angel of the Lord (vs. 5-11). He made his way to the house of Mary, the mother of John Mark, where many were praying. He told them of his miraculous deliverance, and asked them to report the matter to James the Lord's brother, who by this time seems to have become the chief pastor of the church.

The whole incident gives an interesting and illuminating glimpse of early church life in Jerusalem (vs. 12-19). Soon afterwards Herod met his death at Cæsarea, smitten by the hand of God for accepting divine acclaim from the people at a state function (vs. 20-23). In spite of all opposition the Gospel continued to spread and the Church to grow. Meanwhile Barnabas and Saul returned to Antioch from their mission in Jerusalem, taking with them John Mark (vs. 24-25).

THE FIRST GENTILE MISSION
(Chs. 13—14)

The narrative now turns to the church at Antioch in order to take up the story of the evangelization of the Gentile world, which was carried on from that centre. This theme occupies the rest of the book. Barnabas and Saul were sent out on the first missionary enterprise of the Christian Church. These chapters contain the story of their mission.

1. The Origin of the Mission (13:1-4). It was undertaken under the leadership of the Holy Spirit, exercised through the corporate fellowship of a group of preachers and teachers in the church at Antioch. As they waited on the Lord with fasting and prayer, seeking His mind on the subject of evangelizing, the Holy Spirit led them to a unanimous conviction that Barnabas and Saul should be set apart for this work. Accordingly, with further prayer and fasting, these two men were solemnly dedicated by the church. Assured of the leading of the Holy Spirit in their mission, they went down to the port of Antioch and sailed for Cyprus, taking John Mark as their assistant.

2. The Gospel in Cyprus (13:5-12). The plan followed by the missionaries was to preach first in the synagogues of the Jews. They went through the island in this way to Paphos, the seat of the Roman governor. Here occurred their first conflict with the demonic power of the heathen world. They met it in the person of a renegade Jew who was practising sorcery. He opposed the missionaries in the presence of the Roman governor Sergius Paulus, who had sent for them to hear their message. Paul now came to the front as the real leader of the party, and he is called by the new name from this point onward. He at once denounced the false prophet and called down a divine judgment of temporary blindness upon him. All this resulted in the conversion of the governor to the faith.

3. In Antioch of Pisidia (13:13-52). When Paul and Barnabas crossed to the mainland of Asia Minor, John Mark left them and went home to Jerusalem. The reason is not stated, but it was evidently not to Mark's credit (15:38). The two missionaries went up into the highlands of the interior as far as Antioch, a city of Pisidia, which was a district in the southern part of the Roman province of Galatia. As their custom was, they attended the Jewish synagogue on the Sabbath day, and the rulers of the synagogue gave the visiting Jews an opportunity to speak to the people (vs. 13-15).

The address which Paul gave on this occasion is reported at length. He traced the dealings of God with Israel from their deliverance out of Egypt to the reign of David (vs. 16-22). Then he declared that of David's seed God had raised up a Saviour in the person of Jesus, whose coming John the Baptist had proclaimed beforehand (vs. 23-25). The Apostle went on to appeal to his Jewish hearers and the

God-fearing Gentiles among them. The rulers in Jerusalem, in their ignorance of the prophecies, had fulfilled them by condemning Him. Without finding any ground for putting Him to death, they asked Pilate to crucify Him. When He was laid in the tomb, God raised Him up from the dead, and He was seen for many days by His Galilean followers, who were now His witnesses (vs. 26-31).

Paul then proceeded to enlarge upon the fact that Jesus was raised from the dead never to die again, quoting several Old Testament passages to confirm this. On the ground of this fact he proclaimed the Gospel—through this Jesus, forgiveness of sins, and such justification as the Law of Moses could not give, may be had by all who believe (vs. 32-39). He closed with a warning from the Prophets about the peril of despising the work of God (vs. 40-41).

This address made a deep impression, and the people besought Paul and Barnabas to repeat the message on the next Sabbath. Some of them, both Jews and proselytes, showed signs of faith, and the missionaries urged them "to continue in the grace of God" (vs. 42-43).

On the next Sabbath a great throng gathered to hear them, and this roused the prejudice of the Jews, who now proceeded to oppose the Gospel. Paul and Barnabas then deliberately pronounced the divine judgment. It was necessary to proclaim the Word of God to the Jews first, but they had refused it and thus showed themselves unworthy of it. The missionaries would now turn to the Gentiles and offer it to them, for it was God's purpose, as revealed in Isa. 49:6, that this salvation should be for all the world. The Gentiles then heard the news with gladness. "As many as were ordained to eternal life believed"; that is, as many as were disposed for it and fell in with the divine order regarding it. The reference is not to a decree of God ordaining the result, but to the preparation of heart in those that believed (vs. 44-48).

The Gospel began to spread throughout the whole region. But the Jews stirred up a persecution against Paul and Barnabas through the influential Gentile women who attended the synagogue and the leading men of the city, and had them driven out. They departed for Iconium, about eighty miles to the south-east, leaving behind a group of disciples rejoicing in their new life, with the presence of the Holy Spirit in their midst (vs. 49-52).

4. Evangelizing South Galatia (14:1-20). The experience of Antioch was repeated in Iconium. The missionaries preached in the synagogue, with the result that many Jews and Greeks believed; but the unbelieving Jews stirred up the Gentiles against them. Paul and Barnabas remained there a considerable time, their preaching being accompanied by miraculous signs confirming the truth of the Gospel (vs. 1-3). The city was divided over them; and finally, when they were about to be mobbed, they went on into Lycaonia, another district of South Galatia, which contained the cities of Lystra and Derbe; and they proceeded to evangelize that region (vs. 4-7).

At Lystra Paul healed a man who had been a cripple from his birth: and the pagan people, taking the two Apostles for gods come down to earth in the form of men, got ready to offer sacrifice to them (vs. 8-13). The names of the deities which the people applied to Barnabas and Paul throw light on the personal appearance of the two men, for Jupiter was supposed to have a sedate and imposing appearance as the father of the gods, while Mercury was the active messenger of the gods and spoke for them.

When the missionaries became aware of it, they rushed in among the people with their garments rent in grief and dismay, and declared themselves to be only men. They turned the pagan people from their purpose by telling them of "a living God", who created the world, and who left the nations to walk in their own ways but showed His goodness in providing food for them (vs. 14-18). But the Jews from Antioch and Iconium succeeded in turning the friendliness of the heathen people into hostility. Paul was stoned and dragged out of the city, and left for dead. But he rose up and next day went with Barnabas on to Derbe (vs. 19-20).

5. The Return Journey (14:21-28). Although Derbe was within easy reach of Tarsus, Paul's old home, yet the Apostles turned back when they had established a church there, and re-visited their converts in the other cities where they had been, confirming the faith of the disciples, telling them that "through many tribulations we must enter into the kingdom of God", and appointing elders in each church (vs. 21-24). They went back by sea to Antioch, to the church that had sent them out, without visiting Cyprus again. When they arrived they gave a report of their mission, telling what God had wrought through them, and showing how He had made salvation by faith free to the Gentiles. After that they remained some little time with the church in Antioch (vs. 25-28).

This account of the first Gentile mission, which probably covered about two years, showed the methods that Paul followed in his evangelization of the Gentile world. He aimed at the cities and large centres of population along the main highways. He offered the Gospel first to the Jews in the synagogues, proving from their own Scriptures that Jesus was the promised Messiah. But everywhere the Jews as a people showed the same implacable hostility when they found the Gentiles sharing the Gospel. While some accepted it, the mass of the Jews refused it, and stirred up a bitter persecution against the missionaries. The heathen were usually friendly, and their friendship was turned into hostility only through Jewish instigation. The missionaries organized their converts into churches under the care of elders, and left them to evangelize their own districts. The churches were expected to be indigenous and self-supporting.

THE FIRST CHRISTIAN COUNCIL
(Ch. 15)

There was a party in the church at Jerusalem, composed mainly of converts from the Pharisees, who did not agree with the free offer of the Gospel to the Gentiles. Some of them came down to Antioch and opposed the methods of Paul and Barnabas. This was the occasion of the first Christian council, the story of which is recorded in this chapter.

1. The Question at Issue (vs. 1-5). The Judaizers taught that salvation was limited to those who conformed to the ceremonial law, and that Gentiles should be circumcised before they could be saved.

This opposition to Paul and Barnabas, who stood for the liberty of the Gospel and salvation by faith in Christ alone, caused great dissension in the church at Antioch. The question was referred to the Apostles and elders in Jerusalem, and a deputation was sent up with Paul and Barnabas to confer with them about it. On their way the two missionaries told the story of the conversion of the Gentiles to the churches in the districts through which they passed. When they arrived in Jerusalem they told the story to the whole church there.

2. The Question Considered (vs. 6-21). When the Apostles and elders met to consider the matter, all the facts regarding it were first related. Peter told how God had chosen him as the first to preach the Gospel to the Gentiles, and had confirmed their faith by giving them the Holy Spirit, making no distinction between Gentile and Jewish believers; and he added an appeal to put no additional burden on the disciples (vs. 6-11). Paul and Barnabas then rehearsed the story of what God had wrought through them among the Gentiles (v. 12). Finally James, who seems to have presided over the council, summed up the case, stating that the preaching of the Gospel to the Gentiles, which God had used Simon Peter to begin, was in accordance with His purpose as declared in the Prophets.

In support of this James quoted Amos 9:11-12, where the Lord's promise to restore the broken down house of David, which was fulfilled in the birth of Jesus Christ in the family of David, is followed by its purpose: "that the residue of men may seek after the Lord, and all the Gentiles, upon whom my name is called" (vs. 13-18). A Saviour was to be raised up in the house of David for all men, the Gentiles as well as the Jews. James' quotation is a free rendering of the original passage. The phrase, "after these things", does not mean, after the Gospel has been preached to the Gentiles. It is James' paraphrase of Amos' phrase, "in that day", and refers to the day of the Messiah, the age of salvation. He then gave his judgment, that they should not impose the ceremonial law upon Gentile believers, but enjoin them to abstain from the sins and pollutions of their former heathenism and from eating things that would offend their Jewish brethren (vs. 19-21).

3. The Question Settled (vs. 22-34). It was decided to send a chosen deputation back with Paul and Barnabas, with a letter of greeting to the Gentile brethren containing the judgment of the council. The letter shows that the judgment was reached by arriving at unanimity, and not by the vote of a majority. It was therefore regarded as the mind of the Holy Spirit: "It seemed good to us, having come to one accord" (v. 25); "it seemed good to the Holy Spirit, and to us" (v. 28). The letter was received with joy in the church of Antioch; and the deputies from Jerusalem, Judas and Silas, being prophets themselves, gave messages of comfort and exhortation.

4. Preparing for Another Mission (vs. 35-41). After teaching and preaching for some time in Antioch, Paul suggested to Barnabas that they revisit the churches which they had founded on their former mission. Barnabas wished to take John Mark, but Paul thought it unwise to take one who had failed them before. The contention between the two men resulted in their separation. But it was over-ruled, so that two missions went out instead of one. Barnabas took Mark and sailed for Cyprus. Paul chose Silas and set out, with the prayers of the church, on his second missionary journey. Here we see the very strength of Barnabas' character becoming a source of weakness when not balanced by good judgment. Paul was the wiser leader when the interests of the Church as a whole were involved, and apparently the church in Antioch sided with him. Later on Paul and Barnabas were reconciled, and Mark was restored to Paul's full confidence (Col. 4: 10; Philemon 24; 2 Tim. 4:11).

PAUL'S EUROPEAN MISSION
(Chs. 16—18)

The Church had now been established and its character determined. Jews and Gentiles had been brought into one body, united by the common possession of the Holy Spirit. It only remained to tell how this body spread abroad. It came to its full strength, not among the Jews in Jerusalem, but among the Gentiles in Antioch. Peter has been mentioned for the last time, and the Jewish church now recedes out of view. Paul, the Apostle of the Gentiles, occupies the whole field from this time on. The story of his second missionary journey in these chapters tells how he carried the Gospel into Europe, and shows how the Church went on advancing in triumphant conflict with heathenism.

1. Revisiting the Churches in Galatia (16:1-10). Paul and his companion travelled from Antioch through Syria and Cilicia into southern Galatia, revisiting the churches on their way, confirming them in the faith, and delivering the decrees of the council of Jerusalem. At Lystra Paul chose young Timothy to be his companion and fellow-worker. He was the son of a Jewish mother and a Gentile father, and was held in high regard by the churches of the district (vs. 1-5). He had been converted during Paul's first missionary journey, for the Apostle calls him his "true child in the faith" (1 Tim. 1:2), and he had been brought up in a pious family (2 Tim. 1:5). The story of the journey through Asia Minor to Troas shows that Paul recognized and followed the guidance of the Holy Spirit, though we are not told how this was manifested to him (vs. 6-8). At Troas he had the vision that led the missionary party to cross over into Europe (vs. 9-10).

At this point the writer begins to use the first personal pronoun. He drops it when the missionaries leave Philippi (17:1), and continues in the third person till Paul arrives at Philippi again on the return journey of his third mission several years later (20:5). Then he resumes the first person and continues it to the end of the book. This may mean that Luke joined Paul first at Troas on the present mission, remained with the new church at Philippi till the Apostle returned to visit it on his next mission, and then joined Paul again and became his constant companion afterwards. It is just as likely, however, that Luke was with Paul from the very beginning as his medical attendant and was an eye-witness of all his missionary work, and that, while usually writing with a detached attitude, he shows his sympathetic reaction at points of crisis and special importance in the story by re-calling his own participation in what he is recording.

2. Founding the Church in Philippi (16:11-40). The city of Philippi was "a colony" of Rome; that is, it was governed by Roman law on the plan of Rome itself. It had no synagogue, but there was a "place of prayer" outside the city where Jews and God-fearing Gentiles worshipped on the Sabbath day. The missionaries went and spoke to the women that were gathered there (vs. 11-13). As a result Lydia, a devout proselyte, who was an agent for the purple goods of Thyatira, was led into the light of the Gospel as Paul explained it, and she and her household were baptized. It is evidence of her conversion that she constrained Paul and his company to accept her hospitality and make her house their headquarters. She was evidently a woman of means with a home of considerable size (vs. 11-15).

Paul cured a demonized girl one day (vs. 16-18); and her masters, who could make no more gain out of her, dragged Paul and Silas before the magistrates and charged them with disturbing the city. The missionaries were beaten, cast into prison, and put in the stocks (vs. 19-24). There they were praying and praising God at midnight, when an earthquake opened the prison doors and released the prisoners. Seeing this the jailer was about to kill himself, when Paul intervened, calling out that all the prisoners were still there (vs. 25-28).

Then his attitude toward Paul and Silas completely changed. He took them into his house and asked how to be saved. The result was that he and his household were baptized. The fruits of his conversion were manifest in his act of kindness to the missionaries (vs. 29-34). The next day, when the magistrates sent officers to have the missionaries released, Paul told them that their punishment had been illegal because they were Roman citizens, and required the magistrates to set right the wrong by coming themselves to release them. This sobered the Roman magistrates, who, fearing the consequences to themselves, came and besought them to leave the city (vs. 35-40).

3. In Thessalonica and Berea (17:1-15). Passing through the smaller towns, Paul and Silas went on to the large city of Thessalonica, where there was a synagogue of the Jews. There Paul preached Christ on three successive Sabbath days, following his usual method of showing from the Old Testament Scriptures that Jesus was the promised Messiah. Some Jews believed and threw in their lot with Paul and Silas; and so did a large number of the God-fearing Greeks and a considerable number of the chief women (vs. 1-4).

But the Jews stirred up a riot by inciting some of the rabble of the city to attack the home of Jason, where the missionaries were staying. When they could not find them, they dragged Jason himself before the rulers of the city, crying out that he had received into his house "these that have turned the world upside down", and who, they insinuated, were preaching treason. The rulers evidently did not find the missionaries guilty, but they took security from Jason for the good conduct of his guests (vs. 5-9).

The brethren at once sent Paul and Silas away by night to Berea. There they found the Jews "more noble than those in Thessalonica", for they received the word with a ready mind and tested its truth by the Scriptures. The result was that many of the Jews believed, and also many Greeks of high standing, both men and women (vs. 10-12). But the Jews showed their persistent hostility as a people to the Gospel by coming from Thessalonica and stirring up trouble. Then the brethren sent Paul away while Silas and Timothy remained. The Apostle was taken to Athens, and from there he sent back word for Silas and Timothy to join him with all speed (vs. 13-15).

4. Preaching in Athens (17:16-34). While Paul waited in Athens his spirit was stirred by the sight of the idols that filled the city. He reasoned in the synagogue on the Sabbath days and in the market place on other days, preaching Jesus and the Resurrection. Some of the Epicurean and Stoic philosophers, the prevailing schools of the time, came across him and brought him to Mars' Hill, the meeting-place of the Areopagus or court of Athens, to hear what this novel teaching of his meant (vs. 16-21).

Paul began by addressing the Athenians in the style of their own orators: "Ye men of Athens". He noticed as he passed through their city that they were "very religious": they had so many objects of worship. Among these he found one altar erected "To an unknown god". It was the God whom they worshipped without knowing Him that he would set forth unto them (vs. 22-23). Then he went on to sketch natural theology for his cultured audience. The Creator of the world dwells not in temples made by man and needs not the service of man, for He Himself is the source of all life. He made all nations of one race, and set them in their appointed times and places, that they might seek after Him and find Him, though He is not far from us. "In him we live, and move", declared Paul, "and have our being"; and he quoted similar words from two of their own poets (vs. 24-28).

Therefore we ought not to think that the Godhead is like anything that can be made by the art or device of man. He has overlooked this ignorance in the past, but now He calls men everywhere to repent, for He has appointed a day when He will judge the world by a Man whom He has raised from the dead (vs. 29-31). When Paul spoke of the resurrection of the dead, some of his hearers mocked; but others expressed a wish to hear him again. Apparently no church was formed in Athens, but Paul's work was not fruitless, for he left a few believers there, one of whom was a member of the Areopagus (vs. 32-34).

5. Establishing the Church in Corinth (18:1-17). When Paul came to Corinth, he worked at his trade as a tentmaker in the house of Aquila and Priscilla, who had recently come from Rome because the Emperor had banished the Jews from the capital. Every Sabbath day he bore witness to Christ in the synagogue (vs. 1-4). When Silas and Timothy joined him, he became still more zealous in his testimony to the Jews. When they opposed him and railed at the Gospel, he delivered himself of his responsibility for them and turned to the Gentiles, teaching in the home of a certain Titus Justus close to the synagogue (vs. 5-7). Crispus, the ruler of the synagogue, believed and many of the Corinthians besides. Paul was encouraged by a vision of the Lord in the night, and remained a year and a half among them (vs. 8-11).

When Gallio was made governor of Achaia (A.D. 52), the Jews of Corinth brought Paul before him on the charge of teaching an illegal religion. Paul was about to answer, but Gallio dismissed the charge as not being a criminal matter, and drove the Jews from his judgment-seat. The mob of the city then turned against the Jews, and attacked Sosthenes, who had succeeded Crispus as the ruler of the synagogue. Gallio took no notice of the affair, showing that he thought the Jews were getting what they deserved (vs. 12-17).

6. Subsequent Events (18:18-28). Paul remained in Corinth for some time after this, and then set sail for Syria on his return journey. Priscilla and Aquila went with him as far as Ephesus. There he spoke to the Jews in the synagogue, and when asked to remain longer, he promised to return if it were God's will (vs. 18-21). Landing at Cæsarea, he went up to greet the church in Jerusalem, and then went on to Antioch. There he remained for some time before setting out on another journey (vs. 22-23).

In the meantime an Alexandrian Jew named Apollos, a man of culture, well versed in the Scriptures, came to Ephesus. He had a zealous spirit and began to speak in the synagogue, teaching about Jesus, but knowing only John's baptism of repentance. Priscilla and Aquila taught him more fully, telling him, no doubt, of the exaltation of Jesus as the Christ and the subsequent coming of the Holy Spirit. When Apollos went over to Achaia, the brethren commended him to the disciples there. He greatly helped the church in Corinth by publicly proving to the Jews from the Scriptures that Jesus was the Christ (vs. 24-28).

PAUL'S EPHESIAN MISSION
(Chs. 19—20)

The headquarters of Paul's work during what is usually called his third missionary journey were at Ephesus. The church was established in that city, and the whole surrounding country, the Roman province of Asia, was evangelized during his three years' stay there. After that he made a short visit to Greece, and then set his face toward Jerusalem.

1. Establishing the Church in Ephesus (Ch. 19). Paul reached Ephesus, in fulfilment of his promise to return, by going overland and visiting the churches on the way (18:20-23). He found some twelve disciples there who had received only John's baptism of repentance, and had not heard of the Pentecostal gift of the Holy Spirit. They had probably been influenced by the teaching of Apollos before Apollos himself was led into the light. Paul instructed them more fully, and they were baptized "into the name of the Lord Jesus", having now come to believe in Jesus as Lord (vs. 1-7). The representative nature of what happened on this occasion is seen in its similarity to the case of the Samaritans (8:15-17).

Paul taught in the synagogue for three months, and then the usual Jewish opposition to "the Way" forced him to leave it. After that he taught daily for two years in the school of Tyrannus, one of the public halls used by teachers of philosophy. From this centre he carried on a ministry of healing as well as teaching, and the Gospel spread throughout the whole province of Asia (vs. 8-12). The discomfiture of the Jewish exorcists, who tried to imitate Paul in casting out demons, became widely known and produced a feeling of awe regarding the name of the Lord Jesus. Many who practised magical arts burned their books in a great public bonfire. "So mightily grew the word of the Lord and prevailed" (vs. 13-20). The price of the books would be nearly ten thousand dollars in our money.

Paul now made some far-reaching plans. He intended to visit the churches that he had founded in Europe, and he sent two of his companions ahead of him. He would then go to Jerusalem, and afterwards carry out his desire to see Rome (vs. 21-22). His purpose in the meantime was to gather a contribution from the Gentile Christians for the relief of the poor in the mother-church. This would be a manifest demonstration of the spirit of love which bound all Christians, both Jews and Gentiles, into one body.

About that time a riot occurred in Ephesus, stirred up by the silversmiths under Demetrius, whose business of making silver shrines of Diana, the goddess of the Ephesians, was being affected by the spread of the Gospel (vs. 23-28). The people of the city seized two of Paul's companions and rushed into the theatre. Paul would have gone in to speak to them, but was dissuaded by the disciples and by his friends among the Roman officials. The story is told with great vividness. We are shown the characteristic behaviour of the many-headed mob, moved by passion and prejudice, and the wisdom and tactfulness of the town-clerk in appeasing the multitude and finally dismissing the assembly (vs. 29-41). This incident illustrates the fact that the Roman officials were usually friendly to Paul. They did not oppose the Gospel in its early days. Opposition came first from the Jews.

2. Visiting Greece Again (20:1-16). This riot hastened Paul's departure from Ephesus. He went through Macedonia, visiting the churches there, and then spent three months in Corinth. A Jewish plot caused him to change his plan for sailing to Syria, and he returned through Macedonia (vs. 1-3). The men that are mentioned as Paul's travelling companions from the various churches were deputies appointed in connection with the collection that was being made for the church in Jerusalem. This is inferred from Paul's letters to the Corinthians, the first of which was written before Paul left Ephesus and the second from some place in Macedonia on his way to Corinth (1 Cor. 16:1-4; 2 Cor. 9:1-2). The Passover was already past when he sailed from Philippi for Troas (vs. 4-6). Luke resumes the first personal pronoun at this point and continues it to the end of the book.

While at Troas, where he stayed a week, Paul spoke to the disciples and observed the Lord's Supper with them at a gathering which lasted all through the night. During the meeting he raised to life a young man who had fallen down from a window. The story gives us a glimpse of the fellowship of a Christian group in a heathen town (vs. 7-12). Then the party took a coasting vessel down past Ephesus to Miletus, for Paul was hastening to reach Jerusalem by the day of Pentecost (vs. 13-16).

3. Addressing the Elders of Ephesus (20:17-38). Having sent for them to come down to Miletus, he gave them a farewell address of great earnestness and tenderness. He reminded them of his ministry among them in proclaiming the Gospel to Jew

and Gentile alike (vs. 17-21). He was now going to Jerusalem in the face of tribulation that awaited him, intent on finishing the ministry which he had received from the Lord, and they should see his face no more (vs. 22-25). He appealed to them to care for the flock over which the Holy Spirit had made them overseers, and warned them against false teachers, who, he declared, should arise among them after he was gone. He reminded them that for three years he had watched over every one with anxious care night and day (vs. 26-31).

Then the Apostle solemnly commended them to God and the word of His grace, which could "build them up and give them an inheritance among all them that are sanctified". He had not laboured for any remuneration, but had supported himself and his fellow-workers, thus giving them an example of helping the weak (vs. 32-35). The whole address breathes the fine Christian spirit of the Apostle—his earnestness and zeal, his courage and patience, his humility and self-sacrifice. The closing scene reveals the deep affection that existed between Paul and his converts (vs. 36-38).

THE ARREST IN JERUSALEM
(Chs. 21—23)

Paul's purpose in going to Jerusalem was to present the gifts of the Gentile Christians to the Jewish Christians there as a token of their love, and thus help to bind the whole Church together in unity. Luke amplifies his narrative from this point onward, showing his sense of the importance of what he is recording. The work of Paul was approaching a crisis.

1. Journeying to Jerusalem (21:1-16). Paul and his company continued their journey by sea to Tyre. Every stop on the way is carefully noted (vs. 1-3). At Tyre they found a group of Christians and remained with them several days. They urged Paul, through the Spirit, not to go to Jerusalem, and bade him a tender farewell when the ship continued its voyage (vs. 4-6). At Ptolemais, the modern Acre, they greeted the brethren, and stayed with them one day before going on by land to Cæsarea, where they abode for several days with Philip the evangelist and his four daughters (vs. 7-9).

While they were there, a prophet came from Judea and foretold that Paul would be arrested by the Jews in Jerusalem and delivered to the Gentiles. His friends besought him not to go up, but he refused to yield to their entreaties, and they submitted to God's will in the matter (vs. 10-14). Some of the disciples of Cæsarea accompanied Paul and his party to Jerusalem (vs. 15-16).

Every step of the journey from Macedonia is minutely traced in the narrative. The affectionate interest of the Christian community in the Apostle is manifested in every place. The warnings he received through the Spirit about what would happen to him in Jerusalem gave him an opportunity to turn aside from his course if he wished. The way in which the whole story is told goes to show that Paul had counted the cost.

2. Arrested in the Temple (21:17-40). Paul and his company were received gladly by the church in Jerusalem; and the Apostle reported to James and the elders what God had wrought among the Gentiles. They praised God when they heard of it, and then they made a proposal to Paul intended to meet the prejudice of the Jewish believers who still clung to the Law and had heard false reports about him (vs. 17-22). They suggested that he associate himself with four men who were under a Nazirite vow, and undertake the expense of the sacrifices necessary in their case, in order to show publicly that he himself observed the Mosaic Law. To this Paul consented, and he showed himself in the Temple for the purpose (vs. 23-26).

The seven days required for the purification were almost ended, when some Jews from the province of Asia saw Paul in the Temple and raised a cry that he had defiled the holy place by bringing Greeks into it. They had seen an Ephesian with him in the city before that. This roused the Jewish mob to fury, and they dragged Paul out of the Temple precincts and were about to kill him, when the captain of the Roman garrison heard of it (vs. 27-31). Hurrying down with his soldiers from the fort which overlooked the Temple courts, he took Paul out of the hands of the Jews, had him bound with chains, and ordered him to be brought into the fort, while the violent crowd surged after him, crying out for his death (vs. 32-36).

Paul asked for a word with the captain, who was surprised to find that he could speak Greek and was not the notorious Egyptian rebel that he thought he was. Paul declared that he was a Jew of Tarsus, "a citizen of no mean city", and asked permission to speak to the people. When leave was given, he stood on the steps of the fort, and with his characteristic gesture began to speak to them in Hebrew (vs. 37-40).

3. Addressing the Jewish People (Ch. 22). When the crowd heard him speaking in their own tongue, they sobered into silence and listened quietly (vs. 1-2). He told them of his strict Jewish up-bringing and his zeal for the Law, and of his persecution of the Christians (vs. 3-5). Then he described how he saw a vision of the Lord Jesus at Damascus and was converted to the Christian faith (vs. 6-16). When he returned to Jerusalem and was praying in the Temple, the Lord appeared to him in a trance and told him to depart quickly out of the city, for they would not receive his testimony there, and added, "I will send thee forth far hence unto the Gentiles" (vs. 17-21).

As soon as Paul uttered that hated word, the fury of the Jewish mob broke out again. The captain had him brought into the fort, and was about to have him examined by scourging to know the cause of such an outcry against him, when Paul quietly asked the officer in charge of the soldiers if it were lawful to scourge a Roman citizen (vs. 22-25). The officer warned the captain, and an immediate change took place in his attitude towards his prisoner, especially when he found that Paul had inherited his Roman citizenship (vs. 26-29).

4. Before the Jewish Council (23:1-11). Next day the Roman captain summoned the Jewish Council to meet and brought his prisoner before them (22:30). Paul began courteously, but was interrupted by the high priest commanding him to be smitten on the mouth. Probably he had been roused to fury by Paul's first statement, which described a life that was very different from his own. Paul rebuked him at once for his violation of the law as a

judge, and then apologized for not having shown sufficient reverence to the office of the high priest (vs. 1-5). Though spoken with indignation, the Apostle's words were a prophecy, fulfilled some years later in the assassination of Ananias.

When Paul saw that the Council was composed of the two rival parties of Pharisees and Sadducees, he raised a division between them by declaring he was a Pharisee, and that the case against him turned on the question of the resurrection of the dead. The dissension became so great that the Roman soldiers had to rescue Paul from the Jewish Council (vs. 6-10). That night Paul received a message of assurance from the Lord: as he had borne witness at Jerusalem, so he should bear witness also at Rome (v. 11).

5. Taken to Cæsarea (23:12-35). The bitter and implacable nature of Jewish hostility to Paul is shown in the plot to kill him, made next day by a band of more than forty fanatical Jews, with the connivance of the religious leaders (vs. 12-15). Paul's nephew heard of the conspiracy, and came and told him of it. Paul had one of the officers take the young man to the chief captain and disclose to him the nature of the conspiracy (vs. 16-22). The Roman official immediately made arrangements to send Paul to Cæsarea before morning, under a strong guard of soldiers and horsemen, with a letter to Felix the Roman governor describing his case (vs. 23-30). They took him by night as far as Antipatris, more than half way. From there the footmen returned, while the horsemen went on with Paul to Cæsarea and presented him to the governor. Felix questioned Paul, and promised to hear his case when his accusers were come (vs. 31-35).

THE IMPRISONMENT IN CÆSAREA
(Chs. 24—26)

This section covers a period of two years, in which there is little advance. It serves, however, to show how incurable was the hatred of the Jews for the Gospel, and how Paul was finally taken to Rome.

1. Paul and Felix (Ch. 24). Five days after Paul's arrival, the high priest and elders came down with a lawyer to plead their case before the governor. Tertullus the lawyer began by flattering Felix, and went on to accuse Paul of stirring up insurrection among the Jews of the world as a ringleader of the sect of the Nazarenes, and of attempting to profane the Temple (vs. 1-9). When Tertullus had finished his charge, Felix gave a sign to Paul to speak.

The dignified courtesy with which the Apostle began his address is in contrast with the hypocritical flattery of Tertullus (vs. 10-11). He denied the charge of stirring up a crowd anywhere, but confessed himself a Christian, serving the God of his fathers, believing the Law and the Prophets, and looking forward, as his accusers themselves did, to the resurrection, and exercising himself in this faith with a good conscience toward God and man (vs. 12-16). He came bringing alms to his people, and they found him presenting offerings of purification in the Temple with no crowd or tumult. The Jews from Asia, who caused his arrest in the Temple, ought to have been here if they had anything against him. Let these elders say what wrong-doing was found in him before the Council, except that he stood up for the resurrection of the dead (vs. 17-21).

Seeing that no case had been made against Paul, Felix deferred judgment until Lysias the chief captain should come down. While Paul was kept a prisoner, he was given a certain amount of freedom, and his friends were allowed to minister to him (vs. 22-23). Felix, who had a Jewish wife, Drusilla, whom he had recently induced to desert her former husband, sent for Paul again and again to hear about the faith in Jesus Christ. His conscience was deeply moved by the Apostle; but he hoped for a bribe from him, and kept him a prisoner for two years, till he was succeeded in the office of governor by Festus (vs. 22-27).

2. Paul and Festus (Ch. 25). When in Jerusalem, Festus foiled a plot which the Jewish leaders had laid to kill Paul, by declining their request to have him brought to Jerusalem for trial (vs. 1-5). But when Paul was being tried before him in Cæsarea, he sought to gain favour with the Jews by asking Paul if he was willing to be tried before him in Jerusalem (vs. 6-9). Then the Apostle, protesting his innocence of the charges against him, used his privilege as a Roman citizen and appealed to Cæsar's tribunal at Rome (vs. 10-12).

Soon afterwards King Agrippa, a son of Herod Agrippa I (12:1), and the last of the Herods, who reigned over a small state in north-east Palestine, came to pay his respects to Festus with his wife Bernice, who was a sister of Drusilla. The Roman governor laid Paul's case before the Jewish king (vs. 13-16). He told him that the Jews wanted Paul condemned, and yet brought no charge of wrongdoing against him, but only some question of their religion, "and of one Jesus, who was dead, whom Paul affirmed to be alive". He himself was perplexed about these things, and Paul had appealed to Cæsar (vs. 17-21). Agrippa expressed a desire to hear Paul himself; and next day Festus had Paul brought in before a public gathering of high officials and notable citizens, where Agrippa and Bernice were present with great pomp. He then explained the case to Agrippa before them all (vs. 22-27).

3. Paul and Agrippa (Ch. 26). When invited by Agrippa to speak, Paul began his address with his characteristic gesture and his usual courteous approach (vs. 1-3). His manner of life from his youth as a Pharisee was known to all the Jews. He stood there accused by the Jews because of his hope of the promise of God, the hope of all the tribes of Israel, the resurrection of the dead (vs. 4-8). Then he told of his persecution of the followers of Jesus of Nazareth, and of the transcendent light that shone about him at midday on the way to Damascus (vs. 9-13). Jesus whom he had been persecuting called him to be His witness, and sent him to turn men to God that they might receive remission of sins through faith in Him (vs. 14-18). He was not disobedient to the heavenly vision; but, beginning in Damascus, he declared to Jews and to Gentiles that they should repent and turn to God. For this reason the Jews sought to kill him. With the help of God he had continued to that day proclaiming only what Moses and the Prophets had foretold, that through the suffering and resurrection of the Messiah light should be proclaimed both to the Jews and to the Gentiles (vs. 19-23).

This is one of the noblest and most dignified of Paul's defenses. It is marked by courtesy without flattery and directness without rudeness. The Apostle addressed himself personally to Agrippa again and again. He revealed the central principle of his life to be obedience to the light and truth as he saw it (vs. 9, 19); and he brought his defense to a head as usual in a statement of the Gospel message.

Paul's words produced a deep impression on both Festus and Agrippa. Festus thought him mad; Agrippa tried to turn him aside with levity. Paul replied to both men with dignity and deep earnestness (vs. 24-29). When they withdrew and conferred together, Agrippa bore witness to Paul's innocence by remarking that he might have been set at liberty if he had not appealed to Cæsar (vs. 30-32).

THE JOURNEY TO ROME
(Chs. 27—28)

Because of his appeal as a Roman citizen from the Jews to the Emperor's tribunal, Paul must be sent to Rome. These chapters describe in graphic and minute detail the course of the long and perilous journey, and the arrival at last in Rome. In the person of the great Apostle, God's mercy was forsaking His ancient people who had rejected it, and was turning to the Gentile world. The Gospel which went out first from Jerusalem was to continue henceforth from Rome.

1. The Sea Voyage (27:1-26). Paul with some other prisoners was put in charge of a centurion, who first took a vessel sailing to the coast of Asia Minor, and then a ship of Alexandria sailing for Italy. They encountered bad weather off the coast of Crete (vs. 1-8). Paul warned against proceeding further because of the lateness of the season, but the centurion, although he had treated Paul kindly, did not take his advice. They tried to reach a better harbour farther on (vs. 9-13). Very soon the ship was caught in a tempest, and had to give way and be driven before it. The story of the storm, which lasted fourteen days, is told with great vividness. It brings out the influence exerted upon the ship's company by the strong faith of the man of God (vs. 14-26).

2. The Shipwreck (27:27-44). Paul's influence continued to keep up the confidence of the ship's company through his steadfast faith in God. The centurion's respect and concern for Paul are also apparent in the story. The number of persons in the ship shows that it must have been a vessel of very large size (v. 37).

3. The Stay on Malta (28:1-10). The story emphasizes the natural kindliness of the pagan inhabitants, and the courteous hospitality of Publius, the head man of the island (vs. 1-7). Paul healed the father of Publius of a fever by praying and laying his hands on him, and this resulted in many others coming to be cured and showing kindness to Paul and his companions (vs. 8-10).

4. From Malta to Rome (28:11-16). After three months on the island, they set sail on another ship of Alexandria, stopped at Syracuse and Rhegium, and finally landed at Puteoli, where they stayed seven days with the Christians whom they found there. The narrative shows how the interest deepened as the party approached the great capital of the Empire. Every day is accounted for. As they drew near Rome, a group of Christians came out from the city to meet Paul on the Appian Way, and when he saw them, he "thanked God, and took courage". Having arrived in Rome, Paul was allowed to dwell in his own lodging with a soldier to guard him.

5. Paul in Rome (28:17-31). Three days after his arrival, the Apostle called together the principal Jews and reported his case to them. They were impressed by him and wished to get a full statement of his views, for everywhere the Christian sect was spoken against (vs. 17-22). On an appointed day, a large and representative group of the Jewish community came to him. He spent the whole day explaining the Gospel, showing that Jesus Christ was the fulfilment of the Law and the Prophets. But they disagreed among themselves, their general attitude being one of disbelief. Paul gave them a final warning, and declared that "this salvation of God" would be offered to the Gentiles, and they would hear (vs. 23-29).

The importance of this conference with the leaders of the Jewish community in Rome consists in its being the occasion of the rejection of the Messiah by the most representative Jews of the Dispersion. The Acts closes with the same judgment on Jewish unbelief as was pronounced in the Gospels (vs. 25-27; John 12:37-40). Paul remained for two years in Rome before his case was decided, preaching the Kingdom of God and proclaiming the Gospel of Christ without hindrance, to all who came to him (vs. 30-31)

Although the book seems to close abruptly, yet there is a tone of finality in the closing words. Luke uses the full title of the Saviour in his last sentence for the first and only time. He seems to realize that the theme of his whole narrative has come to its climax. Everywhere the Jews have been offered God's salvation first, and everywhere they have refused it. Israel is now to be definitely set aside, and henceforth the Church is to bear its own witness to the Kingdom of God and to the Lord Jesus Christ.

THE NATURE OF THE CHURCH IN ACTS

The essential reality of Christianity as a new creation is seen in the nature of the Church as depicted in the Books of Acts. The Christian Church was not formed by the disciples of Jesus agreeing to unite in a voluntary association. It was brought into being by an act of God. Several marks of its Divine origin and nature are brought out in the narrative of the book.

The Holy Spirit had come to reside in its midst. When the Spirit was poured out upon the disciples on the Day of Pentecost, it was not simply a larger outpouring of an old blessing. What happened was something entirely new. It is true that the event was brought about by the same Divine Spirit who had been moving on the hearts of men in the old dispensation. But since then a new instrument had been prepared for Him to use—the perfect manhood of Jesus Christ. The Holy Spirit came now as the Spirit of the glorified Son of Man, in whose soul He had been residing and in whose life He had been living. He came to establish living and abiding relations between the disciples on earth and their risen Lord in Heaven. The Church was formed as the body of Christ (Eph. 1:24; 1 Cor. 12:27). It was the continuation, as it were, of the Incarnation.

The subsequent experiences of the disciples showed that an entirely new set of spiritual forces had come into operation. These were the powers of the Kingdom of Heaven. The new spiritual order, which was only "at hand" before, was now ready for men to enter. Those who believed had entered it at Pentecost by a new birth from above. A transcendent change had taken place in them. They found their lives charged with a sense of the spiritual presence of the Lord. He was among them again; and he was also in them. His life had become the spirit of their lives. The Holy Spirit had brought them a new kind of life, the eternal life whose quality is love, the life of Jesus Christ Himself.

There was also a new atmosphere about them, the atmosphere of the other world into which their Master had gone. They looked upon this present world from a new point of view. They belonged to a new order of being, whose seat and centre were in Heaven, and whose living springs were there in the glorified Person of their Lord. The new fellowship which they enjoyed on earth was due to their being now members of the Kingdom of Heaven.

The first effect produced upon the community around them was one of surprise and awe—"fear came upon every soul" (2:49). It was recognized that strange new powers, which were not of this world, were at work in the lives of the disciples of Christ and their first converts. The first Christian Church bore manifest marks of an immediate supernatural origin. It had sprung into being by a demonstration of the power of God.

As the community became more accustomed to the presence of the Church in its midst, and more familiar with its characteristics, this first sense of awe passed away; and it was not long before a spirit of enmity took its place. The world came to recognize that the Church was something alien to it. As the gospel spread throughout the world, the Apostles taught their converts to expect opposition and persecution: "Through many tribulations we must enter into the kingdom of God" (14:22). The Church and the world were two radically hostile systems.

The Christians in the Acts of the Apostles manifested a freedom of access to God that was not realized in Old Testament days. After Pentecost prayer assumed a new importance, as though it had entered a new field. There are some thirty different references to prayer in the Acts. When persecution threatened the Church, the disciples turned to God as naturally as children in trouble turn to a father (4:24). Prayer had become a real approach to God and real communion with Him.

It was not so in former days. Prayer in the Old Testament, though always a true expression of religious feeling, was associated with the local manifestation of God's presence in the tabernacle or the Temple. In those days God was not so near. His people could enter only into His antechamber. The congregation of Israel stood in the outer courts. But now the disciples of Christ found the inner sanctuary wide open. They realized at once that they had access to the presence-chamber of God through their crucified and risen Head. They had "boldness to enter into the holy place by the blood of Jesus" (Heb.

10:19). Thus it was that prayer became spontaneously, without the imposition of any new command, the true expression of the life of the Church and the real source of its power.

The Church had no outward organization to begin with. It was simply a new fellowship of a heavenly character. But it had power within itself to develop its own organization and to be self-propagating. The Holy Spirit residing in its midst was the secret of its corporate life. The presence of the Spirit was always recognized in the life of the Church (4:31; 5:3, 32; 9:31; 13:52). The mind of the Spirit was sought in its councils (15:28), the leadership of the Spirit in its work and activity (13: 2-4; 16:6-7), and the supervision of the Spirit in the appointment of its pastors and elders (20:28). There are between fifty and sixty references to the Holy Spirit in the course of the narrative. The Third Person of the Trinity was now in the world, and was operating among men through the Church of Christ.

Herein consists the essential reality of Christianity and the fundamental difference between Israel and the Church. Israel was organized as a nation belonging to the order of the present world. It was developed under a system of law and worship imposed from without by the hand of man. The Church began as a new creation, existing in the midst of the present world, but belonging to the order of the spiritual world. It was to be organized and developed by an entirely new principle of life, which came from Heaven and was implanted within. It was to become "a habitation of God in the Spirit" (Eph. 2:22).

THE GOSPEL THE APOSTLES PREACHED

The original Christian Gospel, the message by which Christianity was established in the world, is found in the addresses of the Apostles in the Book of Acts. The Apostles of Christ did not set out to impose their Master's teaching upon the world; nor did they present Jesus as an example for other men to follow. Their message was of a nature altogether different. They were not propagating new ideas: they were proclaiming new facts. God had done something new: He had provided a Saviour for men. Through the death and resurrection of Jesus of Nazareth, something transcendent had been accomplished, which removed the guilt of human sin and made a new kind of life possible to all men everywhere. The original Gospel was the witness the Apostles bore to this Divine event.

The first Gospel preacher was the Apostle Peter, and the first Christian sermon was delivered to the Jewish people on the Day of Pentecost (ch. 2). It proclaimed and proved the resurrection and exaltation of Jesus, whom they had crucified; and then it came to head in Peter's reply to the question of the convicted Jews: "Brethren, what shall we do?" (vs. 37-38). This reply may be summed up in two words: "Repent and surrender"—repent and turn from your old manner of life, and surrender in faith and trust to the crucified and living Christ. As a result, they should receive remission of sins and a new life should be given to them by the Holy Spirit.

Some days later Peter preached another sermon to the Jewish people (ch. 3). His theme was substantially the same as on the Day of Pentecost, the great Messianic transactions of the Cross and the

Resurrection. He dwelt more fully on the preparatory unfolding of God's redemptive purpose in the Old Testament; but he closed with the same appeal to repent and turn to Christ as the Saviour from sin (v. 26).

On two occasions Peter appeared before the Jewish Council, and each time he proclaimed the Gospel to the rulers in the same terms as he had proclaimed it to the people (4:10-12; 5:30-31). In both cases his theme was salvation from sin, and in each case this salvation was presented as the gift of God on no other ground than the death and exaltation of the Lord Jesus Christ.

Later on in the story of Acts, Peter was called to go to Cæsarea and preach the Gospel to Gentiles (ch. 10). His message was still the same. It was not a teacher, or an example, that Peter presented to Cornelius and his household, but a living Saviour, who had been dead but was now alive for evermore. He closed his address with the same appeal that he had made to the Jews (vs. 40-43).

We have no record of the preaching of any other member of the original Twelve; but as Peter was always their spokesman, there can be no doubt that his preaching represents the preaching of them all. They had but one message to give to the world, and it was entirely concerned with the redemption that Christ had accomplished. It is true that the Apostles instructed their converts in the teaching of Jesus (2:42), but there is no indication anywhere in the New Testament that they ever made any attempt to spread His teaching among the people of the world or propagate it outside the fellowship of the Church. Their one aim was to bring men and women to repentance and faith in the Lord Jesus Christ.

The Apostle Paul presented the Gospel in the Gentile world in exactly the same way as Peter had presented it in Jerusalem. The most complete record that we have of any of his addresses is the sermon he delivered in the synagogue in Antioch of Pisidia (ch. 13). As he was speaking mainly to Jews on that occasion, he naturally made his approach through the Old Testament. He passed over entirely the teaching ministry of Jesus and brought his message to a head in the facts of His death and resurrection. Then he concluded by placing the Gospel message of salvation on the ground of these facts (vs. 38-39). When the Jews in that city rejected the Gospel, Paul turned to the Gentiles; and the record implies that there was no change in his message. It was "the word of God" which the Jews had refused that the Gentiles heard with gladness (v. 48).

Paul had obviously the same message for the Gentiles as he had for the Jews. His method of approach differed, of course, for the Gentiles had not the Law and knew not the Old Testament. But Paul could find a point of contact anywhere in the Gentile world. His superior education and intellectual training gave him an approach to Greek audiences which was beyond the original Apostles of the Lord. But his message was in no essential part different from theirs. It was not something Jesus had taught, but something He had done. Even in Athens, the centre of philosophical teaching, where he might have been expected to say something about what Jesus taught, Paul did not even refer to the fact that He had been a teacher at all. After bringing the one true God who created the world before his cultured audience, his address moved straight forward to an appeal for repentance on the ground of the resurrection of Jesus (17:30-31).

The Gospel which the Apostles preached was something entirely new. It was unlike anything that the world had ever heard before. It was not another religion or another philosophy. Its supreme and unique aspect was its saving power. The Book of Acts reveals a conviction of the universal need of salvation underlying all the apostolic preaching. Peter's exhortation to the Jews on the Day of Pentecost was, "Save yourselves from this crooked generation" (2:40). To their rulers he declared that "neither is there any other name under heaven, that is given among men, wherein we must be saved" (4:12). Cornelius sent for Peter to hear words whereby, he had been told, "thou shalt be saved, thou and all thy house" (11:14). Paul characterized his message to the Jews in Antioch of Pisidia as, "the word of this salvation" (13:26); and the appeal of the jailor in Philippi, which Paul was able to meet at once with the Gospel message, was, "What must I do to be saved?" (16:30).

These incidents also show that a sense of the need of salvation existed in the hearts of men as their reason for receiving the Gospel which the Apostles preached. When the depths of any human life are probed there is always found a restless sense of something wrong, a haunting sense of something missing. This is the evidence that the soul of man has lost the way to God, and that salvation is the one fundamental need of the whole human race. This need the Apostles met by going out into the lost world of their day and preaching salvation by faith—the gift of Divine grace and not the attainment of human effort.

This message surprised the world; it was so radically different from the salvation proposed by the religions of the world and the philosophies of men. It was folly to the Greeks, and an offence to the Jews. But it was this unique feature of the Gospel that gave Christianity the headway it got in the world in that day. It could not have been devised or invented by man, and it was one of the most conclusive proofs of the reality of the Gospel message and the Divine origin of the Christian faith.

THE NEW TESTAMENT

<small>ROMANS TO REVELATION</small>

THE EPISTLES

INTRODUCTION TO THE EPISTLES

THE doctrinal part of the New Testament is composed of a collection of letters. In the Gospels we are given the foundation upon which Christianity rests. In the Acts we are told how it spread from Jerusalem out into the world of the nations around. In the Epistles we see how it began to express itself in a doctrinal form.

And yet this was not the primary purpose of these documents. What we find in them is not so much a system of Christian doctrine as a description of Christian experience. The new kind of life into which the Gospel of Jesus Christ had brought the men and women of the New Testament churches is explained in all its manifold relations, with great fulness and richness of language, in these apostolic letters. This kind of writing was especially fitted for the purpose. In a letter a subject is given much freer treatment than in a formal treatise. The personality of the writer finds fuller expression. More use is made of the circumstances of the readers. There is scope for vividness, warmth, and personal interest. Letters could thus deal most effectively with the varied needs of the Christian communities as these needs arose from time to time. They could best serve the purpose of the Holy Spirit in teaching and training the members of the Church of Christ as it spread throughout the world.

The Epistles were written with special reference to the conditions of the time. They were occasioned by particular incidents and definite circumstances, and were written for various specific reasons. The purpose of the writers was to explain more fully in writing what they had already taught orally, to correct errors into which some Christians had fallen, to meet difficulties and reform abuses which had arisen in some churches, and to comfort and strengthen the believers under trial and persecution. While they were specially intended for particular churches and particular individuals in the apostolic age, they contain the principles of faith and conduct designed by the Holy Spirit for all Christians and all churches in every age.

The authorship of the Epistles is divided among five, or probably six, different writers. Thirteen of the twenty-one letters bear the name of Paul. Another (Hebrews) has been ascribed to him by tradition, but does not bear his name. It cannot be proved to have come from his hand, though it bears the stamp of his teaching and must have come from the circle to which he belonged. These fourteen are known as the Pauline Epistles. Two epistles bear the name of the Apostle Peter. Three were written by the Apostle John, but do not contain his name. One was written by James, the Lord's brother, who was the pastor of the mother-church in Jerusalem. The last epistle bears the name of Jude, the brother of James. These seven are called the General Epistles, because most of them have in view the Church in general, and not some local church.

The readers for whom the Epistles were first intended are widely representative. They include organized churches, scattered groups of Christians, and individual believers. Nine of them were addressed to particular churches in specific localities, seven churches in all (Romans to Second Thessalonians). Two were written for Jewish Christians exclusively (Hebrews and James), and two others for Jewish converts chiefly (First and Second Peter). Two epistles were intended for believers in general, and not for any particular church or Christian group (First John and Jude). Three epistles were addressed to pastors in charge of churches (First and Second Timothy, and Titus), and three others to private Christians (Philemon, and Second and Third John).

The Epistles are not arranged in chronological order in the New Testament. The order in which they do occur, however, bears manifest evidence of the providential guidance of the Spirit of God in the collection and arrangement of the New Testament Canon. As they stand, there is a progressive development of Christian doctrine running throughout. This is shown in the following classification:

I. The Pauline Epistles. These contain the fundamental truths of the Christian faith.

1. The Epistles to Churches. These explain the doctrines on which the Church rests and by which it lives.

(1) The First Group:—Romans, First and Second Corinthians, and Galatians. These epistles explain the significance of the Cross, and deal mainly with the way of salvation from sin.

(2) The Second Group:—Ephesians, Philippians, and Colossians. These epistles explain the significance of the Resurrection and Ascension, and deal mainly with the believer's spiritual union with the Lord.

(3) The Third Group:—First and Second Thessalonians. These epistles have to do with the Second Coming of Christ, and deal with the end of the believer's life on earth and the consummation of the Christian age.

2. The Epistles to Individuals. These deal with the practical side of the Church's life and work in the world.

(1) The Pastoral Group: — First and Second Timothy, and Titus.

(2) The Private Epistle: — Philemon.

3. The Epistle to the Hebrews. This document, with its hidden authorship, explains the relation of the New Covenant to the Old, and deals with the finality of Christianity and its superiority to Judaism.

II. The General Epistles. These seven letters, written by four other apostolic authorities, confirm and supplement the teaching of the Apostle Paul. James shows that faith manifests itself in works. Peter emphasizes hope, and John emphasizes love. Jude deals with the need of maintaining the purity of the Gospel message of the grace of God.

THE EPISTLE TO THE ROMANS

NOTHING is known of the origin of the church in Rome. It had come into existence before Paul, or any other Apostle, visited Rome. Probably some of the "sojourners from Rome, both Jews and proselytes", who were in Jerusalem on the Day of Pentecost and heard Peter's sermon (Acts 2:10), carried the Gospel back with them and started a Christian fellowship. This would lay the foundation of the church. Rome was the capital of the Empire, and the roads of the world led there. Christian travellers from other parts of the Empire, visiting Rome in the interests of business and trade, would encourage the believers and help the development of the church. The story of their faith was already well-known to the other churches throughout the world (1:8).

The Christians in Rome had no central meeting-place, for it seems that groups of believers assembled in private houses in different parts of the city (16:5, 14, 15). Both Jews and Gentiles are addressed in the Epistle, but the general impression it gives is that its readers were mainly Gentiles. Probably the nucleus of the church in Rome, like the nucleus of most of the churches in the Gentile world, was composed of Jewish proselytes, or Gentiles who had been in the habit of attending the synagogue. This would account for the large use that Paul makes of the Old Testament in the course of the Epistle. Even the Gentiles among his readers would be familiar with it.

The Epistle was written in Corinth during the winter of A.D. 56-57, at the time of the Apostle's second visit to that city. This is gathered from a comparison of Acts 20:2-3, 1 Cor. 16:5-6, and Rom. 15:23-26. What gave Paul the occasion for it was his desire to visit Rome, coupled with the intended visit of Phoebe of Cenchreæ, the port of Corinth (Acts 19:21; Rom. 1:11-13; 16:1-2). The fact that she was going to Rome and needed a letter of commendation to the Christians there, gave Paul the idea of sending with her a deliberate letter addressed to the whole church. His friends Aquila and Priscilla had already gone back to Rome (Acts 18:2; Rom. 16:3).

The Apostle's purpose in writing the letter was to set forth for the Christians in the world's capital a full statement of the Gospel of God which he was preaching among the nations. It probably represents the system of Christian instruction that he had been giving in the school of Tyrannus in Ephesus during the two preceding years (Acts 19:9-10). His general theme is the Gospel as God's way of salvation. The special aspect of the Gospel that filled his mind as he wrote is the righteousness of God which it offers to unrighteous man. This theme is unfolded throughout the Epistle in such a systematic way as to make it the most closely reasoned of all the apostolic writings. The plan of its argument may be outlined as follows:

THE INTRODUCTION
(1:1-17)

Writing to a church that he had not founded and had not yet visited, Paul begins with a formal and deliberate salutation. He presents the credentials of his apostleship, and gives a brief outline of the faith which he preaches among the Gentiles. He has been set apart unto the Gospel of God, which was foretold in the Old Testament Scriptures, and concerns His Son, "Jesus Christ our Lord". Thus the full title of the Saviour is brought before the readers of the Epistle at once. He is declared to be both human and Divine. He was a descendant of David in respect of His bodily nature, and was marked out as the Son of God in respect of His spiritual nature, a nature essentially holy, by the omnipotent miracle of the Resurrection (vs. 1-4).

Then Paul goes on to say that it was from Him that he received his commission as an Apostle among all the nations, and that its sphere extends to his Roman readers. They are "beloved of God", because reconciled to Him through Christ; and they are "called to be saints", because converted by the Gospel that they might become holy. The prolonged salutation comes to a head with a benediction of "grace and peace", the characteristic words of the Apostle's salutation in all his Epistles (vs. 5-7).

Paul expresses his thanksgiving to God for what he has heard of the faith of the Roman Christians, and assures them that he constantly mentions them in his prayers, asking that it may be God's good pleasure for him at length to visit them (vs. 8-10). He has long desired to see them that he may share with them some spiritual benefit, and that he, too, may be encouraged by their faith. He would have them know that he has often planned to visit them, in the hope of having some result of his labour among them as among other Gentiles, but hitherto he has been hindered by one thing and another (vs. 11-13). He has a debt to discharge both to civilized Greeks and uncivilized Barbarians, both to the cultured and to the uncultured; and so for his part he is ready to preach the Gospel to those also who dwell in Rome (vs. 14-15).

Thus the Apostle has approached his theme, which he now defines as the righteousness of God revealed in the Gospel (vs. 16-17). God's way of saving men, Jew and Gentile alike, is by the gift of a righteousness provided by Himself and received by faith alone. The subsequent argument of the Epistle shows that what Paul means by the righteousness of God is not the holiness of His character, or His justice in punishing sin, but the perfect fulfilment of the Moral Law, wrought out first by Jesus Christ, and now offered as a free gift to unrighteous man.

RIGHTEOUSNESS NEEDED
(1:18—3:20)

Paul begins the exposition of his theme by showing the need of the Gospel. This is seen in the guilt and moral ruin of the whole race. The world is lost without it. The Apostle takes up the case of the

Gentiles first, before he goes on to deal with the special case of the Jew.

1. The Guilt of the Gentiles (1:18-32). In this passage three facts stand out regarding the moral responsibility of the heathen world.

(1) Natural revelation (vs. 18-20). The moral failure of man is traced to his neglect of the revelation of God as the Creator of the world. The existence of God is revealed to men through the works of nature. Although He is invisible Himself, yet the natural world bears witness to His power and benevolence. In His works of creation God has given enough knowledge of Himself for adoration and gratitude. The wickedness of men is due to ignoring God and suppressing the truth about Him. Hence "the wrath of God is revealed from heaven against all ungodliness and unrighteousness of men". By "ungodliness" Paul means absence of reverence for God. He implies that this is the root of "unrighteousness", by which he means iniquity or wicked conduct between man and man.

(2) Heathen sin (vs. 21-23). Men ignored the revelation of God that was given them in nature. They did not glorify Him by giving Him worship, nor did they give Him the thanks that are due to the Creator. They followed futile speculations, and lost the sense of the spiritual. As a result, their wisdom turned to folly. The religious history of mankind has been a downward course from a primitive knowledge of God into gross idolatry.

(3) Divine judgment (vs. 24-32). Paul now goes on to explain how "the wrath of God is revealed". The principle of Divine judgment is contained in the statement, "God gave them up", which occurs three times in this passage (vs. 24, 26, 28). Refusing to acknowledge God or keep Him in their thoughts, He gave them over to their own thoughts. The consequence of this was the degradation of the whole man—body, mind, and spirit. One evil led to another, till men sank into utter depravity. God's wrath is manifested in giving man his own way. He punishes sin with the consequence of sin. Thus does Paul throw into striking contrast the "revelation" of the righteousness of God in the Gospel (v. 17) and the "revelation" of the wrath of God in idolatry and in the moral state of the pagan world (v. 18).

2. The Righteous Judgment of God (2:1-16). Having shown the guilt of the Gentile world, the Apostle now turns to the Jew, but does not name him at first. The argument at this point takes the form of a dialogue with an imaginary Jewish hearer who poses as a judge of the Gentiles. His judgment recoils upon himself, because he is guilty of the same practices, and the principle upon which God judges men brings him under the same condemnation (v. 1). Then Paul goes on to explain the principle of God's judgment in its various aspects.

(1) The judgment of God is "according to truth". That is, it deals with realities, not with appearances; with what a man is, not with what he professes to be (v. 2). God's goodness and forbearance form no ground of hope for escape from judgment, for His purpose is to give men time for repentance (vs. 3-4). There is a day coming when His forbearance to the impenitent will come to an end and His righteous judgment will be revealed (v. 5).

(2) In that day God will judge every man "according to his works" (v. 6). The fervour of the Apostle's spirit as he poured out his thought has involved his style in some irregularity in the phrases that follow this statement. The balance of the construction would be preserved, and the meaning of the passage clarified, if "eternal life" were taken as an explanation of the preceding words and a full stop put after "unrighteousness".

Then we should read as follows:—God "will render to every man according to his works: both to them that by patience in well-doing seek for glory and honour and incorruption, (that is,) eternal life; and also to them that are factious, and obey not the truth, but obey unrighteousness. Wrath and indignation, tribulation and anguish (shall be) upon every soul of man that worketh evil, of the Jew first and also of the Greek; but glory and honour and peace (shall be) to every man that worketh good, to the Jew first, and also to the Greek" (vs. 7-10). God shows no respect of persons in judgment, and regards no distinction of race, except in giving priority to the Jew (v. 11).

The principle of Divine judgment set forth in these verses is not inconsistent with the Gospel principle of justification by faith which Paul explains afterwards. It is true of the believer that God deals with him according to his works, for the true works of a believer are the evidence of his union with Christ and the manifestation of the righteousness of God in his life.

(3) God will judge men according to the light they have enjoyed—the Jews by the Moral Law and the heathen by the light of nature and the law of conscience. Although the heathen have no prescribed law, yet their conscience bears witness to the Moral Law by reflecting its work in their hearts (vs. 12-15). The word "justified" occurs for the first time in the Epistle in the statement, "the doers of the law shall be justified", and its use here determines its meaning. It cannot mean "pardoned", for "the doers of the law", by which Paul means those who fulfil the law, have nothing for which to be pardoned. Nor can it mean "made just", for the doers of the law are just already by so doing. It must therefore mean, "accounted just", or "declared to be just".

(4) When the day comes for this judgment of the secret thoughts of men, God will execute it through Jesus Christ (v. 16). In adding the phrase, "according to my gospel", Paul did not mean that he had a different Gospel to preach from that of the other Apostles, but that the very Gospel itself implied a background of judgment. It is part of the Gospel message to declare that a day is coming when God shall judge the world by Him whom He has given to be the Saviour of the world (Acts 17:31; Matt. 7:22-23; 25:31-33; John 5:27-29).

3. The Failure of the Jews (2:17-29). The Apostle now takes up the special case of the Jew, and addresses him. As a Jew he may boast of the peculiar privileges that are his through the revelation of the Law, and of his superior position because of it (vs. 17-20). But his conduct shows that he is no better than the Gentile. The list of sins with which Paul goes on to charge the Jews is a revelation of the low state of Jewish moral conduct in that age. So far from fulfilling their true function

in the world, they were dishonouring God. They prided themselves on their aversion to idolatry, yet in many places they were guilty of stealing treasures from the temples of the heathen (Acts 19:37). The name of God was blasphemed among the Gentiles because of them—"even as it is written", adds Paul, referring to such passages as Isa. 52:5 and Ezek. 36:20-23 (vs. 21-24).

The circumcision of the Jew was of value only if he kept the Law. He is not a true Jew, Paul explains, who has only the outward mark. A true Jew is one who has the inward character, whose circumcision is moral and spiritual (vs. 25-29). This is only emphasizing what the Old Testament has already taught about spiritual circumcision (Deut. 10:16; Jer. 4:4; 9:26). In the closing words of the passage, "whose praise is not of men, but of God", there is an allusion to the fact that the word "Jew"—a descendant of Judah—means "praise" (Gen. 29:35; 49:8).

4. The Objections of the Jew (3:1-8). Paul has shown that the judgment of God is concerned with character, and not with the outward form of religion. This puts the Jew who breaks the Moral Law in the same class with Gentile sinners. His Judaism goes for nothing. This raises a series of objections from the Jew's point of view, and these Paul now takes up and answers.

(1) If circumcision does not save, what is the advantage of being a Jew? Much every way, replies the Apostle. The chief advantage is that the Jews have been entrusted with the sacred Scriptures, which contain the revelation of God and the promise of the Messiah (vs. 1-2).

(2) Does the fact that some Jews disbelieve cancel the promises God gave to the Jews as a whole? Does their want of faith mean that God will not keep faith? That can never happen, is the reply. God is always true to His word, but no man can be relied upon. This is what David's confession means in Psa. 51:4 (vs. 3-4).

(3) Well then, if our unrighteousness sets God's righteousness in a clearer light, is not God unjust in punishing wrong-doing? Away with the thought, exclaims Paul. It would mean that God has no right to judge the world. It would also mean that we may do evil that good may come. Some, indeed, lay the slanderous charge against us Christians that we teach this doctrine; but they will be justly condemned (vs. 5-8).

5. The Verdict of the Scriptures (3:9-20). The need of salvation is universal. This has been shown in the sin and guilt of both Gentiles and Jews. Now comes the summing up of the whole case in the light of the Old Testament. This argument from Scripture may be stated as follows: The definite charge is made that all are under sin (v. 9). Then the Scripture proof is adduced. The character of man is described generally, by quoting Psa. 14:1-3, and 53:1-3 (vs. 10-12); then more particularly, by quoting Psa. 5:9, 140:3, and 10:7 in reference to their words (vs. 13-14), and Isa. 59:7-8 in reference to their deeds (vs. 15-17).

Finally, the fundamental cause of their sin is found in Psa. 36:1: "There is no fear of God before their eyes" (v. 18). Man's moral failure is due to his neglect of God. Then comes the general conclusion of the whole argument (vs. 19-20). All the world is under the judgment of God, and the Jew can claim no exemption. His own Law condemns him, for its only effect is to show man's inability to obey it and to prove that man is a sinner. The Law cannot save; salvation must come in some other way.

RIGHTEOUSNESS PROVIDED
(3:21—5:21)

Having concluded the preliminary stage of his argument by showing the need of salvation in the moral ruin of the whole human race, Paul now proceeds to show that God has provided salvation Himself through Jesus Christ, in the free gift of His righteousness to all who believe.

1. God's Gift of Righteousness (3:21-31). This passage contains the germ of the rest of the Epistle. It is marked by intense concentration of inspired thought. Into it the massive mind of the great Apostle has condensed the whole truth regarding the righteousness of God as revealed in the Gospel. Its meaning may be unfolded under two main ideas, by dividing it in the middle of v. 25.

(1) The fact of the Cross (vs. 21-25). In these verses the Apostle explains the central significance of the Cross in human history. His conception is that the Cross of Christ stands, as it were, on the border of the unseen world, at the meeting-place between man and God. It has a two-fold aspect. It is related both to man on the one side and to God on the other. The passage may be paraphrased as follows:

But now, since Christ has come, a righteousness has been provided by God quite independently of the Law. It has been manifested in the facts of the Gospel history, having been foreshadowed and foretold in the Law and the Prophets (v. 21). That is, over against the failure of all human righteousness, Jesus exhibited the righteousness of God by doing the will of God throughout His earthly life and completely fulfilling the Law. The character of Christ is the manifestation of the righteousness of God.

This righteousness which God provides is obtained by personal trust in Jesus Christ on the condition of faith alone, no distinction being made between Jews and Gentiles (v. 22). For all have sinned and have failed to attain to the Divine likeness which man was intended to bear (v. 23). All those that believe are "justified freely by his grace". That is, they are accounted righteous without any cost to themselves, all the cost being borne by God. This is made possible "through the redemption that is in Christ Jesus"—the transaction that He accomplished for our ransom and wrought out in His own Person (v. 24).

This now brings Paul's argument to the Cross (v. 25). In the transaction of the Cross, "God set forth" Jesus Christ on the stage of human history "to be a propitiation"—strictly a place of propitiation, a place where man can meet God and be reconciled to Him. The word contains an allusion to the mercy-seat in the Holy-of-holies where forgiveness was obtained under the Old Covenant. This reconciliation with God is obtained "through faith"— sheer trust in God alone without any human claim. The phrase, "in his blood", should be connected with the words, "set forth to be a propitiation". It indicates the central significance of the Cross, which consisted in Christ's voluntary offering of His own life as an atoning sacrifice. It was through the Cross that the righteousness of God manifested in the life of Jesus was made available to the faith of men. By suffering death as the voluntary end of His own righteous life, Jesus Christ accepted for Himself the inevitable end of man's moral failure. Having achieved a perfect righteousness, He accepted the wages of sin. On the Cross He was "set forth" for all men to behold as the one sacrifice for the sin of the world.

But the Cross looked out also on the Godward side. The form of the original word implies that God "set forth" Christ for Himself also. In the preceding part of the Epistle Paul has pointed out that the wrath of God is the Divine attitude toward all human sin (1:18; 2:5). On the Cross the Righteous One was set forth in the sight of God as the representative of sinful man. And there, in that supreme hour, the righteousness of God met the wrath of God and accomplished "the redemption that is in Christ Jesus". It was an objective achievement, entirely outside the sphere of subjective human experience. But now that it has been accomplished, men may share "the righteousness of God". The Gospel may now be proclaimed to the world. The sinner may be justified "freely"—by way of a gift. Righteousness has now become "the gift of God", which God gives "by his grace", and man receives "through faith in Jesus Christ".

(2) The effect of the Cross (vs. 25-31). In these verses Paul shows how the Cross manifests and vindicates the righteousness and justice of God. It is the key to His moral government of the world. It is the central fact in human history, and casts a revealing light both backward and forward. It explains the forebearance of God in "the passing over of the sins done aforetime". This means that God passed over the sins of His people in the Old Testament dispensation without adequate punishment, because of the redemption that He was going to accomplish through the Cross. It also vindicates His justice "at this present season", that is, in the New Testament age, when He accepts the sinner as righteous who believes in Jesus (vs. 25-26).

The righteousness of God humbles the pride of man. Justification by faith without works leaves no room for human merit (vs. 27-28). It puts Jews and Gentiles on the same footing before God (vs. 29-30). It confirms and fulfils the Law (v. 31). The Law is not abrogated by this method of saving men, for its requirements are fulfilled and its majesty is honoured (Isa. 42:21). It is the moral aspect of the Law, and not its ceremonial aspect, that the Apostle has in mind in all the discussion of righteousness throughout the Epistle.

2. The Faith of Abraham (Ch. 4). Paul now takes up the case of Abraham, the founder of the chosen race, who might plead privilege and merit as the ground of his acceptance with God. He shows that Abraham was accepted because of his faith in God, and not because of any works of his.

(1) Abraham justified by faith alone (vs. 1-8). That he was not justified by works is proved by the statement of Scripture which Paul quotes (Gen. 15:6). The expression, "it was reckoned unto him for righteousness", does not mean that Abraham's faith was accepted instead of righteousness, or as equivalent to it, but that it put him in the right relation with God, so that God could regard him as a righteous man. Compare the phrase "unto salvation" in 1:16, where the preposition in the original is the same (vs. 1-5). The same principle is found in Psa. 32:1-2, where David pronounces blessing upon those to whom God attributes righteousness without any reference to works. Righteousness, therefore, is put to our credit because of our faith; it is not achieved by us because of our works (vs. 6-8). The significant word in this statement about Abraham's faith occurs eleven times in the chapter. It is rendered "counted", "reckoned", and "imputed" in the A.V., but always "reckoned" in the R.V.

(2) Abraham justified before he was circumcised (vs. 9-12). Abraham's personal state or religious standing at the time when he was justified was in uncircumcision; he was in the same position as the heathen. The story in Genesis (ch. 17) shows that circumcision was introduced fourteen years after Abraham was accepted with God. Circumcision was only a sign or seal of the righteousness which he had already received by faith. Thus Abraham is the father of all that have faith and believe in God, whether they be circumcised Jews or uncircumcised Gentiles.

(3) The promise to Abraham based on his faith (vs. 13-16). It was not based upon the Law. Under the general phrase, "the promise that he should be heir of the world", Paul sums up the whole series of promises given to Abraham—that he should inherit the land, and that he should have seed and through his seed blessing should come to the whole world. It included an inheritance in the land of Canaan. But Canaan was only an emblem of the heavenly country, in which alone he could have an eternal inheritance; and this was what the patriarch understood it to be (Heb. 11:8-10). This promise was given to Abraham as justified by faith. Its fulfilment turns on faith, and will be shared as a matter of grace by all who have Abraham's faith, whether they be Jews or Gentiles.

(4) The nature of Abraham's faith (vs. 17-22). It was sheer trust in God to fulfil His own promise. It was not merely the conviction that God exists and that He is good. Abraham believed in God as the One "who giveth life to the dead, and calleth the things that are not, as though they were". That is, he believed that God could introduce a new creation. His faith was superior to all the hindrances and apparent impossibilities that nature put in the way. It gave all the glory to God, believing that He had supernatural power to fulfil what He had promised. Therefore it was reckoned to him for righteousness.

(5) Abraham's faith a type of Christian faith (vs. 23-25). The kind of faith by which Abraham was justified is the model of our faith. Saving faith rests upon the supernatural transaction that God has accomplished in the death and resurrection of Jesus Christ. It believes that God wrought this for our salvation, Jesus Christ having been crucified to atone for our sins and raised from the dead because of our justification. His resurrection proved that He was accepted as our substitute, and therefore that we are accepted in Him.

3. The Security of the Justified (5:1-11). Paul

now goes on to explain the security and permanence of this method of salvation. Those that are justified by faith in Jesus Christ stand in a new relation to God. If the righteousness of God is put to our account, it means that there is reconciliation on God's part toward us and all life is changed for us. The privileges of the justified, and the results that follow from having righteousness imputed to us, are set forth in this passage.

(1) Peace with God (v. 1). The past is changed. There is no hostility on God's part toward us because of our past sin. This brings peace in every sense—peace of mind, heart, and conscience.

(2) Favour with God (v. 2). The present is changed. We stand in a new position before God. We have been introduced by Jesus Christ into a place of favour with God. This means the privilege of access to His presence at any time.

(3) Hope of glory (v. 2). The future is changed. We have the hope of sharing the glory of God—the glory that shall be revealed in us when we are made like Jesus Christ. This is a hope we should rejoice in.

(4) Joy in tribulation (vs. 3-4). Our circumstances are changed. Tribulation seems to be the Christian's lot in the world. But tribulation, says the Apostle, works out Christian character. "We also rejoice in our tribulations" — tribulations considered in their effects, not in themselves. "Tribulation worketh steadfastness" — endurance, the habit of waiting on God and submitting to His will. "And steadfastness, approvedness": it proves the genuineness of the Christian's faith and the reality of the Lord's faithfulness. "And approvedness, hope": our hope of enjoying the glory of God is confirmed when the genuineness of our Christian faith is tested by experience. From the hope of glory in v. 2 the Apostle swings round the circle through tribulation to the hope of glory again in v. 4.

(5) Realization of God's love (vs. 5-8). The inner life is changed. The sense of God's love to us is shed abroad—literally, "poured out"—in our hearts by the Holy Spirit. This is the first mention of the Holy Spirit in the Epistle. In the figure of pouring out water, Paul may be alluding to the promise in Isa. 44:3: "I will pour my Spirit upon thy seed". He points out the wonderful nature of God's love as manifested in the way Christ died for us, when we were neither righteous nor good, deserving neither respect nor affection. Thus God commends His own love toward us as something different from and above all human love.

(6) Assurance of salvation (vs. 9-10). If we have been justified and reconciled to God by the death of Christ when we were enemies, "much more" now shall we be kept safe from the wrath of God by sharing the life of Christ. The emphasis lies on "much more", which occurs twice.

(7) Joy in God (v. 11). This is the final issue of our justification—rejoicing in God Himself, who is the Author and Giver of our salvation. It is joy in God, "through our Lord Jesus Christ". How often the name of the Saviour is mentioned in this passage! It begins with "peace with God through our Lord Jesus Christ", and ends with "joy in God through our Lord Jesus Christ". Every privilege possessed by the justified is secured through Him.

4. The Headship of Christ (5:12-21). This passage draws out the parallel and the contrast between the results of Christ's work and the results of Adam's fall. The general meaning will be seen if we connect v. 12 at once with vs. 18-19, dropping out the intervening parenthesis in the meantime. In Christ, whom God has provided as a new Head for the race, the results of Adam's fall have been overcome and put away. Adam and Jesus Christ are the two representative men of the race. Each is the head of a system or solidarity. Adam was the type of Christ, "a figure of him that was to come" (v. 14); and he sustains a vital relation to those that are united to him.

The destinies of mankind are bound up with these two men because they are corporate personalities. We are descendants of the first Adam by our natural birth, and we inherit the sin and death which his disobedience brought into the world. By our faith we become united with Christ, "the last Adam" (1 Cor. 15:45), and thus we are born by a spiritual birth into a new system of which He is the Head. In Him we recover all that was lost in the first Adam, and much more. The argument is based on the story of the Fall in Gen. 3.

(1) The results of Adam's fall (vs. 12-14). "Through one man"—by Adam's act of disobedience —sin and death entered the world. By "sin" Paul means the tendency and disposition to sin, the active principle of human self-will, working like a malignant force through all mankind. The inevitable effect of sin was death—physical death, carrying with it spiritual death and eternal separation from God. The clause, "for that all sinned", is explained in vs. 13-14. The fact that death prevailed during the age from Adam to Moses shows that even before the Law was given sin was universally present in the race. All died, even those whose sin was not the transgression of a definite command like Adam's, because they had inherited something from Adam that made them sinners by nature.

(2) The power of God's grace (vs. 15-17). "But not as the trespass, so also is the free gift": the gift is very different from the trespass. The grace of God is much more powerful than the sin of man. The good that comes by Christ does "much more" than repair the evil that came by Adam. "By the trespass of the one the many died": by Adam's act of disobedience all his descendants passed under death. "Much more did the grace of God, and the gift by the grace of the one man, abound unto the many": all who belong to Jesus Christ receive all that was lost under Adam, and much more. These verses dwell on the fact that salvation is a gift. It is "the gift of righteousness", and comes by grace. The word "gift" is used five times.

(3) The results of Christ's work (vs. 18-21). These verses sum up the whole comparison between Adam and Christ. The resemblance is set forth in vs. 18-19, and the contrast in vs. 20-21. The results of Christ's redemptive work are available for all mankind; and they are effective for all them that are united to Him by faith. As by one man's disobedience, "the many"—all that are united with Adam as their representative head—were made sinners; so by the obedience of One, "the many"— all that are united with Christ as their representative Head—shall be made righteous. Paul uses

the future here because he is thinking of the process of being made righteous as taking place in one after another of "the many" as they believe.

He then goes on to show that the Law resulted in magnifying the sin, but grace more than met the Law—it provided a glory and bliss which even the keeping of the Law could not give. Finally, the ultimate result in each case is contrasted. The reign of sin issues in death: the reign of grace bestows righteousness and issues in eternal life. Grace reigns "through righteousness"—not merely by the gift of righteousness to them that believe, but by working out righteousness in their lives and enabling them to fulfil the Law "through Jesus Christ our Lord". And with the full name of the Saviour again, the whole section dealing with the salvation which God provides in the gift of His righteousness comes to a close.

RIGHTEOUSNESS APPLIED
(Chs. 6-8)

Now Paul deals with the kind of life that is to be lived by those who are justified by faith and receive the righteousness of God as a gift of grace. In these chapters he shows that God's method of salvation not only justifies, but also sanctifies and glorifies. The principle by which salvation is secured through the work of Christ as our representative Head, which has been explained in the foregoing passage, is also the principle by which salvation is applied and carried out. The righteousness of God, secured by Jesus Christ and put to our credit, is wrought out in our lives by spiritual union with Him as our representative Head.

1. The Believer's Union with Christ (6:1-11). Although this passage begins a new step in the argument of the Epistle, it is closely connected with the last verses of ch. 5. Under Adam sin abounded; under Christ grace much more abounds (5:20). If that is the case, some might say, let us continue in sin that grace may abound. Certainly not, says the Apostle, for in our new representative Head we have died to sin (vs. 1-2). Then he goes on to show how union with Christ gives us complete victory over sin. In the present passage he explains how this union operates. By our spiritual union with Christ we are identified with Him at each stage of His redemptive work. Just as all that happened to Adam passed to us at our natural birth because of our identification with him, so all that happened to Christ passes to us at our spiritual birth because of our identification with Him.

This passage is one of the profoundest in Paul's Epistles. Here he takes us to the inner secret of the Gospel, and describes the spiritual activity that operates at the heart of the Christian system. It is the supernatural reality in Christianity, that element in it which makes the Gospel "the power of God unto salvation" (1:16). His meaning will appear if we understand the four leading ideas which emerge as he goes on with his explanation.

(1) Baptism into Christ Jesus (vs. 3-4). This baptism is the work of the Holy Spirit in uniting us with Christ our federal Head. It takes place when we are born again, or "born from above" (John 3:3 marg.). Paul is referring to the special action of the Spirit of God in regeneration. It is the transcendent operation of the new creation. It began when the Spirit was poured out at Pentecost, and it goes on continually as the Gospel is preached and believers are added to the Lord. He mentions it again and again in his Epistles (1 Cor. 12:13; Eph. 4:5). Having been "baptized into Christ" in this way, we become identified with Him in all that happened to Him. We died in Him when He died, and we were raised to newness of life in Him when He rose. That being so, Paul argues, we are dead to sin and should no longer walk therein.

(2) The likeness of His death (vs. 5-7). This is not death in the general sense, but "his death", the particular death that Jesus died. The first clause of v. 4 rendered literally is, "We were buried therefore with him through the baptism into the death"—through the baptism of the Spirit into the death of Christ. The death of Christ was different from any other death in that it took place by the consent of His own will. He died to Himself, or gave Himself to death. "If we have become united with him in the likeness of his death", means, if we share His way of dying and consent to die to ourselves. "We shall be (united with him) also in the likeness of his resurrection", means, we shall share His new way of living and live in the power of His resurrection.

In the next verse Paul explains how this can take place: "our old man was crucified with him, that the body of sin might be done away". "Our old man" and "the body of sin" both mean our old nature, the nature in which sin has its seat. As Christ's human nature was put to death on the Cross, so, by virtue of our union with Him, our human nature was crucified there. Thus the body of sin, or sin embodied in human nature, has been rendered powerless for the believer.

(3) Living with the risen Christ (vs. 8-10). Here Paul carries out more fully the thought expressed in v. 5, that if we share His way of dying we shall also share His way of living. This means that if we give ourselves to die to self as He did, we shall be quickened by His risen life. We shall live with Him a life over which death has no power. "He died unto sin once"—once for all. Being made sin for our sake, the power of sin culminated in His death; and in His death it came to an end once for all. Now He lives unto God.

(4) Reckoning oneself dead (v. 11). The word "reckon" used here is the same as that so often used in ch. 4 of God's reckoning righteousness to those that believe. There it means that God regards them as righteous, and here it means that we regard ourselves as dead. We reckon ourselves to be dead unto sin but alive unto God when we think of ourselves as having passed through the experience of the Cross with Christ, when we treat our old self as a dead thing and give ourselves to a new life in dependence on Him. Then we find that the life of the risen Christ is supplied to us and gives us life indeed, Paul puts the same thought in other forms in 2 Cor. 4:10, and Phil. 3:10.

2. The Christian's Release from Sin (6:12 — 7:6). This section is an expansion of the injunction in v. 11. Our deliverance from sin is realized, not by our own efforts to overcome it, but by reckoning ourselves dead unto sin in Christ. The Apostle explains that our union with Christ in His death

means that we have been transferred from the old order of life to a new order of life.

(1) A new order of life—under grace (6:12-14). By the death of Christ we have passed from the sphere where sin reigns and the Law is the rule of life to the sphere where grace reigns and the Holy Spirit is the principle of life. Therefore let us not go on yielding to the old tyranny, but dedicate ourselves once for all to the new liberty. Paul then goes on to illustrate the new position of the Christian by means of two analogies, one from the state of slavery and the other from the state of wedlock.

(2) A new service—the service of righteousness (6:15-23). The Christian was a slave of sin; his business was iniquity and his wages were death. But by his union with Christ he has been emancipated from this service to enter another service, that of righteousness, where the end is eternal life. The phrase, "that form of teaching" (v. 17), does not mean a formal statement of doctrine, but the Gospel itself in its power to save from sin. When Paul says, "I speak after the manner of men" (v. 19), he means that he is using a human illustration to express a spiritual truth (Gal. 3:15). There is a significant difference between the two expressions in v. 23, "the wages of sin" and the "gift of God". The sinner earns his wages: the believer receives God's gift.

(3) A new marriage—marriage with the risen Lord (7:1-6). The marriage contract binds a woman only while her husband lives. If he dies, she is free to contract another marriage. So it is with the Christian. Formerly he was married, as it were, to his old nature, the flesh or the self-life, and was subject to the law of that nature. But this old nature has been put to death in the death of Christ. Now the Christian is free to contract a new marriage, a marriage with the risen Christ, the fruits of which will be a life quickened by the Spirit.

3. The Failure of Life under Law (7:7-25). Paul closed the last section by saying that as Christians "we serve in newness of the Spirit, and not in oldness of the letter". He now goes on to describe these two different ways of life, taking the last first. By the phrase, "in oldness of the letter", Paul means, according to the old Law. He is thinking of the Law as a standard of moral authority. The profound analysis of the work of the Law in the heart which this passage contains must have been based on Paul's own experience; otherwise it would have no practical value. It is not only his experience, but the experience of all men who try to overcome sin by their own efforts. Any man, saved or unsaved, regenerate or unregenerate, who tries to become righteous by obeying the Moral Law will be beaten back by the power of sin in his own nature. The passage describes what the Law does for the man who lives under it.

(1) It reveals the fact of sin (vs. 7-8). The Law itself is not sin, but it shows up the presence of sin. Paul would not have known that it was wrong to covet if the Law had not said, "Thou shalt not covet". The very fact that the Ten Commandments are set in prohibitions implies the presence of sin in human nature.

(2) It exposes the sinful nature (vs. 9-11). Paul refers to his experience as a child, before he was conscious of what the Law commanded, as typical of the nature of man when unrestrained by the Law. The commandment of the Law wakens up the sin in man's nature and leads him into the way of death.

(3) It produces conviction of sin (vs. 12-13). The Law in itself is holy and righteous, and intended for man's good; but its effect is to stir up his human nature to sin. Thus it shows him the enormity and exceeding guilt of sin.

(4) It cannot prevent one from doing wrong (vs. 14-17). The secret of the Law's failure in this respect lies in the fact that man by nature is carnal, while the Law itself is spiritual and accords with the Spirit of God. Man by nature is of the flesh, and the flesh is under the power of sin. A carnal man is one who lives by the power of the flesh or the self-life, and not by the power of the Spirit.

(5) It cannot help one to do right (vs. 18-20). When Paul says, "in me, that is, in my flesh, dwelleth no good thing", he does not mean that there is nothing good in human nature, but that there is nothing entirely good. All parts of man's nature have been affected by sin, and it is powerless to achieve righteousness, even with the good that is in it. Paul approves of the commands of the Law, but finds in his human nature no power to get those commands obeyed.

(6) It reveals the bondage of sin (vs. 21-23). Paul mentions four laws here, which fall into two pairs in constant conflict. The Law of God and the law of his mind or higher nature agree, for his mind recognizes the righteousness of the Law of God. The law of his members or lower nature and the law of sin agree, for sin finds something in his lower nature to correspond with it. As the Law of God is opposed to the law of sin, so the law of his higher nature is opposed to the law of his lower nature. There is, therefore, this constant conflict within him, bringing him into bondage to sin.

(7) It drives one to deliverance to Christ (vs. 24-25). At this point Paul utters a heart-rending cry as he recalls the unavailing struggle that he went through as a Pharisee; and then he throws the light of his victorious Christian experience back on it. By union with the Lord Jesus Christ he has been delivered out of the bondage of his old sinful nature, which he calls "the body of this death" as being subject to death. Then he closes with a compressed summary of the state of life under the Law, which reflects the deep feeling with which he has been describing it. In the whole passage the first personal pronoun occurs nearly fifty times. It is a picture of the self-life at work trying to save itself by the Law.

4. The Victory of Life in Christ (8:1-17). The Apostle now turns to the other kind of life referred to in 7:6, "in newness of the Spirit". This phrase means, in a new way which the Holy Spirit makes possible. By our union with Christ in His death and resurrection, the power of sin has been dethroned in the heart and the Spirit of Christ rules there instead. The name of the Holy Spirit, which has been mentioned only once before (5:5), now becomes prominent, being used here fourteen times. Those who are in Christ Jesus live in the power of His Spirit, and not under the Law. They walk not after the flesh, but after the Spirit. They do not follow the mind of the old nature; they respond to the mind of the Spirit of Christ.

(1) They fulfil the Law by the power of the Spirit (vs. 1-4). "The law of the Spirit of life in Christ Jesus", means the power exercised by the Spirit of the risen Christ. "The law of sin and of death", means the power of sin operating in the old nature and resulting in death. God interposed by sending His Son to free us from this power by taking the condemnation of our sin in His own human nature, so that hereafter the same Spirit who fulfilled the Law in Him might fulfil it in us when we walk after the Spirit.

The phrase, "and for sin", looks back to the Old Testament, where it is constantly used for the sin-offering in the Mosaic ritual, occurring more than fifty times in the Book of Leviticus alone. Paul saw in the sin-offering a type of the sacrifice of Christ as the one decisive act by which the sinner is acquitted of the guilt of sin and delivered from its power. The result is stated in v. 4. Those who are in Christ Jesus fulfil the requirement of the Law, not by the outward compulsion of the old commandment, but by the inward constraint of the Spirit of Christ.

(2) They are delivered from the power of the flesh by the power of the Spirit (vs. 5-9). There is a running contrast here between the mind of the flesh and the mind of the Spirit. The reference is to the active principle in each case, the general bent of thought, affection, and motive. The mind of the flesh is self-will: the mind of the Spirit is the will of God. The Christian is not controlled by the mind of the flesh, for in Christ he has passed out of the sphere of the flesh into the sphere of the Spirit. The real test of the Christian is the possession of the Spirit of Christ.

(3) They are assured of immortality by the presence of the Spirit (vs. 10-13). The contrast in v. 10 is between the body and the human spirit, not the Holy Spirit. "The body is dead because of sin": our physical nature is a dead thing because Adam's sin of self-will is rooted in it, and it must suffer the consequences. "But the spirit is life because of righteousness": our spiritual nature is a living thing because the righteousness of Christ has been imparted to us by His Spirit. Our present possession of the Holy Spirit is a pledge of our future resurrection. The same Spirit who raised up Jesus from the dead will also give life to our mortal bodies, because His Spirit dwells within us. With such a destiny before us, we are under obligation to follow the rule of the Spirit and put our bodily tendencies and habits to death.

(4) They became children of God by receiving the Spirit (vs. 14-17). In this passage Paul gives four marks of the sons of God:—being led by the Spirit of God (v. 14); having the spirit of sonship, the spirit that does not fear God but approaches Him as a Father, instead of the spirit of bondage and fear which is produced by the Law (v. 15); the inner witness of His Spirit in our hearts (v. 16); and sharing the sufferings of Christ, that is, suffering because we are Christians (v. 17). If we are children of God, it follows that we are heirs of God, joint heirs with Christ, destined to share His glory. This thought leads on to the final issue of life in Christ, which Paul deals with next.

5. Glorification with Christ (8:18-39). This passage takes us to the consummation of salvation. The final issue of life lived in union with Christ is sharing His glory. The possession of the Holy Spirit is the earnest of our glorification. The passage may be analyzed under five leading ideas.

(1) Through suffering to glory (vs. 18-22). "The sufferings of this present time", are the sufferings that believers have to endure in the present dispensation of distress and tribulation, which is to end with Christ's second coming. "The glory which shall be revealed to us-ward", is the likeness of Christ which is to be manifested in us at His coming, called in the next verse, "the revealing of the sons of God". "The earnest expectation of the creation", means the longing outlook of the whole natural world. The figure is that of an animal stretching its neck eagerly forward because of something it sees in the distance.

"The creation was subjected to vanity": it was put under the curse of futility, so that it could not realize the purpose for which it was created. This seems to refer to the Fall (Gen. 3:17-19). Some change for the worse passed over nature then. Man's sin infected the world around him. This took place "not of its own will", that is, not because of any wrong on its own part. The change took place "by reason of him who subjected it", that is because of the curse which God pronounced on the ground for the greater punishment of man.

"In hope that the creation itself also shall be delivered from the bondage of corruption into the liberty of the glory of the children of God": the natural world is to be released from the curse of futility, and is to share in the glorified state of the children of God. "The whole creation groaneth and travaileth in pain together until now": nature groans in all its parts, expressing a sense of something wrong which it longs to set right, and of something wanting which it strives to supply. We bear witness to the truth of this statement when we speak of the "sighing" of the wind and the "moaning" of the sea. Even the songs of the birds are often in a minor key.

(2) The Christian's hope (vs. 23-25). We Christians, too, who possess the Spirit as a foretaste of future glory, painfully long for the full recognition of our sonship, which will come when our bodies are delivered from their present state of decay and are changed into glory. Our full salvation still lies in the future; it is an object of hope, and we patiently wait for it. It will come with "the redemption of our body" (Luke 21:28; 1 Cor. 15:49-53; Phil. 3:21), the final salvation of that part of our being that links us with the natural world.

(3) The help of the Spirit (vs. 26-27). In our weakness we have the help of the Holy Spirit, who puts a meaning into our groans and aspirations, and brings them into harmony with the will of God. The Searcher of hearts reads the mind of the Spirit in the prayers of the saints.

(4) God working in all things for good (vs. 28-30). God is working through all things toward one end in the lives of those that love Him. The chain of His providential care stretches back into the eternal past and onward into the eternal future. He had a purpose in their call, and He is the Author of every step in the process of their salvation. His purpose is that they should bear the image of His

Son, so that the Son may be the first-born of a great brotherhood, the Head of a vast family of the redeemed. The last step in the whole process is their glorification.

(5) Assurance of God's love (vs. 31-39). With God doing all this for us, we have nothing to fear. Having given His own Son to die for us, He will surely provide everything necessary for our final salvation (vs. 31-32). Who will accuse those whom God has chosen? When God acquits, who can condemn? Will Christ? He died for us, and is now exalted in Heaven as our representative there (vs. 33-34). No troubles or sufferings of any kind can separate us from His love. Though the words of the Psalmist (44:22) might be applied to us, yet all these things turn to our glory, for we triumph over them through His love (vs. 35-37).

Then the Apostle closes this part of his argument with a magnificent sweep of sublime assurance. He is convinced that nothing in all human experience or in the hierarchy of the spiritual world, nothing in the present or in the future, nothing in the heights above or in the depths beneath, nor anything else in the whole creation, will be able to separate us from the love of God which has come to us through Jesus Christ our Lord (vs. 38-39).

RIGHTEOUSNESS REFUSED
(Chs. 9—11)

Paul has finished his main argument and now faces the problem of Jewish unbelief. If this method of salvation is true and is in accordance with the Old Testament, how are we to account for the Jews' rejection of it? Having refused the righteousness of God offered in the Gospel, God has excluded them from its benefits. How can this be consistent with His election of Israel in the past? It seems to mean that His promises to them have failed. The Apostle discusses this question in these three chapters.

1. Paul's Sorrow Over Israel (9:1-5). The glorious prospect of life in Christ which he has been describing brings home to his heart with deep sorrow the fact that his own countrymen are excluded from it. Excluded from it in spite of all the special privileges and promises that were given to them, in spite of the fact that Christ, who is none other than the Lord God Himself, came from them.

The whole passage is one continuous sentence. The phrase, "for my brethren's sake, my kinsmen according to the flesh", should be connected directly with v. 2. The first part of v. 3 is a parenthesis, in which Paul refers to his old attitude to Christ as a Pharisee (cf. Acts 26:9), and it should be rendered literally: "For I myself was wishing (used to wish) to be accursed from Christ". The original contains no sign of a conditional sentence; and besides that, it is inconceivable that after Paul's Damascus vision he could have wished himself accursed from Christ under any condition.

2. The Fact of Israel's Exclusion (9:6-33). The Apostle deals with this question first from the point of the view of the Divine sovereignty, He vindicates God's character from any charge against it.

(1) It is not inconsistent with God's promises (vs. 6-13). Israel's exclusion does not mean that God's word has failed; for the promises to Israel were not based on descent from Abraham, but had in view a true Israel within the nation (vs. 6-7).

This is illustrated by the case of Abraham's children (Gen. 21:12; 18:10). It was no breach of God's promise to Abraham when Ishmael was rejected and Isaac was chosen (vs. 7-9). It was the same with the children of Isaac, who were both born of the same mother. Even before their birth, before they had done anything good or bad, the younger was chosen and the elder rejected (Gen. 25:23). This shows that the purpose of God is independent of man; it depends upon God's choice, and not upon man's works (vs. 10-13). Paul quotes Mal. 1:2-3, where the Jews were reminded of God's unmerited choice of Jacob over Esau to inherit the land.

(2) It is not inconsistent with God's justice (vs. 14-18). Can it be said in view of this that God is unjust? By no means. The Scriptures show that He has the right to confer His favours on whom He will, as He did on Moses, and to withhold them from whom He will, as He did from Pharaoh (Exod. 33:19; 9:16). In v. 18 the emphasis is on the words, "whom he will", in each clause.

Paul's aim is to assert the unconditional sovereignty of the Divine will over against all human arrogance, and he deals with only one aspect of the matter. His argument does not require him to explain how God's will takes man's will into account. As the same sun softens wax and hardens clay because the property of the one is to yield and the property of the other is to resist, so the same Divine will "hath mercy" on the man who yields to it and "hardeneth" the man who resists it. The story in Exodus describes God as hardening Pharaoh's heart (7:3; 9:12; 10:20, 27; 11:10; 14:4, 8), but it also describes Pharaoh as hardening his own heart (8:32; 9:34).

(3) It is not inconsistent with God's mercy (vs. 19-29). Again it may be urged, why should God find fault with one who fulfills His will by refusing His offer? But the creature may not complain against the Creator any more than the vessel against the potter. The Creator is free to do as He pleases and does not explain the ground of His action (vs. 19-21). He uses His freedom for beneficent ends, showing His longsuffering to sinners and His mercy toward us, whom He has called both from the Jews and from the Gentiles (vs. 22-24). Here Paul quotes a number of passages from the Prophets (Hos. 2:23; 1:10; Isa. 10:22-23; 1:9) to show that God had promised to extend His mercy to the Gentiles and to exclude all but a remnant of the Jews (vs. 25-29).

3. The Cause of Israel's Exclusion (9:30—10:21). The Apostle now turns to the other side of the question, and deals with it from the viewpoint of human responsibility. He shows that the Jews have been rejected because of their own fault. They chose the wrong method of salvation, and refused the righteousness that God offered them.

(1) They sought righteousness in the wrong way (9:30-33). While Gentiles came upon a righteousness which they did not seek after, the righteousness of faith, Israel failed to attain to the righteousness which they did follow after, the righteousness of the Law. Instead of accepting righteousness by faith, they tried to accomplish righteousness by works. Instead of believing in the Messiah when He came, they regarded Him as a cause of offence,

as the Scriptures had already foretold (Isa. 8:14; 28:16).

(2) They refused the righteousness of God (10: 1-4). Paul pauses here to reaffirm his intense desire that his own people should be saved. He can testify to their zeal for God, but it is a zeal without spiritual knowledge. Ignoring the righteousness of God by the method of faith, they sought to establish their own righteousness by the method of law; thus they produced self-righteousness. They did not know that the righteousness of the Law has been realized in Christ, that He has fulfilled the Law, and that righteousness may now come to every one who believes in Him. In rejecting Him the Jews have refused God's way of salvation.

(3) God's way of salvation is free and easy to find (10:5-10). Over against the method of righteousness by the Law described by Moses (Lev. 18: 5), which is beyond our reach and impossible to attain, Paul shows that the righteousness of faith is within the reach of all and is easy to obtain. He does this by appropriating to his own use language which Moses used of the Law (Deut. 30:11-14). One does not need to ascend into Heaven, for Christ has come down. Nor does one need to descend into the grave, for Christ has been raised from the dead. All one needs to do is to believe with the heart in Christ Jesus and confess with the mouth that He is Lord (Jehovah).

(4) God's way of salvation is universal and is offered to all (10:11-15). The Apostle goes on to support what he has said about God's method of salvation, by quoting some Old Testament passages, to show that it was intended for all without distinction of Jew or Greek, on the one condition of faith (Isa. 28:16; Joel 2:32). In order to believe in Christ, men must hear about Him; and in order to hear about Him, the Gospel must be preached. By introducing another Old Testament quotation (Isa. 52:7), Paul implies that the messengers of the Gospel have been sent out, and that the conditions necessary for the salvation provided by God have all been fulfilled.

(5) God's way of salvation has been refused by Israel (10:16-21). Paul now proceeds to show that the Jews, having had opporunity of knowing the Gospel, are themselves to blame for not believing it. Even when the Gentiles found God through the Gospel, the Jews persisted in their unbelief, and stubbornly refused all the pleadings of their God. Here Paul continues to weave into his argument further quotations from the Old Testament Scriptures (Isa. 53:1; Psa. 19:4; Deut. 32:21; Isa. 65: 1-2).

4. Israel's Exclusion Only Partial (11:1-10). The Apostle now comes to the question that has been behind his whole argument. Has God really cast away His people? In this passage he shows that God has not rejected His chosen people, for there has always been a remnant of believing and God-fearing Israelites. This is proved, to begin with, by his own case (v. 1). Each of the three chapters in this division of the Epistle begins with a reference on the part of the writer to his own profound sympathy with Israel. In the time of Elijah, when he thought that all the nation had apostatized and he alone was left (1 Kings 19:10, 14, 18),

there was a kernel of seven thousand in Israel still loyal to the Lord (vs. 2-4).

So now there is a remnant of loyal Jews, chosen by His free grace through the Gospel (vs. 5-6). The mass of the nation failed to attain the righteousness which it sought, but those whom God selected have obtained it. The rest have been hardened. These same conditions have prevailed throughout Israel's history, according to the Scriptures quoted (Isa. 29:10; 6:9-10; Psa. 69:22-23). All through their history the mass of the people have been destitute of spiritual insight. Spiritual blindness is God's judgment for unfaithfulness (vs. 7-10).

5. Israel's Exclusion Only Temporary (11:11-16). Having shown that God has not rejected Israel completely, the Apostle now goes on to say that He has not rejected them finally. Israel will yet be restored and saved. Israel's refusal of the Gospel ("their fall") has resulted in its extension to the Gentiles, and Israel's return to God ("their fulness") will bring still more abundant blessing to the world (vs. 11-12). Paul explains to his Gentile readers that he takes pride in his ministry as an Apostle of the Gentiles, not only that the Gentiles may be saved, but also that the Jews may be stirred up to emulation and be saved too (vs. 13-14).

Then he repeats the statement of v. 12 in a stronger form. If the rejection of the Jews has opened the offer of salvation to the world, their restoration to God's favour will mean new life for the world (v. 15). His confidence in the future of Israel is based upon the holiness of the patriarchs from whom they are descended. This he expresses in two different metaphors—that of the first fruit consecrating the whole lump of dough in the offering (Num. 15:20-21), and that of the root of a tree consecrating the branches (v. 16).

6. The Figure of the Olive Tree (11:17-24). The Apostle now takes up his second figure and enlarges upon it to show how Israel is the stock through which life comes to the Gentiles. The figure of the olive tree is taken from the Prophets (Jer. 11:16; Hosea 14:6). The good olive tree is the Israel of the Old Covenant with Abraham as its root, because of whose faith the nation was chosen. The wild olive tree is the Gentile world. Some of the branches of the good olive tree have been broken off. That is, part of Israel has been rejected because of unbelief; but the true Israel remains. A branch from the wild olive has been grafted into the good olive tree, and shares the life of the root. That is, Gentiles have been united to the true stock of Israel because of their faith, and they share the promises and benefits of the covenant made with Abraham (vs. 17-20).

This gives the Gentile Christians no ground for pride, but rather for awe and fear. If God showed His severity by cutting off the Jews who rejected His goodness, He will show His severity by cutting off the Gentiles who do not continue in His goodness. If the Jews turn from their unbelief, He will graft them in again. The Gentile branch was grafted in "contrary to nature", for the natural process is to graft a branch from a cultivated tree into a wild one. How much more easily then will the Jewish branches be grafted into their own olive tree. The restoration of Israel should be an easier process than the calling of the Gentiles (vs. 20-24).

7. A Prediction of Israel's Conversion (11:25-32). Paul now brings his great theme to a close by declaring that a bright future is in store for Israel, notwithstanding the present failure of the nation. Having shown that God's rejection of Israel is only partial and temporary, and that Israel's restoration would take place easily if the nation gave up its unbelief, Paul now foretells the future conversion of the nation. He has received a Divine revelation to this effect, which he now discloses: "I would not, brethren, have you ignorant of this mystery". The present partial blindness and hardening of Israel is to last only "until the fulness of the Gentiles be come in". This does not mean, till all the Gentiles are converted, but until converts are gathered in from the Gentile world and from all nations, and all the Gentile races are represented in the Church of Christ. "And so all Israel shall be saved": this means Israel as a whole, national Israel, but not necessarily every individual Israelite (vs. 25-26).

The Apostle supports his statement by another quotation from Isaiah (59:20-21), saying that the present alienation of Israel from God does not alter the fact that they are still His people, chosen for their fathers' sake. The promises which He made to them still stand (vs. 26-29). Then he draws a parallel between the case of the Gentiles and that of the Jews, to show that mercy is the general principle upon which God deals with all (vs. 30-32).

8. A Final Ascription of Praise to God (11:33-36). Paul has concluded his whole argument—his unfolding of the righteousness of God revealed in the Gospel, and his discussion of God's method of dealing with Israel—and he has been carried away by it. He now breaks out in an impassioned utterance of adoring wonder and praise, and, with a noble doxology, he brings the doctrinal part of his letter to an end.

RIGHTEOUSNESS REALIZED
(12:1—15:13)

This section contains the most complete and elaborate treatment of Christian conduct in all Paul's Epistles. It is the practical application of God's method of salvation to the life of the believer. Though given in the form of precepts and exhortations, it is not a code of ethics or a system of morals. It is a description, rather, of the way the Christian should react to the various conditions of life in which he finds himself. It is the righteousness of God as realized by those who live by faith and walk after the Spirit. It is the kind of behaviour the Gospel produces.

1. The Christian's New Life (Ch. 12). The Apostle begins with an appeal to his readers to surrender their lives to God on the ground of this wonderful redemption His mercy has provided (vs. 1-2). They are not to fashion themselves according to the world's manner of life. They are to be transfigured by the entire inward renewal of their mind through the Holy Spirit, that they may prove by experience what the will of God is—how good, and acceptable, and perfect.

Then Paul goes on to urge them, on the ground of his inspired authority as an Apostle, to cultivate spiritual humility (vs. 3-8). The Church is the body of Christ, and every member in it has some function to perform. Let him not value himself unduly, but remember that his position in the body is dependent, not upon his own merit, but upon the faith by which he received his salvation from God. We should not forget our brethren, and our mutual relation to one another and to Jesus Christ. Paul follows this appeal with a list of spiritual gifts bestowed on different members of the Christian community, telling how each is to be used, in accordance with the renewing of their minds, in the spirit of true humility.

The surrender of life to God for which Paul has appealed will manifest itself also in a spirit of genuine love. This will express itself in brotherly affection and sympathetic understanding among fellow Christians, and in corresponding qualities of character and conduct (vs. 9-16). It will also show itself toward those that are not Christians in not returning evil for evil or avenging themselves against wrong. They are to leave their vindication with God and treat their foes with kindness. In support of these instructions Paul quotes Deut. 32:35 and Prov. 25:21-22. They are not to let the evil of the world get the better of them, but meet the evil by doing good (vs. 17-21).

2. The Christian's Relation to the State (Ch. 13). Surrender of life to the will of God carries with it the fulfilment of one's duties toward the state.

(1) Obedience to civil authority (vs. 1-7). Civil government is a Divine institution, and to resist it is to put oneself in opposition to God (vs. 1-2; 1 Pet 2:13-17). The principle is not invalidated by the abuse of human government, for any government is better than anarchy. The function of civil authority is to restain and punish evil, and to defend the good (vs. 3-4). It is a moral obligation to be subject to it, to pay the taxes required to support it, and to give to all in authority the tribute, respect, and honour that is due to their office (vs. 5-7).

(2) Love the fulfilment of law (vs. 8-10). There is one debt which the Christian must always be paying but can never succeed in discharging, the obligation of love. All particular precepts are summed up in that of love. This makes injury to any man impossible. He who loves his neighbour will fulfil all the commands that concern his duty to his neighbour.

(3) The Christian citizen's motive (vs. 11-14). The Apostle now brings in the supreme motive for the believer's life in the world, the hope of the coming of the Lord. "Now is salvation nearer to us than when we first believed"—in the sense of its completion. "The night is far spent": the corrupt age under the present form of human government is passing. "The day is at hand": the new age of the Kingdom of God is soon to appear. "Let us walk becomingly as in the day"—as if it were now the day of the Lord. "Put ye on the Lord Jesus Christ": walk in the power of His risen life.

3. The Principles of Christian Fellowship (14:1—15:13). In this section Paul applies the principles of the new life to the sphere of Christian fellowship, and deals with matters which in themselves have no moral quality, but about which some members of the Christian community might have conscientious scruples. He points out the way that true Christian fellowship will manifest itself in these matters. Three principles are to be kept in mind.

(1) Personal liberty (14:1-12). In matters of indifference, where no moral issue is involved, the believer is free to follow his own conscience, but he is not to offend those who have scruples. The general Christian principle is stated in v. 1. Conscientious scruples are to be respected and not criticized. The convert who is "weak in the faith" is one who does not fully understand the fundamental principle of faith, and thinks he will make his salvation more certain by the scrupulous performance of something in addition. Paul gives two examples of such scruples, one regarding the eating of certain kinds of food (vs. 2-4), and the other regarding the observance of certain days as religious festivals (vs. 5-6).

The fundamental principle in these cases is that each person must be fully assured in his own conscience that he is doing right. Every Christian is directly responsible to the Lord alone in life and in death (vs. 7-9). By His death and resurrection Christ has become Lord over all alike, both the dead and the living. We must all stand before His judgment seat, and every one shall give account of himself, not of his brother, to God. There is therefore no place for judgment of one another.

(2) Brotherly charity (14:13-23). The Apostle has already addressed himself to those who have no conscientious scruples, and now he points out that the highest and noblest use of personal liberty is to give it up for the good of others. Higher than the principle of personal liberty is the principle of brotherly charity; and this demands consideration for the feelings and consciences of others. Paul applies this to the case of eating meat ceremonially unclean (vs. 13-15). "Let not then your good be evil spoken of": let not your Christian freedom become a cause of reproach in the Christian community. Life in the Kingdom of God does not consist in the personal enjoyment of material things, but in the manifestation of those spiritual qualities of character that spring from the presence of the Holy Spirit. He who serves Christ in this way is pleasing to God and stands the test with his fellow-men (vs. 16-18).

We should follow the things that make for peace and mutual edification, and not pull down the work of God. All things are ceremonially pure, but it is evil for that man who puts a stumbling block in his brother's way by what he eats (vs. 19-20). Let not him that is strong lead him that is weak into sin by following some course of action that his weak brother is not sure is right. The faith that is strong is not for display, but for oneself and God alone. Then Paul states the principle that should guide the Christian in all matters of conscience: "whatsoever is not of faith is sin". To perform some action merely because someone thinks I should do so, while I am not convinced it is agreeable to the will of God—that would be sin for me (vs. 21-23).

(3) Mutual forbearance (15:1-13). The Apostle now reaches the highest reason why the strong should bear with the weak. The strong should act toward the weak in the spirit of Christ, who pleased not Himself. "To bear the infirmities of the weak", is to put oneself under their limitations and to give up one's own rights for their good, as Christ did. Paul quotes Psa. 69:9 in support of this, and justifies his quotation by a statement about the abiding value of the Old Testament Scriptures (vs. 1-4).

Then he prays for unity of mind in the Christian community, and that it may result in unity and harmony in the worship of God (vs. 5-6).

The Apostle concludes his argument by generalizing the principles that he has laid down. All whom Christ has received should be received into His Church without distinction between the strong and the weak, in order to promote the glory of God (v. 7). This applies specially to the division between Jews and Gentiles in the Christian community. By saving both Jews and Gentiles, Christ promotes the glory of God, showing God's faithfulness in the one case and His mercy in the other. The Apostle supports his appeal by a series of passages from the Old Testament (vs. 8-12). His quotations are taken from the Septuagint (Psa. 18:49; Deut. 32:43; Psa. 117:1; Isa. 11:10). Then he brings the whole doctrinal part of his Epistle to an end with a benediction: "Now the God of hope fill you with all joy and peace in believing" (v. 13). This is characteristic of Paul. It is a beautiful habit of his in closing an argument.

NOTE:—The conduct which Paul describes in this section of the Epistle is essentially different from ordinary human righteousness. There is a different atmosphere about it. It is marked by the entire absence of self-will, self-interest, and self-love. Its point of view is always a tender and sympathetic interest in others, and it is pervaded by genuine love. Righteousness of this kind is not the product of natural ethics. Its secret is beyond the reach of psychological analysis. It is found by those alone who follow Christ in the way of the Cross.

Christian life is not self-culture. It is not the result of developing and perfecting one's own life. It is something immeasurably higher and nobler.

The Christian man escapes from evil habits and evil passions, not by the force of his own moral struggles, but by the power of the Spirit of the living Christ. He takes his place with other men in human society, but he holds in his heart a transcendent secret. He shares with other men the duties and tasks of common life, but the quality of his life is entirely different from theirs. While his feet are on the solid earth, the springs of his life are in a higher world.

THE CONCLUSION
(15:14—16:27)

God's way of salvation by the gift of His own righteousness having been fully explained, and the theme of the Epistle being finished, the Apostle goes on with a somewhat lengthened conclusion. It deals with some personal matters and contains some personal messages.

1. Personal Matters (15:14-33). Paul explains that his writing to the Romans does not imply that he is ignorant of their high Christian character and deep spiritual knowledge. But he is fulfilling the ministry with which God entrusted him as the Apostle to the Gentiles (vs. 14-17). His guiding principle has been to preach the Gospel where others had not done so and where Christ was not yet named. He has already fulfilled this ministry in the eastern part of the Empire (vs. 18-21). And again he describes the aim of his mission in words taken from the Old Testament (Isa. 52:15).

He goes on to tell of the desire he has had for many years to visit Rome. He plans a journey into Spain, and he hopes to visit the Romans on the way (vs. 22-24). But at present he must go to Jerusalem with the contribution which the Gentile churches of the two provinces of Greece have raised for the poor among the Jewish Christians at Jerusalem. This gift of theirs is but a just recompense for the spiritual blessings which the Gentiles have received from the Jews (vs. 25-27). When that mission is accomplished, he hopes to visit the Romans on his way to Spain, "in the fulness of the blessing of Christ" (vs. 28-29). Meanwhile he earnestly asks for their prayers, that he may be delivered from the unbelieving Jews in Judea, that the gifts which he bears to Jerusalem may be accepted by the believing Jews, and that it may be the will of God that he should come to the Romans with joy, and find rest in their fellowship. Then comes another benediction: "Now the God of peace be with you all" (vs. 30-33).

2. Personal Messages (Ch. 16). This chapter is a revelation of the brotherly love that existed in the early Church, and of the personal interest which Christians took in one another. In the course of these messages Paul names thirty-three persons, nine of whom are with him in Corinth and twenty-four are in Rome. He also refers to three groups of unnamed brethren and two unnamed women.

Paul begins the list by commending Phoebe to the Roman Christians, who was an active worker in the church at Cenchreæ, the port of Corinth. She was going to Rome, and probably carried the Epistle with her. Nothing else is known about her; but what is said here would indicate that she was a person of some wealth and position, and was thus able to help the Christian community (vs. 1-2).

Next comes a greeting to Priscilla and Aquila. Paul adds a special commendation about them (vs. 3-5). This remarkable couple exerted a wide influence among the churches as they moved from place to place. Paul would doubtless learn a good deal about the church in Rome when he lived with them in Corinth (Acts 18:2-3). They went with him from Corinth to Ephesus, where they remained for some time, making their house a meeting place for the Christians there (1 Cor. 16:19). They were back in Rome now, and here again Paul mentions "the church that is in their house".

Then follows a list of the other Christians in Rome to whom Paul sends salutations (vs. 5-16). Seventeen men are mentioned and seven women, and about almost every one he has something particular to say, showing his sympathetic personal interest in people. When he calls some "kinsmen", he means fellow-countrymen, and not relatives. When he refers to them that are of the households of Aristobulus and Narcissus, he means slaves belonging to the household establishments of these wealthy Romans.

Then the Apostle introduces a warning against false teachers (vs. 17-19). He is probably not referring to teachers actually in Rome at the time, but to such as he knew existed in some of the churches he had founded, and who might yet appear in Rome. They are described as being self-interested in their motives and deceptive in their manners. He gives this warning because he would have the Roman Christians "wise unto that which is good, and simple unto that which is evil"—that is, discreet and wary, and therefore blameless. These teachers who cause divisions and break up the peace of the Church are not serving Christ, but are instruments of Satan.

In allusion to this Paul adds the assurance: "And the God of peace shall bruise Satan under your feet shortly". Then he ends the warning with a benediction, as if he were closing the Epistle (v. 20).

Following this is a sort of postscript with the greetings of Paul's companions in Corinth, ending in another benediction (vs. 21-24). Tertius was the amanuensis who was writing the Epistle at Paul's dictation. It seems to have been the Apostle's general custom to dictate his letters and add a salutation with his own hand (1 Cor. 16.21; Col. 4:18; 2 Thess. 3:17). Gaius, who is described as the host of Paul and of the whole church, is probably the Gaius of 1 Cor. 1:14. The Christian assembly in Corinth met in his house. Erastus held the office of "the treasurer of the city"; which shows that there were at least a few important people among the members of the Corinthian church (1 Cor. 1:26).

The Epistle comes to an end with a noble doxology, which sums up all its great ideas—the power of the Gospel of Jesus Christ which Paul preached, the revelation in it of God's eternal purpose, and the gift of salvation promised in the Scriptures, which God now offers through it to the faith and obedience of all the nations. To its Author, the only wise God, be ascribed through Jesus Christ, glory for ever. Amen (vs. 25-27).

THE FIRST EPISTLE TO THE CORINTHIANS

CORINTH was the largest and most important city in Greece in Paul's time. It had a population of more than half a million people, two-thirds of whom were slaves. It was a great commercial metropolis, lying on the direct route between Ephesus and Rome. For a hundred years it had been steadily growing in size and wealth, and it now occupied a position of great prosperity. It was also the centre of an immoral pagan worship. Its people lived in luxury, and it had the reputation of being one of the most profligate and corrupt cities in the Roman Empire.

The Gospel was introduced into Corinth, and the church was established there, by the Apostle Paul, who laboured in the city for a year and a half during his second missionary journey (Acts 18:1-11). Apollos came later and greatly helped the cause of Christ and the growth of the church (Acts 18:27-28). Its membership contained some Jews, but was composed mainly of poor and unlearned Gentiles who had been converted from paganism (1 Cor. 1:26; 12:2).

The First Epistle was written from Ephesus in the spring of A.D. 56, toward the close of Paul's three years' stay there, not more than five years after the Gospel had first been preached in Corinth. The note at the end of the letter in the A.V., saying that it was written in Philippi, is due to a misunderstanding of Paul's statement in 16:5. The Apostle was already making plans to depart for Macedonia and go on through that province to Corinth, but he intended to remain in Ephesus till the early summer (Acts 19:21-22; 1 Cor. 16:5-9). A deputation from Corinth had visited him (16:17-18), bringing a letter from the church in which several matters were submitted to him for his judgment and advice (7:1). These had to do mainly with the social life and fellowship of the Christian community.

Besides the information contained in that letter, Paul had learned from other sources that serious troubles existed in the church (1:11; 5:1). The members were divided into factions by party spirit and rivalry. Moral disorders had crept in, and spiritual discipline was lacking. Misunderstandings about their social relations existed among them, and these had led to disturbance and confusion in their meetings for worship. The church was noted for its spiritual gifts (1:4-7), but many of its members were manifesting these in wrong ways. The fundamental Christian doctrine of the resurrection was being called in question.

All these matters combined to give Paul the occasion for writing this letter. It was not the first letter he had written to them, for in 5:9 he refers to an earlier one, which has not been preserved. The one comprehensive theme of this First Epistle is the practical application of the Gospel to the life and work of the Church. It falls into the following main divisions:

I. Party Spirit in the Church—Chs. 1-4
II. Moral Disorders in the Church—Chs. 5-7
III. Social Relations in the Church—Chs. 8-11
IV. Spiritual Gifts in the Church—Chs. 12-14
V. The Fundamental Doctrine of the Church— Ch. 15
VI. The Conclusion of the Letter—Ch. 16

PARTY SPIRIT IN THE CHURCH
(Chs. 1—4)

The letter begins with a brief introduction containing Paul's salutation to the church at Corinth (1:1-3), and his thanksgiving for the character and testimony of its members (1:4-9). Probably Sosthenes, whom he associates with himself in the salutation as a "brother", and who must have been well known to the Corinthians, was the ruler of the synagogue mentioned in Acts 18:17, who had played a part in the scene that took place when the Jews brought Paul before Gallio. If so, he was now a Christian and was living in Ephesus. He was probably Paul's host at the time the letter was written.

The Corinthian church was noted for the spiritual endowments which the grace of God had bestowed upon its members. They had been enriched "in all utterance and all knowledge"—inspired utterance and spiritual knowledge. They came behind other churches in no divine gift, while they watched for the coming of the Lord. Christ Himself would keep them steadfast, so that they should be without reproach in that day. God who had called them would not fail them.

After this introduction, the Apostle refers to the divisions among the Corinthians which he has been

told about, and appeals for the spirit of unity. He urges this on several grounds.

1. Christ is the Only Head of the Church (1:10-17). "Now I beseech you, brethren, through the name of our Lord Jesus Christ": this is the tenth time the Apostle has used the Saviour's name in ten verses. Party spirit dishonours Him. Factions arise in the Church when the members attach themselves to human teachers. The Church is the body of Christ, and Christ cannot be divided. It was into His Name, and not into the names of their teachers, that the members of the church were baptized. Paul himself baptized very few, for the mission on which he was sent was not to baptize but to preach the Gospel.

2. The Gospel Manifests the Power of God Alone (1:18—2:5). It leaves no room for glorying in men. Paul bases his argument on this point on three facts.

(1) The story of the Cross (1:18-25). In the eyes of the world the Gospel is an absurdity; but to us who are saved it is a manifestation of the power of God. The word of the prophet has been fulfilled (Isa. 29:14). God has shown the foolishness of worldly wisdom. When the world by its wisdom failed to find God, God Himself provided a way of salvation for those that trust Him, by the proclamation of what seems foolish (vs. 18-21). The Jews demand a miraculous sign, and the Greeks seek philosophical wisdom. The message that we preach is Christ crucified—an offence to the Jews and folly to the Greeks; but to those that believe and accept it, it is both the power of God and the wisdom of God. The "foolishness" and "weakness" of God surpass all the wisdom and strength of men (vs. 22-25).

(2) The membership of the Church (1:26-31). It does not include many that are wise and learned and high-born. It is composed mainly of those that are lowly and despised by the world. Through them God has put to shame the things that are wise and strong. It was not through these things that the salvation of the Corinthians was achieved. Jesus Christ alone is made God-given wisdom for us, our righteousness and sanctification and redemption. And so there is no place for glorying in man (Jer. 9:23).

(3) Paul's ministry in Corinth (2:1-5). The Apostle came to the Corinthians not with oratory or philosophy. He determined to make no display of knowledge among them except of Jesus Christ and Him crucified. He appeared before them in bodily weakness and in timidity, and his message was delivered to them with no plausible arguments of human wisdom, but with the manifestation of the power of the Holy Spirit. Thus their faith does not rest on human philosophy, but on the power of God.

3. The Gospel Contains God's Wisdom not Man's (2:6-16). Paul imparts this wisdom to those that are of ripe understanding. It is a wisdom that is not of this world, and is unknown to its rulers. It is a hidden spiritual truth revealed only by the Spirit of God. The rulers of the world showed their ignorance of it by crucifying the Lord of glory (vs. 6-8). At this point Paul refers to Isa. 64:4 in a free quotation, and goes on to explain that just as a man's secrets are known only by the man's own spirit, so the secrets of God are known only by the Spirit of God. And these are the things that have

been revealed to us, not by the spirit of the world, but by the Spirit of God (vs. 9-12).

It is of these themes that Paul speaks, not in terms of human philosophy, but in terms learned from the Holy Spirit, embodying spiritual conceptions in spiritual language. Man in his natural state cannot understand the revelations of the Spirit of God. They require a spiritual attitude for their appreciation, and only a spiritual man can discern them. The spiritual man is able to bring his own judgment to bear upon all things, while he himself is beyond the reach of the natural man's judgment. Paul then quotes Isa. 40:13 to support his argument that the natural man knows not the mind of the Lord God. It is known only by those who have the mind of Christ (vs. 13-16).

4. Party Spirit Hinders Spiritual Progress (3: 1-9). When Paul was with the Corinthians he could not treat them as spiritual and full grown men. He had to deal with them as "babes in Christ", as immature Christians in whom the carnal nature was still dominant. Their jealousy and strife in preferring one teacher above another arose from their carnal nature, and were marks of their spiritual immaturity (vs. 1-4). The various teachers through whom they believed are but instruments in God's hands, each of them doing the work that God assigned to him. Paul who planted the seed of the Gospel, and Apollos who watered it, are nothing in themselves; it is God who makes the seed grow (vs. 5-7). He who plants and he who waters work together as one instrument. Each shall receive his special wage according to the special work he has done, but the results are God's alone. The ministers of the Gospel are God's fellow-labourers; but the husbandry, the building, is God's, and not theirs (vs. 8-9).

5. Jesus Christ is the One Foundation of the Church (3:10-23). According to the grace that God gave him, Paul laid the foundation of the church in Corinth, and another builds thereon. Each one is responsible for the material he puts into the building. The foundation, which is Jesus Christ, has been laid once for all (vs. 10-11). The work of each builder will be put to the proof in the day of judgment. It will be tested by a fire that will reveal the true quality of every man's work. If his work endures the test, he will receive a reward. A man's work may be destroyed while he himself is saved (vs. 12-15). The members of the church in Corinth form a sanctuary in which God dwells, and God will destroy the man who destroys His holy temple (vs. 16-17).

Let no man therefore deceive himself by boasting of his wisdom to judge between human teachers. The wisdom of the world is foolish and vain, says Paul, and to support his statement he quotes Job 5:13 and Psa. 94:11. Therefore let no one glory in a particular human teacher. All the teachers of the Church belong to the members of the Church. In God's purpose all things—life and death, the present and the future—are made to serve the members of the Church. This is so because they belong to Christ and Christ belongs to God (vs. 18-23).

6. The Lord is the Only Judge of His Servants (4:1-5). The teachers of the Church should be regarded as servants of Christ and stewards of God's revealed truth. They are responsible only to God, and they will be judged according to their faithfulness. Paul is not concerned about man's judgment of him; nor does he judge himself, but leaves his judgment with the Lord. He warns the Corinthians against passing judgments before the Lord comes, who will lay bare the purposes of men's hearts. Then due praise will be awarded to each man from God.

7. Party Spirit Springs from Spiritual Pride (4:6-13). In dealing with the relation of the Corinthians to their teachers, Paul has spoken only of himself and Apollos, that in them his readers may learn not to go beyond the authority of Scripture by glorying in men, and not to be inflated with conceit in their partisanship. Every gift and grace they possess has been received from God, and this gives them no ground for boasting (vs. 6-7). Then Paul proceeds to draw out an ironical contrast between the pride and self-complacency shown by the Corinthians and the labours and privations endured by the Apostles (vs. 8-13).

8. A Final Appeal for Unity (4:14-21). The Apostle's purpose in writing in this way is not to put his readers to shame, but to warn them as his dear children. He reminds the Corinthians that they are his own converts, and therefore they should follow his example. He has sent Timothy to them, his "beloved and faithful child in the Lord", who will remind them of his "ways which are in Christ" —how he conducts himself as a teacher in every church everywhere (vs. 14-17). Probably Timothy was going around by land, and the letter, being sent across the sea, would arrive before him.

They were not to infer from this that Paul was not coming himself. Some of them had assumed an arrogant tone, thinking that he dare not come. But come he would shortly, if it was the Lord's will. And then he would test, not how great is the talk of the arrogant, but how great is their power. The Kingdom of God depends not on talk, but on supernatural power. Let them choose whether he should come with a rod of chastisement, or in love and a spirit of gentleness (vs. 18-21).

MORAL DISORDERS IN THE CHURCH
(Chs. 5—7)

The Apostle now turns to questions affecting the moral conduct of the members of the church. They were in danger of being contaminated by the corrupt state of heathen society around them.

1. The Need of Discipline (5:1-8). A case of gross immorality existed among them; and they were puffed up with self-satisfaction, when they should have been bowed down with grief and should have removed the offender from their fellowship (vs. 1-2). Paul states his own judgment in the matter: the church should solemnly deliver such a person into the hands of Satan, that his body may be afflicted in order that the spirit may be saved in the day of judgment (vs. 3-5). Satan was regarded as ruling the realm of disease and death, but as acting only by God's permission (Job. 2:5-6; Luke 13:16; 22:31; 2 Cor. 12:7). Paul refers to another case of the same kind of punishment in 1 Tim. 1:20.

The Corinthians have little cause for glorying when they allow contagion to remain which would defile their whole society. They should purge out the old leaven, for the fellowship of the Church should be maintained with "the unleavened bread of sincerity and truth" (vs. 6-8). In using this figure Paul has in mind the removal of leaven from the house of the Israelites at the time of the Passover (Ex. 12:15).

2. The Christian Principle of Discipline (5:9-13). The Apostle now turns from the particular case to general rules of conduct on the subject. He refers to what he had told the Corinthians in an earlier letter, now lost. He pointed out that it was impossible for Christians to avoid coming into contact with the immoral and wicked people of the pagan world, for then they should have to withdraw altogether from the active business of life. But if a member of the Church commit such sin, the Christians should refuse to have any fellowship with him. We are to leave the judgment of those that are without the Church to God; it is those within the Church that we are to judge. Therefore Paul commands the Corinthians to put away the wicked man from among themselves.

3. On Going to Law (6:1-11). Christians should settle disputes among themselves within the Church, and not go to law in the courts of unbelievers. The saints are finally to judge even angels; and surely they ought to be able to judge things pertaining to this life (vs. 1-3). Has it come to this that no wise man can be found among the members of the Corinthian church capable of judging between his brethren; so that brethren have to go to law before unbelievers (vs. 4-6)? It is better that Christians should bear wrong and be defrauded rather than go to law before the world (vs. 7-8). This principle applies when no more important matter is at stake than one's own individual loss, or when the rights of others are not involved. On one occasion Paul used his right as a Roman citizen to appeal to Cæsar (Acts 25:9-11).

The Apostle then sums up what he has been saying in this section about moral questions (vs. 9-11). The unrighteous, and those living in wickedness and immorality, will not inherit the Kingdom of God. The Corinthians were once like that. But they have been "sanctified", set apart from sin to God; they have been "justified", freed from guilt and accounted righteous.

4. The Sanctity of the Body (6:12-20). It is true that all things are lawful for me (Paul is probably quoting a saying of his own which some have been misusing), but it does not follow that all things are good for me. All things that are not immoral are lawful for the Christian; but freedom is not licence. The question for him to answer is, are they expedient? He should not indulge in anything that brings his body under its power. Food is intended for the body, and the body is adapted for food; but both shall be destroyed by death. The body is not intended for fornication, for it belongs to the Lord, who gave Himself for our bodies. They have been sanctified by His resurrection, and are destined to be raised up as His body was raised up (vs. 12-14).

Your bodies are members of Christ. Therefore unchastity is to be abhorred; it is a sin against one's own body. Know you not that the Holy Spirit, which you have received from God, dwells in your body as in a temple? You are not your own; you were bought with a high price when Christ suffered.

Therefore glorify God with your body as well as with your spirit (vs. 15-20).

5. The Subject of Marriage (Ch. 7). A number of questions regarding this matter had been referred to Paul for his judgment. Many of them had to do with local conditions of life in Corinth. Paul's answers contain principles of permanent application, and may be summed up as follows:

(1) The unmarried state is good and has special advantages; but marriage is honourable, and should be the general rule in practice (vs. 1-9). Paul gives certain advice "by way of concession" (v. 6)—that is, by way of permission on his part to the Corinthians. He gives it as a concession to their weakness, not as an injunction. He wishes all had the gift of self-control that he has.

(2) The sanctity of the marriage bond should be preserved (vs. 10-16). The Apostle reminds his readers of the Lord's charge prohibiting divorce (Matt. 5:32; Luke 16:18). Then he gives his own advice regarding married couples when one of the parties is an unbeliever. An unbelieving husband or wife may be saved by the Christian life of the other. When one parent is a believer, the family should be taken into the Christian community and the children should be recognized as "holy"—set apart for God. Paul's teaching is, that the Church should recognize the solidarity of the family, and the children of Christian parents, though not yet believers, should be treated as members of the Christian fellowship. This principle holds even if only one parent is a believer. If, however, it is the unbeliever who desires a separation, let the separation take place; for we are called as Christians to live in an atmosphere of peace.

(3) Christianity does not interfere with existing relations in human society (vs. 17-24). Jews and Gentiles should remain Jews and Gentiles when they are converted; they should not abandon their former national and social customs. Bondservants should remain in the position they occupied before being converted, for they are now the Lord's freedmen. Those who were freemen before conversion should now be the Lord's bondservants. The general principle for the Christian is stated twice (vs. 20 and 24). Paul says in effect: do not aim at getting on and getting up in the world, but do God's will wherever you are and leave the rest to Him. This does not agree with the maxims of worldly ambition, but it is spiritual wisdom.

(4) The advantages of the unmarried state (vs. 25-40). Paul now returns to the subject of marriage, and takes up the question "concerning virgins", or unmarried daughters under parental care. Before dealing with their special case, which he does not reach till v. 36, he discusses the general principle that covers it. He begins his discussion of this part of the subject by saying that the Lord has left no command about it, but he will give his own judgment according to the light given him (v. 25), and he ends with a modest claim that his judgment is inspired of God (v. 40).

His judgment may be summarized as follows: There are circumstances in which it is better for men and women to remain unmarried, for in that condition they are better able to serve the Lord. The married state ties one to the things of this world with its joys and its sorrows. The unmarried state leaves one free to "attend upon the Lord without distraction". Paul's advice is based upon the character of the time that is left before the coming of the Lord (v. 29). Christians have no longer anything assured in the present world. They are to live in the world, "as not using it to the full" as if their full enjoyment lay therein; "for the fashion of this world passeth away" (v. 31). It is in the light of this hope they should live, and from this point of view they should treat all earthly questions.

SOCIAL RELATIONS IN THE CHURCH
(Chs. 8—11)

Difficulties had arisen among the Corinthian Christians in their social relations both with their heathen neighbours and among themselves. These had to do mainly with the eating of meat that had been offered in sacrifice to idols (chs. 8—10), and with the conduct of public worship in the church (ch. 11). In the one case Paul explains and applies the principle of Christian liberty, and in the other case the principle of Christian decorum.

1. The Use of Christian Liberty (Ch. 8). There is a general similarity between this chapter and Rom. 14. There the question has to do with the ceremonial difference between clean and unclean meats; here it has to do with eating meat offered in sacrifice to idols and afterwards sold in the market for food. Paul begins by pointing out the two principles that are to be kept in mind in all such cases—knowledge and love. Knowledge tends to spiritual pride: brotherly love leads to spiritual growth (vs. 1-3). Then he states the question in the light of knowledge. Knowledge delivers the Christian from the bondage of heathen superstition. He knows that there is no reality in an idol, and that there is but one true God, the Father, and one Lord, Jesus Christ (vs. 4-6).

But some have not this knowledge, and so Paul goes on to state the question in the light of love. A Christian who acts from love will consider the effect his own conduct may have on his brother. He will limit his liberty so as not to offend the conscience of his weaker brother. To offend the weak conscience of one for whom Christ died is to sin against Christ (vs. 7-12). Finally Paul, speaking for himself, states the true use of Christian liberty in regard to the question under consideration: "If meat causeth my brother to stumble, I will eat no flesh forevermore" (v. 13).

2. The Apostle's Example (Ch. 9). Paul now illustrates the proper use of Christian liberty by describing his own conduct as an Apostle in another matter. Although others might question his apostleship, the very existence of the Corinthian church was a proof of it (vs. 1-2). As an Apostle of the Lord he had certain rights with the rest of the Apostles (vs. 3-6). One of these was the right to receive support from the churches that he had founded—to accept a ministry in temporal things from his converts for his ministry to them in spiritual things. He quotes Deut. 25:4 to show that this principle is recognized in the Law (vs. 7-12). But he did not use this right, even though the Lord ordained that they that proclaim the Gospel should be supported by the Gospel. Paul has been restrained from using this right by his thought of the needs of others, and while preaching the Gospel he has supported himself (vs. 12-18).

His general principle in preaching the Gospel has been that of sympathetic approach. He put himself in the position of those to whom he preached that he might win them for Christ—becoming "all things to all men, that I may by all means save some" (vs. 19-23). He then goes on to emphasize the need of self-restraint in Christian life by an illustration taken from the Greek games, which were held on the Isthmus a few miles from Corinth. The athlete who contends in the race must observe self-control in all things. The crown of victory is won only by rigid discipline (vs. 24-27).

3. The Failure of the Israelites (10:1-22). Paul now turns to Old Testament history, and bases a warning for the Corinthians upon the failure of the Israelites in the wilderness. All the members of the nation shared alike in the high privileges bestowed on them when they were delivered from Egypt through Moses (vs. 1-4). The emphasis is on the word "all", which is repeated five times. The Apostle treats the historic events of the Exodus as the frame of spiritual realities. He regards the salvation wrought for Israel through Moses as one and the same work with the salvation brought in by Christ. The principles of Divine action which were at work in the redemption from Egypt are the same as those that wrought out the final salvation from sin.

The means of grace provided by God—"the same spiritual food, and the same spiritual drink"—were enjoyed by all the Israelites after they came out of Egypt, but the majority of them perished in the wilderness because of their self-indulgence (v. 5). Their fate is a type of the lot that threatens the Corinthians if they act in the same way (vs. 6-10). Their lot is a lesson and warning to us. The things that happened to them are historical types of spiritual realities belonging to the present Christian age (v. 11).

The Apostle proceeds to warn the Corinthians against the over-confidence that was too common among them, and adds a comforting assurance of Divine help to encourage their dependence on God (vs. 12-13). Then he returns to the main argument of ch. 8, and gives his converts a tender and solemn warning against taking part in the sacrificial feasts of their heathen neighbours (vs. 14-22). He draws a parallel between these feasts and the feast of the Lord's Supper. The Christian feast means communion with Christ and sharing the benefits of His sacrifice. The heathen feast means communion with demons, for although the idol is nothing in itself, there is a demonic power at work behind the worship of idols.

4. The Limits of Christian Liberty (10:23-33). The whole discussion of the question is now summed up in these verses. Paul begins with a repetition of the words in 6:12, which were probably his own but had been used by some in Corinth in a sense he did not intend. The Christian is free to enjoy anything and everything that belongs to this world of God's. For the earth is the Lord's and the fulness thereof (Psa. 24:1). But that freedom of his is to be used in accordance with other Christian principles. He is to seek not his own but his neighbour's good, respecting the conscience of his weaker

brother without weakening his own. The promotion of the glory of God is to be the rule of Christian conduct in all matters. No stumbling blocks should be put in the way of any by offending their scruples, whether Jews or Greeks or fellow-members of the Church of God.

5. Decorum in Public Worship (11:1-16). The Apostle now deals with some disorders that had appeared in the public services of the Corinthian church. These arose from the women thinking that their Christian liberty gave them equality with men. He first points out the system of subordination in the divine order of creation (vs. 1-3). As Christ is dependent on God, and man is dependent on Christ, so woman is dependent on man. This order of subordination is to be maintained in the Church and in its worship (vs. 4-6). It is manifested by proper respect for the recognized differences of dress on the part of men and women, and by proper deportment befitting each sex, according to the conventional customs of the social order. Greek women wore a veil in public, and Christian liberty did not give them the right to discard it when they were converted. Only women of low reputation appeared in public unveiled. What Paul describes in these verses practically means that a man with his head covered worshipped as a woman, and a woman with her head uncovered worshipped as a man.

Paul now confirms his teaching in this matter by a direct appeal to the divine order of subordination in the creation (vs. 7-10). Man with his face uncovered represents the image and glory of God. Woman represents the image and glory of man, because she had her being originally through the man, and not directly from God like the man. She was made subject to the man, and therefore she should have "a sign of authority" on her head, showing that she modestly accepts her place as subordinate to man in the Divine government. And this, "because of the angels". They are present unseen in the worship of the Church of God (Heb. 12:22; 1 Tim. 5:21), and are offended when any dishonour is shown to the Divine majesty.

This difference between men and women in the order of creation does not affect their equality in the Lord. They both share the same privileges in the Church (vs. 11-12). Finally, Paul appeals to the natural feelings of humanity and the fitness of things in general (vs. 13-16). Christianity recognizes the established rules of decorum in every country, and never violates the natural instincts of any people.

6. The Observance of the Lord's Supper (11:17-34). Even this sacred feast had been affected by the factions and social disorders in the Corinthian church. The Apostle now deals with its proper observance. He first rebukes his readers for their abuse of the feast. The service that was intended to be the very symbol of union and communion in the Church was being made the occasion for exhibiting the differences and divisions among the members (vs. 17-19). They also turned the spiritual feast into a material one, treating it as an occasion for satisfying their own hunger, as in the idolatrous feasts of their former heathenism (vs. 20-22).

Then in simple and stately language Paul tells of the original institution of the Supper as he had received it from the Lord, and adds his comment upon it (vs. 23-26). It is the Church's way of proclaiming that the ground of its salvation lies in the sacrificial death of the Lord Jesus Christ, and it is to be continued till He comes again. There is therefore need of self-examination, lest one commit an offence against the Lord Himself by coming to His table in an irreverent spirit, and by failing to see the Lord's body in the symbols of bread and wine (vs. 27-29). This is the reason why bodily chastisements have been visited upon some members of the Corinthian church. Chastisements are intended for our spiritual discipline, that we may not be involved in the world's judgment (vs. 30-34).

SPIRITUAL GIFTS IN THE CHURCH
(Chs. 12—14)

The Corinthian Christians were displaying a personal rivalry in spiritual matters. They were more concerned about gifts than about grace. The Apostle now turns to this aspect of their church life. "Now concerning spiritual gifts" (12:1): the word "gifts" is not in the original, but it expresses as well as any word can what the Apostle has in mind. He means the different ways in which the Holy Spirit manifests His presence in the Church.

1. The Origin and Purpose of Spiritual Gifts (12:1-11). After referring to the frenzies of idol worship by which they were carried away in their former paganism (vs. 1-2), Paul explains to the Corinthians that the presence of the Holy Spirit is the governing principle in the worship of the Church. It is through Him that we recognize the Deity of Jesus and call Him Lord, thus giving Him the Old Testament title of Jehovah (v. 3).

There are different kinds of spiritual gifts and they have different functions, but they are distributed to the various members of the Christian community for the common good (vs. 4-7). Paul illustrates this with a list of nine gifts of the Spirit, given for different purposes (vs. 8-10). It is not implied that these were all the spiritual gifts that were given; nor that they were all given to every church. They are mentioned to show that the Spirit is always sovereign in their disposal—"dividing to each one severally even as he will" (v. 11).

2. The Mutual Relation of Spiritual Gifts (12:12-31). The Church with its members is like the human body. Believers with their different gifts are related to one another as the different members of the body. The Church is the spiritual body of Christ, created such by the baptism of the Holy Spirit at Pentecost. It is one spiritual organism, with many members, sharing one and the same Spirit (vs. 12-13). In the body every member is needed for the sake of the whole body; and each member needs the other members in order to fulfil its own function (vs. 14-21). Even the weaker members are necessary; and we bestow more care upon them and show them more honour, so that there may be no schism in the body, but sympathy and harmony between all its members (vs. 22-26).

The direct application of this analogy follows in the rest of the passage (vs. 27-31). Christians are the body of Christ collectively and His members individually. God has assigned different functions to different members of the Church, but none of these functions is common to the whole Christian body.

A list of functions is given in the order of their rank or importance in the Church. The first is that of the Apostles; next, that of the prophets, or inspired preachers; third, that of the teachers, or expounders of the truth. Then come certain supernatural functions given to various members—the working of miracles and gifts of healing—followed by certain functions for giving help and giudance. The gift of tongues comes last in the list. The Apostle closes with an injunction to his readers to seek after the best gifts, those that minister to the edification of the Church.

3. The Supreme Gift of Love (Ch. 13). This chapter is connected with the last verse of ch. 12, the second part of which should belong to it and may be paraphrased as follows: Moreover I show unto you the most excellent way to attain spiritual greatness, the greatest gift of all, the grace of love The old word "charity" (A.V.) is now commonly limited to almsgiving, or kindly judgment of others. Paul is describing something larger than that, something that is not merely an emotion but an attitude of mind and heart requiring constant expression.

(1) The pre-eminence of love (vs. 1-3). Love is supreme over the emotional gift of eloquence, over the intellectual gift of knowledge, over the practical gift of faith, and over the heroic gift of self-sacrifice.

(2) The properties of love (vs. 4-7). In this analysis of the grace of love, Paul presents an ideal of the same kind as the beatitudes in the Sermon on the Mount (Matt. 5:3-9). It is another description of the character of Jesus. Here the mark of the Cross is unmistakable; self-will and self-seeking have completely died away. Its supreme quality is the surrender of self-interest for the sake of others.

(3) The permanence of love (vs. 8-13). Love always holds its place and will never cease to function. Other spiritual gifts have temporary purposes and are only fragmentary. They are suited for a state of imperfection. like that of childhood, and will make way hereafter for that which is full grown. In the present life we have only imperfect vision, but in the next life we shall have perfect knowledge. The abiding graces are faith, hope, and love; and the greatest of these three is love.

4. The Relative Value of Spiritual Gifts (14:1-19). Paul now takes up the two gifts that seem to have caused most rivalry in the Corinthian church, prophecy and tongues, and discusses their relative importance. He points out that the value of a gift depends on what it does for the edification of the Church. Hence prophesying, which edifies men, is more important than speaking with tongues, which edifies oneself and is not understood by others (vs. 1-5). The gift of prophecy was evidently that of proclaiming Christian truth and bearing Christian witness.

The Apostle proceeds to explain that speaking with tongues should be accompanied by interpretation, for without that it is useless (vs. 6-12). Tongues could be interpreted by those who had a sympathetic understanding of what they expressed. Their meaning was felt by the emotional nature rather than understood by the intellect. This gift, therefore, was evidently something of the nature of music, something intermediate between speaking and singing. It was not the power to speak in other languages. It was the ecstatic and spontaneous expression of those feelings of joy and praise that sprang up in the heart of the convert from heathenism because of his new life in Christ. It was the result of the Holy Spirit's presence within his soul overflowing his human nature.

The spiritual gift of speaking with tongues has passed into the ordered worship of the Church in the form of sacred song and praise. This gift, Paul explains, should not be exercised without interpretation, for those who do not understand what praise and thanksgiving is being expressed are not edified. Paul himself speaks with tongues privately more than they all do. But in a church service he would rather speak five words for the instruction and edification of others than ten thousand words in a tongue that they did not understand (vs. 13-19).

5. The Right Use of Spiritual Gifts (14:20-40). In the use of the gift of tongues the Apostle appeals for common sense (v. 20). Tongues are a sign of God's presence to the unbelieving; and Paul quotes Isa. 28:11-12 as an illustration of God's use of the strange tongue of the Assyrian invaders to warn His own unbelieving people, who would not listen to His prophets speaking to them in their own tongue. But if tongues are unregulated in the services of the church, unbelievers will think you are mad (vs. 21-23). Prophecy, on the other hand, searches the heart of the hearer and brings him face to face with God (vs. 24-25). Let all parts of church worship be carried on for edifying. Those who speak in a tongue should do so in regular order, and only when there is someone present who can interpret (vs. 26-28).

The prophets also should limit themselves to two or three at a meeting, and the congregation should discern the spiritual value of what they say. If a revelation comes to one sitting in the audience, the first speaker should bring his address to a close. It is quite possible for all to speak in turn under inspiration for the instruction and comfort of all, because the spirits of the prophets are under their own control, and God is not a God of confusion but of peace (vs. 29-33). Then comes a prohibition forbidding women to speak in the churches. They are to recognize the subordination in which they are placed according to Gen. 3:16 (vs. 34-36). This cannot be a contradiction of 11:5, which implies that women have the right to pray or prophesy in the church if they are veiled.

The Apostle's prohibition is probably directed against unseemly outbursts of emotional excitement to which the women were especially prone. The warning occurs in connection with Paul's discussion of the gift of tongues, and immediately after his warning about confusion. Then he concludes his discussion with final admonitions addressed to the prophets and others endowed with spiritual gifts (vs. 37-38), and to all the members of the church (vs. 39-40). The gift of prophecy is to be earnestly desired, and speaking with tongues is not to be forbidden. But whatever gifts are exercised, church services should be carried on "decently and in order".

THE FUNDAMENTAL DOCTRINE OF THE CHURCH
(Ch. 15)

Some members of the Corinthian church had been

declaring that there is no resurrection of the dead. Paul now deals with this error by showing that the Resurrection is the fundamental doctrine of the Christian Church, because the Church is based on the resurrection of Christ.

1. The Fact of Christ's Resurrection (vs. 1-19). Paul reminds the Corinthians that the Gospel which he preached unto them, and by which they are saved, is the story that Christ died for our sins and was raised from the dead; and all this was in fulfilment of the Scriptures (vs. 1-4). The fact of His resurrection is proved by the many witnesses to whom He appeared, of whom Paul himself was the last (vs. 5-8). The change that took place in Paul's life, from being a persecutor of the Church to becoming an Apostle of Christ, and his abundant labours afterwards, are evidence of the reality of the risen Lord's appearance to him (vs. 9-11). The Gospel of Christ's resurrection implies the resurrection of the dead; for if the dead do not rise then Christ is still dead, the preaching of the Gospel is useless, and the Apostles are false witnesses (vs. 12-15). If Christ has not been raised, then faith in Him is empty, Christians are yet in their sins, those who have died in Him have perished, and Christian life is a pitiful delusion (vs. 16-19).

2. The Place of the Resurrection in the Plan of God (vs. 20-28). Christ's resurrection is the firstfruits of a great harvest. The same principle that brought death brings life from the dead. As all who are in Adam and have his nature share his death, so all who are in Christ and have His nature will share His resurrection (vs. 20-22). Christ's resurrection is the first in order, then at His coming the resurrection of those that are His. Finally, when He has put all His enemies under His feet and abolished all the foes of God, He will abolish death itself, the last enemy (vs. 23-26). Then He will deliver up the Kingdom to God, with all things put in subjection to Him, that God may be all in all—that is, that God's sovereignty in the universe may be complete, the life and power of God the Father filling every part and member of it (vs. 27-28).

3. The Hope of the Resurrection in the Life of the Christian (vs. 29-34). Here Paul abruptly changes the course of his thought and brings in another argument for belief in the Resurrection. It is the supreme motive for Christian hope. This is shown by those who are "baptised for the dead" (v. 29). This obscure expression, which has been explained in numberless ways, most probably refers to those who became converts to Christianity "for the sake of the dead", their own beloved dead. They turned to Christ and were baptized in the hope of reunion with them through the resurrection of the dead. This belief is also the motive of those who "stand in jeopardy every hour", and suffer for Christ, as Paul himself did at Ephesus (vs. 30-32). Then the Apostle quotes a Greek proverb to warn his readers that they had been contaminated by a bad moral atmosphere and a false philosophy. They should awake out of their stupifying self-indulgence to righteousness of life. The hope of the Resurrection should impel them to live for spiritual things and avoid worldly pleasures (vs. 33-34).

4. The Nature of the Resurrection Body (vs. 35-49). The Apostle takes up the question raised by some as to the kind of body with which the dead

are raised up (v. 35). He first points out some analogies to illustrate bodily changes and varieties of bodily manifestations (vs. 36-41). These are intended to show that while there will be a continuity of the personality in the resurrection, there will be a difference in the body. He then describes the resurrection body as a spiritual body, and explains the difference between that and the natural body (vs. 42-49). The natural body is the body governed by the animal life. It belongs to the earthly order, and is subject to corruption. The spiritual body belongs to the heavenly order. It is adapted for, and under the control of, the spirit, and is not subject to the present world. As we have borne the image of the earthly in our natural bodies, so we shall bear the image of the heavenly in our spiritual bodies.

5. The Manner of the Resurrection (vs. 50-58). It will be the changing of corruptible and perishable bodies into incorruptible and immortal bodies, so that they may become fit organs of the spirit in the Kingdom of God (v. 50). The change that will take place in the resurrection of the dead saints will be accompanied by a similar change in the living saints This will all happen as a sudden, momentary event at the second coming of the Lord. Paul announces this as a Divine revelation made to him (vs. 51-53). It will mean the complete triumph over death and the power of sin, and the fulfilment of Isa. 25:8 and Hos. 13:14. The praise for this victory we owe to our Lord Jesus Christ (vs. 54-57). Paul closes his discussion of the Resurrection by summing up the practical bearing of this doctrine on the life and work of the Christian Church (v. 58).

THE CONCLUSION
(Ch. 16)

Having dealt with the various questions that had been referred to him relating to church life in Corinth, the Apostle now takes up some local and personal matters, and brings his letter to a close.

1. The Collection for the Poor (vs. 1-4). Paul was gathering a fund from the churches of the Gentile world to help the Christians in the Jewish church of Jerusalem, who were in poverty and suffering. Christianity gained the mass of its adherents in Palestine from the poorer classes of the people, and they would suffer still further oppression from the richer classes and from the official leaders among the Jews, who hated the Gospel. The instructions which Paul gives in this passage contain some principles of Christian giving. Giving should be systematic ("upon the first day of the week"), universal ("every one of you"), and proportionate ("as God hath prospered you"). The Apostle also suggests the appointment of delegates to carry the money to Jerusalem. Under no circumstances would he take charge of it himself; he would avoid all suspicion of appropriating any of it to his own use.

2. Paul's Approaching Visit (vs. 5-9). He tells the Corinthians of his plans. He intends to make a journey through Macedonia and then visit Corinth, and perhaps spend the winter there. In the meantime he intends to stay in Ephesus till the early summer—until Pentecost: "for a great door and effectual is opened unto me, and there are many adversaries". He would take advantage of such an

opportunity for work, especially because many were trying to close the door upon him.

3. News of His Companions (vs. 10-12). Paul had mentioned Timothy's visit before (4:17). Here he speaks of it with some uncertainty. What is said of Timothy here agrees with what we learn of his character elsewhere. He was comparatively young (1 Tim. 4:12) and perhaps a little timorous, but his work claimed the same respect as Paul's work. Apollos steadfastly declined Paul's earnest request that he should go to Corinth, probably because he feared that his presence there would stir up party spirit again.

4. Final Exhortations (vs. 13-18). The Apostle is preparing to close, and he sums up the message of the whole Epistle in the concise exhortations contained in vs. 13-14. The names mentioned in vs. 15-18 are those of the Corinthian deputies who had brought the letter from the church to Paul. In the fellowship of these three men he felt himself in fellowship with the whole church. They served as a link of sympathetic understanding between himself and them.

5. Final Salutations (vs. 19-24). The salutations that Paul attaches to his letters manifest his personal interest in his fellow Christians and his careful attention to the courtesies of life. The churches of Asia were those that had been founded in that province during Paul's ministry in Ephesus. Aquila and Priscilla had been with Paul in Corinth when he was establishing the church there (Acts 18:1-3), and they were now with him in Ephesus. "All the brethren salute you"—that is, the whole Ephesian church (vs. 19-20). The "holy kiss", or the kiss of peace, formed a prominent part in the ritual of the early Church as a token of Christian brotherhood (Rom. 16:16; 2 Cor. 13:12; 1 Thess. 5:26; 1 Pet. 5:14).

As the Apostle closes the Epistle with his own hand, after all its argument and controversy, he brings back the thoughts of the Corinthians to the true test of Christianity—personal love for the Lord Jesus Christ. If any one does not love the Lord— the word "not" is emphatic—he should be accursed. The word "Maranatha" is an Aramaic expression, standing by itself. It means "the Lord is at hand" (Phil. 4:5), and fittingly seals the whole message of the book. With a simple benediction and a tender expression of the Apostle's affection for his readers, the letter comes to a close. As it had begun, so it ends, with the emphasis on the Saviour's name (vs. 21-24).

THE SECOND EPISTLE TO THE CORINTHIANS

AFTER writing the First Epistle, Paul sent Titus to Corinth to see if its instructions had been carried out and if the troubles in the church had been settled (2 Cor. 8:6; 12:18). Before Titus returned with his report, the riot took place which hastened the Apostle's departure from Ephesus (Acts 20:1). He set out on his journey into Greece, hoping to meet Titus on the way, and anxiously looking for him. When he reached Troas and found that Titus had not arrived there yet, his anxiety was greatly increased. Although a door was opened for him to preach the Gospel there, he did not stay, but hurried on into Macedonia (2 Cor. 2:12-13). While he was in that province, probably at Philippi, Titus arrived, and Paul's fears were relieved by the tidings he brought (2 Cor. 7:5-7).

Although the situation that Titus found in Corinth was mainly favourable, yet there was a painful element in it. The majority of the members of the church had shown a godly sorrow for their sin and a warm affection for the Apostle. But a new danger had arisen. Emissaries of the Judaizing party, bearing credentials from leaders of the church in Jerusalem, had stirred up a faction opposed to Paul. They denied his apostolic authority, criticized his actions, and asserted that he had no right to the status of an Apostle. It was necessary to meet these charges at once, and this was the occasion of the present letter. It was written somewhere in Macedonia during the summer of A.D. 56.

Paul's purpose was to encourage the faithful and obedient members of the church, and at the same time to defend and vindicate his apostolic authority against the accusations of his foes. It is the least doctrinal and most personal of all the Apostle's letters. It is an unstudied outpouring of his heart. The one theme that gives it unity is the practical application of the Gospel to the work of the Christian ministry.

Although there is no systematic development of thought, yet there are three clearly marked divisions in the Epistle. The first part (Chs. 1—7) deals with the past. It contains an explanation of the principles and methods that Paul followed in carrying on his apostolic work. It presents an apostolic example for the Christian ministry. The second part (Chs. 8—9) is concerned with the present. It has to do with the collection that was being made at that time by the churches in the provinces of Greece for the poor Jewish saints in the mother-church at Jerusalem. It contains the Apostle's appeal to his Corinthian converts regarding it. In the third part (Chs. 10—13) Paul turns to the future. Looking forward to his approaching visit to Corinth, he proceeds to establish his independent apostolic authority in the eyes of the church. This could only be done by speaking of himself, and it was most painful to him. He shrinks from the task of making his own defence, but it has to be done.

CONCERNING THE PAST—AN APOSTOLIC EXAMPLE
(Chs. 1—7)

Reviewing his relations with the Corinthians in

the past, Paul explains the principles and motives that guided him in his apostolic ministry. This account of his own ministry sets an example for all ministers of the Gospel.

1. His Recent Affliction in Asia (1:1-14). The Apostle begins with a brief salutation in which he includes his companion Timothy, and he addresses it both to the church in Corinth and to the scattered Christian communities in the whole of Achaia, the southern province of Greece (vs. 1-2). He gives thanks for the comfort he found in the sufferings through which he had recently passed (vs. 3-7). The word "comfort" is repeated again and again; and the whole passage throws light on the value of suffering in the life of the Christian. Paul found in his experience the comfort of God. He had the comfort of sharing in the sufferings of Christ, and being fitted to comfort others in their sufferings.

He then describes the nature of the affliction which befell him in Asia, and tells how God delivered him out of it (vs. 8-11). It brought him the testimony of a good conscience and strengthened his hope in God (vs. 12-14). What particular affliction Paul means, we do not know; but his readers must have known. If he refers to the Ephesian tumult, then that was a more serious attempt on his life than appears from Luke's account in Acts. On the other hand, it is possible that the Apostle is describing the effect of some serious illness that may have occurred elsewhere which brought him down to the gates of death.

2. His Delay in Visiting Corinth (1:5—2:13). Paul's first intention was to visit Corinth twice, once on his way from Ephesus to Macedonia and again on his way back from Macedonia to Judea. The change in his plan was not due to fickleness or caprice, for he was not following the will of the flesh like a double-minded man (vs. 15-17). The Gospel of the faithful God, the message about His Son, Jesus Christ, which Paul and his companions preached among the Corinthians, was not changeable and unreliable. For in Him all the promises of God are fulfilled and ratified, and thus through the Apostle's preaching God is glorified (vs. 18-20). Such a result does not come from fickleness, but from a steadfastness that is due to God Himself, and from the anointing of the Spirit which God Himself has given (vs. 21-22).

Paul delayed his coming to the Corinthians in order to spare them a painful visit. He did not want to come to them in sorrow, and he waited till they themselves had put away the sin in their midst. He had written to them about it in great grief, that they might know his overflowing love for them (1:23—2:4). Now that the sin has been put away, he appeals to them to forgive the erring member of the church and show him their love, lest he be overwhelmed with sorrow and Satan get the advantage (2:5-11). Then he tells them of his anxiety in not finding Titus in Troas, and of his going on at once to meet him in Macedonia (2:12-13).

3. The Character of the Gospel Ministry (2:14—3:18). In what Paul says here of his own apostolic ministry we have the characteristic qualities of a true Gospel ministry.

(1) It diffuses the knowledge of Christ as a sweet savour (2:14-17). The terms used in this passage allude to the triumphal procession of a Roman general returning home with a train of captives taken in war. Paul uses this as an illustration of the triumph of Christ in which His ministers share. The phrase, "the savour of his knowledge", is a reference to the fragrant clouds of incense that accompanied the triumphal march as an essential part of it. In the statement, "we are a sweet savour of Christ unto God", Paul claims to be, as it were, an incense-bearer in the procession of the Conqueror.

Such is the work of the ministers of the Gospel. To some they are "the savour from death unto death", and to others "the savour from life unto life". These phrases refer to what was done with the captives at the end of the trimphal procession. Some of them were led off to execution, while others were given their liberty. Thus does Paul indicate the result of the preaching of the Gospel "in them that are saved, and in them that perish". He was not corrupting the word of God like the Judaizing teachers, but was proclaiming it with a sincerity inspired by God.

(2) It manifests the life-giving power of the Spirit (3:1-6). Paul disowns any desire to commend himself. He does not need, "as do some,"— a reference to the Judaizing teachers—any written credentials, "epistles of commendation". The Corinthians themselves, as his converts, are his recommendation, written on his heart, for all men to recognize. They are an epistle of Christ, written through his ministry, not with lifeless ink, but with the Spirit of the living God (vs. 1-3).

As Paul writes this there rises before his mind the Old Testament promise that the Law should be written on the heart (Jer. 31:33). This was to be the special function of the New Covenant, and it is being carried on by the Spirit through those who are qualified to be ministers of the New Covenant, and whose "sufficiency is from God". Paul states the essential difference between the two Covenants in these words: "the letter killeth, but the Spirit giveth life". All that the Law can do is to make men conscious of sin, to show that they are dead in sin. The Holy Spirit alone has the power to give life (vs. 4-6).

(3) It possesses an abiding glory (3:7-11). Paul's thoughts now go back to the story of the giving of the Law. When Moses came down from the mount with the tables of stone, his face shone with a glory that he carried from the presence of God. (Exod. 34:29-35). But that glory gradually passed away, and Moses wore a veil on his face that the people might not see it fading. Such was the Old Covenant, which ministered condemnation. It had a glory of its own, but it was a glory that could not abide. Much more glorious is the New Covenant, which ministers righteousness. It has "the glory that surpasseth".

(4) It reveals the transforming power of the Lord (3:12-18). Paul now speaks without reserve. He declares that just as the veil over Moses' face prevented the Israelites from seeing that the glory there was passing away, so the veil over their hearts to-day prevents them from seeing that their Law was not permanent, but has been fulfilled and done away in Christ (vs. 12-15). But whenever the heart

turns to the Lord, then the veil is taken away (v. 16).

Then the Apostle reverts to what he had said in v. 6 about the Spirit, and declares that "the Lord is the Spirit". He means that it is from Jesus Christ in His glorified state as the risen and ascended Lord that the ministry of the Spirit is carried on. Then he adds, "where the Spirit of the Lord is, there is liberty", with an allusion to the bondage of the Jews who are still living under the letter of the Law (v. 17). Finally he describes the way that the Spirit of the Lord carries on His ministry in the lives of believers. We Christians, he says, "with unveiled faces reflecting as a mirror the glory of the Lord" (marg.), are being transformed into His likeness from one degree of glory to another, by the influence of His Spirit (v. 18).

4. The Spirit of the Gospel Ministry (4:1-5: 10). This section may be summarized under two expressions, each of which occurs twice in the course of it: "we faint not" (4:1, 16), and "we are of good courage" (5:6, 8).

(1) Fainting not in tribulation (ch. 4). The fact that the ministry of so glorious a Gospel has been entrusted in mercy to us, says Paul, makes us renounce all dishonest and underhand practices (such as those his enemies used at Corinth), and leads us to recommend the truth to the conscience of every man by our lives (vs. 1-2). The god of this world blinds the unbelieving, and prevents them from seeing that the light of the Gospel reveals the image of God in the glory of Christ (vs. 3-4). The true God, who called light to shine out of darkness at the beginning (Gen. 1:3), has given us light to see the glory of God revealed in Jesus Christ (vs. 5-6).

But we carry the treasure of this ministry in frail vessels, showing that the power by which we are able to fulfil it is God's, and not our own. We are subjected on every side to suffering and persecution, but this does not break us down. While the dying of Jesus is repeated in the wearing out of the body, the triumphant life of Jesus is also manifested in us (vs. 7-10). While we live, we are continually exposed to death for Jesus' sake. The faith expressed by the Psalmist (116:10) enables us to carry on this ministry for your sakes (vs. 11-15). Though the body keeps decaying, the spirit is being constantly renewed. Our present suffering, which is only momentary, is light in comparison with the weight of the coming glory. We keep our eyes on the unseen world, which is eternal, and not upon the visible world, which lasts only for a season (vs. 16-18).

(2) Of good courage in view of the coming glory (5:1-10). Paul now explains the secret of his calmness and courage in the midst of his afflictions. He looks beyond them to the glorified body in which he will dwell, as in an eternal habitation, when his present earthly tabernacle has been dissolved. In the present earthly body we feel the burden and weariness of life, and we long to have the heavenly tabernacle put on over the earthly house. Then we shall not be left through death without a body. God Himself has made us ready for this transformation by putting the Holy Spirit within us as a partial fulfilment and pledge (vs. 1-5).

Confidence in God and in the pledge He gives us makes us of good courage in the face of death. While we are in the body we are absent from the Lord, walking by faith in Him without seeing Him. We are of good courage even in prospect of death, preferring to be absent from the body and present with the Lord. Therefore, whatever befalls us, whether at home with the Lord or absent from Him, our ambition is to be acceptable to Him when the day of testing comes. For we must all appear before His judgment-seat, that each of us may receive the due reward of what his bodily life has wrought (vs. 6-10).

5. The Motive of the Gospel Ministry (5:11—6:10). In the light of this coming judgment-day, the Apostle goes on to speak of the motives of his ministry. They may be summarized as follows:

(1) The fear of the Lord (5:11-13). Knowing how the Lord is to be feared, Paul goes on pleading with men. God knows that his motives are unselfish and genuine, and he hopes that the Corinthians also know this, that they may be able to defend him against his opponents, who have only the outward appearance of things to glory in and not inward sincerity.

(2) The love of Christ (5:14-15). Christ's love for men constrains Paul and holds him to his ministry. Paul had come to see that if Christ died as representing all, then all died in Him. If He died for all, we should further the purpose of His death by living for Him and not for ourselves.

(3) The new creation (5:16-17). When Paul says, "even though we have known Christ after the flesh", he seems to admit that he had seen and known Jesus of Nazareth before his conversion. To be a true witness that Jesus had risen from the dead, the Apostle must have seen Him before His resurrection. But Paul goes on to say, "yet now we know him so no more"; that is, he is not preaching the Christ of the flesh, but the risen Christ, the Christ of the new creation.

(4) The reconciling work of Christ (5:18-21). The Gospel is a message of reconciliation. It contains the good news that God has been reconciled to men through Christ, together with an appeal to men through the ambassadors of Christ to be reconciled to God. This passage is one of the finest definitions of the Gospel in the whole New Testament. The gospel is "the word of reconciliation". There was a two-sided estrangement between God and man. In the death of Christ, God accomplished something which put away the cause of estrangement on His side. It is the story of what God has done that constitutes the Gospel. It appeals to men to believe in the love of God and put away their distrust of Him.

(5) The grace of God (6:1-10). Because of the reconciling work of Christ, the grace of God is now extended to men. By quoting Isa. 49:8 Paul leads up to his own statement, that this is the day in which to obtain salvation (vs. 1-3). As one of those who are "working together" with Christ, Paul seeks to commend his ministry of the grace of God by an irreproachable life under all kinds of circumstances (vs. 4-10). In this glowing passage Paul heaps phrase upon phrase—there are twenty-eight of them—to describe the character of his life as a minister of the Gospel. They depict it in both its physical and its spiritual aspect, on its passive and its active side. In their variety and their contrasts

they give us a vivid idea of the range of the Apostle's experiences.

6. A Plea for Consecration (6:11—7:16). Declaring his affection for his converts (6:11-13), the Apostle appeals for separation from all the iniquity and defilement of the heathen world around them, and he supports his appeal by quoting Lev. 26:12, Isa. 52:11, and Jer. 31:1 (6:14—7:1). Then he goes on to appeal for confidence in himself (7: 2-4). He tells them of his meeting with Titus in Macedonia, and of the comfort that he got from his presence and from the news he brought (7:5-7).

He did not regret the sorrow that his first letter gave the Corinthians, for it led them to a repentance that was not to be regretted. It was a godly sorrow, not the sorrow of the world which is only remorse, and it resulted in works of reformation among them and in proving them innocent of complicity in the sin. Thus the effect of his letter was to bring out their real feeling for Paul (7:8-12). Then he refers again to the comfort that the news from Corinth gave him, which was all the greater when he saw the joy of Titus and his affection for the Corinthians because of the way they had received him (7:13-16).

CONCERNING THE PRESENT—AN APOSTOLIC APPEAL
(Chs. 8—9)

This section deals with the collection for the Jewish saints in the church at Jerusalem, to which Paul had referred at the close of his First Epistle (16:1-4). He desired that this should be completed before his arrival in Corinth, so that it might not seem to be done under compulsion. He regarded this collection as a matter of great importance. It was an evidence of the unity of the Spirit that bound all the churches together, and a conspicuous proof of the reality of the Christian faith. The Apostle discusses the matter in these chapters with fine, delicate consideration, and shows us what Christian liberality really is.

1. The Grace of Liberality (8:1-15). Paul first tells the Corinthians what the churches of Macedonia had done in circumstances of great affliction and deep poverty (Macedonia was the northern province of Greece. cf. 1:1). The grace of God was manifested in their liberality. They gave with joy, to the limit of their ability and of their own accord, having first put themselves at the service of the Lord and of the Apostle in the matter (vs. 1-5). Paul has urged Titus to complete this same grace among the Corinthians which he had already begun. As they abound in other graces, let them abound in this grace also, and prove their own sincerity. The great incentive to it is the grace of our Lord Jesus Christ in becoming poor that we might be rich (vs. 6-9).

The grace of liberality does not end in good intentions; it is completed when the doing is added to the willing. The giving is acceptable to God according to a man's willingness to give in proportion to his means, not according to the intrinsic value of the gift (vs. 10-12). The purpose of Christian giving is to bring about "equality", or a balance—the abundance of those who have supplying the need of those who have not (vs. 13-15).

2. The Deputation Sent to Corinth (8:16—9:5). Paul has sent Titus to Corinth to care for the collection, and Titus has accepted the mission willingly (8:16-17). Along with him he has sent two others who are unnamed and whose identity is unknown. One of these, "the brother whose praise in the gospel is spread through all the churches", was chosen by the churches to be Paul's travelling companion in the matter of the contribution he was gathering, so that there would be no doubt of the Apostle's honesty regarding it (8:18-21). The other unnamed deputy, whom Paul speaks of as "our brother, whom we have many times proved earnest in many things", seems also to have been appointed by the churches; for in commending them all, Paul refers to these two as "the messengers of the churches" (8:22-24).

The Apostle goes on to say that he does not need to write to the Corinthians about the general question of ministering to the saints; for he has told the Macedonians of their zeal, and it has stirred them up to emulation (9:1-2). But he has sent the deputation to them, that his glorying about them may not be in vain, and that their gifts may be ready when he arrives (9:3-5).

3. An Appeal for Liberality (9:6-15). The Apostle now proceeds with a final exhortation. He assures them that the exercise of liberality yields a rich harvest. Let each man give with deliberate purpose, not grudgingly or reluctantly, but cheerfully (vs. 6-7). God is able to repay them in kind and enrich them for the increasing exercise of liberality, and he quotes Psa. 112:9 to support his plea (vs. 8-11). Their liberality will confer both material and spiritual blessings upon the saints, and will bring glory and thanksgiving to God; for it will prove to the Jewish saints the reality of the Christian love which the Corinthians have, and it will deepen the warm sense of fellowship between Jews and Gentiles (vs. 12-14). This section of the Epistle comes to a close with a jubilant utterance of praise for God's "unspeakable gift" (v. 15).

CONCERNING THE FUTURE—AN APOSTOLIC DEFENCE
(Chs. 10—13)

The opening words of ch. 10 — "Now I Paul myself" — indicate that the Apostle is coming to a new and more personal matter. The third and last division of the Epistle begins here. In view of his approaching visit to Corinth, and in preparation for it, Paul now proceeds to defend and vindicate his apostolic authority against the criticisms of the Judaizing faction in the church who still opposed him. This accounts for the marked change of tone in what follows.

1, His Opponents' Charges (Ch. 10). This chapter reflects the kind of opposition that Paul had to meet from the Judaizers, and reveals his own bearing in the face of it. They said that he was very bold and courageous when absent, but very meek and subdued when present among the Corinthians (v. 1), and that he was a man of the world, walking according to the flesh (v. 2). He could write weighty and powerful letters, but his personal appearance was insignificant and his oratory was of no account (v. 10). They claimed that they themselves were the true Christians (v. 7): they belonged to the Christ party (1 Cor. 1:12). They commended one another, making themselves the standard of measurement (v. 12).

In the face of all this, Paul takes the meekness and gentleness of Christ for his example, but he begs his readers not to drive him to act, when he visits them, with that fearless decision with which he is quite prepared to confront his foes (vs. 1-2). Though living in the flesh and within human limitations, he does not war after the flesh. The weapons he uses are spiritual, and are of mighty power against the self-sufficiency and pride of man. He is ready to execute justice upon the disobedient when the loyalty of the church is restored (vs. 3-6).

If there is any one in Corinth who assumes that he belongs to Christ's party, let him reflect that Paul can make the same claim. The Apostle's authority rests in the commission that Christ has given him. It is an authority to build up the church and not to break it down, as his opponents are doing (vs. 7-9). Let those who say that Paul claims this authority only in his letters, and not in person, reflect that when he comes in person he will manifest his authority no less strongly in action (vs. 10-11). He does not measure his claims by their standard. The measure of the commission given him by God over the Gentile world extends to the Corinthians (vs. 12-14). He is not building his work on the labours of other men, and he hopes to take the Gospel into regions beyond Corinth. With a reference to Jer. 9:24, Paul declares that the only true commendation is that which comes from the Lord (vs. 15-18).

2. The Apostle's Reply (11:1-15). He appeals to his readers to bear with him in the foolish thing he is about to do. He is driven to it by his jealousy for the honour of God and his concern for his converts. He betrothed them to Christ through the Gospel at their conversion, that he might present the church of Corinth to Him as a true bride. But he fears lest they should be turned away from the simplicity and purity of their devotion to Christ, as Eve was deluded by the craftiness of the serpent (vs. 1-3). If some one comes proclaiming a different Jesus from Him whom Paul proclaimed, or if they are presented with a different kind of spirit from the one they received from Paul, or a different kind of Gospel from the one they accepted from him —then they submit to it well enough (v. 4).

The Apostle now proceeds to make his defence with no mock modesty. As to his credentials, he counts himself in no respect inferior to his opponents—those pre-eminent apostles. Though untrained, as compared with them, in the arts of speech, he is not behind them in true knowledge, the knowledge of divine things. He has shown this in all details of his work among the Corinthians (vs. 5-6). Did he commit a wrong in preaching the Gospel among them without charge, humiliating himself that they might be uplifted? He accepted from other churches more than was their share of his support, that he might serve the Corinthians without laying any burden on them (vs. 7-9). He boasts of his independence in doing this in the province of Achaia; for he did it because of his love for the Corinthians, and because of his desire to give no occasion to false teachers to prey upon them in the guise of Apostles of Christ (vs. 10-13). It is not surprising that they should do this, for even Satan himself is wont to masquerade as an angel of light (vs. 14-15).

3. The Apostle's Labours (11:16—12:13). He asks his readers to bear with him in his foolishness as he goes on to boast in his own behalf. He shows very great reluctance in doing this. He confesses that he is not speaking by inspiration from the Lord, but following the example of his opponents (11:16-21). They were of the Judaizing party, and Paul first compares himself with them on their own ground. And then he goes on to give a summary of his labours and sufferings for Christ, which were such as none of them had ever endured (11:22-27).

These few verses throw a flood of light on Paul's career. The incidents he mentions are passed over almost entirely in the Book of Acts. Besides all these outward things, he goes on to say, there is the spiritual burden he carries daily, his care for all the churches and his sympathy for all his converts (11:28-29). Paul then turns away from apparent self-praise to the praise of God, and boasts of his natural weakness, which would make his work impossible but for the strength and protecting care of God (11:30-33).

With a fresh apology he proceeds to boast of heavenly visions and revelations, especially of one that was given him fourteen years before, in which he heard things unlawful for a man to utter (12: 1-6). The date of this experience would be about A.D. 42, when Paul was in Tarsus or Antioch before he had entered upon his missionary labours (Acts 9:30; 11:25-26). That he might not be unduly exalted by these revelations, he was given "a thorn in the flesh", some physical infirmity which he had to suffer continually. What this was we have no means of knowing, and it is futile to speculate about it. Paul regarded it as "a messenger of Satan" sent to buffet him, and petitioned the Lord three times that it might depart from him. But instead of removing it, the Lord gave him strength to bear it, thus showing the sufficiency of His grace.

Therefore Paul glories in his weaknesses for Christ's sake, for through them the strength of Christ is revealed as dwelling in him (12:7-10). He finally declares that this foolishness of his in boasting was made necessary by the failure of the Corinthians to recognize the signs of an Apostle that had been wrought when he was among them (12: 11-13).

4. His Approaching Visit (12:14—13:10). The Apostle now tells the Corinthians that for the third time he has been in a state of readiness to go to them, and when he does go he will continue to labour in their interest without accepting support at their hands. His actions are prompted by love for them, and he would gladly be spent for their souls (12: 14-15). He then refers to the insinuation of his enemies that he made use of the agents whom he sent to take advantage of the Corinthians. He answers the charge by appealing to what they themselves know of Titus and the messengers who accompanied him. Did Titus over-reach them? Was not his spirit and conduct the same as Paul's? (12: 16-18). He is not excusing himself, but aiming at their edification. He is preparing them for his coming, lest he find sins of self-will and self-indulgence among them, lest he be humbled by seeing the failure of his work, and have to mourn over many who have previously lived in sin and have never repented of their former wickedness and impurity (12:19-21).

He reminds them again of his approaching visit, which is the third time he has planned to come; and he warns them that it will not be in vain. If they seek a proof of the power of Christ speaking in him, they shall have it (13:1-4). Let them put their own selves to the proof that they are in the faith. Paul hopes that they will come to know that he, at all events, is not a false disciple of Christ (13:5-6). He prays that they may take no false step this time. It is not their good opinion he seeks, but the purity of their lives. He has no ambitions for himself, but only for their perfecting (13:7-9). He writes these things while absent, that he may not have to deal sharply with them when present (13:10).

5. The Conclusion (13:11-14). The letter has come to an end. Much of it has been written in a tone of severity and indignation. But the love of the Apostle for his converts has been behind it all. And now that love speaks out in a few farewell words. They are brief, disconnected exhortations; but they sum up the practical message of the Epistle. Paul closes the letter with the apostolic benediction in its most complete and perfect form. It refers to the three Persons of the Godhead, and corresponds with the high-priestly benediction of Num. 6:24-26.

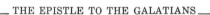

THE EPISTLE TO THE GALATIANS

THE churches to which this letter was written were those established in the cities of Antioch, Iconium, Lystra, and Derbe during Paul's first missionary journey. The story of this mission is told in Acts 13—14. The region in which these cities lay was the southern part of the large Roman province of Galatia, which occupied the centre of Asia Minor. Hence the Apostle addressed the churches as a group under the name of the province—"the churches of Galatia" (1:2).

Another view, which was once widely held but is now largely given up, regards these churches as belonging to "the region of Galatia" mentioned in Acts 16:6, through which Paul passed on his second missionary journey. This district was in the northern part of the province, to which it had given its name, and was so called because it was inhabited by a Gallic people whose ancestors had entered Asia Minor in the third century B.C. Luke gives no hint in Acts that Paul carried on any mission in North Galatia, while he gives a detailed account of the Apostle's work in South Galatia. And besides, Barnabas, who was Paul's companion in South Galatia but was not with him when he passed through North Galatia, is mentioned in the Epistle as personally known to the Galatians (2:13). The very deep concern which Paul shows in this letter for his beloved converts in the Galatian churches

falls in best with the idea that these were the first churches that he had founded in the Gentile world rather than churches of which no account at all has been given in the story of his missionary labours.

During Paul's absence from the churches of Galatia, Judaizing teachers had visited them and declared that there was no salvation for the Gentiles unless they were circumcised and observed the Law of Moses. When Paul heard that his converts were beginning to depart from the Gospel of salvation by faith in Christ alone which he had preached among them, he wrote this letter to correct this false teaching and arrest their apostasy. A reference that he makes in the course of it to the occasion when he preached the Gospel to them "the first time" (4:13), implies that he had already made two visits to Galatia, for the word used strictly means "the former time," as the margin indicates. It would seem, therefore, that the Epistle was written after the Apostle's second missionary journey. He probably wrote it before he set out from Antioch on his third journey in the summer of A.D. 53 (Acts 18:22-23).

The theme of the Epistle is the liberty of the Gospel of Christ. Paul shows that the Gospel is entirely free from the Law, and that the Cross of Christ liberates the believer from bondage to law and ritual. All Christianity is explained by the Cross. The Cross is the principle of everything in the Christian's life. The Epistle is the severest in tone of all Paul's letters. It is the only one of his letters to the churches that contains no thanksgiving for its readers. Instead of that, there is an indignant expression of surprise that his converts are departing from the faith, and an emphatic curse is twice pronounced upon those who have been leading them astray (1:8-9).

The Epistle is in three equal parts. In the first part, which is personal (Chs. 1—2), Paul asserts and defends his independent apostolic authority for preaching the Gospel. In the second part, which is doctrinal (Chs. 3—4), he explains and illustrates the doctrine of salvation by faith apart from the Law. In the third part, which is practical (Chs. 5—6), he describes the kind of life that results from the freedom which salvation by faith in Christ gives.

THE APOSTLE OF LIBERTY
(Chs. 1—2)

Paul prepares to vindicate the Gospel of free grace which he has preached among the Galatians by asserting and defending his independent apostolic authority. He received the Gospel and his commission to preach it directly from God.

1. The Introduction (1:1-10). The Apostle strikes his key-note at once in the opening salutation, He expands his official title into a statement of his direct commission from God, and when he mentions the name of the Lord Jesus Christ he dwells on His redeeming work (vs. 1-5). Instead of the usual thanksgiving, which comes at this point in his other letters to the churches, Paul proceeds, in the tone of rebuke, to explain his reason for writing. He marvels that so soon after their conversion the Galatians are turning away from the grace of God to another gospel. There cannot be two Gospels; but certain men are attempting to pervert the Gospel of Christ. The Apostle then pronounces a solemn curse upon them (vs. 6-8). And he repeats it, thus

showing that, as a servant of Christ, he is not looking for the favour of men (vs. 9-10).

2. Proof of his Apostleship (1:11—2:21). He now proceeds to support his independent apostolic authority by three personal arguments.

(1) The manner of his conversion to Christ (1: 11-24). The Gospel which he preached was not received from man. It came to him "through revelation of Jesus Christ". Paul is referring to his Damascus vision (vs. 11-12). They have heard of his former manner of life, how he persecuted the Christian Church above measure, and how he excelled his contemporaries in zeal for the Jew's religion. He was a fanatic in defence of the traditions of his fathers (vs. 13-14). His conversion was foreordained before he was born, and was a work of God's grace. When it did take place, he did not confer with human advisers, but went away into retirement in Arabia and then returned to Damascus (vs. 15-17).

Three years afterwards he went up to Jerusalem to see Peter, and stayed with him only a fortnight. He saw none of the other Apostles except James the Lord's brother (vs. 18-20). After that he went to the distant regions of Syria and Cilicia, and thus was personally unknown to the Christian community in Judea. They had only heard that their former persecutor was now preaching the faith which he had once tried to destroy, and they glorified God for his conversion (vs. 21-24).

(2) His reception by the brethren in Jerusalem (2:1-10). After an interval of fourteen years Paul went up again to Jerusalem along with Barnabas, his fellow-labourer among the Gentiles, taking Titus with him, who was an uncircumcised Greek. This journey was prompted by a direct revelation from God; and he laid before the leaders of the church, in a private conference, the terms of the Gospel he was preaching among the Gentiles, lest his work should be discredited (vs. 1-2). While he held conference with the Apostles of the circumcision, Paul did not yield to the Judaizing agitators in their attempt to have Titus circumcised. They had insinuated themselves into the midst of the brethren and were striving to subvert the liberty of the Gospel by fraudulent methods (vs. 3-5).

The reputable leaders of the Jewish church — their reputation made no difference to him—taught Paul nothing new. And they had no fault to find with him. On the contrary, they received him as an equal, and recognized that he had been given a mission among the Gentiles, as Peter had been given a mission among the Jews (vs. 6-8). The pillar Apostles, James, Peter, and John, gave Paul and Barnabas the right hand of fellowship, recognizing that their respective spheres of labour were to be separate, and only asking them to remember the poor brethren of Judea (vs. 9-10). The visit to Jerusalem to which Paul makes reference here was at the time of the council described in Acts 15.

(3) His rebuke of Peter at Antioch (2:11-21). On the occasion of Peter's visit to Antioch, Paul had to withstand him. Peter at first ate with the Gentile Christians, but afterwards drew back for fear of the Jewish brethren from the church in Jerusalem. The other Jews, and even Barnabas, were carried away by his example (vs. 11-13). When Paul saw that the liberty of the Gospel was being compromised, he rebuked Peter before them all, pointing out that the Jews themselves, by believing in Christ for justification had acknowledged that no man can be justified by the works of the Law (vs. 14-16). If after seeking justification in Christ, we should turn again to the Law for justification, it would mean that Christ had only led us deeper into sin. Such a thought is not to be tolerated. On the contrary, sin is seen, not in leaving the Law for Christ, but in going back from Christ to the Law (vs. 17-18).

Now Paul goes on to say that it was the Law itself that led him to abandon the Law and become dead to it, that he might live a life consecrated to God. He has got beyond the reach of the Law by sharing the crucifixion of Christ. It is the life of Christ that now lives in him. His own earthly life is lived by personal faith in the Son of God, the Saviour who loved him and died for him. If he went to the Law for righteousness like the Judaizers, he would be declaring the death of Christ to be useless (vs. 19-21). In these verses we have the same idea of spiritual union with Christ that the Apostle develops in Rom. 6:1-10.

THE GOSPEL OF LIBERTY
(Chs. 3—4)

Having established his right to preach the Gospel, the Apostle proceeds to establish the doctrine of salvation by faith alone. The Gospel means that salvation comes from the grace of God, and not from the observance of the Law.

1. The Doctrine Proved (Ch. 3). Paul builds up his argument on the basis of the following facts:

(1) The conversion of the Galatians (vs. 1-5). When Paul proclaimed Christ crucified among them and set Him forth before them, did they receive the gift of the Spirit then by obeying the commands of the Law, or by believing the word he preached? Having begun their new life in the Spirit, are they so foolish as to seek perfection through the observance of an outward rite? Have their past sufferings for Christ been in vain? Is the mighty work of the Spirit which is going on among them due to their observance of the Law, or to the faith with which they hearkened to the Gospel?

(2) The experience of Abraham (vs. 6-9). He was accepted as righteous because of his faith (Gen. 15:6). Only those that exercise faith are the true children of Abraham. It is they who receive his blessing. This was the blessing of salvation which God intended for the Gentiles when He gave Abraham the promise: "In thee shall all the nations be blessed" (Gen. 12:3).

(3) The failure of the Law to justify (vs. 10-14). The Law only lays us under a curse, for it is impossible to fulfil its requirements (Deut. 27:26). The Scripture shows that no man is held righteous before God by his observance of the Law, for it says, "The righteous shall live by faith" (Hab. 2:4); and the Law does not depend on faith, but demands the fulfilment of its commands (Lev. 18:5). Christ has redeemed us from the curse that the Law lays upon us (Deut. 21:23). He has assumed the curse for us, so that the blessing of justification given to Abraham might pass to the Gentiles through Jesus Christ, and that we might receive the gift of the Spirit through faith.

(4) The place of the Law in the plan of God (vs. 15-18). Here Paul introduces a human illustration drawn from a social contract between men. God made a covenant with Abraham, giving certain promises to him and to "his seed". This had special reference to Christ. The Law came in long afterwards, before the promise was fulfilled, and as distinct from it. It did not annul the covenant or change the terms of the promise. If our share of what was given to Abraham by promise depends on our observance of the Law, then it has ceased to be a matter of promise.

NOTE:—Paul's argument in v. 16, that the promise to Abraham's seed refers to Christ, does not rest upon the mere use of the singular word "seed" instead of the plural "seeds", but upon the fact that the word used is a singular collective noun. The Apostle is pointing out that the covenant with Abraham restricted his seed to one line. The descendants of Hagar and Keturah were not included. A similar argument is used in Rom. 9:6-8. The seed of Abraham means, in the first place, the Jewish people. But the Jewish race was summed up and fulfilled its purpose in the Messiah. He was the true seed of Abraham as the representative and embodiment of the people, and through Him they became a blessing to the whole earth. In accordance with the analogy of Scripture interpretation, the natural in the Old Testament is replaced by the spiritual in the New Testament. The seed of Abraham becomes the spiritual seed, who are gathered up in their one Head and Representative, Jesus Christ.

(5) The real purpose of the Law (vs. 19-24). It was added to the promise in order to reveal sin and show the need of a Saviour, and it was designed to operate until the coming of the promised Seed. It was given through a mediator, being enacted by angels as a contract between God and Israel. But in the case of the promise, there is no contract through a mediator; everything depends on God alone (vs. 19-20). The Law is not opposed to the promises of God. It cannot give life, but it condemns all alike, and so prepares the way for the fulfilment of the promise to those that believe in Christ (vs. 21-22). Before faith came, the Jews—Paul refers to them as "we" — were kept under guard by the Law. It watched over them as a moral guardian till Christ should come, so that they might be justified by faith (vs. 23-24).

(6) The freedom that faith brings (vs. 25-29). It sets us free from guardianship. By faith in Jesus Christ, and by our spiritual baptism into Him, we are all united together in the one body of Christ. In union with Christ Jesus there is no difference beween Jew and Greek, bondslave and freeman, male and female. If we belong to Christ we are Abraham's seed and heirs of the promise of salvation.

2. The Doctrine Illustrated (Ch. 4). Paul now brings in two analogies to illustrate the difference between the Law and the Gospel, and to show that they are two stages in the development of God's plan of salvation.

(1) The analogy of the heir (vs. 1-20). Every heir during his childhood is under guardians like a bondslave. When he comes of age he is free and has the privileges of a son. The first state is like that of the Jews under the Law during the old dispensation. The second state is like that under the Gospel during the new dispensation. When the time was ripe, God sent His Son, born under human conditions subject to the Law, that He might ransom all who were under the Law, and introduce us to the state of sonship. And to prove that we are His sons, He has sent the Spirit of His own Son to come into our hearts, prompting us to cry to God as our Father (vs. 1-7).

You Gentiles in your former condition were bondslaves to idolatry, and you have now come to recognize God as your Father, or rather to be recognized by God as members of His family. How is it that you are turning back again to what are mere elementary and impotent things, and are willing to become slaves to them again? You are observing all the seasons of the Jewish dispensation and the Mosaic Law. I fear that all my labour among you may have been in vain (vs. 8-11).

I beseech you to become free as I am by shaking off all this formalism. You have never wronged me yet; do not do it now. You remember how it was owing to a physical infirmity that I came to preach the Gospel among you the first time. My bodily affliction was a trial to you; yet you did not loathe me, but received me as an angel of God, even as Christ the Saviour Himself. What has become of the happiness you showed then? I can testify that you would have plucked out your very eyes and given them to me (vs. 12-15).

Am I your enemy when I tell you the truth? These false teachers are trying to win you, but for no good end. They want to shut you out from Christ, that you may seek their favour. It is well that your good should be earnestly sought at all times, even when I am absent from you (vs. 16-18). My own little ones, for whom I am in travail again until the likeness of Christ be formed in you, I wish that I might be present with you now and speak in a different strain from this. I am at a loss to know how to deal with you (vs. 19-20).

(2) The allegory of Abraham's two sons (vs. 21-31). Paul now turns to the case of Abraham's two sons, Ishmael and Isaac, to illustrate the difference between the bondage of the Law and the freedom of the Gospel. The difference is drawn out as follows: Hagar, the bondwoman, represents the Covenant of the Law; and her son Ishmael, born after the flesh, represents the state of bondage under the Law; Sarah, the freewoman, represents the Covenant of promise; and her son, Isaac, born according to the promise, represents the state of freedom under the Gospel (vs. 21-24).

The Apostle carries the analogy further by explaining that the Old Covenant belongs to the earthly order and the New Covenant to the heavenly order (vs. 25-27). Hagar represents Mount Sinai, from which the Covenant of the Law came, and answers to the earthly Jerusalem. Correspondingly, Sarah represents Mount Zion and the heavenly Jerusalem (Heb. 12:22). She is our mother according to the Gospel, and of her Isaiah wrote (54:1). Paul completes the application of the allegory by pointing out that just as the natural son was wont to persecute the son born after the Spirit, so it is now. As the bondwoman and her son were cast out, and as her son did not share the inheritance with the son of the freewoman, so, the analogy implies, the Covenant of the Law was ultimately to disappear. Then Paul draws the final inference: we should act as children of the freewoman (vs. 28-31).

The Apostle now applies the doctrine of salvation by faith to practical conduct, and describes the kind of life that results from the freedom which the Gospel gives. The teaching of this part of the Epistle may be summarized under the following main ideas:

1. Standing Fast in the Liberty of Christ (5:1-12). Paul appeals to his converts not to be entangled in bondage again. If they submit to circumcision, they are placing themselves under obligation to observe the whole Mosaic Law. Christ will not avail them, for they are severing themselves from Him. If they seek righteousness by the observance of the Law, they have fallen away from the grace of God (vs. 1-4). We Christians, he says, living in the Spirit, wait by faith for the final state of righteousness that we hope for. It makes no difference whether we are circumcised or uncircumcised. Faith in Christ is the one principle of life, and faith shows its efficacy through love (vs. 5-6).

Who tripped you up in the race you were running so well, so that you are turning away from the truth? The influence you are yielding to does not come from God who called you. The leaven introduced by the false teachers, though it seems little, will affect the whole Church. I have confidence in you as a whole, but whoever is disturbing you will have the judgment of God visited upon him (vs. 7-10).

At this point Paul alludes to the malicious charge of his enemies that he was doing the very thing he condemns them for: he had Timothy circumcised, who once belonged to the Galatian churches (Acts 16:1-3). To this he replies that the persecutions he suffers from the Judaizers show that he does not preach circumcision. If he did preach circumcision, there would be no need to preach the Cross. Paul wishes that those who are causing trouble would openly secede from the church (vs. 11-12).

2. Serving One Another in Love (5:13-15). You have been called to freedom; only do not make it a pretext for self-indulgence. There is one servitude we may submit to—the service of love to one another. The whole Law is fulfilled in the command to love one's neighbour as oneself (Lev. 19:18). Dissensions, on the other hand, would be fatal to all who took part in them.

3. Walking in the Spirit (5:16-26). The way to overcome the power of the flesh is to order your lives by the guidance of the Spirit and live in the power of the Spirit. The Spirit and the flesh are mutually antagonistic, and if you surrender to the Spirit you have escaped from the dominion of the Law (vs. 16-18). The Apostle follows this instruction with a list of "the works of the law", with which he contrasts "the fruit of the Spirit" (vs. 19-23). The change of terms from "works" to "fruit" is significant. The flesh is a rank weed which produces no fruit properly so called. The fruit of the Spirit is the product of the new life that has been planted within.

The fruit of the Spirit is composed of three groups of three graces each. The first three—"love, joy, peace"—have a general character. The second three — "longsuffering, kindness, goodness" — are special qualities that concern the Christian's attitude to his neighbour. The third three—"faithfulness, meekness, self-control"—are general principles of Christian conduct. "Against such there is no law", says Paul, for the Law is not needed when there is nothing to restrain. The Christian has crucified the old life of the flesh, so there should be nothing in him to make him act differently from these graces. We should therefore conform our conduct to the new life of the Spirit and not yield to the pride and jealousy of the flesh (vs. 24-26).

4. Bearing One Another's Burdens (6:1-5). The Apostle appeals to his readers to act in a brotherly spirit, and to be sympathetically helpful to one another. Let those who profess to be spiritually-minded tenderly correct those who may have fallen into error, remembering their own weakness. The injunction to "bear one another's burdens" (v. 2) has reference to the burdens of mutual sympathy, the sorrows and sufferings of others. The statement that each man shall "bear his own burden" (v. 5) has reference to the burden of personal responsibility, which each must bear for himself.

5. Not Growing Weary in Well-doing (6:6-10). The instruction to provide for the temporal wants of their teachers is a special application of the command to bear one another's burdens. Let them not deceive themselves; God is not to be treated with contempt. According as a man sows in this world, so will he reap at the end of the world. He who sows to satisfy his sensual nature will reap from that nature a harvest of moral corruption. He who sows to serve the Spirit will reap from the Spirit a harvest of life eternal. Let us not grow weary in doing what is right, for at the proper time we shall reap the harvest. Let us do what good we can, whenever an opportunity is given to us, especially to our fellow-Christians.

6. Summary and Conclusion (6:11-18). The last section of the Epistle is written in the Apostle's own hand: "See with how large letters I write unto you with mine own hand". Thus does he express the emphasis and authority which he wishes the letter to carry. The Judaizing teachers desire to have his readers circumcised, in order to disguise their own professed Christianity and to escape persecution from their fellow-Jews. But they are not keeping the Law themselves (vs. 11-13). The true ground for glorying is not the flesh, but the Cross of Christ. By that Cross we are completely separated from the world.

In Christ Jesus what counts is neither circumcision nor uncircumcision, but the creation of a new nature. All who walk by this rule are the true Israel, and the Apostle invokes peace and mercy upon them. He dismisses the attacks upon himself and his authority with this final word: he bears upon his body the scars he has received in his Master's service. Then he ends the letter with a brief benediction, which he addresses to them as "brethren" (vs. 14-18).

THE EPISTLE TO THE EPHESIANS

EPHESUS was the chief city of Asia Minor and the metropolis of the Roman province of Asia. It was a centre of idolatrous worship among the Greeks, being celebrated for its temple of Diana, which was regarded as one of the wonders of the world. It also possessed a large theatre, which was excavated on the side of the hill to the east of the city, and was capable of seating 25,000 spectators. Both of these places are mentioned in the story of the riot that brought Paul's mission in Ephesus to a close (Acts 19:27-29).

Paul proclaimed the Gospel in Ephesus for the first time during a brief visit to the city on his voyage from Corinth back to Syria at the end of his second missionary journey. He took Aquila and Priscilla with him and left them there, promising to return if it was God's will (Acts 18:18-21). During his absence Apollos came to Ephesus as a disciple of John the Baptist, and he was led into the fuller knowledge of the Christian faith by Aquila and Priscilla before passing on to Corinth (Acts 18:24-28).

On his third missionary journey, Paul returned to Ephesus by way of the interior (Acts 19:1), and remained there between two and three years. During that time the Gospel was firmly established in the city, and also spread throughout the whole of Asia (Acts 19:10). This province took in the whole western coast of Asia Minor and a considerable portion of the interior. It was then that "the seven churches of Asia" had their beginning (Rev. 1:11).

The Epistle to the Ephesians, and the Epistles to the Philippians and the Colossians, together with the Epistle to Philemon, were all written at Rome during Paul's first imprisonment (A.D. 60-62). They all bear evidence of having been written in prison (Eph. 3:1; 4:1; Phil. 1:7, 13, 14 17; Col. 4:3, 18; Philemon 9-10), and the circumstances referred to in them harmonize better with the Apostle's stay in Rome than with his imprisonment in Cæsarea. There is no decisive evidence as to the order in which they were written.

The present Epistle does not seem to have been called forth by any local circumstances. There are no references to conditions in Ephesus, no salutations to individuals. It was probably written as a circular letter, intended not only for the church in Ephesus, but also for all the other churches in the province. This inference is supported by the fact that two of the oldest manuscripts omit the phrase "at Ephesus" in the opening verse, and leave a blank in its place, which could be filled in with the name of the particular church for which the copy was intended. The reference in Col 4:16 to "the epistle from Laodicea" points to the Ephesian letter, which would be going around from church to church throughout the province, and would reach Laodicea, only a few miles away, about the time the Colossians received their letter. These two letters were carried by the same messenger, Tychicus (Eph. 6:21; Col. 4:7).

The wide destination of the Epistle accounts for the general character of its theme. It concerns the whole Church of Christ, and has in view all Christians everywhere. It was written to explain the heavenly nature of the Christian life. Of all the New Testament Epistles, its tone is the most exalted and its outlook the most sublime. The key-note is struck in the third verse, and the theme may be stated in Paul's own words: "spiritual blessing in the heavenly places in Christ". The Apostle's mind seems to have been filled with the transcendent privileges that believers enjoy because of their union with Christ. Oneness with Him is the underlying thought of the whole Epistle, and it is set in a framework of praise. It falls into two equal parts. The first part (Chs. 1—3) is doctrinal, and explains the character of the Church's calling. The second part (Chs. 4—6) is practical, and deals with the character of the Church's life.

THE CHURCH'S HEAVENLY CALLING
(Chs. 1—3)

These three chapters reach the sublimest heights of Christian thought. Here the Apostle unfolds his conception of the Church as the body of Christ, or the new humanity created in Him. After beginning the Epistle with an introductory salutation (1:1-2), he takes up his theme by going back to the Church's origin, which he finds in the eternal purpose and love of God, and he strikes his key-note at once in an ascription of praise to "the God and Father of our Lord Jesus Christ" for the blessings of redemption which He has bestowed upon us.

1. Praise for the Blessings of Redemption (1: 3-14). This passage is one continued and sustained sentence. Beginning with an expression of praise to God, "who hath blessed us with every spiritual blessing in the heavenly places in Christ", Paul goes on describing these blessings till his inspired and illumined thought has traced the whole movement of God's redeeming grace from its origin in the Divine mind to its final consummation. He begins in the eternal past with God's choice of us in Christ "before the foundation of the world", and he ends in the eternal future with the full enjoyment of our inheritance in "the redemption of God's own possession". Between these two eternities stretches a series of blessings in one unbroken chain.

These spiritual blessings are described as belonging to "the heavenly places", or "the heavenlies" (v. 3). This peculiar expression occurs four more times in the Epistle (1:20; 2:6; 3:10; 6:12) and nowhere else in the whole New Testament. It means the realm that lies outside of time and space, the supersensible world. It may be defined simply as "the unseen world", the sphere of ultimate reality as over against the present visible world of man's abode which is but the sphere of relativity (2 Cor. 4:18). Blessings "in the heavenly places" are not so much blessings coming from those places as blessings that lift us into that realm and give us a place in the world of God and the angels.

These blessings are also described as being "in Christ". This is the essential and decisive element in the Apostle's conception. The phrase occurs, in one form or another, ten times in the present passage. The blessings of redemption are not separate and individual endowments bestowed upon the believer, but different aspects and manifestations of the one great gift of God, which is Jesus Christ Himself.

Paul's account of these blessings moves through three progressive stages, marked by a note of praise three times repeated (vs. 6, 12, 14). These three stages are apparently related in the mind of the Apostle to the three Persons of the Godhead. Thus we have the Father's purpose of love (vs. 4-6), the Son's work of grace (vs. 7-12), and the Spirit's ministry of fellowship (vs. 13-14). In each case two blessings are described. The six may be set forth as follows:

(1) Election (v. 4). We have been chosen in Christ before the creation of the world. Redemption is not an afterthought on God's part, or a piece of patchwork in the universe. It is rooted in His eternal purpose; it is part of one system with creation. In that purpose, and in that system, Christ is the supreme and all-inclusive Object of God's choice. And "in him" our election was provided for even before the foundation of the world.

(2) Adoption (vs. 5-6). Provision was also made for our adoption from out the human family into the divine fellowship, where we have the position and privilege of sonship. This, too, comes "through Jesus Christ", the only begotten and beloved Son, through whom we have been accepted.

(3) Reconciliation (vs. 7-8). Those whom God chose and adopted must be redeemed and reconciled to Him. This brings us to the one pivotal event upon which the whole movement of spiritual blessing turns. Redemption has been accomplished, "through his blood". This phrase marks the achievement of God's eternal purpose. The Cross is the one point in the course of Christ's life on earth to which Paul links the chain of spiritual blessings that stretches between the eternities. He regards the Cross not only as an historic event but also as an eternal fact.

(4) Knowledge of His will (vs. 9-12). God has made His purpose for the world known to us. The divine secret which lay behind the creation of the world has been brought to light by the presence of Jesus Christ in the world. The redemptive purpose of God is to reach a consummation and have a triumphant issue ultimately. The whole universe of the heavens and the earth, of angels and men, is to be brought into one harmonious system under the Lord Jesus Christ. The operation of God's will through the ages has one thing in view, the glorifying of Christ as the Head of the universe. As we belong to Christ we share in that divine event. Because of our trust in Him we have been allotted a portion in the inheritance to be realized at that time.

(5) Assurance of salvation (v. 13). We have been sealed with the Holy Spirit of promise. The gracious gifts and powers of the Comforter, promised by the Lord to His disciples, and realized by believers since the Day of Pentecost, are the true evidence of salvation.

(6) Foretaste of Glory (v. 14). The sealing of the Spirit which we receive when we believe is only a partial gift. But it is "the earnest of our inheritance", a pledge of what awaits us in the future.

2. Prayer for the Realization of Redemption (1: 15-23). Because such is the greatness of the blessings of redemption, Paul gives thanks for the evidences of it in his readers—their faith in the Lord and their love to the saints (vs. 15-16). Then he prays that the Father of glory, in bestowing the full knowledge of Himself upon them, may give them divine illumination and spiritual insight. So shall they know the hope opened up when they were called, the rich and glorious life that awaits the saints, and the surpassing greatness of the power that He is exercising in the process of their salvation (vs. 17-19). This is the same power that He put forth when He raised Christ from the dead and enthroned Him at His own right hand in Heaven, far above all ranks and orders of power in this age or the next (vs. 20-21). Thus He put the whole universe under the feet of Jesus Christ, and made Him the Head of the Church, which indeed is His body, and is filled with the presence of Him who fills all that there is in the universe (vs. 22-23).

3. The Salvation of the Saints (2:1-10). The Apostle now goes on to show that the Church is composed of sinners, saved by the grace of God, and united into one spiritual temple. In their original state by nature his Gentile readers were dead in trespasses and sins, walking according to the course of the present world, under the influence of Satan, the spirit that is now at work in the fallen human race (vs. 1-2). The Jewish Christians also shared their life, and were by nature children of wrath, like all other men (v. 3). But because of His great love for us, God has saved us by uniting us with Jesus Christ. What He did in Christ, that He has done in us—quickened us together with Christ, raised us up with Him, and made us sit with Him in the unseen spiritual world (vs. 4-6).

His purpose in all this was to demonstrate in future ages the overabounding wealth of His grace in kindness to us through Christ, by whom we have been saved. For our salvation is entirely the gift of God, which we receive by relying on Him, and not the result of any works about which we might boast (vs. 7-9). We are His workmanship. We are a new creation, which He has wrought in Christ Jesus. His purpose was that we should walk in good works which He prepared beforehand (v. 10).

4. The Union of the Saints (2:11-22). Paul reminds his Gentile readers again of what they once were—separate from Christ and isolated from the redeemed people, without hope and without God in the world. But a great change has been wrought by the death of Christ. The Gentiles have been brought into the same position before God as His chosen people (vs. 11-13). Christ has made peace between Jew and Gentile by breaking down the barrier of the Law which made a partition between them. He has also made peace between man and God by abolishing the claims and demands of the Law. Through Christ Jesus both Jew and Gentile have access to the Father (vs. 14-18). The Gentiles are now fellow-citizens with the saints, members of the family of God, incorporated into the Church of God, which is being built up as a holy temple for God to dwell in by His Spirit (vs. 19-22).

5. The Mystery of Christ (3:1-7). In this passage the Apostle digresses from the main line of his thought to refer to the divine commission that was given to him for preaching the Gospel. He declares that it contains the revelation of "the mystery of Christ", a divine secret which was not known in former times but has now been revealed to all the

founders of the Church (vs. 1-5). This new truth is the union of the Gentiles with the Jews into one body in Christ by the Holy Spirit. The mystery is not the fact of the Church's existence, but the nature of the Church's life. All the saints together form with Christ one spiritual organism, of which the Head is Christ and the body is the Church. This means that the Gentiles are members of the same body and partakers of the promise in Christ through the Gospel, which Paul has been empowered by the grace of God to preach to them (vs. 6-7).

6. The Purpose of the Gospel (3:8-13). The Apostle felt himself unworthy of his commission—"less than the least of all saints"—in view of its wide field and high purpose. The preaching of the Gospel among the Gentiles has a two-fold purpose. It is intended to enlighten all men regarding this divine secret which, during all the past ages, has been hidden in the mind of the Creator. Thus it gains converts for Christ among men and builds up His Church on earth (vs. 8-9).

But it has also a wider scope than that. It serves to display the wisdom of God to the angelic hosts in Heaven—"to the intent that now unto the principalities and the powers in the heavenly places might be made known through the church the manifold wisdom of God". The Church on earth is an object lesson to these high intelligences in the heavenly world. It shows what the love and wisdom of their God can do with the members of a ruined race through our Lord Jesus Christ (vs. 10-11). It is through Him, and through our faith in Him, that we have courage and confidence. And so the Apostle begs his readers not to lose heart when they hear of the afflictions that befall him in their cause, but rather count them something to glory in (vs. 12-13).

7. Prayer for the Church (3:14-21). Here Paul resumes the prayer that he was about to offer at the beginning of the chapter. It arises out of the truths contained in the preceding chapters — "for this cause" (vs. 1, 14). Addressing himself to God as the Father of angels and men (v. 15), he asks that God would endow his readers "according to the riches of his glory"; that is, that His gifts may be worthy of the glorious revelation of Himself which He has now made in the Gospel. Then the prayer unfolds in a series of great petitions:

(1) First for the inward power of the Holy Spirit: "That ye may be strengthened with power through his Spirit in the inward man" (v. 16). This will result in

(2) The permanent indwelling of Christ Himself: "That Christ may dwell in your hearts through faith" (v. 17). Thus they will become firmly grounded in love, and will be enabled to obtain

(3) A comprehensive grasp of God's plan for the Church: "That ye may be strong to apprehend with all the saints what is the breadth and length and height and depth" (v. 18). This is a collective idea, and can be understood only in conscious fellowship with the whole Church of God—"with all the saints". Then they will come to have

(4) A knowledge of the surpassing greatness of Christ's love: "To know the love of Christ which passeth knowledge" (v. 19). The idea is that of getting to know a love which is so transcendent that every step in our apprehension of it reveals profound depths unperceived before. This carries with it

(5) The partaking of the Divine nature: "That ye may be filled unto all the fulness of God" All the qualities that go to make up the character of God are available for us, and He can bestow them upon us up to the limit of our capacity to receive them.

Then the prayer passes into a rapturous ascription of adoring praise to God (vs. 20-21). What He is able to accomplish transcends all that we can ask or imagine. "According to the power that worketh in us"—the power of the indwelling Spirit, the same power that raised Jesus Christ from the dead (1:19-20).

THE CHURCH'S HEAVENLY WALK
(Chs. 4—6)

With another reference to his imprisonment, Paul appeals to his readers to walk worthily of their heavenly calling; and in these chapters he applies to their practical life and conduct the great truths regarding the Church which he has explained in the first part of the Epistle. He uses the word "walk" frequently, marking the importance of the steps and details of conduct in the Christian life.

1. The Life of the Corporate Body (4:1-16). The idea of the Church as the body of Christ pervades this passage. For the proper growth of the corporate life of the Church, three things are involved:

(1) The unity of the Spirit (vs. 1-6). This is to be maintained by the manifestation of those qualities of character in which all self-will and self-interest are suppressed in an atmosphere of love and peace (vs. 1-3), and by the recognition of the fundamental unities that make the Church one living organism, spiritually united with Christ by faith, under one God and Father of all (vs. 4-6).

(2) The diversity of grace (vs. 7-12). The members of the Church have different functions and offices, according as Christ has distributed the gifts of His grace (v. 7). The inspired Apostle quotes Psa. 68:18 from the point of view of the New Testament dispensation, changing "received gifts for men" into "gave gifts unto men". The reference is to the Ascension and to the spiritual powers which Christ triumphed over on the Cross (Col. 2:15). By so doing He received spiritual gifts as man, and was enabled to give them to men when He ascended (v. 8). He could not have done this if He had not first come down and taken part among men; for the Ascension was based upon the Incarnation and the descent into death (vs. 9-10). Then comes a list of the various offices in the Church, for which Christ has bestowed special endowments upon different members, with a view to the spiritual growth of individual believers, and the building up of the Church as His own body (vs. 11-12).

(3) Growth into Christ (vs. 13-16). The mission of the Church is to bring all believers to a full knowledge of Christ and to the spiritual stature of His perfect manhood. We should not be children, yielding to every kind of false teaching; but following divine truth in the spirit of love, we should grow up in all things into Christ our Head. It is thus the corporate body of the Church, vitalized in all its parts by spiritual union with Christ, keeps on growing and building itself up in love.

2. The Life of the Individual Believer (4:17—5:21). In applying the truth to individual life, Paul first states the general principle of Christian conduct and then makes the particular application.

(1) The general principle (4:17-24). He urges upon his readers that their new life must be marked off entirely from that of their heathen neighbours (vs. 17-19). They did not so learn Christ, but were taught "even as truth is in Jesus"; that is, that spiritual truth is incarnate in Him (vs. 20-21). They are to "put away the old man", and "put on the new man", the new human nature of righteousness and holiness which has been created in Christ Jesus (vs. 22-24).

(2) The practical application (4:25—5:21). The Apostle enlarges upon the truth that he has stated by proceeding to give a series of practical instructions. In doing so he draws out the difference between the old life and the new in a number of contrasts. These may be summarized as follows: Falsehood and truth (4:25-30); malice and love (4:31-5:2); darkness and light (5:3-14); folly and wisdom (5:15-21).

3. The Christian Household (5:22—6:9). The family is the first divine institution in the world. It came into existence before the state, and stands above it. Paul deals with the Christian family in three pairs of relationships, taking the weaker members of each pair first.

(1) Wives and husbands (5:22-33). In this passage the Apostle make a tender and beautiful reference to the mystical union between Christ and the Church, using the one as the analogy of the other.

(2) Children and parents (6:1-4). The primary duty of children is obedience to their parents. Fathers are to train their children according to the Lord's method of discipline.

(3) Servants and masters (6:5-9). Servants were all bondslaves in the ancient world. They formed a large section of the early Church. The Gospel did not directly condemn slavery, but introduced principles which mitigated its evils and were ultimately to eliminate it altogether.

4. The Spiritual Conflict (6:10-20). Paul's survey of the conditions of Christian life in the world leads him now to consider that which lies behind it. The Christian has to stand against the wiles of the devil. His foes are not mere flesh and blood, but the whole hierarchy of evil—"the world-rulers of this darkness, the spiritual hosts of wickedness in the heavenly places" (vs. 10-12). The New Testament assumes the personality of Satan. But Satan does not stand alone. There is a hierarchy of evil spirits in the unseen world. They exercise a mysterious domination over the fallen human race in the darkness of ignorance and sin. The conflict with them is essentially a spiritual one, and the Christian must be armed with spiritual weapons—"the whole armour of God" (vs. 13-18).

The armour which Paul bids his readers put on is described in terms of the equipment of a Roman soldier. It consists of seven weapons, if we count prayer as one of them. With truth as a girdle, righteousness as a breastplate, the foot-hold of peace for sandals, faith as a shield, and salvation as a helmet, the defensive armour of the Christian soldier will be complete. His only offensive weapons are the Word of God for a sword and the continual practice of prayer in every form. Then Paul adds a request for prayer for himself, that he may be able to proclaim the Gospel boldly in his imprisonment (vs. 19-20).

5. The Conclusion (6:21-24). The Apostle has finished his message for the churches of Asia, and he makes only one personal reference. It is a commendation of Tychicus, whom he is sending with the letter. Then he closes with a benediction, which is written in the third person, and is more general in form than his usual benedictions as more suited for a circular letter. Its closing word is especially appropriate, because of its suggestion of the spiritual and the eternal: "Grace be with all them that love our Lord Jesus Christ with a love incorruptible."

THE EPISTLE TO THE PHILIPPIANS

THE city of Philippi lay on the great highway that ran through Macedonia from sea to sea. It had been raised to the dignity of a "colony" of Rome by Augustus Cæsar, in honour of the decisive victory which he had won there over the armies of the Republic in 42 B.C., and which marked the beginning of the Roman Empire. This meant that it had the same privileges and was governed in the same way as the city of Rome.

Philippi was near the Aegean Sea, and it was the first city in Europe in which Paul proclaimed the Gospel after crossing over from Asia on his second evangelizing journey. The story of his work in Philippi, and of the way the church was established there, is told in Acts 16:11-40. The most notable converts were Lydia and the jailor, with their households. The date of that first visit was A.D. 50 or 51. Twice after that, within the period covered by the Book of Acts, we find Paul at Philippi. During his third evangelizing mission he visited Philippi on his journey from Ephesus to Corinth in the summer of A.D. 56, and also on his journey back again early in the next year (Acts 20:1-6).

The Philippian church was mainly Gentile. The absence of a synagogue in the city would mean that there were but few Jews among its people. Women occupied a prominent place in the church (Phil. 4:2-3). The members were noted for their liberality

(2 Cor. 8:1-5), and they had sent generous gifts to Paul more than once (Phil. 4:10-18). The Judaizers had not disturbed the loyalty of the Philippians to the Apostle, and no church held a deeper place in his affection. The occasion of the Epistle was a gift which they had sent to him during his imprisonment in Rome (4:18). Epaphroditus, the messenger who had brought the gift, fell sick in Rome and came near death. News of this caused great distress among his friends in Philippi. He had recovered and longed to get home, and Paul sent this letter with him to thank the Philippians for their gift.

It is full of praise and thanksgiving. The note of joy rings through it. Its reiterated call is "rejoice" —"Rejoice in the Lord"; "Rejoice in the Lord always" (3:1; 4:4). The word "joy" occurs, in one form or another, fourteen times. Its theme may be defined as the joy of Christian experience, or joy in Christ. It is entirely devoid of censure, and the word "sin" is not used once.

Being a familiar letter, it does not lend itself to logical analysis. Its contents are not arranged systematically, but alternate between personal matters and doctrinal instruction. A key-verse may be taken from each of the four chapters, thus setting forth four main features of Christian life and experience. The secret of the Christian life is Christ Himself: "For to me to live is Christ" (1:21). The motive of the Christian life is the mind of Christ: "Have this mind in you, which was also in Christ Jesus" (2:5). The goal of the Christian life is likeness to Christ: "I press on toward the goal unto the prize of the high calling of God in Christ Jesus" (3:14). The support of the Christian life is the strength of Christ: "I can do all things in him that strengtheneth me" (4:13).

For purposes of study, however, the contents of the Epistle are best divided into separate sections under the general idea of the joy of the Christian life.

1. Joy in Prayer (1:1-11). Timothy is associated with Paul in the opening salutation (vs. 1-2). He had been with Paul when the Apostle first entered Macedonia and established the churches there. He had visited the province since then (Acts 19:22), and was about to be sent again to Philippi as the Apostle's representative (2:19). The omission of Paul's official title is an indication of his friendly relation with the Philippians; he does not need to emphasize his authority. The inclusion of "the bishops and deacons" in the greeting marks the advanced state which the organization of the Church had reached at the time the Epistle was written. There were now two different kinds of office-bearers.

In his thanksgiving for his readers (vs. 3-8), Paul mentions the help which they had always given him in preaching the Gospel. He is confident that God will go on perfecting the good work that He has begun in them until its consummation at Christ's coming. His love goes out to them because of their sympathetic fellowship with him in his imprisonment and in his Gospel ministry, and he longs to see them. This is followed by the petitions of his prayer for them (vs. 9-11). These include abounding and increasing love, spiritual knowledge and discernment, singleness of heart and freedom from offence, and fruitfulness in life and witness.

2. Joy in Suffering (1:12-30). Paul now refers to his own circumstances in Rome. His imprisonment has been the means of spreading the Gospel, and therein he rejoices. He takes each of the darkest facts of the situation and makes it minister to his joy: his bonds have made the Gospel known among the soldiers of the imperial household, and among other people in general; and most of the Christians in Rome have been encouraged to proclaim the Gospel fearlessly (vs. 12-14). His rivals, who are animated by party-spirit and personal hostility instead of the good-will which the others show, have been stirred up to increased activity in preaching the Gospel (vs. 15-18). The danger in which he stands, and the uncertain issue of his imprisonment, only make him confident that Christ will be magnified in his body, whether it be by his life or by his death (vs. 19-20).

His own desire would be to depart and be with Christ. But for their sake it would be better for him to go on living, and for this reason he has the conviction that he will be with them again (vs. 21-26). He appeals to them to let their life be worthy of the Gospel, and he hopes to hear that they are standing firm and working together for the faith of the Gospel, undaunted by their adversaries. This is a sign that destruction awaits their foes, but that salvation is theirs. It is their privilege, not only to believe on Christ, but also to suffer for Him. In this experience they are maintaining the same conflict as the Apostle himself (vs. 27-30).

3. Joy in Humility (2:1-11). Paul makes an affectionate appeal to the Philippians to cultivate unity of spirit and lowliness of mind, and to think of others without any selfish interest (vs. 1-4). They should have the attitude of mind shown by Christ Jesus in the Incarnation, and follow His example. Existing originally in the essential form of God, He did not set His mind upon His own equality with God as a prerogative to be jealously retained. He emptied Himself of all that glory, and took upon Himself the nature of a servant in the form of man, and lived in the world like other men. As man, He humbled Himself still further, being continually obedient to God. He maintained this spirit of obedience to the utmost length of death, even consenting to die the death for sin (vs. 5-8).

For this reason, because He looked to the interests of others and not His own, God has exalted Him, and bestowed upon Him the Name that is supreme over every name. He is invested now with the transcendent glory and greatness of Jehovah. In that Name, which belongs to Jesus, every creature in the universe, of all ranks and orders, wherever they dwell, shall bow in prayer and worship; and every one shall acknowledge that Jesus Christ is nothing less than Lord in the supreme and highest sense. The worship given to the Son is glory given to God the Father (vs. 9-11).

4. Joy in Service (2:12-30). Addressing his readers with a term of affection, the Apostle goes on to exhort them to work out their own salvation in his absence with reverence and watchfulness. They should do this because the energy of God, operating in their inmost being, gives them both power to will and strength to perform His own good pleasure (vs. 12-13). The outward result of this inner life will be such conduct and character as will

show them to be children of God, and will make them seen as lights in the world, holding forth the message of life, so that Paul may rejoice that his work among them was not in vain (vs. 14-16). Even if his life should be poured out as a libation, while they offer themselves by faith as a living sacrifice to God, he and they will rejoice together (vs. 17-18).

The Apostle then informs them that he intends to send Timothy to visit them as soon as he sees what the result of his trial is to be; and he tells them that the faithful and devoted service which Timothy has given him has been that of a son to a father (vs. 19-24). Meanwhile he is sending Epaphroditus back, the messenger who brought their gift. He had been seriously ill, and was troubled because they had heard about it; but God mercifully restored him. They should receive him gladly and hold him in high esteem, for he risked his life in rendering the service to Paul which they were unable to give (vs. 25-30).

5. Joy in the Knowledge of Christ (3:1-11). The Apostle seems to be approaching the end of his letter when he writes, "Finally, my brethren, rejoice in the Lord". And then he thinks of the Judaizers, who were disturbing the Church in so many places and might yet appear at Philippi, and he proceeds with a warning against them (vs. 1-2). It is the Christians that are the true Israel, who worship God by His Spirit, glory in His gift of the Saviour, and put no confidence in anything of the flesh (v. 3). Then Paul points out that he has more reason to glory in the flesh and in the observance of the Law than any other man. He is a thorough Israelite, of pure and unmixed descent, and he was a zealous and blameless Pharisee (vs. 4-6).

But he renounced all that for Christ's sake. Yea more, he considers all things to be but loss in comparison with the transcendent blessedness of knowing Christ Jesus his Lord. For Christ's sake he let everything go, counting it as refuse, that he might gain Christ and be united with Him, possessing no righteousness of his own derived from the Law, but that alone which is received by faith in Christ, the righteousness provided by God (vs. 7-9). Then he goes on to enlarge upon this, explaining the Christian life in terms of his own experience of knowing Christ: That I may know Him, may know the power that flows from His resurrection, may know what it is to share His sufferings; that I may become conformed to His way of dying—His self-surrender to death—if by any means I may attain to the resurrection from among the dead (vs. 10-11).

Paul does not mean to imply that he is uncertain about the resurrection. His mind is filled with the thought of Christ's resurrection, which was a resurrection "from the dead", a new life out of death, and he is expressing the modest hope that, as his life is being conformed to the death of Christ, it may also show the power of the resurrection of Christ. Becoming conformed unto His death means dying to sin, being crucified with Christ, or bearing about in the body the dying of the Lord Jesus (Rom. 6:2; Gal. 2:20; 6:14; 2 Cor. 4:10). Attaining unto the resurrection means living in union with Christ in the power of His resurrection (Rom. 6:5).

6. Joy in Spiritual Progress (3:12-21). It is

not that the Apostle has obtained the prize yet, or been already made perfect, but he is pressing on to lay hold of that for which Christ laid hold of him. As for himself, he does not claim to have laid hold of it; but one thing he can say is this: Forgetting all that is behind, and stretching on toward what is before, he presses on to the goal for the prize to which God has called him upward in Christ Jesus (vs. 12-14). Let us, therefore, he goes on to say, who are full-grown in faith, be of this mind. And if any of them are differently minded in any particular, God will make the matter clear to them. Only, whatever progress we have succeeded in making, let us continue in the same path (vs. 15-16).

The Apostle then appeals to his readers to take him for their example, and to take note of those who follow the same path. For there are many, of whom he used to warn them and now warns them again with tears, whose conduct shows them to be enemies of the Cross of Christ. They are doomed to destruction, for they worship their sensual appetites, and shame their Christian profession (vs. 17-18). Our citizenship, our true home, says Paul, is in Heaven, out of which we are waiting for the Saviour to appear, who will transfigure the body of our humiliation that it may be like the body of His glory, by virtue of the power that He has to subject all things to Himself (vs. 19-21).

7. Joy in the Peace of God (4:1-9). In view of the warning he has just given, the Apostle, using terms of deep affection for his Philippian converts, appeals to them to stand firm in their union with the Lord (v. 1). He makes a special appeal to two women, whom he names, to work harmoniously in the service of the Lord (v. 2). He makes another special appeal to one whom he calls a "true yokefellow", but does not name, to help these women, and to do so along with the rest of his fellow-workers (v. 3). This was probably the presiding elder of the church, to whom the letter would be delivered, and who would read it to the congregation.

Then he takes up the appeal with which ch. 3 began, and calls them again, with still more emphasis, to rejoice in the Lord; and to this he adds further instructions (vs. 4-6). They are to let their life-principle of "forbearance" be evident to all men who have any dealings with them (vs. 4-5). We have no exact English word for the term Paul uses here. The A.V. renders it "moderation" and the R.V. puts "gentleness" in the margin. What the Apostle has in mind is the essential and fundamental element in Christian character shown in yielding all self-interest for Christ's' sake. Then he reminds his readers that "the Lord is at hand". He is always near, not only in the future but also in the unseen world, and will take care of their interests Himself. They are not to be anxious about anything; but in every matter they are to let their needs be made known to God by prayer and definite requests, linked with thanksgiving. And then the peace of God, which surpasses all human thinking, will be a garrison for their hearts and minds in Christ Jesus (vs. 6-7).

As a final instruction, the Apostle begs his readers to give their minds, thus safe-guarded by the peace of God, all possible material of the proper kind to work upon. He gives a summary of the things they should occupy their thoughts with — whatever is virtuous, and whatever is worthy of praise. Then follows a more personal word, reminding them again that in his life they have an example to follow, and assuring them that God, who gives peace, will be with them (vs. 8-9).

8. Joy in the Strength of Christ (4:10-23). Paul now turns from teaching the Philippians to thanking them for the gift that they have sent him, and again he does it with a note of joy. This gift had come after an interval in which they had no opportunity for sending it (v. 10). He would not have them think that he spoke thus because he was feeling in want, for he had learned to be independent of his circumstances. He had learned the secret of being filled and being hungry, of having abundance and suffering need. He is able for anything through Him who gives him inward strength (vs. 11-13).

But the Philippians had done nobly in sharing the burden of his affliction. In the early days of his mission work, when he left Macedonia, they alone among the churches participated with him by giving him material aid for the spiritual help they had received. Even in Thessalonica they had sent him aid twice over. Not that he is seeking for the gift, but he seeks for the interest that is accumulating to their account (vs. 14-17).

Now he has all that he needs, and more than enough, since he has received from Epaphroditus what they have sent. It is sweet-smelling incense, an acceptable sacrifice, pleasing to God. He assures them that his God, the God who has supplied his need, will fill up every need of theirs, according to His riches in glory. Then he adds an ascription of praise to God (vs. 18-20). The salutations follow and the final benediction. The saints "that are of Cæsar's household", who sent their greetings to the Philippians, were not members of the imperial family, but slaves and freedmen attached to the palace of the Emperor (vs. 21-23). The Gospel had spread among them from Paul's presence as a prisoner, and evidently a group of earnest converts had been gathered out, who probably found a welcome meeting-place in the Apostle's lodging, where he was writing the Epistle.

THE EPISTLE TO THE COLOSSIANS

THE city of Colossæ was in the interior of Asia Minor, about a hundred miles east of Ephesus. It was one of a group of three cities in the Lycus valley on the great highway connecting Ephesus with the Euphrates. The other two, Laodicea and Hierapolis, were larger and more important places; and there were Christian communities in them also (4:13).

These three churches were no doubt established during Paul's long stay in Ephesus, when the Gospel spread throughout the whole province of Asia (Acts 19:10, 26). The Apostle had not been in Colossæ himself (2:1), but the chief agent in the founding of the church there, and also in the other cities of the group, was Epaphras, his companion and fellow-labourer, and probably one of his converts (1:7; 4:12-13). The Colossian church was mainly Gentile (1:21, 27). It was one of the smaller churches, for Colossæ was little more than a country-town. And yet the letter that Paul sent it contains some of the most important truths in the New Testament.

The Epistle to the Colossians was written during the Apostle's imprisonment in Rome, at the same time as the letter to the Ephesians. Both letters were carried to their destination by the same messenger (Col. 4:7; Eph. 6:21). Epaphras had visited Paul in Rome bringing news from Colossæ. There were many tokens of divine grace among the Christians, but a serious danger was threatening the church. It was a new teaching, an incipient Gnosticism, containing a mixture of Judaism and oriental mysticism (2:8, 16-17). This heresy minimized the work of the Saviour and obscured His glory, by introducing other things into the plan of salvation, such as the mediation of angels, ritualistic observances, and ascetic practices (2:18, 20-23). Paul wrote the letter to refute these errors; and he did this by exalting Jesus Christ as the one sufficient Saviour and Lord.

There is great similarity between the Epistles to the Ephesians and the Colossians in language and thought, and yet there are also striking differences. The aim of Ephesians is to build up Christians in the truth; the aim of Colossians is to guard them against error. The subject of Ephesians is the Church as the body of Christ, which He fills with His Divine fulness; the subject of Colossians is Christ as the Head of the Church, from whom the body derives its life. The message of Ephesians is that the saints are one in Christ; the message of Colossians is that they are complete in Christ.

The Epistle to the Colossians, like that to the Ephesians, is in two equal parts. The first part (Chs. 1-2) is mainly doctrinal. It reveals the supreme greatness and glory of Jesus Christ in His person and work. The second part (Chs. 3—4) is mainly practical. It unfolds the necessary issue of this great fact in the fulness of life provided for the believer in Christ.

THE GLORY OF THE PERSON OF CHRIST
(Chs. 1—2)

These chapters show that the surest test that can be applied to any teaching that claims to be Christian is this: Where does it place Jesus Christ? Over against the Colossian heresy Paul sets the pre-eminence and supremacy of the Lord.

1. Paul's Prayer for the Saints (1:1-14). The Apostle begins in his usual way, with a salutation of grace and peace (vs. 1-2), followed by a thanksgiving for the Colossian Christians (vs. 3-8). In this he mentions their faith in Christ Jesus, their love toward all the saints, and the hope laid up for them in Heaven, which they heard of first in the Gospel when Epaphras proclaimed it among them. Then come his special petitions for them (vs. 9-14). He prays that they may be filled with true spiritual knowledge, that their conduct may be worthy of the Lord, that they may bear fruit in every good work, that they may realize the power of Christ to keep them patient and joyful under trial and provocation, and that they may be continually thankful to God the Father for delivering us out of the power of darkness and transferring us into the kingdom of His own Son.

2. The Pre-eminence of Christ (1:15-23). At this point the Apostle passes on without a pause to his main theme. Having mentioned the Son of the Father's love and referred to our redemption through Him, he goes on to explain that all the Divine fulness dwells in Him.

(1) The supreme dignity of His Person (vs. 15-18). This is brought out in a three-fold personal relationship. In relation to God: Christ is the visible manifestation of the unseen God, antecedent to all creation (v. 15). In relation to the Universe: He is its Creator. All things, heavenly and earthly, seen and unseen, came into existence through Him and for Him. By Him they are held together in one ordered system. Thus He is the secret of all things (vs. 16-17). In relation to the Church: He is its Head, the origin of its life, being the first to pass through death in triumph, so that in all things, in grace as well as in nature, in salvation as well as in creation, He might hold the first place (v. 18).

(2) The glorious purpose of His work (vs. 19-23). This is first described generally, as the reconciliation of the Universe. It was the Father's good pleasure that the fulness of the Godhead should dwell in Christ, and that through Him all things, both on earth and in Heaven, should be reconciled to Himself. The means of this reconciliation was the peace made by the transaction on the Cross (vs. 19-20). Then the application is made to the special case of the Colossians. They have been reconciled to God by the death of Christ from their former evil ways of life and thought, that they might be presented to Him without blemish or blame. And so let them continue steadfast and unmoved in the faith and hope of the Gospel, which was given by the Lord to be proclaimed in the whole world (vs. 21-23).

3. Paul's Work for the Saints (1:24—2:7). Having referred to the fact that the Colossians had received the Gospel and that he himself was made a minister of it, the Apostle now goes on to tell of the way he has been carrying out his ministry. It comprises the following elements:

(1) Suffering (1:24). He rejoices in the sufferings that he is undergoing for the sake of the Church, for thereby he is filling up what is lacking of the afflictions which Christ began, and left to be completed by the members of His body.

(2) Preaching (1:25-29). The stewardship of the Gospel was committed to him that he might proclaim among the Gentiles its divine secret, which has been hidden for ages, but has now been made manifest to believers. That secret is this: the indwelling of Christ within you is the hope of coming glory. So Paul toils on in dealing with men that he may present every man perfect in Christ.

(3) Praying (2:1-3). He would have them know how he wrestles in prayer for the believers in Colossæ and Loadicea, and for all whom he has never visited. He prays that they may be knit together in love, and have the sure and satisfying knowledge of the secret which God has disclosed for our salvation —the fact that in Christ are hidden all the treasures of His wisdom and knowledge.

(4) Warning (2:4-7). He tells them this so as to warn them against the danger of being allured and misled by a different kind of teaching from that which they received. They should continue in the exercise of the faith in Christ which they were taught, getting built up in Him, and living a life of thanksgiving.

4. The Sufficiency of Christ (2:8-23). Following his appeal to his readers to continue their walk in Christ as they were taught, the Apostle proceeds to point out that in Him the Church has all its needs supplied. Through Him all the resources of the Godhead are communicated to the saints. Over against the false teaching which had invaded the Colossian church, Paul sets two great spiritual facts:

(1) The believer's completeness in Christ (vs. 8-15). Warning his readers against being captivated by the philosophy of the false teachers, which was but an empty delusion, and their mode of teaching, the Apostle goes on to declare that in Christ "dwelleth all the fulness of the Godhead bodily"— that is, in bodily form through the Incarnation. "And in him ye are made full"—filled full of the fulness of God by virtue of union with Christ, who is the Head of all the ranks and orders of God's government (vs. 8-10). He carries out the idea of union with Christ by representing it as spiritual circumcision, which means putting off the carnal nature so as to receive Christ's nature, and as spiritual baptism, which means having the old self-life buried with Christ so as to share His resurrection-life (vs. 11-12).

Then Paul goes on to point out the results of Christ's work that come to us through our union with Him. It delivers us from the power of sin, because we are forgiven and have a new life in Christ; from the claims of the Law, because He has abolished them; and from the fear of evil spirits, because of His victory over them on the Cross (vs. 13-15).

Two phrases in these last verses need explanation: (a) "Having blotted out the bond written in ordinances". The "bond" is the same as the "law of commandments" in Eph. 2:15. It means the will of God expressed in formal commands and enforced by penalties on disobedience. Christ cancelled this bond that was against us, by fulfilling its commands for us, and by suffering its penalties which our disobedience had incurred. (b) "Having despoiled the principalities and the powers". The reference is not to putting off the body, but to the final defeat of the powers of darkness. The conflict with them which began with Satan's attack upon Him in the wilderness came to a crisis at Calvary (Luke 22:53; John 12:31). What seemed to be their triumph over Christ on the Cross was His complete and eternal triumph over them.

(2) The believer's freedom in Christ (vs. 16-23). In view of this deliverance which Christ has wrought for us and of our spiritual union with Him, the Apostle warns his readers against losing their freedom in Christ. In this section he is referring to the special features of the heresy which was threatening the Colossian church. They should allow no man to call them to account for not following the Jewish ceremonial system of meat offerings and drink offerings, of feast days and holy days. These were only types and shadows of the reality that is in Christ (vs. 16-17). Nor should they let any one rob them of their heavenly prize by a self-willed humility, which displays itself in worshipping angels and in dealing presumptuously with the mysteries of the unseen world. Instead of this they should continue to hold fast the one Head from whom the whole body, vitally linked together with Him, keeps growing with the growth that God supplies (vs. 18-19).

If they have been set free by their death in Christ from the world's rudimentary ordinances, why do they still subject themselves to the tyranny of ordinances? Rules prohibiting this or that in conduct and practice have no moral value, and rest on the precepts of men alone. Such things, indeed, have a pretense of religious devotion and an affectation of humility, but they have no real value in checking the indulgence of the flesh (vs. 20-23).

THE FULNESS OF LIFE IN CHRIST
(Chs. 3—4)

The practical part of this Epistle follows the same line of thought and teaching as in the Epistle to the Ephesians. The truth unfolded in the first two chapters is now applied to the life and conduct of the Christian. The Apostle first states briefly the fundamental principle, and then draws it out in a general and a special application.

1. The Fundamental Principle (3:1-4). This consists in our complete identification with Christ. Having been raised with Christ, we belong to Heaven and should seek the things that are there, where He sits enthroned. We are to set our heart and mind on things above, not on things on the earth. We died when Christ died for us, and our life lies hidden with Him in God. When He who is our life is manifested at His coming, we also, because of our living union with Him, will be manifested in glory.

2. The General Application (3:5-17). Now comes the practical application of this principle. Paul appeals to his readers to put to death the old man, or count it a dead thing, and to put away the vices in which they formerly walked and for which the wrath of God is coming upon the disobedient world (vs. 5-9). Having put off the old man, they have put on the new man, which is being renewed after the image of God, who is the Author of the new creation as of the old. In this there is no distinction of race or language or social position, but Christ is embodied in all (vs. 10-11).

They are to put on therefore all His virtues, and over them all to put on love as the bond and mark of perfectness (vs. 12-14). They are to let the peace of God rule in their hearts, and to be more and more thankful. They are to let the Word of Christ dwell in them richly, and encourage and teach one another with psalms and hymns of praise to God. And let everything they do be done in the Name of the Lord Jesus, giving thanks to God, His Father, through Him (vs. 15-17).

3. The Special Application (3:18—4:6). The relations of the Christian household are dealt with in the same way and in the same order as in Ephesians, but in shorter form: wives and husbands; children and parents; servants and masters (3:18—4:1). Then follow some instructions for individuals: the duty of prayer and thanksgiving, with special intercession on the Apostle's behalf, and the duty of proper behaviour toward the unconverted (4:2-6).

4. The Personal Conclusion (4:7-18). The letter draws to a close, and the Apostle tells the Colossians of the mission of Tychicus whom he is sending with it, and of Onesimus who is to accompany him (vs. 7-9). Onesimus carried the Epistle to Philemon, who was a member of the Colossian church. Then come greetings from Paul's companions in Rome (vs. 10-14), the salutations, a message regarding the church at Laodicea, and the final word by Paul's own hand (vs. 15-18).

THE FIRST EPISTLE TO THE THESSALONIANS

THE Epistles to the Thessalonians are the earliest of Paul's letters that have come down to us. They were both written in Corinth during the Apostle's first visit there in A.D. 51-52, not many months after the Thessalonian church had been founded.

Thessalonica was a large and important mercantile city on the great highway that ran through Macedonia between the east and the west. It was situated at the head of a gulf of the Aegean Sea and had an excellent harbour. It has preserved its existence to the present day, and is now called Saloniki. In Paul's day it was the capital of the province, and its population had a large proportion of Jews. The Apostle planted the church there, with the help of Silas and Timothy, during his second missionary journey (Acts 17:1-9). It contained a few Jews, but was composed mainly of Gentiles (1 Thess. 1:9).

Paul and Silas were sent away from Thessalonica because of a riot stirred up by the Jews, and they went on to Berea. The Jews followed them, and stirred up trouble there also. Leaving Silas and Timothy behind, Paul went on alone to Athens, and then to Corinth (Acts 17:10, 14-15; 18:1). When they joined him again in Corinth, they brought news from Thessalonica.

The members of the church had been faithful in the face of continued hostility and persecution. But their minds had been disturbed and their lives disorganized by some misunderstanding regarding the coming of the Lord. Believing it to be imminent, some of them were beginning to neglect their daily occupations and were waiting in idleness for the event. Some of them also were distressed by doubt and sorrow regarding fellow-members of the church who had died since their conversion. They feared that these friends of theirs might be deprived of a place among the saints at the Lord's return. It was to meet this situation that Paul wrote the First Epistle.

It is in two main parts. The first part (Chs. 1—3) is personal, and contains Paul's account of his work among the Thessalonians. The second part (Chs. 4—5) is practical and doctrinal, and contains his instructions to the Thessalonians. Each of the five chapters ends with a reference to the Lord's coming, and each of the two main divisions closes with a prayer.

PAUL'S WORK AMONG THE THESSALONIANS
(Chs. 1—3)

The simplicity of the opening address and salutation in the first of Paul's letters to the churches is significant (1:1). He does not introduce himself as an Apostle, as he does in most of the later letters; nor does he style himself "a servant of Jesus Christ", as he does in Romans and Philippians. He approaches the Thessalonians with the affectionate intimacy of a friend who does not need to bring his credentials. He has no reason yet to assert his claims, for the opposition of the Judaizing Christians had not yet risen when he wrote these letters. With his usual delicate feeling for others, he associates Silas and Timothy with himself in the salutation because they had been with him in Thessalonica.

1. His Thanksgiving for his Converts (1:2-12). Paul thanks God for the Christian graces seen in them, which prove the reality of their conversion and show that his work among them has been effectual. The three features which he notes in their Christian life may be described in this way: Remembering how your faith works, how your love toils, and how your hope endures (vs. 2-3). Then he notes four elements in their conversion as signs of their election.

The Gospel came home to them with four-fold strength: in the preaching of the Word, in the power of conviction, in the quickening power of the Holy Spirit, and in assurance of salvation (vs. 4-5). They had become an example to believers throughout both provinces of Greece, because of the joy they manifested in spite of the persecution they suffered, so that the Gospel had sounded out from them everywhere (vs. 6-8).

Wherever he went Paul heard the story of their conversion, which he describes as turning to God from idols (their work of faith), to serve the living and true God (their labour of love), and to wait for His Son from Heaven (their patience of hope). Then he adds a reference to the Resurrection as a proof of the Sonship of Christ, and an allusion to the Second Coming (vs. 9-10).

2. His Mission in Thessalonica (2:1-12). The Apostle now describes how he and his companions came to Thessalonica fresh from the persecution in Philippi, and how he laboured to proclaim the Gos-

pel to the Thessalonians. His ministry was characterized by boldness of speech (vs. 1-2), sincerity and singleness of purpose (vs. 3-6), gentleness and tenderness (vs. 7-8), unselfishness and blamelessness (vs. 9-10), and fatherly concern for them individually (vs. 11-12).

3. The Persecution of the Thessalonians (2:13-20). Paul tells them how he thanks God continually that they received his message not as a mere message of men, but as the effectual message of God. They suffered for it from their own countrymen, as their fellow-believers in Judea did from the Jews (vs. 13-14). The killing of the Lord Jesus by the Jews was the crime that consummated their murder of their prophets. They have become enemies of God and man. They have filled up the measure of their sins by refusing the Gospel themselves and forbidding its proclamation to the Gentiles. God's wrath has overtaken them at last (vs. 15-16). This is the only place in Paul's letters where such an outburst against the Jews occurs. It is in striking contrast with Rom. 9:1-5.

The Apostle then tells his readers of his longing to see them again after his enforced departure from them. Satan hindered the attempts he made to return. In words of tender affection for them as his converts, he expresses his joy in them, and the glory he hopes to have in them before Christ at His coming (vs. 17-20).

4. Timothy's Mission to Thessalonica (Ch. 3). When Paul could no longer bear his separation from his converts without news from them, he remained at Athens alone and sent Timothy to encourage them in the faithful endurance of persecution. He himself had told them before that tribulation is the common lot of Christians, even as it has happened to them. He was anxious to know if they stood firm under it (vs. 1-5).

Timothy has come back with good news, both of their faith and love for one another, and of their affectionate remembrance of Paul. He was greatly cheered. It was his very life to know that his converts stood fast in the Lord (vs. 6-8). He thanks God because of this good news. His constant and earnest prayer is that he may see them again and supply what is lacking in their knowledge of the truth (vs. 9-10).

Now comes a fervent prayer that God may direct his way to them, and that they may abound in love to one another and to all men, so that they may be established blameless in holiness "at the coming of our Lord Jesus with all his saints" (vs. 11-13). Thus for the third time in the course of the letter Paul brings the glorious appearing of the Lord into view as the consummation of salvation and the object of the Christian hope. The saints referred to are the angelic hosts, and not the departed dead. The latter is a possible meaning; but Paul always writes with the Old Testament in his mind, and in the light of such Scriptures as Deut. 33:2, Dan. 4:13, and Zech. 14:5 (cf. Matt. 13:41; Mark 8:38; 2 Thess. 1:7), the former meaning is the more probable.

PAUL'S INSTRUCTIONS TO THE THESSALONIANS
(Chs. 4—5)

The teaching contained in these chapters is based

on Timothy's report about the condition of the Thessalonian church.

1. The Christian's Walk (4:1-12). In this passage Paul emphasizes the instruction that he had given them before about the kind of life that pleases God (vs. 1-2). It has a three-fold relation:

(1) In relation to oneself—personal purity (vs. 3-8). In heathenism there was no connection between religion and morality. Ancient philosophy saw no wrong in acts which the Christian mind regards with abhorrence.

(2) In relation to one another—love of the brethren (vs. 9-10). In the New Testament the word "brethren" means fellow-Christians and not fellowmen. The one outstanding characteristic of the early Christians which attracted attention from the Gentile world, besides personal purity, was their love for one another.

(3) In relation to the world—quiet, self-possessed, and honourable independence (vs. 11-12). Some of the members of the church seem to have been giving up their daily occupation under the influence of religious fanaticism. Paul urges the duty of the Christian to support himself by his own work and to be loyal to the ordinary duties of life. Excitement, idleness, and want of common sense are inconsistent with the dignity of Christian character.

2. Concerning the Christian Dead (4:13-18). The Apostle's purpose in this passage is not to give a program of the Lord's coming, but to assure the Thessalonians that the dead and the living saints will be united, and will share alike in the trancendent change which that event will bring about. They need not sorrow over their dead friends as the heathen do, who are without God and have no hope in the future. And so Paul concludes what he says about the matter with this practical advice: "Wherefore, comfort one another with these words". A number of phrases used by the Apostle in the course of the passage should be noted:

"Them that fall asleep"; "them that are fallen asleep in Jesus":—Jesus looked upon death as a sleep (Mark 5:39; John 11:11), and the Apostles, following Him, describe the state of believers after death as being asleep. Christ having conquered death for them, all that death can do to them now is to put them to sleep in Him.

"For if we believe that Jesus died, and rose again":—Paul's argument here means that the place of believers at the Lord's coming is assured by their union with Him. If we are in Christ now, we shall still be in Him after death, and with Him when He comes. Our destiny is linked with His.

"This we say unto you by the word of the Lord": —This does not mean that Paul had received some direct revelation from the Lord about His return, but that he is basing his teaching on what the Lord had taught. There are sayings in the Gospels which bear a striking resemblance to Paul's words here (Matt. 24:31; John 6:39). Jesus had given His disciples to understand that at His coming He would raise the dead, and that the dead no less than the living would share in His Kingdom.

"We that are alive, that are left unto the coming of the Lord":—Paul does not necessarily mean that he expects to be alive when the Lord comes, for elsewhere he ranks himself among those that will be raised from the dead (1 Cor. 6:14; 2 Cor. 4:14;

Phil. 3:11). In other places he writes as if undecided (2 Cor. 5:6-10; Phil. 1:21-24; 2:17). What he means is that there will be two classes of believers, undergoing different changes, at the Lord's coming—those that are dead, who will be raised, and those that are living, as "we" are now, who will be translated.

"To meet the Lord in the air":—By this phrase we are not to understand the atmosphere above us, but the supersensible world, the realm of spiritual beings, where Satan now holds sway (Eph. 2:2). The error of the Thessalonians arose from thinking that the Lord's coming would be a return to the conditions of this world. The Apostle corrects this wrong idea, and tells them that it will introduce them into another world altogether, a world where the Lord will meet them. Then Paul states the spiritual significance of the event for us: "And so shall we ever be with the Lord". Nothing more is said as to what will happen then. This is bliss enough for our comfort and hope.

3. Preparation for the Lord's Coming (5:1-11). The Apostle now proceeds to give some instructions as to how the living should prepare themselves for the coming of the Lord. He had already taught his readers what the Lord had told His disciples about His coming as a thief in the night (Matt. 24:43), that the day of the Lord should come upon the world without warning, unobserved and unexpected, bringing sudden destruction that none could escape (vs. 1-3).

The day of the Lord was one of the themes of the Old Testament prophets. They used the phrase for the time when God would put forth His power to deliver His oppressed people and destroy their foes, or to bring judgment upon Israel. In the New Testament the phrase is always applied to the time when the supreme manifestation of the Lord's power will take place, which is to be ushered in by the Second Coming.

The day of the Lord should not come upon his readers, Paul tells them, like a thief in the night, for they are all children of the day, living in the light, not in moral darkness (vs. 4-5). Therefore we should not sleep in a moral stupor as other men do, but keep watch and live in a calm and collected spirit, manifesting the graces of faith, love, and hope (vs. 6-8).

Thus Paul explains how to watch for the Lord's coming in a world that is utterly insensible of the approach of such an event. The destiny God will have for us then is not the wrath that He will visit upon the world, but the consummation of the salvation that Christ secured for us by His death. Whether we are awake or asleep when He comes, whether we are among the living or among the dead at that time, we shall be forever with the Lord. Therefore take comfort and encouragement from this truth (vs. 9-11).

4. The Sanctified Life (5:12-28). In these two chapters Paul has been keeping in view the sanctification of his readers (4:3). The present section contains a number of specific instructions for the sanctified life, leading up to a final prayer for entire sanctification. The pastors and leaders of the church are to be honoured, and the brethren are to live at peace among themselves, exercising discipline over the disorderly, and admonishing and encouraging one another. They are to see that there is no revenge,

the most natural and instinctive of all vices; they are always to confer good upon others (vs. 12-15). Then follow a number of short rules for their religious life, which is to be joyful, prayerful, and grateful (vs. 16-18). The spiritual gifts of the various members of the church are not to be checked, but are to be tested and proved, the good held fast and all kinds of evil rejected (vs. 19-22).

Then comes the Apostle's final prayer for the entire sanctification of his readers, to which he adds the ground of his confidence in its fulfilment (vs. 23-24). He makes a three-fold division of human nature. Sanctification begins in the spirit, that part of our nature which makes us conscious of God. It extends to the soul, the seat of our separate personalities, and to the body, which links us with the physical world. The conclusion of the letter is very brief (vs. 25-28). Besides the benediction, it contains an urgent request that the Epistle be read to all the members of the church. This was probably due to Paul's concern that none of them should miss the consolation it contained for the bereaved. The custom of reading apostolic letters to the whole congregation had not yet been established.

THE SECOND EPISTLE TO THE THESSALONIANS

THIS letter was written while Silas and Timothy were still with Paul in Corinth (1:1). The First Epistle had quieted the fears of the Thessalonians regarding their departed friends, but the excitement caused by the expectation of an immediate coming of the Lord still remained. This was aggravated by the claims of some to have received prophetic revelations, and by a message alleged to have come from Paul agreeing with them (2:2). Hence the Christian community in Thessalonica was becoming more and more disturbed. When the Apostle heard of this, he wrote the Second Epistle, to put a stop once and for all to these mistaken views about Christ's coming. Only a short interval could have elapsed between the two letters.

The First Epistle had dealt with the Second Coming in its relation to the Christian Church. The Second Epistle deals with the event mainly in its relation to the world and the foes of the Church. It may be taken in three parts. The Apostle first explains the Lord's purpose in His coming. It is to bring retribution on the foes of the Gospel as well as to bring deliverance to believers (Ch. 1). Then he declares that before that takes place certain intervening events will happen, and the movement which will bring them about has yet to develop and run its course (Ch. 2:1-12). Finally, on the basis of this

revelation, some further instructions and warnings are given (Chs. 2:13—3:18).

THE PURPOSE OF CHRIST'S COMING
(Ch. 1)

After beginning with the same kind of salutation as in the first letter (vs. 1-2), Paul continues with an extended thanksgiving, in the course of which he states the general purpose of the Second Coming. He thanks God that his readers continue to manifest increasingly the three graces he mentioned in 1 Thess. 1:3. Hope is not mentioned by name, but that grace is involved in their patience in enduring persecution. They are to regard these afflictions as a token that God counts them worthy of His Kingdom, and is preparing them for it (vs. 3-5). This leads to the thought of the Lord's return, and the passage goes on to unfold the objects to be achieved at that time.

It is God's purpose to bring righteous retribution upon those that refuse the Gospel and persecute His people (vs. 6-9). This will take place at the revelation of the Lord from Heaven attended by the angels of His power. The phrase, "in flaming fire", probably marks the robe of glory in which the Lord appears. But in the light of 2 Pet. 3:10-12 it is possible to interpret it as describing the instrument of judgment in the day of the Lord. Vengeance is to be visited both upon "them that know not God" (the Gentiles who have refused the Gospel), and upon "them that obey not the gospel of our Lord Jesus" (the Jews to whom the Gospel came first). The punishment to be inflicted upon them is "everlasting destruction from the presence of the Lord". They are cut off from God for ever. This is the antithesis of everlasting life.

It is also God's purpose to give rest to His afflicted people. As a result of the revelation of the Lord, His glory will be exhibited in His saints. What He has done in the case of those that have accepted the Gospel will be a source of wonderment in that day (v. 10). Paul then adds his constant prayer that God would count his readers worthy of their calling, and fulfil in them all that goodness desires and all that faith can effect, so that through them the Name of the Lord Jesus Christ may be glorified; that is, that He may be shown to be Jehovah (vs. 11-12).

THE INTERVENING EVENTS
(2:1-12)

The Apostle now comes to the main theme of his letter. It has to do with "the coming of our Lord Jesus Christ, and our gathering together unto him" (v. 1)—the special subject about which he had written in his former letter (4:15-17). He begs his readers not to give way to excitement, or to allow themselves to be deceived by some pretended revelation, or some letter purporting to come from him, to the effect that the day of the Lord is just upon us. Because it will not come, he goes on to declare, until two other events have happened. These are closely related—"the falling away", and the revelation of "the man of sin, the son of perdition" (vs. 2-3).

The man of sin is described in terms which mean that he presents himself instead of God as the object of divine worship, and usurps the place of God in the Christian Church (v. 4). Paul uses the phrase, "the temple of God", for the Church in 1 Cor. 3:16-17 and 2 Cor. 6:16, and he cannot mean the Jewish temple here. That could no longer be called the temple of God when its typical significance had been fulfilled in Christ. It is never mentioned elsewhere in Paul's letters except in 1 Cor. 9:13, and there he uses another Greek word to describe it.

This prophecy should be interpreted in the broad light of Christian history. The nineteen centuries through which the Church has passed have something to say about it. Any other method of dealing with it can only result in speculation. The use of the article with "falling away" indicates that no local or temporary apostasy from the faith is meant, but something that affects the whole Church and stands out in its history. It is not said to be a falling away from belief in the Lord Jesus Christ. Apostasies of that kind have been temporary and have never affected the Church as a whole. What is meant is the falling away from the spiritual constitution of the Church and the unseen leadership of the Holy Spirit. This "falling away" began very early, and is the most significant movement in the ecclesiastical history of the first five centuries. What is seen in the Book of Acts as the Church of the Spirit gradually became the Church of the Bishops, and finally the Roman Catholic Church with the Papacy at its head.

There is a striking parallel in this respect between the history of Israel and the history of the Church. Israel fell away from Jehovah when they demanded a king "like all the nations" (1 Sam. 8:4-7). It was not that they denied His Deity, but that they rejected His invisible Kingship. This started the nation on a path which led her away from her covenant God and ended in her overthrow in judgment. The organized Church has followed a similar course, and out of "the falling away" has arisen "the man of sin".

This phrase does not indicate a man in whom the sin of the world will be consummated, but the man in whom the sin of the Church, its falling away, comes to a head. He is called "the son of perdition" in the same sense as Judas Iscariot (John 17:12). The prophecy does not point to any particular Pope, but to the Papal hierarchy as a whole. The Papacy is to be distinguished from the Church of Rome, for it is a distinct system by itself. It is the consummation of "the falling away", for it puts the Pope in the place of the Holy Spirit as the representative of God in the Church of Christ.

Paul reminds the Thessalonians that he had told them about these things when he was with them (v. 5). It seems that on this subject he was drawing out teaching that he found in the Old Testament Scriptures. By "the man of sin" he meant "the little horn" in Daniel's vision of the four beasts (Dan. 7:8). The career of this horn symbolizes prophetically the rise of the Papacy as a political power among the various national powers that developed out of the Roman Empire (See pages 214-216 in Vol. II of this series). Paul does not use the term "Antichrist", but the phrase, "the man of sin", or according to another reading, "the man of lawlessness", may contain an implied allusion by contrast to "the Son of man" in whom righteousness is embodied and the Law is fulfilled.

The Apostle goes on to refer to a restraining power and a restraining person holding back the revelation of the man of sin until his time comes— "that which restraineth" and "one that restraineth now" (vs. 6-7). Paul had to use guarded terms, for he was referring to the Roman Empire and its ruler. As long as the seat of Empire was in the city of Rome the power of the Pope was limited; but when that was moved to Constantinople early in the fourth century, then Papal power began to develop rapidly.

"The mystery of lawlessness doth already work". This was the tendency in the Church to fall away from the headship of Christ which began even in the days of the Apostles (Rev. 2:4). "Then shall be revealed the lawless one" (v. 8)—so called as departing from the law of Christ and as disobedient to Him. "Whom the Lord Jesus shall . . . bring to naught by the manifestation of his coming." This seems to be a prophetic indication that the Papacy will continue to oppose the progress of the Word of God in the world until the coming of the Lord Himself.

The next verses (vs. 9-10) contain a prophetic description of the rise and appearance of the Papacy — its "coming" — on the stage of world history, which corresponds exactly with historic fact. It is literally true that this took place "according to the working of Satan", and that its whole course is marked by "lying wonders"—pretended miraculous signs.

In all the long history of Christianity, nothing has ever appeared that answers so closely to all the characteristics described in this passage as does the Papal system of the Roman Catholic Church. No other institution in the world has exerted such a universal and long-sustained influence in preventing men from knowing the truth "that they might be saved". Paul then goes on to declare that all this was permitted to happen as a Divine judgment upon men for their aversion to the Gospel and their delight in unrighteousness (vs. 11-12).

CHRISTIAN DUTY IN VIEW OF CHRIST'S COMING (2:13—3:18)

Paul follows up the new light he has given about the Second Coming with further instructions of the same kind as those contained in his first letter.

1. Words of Encouragement (2:13-17). While there is a principle of iniquity secretly at work in the world, deceiving men and carrying them on to ruin, there is also a work of God leading men to salvation. Paul gives thanks for the part that the Thessalonians have in this through the Gospel message which he brought them. He urges them to stand fast in it, and invokes the comfort and strength of God to keep them faithful.

2. Prayer for the Progress of the Gospel (3:1-5). Paul's request of the Thessalonians to pray for him reveals how his own heart was burdened about the work in Corinth. But in a moment, he thinks again of their need and offers prayer for them. This is characteristic of the Apostle. How easily and often he breaks into prayer as he writes (1-11; 2:13, 16; 3:5, 16).

3. Discipline in the Church (3:6-15). Some members of the church, under a mistaken notion that the Lord was to be expected at any moment, were giving up their daily work and were waiting for Him in idleness. Paul condemns their conduct as

"disorderly", and calls them "busybodies". They have a false Christian spirit and a wrong attitude toward the Lord's coming. The thrice repeated expression about "walking disorderly" does not mean that these persons were causing a disturbance or living in open sin, but that they were shirking their personal responsibilities.

Working for one's own living is essential to Christian character, and the true attitude of waiting for the Lord is that of earnest attention to present duty. If one is not willing to work, he is not worthy to eat. Such a Christian is to be disciplined, but not treated as an enemy. The Christian community has a character to keep, and he is to be excluded from it till he comes to see that he is out of fellowship with it. Discipline in the Church is necessary in order to preserve its true character and witness in the world, but it should be exercised in the spirit of love.

4. The Conclusion (3:16-18). In contrast with the excitement and disorder which a false view of the Second Coming had brought into the church, Paul brings his letter to a close with this significant prayer: "Now the Lord of peace himself give you peace at all times in all ways". Having dictated the Epistle, he adds the salutation and benediction with his own hand as his own personal mark and token.

```
┌─────────────────────────────────────────┐
│                                         │
│                                         │
│                                         │
│                                         │
│                                         │
└─── THE FIRST EPISTLE TO TIMOTHY ────────┘
```

PAUL'S letters to Timothy and Titus form a group by themselves. They are known as the Pastoral Epistles, because they were written to pastors in charge of churches and are concerned chiefly with the qualifications and duties of ministers and office-bearers. It is not likely that they were intended to be read aloud to congregations. They belong to the closing years of the Apostle's life, and lie beyond the narrative of the Book of Acts.

According to an early and general tradition, Paul was released from the imprisonment with which Acts closes, and subsequently resumed his evangelizing work and his visitation of the churches, and suffered martyrdom five or six years afterwards in a second imprisonment at Rome. The First Epistle to Timothy and the Epistle to Titus were written in the interval between the two imprisonments, and the Second Epistle to Timothy was written during his second imprisonment.

These letters reveal the Apostle's deep concern for the welfare of the Christian Church. It had now been for many years a visible institution in the world, with an organization and office-bearers of its own in each locality where it existed. The doctrines upon which it was founded, and by which it lived, had been explained and established. To preserve the purity of its teaching and the sanctification of its fellowship, and to provide for the supervision and maintenance of its well-ordered life after

he and the other Apostles had passed away, was Paul's object in writing these letters.

Timothy was the most tenderly loved and the most thoroughly trusted of all Paul's companions and fellow-workers. He was the Apostle's "true child in faith" (1 Tim. 1:2), having been converted during his first missionary journey. He had been continuously employed by Paul ever since he was chosen "to go forth with him" from his home in Lystra during the second missionary journey (Acts 16:1-3). Timothy accompanied Paul and Silas during the rest of that mission, was associated with Paul during his third missionary journey, and was with him during his first imprisonment in Rome (Phil. 1:1; Col. 1:1).

After his release, Paul entrusted Timothy with the supervision of the church in Ephesus; and he was there when this First Epistle was written to him. It is a charge to a chief pastor concerning the oversight of a church. Its purpose is definitely stated: "that thou mayest know how men ought to behave themselves in the house of God" (3:15). The word "charge", as a noun or a verb, occurs seven times in the course of the Epistle. It is best taken chapter by chapter.

1. The Gospel in the Church (Ch. 1). After the opening salutation, in which Paul adds "mercy" to his usual greeting of "grace and peace" (vs. 1-2), he exhorts Timothy to be faithful in the ministry which he had left him to carry on at Ephesus, maintaining the true doctrine of the Gospel, for there were certain men teaching a different doctrine (vs. 3-4). The practical aim of the teaching contained in "the gospel of the glory of the blessed God" is a life of love springing from a pure heart, a good conscience, and a sincere faith (vs. 5 and 11). But some have turned aside to vain talking, desiring to be teachers of the Law, although they fail to understand the purpose of the Law. We understand that the Law was made not for the righteous but for the wicked, and for whatever is opposed to "the sound doctrine" (vs. 6-10).

This expression is characteristic of the Pastoral Epistles. It means "healthful teaching", and was probably suggested by the growing heresies of the time, which were harmful forms of thought. The word "doctrine" or "teaching", in the sense of the substance of teaching as distinguished from the act, occurs fifteen times in these Epistles, more often than in all the rest of the New Testament. The heretical teachers to whom Paul refers seem to have belonged to the Judaizing party, who gave the Apostle lifelong trouble.

The Apostle goes on to remind Timothy of his own call to preach the Gospel and of the grace bestowed upon him in carrying out his commission (vs. 12-14). His conversion was a supreme example of the longsuffering of God, and of the power of the Gospel to save sinners, of whom he counts himself to be the chief (vs. 15-16). This thought evokes from his heart a doxology of adoring praise (v. 17). Then he solemnly commits the same charge to Timothy, recalling the prophecies that were uttered over him, probably at his baptism or his ordination, and reminding him of some teachers who had made shipwreck of their faith (vs. 18-20). The expression "faithful is the saying" (v. 15) is used five times in these Epistles and in each case it introduces or describes some statement regarding the Christian faith (1 Tim. 3:1; 4:8-9; 2 Tim. 2:11; Titus 3:8). These may have been extracts from early Christian hymns.

2. The Public Worship of the Church (Ch. 2). Prayers of intercession are to be made for all men, with thanksgiving, especially for kings and all who are in authority (vs. 1-2). The reason for this is that God desires the salvation of all men, and there is but one appointed Mediator for the race (vs. 3-5). The ransom He gave is now available for all, and this redemption, which Paul was appointed to proclaim among the Gentiles, was to be announced when the time of its accomplishment had come (vs. 6-7).

These public prayers are to be offered only by men, and in a devout spirit (v. 8). Women are to have a place in public worship, but a subordinate one. They are to worship in silence, and their dress and behaviour should be consistent with their Christian profession (vs. 9-12). This subordination of women in the public worship of the Church is based upon the order of creation and the facts of the Fall. The woman was the second in creation and the first in transgression; yet through her function of motherhood she has an honoured place in the Church (vs. 13-15). Paul has in mind here both the curse and the promise of Gen. 3:15-16.

3. The Office-bearers of the Church (Ch. 3). Now come instructions regarding the character and qualifications of those who hold office in the Church. The first office mentioned is that of bishop, which is the same as that of pastor or elder. This office has to do with the spiritual oversight of a church, and it is described as "a good work", in the sense of being noble or honourable (v. 1). The necessary qualifications of the bishop are described as to character (vs. 2-3), temperament (vs. 4-5), experience (v. 6), and reputation (v. 7).

The qualifications of deacons are given next (vs. 8-13). This office had to do with the temporal welfare of the members of a church, especially with the care of the poor, who formed by far the largest class among the early Christians. The office of deacon may have been suggested by the appointment of the Seven to care for the poor widows among the Grecian Jews in the church at Jerusalem (Acts 6: 1-6), although they are nowhere called deacons. It was held by women as well as men, as v. 11 indicates, which refers to women as deaconesses and not to wives of deacons. The qualifications required for this office are similar to those of the bishop.

Paul now goes on to emphasize the importance of these instructions. He hopes to join Timothy shortly, but in case of delay he wishes him to know "how men ought to behave themselves in the house of God, which is the church of the living God, the pillar and ground of the truth" (vs. 14-15). The house of God is not the building but the household, the society of believers. A proper order is to be maintained in it, because it is the assembly where the living God is worshipped, and the mainstay of divine truth in the world.

Then the substance of the truth which a church has to maintain is given in a number of succinct parallel phrases (v. 16). They appear to be in poetical form, as though they were taken from a Christian hymn. The "mystery of godliness" is the revelation of God in Christ, and is so called because it is the secret from which vital godliness springs (Col. 1:27). The word "godliness" is used eleven times in the Pastoral Epistles, and elsewhere only in 2 Peter. By the time these letters were written it had become a compendious expression for Christian faith and practice.

4. The Testimony of the Church (Ch. 4). From the idea of the Christian society as the pillar and prop of the truth, the Apostle passes on to warn Timothy of the error against which the truth will have to be maintained (vs. 1-3). He had been taught by the Spirit that in future times some would "fall away from the faith", and be led astray by the hypocrisy and deceitful teaching of men who would fain impose a false asceticism upon believers. In the New Testament, "the faith" does not mean a body of doctrine, but the attitude of trust in the incarnate Redeemer alone for salvation. This is the truth for the Church to maintain, and Paul declares that those who know it can receive with thanksgiving all that God has created for food (vs. 4-5).

Timothy will be a good servant of Christ Jesus if he reminds the brethren of these things. Let him oppose all vain and false teaching, and give an illustration of godliness in the discipline of his own life. This is beneficial both for the present life and for the life to come (vs. 6-9). This is the end of the trials we endure, because our hope is set upon the living God. He is "the Saviour of all men"—in having made propitiation for the sins of the world through Jesus Christ (1 John 2:2)—, but "specially of them that believe", for salvation can only be realized through faith. This is what Timothy is to teach in the church (vs. 10-11).

Then follow some directions for Timothy regarding his own personal conduct (vs. 12-16). He is to be an example to believers in all respects, and to conduct himself in such a way that the church cannot but respect and honour him notwithstanding his youth. "Give heed to reading"—the public reading of the Scriptures; "to exhortation"—the sermon following the reading; "to teaching" — the teaching that accompanied the exhortation. "Neglect not the gift that is in thee"—the special equipment of the Holy Spirit for the office to which he was ordained.

5. The Administration of the Church (Ch. 5). Special instructions are now given Timothy to guide him in his pastoral care of the church and his treatment of the different classes of its members. He is to act toward the older men and women as he would toward his father and mother, and toward the younger men and women as he would toward his brothers and sisters (vs. 1-2).

Careful directions are then given regarding widows, for they were a large class, and their condition in the pagan world was solitary and helpless. Christian widows were the special care of the corporate body of a church (Acts 6:1). Paul explains the principles to be observed in dealing with them. Children should make some return to their parents and should provide for widows who belong to their own family. Those who are destitute of support, "widows indeed", should be taken under the special care of the church, but only if they are living devout and blameless Christian lives (vs. 3-8). Then follow special instructions for an order of widows who were to be enrolled as church servants. This was to include only women of mature age and experience, and of tried Christian character (vs. 9-16).

Instructions are given also for the treatment of elders (vs. 17-25). Special honour was to be paid to them, and the quotations from Deut. 25:4 and Matt. 10:10 mean that they were entitled to financial remuneration for their labour. Paul realized the serious responsibility of the judicial functions involved in his instructions to Timothy regarding the elders, and hence the solemn charge of v. 21 thrown in as a kind of parenthesis.

Another parenthesis occurs in v. 23, suggested by the last words of v. 22. In disciplining himself in purity, Timothy is to exercise sanctified common sense and not let his health be injured. The injunction implied that Paul regarded wine as a medicine for the infirm, and not as a beverage for the strong. In the next verses he reverts to the judicial position of Timothy in dealing with the office-bearers of the church. The instructions contained in this chapter indicate that Timothy was acting as Paul's representative in Ephesus, and not as the ordinary church pastor.

6. Closing Charges (Ch. 6). Paul gives some wise advice regarding bondservants, of whom there were many in the New Testament churches (vs. 1-2). The tendency of the Christian slave in a household would be to treat his unbelieving master with contempt; and on the other hand, if his master was a Christian, to treat him with undue familiarity.

Then comes a further warning against false teachers, who are puffed up and ignorant, and whose motive is gain—"supposing that godliness is a way of gain" (vs. 3-5). This leads the Apostle to say that contentment is the mark of the pilgrim life in the world (vs. 6-8), and to point out the peril of covetousness (vs. 9-10). The desire to be rich brings on temptation and the snares of sin, and often results in moral ruin. The love of money is a root of all kinds of evil, and has led some astray from the faith and into many sorrows.

Turning from the conduct of false teachers, Paul describes the life of the true teacher in a beautiful and dignified appeal to Timothy, beginning, "But thou, O man of God, flee these things" (vs. 11-16). He describes the character that he should follow after in three pairs of virtues, and summons him to fight the noble fight of faith and lay hold on the life eternal which he has professed. Then Paul adds a solemn and impressive charge, urging Timothy to keep his sacred commission without spot and without reproach, in view of the inspiring hope of the appearing of the Lord Jesus. This sublime passage closes with a majestic description of the living God, who in due time is to bring in the Lord Jesus Christ.

The prospect of the Lord's coming leads Paul to think of the rich again, and he gives Timothy a further charge about them. They are to be told to use their wealth in such a way as to lay up in store for themselves "a good foundation against the time to come" (vs. 17-19). After that the letter comes to an end with the closing exhortation of warning to Timothy himself, and a brief benediction (vs. 20-21).

THE SECOND EPISTLE TO TIMOTHY

THIS is Paul's farewell message. When it was written the Apostle was a prisoner in Rome under close guard (1:8, 16-17). This was a different kind of confinement from the imprisonment mentioned at the end of Acts. He had already had a preliminary trial, and was remanded (4:16-17). The persecution of the Christians in Rome, following the great fire of A.D. 64, had been so severe that no one now dared to stand by him in the court. He expected to suffer death very soon (4:6-8). He was almost quite alone; only Luke remained with him; and he longed to see his "beloved child" Timothy before the end (1:2; 4:9-11).

Timothy was still at Ephesus where Paul had left him, bearing the heavy burden of his responsibility in the church there. His difficulties had been increased by the activity of false teachers. Paul seems to have felt that he would need all the encouragement and advice that the Apostle could give him, for henceforth he should have to stand alone. This is the main purpose of the letter. But the Apostle also appeals to Timothy to come to him with all haste, and if possible before the winter (4:9, 21). The probable date of the Epistle is the fall of A.D. 67.

It is a purely personal letter, and its value does not depend so much upon its doctrinal and ecclesiastical teaching as upon its human interest. It is a revelation of the passionate attachment that Paul felt for Timothy, and also of the profound nature of the Apostle's faith as he reviewed his Christian experience in the face of death. His personal interest in people still remained, for twenty-three persons are mentioned by name. The Epistle may be taken chapter by chapter.

1. Timothy Encouraged (Ch. 1). After the opening salutation, Paul expresses his thanksgiving to God as he prays for Timothy and remembers his genuine faith and the religious influence of his early home (vs. 1-5). He reminds him to stir up the gift of God that he received at his ordination, and encourages him not to be ashamed of the ministry of the Gospel, but to share its hardships (vs. 6-8). Then the Apostle goes on describing the power and grandeur of the Gospel which he was appointed to proclaim and teach among the Gentiles (vs. 9-11). He declares that he himself is not ashamed of the sufferings he has endured in this ministry of his; for he knows Him in whom he has put his trust, and is sure that He is able to guard what he has laid up in his keeping until the great day (v. 12).

Paul bids Timothy adhere to the doctrine of the Gospel that he taught him, "the pattern of sound words", and guard the deposit of truth entrusted to him by the help of the Holy Spirit (vs. 13-14). He then holds up before him two instances, one as a sad warning, and the other as a bright example. The Christians of Asia deserted the Apostle; this Timothy knows. Onesiphorus, on the other hand, a prominent Christian of Ephesus well known to Timothy, sought Paul out in his imprisonment when he was in Rome, and often cheered him. Paul twice invokes mercy upon him (vs. 15-18).

2. **Timothy Exhorted (Ch. 2).** Paul now gives Timothy a personal exhortation. Finding his strength in the grace of Christ, he is to take practical measures for preserving the truth which the Apostle has taught him, by transmitting it to faithful men who will be able to teach it to others (vs. 1-2). Then he urges him to fidelity in the hardships and difficulties of his service for Christ by illustrations from the life of the soldier, the athlete, and the husbandman. The Lord will make all these things clear to him, Paul adds (vs. 3-7). The highest motive in the ministry of the Gospel of salvation consists in keeping the risen Christ before his mind (vs. 8-10). Then comes another "faithful saying", confirming the foregoing statement. It dwells on the fact that faith in Christ identifies us with Him in everything, and it ends with a warning against denying Him (vs. 11-13).

The Apostle now turns to the condition of the church, and gives Timothy some instructions in view of it. He tells him how to deal with those who carry on worthless disputes about doctrine (vs. 14-18). He is to take good heed that his own manner of presenting the truth is such as will receive the blessing of God. He is to show himself a workman who is not to be put to shame, marking out aright the word of truth; and he is to keep aloof from the profane babbling of false teachers. They will go to more daring lengths in impiety; and their teaching will work deeper and deeper like a gangrene. There follow two instances of teachers who had gone utterly astray about the Resurrection.

But the foundation of the Church of God stands firm in spite of the false teaching of some (v. 19). It has as its seal two correlative truths: the sovereign care and love of God for His own children ("The Lord knoweth them that are his"), and their responsibility to be separate from sin ("Let every one that nameth the name of the Lord depart from unrighteousness").

Although the Church in its ideal condition is a society of believers, yet its condition as actually found in the world is like a large mansion, in which there are vessels made of precious metals which are used for honourable purposes, and other vessels of perishable material which are put to an ignoble use. If a man cleanse himself from the pollutions of false teaching, he will be a vessel for a noble use, prepared for every good work in the service of his Master (vs. 20-21).

Then Paul exhorts Timothy to look to the cultivation of his own spiritual life, in fellowship with sincere followers of the Lord, and to avoid questions that engender strife in the church (vs. 22-23). As the servant of the Lord, he should be gentle and patient with all. He should in a kindly spirit instruct those who are contentious, in the hope that God may bring them to repentance, so that they may acknowledge the truth and come to themselves again out of the snare of the devil (vs. 24-26). The last words of the passage, "unto his will", refer to the restoration of the sinner to do the will of God.

3. **Timothy Warned (Ch. 3).** From the false teaching and its results which Timothy was meeting in his day, Paul turns to the future and warns him of more grievous things to happen "in the last days" (vs. 1-5). By this phrase he refers to the close of the Christian age. He had said that profane babblings would lead to still more impiety, and here he describes the results. The immoral features by which life would be marked make it more akin to paganism than Christianity. He does not mean that all these vices would appear in the same persons, but that they would characterize human society; and it is to society within the sphere of Christendom that he refers. There would be a superficial form of Christianity without the inward reality.

The prediction has been fulfilled at different times in the course of the centuries, but the fulfilment has not yet reached its climax. The reason why Timothy was warned about this is stated in the next verses (vs. 6-9). Signs of it had already begun to appear in some Christian communities. An indication of the real character of these deceivers is given in the example of Jannes and Jambres. According to Jewish tradition these were the two chief magicians who withstood Moses in the court of Pharaoh. A word of encouragement is added, based on the failure of these men. And then Paul reminds Timothy of the privilege he has had in the company of the Apostle on his missionary journeys, in following his manner of life and his methods of work, and in seeing what persecutions he endured and how the Lord delivered him out of them (vs. 10-11).

Those who live a godly life, Paul declares, will suffer persecution, but impostors will go on their way of destruction (vs. 12-13). He bids Timothy abide in the truth that he has learned from his teachers. From his childhood he has known the sacred Scriptures, which can give him the wisdom that leads to salvation through faith in Christ (vs. 14-15). Every Scripture is inspired of God, and is fitted to prepare one for the work of the ministry, so that the man of God may be fully equipped for every good work (vs. 16-17). This passage contains the most definite statement in Paul's writings of the inspiration of the Old Testament and of its authoritative value for the Christian minister. Paul evidently believed that these Scriptures testify of Christ, and can lead men to a knowledge of the truth which was fulfilled in Him.

4. **Timothy Charged (Ch.. 4).** Now comes the aged Apostle's last charge. It is marked by a tender and solemn dignity, and is urged in the light of the Lord's appearing. Timothy's chief work was to preach the Word, the Divine message of the Gospel, and he was to be ever on the alert for opportunities of enforcing the truth (vs. 1-2). The time should come when men would not endure "the sound doctrine", the healthful truth of the Gospel, but would gather teachers to satisfy their self-willed notions and their itch for novelty, who would turn them away from the truth. But Timothy was to remain calm and sane in all things, enduring hardship, doing the work of an evangelist, and thus fulfilling his ministry (vs. 3-5).

Paul's life-work was ended, and his departure was at hand. He had fought the good fight, finished the race, and kept the Christian faith. He now faced death with triumphant assurance. The victor's crown of righteousness was laid up for him, which the Lord, the righteous Judge, would award him in the great day of His appearing (vs. 6-8). This passage regarding Paul's finished course and coming reward is more than an outbreak of personal joy; behind it is his strong desire to encourage Timothy to fight his own fight and run his own course with a view to the crown.

Then follow some personal messages (vs. 9-15). He appeals to Timothy to come to him soon, and bring Mark along with him. He is lonely; some have forsaken him, and others have gone to their homes or fields of labour. Luke alone is with him, faithful to the end. Paul left a cloak at Troas; Timothy is to bring that, for winter is coming on, and it can be terribly cold in the prison. He is also to bring the books, but above all the parchments. These may have been portions of the Scriptures, but we have no means of knowing.

Then Paul interposes a touching notice of the first stage of his trial (vs. 16-18). None of the Christians in Rome appeared as his advocate; all deserted him. May God not record it against them. But the Lord stood by him and gave him strength to make the Christian message known to all the Gentiles there. He was delivered from death on that occasion, and he is assured that the Lord will deliver him from every evil work and will bring him safely into His heavenly Kingdom. The Epistle then comes to an end with another appeal to Timothy to come soon, set in the midst of a few salutations and a closing benediction (vs. 19-22).

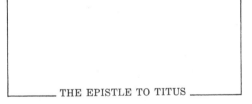

___ THE EPISTLE TO TITUS ___

TITUS was a Gentile who had been converted at an early period in Paul's ministry, his "true child after a common faith" (1:4). He had been associated with the Apostle longer than Timothy, but did not hold the same place in his affections. He is never mentioned in the Book of Acts, but from the references Paul makes to him in his Epistles it would seem that he was one of the ablest and most reliable of the Apostle's fellow-workers. He appears first as accompanying Paul and Barnabas to Jerusalem after the first missionary journey (Gal. 2:1-3), and next as sent by Paul on important missions to Corinth during the third missionary journey (2 Cor. 2:13; 7:6; 8:6; 12:18).

Some time after the Apostle's release from Rome, he took Titus with him to the island of Crete, and left him there in charge of the organization of the churches. He was engaged in that ministry when this Epistle was sent to him. He evidently possessed a rare combination of firmness and tact, and was fitted for delicate and difficult tasks. Paul reminds him that the Cretans had a bad reputation, and even after conversion they needed firm and resolute oversight (1:10-13). He quotes a Cretan poet of about 600 B.C. to support his description of them. It is not known how the Gospel reached Crete. Probably the Cretans who were in Jerusalem on the

Day of Pentecost (Acts 2:11) carried it back to the island.

The Epistle to Titus is very similar to First Timothy, and was probably written about the same time. It may be described as a charge to a missionary superintendent. It deals with three main themes.

1. The Church and its Elders (Ch. 1). Paul begins with a much more elaborate salutation than in the letters to Timothy (vs. 1-4). He evidently feels a deep sense of responsibility, and wishes to impress Titus with the important place the Gospel occupies in God's eternal purpose. He instructs him first about the appointment of elders in the churches (vs. 5-9). Elders were to be appointed in each congregation—"in every city". The elder, or bishop, should be blameless in his family life, in his personal character, and in his social relations. As a special qualification he must hold fast the truth which he has been taught and be able to proclaim it and explain it to others.

The Apostle goes on to point out the need for these office-bearers (vs. 10-14). False teachers, especially of the Judaizing party, were threatening the Christian communities. The Cretans were of an unruly disposition, and firmness was needed in dealing with them. Then Paul states some important maxims about human nature fitted to guide Titus in his teaching (vs. 15-16).

2. The Church and its Members (Ch. 2). The Apostle now turns to the "things which befit the sound doctrine" (v. 1), and instructs Titus about the behaviour expected of the various classes of Christians—the aged men and women (vs. 2-3), the young women and the young men (vs. 4-6). In connection with the last class, Paul points out the special responsibility resting upon Titus to set a good example in his conduct and teaching (vs. 7-8). The duties of household slaves are next set forth (vs. 9-10).

And then Paul gives a grand outline of the grace of God in the Gospel itself as it bears upon the life of Christians in the world (vs. 11-14), and adds a pointed exhortation to Titus to proclaim these things, and to maintain such authority in his ministry that no man can despise him (v. 15).

3. The Church and the State (Ch. 3). Paul now instructs Titus regarding proper conduct toward those who are in authority in the state, and those who belong to the world outside the Church. It is the duty of all Christians to be in subjection to the civil authorities, and to contribute to the well-being of the state by following proper callings in life. They are to speak evil of no man, and show gentleness and meekness to all men (vs. 1-2). These were new virtues, and were peculiar to Christianity. The motive for them consists in recognizing what we once were in our sinful state (v. 3), and what God did to save us from our sins (vs. 4-7). Here we have another fine summary of the Gospel similar to 2:11-14.

Titus was to insist on these essential things, that believers might be careful to show their Christian character in honest occupations (v. 8). He was to avoid unprofitable controversies, especially those about the Law which Judaizers raised, and shun any man who persisted in being factious after repeated warnings (vs. 9-11). Then the Epistle comes to a close with a few personal messages and the final salutations, in the midst of which Paul reminds Titus again that Christians are to "learn to maintain good works" (vs. 12-15).

This is the eighth time in the course of these pastoral Epistles that the Apostle emphasizes the duty of Christians to manifest their faith by "good works". Two different adjectives are used in the original Greek. One marks the intrinsic character of the works; they are essentially good (1 Tim. 2:10; 2 Tim. 3:17; Tit. 3:1). The other marks their effect upon others: they have a nobility that attracts (1 Tim. 3:1; 5:10, 25; 6:18; Tit. 2:7; 3:14).

_____ THE EPISTLE TO PHILEMON _____

PHILEMON was a Colossian Christian who had been converted to Christianity through Paul (v. 19). He was a man of considerable means, and was noted for his charity and devotion (v.7). His house was a meeting-place for the church in Colossæ (v. 2).

Onesimus, a household slave belonging to Philemon, had robbed his master and run away from home. He had found his way to Rome when Paul was a prisoner there, and by some strange coincidence he had come within the sphere of the Apostle's influence and had been converted (v. 10). Paul then sent him back to Philemon with this letter. It was written at the same time as the Epistle to the Colossians. Onesimus accompanied the messenger who carried that letter to Colossæ (Col. 4:8-9).

The Epistle to Philemon is a private letter, written by one Christian to another. It is a model of Christian courtesy, tact, and delicacy. Paul's purpose was to restore the penitent slave to his master, and to commend him as a fellow-Christian. The letter shows how Christianity deals with the evils of human society. The system of slavery was the main foundation of social life when the Gospel entered the world. It was not attacked openly from without, but the Spirit of Christ was brought to bear upon it from within. The letter also illustrates the human interest which the Gospel creates. On its single

page eleven different persons are mentioned by name, and in most cases portraits of them drawn.

Paul begins the Epistle with his usual greeting of "grace and peace", but does not use his official title. To Philemon he is simply "a prisoner of Jesus Christ" (vs. 1-3). Apphia was probably the wife of Philemon, and Archippus his son. Then, as usual in Paul's letters, comes a thanksgiving. This time it is for the character of Philemon—his love and faith toward the Lord Jesus, and his charity and kindness toward all the saints (vs. 4-7).

The case of Onesimus is put before Philemon. The Apostle might enjoin him by his authority, but he rather beseeches him for love's sake, on the ground of his age and imprisonment, for his son whom he has begotten in his bonds (vs. 8-10). Then he plays on the slave's name, which means "serviceable", "good for something". Onesimus once was Little Good to Philemon; but now he is Great Good both to Philemon and to Paul (v. 11).

Paul is sending him back in his own person as one with himself. He would fain have kept him that he might serve himself on Philemon's behalf in the bonds of the Gospel. But he would do nothing without Philemon's consent, that his kindness might not be compulsory, but wholly of his own free will (vs. 12-14). Perhaps Onesimus was parted from him for a little that he might have him for ever, no longer as a slave, but as a brother beloved. Such he is to Paul; how much more to Philemon (vs. 15-16).

Next Paul appeals to Philemon as his partner to receive Onesimus as himself, and pledges himself to repay whatever Onesimus owes him. He might urge the plea that Philemon owes to Paul all that he is, but he will not. But he pleads with him to do one piece of joyful service, and thus refresh his heart (vs. 17-20). This is probably a delicate suggestion to Philemon to set his slave free. He has written thus because he is sure that Philemon will yield to his appeal, and even do more than he requests. But he asks him now to prepare a lodging for him in Colossæ for he hopes to be able to visit him in answer to his prayers (vs. 21-22).

The letter comes to an end with a salutation from Epaphras, who had come to Rome from Colossæ (Col. 1:7) and seems to have shared the Apostle's imprisonment, and also from four of his fellow-workers, followed by a simple closing benediction (vs. 23-25).

THE EPISTLE TO THE HEBREWS

THIS Epistle is anonymous, and there is no indication of the writer's identity in it. The tradition of the Church ascribes it to Paul, but not uniformly. The Eastern Church accepted it as Paul's from the beginning, but in the West its authorship was disputed. It was not till the fourth century that the Pauline tradition was generally received. It differs considerably in style and manner from the Epistles known to be Paul's, and is more like an ordered treatise than a familiar letter. Because of these features, the prevailing modern view denies the Pauline authorship. It assumes that no man, even with the versatility and mental ability that Paul had, could write in such different styles on different occasions.

While the authorship must remain hidden, yet no one was better fitted by training and ability to write such a letter, and the probabilities in Paul's favour are quite as strong as in the case of any other apostolic author whose name has been suggested. Whoever wrote the book must have been a man of massive mind. The mention of Timothy in Heb. 13:23, and the reference in 2 Pet. 3:15 to a letter that Paul had written to Hebrew Christians, would fall in with the Pauline authorship.

Assuming that the Apostle to the Gentiles was the writer, it is quite easy to see why he should omit a personal salutation and a reference to his apostolic authority in writing to Jewish Christians. The chief difficulty lies in a difference in the view-point. In Hebrews the writer's point of view is within Israel, while in Paul's known letters it is outside Israel. This could be explained by the fact that the readers of Hebrews belonged entirely to Israel, while in the other letters Paul was writing to churches that were very largely Gentile.

The Epistle bears the title, "To the Hebrews". It was apparently addressed to a community of Christian Jews in some particular locality, most probably Jerusalem, or Palestine in general; but it was no doubt intended for a wider circle also. They were undergoing persecution and were tempted to lapse into Judaism on account of it (10:23-25, 32-33; 12:3). The believing Jews in Jerusalem and Judea were especially subjected to this temptation, because of the presence of the Temple and the splendour of the Levitical ritual. The author speaks of these ceremonies as still carried on, which shows that he was writing before the destruction of the Temple in A.D. 70.

The Epistle was written to show that Christianity is better than Judaism, that the new dispensation is better than the old. The word "better" occurs thirteen times, more often than in all the rest of the New Testament. The writer shows that the whole system of types and ceremonies has been fulfilled in Christ, that Christianity is the completion and goal of the Old Covenant, and that it introduces a New Covenant. The argument may be divided into five main parts:

I. Jesus as the Mediator of the New Revelation Better than Angels—Chs. 1—2

II. Jesus as the Founder of the New Dispensation Better than Moses—Chs. 3—4
III. Jesus as the High Priest of the New Covenant Better than Aaron—Chs. 5—7
IV. The Work of the Great High Priest—Chs. 8—10
V. The New Life Under the New Covenant—Chs. 11—13

JESUS BETTER THAN ANGELS
(Chs. 1—2)

The Epistle begins with a note of finality. There is a majestic march in the opening sentence. Jesus Christ the Son is brought into view at once, seated at the centre of power in the heavenly world, in the repose of a finished work. This transcendent fact dominates the whole book. The present section shows that Jesus, through whom the new revelation of God was given, is superior to the angels, through whom the old revelation was given (2:2; Gal. 3:19).

1. Jesus the Revealer of God (Ch. 1). God has made His final revelation to man in a Son. The old revelation through the prophets is contrasted with the new revelation in Jesus Christ. He is all that God is, "being the effulgence of his glory, and the very image of his substance". He is therefore the perfect Prophet. He has "made purification of sins", and has therefore accomplished the work of the Priest. He now sits as King, "on the right hand of the Majesty on high" (vs. 1-3). There He occupies a place of pre-eminence over the angels (v.4).

This is proved by Scripture references to the supreme dignity of His person (vs. 5-6; Psa. 2:7; 2 Sam. 7:14; Psa. 97:7), of His office (vs. 7-9; Psa. 104:4; 45:6-7), of His work (vs. 10-12; Psa. 102:25-27), and of His position (vs. 13-14; Psa. 110:1).

2. A Warning to Give Heed (2:1-4). This is the first of a number of digressions in the form of warnings or exhortations that occur throughout the Epistle. It is a warning against neglecting the great salvation which has come through the new revelation, and has been proclaimed through the preaching of the Gospel.

3. Jesus the Representative Man (2:5-18). Man's true destiny, as revealed in the quotation from Psalm 8, is fulfilled in the exaltation of Jesus (vs. 5-9). He was made lower than the angels that He might share man's death: He was exalted that man might share His victory. Man has not yet attained this destiny. But we see Jesus, "because of the suffering of death crowned with glory and honour, that by the grace of God he should taste death for every man".

It makes no difference to the author's argument whether we take the crowning of Jesus with glory and honour as preceding the Cross so as to qualify Him to taste death for every man, in which case it would refer to the Transfiguration, or as following the Cross so as to make the benefits of His death available for every man, in which case it would refer to the Ascension. In either case the central fact remains, that Jesus passed through death as the perfect and ideal representative of the human race.

Having made this point, the writer goes on to show that, as the representative man and the author of our salvation, Jesus was made perfect through suffering (vs. 10-15). The manhood which He carried to the Cross and on into glory was an achievement, wrought out under those conditions which the sin of man had imposed. He was incorporated voluntarily in the human race. He assumed the nature of man and consented to live as men live, subject to the limitations of existence on earth. And this He did for the ultimate purpose of redeeming men: "That through death he might bring to nought him that had the power of death, that is, the devil; and might deliver all them who through fear of death were all their lifetime subject to bondage".

It was not the nature of angels, but the nature of men, that He took upon Himself, for it was necessary that, as the representative man, He should be made like those who were to be redeemed (vs. 16-18). It was thus that He became a true High Priest "in things pertaining to God", that is, on the Godward side of the veil, in order to make atonement for the sins of men. And He is also able to help those who are tempted on the human side.

JESUS BETTER THAN MOSES
(Chs. 3—4)

As the founder of the new dispensation, Jesus is shown to be superior to Moses, the founder of the old dispensation. The real purpose of God in redeeming His people out of Egypt and bringing them into Canaan remains to be realized through Jesus.

1. Jesus Compared with Moses (3:1-6). On the ground of what he has just said, the writer now calls upon his readers as "partakers of a heavenly calling"—members of the spiritual dispensation— to fix their attention on Jesus. He is both Apostle and High Priest of the faith they acknowledge, that is, the representative of both God and man. He was faithful in founding the new economy, as Moses was faithful in founding the old (vs. 1-2). The phrase, "in all his house", is a reference to the Lord's statement about Moses in Num. 12:7: "he is faithful in all mine house".

The writer then establishes the superiority of Christ by two considerations. Moses represents a "house", the house in which God dwells, but Christ represents the builder of the house, God Himself (vs. 3-4). Moses held the position of a servant, and bore witness to truths that were to be made plain afterwards. But Christ holds the position of a Son, and the blessings that He introduced are realized by us now (vs. 5-6).

2. Israel's Failure under Moses (3:7-19). This comparison of Christ with Moses leads naturally to a comparison of the people under the two dispensations. Israel failed in the wilderness because they hardened their hearts against God, and the writer quotes Psa. 95 to point the lesson he draws (vs. 7-11), and then makes a personal application of it to his readers (vs. 12-15). The Holy Spirit in the Psalm announced a new revelation and exhorted those to whom it was coming to be mindful of the fate of their fathers, who disbelieved God and missed the rest that was promised them.

The passage goes on to draw out the lesson in detail by a series of questions and answers showing the danger of backsliding (vs. 16-19): Who, when they heard, did provoke? Was it not the very people that came out of Egypt? With whom was He grieved forty years? Was it not with those that sinned and died in the wilderness? To whom sware

He that they should not enter into His rest? Was it not those that believed not? Thus the apostolic writer shows his readers that faith is the condition of enjoying the Divine blessing.

3. The Blessing Provided under Jesus (Ch. 4). It follows from this review of the history of Israel that the promise of God to His people was not fulfilled in Canaan, but remains to be fulfilled in Jesus Christ; and there is reason to fear that we may miss it because of unbelief, as they did.

(1) The promised rest of God (vs. 1-10). This rest is proclaimed in the Gospel. It is entered by faith, and it has been prepared from the foundation of the world (vs. 1-3). The writer describes it by a further exposition of Psa. 95. It is a rest from one's "own works", from all that man does of himself (vs. 4-5, 10). It is a rest for "to-day", the present age of grace, a day long after the entrance into Canaan under Joshua (vs. 6-8). It is "a sabbath rest", a fellowship with God in His rest (vs. 9-19).

This means that state of divine bliss and satisfaction which followed the creating of the world, when the Creator proceeded to repose in the perfect enjoyment of His own handiwork. It was God's purpose that man should share this rest of His, entering into fellowship with Him in the full enjoyment of the creation, of which man himself is the crown. The writer of Hebrews declares that this blissful privilege is now offered to men through Christ; it is part of the Christian system.

(2) An appeal to enter into this rest (vs. 11-16). Let us therefore give diligence to enter into that rest; let us seek to make sure of it, lest we fail like the Israelites (v. 11). For this purpose we have the living and active Word of God, which goes to the secrets of each man's heart, and lays everything open in His sight (vs. 12-13). We have also a great High Priest in Heaven, who has Himself entered into the rest of God, who knows our infirmities and can sympathize with us, so that we ourselves can draw near to God for the mercy and grace that we need (vs. 14-16). These verses form a transition to the main theme of the Epistle, which deals with the High-priesthood of Christ.

JESUS BETTER THAN AARON
(Chs. 5-7)

This section deals with the general conception of Christ's High-priesthood. As our great High Priest, He is shown to be superior to the high priest of the order of Aaron.

1. The Aaronic Priesthood of Jesus (5:1-10). The qualifications of the old high priest are first laid down (vs. 1-4). These were threefold: (a) His office was to act for men before God and offer sacrifices for sins. (b) He was chosen from among men, so as to sympathize with them and be their true representative. (c) He was called and appointed by God to his office, so that he had authority to act for men in things that relate to God.

Then it is shown that these qualifications were perfectly fulfilled in Christ. They are described in His case in the reverse order (vs. 5-10). He was appointed by God to His office, as the Word of God bears witness (Psa. 2:7; 110:4). He suffered in the days of His flesh and can sympathize with men, having learned through actual experience the deepest needs of human weakness. The reference in v. 7 is primarily to Gethsemane, where His perfect obedience to the will of God was consummated, and in v. 8 to the discipline of having His manhood perfected by obeying the will of God. Then by His perfect sacrifice for the sins of men, He became "the author of eternal salvation", and was named a High Priest after the order of Melchizedek.

2. The Need of Making Progress (5:11—6:8) The mention of Melchizedek calls up the difficulty of unfolding the truth of Christ's High-priestly office to the Hebrews, whose spiritual intelligence is so backward that, though by this time they ought to be teachers, they need to be taught the rudiments of Christianity (5:11-14). The Apostle will not speak of the elementary teaching about Christ and have them begin the Christian life over again, but will go on with his original design, for there is need that they press on toward maturity (6:1-3).

Meanwhile he gives them a warning about the peril of relapse (6:4-8). It is impossible to renew again unto repentance those who were once for all enlightened with the Christian revelation and had a real spiritual experience and then go back to Judaism, seeing they have crucified the Son of God again to their own ruin. Having rejected Him, there is no other Gospel for them. Nature itself teaches that divine gifts and opportunities must be used in order to be retained and enjoyed.

3. Reasons for Encouragement (6:9-20). Addressing his readers with a term of affection, "beloved", used only here in the Epistle, the Apostle tells them that he is persuaded they are not in the condition he has described, but are in the way of salvation. The Christian love which they show in ministering to the saints is an evidence of this, and God will not forget it (vs. 9-10). Let each of them persist to the end in the same zeal and full assurance, and show themselves to be true imitators of those who by faith and patient waiting attained the fulfilment of the promises (vs. 11-12).

Then he goes on to speak of the promise that God made to Abraham, which the patriarch obtained after patient endurance, and to show that God confirmed it in the strongest possible way—by His oath (Gen. 22:15-18), as well as by His word (vs. 13-16). Thus we who inherit the promise have these two immutable things on which to rest our faith (vs. 17-18). The reference to the oath by which God confirmed the promise after the sacrifice of Isaac carries the thought to the oath by which the priesthood of Jesus was confirmed (Psa. 110:4). He received this priesthood when He entered as our representative and forerunner into the heavenly world within the veil. Our hope can now reach into the very presence of God where Jesus is, who has become "a high priest for ever after the order of Melchizedek" (vs. 19-20).

4. The Greatness of Melchizedek (7:1-10). At this point the writer enters upon the main argument of the Epistle, the explanation of the priesthood of Jesus in the Christian system. He first points out the significance of Melchizedek as a type of Christ (vs. 1-3). When Melchizedek comes into the story of Abraham in Gen. 14:18-20, he is called a king as well as a priest. He was "king of righteousness" by the meaning of his name, and "king of peace" by the meaning of Salem. He is introduced into the record without any mention of his birth or

his death: "having neither beginning of days nor end of life". Thus he foreshadows the Son of God in His eternal beginning and endless life.

Then the writer goes on to show "how great this man was" (vs. 4-10). He was greater than Abraham, for he blessed the patriarch and received tithes from him. He was therefore greater than Levi, the head of the Aaronic order of priests, for Levi was but a descendant of Abraham and was not yet born.

5. The Melchizedek Priesthood of Jesus (7:11-28). The main significance of the analogy between Jesus and Melchizedek consists in Jesus becoming a High Priest "forever". The superiority of the Melchizedek priesthood over the Levitical is drawn out in this passage as follows: It is a new priesthood of another order, introduced because the Levitical priesthood could not make salvation perfect. This is seen in the fact that our Lord came from another tribe (vs. 11-14). It is based on an eternal principle, the power of an indissoluble life, instead of the law of an external command. Thus it gives us a better hope, by which we can draw near unto God (vs. 15-19).

It is final and immutable, being confirmed with the oath of God and establishing a better covenant (vs. 20-22; Psa. 110:4). It is an unchangeable and perpetual priesthood, embodied in one Priest who lives for ever, and is thus able to secure salvation to the uttermost for them that draw near to God through Him (vs. 23-25). This Melchizedek priesthood is completely realized in Jesus Christ, because of His personal qualifications (v. 26), because of His priestly work (v. 27), and because of His Divine appointment (v. 28).

THE WORK OF THE GREAT HIGH PRIEST
(Chs. 8—10)

Having shown the superiority of the priesthood of Christ to that of Aaron, the writer now proceeds to compare the two ministries. He shows that our High Priest ministers in the true sanctuary, and that He is the Mediator of a better covenant.

1. The Minister of the True Tabernacle (8:1-5). His place of service is the unseen world of the eternal realities. This is the real sanctuary, while the old tabernacle of the Law, which Moses made at God's command, was only a copy and shadow of the true. In this heavenly world the work of our High Priest is kingly: He "sat down on the right hand of the throne of the Majesty in the heavens". He has entered into the full and permanent participation of the Divine glory and power. It is also priestly: He "has somewhat to offer". What He has to offer is not stated yet. It has been referred to in 7:27, and will be taken up again in 9:11-14. He offered up Himself, and on the ground of this offering He exercises His priestly work in Heaven. The tabernacle in which the priests of the Law served was only a copy and shadow of Heaven.

2. The Mediator of the New Covenant (8:6-13). In this heavenly tabernacle—the true tabernacle of the unseen world—Jesus is carrying on a more excellent ministry. He is the Mediator of a better covenant, which has been established on better promises (v. 6). A New Covenant was needed, for the first Covenant was not faultless. It had no power to achieve its object; it could not secure obedience on the part of the people (v. 7). And so the Lord promised a New Covenant which would be

different from the Old (vs. 8-12). This whole passage is quoted from Jer. 31:31-34. By this Covenant the Law would be written on the heart, and there would be personal knowledge of God for everyone and complete forgiveness of sins. The promise of a New Covenant implied that the first was old and would vanish away (v. 13).

3. The Typical Service of the Old Tabernacle (9:1-10). The first Covenant had divine services and a sanctuary of this world; but they were typical only, and did not avail for redemption (v. 1). The Mosaic tabernacle was a material one, with two parts, the Holy Place and the Most Holy Place, each with its special sacred vessels (vs. 2-5). The priests ministered in the Holy Place continually, but in the Most Holy Place only the high priest ministered; and he could enter only once a year, on the annual Day of Atonement, and only with the blood of the sacrifices (vs. 6-7).

The spiritual significance of this is then explained. It meant that the true sanctuary was not yet open. Immediate access to God was not yet possible, because the old rites and ceremonies could not purify the conscience. They could not "make the worshippers perfect". Redemption was not yet achieved (vs. 8-10).

4. The Eternal Redemption of the New Covenant (9:11-28). The Apostle now sums up Christ's high-priestly work in a general description (vs. 11-12). He has secured "eternal redemption" for us by two transcendent acts: His sacrifice on the Cross ("through his own blood"), and His entrance into Heaven ("once for all into the holy place"). Then he takes each of these acts separately and explains them.

(1) The efficacy of the Cross (vs. 13-22). Through it Christ made a final atonement for sin. This was the voluntary sacrifice of His own perfected human nature. The writer emphasizes the fact that it was "through his own blood": it was "the sacrifice of himself" (v. 26). It was also made "through the eternal Spirit". That is, Christ's own Spirit which found expression in the sacrifice is independent of time, and this gave it permanent validity. It has therefore power to cleanse from sin (vs. 13-14). It ratifies the New Covenant and secures the eternal inheritance for us (vs. 15-17), thus corresponding with Moses' ratification of the Old Covenant by the typical sacrifice of calves and goats (vs. 18-22; Exod. 24:8).

(2) The significance of the Ascension (vs. 23-28). The high priest's entrance into the innermost shrine of the earthly tabernacle was a type and shadow of Christ's entrance into Heaven (vs. 23-24). There He appears in the presence of God for us, on the ground of His own finished sacrifice, by which He put away sin once for all (vs. 25-26). Having finished His earthly work by offering Himself for the sins of many, He has nothing further to do with sin. But He will appear a second time to complete the salvation of them that wait for Him (vs. 27-28).

5. The Perpetual Efficacy of Christ's Sacrifice (10:1-18). The writer goes on with his argument to show that the sacrifice of Christ does what the old sacrifices could not do. It perfects those who come unto God through Him, by cleansing them from sin, and bringing them into communion with God. The old sacrifices were inadequate, because they were the shadow, not the substance (vs. 1-4). They required to be repeated, and thus maintained a consciousness of sins, instead of providing a remission and cleansing of sin. They meant a yearly remembrance of sins and not their removal.

Christ's sacrifice is adequate, because its source was in the will of God. Psa. 40:6-8 is quoted with a free rendering which explains the original text, to show that the essence of the Messiah's sacrifice consisted in His willingness to do the will of God (vs. 5-7). He came into the world with this deliberate purpose. This voluntary obedience gave His sacrifice a moral quality, which was not possessed by the Levitical sacrifices. Thus it could sanctify us in the will of God by removing all hindrance to our fellowship with God (vs. 8-10).

That the one sacrifice of Christ has eternal efficacy is shown by His present exaltation. The priests of the Old Covenant continually repeated the same sacrifices. Our High Priest, having offered one sacrifice for sins for ever, now occupies the place of power in Heaven, and is waiting until His enemies are put under His feet (vs. 11-14). The Holy Spirit also bears witness that under the New Covenant our sins are not remembered by God, and there is no longer any need of another sin offering (vs. 15-18). Here Jer. 31:33-34 is quoted again.

6. The Sacred Privileges of the New Covenant (10:19-39). The whole preceding argument of the Epistle is now summed up in the privilege of direct access to God. Through the work of our Great High Priest we have "boldness to enter into the holiest".

The Cross has made for us "a new and living way" into the presence-chamber of God (vs. 19-21). But this privilege has corresponding duties. We should draw near "in fulness of faith"; we should hold fast "the confession of our hope"; we should provoke one another "unto love and good works"; and we should maintain our Christian fellowship by "not forsaking our own assembling together" (vs. 22-25).

Probably the writer thought that some were already forsaking the Christian assemblies, and he felt that this was ominous of an approaching lapse from the faith. There was a special reason for maintaining their fellowship and exhorting one another—"so much the more, as ye see the day drawing nigh". They were apparently on the eve of the great catastrophe of A.D. 70, the destruction of Jerusalem, and to disregard their corporate fellowship was to incur great spiritual peril, especially the peril of apostasy.

Wilful sin under the Old Covenant was punished by death; no sacrifice was provided for it. If he who despised Moses' Law was deemed worthy of death, "of how much sorer punishment" shall he be thought worthy who rejects the sacrifice of Christ and despises the gracious Spirit of God (vs. 26-29). The writer quotes Deut. 32:35-36 to remind his readers that the punishment of this sin is in the hands of the living God, and He will not lightly pass over such conduct in His people (vs. 30-31).

But the past experience of the Hebrews, the way they endured suffering and persecution after they received the Gospel, gives encouragement for the present (vs. 32-34). Let them have confidence and patience. The memory of the past should encourage them to still further endurance for the future. By a quotation from Hab. 2:3-4 the author reminds them of the coming of the Lord; and he is sure they will not fall back to perdition, but will go on to salvation (vs. 35-39).

NOTE:—In order to understand the full significance of this part of the Epistle, we need to transport ourselves back across the ages to the point of view of the Old Covenant. The whole explanation of the work of Christ is given under the symbols of the Mosaic tabernacle and in terms of the high priest's work on the Day of Atonement. That old Levitical sanctuary was expressly made, says the writer, to be "a shadow of the heavenly things" (8:5). It was far more than Israel's meeting-place for worship. Made after the pattern shown to Moses, its very structure was planned to represent the unseen world in which God dwells. In its courts only the priests could minister; the congregation of Israel stood outside. It was a type and prophecy of the world of eternal realities, which the Old Testament worshipper could see only afar off but could not enter. For him there was no access into the presence of God.

To appreciate the full force of the writer's argument, we should stand in imagination with the congregation of Israel at the gate of the tabernacle where the ceremonies of the Day of Atonement are taking place, and watch the high priest making propitiation for the sins of the people (Lev. 16). We look across the outer court past the altar of sacrifice, where the victim has been offered, toward the curtains of the tent of meeting. Behind those curtains is the Holy Place, and behind that again is the Most Holy Place, the heart of the whole Levitical system, containing the sacred Ark of the Covenant.

To the devout Israelite, that dark and mysterious chamber, so far beyond his reach, into which no man could go save the high priest, and he only on this one occasion in all the year, was the dwelling place of God. The high priest, with the blood of the victim, disappears behind the curtains of the tent. Passing through the first inner court, he enters into the Holiest of all. There, before the sacred symbol of the Divine presence, he presents the blood that bears witness to the sacrifice offered without, and makes atonement for the sins of the people.

That ceremony was the consummation of the Old Testament system of sacrifice, but it had to be repeated year by year. High priests came and passed away, but none of them could abide in that sanctuary, or open it for anyone else to enter in. That old Levitical system could never make the worshipper "perfect"; it could not bring him into the presence of God. It was but "a shadow of the good things to come" (10:1).

And so we turn to a later day, when our High Priest, having offered Himself as the one perfect and sufficient sacrifice, passed by way of the Ascension into the immediate presence of God. There we behold Him now, in the greater and more perfect tabernacle not made with hands, enthroned at God's right hand. From that place of power and dignity, which He has reached by His own merit, he administers for men an atonement that is final and complete, being "able to save to the uttermost them

that draw near unto God through him, seeing he ever liveth to make intercession for them" (7:25).

That is the transcendent truth to which the massive argument of the Epistle has conducted us. In the unseen realm behind the vast visible universe, in the secret place of its life and power, where God is, there is a Man who has been tempted in all points like as we are and can be touched with the feeling of our infirmities (4:15). It is the glory of Christianity that it presents to the world "so great salvation" (2:3). It draws the veil aside from the unseen and reveals at the centre of ultimate reality, not only the Father-heart of God, but also the Brother-heart of Jesus; not only an infinite and eternal love, but also a comprehending and redeeming sympathy.

THE NEW LIFE UNDER THE NEW COVENANT
(Chs. 11—13)

These chapters form the practical part of the Epistle. The writer takes up the three ideas of faith, hope, and love in the special duties mentioned in 10:22-24, and enlarges upon each separately.

1. The Exercise of Faith (Ch. 11). Faith is first explained as the sense that realizes the unseen. It knows that there is substance in what we hope for and reality in transactions that belong to the unseen spiritual world (v. 1). It was because of their faith that the ancient fathers of Israel were accepted of God (v. 2). Faith sees in the visible world the evidence of an invisible world. By faith we understand that God did not make the world out of things that are seen, but out of things that are not seen (v. 3).

Then faith is illustrated in the ancient world (vs. 4-7). It was by faith that Abel offered "a more excellent sacrifice" than Cain. The idea is that there was something more in his offering, something based on faith (Gen. 4:4). It was because of his walk of faith that Enoch pleased God and was translated (Gen. 5:24). It was because of his faith that Noah, when warned of God about the future, carried out the work that God commanded him to do (Gen. 6:22).

Faith is next traced among the patriarchs. In the case of Abraham, we see the obedience of faith and the pilgrim spirit, which looks for a heavenly country and the eternal city of God (vs. 8-10). In the case of Sarah, we see faith trusting in the power and faithfulness of God (vs. 11-12). The patriarchs all died in faith, confessing that they were strangers and pilgrims on the earth, and that they desired a heavenly country (vs. 13-16). To illustrate this fact further instances are given of the faith of Abraham, Isaac, Jacob, and Joseph (vs. 17-22).

This is followed by showing how faith was at work in the life of Moses (vs. 23-28). It is significant that more prominence is given to the founder of the old dispensation than to any other in this list of men and women of faith. In the events of the exodus from Egypt and the conquest of Canaan, faith was still manifested (vs. 29-31).

Finally, the writer sums up the history of Israel in the Land, and gives illustrations of faith both in its power of heroic achievement in action (vs. 32-34), and in its power of patient endurance in suffering (vs. 35-38). The chapter closes with a statement about all these worthies, whose faith was acknowledged by God though they did not obtain what was promised. They had to wait until they could share with the believers of the new dispensation the spiritual blessings provided by God through Jesus Christ (vs. 39-40).

2. The Exercise of Hope (Ch. 12). The apostolic writer now makes the general application of the lessons of the past to the present season of trial through which the Hebrews were passing. These examples of faith in the past present a motive for endurance in our Christian life and experience (vs. 1-3). The writer imagines himself and his readers as contending in the arena for the prize of the race, and as surrounded with a great multitude in the seats of the amphitheatre. These are the men and women of faith who have lived and gone before. They are not regarded as spectators of our lives on earth, but as "witnesses" to the power of faith. By "the sin which doth so easily beset us" is probably meant unbelief. Our supreme motive for endurance consists in the contemplation of Christ Himself— "the author and perfecter' 'of our salvation—in His triumphant entrance into Heaven after the suffering of the Cross.

The writer goes on to explain the value of the discipline of suffering. It is God's method of fatherly chastening, and it is the portion of all true children of God (vs. 4-8). Its purpose is that we may be partakers of His holiness, and after it has been endured it issues in peace and righteousness (vs. 9-11). Then the Apostle states the practical conclusion for the Hebrews in their trial. They should encourage those that are disheartened, and put every hindrance out of their way (vs. 12-13).

This leads to some general instructions for following peace with all men, and for maintaining the purity of the Christian community lest it be compromised by the apostate, the sinful, or the unspiritual (vs. 14-17).

Then there comes a splendid passage which presents a striking contrast between the two Covenants. The writer first describes the scene at Sinai, bringing out the terrifying manifestations which attended the making of the Old Covenant and the overwhelming awe which the sight caused. It was material and earthly in its character, and it barred approach to God (vs. 18-21). Then he describes the position of Christians under the New Covenant in a magnificent scene. Over against the material and earthly is set the spiritual and heavenly (vs. 22-24).

In the spiritual reality, Mount Zion represents the divine foundation of the new order, while the city of Jerusalem represents the heavenly fellowship based upon it. In this God dwells, surrounded by angels and redeemed men in a vast general assembly. Then the scene turns to the human side. The "church of the first-born who are enrolled in heaven" refers to Christians still living on earth while their names are known in Heaven. And now the two great ideas of the final judgment of God and the redemption wrought by the Mediator of the New Covenant are made prominent.

This passage is followed by a warning from the fate of the disobedient Israelites. It should remind Christians of their responsibility. Heaven and earth will soon be shaken by the judgment of God. The Kingdom to which we belong will abide. Let us have grace therefore to serve God with reverence and awe (vs. 25-29).

3. The Exercise of Love (Ch. 13). The Apostle proceeds to give his readers some particular instructions regarding their social and religious duties. They are to practice love of the brethren, hospitality to strangers, care for the persecuted, purity, contentment, and freedom from avarice (vs. 1-6). They are to remember their former leaders in the faith, and imitate them. The reference seems to be to teachers of the Word among the Christian Jews who had passed away, who had perhaps died by martyrdom —Stephen, James the Apostle, and James the Lord's brother. Jesus Christ does not pass away; He always remains (vs. 7-8).

Let them not be carried away by strange doctrines, but guard against this by being established in grace (v. 9). Our altar is the Cross of Christ, represented in the Lord's Supper, of which those who follow the old tabernacle worship have no right to partake; and this is the means of our sanctification (vs. 10-12). Therefore let us be separated unto Him. We must go without the camp and share His reproach, becoming homeless on earth as He was. The reference is to the fact that Christian Jews had to break with Judaism and bear the ignominy of the Cross (vs. 13-14).

The true sacrifice of believers is the offering of praise and thanksgiving to God, and helpful service to their fellow men (vs. 15-16). Then the writer, having told his readers to remember those that "had the rule" over them in the past (v. 7), adds a word instructing them to obey those that "have the rule" over them now (v. 17).

The Epistle closes with the Apostle's personal messages. He asks for the prayers of his readers, and then he pours out his heart for them in a prayer which sums up the message of his letter (vs. 18-21). To this he adds a final exhortation and a personal word about Timothy. Then he ends with the salutations and a brief benediction (vs. 22-25).

NOTE:—This book occupies a unique place in the New Testament. In the preceding Epistles the main emphasis has been on the presence of Christ in the heart of the believer. They interpret the meaning of Pentecost. They unfold the profound significance of the event that took place on earth when the Spirit of Christ came down to dwell in the midst of the Church. The Epistle to the Hebrews, on the other hand, interprets the meaning of the Ascension. It draws aside the veil, and discloses the equally profound significance of the event that took place in Heaven when the Man Christ Jesus entered in to sit at the right hand of God.

As Pentecost made a change on earth, so the Ascension made a change in Heaven. A new world, the unseen world of abiding reality with the Saviour of men at the heart of it, is now open for us to contemplate. We may draw near to it "in fulness of faith". Faith in this Epistle has a richer meaning than in the other Epistles. It is more than trust in God for salvation. It is that attitude of soul which stands face to face with the unseen and gives substance to the things that are there, which counts upon them as more sure and real than if they were apprehended by the senses.

The writer of Hebrews points out that this was the essential element in the faith of the Old Testament saints. They looked beyond the physical world. They knew that there were matters of far deeper importance than the possession of Canaan. They sought a better country, a heavenly one. And yet all these Old Testament believers died without receiving the promise. They could only see it from afar. Their faith looked down the ages toward the true promised land, which was not ready yet for the redeemed to enter. All they could do in the meantime was to "wait upon the Lord", to wait for Him to accomplish the work of redemption.

But now that our great High Priest has entered in, our faith may look through the veil into the new world where He is gone. The words of the prophet have been fulfilled for us (Isa. 33:17). Now we can "see the king in his beauty, and behold a land that reacheth afar". To the saints of the old dispensation that land lay in the future: for us it lies in the unseen. This is the spiritual world of the Bible; and there lie the springs of spiritual power.

The message which this book brings us about the reality of the unseen in the Christian system is needed by the Church in every age. Its value did not cease with the early Hebrew Christians to whom it was addressed. The indwelling presence of Christ in the heart of the believer is the very secret of Christian life; but the secret that is within the heart needs the anchor that is within the veil. The immanent Spirit does His work here because the transcendent Priest does His work there. The nerve centres of Christianity are not in the human mind or the human heart. A subjective approach can never discover them. They lie elsewhere, deep-seated in the unseen verities, where faith alone can find them. All the springs of the Christian Church are there.

THE EPISTLE OF JAMES

Two of the Twelve Apostles bore the name, James; but the author of the Epistle does not call himself an Apostle. He was the other James mentioned in the New Testament, a brother of the Lord, who became the head of the church in Jerusalem after the martyrdom of James the brother of John and the dispersion of the other Apostles. He was probably the oldest of the four brothers named in Matt. 13:55 and Mark 6:3. They did not believe the claims of Jesus during His ministry (John 7:5), but after the Resurrection they are found among His disciples (Acts 1:14). Their conversion was doubtless due to the appearance of the risen Lord to James (1 Cor. 15:7). That brought James to see the true nature of Him who was his brother according to the flesh, and he was then ready to worship and serve Him. In the Epistle he calls himself "a servant of God and of the Lord Jesus Christ" (1:1).

Among the Christians in Jerusalem James took a prominent part and was counted among the Apostles (Gal. 1:19). He presided at the council held there after Paul and Barnabas had carried the Gospel into the Gentile world (Acts 15:13). James did not break with Judaism, and he was held in high esteem by the Jews generally, being known among them as James the Just. During the times of trouble that preceded the outbreak of the war with Rome, he was stoned to death in the Temple court for proclaiming his belief that Jesus was the Messiah.

His Epistle is a circular letter addressed to the Jewish Christians outside Palestine—"the twelve tribes which are of the Dispersion". Jews were found in all parts of the Roman Empire, but especially in the East (Acts 2:5, 9-11). Christian groups had already appeared among them when this letter was written, which was probably in the fifth decade of the century. It was fitting that the recognized head of the Jewish church in Jerusalem should send a message to the Christian Jews in other parts of the world.

The letter was written to strengthen the believing Jews in the midst of suffering and persecution, and to give them instruction in the Christian life. There is no development of doctrine. The purpose of the writer is practical throughout, and he takes up one topic after another without any unifying plan.

1. Trial and Temptation (1:1-18). After the introductory greeting (v. 1), James tells his readers that trials from without are to be received with joy, because they are a test of faith. They work out patience, and result in a fully rounded Christian character (vs. 2-4). If any of them lack wisdom, let them ask of God, for it is a divine gift and is given to those who trust God and are steadfastly devoted to Him (vs. 5-8). What James means by wisdom is not essentially different from the gift of the Holy Spirit (Luke 11:13). This wisdom may be given to rich and poor alike. It will lead them both to look at this present life and its varying conditions in the light of the world to come (vs. 9-11). The result of endurance in trial is the reward of the crown of life (v. 12).

Temptation from within does not come from God, but from some uncontrolled desire in one's own heart. No trial from without can become a temptation to sin apart from something in oneself (vs. 13-15). God cannot tempt us to evil, for His gifts are always good. He is "the Father of lights", like the sun among the stars; His glory is never obscured or cast into a shadow (vs. 16-17). The fact that He has redeemed us and made us His children shows that He does not tempt us (v. 18).

2. Hearing and Doing (1:19-27). James now exhorts his readers, on the ground of what he has stated, to be meek hearers of the Gospel of salvation, and to refrain from hasty speaking and unruly passion. "The implanted word" is the seed that has life in it and springs up into righteous and holy living (vs. 19-21). They are to be doers of the word also, for hearing without doing is only to deceive oneself with a mere passing impression (vs. 22-24).

It is only active obedience to the word that brings blessing. "The perfect law of liberty" is a fine description of the Gospel. In the Christian Gospel there is a law requiring a higher perfection than the Old Testament Law. But the Gospel sets us free to obey the Law by the power of the Spirit, and is therefore "a law of liberty" (v. 25). True religion —the external manifestation of true faith and real worship of God—consists in being courteous and kindly in speech, in doing acts of mercy, and in keeping oneself pure (vs. 26-27).

3. Respect of Persons (2:1-13). To give preference in a Christian assembly to a man of wealth or worldly position over a poor man, is inconsistent with faith in the Lord Jesus Christ. In view of His glorious position in the heavenly world, all distinc-

tions in this world disappear (vs. 1-4). It is the poor who are most often rich in faith, and it is the rich who oppress and persecute the Christians. James refers to the fact that the wealthy Jews bitterly opposed the Gospel and blasphemed the name of Christ (vs. 5-7).

We cannot fulfil "the royal law", the law of love, and have respect of persons. This law may have been so called by the writer because it has the highest place among all the commandments. But the expression he uses may mean the law "of the Kingdom", and may allude to the law of love being the one law of the Kingdom of Heaven (vs. 8-9). To violate this law is to be guilty of breaking the whole Moral Law (vs. 10-11). Our behaviour should be regulated by the free spirit of Christian love, which is "the law of liberty". This law condemns the man who has respect of persons and no compassion for the poor (vs. 12-13).

4. Faith and Works (2:14-26). Faith that has no practical influence on conduct is not the faith that saves (vs. 14). James proves that faith is dead without works by showing how useless benevolence is that does not go beyond words (vs. 15-17), and how empty an intellectual belief is that is shared by demons (vs. 18-20).

Then he proves from Scripture that saving faith is manifested in works by showing how faith wrought in the cases of Abraham (vs. 21-24), and Rahab (v. 25). He concludes his argument with the statement that faith without works is like a dead body without an animating spirit (v. 26). He does not mean that works answer to the inner spirit, but rather to the activity of the living body. Their absence is a proof that there is no life in the body.

5. Control of the Tongue (3:1-12). James now goes back to the subject touched in 1:19. Sins of the tongue seem to have been so common among Jewish Christians that James refers to them several times in the course of the Epistle (1:26; 2:12). He begins here by warning them against eagerness to teach: "Be not many teachers, my brethren" (v. 1). Large freedom of speech existed in the early Church; private members were at liberty to speak and teach in the meetings of the Christians. James goes on to point out that those who undertake to teach assume a great responsibility. Control of one's speech is the test of Christian perfection (v. 2). He means the ability to say the right thing in the right way at the right time.

Then he gives illustrations of the power of the tongue as a little thing (vs. 3-5), and goes on to describe the evil influence of the tongue when uncontrolled. "It setteth on fire the wheel of nature": it sets a destructive power to work through the whole course of human life. "It is set on fire of hell": the destructive power exerted by the tongue is inspired by Satanic passion. "The tongue can no man tame": it can be controlled by the Holy Spirit alone (vs. 6-8). There is inconsistency and duplicity in the tongue, for it utters both blessing and cursing (vs. 9-10). James goes on to point out that the real cause of these things is an unregenerate nature. Christian faith and an uncontrolled tongue are incompatible (vs. 11-12).

6. True and False Wisdom (3:13-18). True wisdom will show itself in a good life and a meek spirit (v. 13). It is a false wisdom, a wisdom of the earth and of the flesh, that leads to jealousy of the brethren and creates factions among them (vs. 14-16). The true wisdom of God, "the wisdom that is from above", is first of all pure, because its object is not the gratification of self-will; and so it is peaceable and gently reasonable. The man that is governed by this wisdom will show it in works of mercy without any partiality or hypocrisy. Those that possess this wisdom will cultivate peace and then righteousness will come to prevail (vs. 17-18).

7. The Spirit of Worldliness (4:1-10). In contrast with the peace that true wisdom brings (3:18), war and strife arise from a self-seeking spirit (vs. 1-2). Here we have a terse and impressive description of the life of self and its evil results. The first part of v. 2 may be read thus: "Ye lust and have not, so ye kill; ye covet and cannot obtain, so ye fight and war". Even in their prayers they asked amiss, because their heart was set on self. In so doing they showed the spirit of worldliness. Did they not know that friendship with the world is enmity with God (vs. 3-4)? The Spirit which God made to dwell in us jealously yearns for the entire devotion He requires (vs. 5-6).

Then James makes a plea for humble submission to God. The order of the injunctions should be noted. "Submit yourselves to God"—then "resist the devil". The devil will only flee from one who has submitted to God. "Draw near to God"—then "cleanse your hands and purify your hearts". God will only draw nigh to one who sincerely desires clean hands and a pure heart (vs. 7-8). In this approach to God they were to express their repentance both inwardly and by appropriate outward signs, and they would find that those who humble themselves in the sight of God will be exalted (vs. 9-10).

8. The Spirit of Humility (4:11-17). James now follows up his appeal for humility with a warning against three things that are opposed to it. The first is the habit of fault-finding and judging one's brethren. To set themselves up as judges is to offend against the majesty of the divine law, and to take the place of the one Lawgiver (vs. 11-12). The next is the habit of making one's plans without God. It shows a spirit of proud indifference to God's will (vs. 13-15). This leads to presumption and the habit of boasting, which is the third thing James warns them against. Then he adds that it is not enough for them to know what is right to do. To know it and fail to do it is sin (vs. 16-17).

9. Patience in Suffering (5:1-11). The suffering of the Jewish believers in the early Church was due largely to their oppression by the wealthy Jews, who hated the Gospel. James now pronounces the doom of these rich men, and foretells their coming miseries—a prophecy which was fulfilled for the Jews of that day when their wealth was destroyed in the fall of Jerusalem in A.D. 70 (vs. 1-3). The cries of the labourers whom they have oppressed and defrauded of their hire have gone up to Heaven, while they have lived in luxury and self-indulgence on earth, fattening themselves like sheep for a day of slaughter (vs. 4-5). They persecute the followers of Jesus, who, like their Master, do not resist (v. 6).

Then James turns to his readers, the oppressed Christians among the Jews, and encourages them to be patient and steadfast in view of the coming of the Lord. Let them guard against murmuring and discontent among themselves; for they, too, are to be judged, and the Judge is at hand (vs. 7-9). As examples of patient endurance in suffering, he reminds them of the prophets, and of the experience of Job and the issue in his case (vs. 10-11).

10. Precepts for Christian Fellowship (5:12-20). This section is a kind of postscript to the letter. It contains some final instructions and precepts suggested by special circumstances among the Jewish Christians. Above all things they should not use oaths in common speech, for their intercourse with one another should have a sanctified character. Then he tells them how to sanctify every experience, whether of sorrow or of joy (vs. 12-13).

This is followed by instructions for cases of sickness. What James has in mind is the healing of sickness that has come as discipline and chastening for sin. In such cases the Church has the right to seek and pray for Divine healing (vs. 14-15). Christians should share with one another in the confession of sin and in prayer for healing. James recommends this for the strength it would give to their mutual fellowship, and adds: "This supplication of a righteous man availeth much in its working". The literal meaning is "inwrought", being inspired and energized by the Holy Spirit. And he illustrates it by citing the case of Elijah (vs. 16-18).

Prayer may result in the conversion of one who has wandered from the truth and fallen into sin, and thus one saves a soul from spiritual death (vs. 19-20). With this message of blessing, the Epistle ends abruptly, on the same strong, earnest note that marks it throughout.

THE FIRST EPISTLE OF PETER

THIS Epistle claims to have been written by the chief of the Twelve Apostles of the Lord. It bears the stamp of his mind, and contains many traces of his experience. The last appearance of Peter in the New Testament was at the council in Jerusalem in A.D. 50 (Acts 15:7). The only light we have on his intervening movements is given in a reference of Paul's to the fact that Peter used to go on missionary journeys and take his wife along with him (1 Cor. 9:5). The only indication of the place from which he wrote this letter is contained in the phrase, "she that is in Babylon", in the salutation of 5:13, which probably means a church and not Peter's wife. Babylon might be the city on the Euphrates, but there is more reason to believe that Peter meant the capital of the Empire. Babylon was coming to be used by the Christians as a cryptic name for Rome. It is so used in the Book of Revelation.

The letter is addressed "to the elect who are sojourners of the Dispersion" throughout the northern provinces of Asia Minor (1:1). This would naturally mean the Jewish Christians in those regions. The term "Dispersion" was used to describe the Jews who had been scattered among the nations since the time of the Captivity (Jas. 1:1). Gentile churches had been established in this district by Paul. Jews from some of the provinces Peter names heard his sermon in Jerusalem on the Day of Pentecost (Acts 2:9), and may have carried the Gospel

back and established churches of Jewish believers in their own home-towns. This would account for the Apostle of the circumcision writing to churches in a district evangelized by Paul. While Peter wrote more particularly for Jewish Christians, several passages in the letter show that he had Gentile readers also in mind (1:14; 2:9-10; 4:3).

The occasion of the letter was some special outbreak of persecution whereby the Christians of Asia Minor were being severely tried. The churches in the provinces were beginning to feel the effect of the Neronian persecution which began in Rome in the fall of A.D. 64. The date of the letter would be soon after that. The messenger who carried the letter was Silvanus (5:12), who may have been Paul's companion, better known as Silas.

Peter regards his readers as "sojourners" in the world (1:1, 17; 2:11). In the light of this the Epistle may be taken as a message to Christians as pilgrims. It falls into three parts, the second and third divisions each beginning with a tender appeal. The first division (Chs. 1:1—2:10) deals with the blessings and privileges of Christian pilgrims; the second (Chs. 2:11—4:11) with their duties and responsibilities; and the third (Chs. 4:12—5:14) with their trials and sufferings.

THE BLESSINGS OF CHRISTIAN PILGRIMS
(1:1—2:10)

In his greeting (1:1-2) Peter uses the new name which the Lord had given him. It has replaced in his own mind, as in that of others, the old name by which he had once been known (John 1:42; Matt. 16:18). He describes his readers as "the elect who are sojourners", terms which are applicable to all Christians. They are elect, as chosen of God (Eph. 1:4), and sojourners, as pilgrims who have their citizenship in Heaven (Phil. 3:20). Then he begins the body of his letter with a doxology to God, who, as the Father of the Lord Jesus Christ, is the source of all our blessings.

1. The Joy of Salvation (1:3-12). This passage is really one continued sentence, like that of Eph. 1:3-14. Its key-note is in the words, "ye rejoice", twice repeated. In the course of it, Peter refers to a number of topics connected with salvation. The beginning of the Christian life consists in being born by the resurrection of Christ into a living hope, the hope of an inheritance reserved in Heaven which is eternal and cannot decay (vs. 3-4). For the realization of this inheritance, when it is revealed, we are being preserved by the power of God through our faith (v. 5). The assurance of this salvation is a source of joy in the midst of trial, and an incentive to perseverance under persecution (vs. 6-7). It is a joy inspired by love for the unseen Christ and the hope of His glorious appearing, when our salvation will be consummated (vs. 8-9).

This salvation was made known to the prophets, but its time and circumstances were hidden from them. Their predictions of the sufferings of the Messiah, and the blessings of salvation that should result from them, were not to be fulfilled in their own generation. They were ministering for those who belong to the present dispensation of the Holy Spirit, in which the Gospel of Christ is being preached (vs. 10-12).

This passage shows how the Apostles of the Lord

linked their preaching of the Gospel with the preaching of the Old Testament prophets. They identified the Spirit of Christ, by whom they were anointed, with the Spirit of Jehovah, who inspired the prophets. They proclaimed the events connected with the life, death, and resurrection of Jesus, and the salvation enjoyed by those who believed on Him, as the fulfilment of the predictions of the prophets regarding the sufferings and glories of the Messiah.

2. The Fruit of Salvation (1:13—2:10). The Apostle now makes the practical application of the message of salvation. The passage begins with "wherefore". Salvation should be manifested in life.

(1) Holy living (1:13-21). Peter exhorts his readers to be steadfast and consistent in their hope. They should keep their minds firmly set upon the coming revelation of the Lord, and show in the pure moral character of their lives that they are separated unto Him (vs. 13-16). Here Peter quotes Lev. 11:44-45 to support his appeal. As children of God, the righteous and impartial Judge, they should pass the time of their pilgrimage in the world with godly fear, remembering that they have been redeemed with the precious blood of Jesus Christ (vs. 17-19). He was fore-ordained for this purpose before the creation of the world, but was manifested in this last age. His resurrection and glorification are the ground of their faith and hope (vs. 20-21).

(2) Brotherly love (1:22-25). This is the natural expression of a holy life, and it comes from a pure heart (v. 22). It is the quality of that new life which all share together who have received the living Word of God, the word contained in the Gospel (vs. 23-25). Here Peter quotes Isa. 40:6-8. There the word of the Lord is the prophetic announcement of God's purpose for Israel's redemption and restoration; and here Peter applies it to the redemption wrought out through Jesus Christ.

(3) Spiritual growth (2:1-10). In speaking of his readers as "newborn babes", Peter carries on the thought of the regeneration of believers expressed in 1:3 and 23. As such they are to desire the pure Word of God for their spiritual growth (vs. 1-3). Then the figure changes to that of a temple. By coming to Christ, to a living stone, rejected of men but chosen of God, they are being built up as living stones into a spiritual house for the offering of spiritual sacrifices to God through Jesus Christ (vs. 4-5).

Then Peter quotes again from the Old Testament (Isa. 28:16; 8:14; Psa. 118:22), as he goes on to point out the blessedness of believing in Christ, and the consequence of disbelief (vs. 6-8). He explains that Christian believers inherit the privileges of Israel as a nation of kings and priests, separated to God. They are to show forth His praise, for He called them out of darkness into light, and made them His own people (vs. 9-10).

THE DUTIES OF CHRISTIAN PILGRIMS
(2:11—4:11)

With a word of affection for his readers, Peter begins a new section of his letter. He now gives more particular instruction about their duties "as sojourners and pilgrims".

1. In the Common Relations of Life (2:11—3:12). The outward expression of their life in the eyes of unbelievers should be blameless and seemly.

Their good works should lead others to praise God (2:11-12). They should submit to the laws of the state, and show due honour to every one in an official position. They should show proper respect for all men, and love their fellow-Christians (2:13-17).

Household servants should serve their employers faithfully, even when ill-treated. Patient endurance of wrong is acceptable to God (2:18-20). We are called to follow the example of Christ in this respect. He suffered unjustly; but He met the reviling of His foes with silent patience, and committed His cause to God (2:21-23). He has a right to require this from us, because He suffered on account of our sins and brought us back to God (2:24-25).

In their household relations, wives should obey their husbands, even if the husbands are not Christians, for such behaviour may lead to their conversion. They should have the outward adornment of a meek and quiet spirit, like the holy women of old (3:1-6). On the other hand, husbands should consider the weakness and dependence of their wives, and give them due honour as fellow-Christians; otherwise their fellowship with God would be hindered (3:7).

Finally, Peter sums up the foregoing instructions regarding Christian duty by urging his readers to show the spirit of unity, sympathy, and humility in all their relations in life (3:8-9). Then he quotes Psa. 34:12-16 as a description of the true life to be exemplified by the Christian (3:10-12).

2. In Suffering and Persecution (3:13—4:11). Those who live upright lives are usually not harmed. But persecution may arise, and it is blessed to suffer for righteousness' sake (3:13-14; Matt. 5: 10-12). Therefore be not afraid, but reverence in your hearts Christ as Lord, and be prepared to give a courteous but confident answer to anyone who asks about the ground of your faith, supporting your testimony by your good manner of life. If it should be God's will that you suffer, it is better to be persecuted for uprightness than to provoke ill-treatment by bad behaviour (3:15-17).

Then the Apostle turns to Christ as an example of the suffering of the righteous and its blessed results. The passage is full of difficulty caused by Peter's compressed and allusive style (3:18-22). Its meaning will unfold as we consider the significance of some of its phrases:

"Being put to death in the flesh, but made alive in the spirit":—There is the same antithesis here between the flesh and the spirit as in Rom. 1:3-4, where the reference is to the Resurrection. Being "made alive in the spirit" is the same as being "declared to be the Son of God with power according to the spirit of holiness by the resurrection from the dead. In the Person of Jesus Christ, "the spirit of holiness" cannot be distinguished from the Holy Spirit.

"In which (spirit) also he went and preached unto the spirits in prison":—This preaching must have occurred after the Resurrection, for only then was He made alive in the spirit. It was the proclamation of the Gospel by the Lord through His Spirit in the Apostles to those who were in the prison-house of sin (Isa. 42:5-7; 49:8-9; 61:1). Of this sinful race the people of Noah's day were examples. The result of Noah's preaching while the ark was being prepared was only eight souls saved

(v. 20), but the result of the Lord's preaching after the spiritual quickening of the Resurrection was three thousand souls saved in one day (Acts 2:41).

The reference to Noah suggests to Peter an analogy between the Flood and Christian Baptism. As the Flood meant the washing away of the corruption of the old world and a new beginning of life for it, so baptism symbolizes the washing away of the defilement of the flesh and the receiving of the new life of the Spirit from the risen Christ, now enthroned in Heaven.

With this example of Christ before them and the blessed results of His suffering in the flesh, Peter goes on to urge his readers to arm themselves with the mind of Christ, the mind that consents to suffer in the flesh in order to cease from sin and live to the will of God (4:1-2). Let their past suffice for living in the sinful ways of the Gentiles. Their former companions are surprised that the Christians do not join them in their wickedness, and so they revile them (4:3-4). But they will give account in the coming judgment of all mankind, and then the Christians will be vindicated. For those who have suffered death since the Gospel was preached to them are sharing the life of God in the spirit (4:5-6).

The Apostle now summarizes this whole section of the Epistle in the light of the approaching "end of all things". He makes an appeal for soberness and prayerfulness, for brotherly love and hospitality, and for the active ministry of the manifold grace of God which has been given to them in various ways, so that God may be glorified through Jesus Christ (4:7-11).

THE TRIALS OF CHRISTIAN PILGRIMS
(4:12—5:14)

The Apostle introduces another main division of his letter with the same tender appeal to his readers as in 2:11. He deals now more particularly with "the fiery trial" of persecution which has come upon them.

1. Suffering for Christ's Sake (4:12-19). He exhorts them to steadfastness and joy, because in being persecuted for bearing the name of Christ they are sharing His sufferings, and so they will share His glory (vs. 12-14). Let no one of them bring dishonour on Christ by suffering for committing a crime, but let him glory in suffering "as a Christian" (vs. 15-16). The word "Christian" is found in only two other places in the New Testament (Acts 11:26; 26:28). The present sufferings are a sign that the time of judgment is at hand, and is beginning with God's own people. If it begins with us as a test of our faithfulness, and the righteous are barely saved, what about the unbelieving and the ungodly (vs. 17-18)? God permits persecution in working out His will; therefore let those who suffer commit their spiritual interests to Him (v. 19).

2. Fidelity in Service (5:1-4). Now comes a tender and sympathetic appeal on Peter's part to his fellow-elders in the Church to be faithful in their oversight of the particular flock committed to their care. He gives a twofold description of the Church: "the flock of God", and "the charge allotted to you". The latter expression is literally, "the lots", and refers to the different congregations or separate churches allotted to the oversight of the different elders. Peter then tells of the reward that faithful shepherds will receive when the Chief Shepherd comes.

3. Humility and Watchfulness (5:5-11). The charge to the elders of the churches is followed by a charge to all the members, emphasizing first the grace of humility. Humility has a double reference, both toward their fellow-Christians and toward God (vs. 5-7). Next the need of watchfulness is emphasized, because of the opposition of the devil, the special adversary of believers. They are to resist him by being steadfast in their faith in Christ (vs. 8-9). Then Peter brings this part of his Epistle to an end with a prayer for his readers, contrasting their brief period of suffering with the eternal glory, and with a doxology repeated from 4:11 (vs. 10-11).

4. The Conclusion (5:12-14). Silvanus is mentioned as the messenger who was to carry the letter to its destination. Instead of "I have written", we would say, "I am writing". The terms in which he describes his letter recall the special commission the Lord gave him: "When once thou hast turned again, establish thy brethren" (Luke 22:31-32). The salutations are sent from the church where Peter was writing, and from Mark, his convert and friend, who was with him at the time. It is much more likely that Babylon means the capital of the world than the city of that name. We never hear of Peter having been in the East, while tradition connects him with the city of Rome. What Babylon meant to Israel, that Rome meant to the Christian Church.

THE SECOND EPISTLE OF PETER

THE genuineness of this Epistle has been questioned more than that of any other book in the New Testament. The external evidence for it is very meagre. But to deny the Petrine authorship raises greater difficulties than to take the letter at its face value. It claims to come from Simon Peter, and to be the second letter written by him to its readers (1:1; 3:1); and the author declare that he was an eyewitness of the Transfiguration (1:16-18). If it was the work of a later writer, who used the name of the Apostle to get his message accepted by the Church, then its presence in the sacred Canon cannot be explained. The Church of those early days was not so devoid of spiritual discernment.

This Epistle was apparently intended for the same circle of readers as the First Epistle, although it nowhere expressly defines them. There is no indication as to where it was written; but the use of the Apostle's Hebrew name in the greeting, and the manifest influence of Jude in the body of the letter, would suggest a Palestine background. The Epistle has no definite plan, and the best way to take it is by chapters.

1. The Knowledge of Christ (Ch. 1). In the opening salutation, the Apostle greets his fellow-Christians with a prayer that the blessings they enjoy may be increased "in the knowledge of God and of Jesus our Lord" (vs. 1-2). The word "knowl-

edge", which occurs five times in the chapter, strikes the key-note. It is in the knowledge of Christ that provision has been made for our spiritual life. Through His promises, we are made partakers of the Divine nature and delivered from the corruption of the world (vs. 3-4). Then Peter instructs us how to grow in the knowledge of our Lord Jesus Christ and become fruitful by adding to our faith a list of graces, each of which grows out of the preceding one, all being rooted in faith (vs. 5-9).

But the growth is not spontaneous. Progress in the Christian life is made only by the co-operation of the human will with the Divine will. And so Peter goes on to urge his readers still further. "Wherefore, brethren, give the more diligence to make your calling and election sure". If these Christian graces are being developed and knowledge is increasing, we shall not stumble, and we shall be assured of a glorious entrance into the eternal Kingdom of our Lord and Saviour Jesus Christ (vs. 10-11).

Then the Apostle proceeds to state the grounds on which this knowledge of Christ rests. He thinks it right to remind his readers, while he is living, of what they already know, for he is conscious that his death as foretold by the Lord is not far off (vs. 12-14). In the meantime he will make an earnest effort to provide for their calling these things to remembrance after his departure (v. 15)—a promise which may have had its fulfilment in the Gospel according to Mark. Then Peter gives his personal testimony as an eyewitness of the glory of Christ on the mount of the Transfiguration. He seems to regard the event as an anticipation and foregleam of the glorious appearing of the Lord, for he calls it "the power and coming of our Lord Jesus Christ" (vs. 16-18).

The certainty of the coming of Christ is further confirmed by Old Testament prophecy, to which Peter urges his readers to take heed, for it gives us light in the gloom of the present world. The phrases, "until the day dawn, and the day-star arise", both refer to the objective event of the coming. The phrase, "in your hearts", was perhaps intended to go with, "ye do well that ye take heed"; otherwise the rise of the day-star becomes a purely subjective experience (v. 19).

"No prophecy of Scripture is of private interpretation":—No prophecy is to be interpreted by itself, but in the light of the whole body of prophecy, and under the guidance of the Holy Spirit. "For no prophecy ever came by the will of man":—Prophecy did not spring from the prophet's own promptings, but all the prophets spoke the mind of God as they were moved by the Holy Spirit (vs. 20-21).

2. The Teachers of Error (Ch. 2). Having shown how the words of the prophets have been confirmed, the Apostle goes on to say that false prophets also arose among the people in Old Testament times, and so false teachers will arise among the Christians now. The whole chapter is one unbroken paragraph, but there are certain stages which mark the course of the thought about these false teachers.

(1) Their rise and motive (vs. 1-3). The fundamental root of their destructive heresies consists in their "denying even the Master that bought them", setting at naught the redemption provided by God in Jesus Christ. They carry on their work "in covetousness"; that is, their real motive is self-interest, personal gain.

(2) Their coming doom (vs. 4-9). The certainty of the punishment of the false teachers, and the deliverance of the faithful, is shown from examples of God's judgments in Old Testament history:—His casting the wicked angels down to hell, His bringing the flood upon the old world and saving Noah, His destroying Sodom and Gomorrah and delivering righteous Lot.

(3) Their character and conduct (vs. 10-16). The secret of their character lies in the first words describing them: they "walk after the flesh". In them the evil of man's self-will and fleshly nature finds full development in all kinds of infamy.

(4) Their evil influence (vs. 17-22). They profess to be sources of spiritual life, but they are "springs without water". They make boastful promises of liberty, but lead astray into sin and bondage. Those who are enticed by them are in a worse state than if they had never known the way of righteousness.

3. The Coming of Christ (Ch. 3). Peter has been moved to write this—his second letter to his readers—to remind them of the teaching of the Prophets and the Apostles (vs. 1-2); and especially of their warnings that, as the present age draws to a close, false teachers should arise ridiculing the doctrine of the Lord's return.

(1) The objections to the doctrine (vs. 3-4). These false teachers oppose the doctrine on two grounds—the long delay since He promised to return ("Where is the promise of his coming?"), and the uniformity of natural law ("All things continue as they were"). The Apostle then proceeds to answer these objections, taking the second first.

(2) The answer to the objections (vs. 5-9). As to the uniformity of nature, it is not true that there has been no intervention in the course of nature. The ancient world was destroyed by a deluge of water, and the present world awaits a judgment of fire (vs. 5-7). As to the long delay, what seems long to us is not long to the Lord. With Him there is no such thing as the passing of time: the issues of a single day are permanent and endless, and the events of a thousand years are present and real at once. The delay is due to the Lord's long-suffering. His purpose is to give men a chance of repentance (vs. 8-9).

(3) The final day of judgment (vs. 10-13). The day of judgment to be ushered in by the Lord's return will come "as a thief", breaking in upon the world unannounced and unexpected. Here Peter gives a more explicit prediction of the judgment he announced in v. 7. This picture of the elements dissolving with fervent heat has been made vividly and terribly real, and its fulfilment has been brought ominously near, by the atomic bomb. Beyond the judgment lies the promise of a new world.

(4) The practical lessons (vs. 14-18). The Apostle's purpose is practical. He urges his readers, in view of the coming of the Lord, to seek earnestly to be blameless in His sight and preserve a quiet confidence; and he reminds them of what Paul wrote to them about the Lord's long-suffering as giving further opportunity of salvation (vs. 14-15).

Speaking of Paul's Epistles, Peter says that some

men, in their ignorance of the truth, wrest some passages in them from the meaning intended with disastrous results; and he warns his readers against being led away into the same wickedness (vs. 16-17). This is perhaps a reference to those who perverted Paul's teaching of justification by faith into antinomianism (Rom. 3:8). What Peter says here about the Epistles of Paul implies that their inspiration was recognized, and that they were being read in the churches as having the same Divine authority as the Old Testament Scriptures. The Apostle then sums up the whole practical purpose of his letter in a final appeal on the note with which he began: "Grow in the grace and knowledge of our Lord and Saviour Jesus Christ" (v. 18).

THE FIRST EPISTLE OF JOHN

THIS Epistle was evidently intended to be a companion to the Fourth Gospel. The Gospel was written that men might believe on Jesus Christ as the Son of God and have eternal life through Him (John 20:31). The Epistle was written unto those that do believe on the Son of God that they might know that they have eternal life (1 John 5:13). The name of the writer does not appear, but the Epistle leaves no doubt that he was the same person as the author of the Gospel, none other than the Apostle John. The two books are closely related in thought and feeling as well as in style.

The Epistle came from an eyewitness of the life of Christ (1:1-4; 4:14), and its tone of authority is such as only an Apostle would use. It was doubtless written soon after the Gospel, and was probably addressed first to the churches in Asia, among whom John spent the last years of his life. The closing warning (5:21) would have special significance in Ephesus and the neighbouring churches. There is no reference in the letter to the Old Testament, and its first readers seem to have been mainly Gentiles.

The theme of the Epistle is fellowship with God in the life eternal. There are two key-notes: "God is light" (1:5), and "God is love" (4:8, 16). These enable us to divide the book into two main parts. Fellowship with God means walking in light (Chs. 1—2), and walking in love (Chs. 3—5).

WALKING IN LIGHT
(Chs. 1—2)

1. The Introduction (1:1-4). There is a simple but solemn majesty in the opening sentences. The great fact is stated of which John and his fellow-disciples were witnesses, that eternal life was manifested in the flesh in the person of Jesus Christ (vs. 1-2). The wonder of that fact, and the profound impression that John received from his fellowship with Jesus, can be felt in the very tone in which he writes, even after more than half a century has passed. Then he states his purpose. It is that his readers also may share this fellowship, which is truly fellowship with God the Father and with His Son Jesus Christ (vs. 3-4).

2. What Walking in Light Involves (1:5—2:11). This fellowship means walking in light, for God is light (v. 5). This simple but profound statement defines the moral character of God. Light is pure and clean, and it cannot be contaminated or defiled. It dispels darkness, and it reveals everything it touches. Then John goes on to explain what it means to walk in the light and have fellowship with Him who is light.

(1) Being cleansed from sin (1:6-10). This passage explains how we are kept free from moral defilement in our walk in the world. Its meaning becomes clear as its various expressions are understood. Walking "in darkness" means living in sinful ways or habits. "The blood of Jesus his Son cleanseth us from all sin": the efficacy of His atoning work on the Cross keeps cleansing us, and the work of sanctification goes on. "If we say that we have no sin"—no sinful nature, the principle of sin that is rooted in the flesh. "If we confess our sins"—our acts or words of sin as we discover them, as they are revealed to us in His light. "He is faithful and righteous"—because of the atonement accomplished in the Cross. "If we say that we have not sinned"—that we are not sinners and have not fallen into sin.

(2) Abiding in Christ (2:1-6). This is the main idea behind this passage. The Apostle makes a tender appeal to his readers: Christians are not to sin. Then he explains the provision that God has made for us in case any one should sin. It lies in the work of the Advocate whom we have with the Father, the great High Priest of Heb. 7:25, who deals with the the sins of His people on the ground of the atonement that He has made for the sins of the whole world (vs. 1-2).

It is implied, of course, that the one who sins acknowledges his sin and commits his case to Christ, but nothing is said as to how Christ pleads with the Father. If this divine remedy for sins has been effective in our lives, it will be shown in obedience to Christ (vs. 3-4). It is thus that love for God is perfected in us, and that we keep abiding in Christ, walking as He walked (vs. 5-6).

(3) Loving the brethren (2:7-11). The "old commandment" to which John refers is the commandment of love, which was included in the first message of the Gospel as the rule of the Christian life. It is also a new commandment: it was new to the Apostles when given to them by the Lord (John 13:34); and it receives new meaning with every fresh experience of the power of the Gospel in Christian life (vs. 7-8). Loving one's brother is a

proof of being in the light. It puts no cause of offence in one's own way or in another's. Hating one's brother, on the other hand, involves complete ignorance of the way and the end of life (vs. 9-11).

3. What Walking in Light Excludes (2:12-29). The Apostle now deals with the perils that beset the Christian's walk in fellowship with God in light.

(1) The love of the world (vs. 12-17). He first explains that he is writing thus, not because of any doubt of his readers' Christian character or standing, but rather to caution them against temptations from which even they cannot be free, and also to encourage them to further achievement (vs. 12-14). In these verses there are six statements, arranged in two parallel series of three each. The first statement in each series is addressed to his readers generally. "Little children" is John's affectionate term for all the members of his flock. "I write unto you"—in the present letter. "I have written unto you"— probably a reference to the Gospel.

Then comes a solemn command in the form of a prohibition: "Love not the world". The love of the world is incompatible with the love of the Father (v. 15). By "the world" John means the whole system of human life on earth, the society of unbelieving men and women. He sums up "all that is in the world" under three false tendencies, which cover all the temptations that appeal to men to make the creature instead of God the end of life—"the lust of the flesh, the lust of the eyes, and the vain-glory of life" (v. 16). These three tendencies correspond with the three temptations of the Lord as recorded in Luke (4:1-11), and with the three points on which Eve yielded to the temptation in Eden (Gen. 3:6).

Then John adds a further reason for not loving the world. All that belongs to it—the whole external system of the present order of life—is fleeting and unsubstantial. But the Christian, "he that doeth the will of God", belongs to another system, another order of life, which has an eternal character and will abide for ever (v. 17).

(2) The spirit of antichrist (2:18-29). Now John goes on to speak of another peril, which he calls antichrist, and which was to arise within the Christian society. For there were those in the Church who did not belong to Christ, and were not really members of the Christian fellowship (vs. 18-19).

John is the only New Testament writer who uses the term "antichrist". It occurs again in 2:22; 4:3; and 2 John 7. The Old Testament knows nothing of an Anti-Messiah. (The prince who is announced in Dan. 9:26-27 is not the Antichrist, but the Messiah himself. See page 222 in Vol. II of this series). But the Lord had foretold the coming of false Christs (Matt. 24:5; Mark 13:6). John is not referring to these, however, but to the doctrine of a future Antichrist, which had arisen from a misunderstanding of these predictions, and which he now proceeds to correct.

So far from being a future event, the coming of antichrist has already taken place; and instead of there being only one Antichrist, there are many antichrists now in the world. These are not regarded by John as forerunners of a future Antichrist, for he says that their presence in the world proves that it is already "the last hour". They had appeared in the Church, but they had gone out from it, showing that they did not belong to the Christian fellowship (v. 19). His readers have the power of discerning the real character of antichrists, for they have the anointing of the Holy Spirit. Because of this they know the essential nature of the truth, and no false teaching can deceive them (vs. 20-21).

The Apostle goes on to explain the meaning of the term. "This is the antichrist, even he that denieth the Father and the Son". In other words, "antichrist" meant for John the denial of the Incarnation (vs. 22-23). Whoever denies that Jesus is the manifestation of God in the flesh, is antichrist. Antichrists existed in John's day, and will always exist as long as the Divine Saviour is proclaimed in the midst of a gainsaying world.

It is possible that antichrists may increase in malignancy and in hostility to Christ until at last all that can be called antichrist is summed up in one great anti-Christian movement or in one great anti-Christian person—but if such is to be the case John does not refer to it. Paul's teaching about the man of sin in 2 Thess. 2 is not the same as John's teaching about antichrist here. In both cases, however, the result is the same—the suppression of the message of the Gospel.

The Apostle tells his readers that belief in the Incarnation is involved in the Gospel which they heard at the first. It is the foundation of the Christian life, and the source of eternal life (vs. 24-25). In view of the peril of being led astray by the spirit of antichrist, John reminds them that their security rests upon the presence of the Holy Spirit in their hearts—"the anointing which ye received of him". Let them recognize the voice of the Spirit and abide in His teaching (vs. 26-27). Then the Apostle closes this part of his letter with another tender and practical appeal to his readers based upon it, which also contains ideas that he is about to develop in the next part (vs. 28-29).

WALKING IN LOVE
(Chs. 3—5)

1. As Children of God (3:1-12). The Father's great love has been shown in calling us His children, and He has made us such in reality by the Divine birth mentioned in the last words of the preceding chapter. For this reason men who live for this world do not understand us, because they did not understand God when He was revealed in Jesus Christ (v. 1). The fact that we share His nature in our present sonship, means that we shall share His likeness when He appears, for then we shall see Him in His glory. This great hope encourages us to strive after the purity of life that is His. John refers to the purity of the Lord's humanity, which was the result of His earthly discipline, and still abides in His glory (vs. 2-3). This is the only passage — beginning with 2:28 — where John speaks expressly of the Christian hope, which both Paul and Peter refer to so often.

The character of the children of God is seen in their separation from sin. Every one that commits sin violates the divine law of his being, and also sets at naught the mission of Christ (vs. 4-5). Sin is inconsistent with Christianity. He that is in fellowship with Christ does not practise sin; and he that practises sin has not known Him (v. 6). The character of the children of God is also seen in their righteousness. They practise righteousness because they have the righteous character of Christ Himself (v. 7).

It is in this relation of theirs to sin and righteousness that the children of God are distinguished from the children of the devil (vs. 8-10). Here John brings out the nature of the conflict between Christ and Satan: "To this end was the Son of God manifested, that he might destroy the works of the devil". The works of the devil are gathered up in sin which the devil has wrought in men. They are described elsewhere as "works of darkness" (Rom. 13:12; Eph. 5:11), and "works of the flesh" (Gal. 5:19).

The Christian's antagonism to sin is brought out in two statements: he "doeth no sin", in the sense of practising it; and "he cannot sin", because sin cannot become the habit of one who shares the Divine nature. Then John goes on to state that the infallible mark of righteousness is love for the brethren, and hatred shows that righteousness is absent, as it was in the case of Cain (vs. 11-12).

2. With Love for the Brotherhood (3:13-24). The mention of Cain leads to the thought of hatred as the characteristic mark of the world. Love among Christians is a sign that we have passed out of death into a new life, a life that is eternal (vs. 13-14). This love should be patterned on the love of God, which is revealed in the sacrifice that Christ made for us (vs. 15-16). It should go out in compassion toward them that are in need, and should be expressed not only in word but also in act (vs. 17-18).

Having spoken of the pattern of love, John goes on to speak of its fruit. It results in the assurance that our lives are surrendered to the truth of the Gospel (vs. 19-21). It finds expression in prayers that are answered, because they arise from obedience to God and faith in His Son (vs. 22-23). This obedience issues in abiding fellowship with God through the Holy Spirit (v. 24).

3. In the Fellowship of the Spirit (4:1-6). Having referred to the gift of the Holy Spirit, the Apostle begins a new step in his argument by explaining how the Spirit of God is to be known, and how false spirits are to be recognized. The test of spirits lies in their attitude to the Incarnation. The teacher who is inspired by the true Spirit confesses Jesus Christ to be God manifest in the flesh. The teacher who denies this is inspired by the spirit of antichrist (vs. 1-3). The test of men lies in their attitude to the truth. John's readers, being true Christians, have the Spirit of God, and are ready to hear the truth taught by Christian teachers. But they that are of the world listen only to those who express the thoughts of the world. They are possessed by the spirit of error (vs. 4-6).

4. In the Love of God (4:7-21). Love is the very nature of God, and love should characterize those who are the children of God and are born of Him. We should love one another, for love comes from knowing God (vs. 7-8). God's love toward us was manifested in the Incarnation and in the Cross—God sending His Son, that He might share His life with us (v. 9), and that he might bear the penalty of our sins (v. 10).

Our consequent duty and privilege is to love one another. Thus we show that God dwells in us, and that His love finds its fulfilment in us. It is by the gift of His Spirit that He dwells in us and we have fellowship with Him (vs. 11-13). The Apostle bears witness to the love of God in the gift of His Son, and declares that those who confess that Jesus is the Son of God dwell in God and have the love of God in themselves (vs. 14-16). In no other book of the Bible does the noun "love" occur so often as John uses it in these chapters dealing with walking in love.

As regards the future, we can await the day of judgment in confidence, because we share with Christ a mutual love and a common hostility to the world. This love delivers us from all fear of punishment. Fear implies some ground for alarm, and that cannot exist where love is perfect (vs. 17-18). By loving us, God made it possible for us to love Him. The result of this love for God in our hearts is a love for our brethren also. Hatred of our brother is incompatible with love for God; and besides this, we have God's command to love both Himself and our brother (vs. 19-21).

5. In the Power of Faith (5:1-12). John now shows that the ground for the love of the brethren which accompanies the love of God is a common faith in Jesus Christ. Love for God carries with it love for the children of God and obedience to the commandments of God (vs. 1-3). Those who believe that Jesus is the Son of God have the faith that overcomes the world. This faith introduces them into the spiritual and the eternal, and so lifts them above the earthly and the temporal (vs. 4:5).

The grounds of this faith are the historic facts of the Gospel: "This is he that came by water and blood, even Jesus Christ". By these phrases John means the Baptism and the Cross, the beginning and the ending of the earthly ministry of Jesus. The coming of the Spirit at Pentecost confirmed and sealed the redemptive work of Jesus, and the inner witness of the Spirit agrees with the faith that rests on these redemptive facts (vs. 6-8).

The first words of v. 7 in the A.V., "For there are three that bear record (witness)", should be connected at once with "the Spirit and the water and the blood" in v. 8. The intervening words contain a statement that is true in itself, but is irrelevant. The passage does not belong to the original text and is omitted in the R.V. It is a theological gloss, which crept into the Latin Bible and made its way into the later Greek manuscripts.

John goes on to say that we have also the witness of God to Christ which is greater than that of men; and those who believe have this witness within themselves (vs. 9-10). Then he sums up the Christian witness in its effect in them that believe. It is realized in their possession of eternal life and in their fellowship with the Son (vs. 11-12).

6. The Conclusion (5:13-21). The Apostle now restates the aim of his letter. His purpose is that his readers may know that they have eternal life (v. 13); and he proceeds on this note of assurance. This will give them boldness in prayer (vs. 14-15). This boldness will find expression in intercession for a brother who is seen committing a sin. Yet there is a limit to this kind of intercession. John cannot bid his readers intercede for a man in the case of "a sin unto death". The article in this phrase

should be omitted. What is meant is not some particular sin, but a course of sin producing a fixed attitude of the soul in opposition to God (vs. 16-17).

Finally, the Apostle summarizes the truths which his letter is intended to teach in three statements, each of which begins with "we know" (vs. 18-21). These are: (1) The sinless nature of the Christian life, the life that is born of God, and its safety from the attack of the evil one. (2) The divine nature of the Christian fellowship, and the evil nature of world fellowship. (3) The revelation of the true God in the presence among men of His Son Jesus Christ, and its profound effect in the lives of them that believe. Then John gives one last warning: "Guard yourselves from idols". The word was to be taken literally by John's readers. But in our day it means all that would seduce us from loyalty to the Lord Jesus Christ.

THE SECOND AND THIRD EPISTLES OF JOHN

THE writer of these two short letters calls himself "The elder", which implies that the title identified him and that he was well known. It marks his unique pre-eminence rather than his official position. It was probably the way that the last remaining Apostle had come to be known through the Church because of his great age. These letters reveal him in a new aspect, as the shepherd of individual souls. They also give momentary glimpses of church life in the province of Asia toward the close of the first century. One is mainly a letter of warning, and the other mainly a letter of encouragement.

The Second Epistle is addressed to "the elect lady and her children". This might be taken figuratively, as meaning a church and its members. But it is simpler and more natural to take it literally, and to think of John as writing to a Christian household. The salutation follows the usual type; the Apostle greets his readers in the fellowship of the truth (vs. 1-3). Then he states the occasion of this letter. He has met some members of the lady's family, and his joy in their Christian life and their fidelity to Christian truth prompted him to write to her (v. 4).

He urges the need of Christians continuing in love to one another and obedience to God, because there are many false teachers abroad who deny the Incarnation. They have the spirit of antichrist (vs. 5-7). Because of the presence of such deceivers among the churches, his readers should practise watchfulness and self-examination, so that they may not lose ground in their Christian life, but abide in "the teaching of Christ" (vs. 8-9). They are not to give hospitality to any one who does not teach this doctrine, for that would be sharing in his evil influence (vs. 10-11). Then John closes by telling them that he hopes to visit them soon, and have the joy of speaking with them face to face (vs. 12-13).

The Third Epistle is addressed to "Gaius the beloved", who seems to have been a man of position and influence in the Christian community to which he belonged. The Apostle prays that his prosperity and his health may be equal to his spiritual condition; for he rejoiced greatly when brethren told him of his devotion to the truth (vs. 1-4). Then he commends Gaius for his hospitality to Christian strangers and travellers. These were probably itinerant evangelists, and John says that it is the duty of Christians to receive such as guests in order to help forward the truth (vs. 5-8).

John had written to the church; and he now writes to Gaius personally, condemning Diotrephes, whose ambition led him to oppose the Apostle and usurp authority, and even to go to the length of excluding true believers from the church (vs. 9-10). John bids Gaius beware of imitating such conduct. If an example of Christian conduct is needed, there is Demetrius, whose devotion to the truth is known to all, and who has the Apostle's commendation also (vs. 11-12). The letter closes in the same way as the second one. John hopes to visit Gaius soon and speak with him face to face. He adds a greeting of peace, and the salutation of friends (vs. 13-14).

THE EPISTLE OF JUDE

THE writer calls himself, "Jude, a servant of Jesus Christ, and brother of James" (v. 1). This must be the well-known James, the author of the Epistle. Jude was therefore a brother of our Lord (Matt. 13:55; Mark 6:3). Nothing more is known of him.

His Epistle is addressed to Christians generally— "them that are called, beloved in God the Father, and kept for Jesus Christ". The Jewish features it contains would show that Jude had in mind chiefly Hebrew Christians. Probably his readers were the same as those to whom the Epistle of James had been sent. Jude survived James, and perhaps in some measure succeeded to his authority and influence among the Christian Jews. It may have been thus that he came to write this letter.

There is no indication in it as to the time and place. Most probably it was written in Palestine. From the absence of any reference to the destruction of Jerusalem it may be inferred that it was written before A.D. 70, when that catastrophe occurred.

There is a close resemblance between Jude and 2 Peter 2:1-3:3, so much as to indicate that one writer must have borrowed from the other. A comparison of the two gives the impression that Jude's letter was the original one, and that Peter was influenced by the language he used, but it is impossible to decide. Another remarkable feature of Jude is the large use made of historical matter taken from non-canonical books. We are not to infer from this that Jude regarded these books as inspired and authoritative. His references to them are like the mention of the Book of the Wars of the Lord and the Book of Jashar in the Old Testament (Num. 21:14; Josh. 10:13; 2 Sam. 1:18).

Jude begins with a threefold greeting of mercy, peace, and love (vs. 1-2), and then gives his reasons for writing. He was eager to write about the salvation of which he and his readers were alike partakers, and he felt constrained to exhort them "to contend earnestly for the faith", for there had crept in among them ungodly men whose coming had long been foretold, and who were "turning the grace of our God into lasciviousness" (vs. 3-4).

What is meant by "the faith which was once for all delivered unto the saints", is not a body of doctrine, but the Gospel principle of salvation by faith in Christ alone. What is meant by contending for the faith, is not defending the Gospel against false teachers by controversy, but striving to exercise in their Christian warfare and illustrate in their Christian life the grace of God which they received when they put their trust in Christ". This grace transferred the control of life from external rules to the indwelling Spirit; but these ungodly men to whom Jude refers were turning the Christian liberty which faith gives into licentiousness. This was an incipient Antinomian heresy.

Jude goes on to give examples of the certain doom of such men from the destruction of the unbelieving Israelites, the eternal captivity of the fallen angels, and the overthrow of Sodom and Gomorrah (vs. 5-7). These ungodly men not only set at naught the principles of Christian morality, but also attack the constituted authorities in the Church —they "rail at dignities". Yet even Michael showed self-restraint in his controversy with Satan over the body of Moses (vs. 8-9). The words attributed to Michael here are recorded in Zech. 3:2 as spoken by the Lord to Satan. The incident that Jude relates was found, according to some of the early Greek Fathers, in a Jewish apocryphal book known as the Assumption of Moses, which existed in their day but is no longer extant.

These ungodly men whom Jude describes rail, not only at persons in authority above them, but also at truths that are above their knowledge. They follow in the footsteps of Cain and Balaam and Korah, and so will share their doom (vs. 10-11). A figurative and graphic description of them follows. They are "hidden rocks", sources of unsuspected peril, or "spots" (marg. and A.V.), spoiling the fellowship of Christians, like blight in vegetation. They are like clouds that bring no refreshing showers, like trees that wither without bearing fruit, like waves of the sea that cannot rest, and like shooting stars of the sky that go out in darkness (vs. 12-13).

Jude quotes a prophecy of Enoch about the coming of the Lord to execute judgment upon ungodly sinners, which would have its fulfilment in the case of such men as these; and he follows it with a further description of them (vs. 14-16). This prophecy was contained in a Jewish apocalypse called "The Book of Enoch" which probably preserved an authentic tradition about him.

Jude then reminds his beloved readers that the Apostles of the Lord had foretold the appearance of such men "in the last time", whose evil character and influence would be due to their being "sensual, not having the Spirit" (vs. 17-19). Jude is dealing with symptoms which show that the tide of spiritual force in the Church had begun to ebb and reaction had set in. This condition has appeared again and again in the history of Christianity, and the prophecy may await a further fulfilment. Jude continues his affectionate appeal by urging his readers to build up their character on the foundation of their faith, letting the Holy Spirit inspire their prayers, and committing themselves to the safe-keeping of the Father in the hope of eternal life through the mercy of the Lord Jesus Christ (vs. 20-21).

The meaning of the next verses is doubtful. They may be paraphrased thus: As for the ungodly men among you, have mercy on those who are deluded by them and are in doubt; save those whom you can snatch from their influence, as from a consuming fire; and let your compassion watch for opportunities of helping others, but take care lest you become in any way tainted with their impurity (vs. 22-23). Then Jude brings his letter to an end with a noble and beautiful doxology, which not only sums up the message of this Epistle, but also makes a fitting conclusion to the whole group of the New Testament Epistles (vs. 24-25).

THE REVELATION

PROPHECY IN THE NEW TESTAMENT

THE New Testament age was marked by a revival of prophecy. It began with the ministry of John the Baptist, the last prophet of the old order. The ministry of Jesus was regarded by the people as that of a prophet (Matt. 16:14; John 4:19; 6:14), and He accepted their view of His mission (Mark 6:4; John 4:44). An order of prophets arose in the early Church soon after Pentecost, and prophetic gifts were apparently exercised everywhere (Acts 11:27-28; 13:1; 15:32; 21:9-10). Paul's letters show that prophecy was very common in the Gentile churches (1 Thess. 5:20; 1 Cor. 12:28; 13:2; 14:3; Rom. 12:6). Next to the Apostles, the prophets were the greatest gift bestowed upon the Church by the ascended Lord. Their function was to build up the churches which the Apostles had established (Eph. 2:20; 4:11).

The Revelation is the only book of prophecy in the New Testament, and the only prophetic work that has come down from the apostolic age. It claims to be a prophecy (1:3; 22:7, 10, 18), yet it differs from prophecy in the ordinary sense. It is an Apocalypse, an "unveiling". A number of books belonging to the general class of Apocalypses had appeared among the Jews during the centuries immediately before Christ. This apocalyptic literature attempted to unveil the future. It had arisen from a misunderstanding of Messianic prophecy. Israel had lost sight of the redemptive element in the work of their promised Messiah. The Book of Revelation, on the other hand, is the true Apocalypse. It is the proper consummation of Messianic prophecy. It breathes a different spirit from that which pervades the Jewish apocalypses. The mark of the Cross is in it, and the unmistakable note of inspiration. As the last book of Scripture, it forms a fitting close to the Divine revelation of redemption, the true theme of the Bible.

The title of the book is literally, "The unveiling of Jesus Christ". The reference is not to the unveiling of events hidden in the future, but to the unveiling of the hidden glory of the ascended Lord. On the Mount of Olives Jesus had disappeared from the eyes of His disciples into the unseen world of Heaven. Ten days afterwards the Holy Spirit came down to take His place. This did not mean that Christ had resigned His active function in the redeeming purpose of God to the Holy Spirit, and had retired into a state of passivity, waiting for the time of His return. Much less did it mean that the Person of the Son of God had been dissolved into the Third Person of the Trinity. Jesus Christ, the Saviour of the world, was active still. The very atmosphere of the Acts and the Epistles vibrates throughout with a sense of power, a power proceeding continually from the exalted and glorified Lord Himself.

Peter told the Jews on the Day of Pentecost that Jesus of Nazareth had been exalted to the throne of God in Heaven (Acts 2:33). Paul told his converts that He must reign till He has put all His enemies under His feet (1 Cor. 15:25). But no-where are we shown how He was using the authority that had been given Him; nowhere do we see the procedure of His reign. Glimpses of His heavenly glory were given to Stephen at his martyrdom and to Paul at Damascus. But the veil was never drawn aside. Throughout the Acts and the Epistles, the Lord Jesus Christ remains hidden behind the cloud that received Him on the Mount.

And now comes the Book of Revelation to unveil Him. He is seen at last in the glory which He entered on that ascension day. Jesus Christ is the central figure of the whole vision that is unfolded, and He dominates the whole book. This is the first and most important thing to remember as we approach it. It was not intended to be an obscure and cryptic prediction of earthly events, but to show us the spiritual forces and mighty movements in Heaven which are the springs of earthly events.

The Revelation was given to John in the form of visions, and these visions compose the book. In the opening verses he declares that he bare witness "of all things that he saw"; and in the course of the book he uses the expression, "I saw", about forty times. It is obvious that the writer was occupied, not with events that were to happen in the future, but with visions that had passed before his eyes. His entire concern was to describe accurately and completely what he saw. If then we are to understand the significance of the book, we must read it primarily as a record of visions; we must see what John saw. We must see the visions also as he saw them, in their orderly sequence, and from the point of view which he occupied. Their sequence is not that of consecutive time, but of progressive movement. It is the sequence of spiritual forces, not of earthly events.

The Revelation was shown to the Seer by the use of representative symbols. The Lord "sent and signified it by his angel unto his servant John" (1:1). The word "signify" properly means to show by some sort of sign. John uses it three times in the Gospel (12:33; 18:32; 21:19). It has therefore special force in a book of symbolic visions. The Revelation is symbolical through and through. Its symbolic nature is due to the impossibility of describing in ordinary language and in concrete terms the things that belong to a world beyond the reach of human sense and sight. The symbols are taken entirely from the Old Testament, and are to be interpreted according to the significance that Scripture has already given to them.

A prominent feature of the book is the frequent occurrence of numbers, which are manifestly intended to carry a symbolic meaning. The predominant number is "seven", which occurs fifty-four times. It signifies completion, or fulness of development. Many of the visions occur in series of sevens. These sevens are all arranged in the same systematic order, a group of four visions which are always similar, and a group of three which always vary.

It is obvious that visions such as these cannot represent events occurring in the course of history, for historic events do not happen in that systematic way. They represent, rather, the hidden movements that give rise to earthly events, the spiritual forces that operate behind world history. As "four" is the number of the world and "three" the number of the Godhead, it would seem that the series of sevens represent movements in which earthly and heavenly forces are both in operation. Each series comes to a head in a culminating crisis, which is described in such a way as to suggest the coming of the Lord. This is the ultimate consummation toward which all the visions of this prophetic book converge. It comes to a close with this promise and hope (22:20). New Testament prophecy, therefore, has one final event in view, the Second Coming of Christ.

THE BOOK OF REVELATION

THE writer of this book calls himself John, with no other designation, as though that name was well enough known to identify him (1:1, 4, 9; 22:8). This can be none other than the Apostle. The style differs very considerably from that of his Gospel and his Epistles, but the tone of authority indicates an apostolic author. No other writer in the early Church would have used this name without distinguishing himself from the Apostle John. And besides that, under the marked diversity of style there are some deeper features of resemblance which can scarcely be accidental, such as a similarity in language and imagery, and in the terms used to describe our Lord.

The Revelation which the book records was given to John during his exile on the isle of Patmos in a time of persecution (1:9). According to an early tradition, this occurred in the last years of the reign of Domitian, between A.D. 92 and 96, and this is the generally accepted view for the date of the book. The tradition, however, is not altogether unanimous, and there are other indications which point to the closing years of Nero's reign. This would date the book before the fall of Jerusalem in A.D. 70. With this would agree the apparent implication in 11:1-2 that the Temple had not yet been destroyed. This is not decisive, however, for the measuring of the Temple is symbolical.

But what would be explained by the early date, are the Hebrew features in the style of the book, and its difference from the style of the Gospel. At that time John still retained the Jewish influences of his life in Palestine, while at the time the Gospel was written he had been under Greek influences in Ephesus for twenty or twenty-five years. The book breathes an atmosphere which fits the last days of Nero and the time immediately following, in which Rome and the whole Empire were in a state of chaos and confusion.

The book is addressed "to the seven churches that are in Asia", and they are named afterwards (1:4, 11). They were seven churches then existing in the proconsular province of Asia, whose chief city was Ephesus. As the number "seven" signifies completeness, the seven churches are meant to represent all the separate congregations that make up the whole Church. The Revelation was written at the command of the Lord (1:11, 19), and was intended for the warning and comfort of His people (22:16). There is a repeated refrain in the separate letters to the seven churches in chs. 2—3, which emphasizes the solemn importance of the message of the book: "He that hath an ear, let him hear what the Spirit saith to the churches".

The structure of the book is indicated in the words used by the Lord in commanding John what to write (1:19). This command was uttered after John had seen the first vision which the book describes, and it may be rendered as follows: "Write therefore the things which thou sawest (the vision already described), and the things which they are (which they signify), and the things which shall come to pass hereafter (in another vision to be seen hereafter)". The entire reference of the command is to things that are seen in visions; none of it refers to things that happen in events. To take it otherwise is to break the logical unity of the sentence.

The phrase in our English Version, "the things which are", is a literal rendering of the original Greek, but the rendering given above is equally correct and is more consistent with the general sense and feeling of the passage. The Lord goes on in the next verse to define the things which John saw more particularly, and then to explain what they "are", using the same word as in v. 19, and in each case "are" means "signify".

Had the Lord intended John to write "the things which are" in the sense of the existing things, it is more than probable that a different form of words would have been used in the original Greek. There are two other passages in the New Testament where the words, "the things that are", occur in that sense (Rom. 4:17 and 1 Cor. 1:28), and in both cases the Greek expression is different from the one used here. In the two former cases, transliterated, it is "ta onta", while in Rev. 1:19 it is "ha eisin".

John was commanded to write an account of two visions, and this gives the book a twofold division. One was the vision described in ch. 1, to which he was to add its significance, making the first division of the book (Chs. 1-3). The other vision, which he saw afterwards, is described in the rest of the book, but nothing is said about its significance. It is composed of a continuous series of visions and makes the second division of the book (Chs. 4-22). These visions are seen from two different points of view and present two different aspects of the glorified Lord. In the first vision the Seer is on the earth and beholds Christ in the midst of the churches as represented by the seven golden candlesticks. In the second vision he is caught up into Heaven and sees Christ in the midst of the Throne. On this basis the book may be analyzed as follows:

I. Jesus Christ in the Midst of the Church—
    Chs. 1—3
    1. The Glorified Son of Man (Ch. 1)
    2. The Letters to the Seven Churches
       (Chs. 2—3)
II. Jesus Christ in the Midst of the Throne—
    Chs. 4-22
    1. The Throne in Heaven (Chs. 4—5)
    2. The Opening of the Seven Seals
       (Chs. 6—7)
    3. The Sounding of the Seven Trumpets
       (Chs. 8—11)
    4. The Foes of Christ and His Church
       (Chs. 12—14)
    5. The Seven Bowls of the Wrath of God
       (Chs. 15—16)
    6. The Doom of the Foes of Christ
       (Chs. 17—20)
    7. The New Heaven and the New Earth
       (Chs. 21—22)

THE GLORIFIED SON OF MAN
(Ch. 1)

1. The Introduction (vs. 1-8). The opening words contain the title of the book and state the theme (v. 1). The phrase, "the revelation of Jesus Christ", when used elsewhere, always means the unveiling of the glorified Lord (1 Cor. 1:7; 2 Thess. 1:7; 1 Pet. 1:7, 13). Even in Gal. 1:12 Paul uses the word "revelation" in the same sense. He means that he came to understand the Gospel through the unveiling of Jesus Christ in his Damascus vision. The words, "even the things which must shortly come to pass", are a further explanation of the theme. The unveiling of the hidden Lord in Heaven involved the revelation of what would happen in the world because of His enthronement there. The visions would show that the passing scenes on earth depend on the eternal scene in Heaven. The words, "which God gave him", do not mean that God gave Christ something to reveal, but that God gave Him this work to do. The angel who showed John the visions is mentioned again in the last chapter (vs. 6. 8, 16).

The words, "the testimony of Jesus Christ" (v. 2), probably mean the message of the whole book. But possibly John is referring to the general character of his teaching. As an Apostle he had been an eyewitness of the life of Jesus Christ on earth; now he was to be a witness of His glory. The peculiar importance of the message of the book is emphasized by the special blessing attached to it (v. 3). It was to be publicly read in the churches, and both the reader and the hearers would be blessed. Six other blessings are promised in the course of the Revelation (14:13; 16:15; 19:9; 20:6; 22:7, 14).

The dedication of the book (vs. 4-6) includes a threefold salutation from the Persons of the Trinity. Jesus Christ is described in His three offices of Pro-

phet, Priest, and King—as the Revealer of God, the Redeemer of men, and the Ruler of the world. Then comes an ascription of praise to Him. It is a twofold doxology, the first of four doxologies in the book. There is a threefold doxology in 4:11, a fourfold doxology in 5:13, and a sevenfold doxology in 5:12 and 7:12. The next verses give a summary of the truth contained in the book in two fundamental declarations regarding the Lord Jesus Christ—the coming event of His glorious appearing (v. 7), and the present fact of His almighty power (v. 8).

2. The Occasion (vs. 9-11). John was an exile on Patmos for Christ's sake, sharing with his readers the tribulation endured by the followers of Jesus Christ. It was a time of persecution, and all Christians were suffering. He "was in the Spirit on the Lord's day". It was the first day of the week, and the Apostle was in an exalted spiritual state, probably thinking of the churches of Asia assembling for worship as they were accustomed to do on the day of the Resurrection. The Christians were beginning to call their day of worship, "the Lord's Day". Then there came a sudden voice, so strong and clear and authoritative as to claim his whole attention. The command to write, which is given here for the first time, occurs twelve times in the book.

3. The Vision (vs. 12-16). John turned in the direction of the voice and saw seven golden candlesticks, each one no doubt like the seven-branched candlestick of the Temple. In the midst of them stood the Son of Man, clothed in royal dignity and heavenly glory. His personal appearance, which is described by symbolic features, was so awe-inspiring that the Apostle fell at His feet as dead. It was a vision of the glorified Lord, the Head of all the churches, standing among them as the source of their life and power, upholding and superintending their work and ministry. There are seven features in the vision, and each one has its own special significance in revealing the perfect glory of the Lord's Person. These features are referred to separately in each of the letters to the seven churches.

4. The Voice (vs. 17-20). The first words spoken by the Lord were for John's encouragement, and may be rendered thus: "Fear not; it is I, the first, and the last, and the Living One". Then He describes His redemptive work: He went down into death, and now He is alive for evermore. As a result, He has the keys of death and of Hades. He has power and authority over the realms that hold the bodies and the souls of men.

Then follows the command to write, which gives the plan on which the book is arranged. This is explained on page 273. The last verse explains the secret significance of the seven stars and the seven golden candlesticks. The stars are the angels of the churches, their inward and prevailing spirit; while the candlesticks are the churches in their outward and visible form. In this book every person and every element in nature has its angel (7:1; 9:1; 14:18; 16:5). This is required by the symbolic and dramatic character of the Revelation.

THE LETTERS TO THE SEVEN CHURCHES
(Chs. 2—3)

There is no break between chs. 1 and 2. The voice which began to speak in 1:17 keeps on speaking through chs. 2 and 3, and commands John to write these letters. They explain the significance of the vision in ch. 1 to each of the seven churches. They are addressed in each case "to the angel of the church", but are intended for the actual church itself and describe its characteristic spirit.

These seven letters have a peculiar tone of majesty and finality. They are the Lord's last messages to His Church on earth till He comes again. They are intended to encourage and strengthen His redeemed people while carrying on their witness for Him in the world. They are all constructed on the same general plan. There is first an impressive introduction, containing a command to write and a title of Christ: "These things saith he that—". Each title is taken from some feature of the vision in ch. 1, and is specially fitted to the condition of the church addressed.

The body of each letter is an appropriate message in three parts. The Lord usually begins with commendation: "I know—". There is an exception in the last epistle; in the church at Laodicea He finds nothing to praise. This is usually followed by condemnation: "But—". The searching eyes of the Lord find the faults of the church. There are exceptions in the second and sixth epistles: the Lord gives no rebuke to the churches in Smyrna and Philadelphia. Then comes His counsel: "Remember therefore—", or "Repent therefore—". He gives a warning to each church to prepare for His coming, which is always implied, and is explicitly mentioned in the last four letters.

Each letter ends with a solemn conclusion, containing both an appeal and a promise. The appeal is always the same, and there is an impressive solemnity in its sevenfold repetition: "He that hath an ear, let him hear what the Spirit saith to the churches". The promise is given "to him that overcometh", which implies that the church is engaged in a conflict, and that each member is to overcome. The rewards promised form a chain of blessings, linking together all the stages of redemption from the Garden of Eden to the Throne of God (2:7, 11, 17; 26-28; 3:5, 12, 21). In the first three epistles the appeal comes first, and in the last four it follows the promise. This divides the seven letters into two groups of three and four.

The seven churches were local congregations in the province of Asia in John's day. Each letter describes the conditions that actually existed in the church addressed. The letters, therefore, have a special application to individual churches. But they have also a general application. Taken separately, the seven churches represent different aspects of the Church of Christ. Taken collectively, they represent the whole Church in all the world. It is possible also that, taken consecutively, they may represent successive stages in the history of the Church through the whole Christian age.

1. Ephesus (2:1-7). This church had a splendid record for patient and persevering toil, intolerance of evil, and zeal for the truth. But its devotion of heart to Christ Himself had cooled: "Thou didst leave thy first love". The Lord counsels it to remember its former devotion, and "do the first works", the things it used to do for Jesus' sake. Then love for Christ would be kindled again, and the heart would grow warm to Him. The Nicolaitans, whose

works were hated by the church in Ephesus, were probably Antinomians, the special class of heretics described by Jude. The reward promised in the letter is restored access to the source of life that was lost in Eden.

2. Smyrna (2:8-11). This church's testimony consisted in suffering, of which she endured three kinds—tribulation, poverty, and calumny. The Lord sees the malice of His own great adversary behind the persecutions suffered by His people. The outlook before them was still more suffering; but the ultimate reward would be the crown of life. This letter is full of praise, and is instinct with life and joy. Its promise is a life beyond the reach of the second death (20:6).

3. Pergamum (2:12-17). This church was in a difficult position—"where Satan's throne is". Pergamum was an official centre of Roman authority, a great stronghold of heathen worship, and a city of wealth and fashion. In the midst of it the church had been loyal to the Person of Christ—"my name"—and to the truth of the Gospel—"my faith". It had maintained its loyalty in the face of persecution; one of its members had died for the faith. But it failed in the matter of discipline. It tolerated some who compromised with the world and followed the teaching of Balaam (Num. 31:16), and also some who were Antinomians.

The "hidden manna" in the promise to this church is an allusion to the manna which was laid up in the sanctuary (Exod. 16:33-34; Heb. 9:4). The "white stone" with a new name written upon it is probably a reference to the Urim and Thummim carried by the high priest under the precious stones of his breastplate (Exod. 28:30).

4. Thyatira (2:18-29). This was the city from which Lydia came (Acts 16:14). As she is not mentioned in the letter to the Philippians, she may have gone back to Thyatira and taken the Gospel with her. The church is commended for its abounding ministry of love and faith and patience. Its last works were more than the first.

But an evil thing had been allowed in the church: "Thou sufferest the woman Jezebel". A woman in the church, whom the Lord calls by that name because of her Old Testament prototype (1 Kings 16:31), claimed to be a prophetess and was teaching what the Lord calls, in irony, "deep things of Satan". Some members of the church, allured by her pretence of deeper knowledge, were being seduced from Christian living into pagan immorality. The Lord warns that she and her followers would be thrown into deep tribulation unless they repented.

The others in Thyatira were to hold fast the one burden of responsibility which Christ had laid upon His servants, that of witnessing for Him. The promise given in this letter takes us down to the time of David. It is that of sharing in the Messianic Kingdom (Psa. 2:9), and in the glory of the new day to be ushered in by the morning star.

5. Sardis (3:1-6). This church apparently had great advantages. There is no reference in the letter to persecution or to heresy. The church had a good name; but it lived on its reputation, and was spiritually dead. Its ministry was carried on in the eyes of the world, and not in the eyes of God: "I have found no works of thine perfected before my

God". And yet some of its members kept themselves unspotted from the world; they had not defiled their garments by compromise with it. The "white garments" mentioned in the promise allude to the white robes of the priests, whose names were enrolled for service in the temple of Solomon; and the blessing promised is that of fellowship with God in the heavenly temple.

6. Philadelphia (3:7-13). This was one of the weaker churches: it had "a little power". But it was faithful to the open door of opportunity set before it. It was also loyal to Christ: "Thou didst keep my word, and didst not deny my name". Because of its faithful testimony, some of the Jews who were hostile to Christ would be brought to acknowledge Him. Because they had kept His word, the Lord pledges Himself to keep them in the time of trial that was to come upon the world. The reward promised in the letter is a place of honour in the heavenly temple, and eternal fellowship with God in the heavenly city. The background of this promise is the return from the Exile, when the temple and the city were rebuilt.

7. Laodicea (3:14-22). This was a lukewarm church — "neither cold nor hot". It was not untouched by grace, but it had no enthusiam. It was self-satisfied and self-complacent—"I am rich, and have need of nothing". The Lord's attitude toward it is twofold. The church as a whole, He treats with stern severity and loathing—"I will spue thee out of my mouth". And then He describes its true condition, of which it was unaware. "The wretched one and miserable and poor and blind and naked".

To the individual members of the church, He gives a tender entreaty to let Him in and sup with them—"Behold, I stand at the door and knock". This letter is the saddest of the seven, and yet the most tender and beautiful. None of them makes more evident the yearning compassion of the great heart of the Son of Man. The promise it contains is the highest reward in His possession to give—a share in His throne.

THE THRONE IN HEAVEN
(Chs. 4—5)

Here the second main division of the book begins. The Seer is taken to a new point of view, from which he is to behold the rest of the scenes. The same voice that introduced the first vision (1:10), now introduces the second vision (4:1), which continues to the end of the Revelation. The voice spoke to John from a door set open in Heaven, calling him to come up hither and be shown "the things which must come to pass hereafter". The reference is not to events that were to happen in the future, but to the second vision announced in 1:19. The scenes of this vision were to pass before his eyes after the first vision had passed away. At once he found himself in the heavenly world, and in the presence of the Throne (Psa. 103:19). From this point onward he is to see things as the angels see them. The Throne is the background of all that follows. The word is used thirty-five times.

1. The Creator on the Throne (Ch. 4). "There was a throne set in heaven, and one sitting upon the throne" (v. 2). The scene is described with reverent awe and dignified restraint. It breathes an atmosphere of calm and majestic peace. John was conscious of a Presence on the Throne, but he saw no form. His eye was arrested by the flashing of gemlike colours which symbolized the glory of the Throne (v. 3). The jasper stone was probably the diamond, the pure sparkling whiteness of which fittingly set forth the holiness of God, His essential glory (21:11). The fiery red of the sardine stone would set forth the justice of God. The rainbow of emerald green encircling the Throne would be a symbol of the Creator's everlasting covenant with the earth (Gen. 9:11-17). The elders seated around the Throne represented the redeemed of Old and New Testament times (v. 4). This is evident from their number, which is twice twelve, the number of the patriarchs of Israel and the Apostles of the Church.

A further description of the central Throne is given in symbolic terms, which suggest the sovereign and almighty power that proceeds from it and the presence of the Holy Spirit in its operations (v. 5). The shining surface of the sea of glass would suggest to the Seer the vast distance that separated him from the Throne (v. 6). Round about the Throne were four "living creatures" (not "beasts" A.V.), which combined features of the seraphim in Isa. 6 and the cherubim in Ezek. 1. They represented the fulness and variety of life in the natural world, and its ceaseless activity under the Creator's rule (vs. 6-8). Their hymn of praise, which was that of Isa. 6:3, was followed by the worship of the elders. They, too, joined in the praise of the Creator on the Throne (vs. 9-11). As yet there was no word about redemption.

2. The Sealed Book (5:1-5). This book, like all ancient books of that time, was in the form of a scroll. It was rolled up and sealed on the back. The words describing it should probably be punctuated as follows: "written within, and on the back close sealed with seven seals". Scrolls were not usually written on the back. The words mean that what the book contained was written within, and could not be read till every seal on the back was opened.

In order to understand what the book symbolizes, we should keep in mind all the circumstances of the scene. Being in the right hand of the Creator on the Throne, it must have something to do with the world over which He rules. The symbol should be sought in the Old Testament, if it is to be interpreted in the light of Scripture. The story of Jeremiah's purchase of a field in his home-town of Anathoth (Jer. 32:6-14) mentions the sealing of the document that contained the title-deeds of the property, and a sealed copy was laid up for safe-keeping. To take the sealed book in this vision as containing the title-deeds of the world, and as representing the right to the kingdoms of the world, meets all the conditions of the scene.

A challenge is issued in Heaven: "Who is worthy to open the book?" The challenge goes unanswered. No one was found worthy in all the universe, and John was profoundly grieved. Obviously what was written in the book was of great concern to him. Then one of the elders, representing the redeemed who also were concerned in the matter, comforted the Seer with the announcement that "the Lion that is of the tribe of Judah, the Root of David, hath overcome (hath won a victory which gives Him the right) to open the book and the seven seals thereof".

This scene can be set in the frame of our Lord's

life. During His temptation in the wilderness, Satan offered Jesus the kingdoms of the world on one condition (Matt. 4:8-10). He must have had the right to make the offer, for otherwise it would have been no temptation to Jesus. In some strange way, unrevealed to us, authority over this world was given to Satan at the beginning, undoubtedly before his fall. The Lord Himself recognized him as "the prince of this world" (John 12:31; 14:30; 16:11). But Jesus rejected Satan's offer and undertook to win the right to the kingdoms of the world by a victory over him. That victory was won on the Cross.

3. The Lamb in the Midst (5:6-7). Now John saw something that had not appeared before. In the midst of the Throne there was "a Lamb standing, as though it had been slain". Here is a manifest and unmistakable symbol of Jesus Christ, fresh from the Cross and newly ascended. He has just taken His place on the Throne. The symbol also represents the Redeemer in the fulness of His Divine power and world-wide energy. The Lamb had "seven horns, and seven eyes, which are the seven spirits of God". It is from Him that the operations of the Holy Spirit are "sent forth into all the earth". When the Lamb took the book "out of the right hand of him that sat on the throne", it meant that the title-deeds it contained were now His, and He claimed the right to the kingdoms of the world. From this time on, "the Lamb" dominates the whole Revelation. The name occurs twenty-nine times.

This scene representing Christ taking His place in the midst of the Throne in Heaven takes us to the Ascension. This is the pivotal event upon which the whole Book of Revelation turns. This is the point of time from which all its scenes proceed. What the Seer was shown is the change that was made in Heaven by the exaltation and enthronement of the Son of Man. In that light, and from that point of view, the book reveals the significance of the Cross in human history.

4. The Praise of the Lamb (5:8-14). This sublime scene, with the grandeur of its magnificent symbolism, is a revelation of what took place on the heavenly side of the cloud that received the Lord on the day of His Ascension. It is Heaven's welcome to the triumphant Redeemer. Volumes of adoring praise, in which all the heavenly hosts engage, sweep out from the central Throne in ever widening circles. It begins with the four living creatures and the twenty-four elders, who sing "a new song", the song of redemption (vs. 8-10). It is taken up by the voice of the angels, whom John now sees in their myriads (vs. 11-12). It is continued by the whole creation in all its parts. Creation's doxology is fourfold, as that of the angels is sevenfold (v. 13). The theme of the universal anthem is, "Worthy is the Lamb that hath been slain". The work of God's redeeming grace has been accomplished. When at last the sounds of praise die away, John sees the elders, representing all whom the Lamb has redeemed, fall down before Him in silent adoration (v. 14).

THE OPENING OF THE SEVEN SEALS
(Chs. 6—7)

The opening of the seals does not mean the unfolding of the roll. Every seal must be opened before it can be unfolded at all. The final purpose is to see what is written therein. By opening the seals Christ is making His claim to the title-deeds of the world and declaring His right to the rule of its kingdoms. As each seal is opened in Heaven, a corresponding scene takes place on earth, representing what is happening there. The Seer is shown how things on earth appear in the light of Christ's redemptive work and from Heaven's point of view.

There is an evident parallel between ch. 6 and Matt. 24, which contains the Lord's answer to the disciples' question, "What shall be the sign of thy coming?" and describes the character of the present Christian age. The vision of the seals, therefore, may be taken to set forth the signs of Christ's coming in the sense of showing the world's need of Him. They describe the conditions that prevail on the earth while Satan continues to rule and Christ is still rejected. Their sequence is not that of events in time, but that of movements in operation. The first four seals form a group by themselves. After the sixth seal there is a pause before the last seal is opened.

1. The First Four Seals (6:1-8). As these seals are opened one by one, the four living creatures cry, "Come!" not "Come and see" (A.V.). It is the cry of creation for the coming of Christ. It corresponds with the groaning of the whole creation as it waits for the manifestation of the sons of God, which Paul describes in Rom. 8:19-22. As each seal is opened in Heaven, a horseman appears on earth. We have here the reaction of the kingdoms of men to Christ's claim to be the Ruler of the world.

The horses are all of one kind, though of different colours. The white horse here is very different from the white horse of 19:11. His rider was given a crown, and "he came forth conquering, and bent on conquest", as the word may be rendered. He appears as a splendid and imposing figure, a fit symbol of man's self-will going into action in the cause of self-interest. This is the spirit that has pervaded the human race since the Fall, and has always inspired the kingdoms of this world. In its final form it is the lust of conquest, the desire to dominate the world.

The white horse is followed by the red horse of war, the black horse of famine, and the pale horse of plague. This grim procession represents the dire consequences that inevitably flow from the pride of conquest in human history. This is what the rejection of Christ's claims has brought upon the world. Creation's sympathy with suffering humanity in the midst of all this is shown in the protest against hunger that comes from the living creatures (v. 6). It is a pleading request that a day's wage may provide a day's sustenance, and that a limit may be set to want.

2. The Fifth Seal (6:9-11). The martyrs represent the whole Christian Church, which is always presented in the Revelation in its ideal condition, as God sees it. During the present age, the true Church is characterized by tribulation (1:9). It is a martyr Church. The cry of the martyrs corresponds with the cry of creation, and represents the prayer of the Church for the coming of Christ (Luke 18:7-8).

3. The Sixth Seal (6:12-17). Here is an ac-

cumulation of spectacular and portentous symbols taken from Old Testament prophecy, and arranged so as to lead to a climax that is terrifying in its awful sublimity. It is the symbolism used by the prophets in foretelling the overthrow of world kingdoms (Isa. 2:17-22; 13:9-13; 34:4). The vision represents the collapse of the kingdoms of this world, and the utter failure of all human efforts to build a world order without Christ. This has never had a better illustration than in the world of our own day. The sixth seal brings us to the eve of Christ's coming, the day of the wrath of the Lamb. In view of that day the question is asked, "Who is able to stand?"

4. An Interlude (Ch. 7). This chapter contains a parenthesis between the sixth and the seventh seals. It answers the question with which ch. 6 ends, by describing two scenes representing the redeemed people of God.

(1) The sealing of the servants of God (vs. 1-8). John saw four angels on the earth holding back the winds of judgment, that the day of grace might be prolonged and the servants of God might all be sealed (vs. 1-3). The scene has its Old Testament parallel in Ezek. 9:3-4. The seal is the Holy Spirit (Eph. 1:13), and the vision represents the salvation and separation of the people of God by the preaching of the Gospel during the present age.

This is signified and emphasized by the precise and elaborate account of "the number of them that were sealed" (vs. 4-8). Israel is used in this book in a representative sense for all the people of God on earth. It is Israel after the spirit, not Israel after the flesh (Gal. 3:7; 6:16). Their number is represented as being complete and all-inclusive. A hundred and forty-four thousand is the number of redemption, squared and multiplied by a thousand. As a number, a thousand is always associated in this book with that over which God rules. It is ten, the number of world rule, raised to the third power, that is, made divine.

Then the passage goes into particulars. Twelve tribes are named one by one, and twelve thousand is the number mentioned as sealed in each tribe. Taken literally, this gives no reasonable meaning; but taken in the spirit of the Revelation, it makes this one of the most comforting visions in the book. It is a symbolic way of magnifying the grace of God. It sets Him forth in His patience and long-suffering, not willing that any should perish, but waiting until all His redeemed have been sought and found in all parts of the world, not one missing.

(2) The great multitude before the Throne (vs. 9-17). The Seer next beheld a vast company in Heaven, so great that it could not be counted. They were gathered from all nations and tongues in all the world, and were robed in white. With palms in their hands, they were keeping the true Feast of Tabernacles, and they were praising God and the Lamb for their salvation. The angelic host around the Throne took up the song with a sevenfold ascription of praise (vs. 9-12). Then one of the elders intervened to explain the vision to John. He described the white-robed throng in terms which express their complete and perfect bliss (vs. 13-17).

"These are they that come out of the great tribulation". The expression in the original is timeless, and does not refer to any special event or any par-

ticular period. In the Revelation the Christian age is always described from the heavenly point of view. It is the period of "the great tribulation" for the saints on earth. Some of the imagery here is taken from the Old Testament (Isa. 49:10; 25:8). The vision represents the innumerable company of the redeemed of all the ages, who have borne their witness to Christ amid the trials of the world, and have passed on into His immediate presence. They have fallen asleep in Jesus (1 Thess. 4:13-14). Their spirits are now with Him (Phil. 1:23; Heb. 12:22-23), and their entire occupation is worship. This passage throws light on the state of the soul after death.

THE SOUNDING OF THE SEVEN TRUMPETS
(Chs. 8—11)

The trumpet visions issue from the seventh seal (8:1-2). When the last seal was opened, "there followed a silence in heaven about the space of half an hour". To get the significance of this silent pause, we must keep in mind the dramatic character of the Revelation. It is not a static series of isolated visions, but a progressive movement of living scenes that develop one into the other. When the seventh seal was broken the scroll lay open, and what was written therein could be read. That was what John, and all Heaven, had been waiting for since the challenge of 5:2 was issued and the Lamb undertook to open the book. The silence, therefore, is dramatic in its suggestiveness. What the roll contains is being read. The claim of the Lamb is vindicated; the title-deeds of the world are proved to be His. This means that Satan is now a usurper and must be dethroned. Hence the trumpet visions announce the conflict with him.

Trumpets are signals of war and judgment. The sounding of the seven trumpets signifies that the sovereignty of Christ in the world is to be established only after a long-drawn-out conflict, and through a series of judgments. Corresponding with each trumpet blast in Heaven, something is seen to take place on earth. The first four trumpets form a group by themselves. They announce judgments affecting the natural world, the sphere of man's life. The other three are called "woes" (8:13), and are judgments of a spiritual kind. The purpose of these judgments is to call mankind to repentance; but men do not repent (9:20-21). Because the world does not repent, the final judgment comes (11:14). Between the sixth and seventh trumpets another pause occurs. At the seventh and last trumpet, Heaven announces that "the kingdom of the world is become the kingdom of our Lord, and of his Christ" (11:15). His reign on earth begins.

1. The Commission of the Angels (8:1-6). This scene sets forth the heavenly preparations for the judgments on the earth. There is a calm and solemn deliberation about it. God's judgments are not arbitrary. They are His answer to the prayers of His saints (6:10), which are mingled with the prayers of Christ Himself. This is signified by the way the incense given to the angel was offered upon the golden altar before the Throne. The casting of fire from the censer into the earth means that, in answer to the prayers of His suffering people, the fire of God's judgment is about to descend upon the world. The lightnings and voices and thunders

which proceed from the Throne in 4:5 appear here again. They may mark the real conclusion of the vision of the seven seals, for the same signs occur in 11:19 and 16:18, where the two series of the seven trumpets and the seven bowls are ended. The seven trumpets, like the seven seals, cover the whole Christian age.

2. The First Four Trumpets (8:7-13). These trumpets introduce destructive plagues falling successively upon the earth (v. 7), the sea (vs. 8-9), the rivers and streams (vs. 10-11), and the sky and the heavenly bodies (v. 12). These four realms make up the whole natural world as the sphere of man's life. A third part in each case was smitten by the plague. They are warning judgments, similar to the plagues of Egypt. As God was warning Pharaoh then, so these plagues symbolize warnings which He gives to the world by smiting the natural surroundings of man's life on earth and turning into a curse what was intended for man's blessing.

The character of these symbolic plagues indicates that God's judgments come as the natural consequences of misusing His gifts. The warning voice that followed these four trumpets (v. 13) announced more terrible judgments to come upon "them that dwell on the earth". This expression is used hereafter to distinguish the unrighteous and ungodly world from the saints of God.

3. The Fifth Trumpet and First Woe (9:1-12). This is an appalling judgment manifestly of a demonic character. John saw a star from heaven which had fallen to the earth. The words do not mean that he saw it fall. It was the symbol of a fallen angel, probably Satan himself (vs. 11; Isa. 14:12; Luke 10:18). The "pit of the abyss" represents the abode of the devil and his angels. Swarms of locusts came out of it to attack those who had not the seal of God upon their foreheads (7:2-3). This means that only they that are sealed with the Holy Spirit are immune from their attack.

Here obviously is the demonic plague of spiritism. The clouds of smoke out of the pit symbolize the spiritual darkness in which it makes its way. The description of the power and appearance of the locusts has frightful significance as indicating the supernatural nature of spiritism and its deadening effect upon the soul. Physical death is no escape from it. The "five months" may allude to the five midsummer months in which the locusts usually commit their ravages, and may be intended to signify that this spiritual judgment would be limited in its duration.

4. The Sixth Trumpet and Second Woe (9:13-21). Another judgment of a similar kind, but coming from an earthly origin. An army of horsemen, whose number is so great that it cannot be a literal army, is set loose from the Euphrates to overrun the world and destroy a third part of men. This means another divine warning of terrible import. In the Old Testament the Euphrates was the seat of the great heathen powers which God used for the chastisement and judgment of Israel. The Euphrates, therefore, may be taken to represent the pagan or godless world. The description of the horses and their riders shows that we have here another judgment of an infernal character, which sweeps over the word. It is a revival of paganism, releasing forces of spiritual evil that have hitherto

been hidden and held in check behind the curtain of the pagan world. The world that refuses to be Christianized cannot but become paganized. Both of these woes have broken out upon the human race in the two world wars of our generation.

The purpose of all these plagues and judgments is to warn the world and lead it to repentance. They are divine warnings, becoming more ominous and terrifying all the time. And yet men will not repent and turn to God. And so the third woe must come. In the meantime another pause occurs, and another interlude is introduced into the progress of the Revelation.

5. An Interlude (10:1—11:14). This section corresponds to the parenthesis between the sixth and the seventh seals. It makes a pause in the movement of the trumpet visions in order to explain the preparations for the seventh and last trumpet. These preparations are shown first on the heavenly side, in the descent of the strong angel (ch. 10), and then on the earthly side, in the prophetic ministry of the two witnesses (11:1-14).

(1) The strong angel (ch. 10). John saw an angel of overpowering aspect descend from Heaven and set one foot upon the sea and the other upon the earth, as if he were taking possession of the world (vs. 1-2). All the features of the vision suggest the glory of the Son of Man in ch. 1. The great voice as of a lion roaring, and the seven thunders (vs. 3-4), whose voice John heard but was forbidden to record, suggest that here we have a prophetic picture of Christ coming to administer the final judgments of God (John 5:22-29; Acts 17:31). The angel's oath also points in the same direction (vs. 5-7). Its import is contained in the words, "there shall be delay no longer". The prayer of the suffering Church in 6:10-11 is now to be answered. "The mystery of God" is now to be finished; that is, the manifestation of God in Christ has come to its consummation.

All this symbolism means that the developing Revelation has reached the eve of the Coming of the Lord. The angel had in his hand "a little book open" (v. 2). This was the book of 5:1, which has had its seven seals all broken and is now held open, in order to show that the title-deeds of the world are Christ's, and to proclaim His right to its dominion. The Seer was commanded to take the book and eat it up, which meant that he was to receive and appropriate the revelation it contained (Ezek. 2:8; 3:3). It was sweet to his taste, but bitter when he digested it (vs. 8-10). The hope it gave brought joy to John, but there was bitterness in realizing that judgments were involved in it. He was told that he "must prophesy again over many peoples and nations and tongues and kings" (v 11). This refers to the contents of chs. 12—22.

(2) The two witnesses (11:1-14). The account of these witnesses is introduced by a command to the Seer to "measure the temple of God, and the altar, and them that worship therein" (vs. 1-2). This meant that the true Church, represented by the sanctuary, was to be set apart for security, and was to be preserved from the judgment that was coming. The outer court was not to be measured: "for it hath been given unto the nations". Possibly it represents the visible and organized framework of the Church, which does not belong to the spiritual order, but rather to the present world. But more

probably it represents the old Jewish system in the midst of which the Church began. The next statement would agree with this: "The holy city shall they tread down forty and two months". These words no doubt refer to, and are a repetition of, our Lord's prophecy in Luke 21:24: "Jerusalem shall be trodden down of the Gentiles, until the times of the Gentiles be fulfilled". This covers the whole Christian age.

Here, then, we get the key to the symbolical period during which the two witnesses were to prophesy (v. 3). It is the present Gospel age. A thousand two hundred and threescore days are the same as forty-two months, the month being counted as thirty days. It is a period of three years and a half, and corresponds to the second half of the last week of Daniel's prophecy of the seventy weeks (Dan. 9:27). The ministry of Christ fulfilled the first half of that week, (See page 223 in Vol. II of this series). The second half of the week would represent the period in which Christ's witnesses were to finish His work in the world. Thus it becomes a symbol of the age of the Church. It is mentioned again in 12:6 and 13:5, and is described in 12:14 as "a time, and times, and half a time" (Dan. 7:25; 12:7).

The two witnesses are described in terms which show that they are to be taken symbolically (vs. 4-6). The olive trees and the candlesticks refer to the vision in Zech. 4, and indicate the spiritual qualities and functions of the witnesses. The miraculous powers with which they are equipped recall incidents in the history of Moses and Elijah, and represent the supernatural forces that are put in operation by prayer. All this goes to emphasize the fact that these two witnesses represent the Christian Church during the present age. The Lord calls them "my two witnesses", because of the two Divine elements in the witness of the Church—the Word of God and the Holy Spirit. They are to carry on their ministry "clothed in sackcloth", because the Church bears witness to a Saviour whom the world has crucified and rejected.

The account of the end of their ministry contains a symbolic prophecy of remarkable significance. They are to be slain by the beast out of the abyss, and "their dead bodies lie in the street of the great city" (vs. 7-8). This would seem to indicate that a time should come when a Satanic attack upon the Church would destroy its spiritual power and leave it in the world as a lifeless organization, with no more power to touch the conscience or convict of sin. The expression, "the great city", is used seven times after this, and never of Jerusalem. Its description as "spiritually called Sodom and Egypt, where also their Lord was crucified", marks the godless world in its threefold character as morally corrupt, defying God, and rejecting the Saviour. The passage goes on to give a graphic account of its patronizing attitude toward the organized Church, and of the relief it would manifest when the authority of the Word of God and the sense of the Spirit's presence should die out of the Church's witness (vs. 9-19).

But this condition is described as lasting for a very brief period—"three days and a half". The victory of Satan and the world would be transitory. Then the writer reverts to the past tense, and describes the culminating event as if it had already

taken place (vs. 11-12). It is symbolical of a great spiritual revival of the Church and its profound effect upon the world, and of the rapture of the Church, as following immediately afterwards. The breath of life entered into the witnesses and they stood upon their feet. Then a voice called them up into Heaven, and their enemies beheld their ascension. Thus the scene brings us at last to the Coming of the Lord (1 Thess. 4:16-17). The whole section dealing with the interlude closes with a great earthquake and its effect upon "the city", and we are prepared for the last trumpet and the final judgment (vs. 13-14).

6. The Seventh Trumpet and Third Woe (11:15-19). This corresponds with the last trump of 1 Cor. 15:52. A proclamation is made in Heaven that the Kingdom has been established on earth and the reign of Christ has begun. The twenty-four elders respond with an ascription of praise to God because the time of judgment and rewards has come. But having reached this point, the vision suddenly comes to an end without disclosing any of the accompanying or subsequent events. Instead of that, we are told that the temple of God was opened in Heaven; and we are thus prepared for another series of visions, for out of this temple the subsequent judgments proceed (14:15, 17; 15:5; 16:17). Then is heard again the artillery of Heaven, which brings each of the series of seven visions to a close (8:5; 11:19; 16:18).

THE FOES OF CHRIST AND HIS CHURCH
(Chs. 12—14)

From ch. 4 to ch. 11 inclusive we have had a continuous series of scenes, which represent the progressive development of spiritual forces that began with the Ascension of Christ and come to a climax at His Second Coming. They show how His claim to the sovereignty of the world is vindicated, and how His dominion over the world is finally established. The special theme of this part of the Revelation may be defined as Jesus Christ making the world His Kingdom. A break occurs at the end of ch. 11, and a new series of visions begins with the Ascension again. It comes to a climax at the end of the book with a vision of the Church as the Bride of the Lamb, sharing with Him the glory of His reign. In this series we are shown how He fulfils the promise of 3:21, and prepares the Church to share His throne. The special theme of this part of the Revelation may be defined as Jesus Christ making the Church His Bride. The scenes in the present chapters show us the foes who must be overthrown, and the nature of the conflict with them.

1. The Great Red Dragon (Ch. 12). John first describes the sign of a woman arrayed with the sun, who represents Israel as invested with heavenly glory, and as the mother of the promised Messianic King (vs. 1-2). Then Satan appears as a great red dragon in the fulness of his power over the kingdoms of the world; and, having dragged a third of the angelic hosts in his fall, he now waits to destroy the Messiah when He comes (vs. 3-4). His attempt on the life of Jesus is frustrated, and we are brought again to the Ascension of Christ in the statement, "her child was caught up unto God and unto his throne" (v. 5). The flight of the woman into the

wilderness, where she is kept and nourished for twelve hundred and sixty days, represents the preservation of national Israel during the present Christian age (v. 6).

The war in Heaven against the dragon results in the expulsion of Satan from the presence-chamber of God (vs. 7-9). This event occurred at the Ascension. Since the return of the Saviour there, Satan has no longer any right to accuse the saints at the bar of God (John 12:31; Rom. 8:33-34). A song of triumph is then heard in Heaven, announcing that the work of salvation has been accomplished and the accuser of the brethren has been cast out. Their victory came through the sacrifice of the Lamb, but "those who dwell on the earth" are to feel the wrath of the devil, for only a brief opportunity is left to him (vs. 10-12).

The dragon proceeds to persecute the woman who gave birth to the man-child. But she is preserved from his attempts to destroy her. Israel has never been overwhelmed by the floods of persecution and tribulation that have pursued her throughout the Christian centuries (vs. 13-16). Then the dragon in his rage turns his attention elsewhere. He "went away to make war with the rest of her seed, that keep the commandments of God, and hold the testimony of Jesus" (v. 17). This is clearly a reference to the persecution of the Christian Church.

2. The Beast out of the Sea (13:1-10). The first words of this chapter belong to the preceding chapter, and should read: "and he stood upon the sand of the sea". The dragon halts upon the shore to call up his great ally out of the sea of the nations. This monster, which is a combination of the four beasts of Daniel's vision (Dan. 7:1-8), is endowed with the power and authority of the dragon (vs. 1-2). The beast is a symbol of world power in the course of its historical development. As a system, the political power of the nations of the world is inspired and energized by Satan. Under the guidance of the prince of the world, it constantly opposes and often persecutes the Church of Christ. It is the devil's policy to disguise his operations under the forms of the world. In John's time that power was centred in Rome; and the fascination which the Empire has imposed upon the human race even in its fall is vividly portrayed in the next verses (vs. 3-5).

The awful influence of this beast was to continue throughout the whole Christian age ("forty and two months"), and to extend over the whole world ("every tribe and people and tongue and nation"). It would oppose the cause of the Lord Jesus Christ and persecute His people (vs. 6-7). The human race as a whole, the unregenerate among men, would yield to the spell of this world power (v. 8). Then there comes a warning which is somewhat obscure, but probably means that believers are to suffer with patience and without resistance (vs. 9-10). The patience and faith of the saints will be displayed in their confidence in God and in their meek endurance of persecution.

3. The Beast out of the Earth (13:11-18). "He had two horns like unto a lamb, and he spake as a dragon"; that is, he looked like Christ, but was inspired by Satan (v. 11). This beast uses the power of the first beast, and counterfeits divine miracles (vs. 12-13). It represents a religious power

in alliance with political power. This symbolism has its historical parallel in the rise and progress of the Papacy. It casts a glamour of deceit over "them that dwell on the earth", as the Papacy has done over the unregenerate human race (v. 14). It revived the life of the first beast, as Papal Rome revived the power and influence of pagan Rome (v. 15).

This beast exerts a controlling influence over the ordinary life of all classes of men by putting its own mark of identification upon them (vs. 16-17). Here we have an apt symbol of the subtle and sinister tyranny which Papal Rome exercises through its world-wide secret organization. John closes his account of the beast by calling attention to its number, in order that its significance may be considered. "It is the number of a man, and his number is Six hundred and sixty and six" (v. 18). If any number could represent the Deity, it would be seven hundred and seventy-seven, the threefold seven. Six hundred and sixty-six aims at that but comes short of it. This number therefore represents an attempt to usurp the place of God. No institution in all human history answers to this description as the Papacy does. And the Papacy is always centred in "a man," the reigning Pope of the time.

4. The Followers of the Lamb (14:1-5). Opposing these three foes whom he has described, the Seer beheld the Lamb standing on Mount Zion, and with him a hundred and forty-four thousand (v. 1). This is the same company that were sealed in 7:1-4. They represent the true Church of Christ on earth, standing on the sure foundation (Psa. 2:6; Heb. 12:22-24). They have "his name, and the name of his Father, written on their foreheads", in contrast with those that have received the mark of the beast (13:16). Then John heard a song from Heaven of mingled majesty and sweetness, a new song which only that redeemed company could learn to sing (vs. 2-3). Their character is described in terms which signify complete separation from the defilement of the world, entire devotion to the service of Christ, and blamelessness in the sight of God (vs. 4-5) They represent the redeemed people of God, the "firstfruits of his creatures" (Jas. 1: 18).

5. The Heavenly Proclamations (14:6-13). In this passage John records four angelic announcements, which reflect the nature and course of the conflict between Christ and His foes.

(1) The everlasting Gospel (vs. 6-7). The preaching of the Gospel is a testimony to the nations of the world against a background of judgment (Matt. 24:14; Mark 16:15; Acts 17:30-31).

(2) The fall of Babylon (v. 8). This announcement anticipates the judgment described in chs. 17—18. The imagery is taken from Jer. 51:7-8. Babylon represents the godless world, as Jerusalem represents the Church.

(3) The fate of the godless (vs. 9-12). This symbolic scene is the most appalling picture of the punishment of the wicked in all Scripture. It is represented as taking place, "in the presence of the holy angels, and in the presence of the Lamb". This signifies their acquiescence in the justice and necessity of God's awful judgments. "Here is the patience of the saints": knowing the terrible judgment of the Lord, they endure the terrible persecution of the beast.

(4) The blessedness of the holy dead (v. 13). "The dead who die in the Lord from henceforth", mean all believers who die during the present Christian age, or since the Lord's Ascension, the point of time from which the Revelation begins. The message, however, was specially intended for the comfort of those who were enduring persecution in that day.

6. The Harvest and the Vintage (14:14-20). The issues of the conflict are now set forth in two symbolic scenes of sublimity and grandeur.

(1) The harvest of the earth (vs. 14-16). This means the reaping of the good, the gathering out of the righteous. The Son of Man is represented as doing this Himself, and the imagery suggests His Coming in glory. A message from God out of the innermost shrine of Heaven tells Him that the time of the harvest has come (Matt. 13:30).

(2) The vintage of the earth (vs. 17-20). This means the gathering and punishing of the wicked, and an angel is commissioned to perform the task. The imagery is that of a winepress, so deep that the juice of the grapes, which appears like blood, comes up to the bridles of the horses trampling them. A symbolic number is introduced to indicate the world-wide nature of the judgment: "As far as a thousand and six hundred furlongs". This is the number of the world multiplied by itself to express intensity, and then by a hundred, the number of the world's kingdoms multiplied by itself. There is no escape from the universal efficacy of the sharp sickle by which the wicked are gathered to their doom.

THE SEVEN BOWLS OF WRATH
(Chs. 15—16)

The Revelation is now approaching the end of the long conflict between Christ and His foes, between the Church and the world. There is a sense of finality and completeness in these chapters. The judgments described here are distinguished from all that came before them as being "the last". They complete the manifestation of the wrath of God.

1. The Preparation (Ch. 15). There is a sense of sublime and awful significance in this scene. It is marked by calm and majestic leliberation. It introduces seven angels who are to execute the final judgments (v. 1). John saw first "them that come off victorious" in the conflict with the beast. The same word is used here as in the promise "to him that overcometh" in chs. 2-3. They were standing beside the sea of glass before the throne (4:6), singing the song of Moses and the Lamb—the song of the saints of both dispensations—and praising the Lord God almighty for His righteous judgments (vs. 2-4).

After that John saw coming out from the innermost sanctuary of Heaven—the presence-chamber of God—the seven angelic agents of these divine judgments, magnificently arrayed. They were given seven golden bowls full of the wrath of God (vs. 5-6). These were not narrow vials (A.V.) but wide bowls, whose contents could be poured out in one sudden action. The fact that these bowls were presented by one of the living creatures would indicate that the plagues were to be inflicted on the natural world of man's abode. The cloud of smoke that filled the sanctuary closed all access to the Divine presence. These judgments would bring man's day of grace to an end (vs. 7-8).

2. The First Four Bowls (16:1-9). These four judgments are parallel with those of the first four trumpets (8:7-12). They fall upon the same objects, and in the same order. But there is an important and significant difference. In the case of the trumpets, a third of each object was smitten: in the case of the bowls, the whole of each object is smitten. The trumpets were warning judgments: the bowls are final judgments. This would indicate that when judgments or signs that were formerly local and partial become universal and affect the whole world, then the day of God's wrath has come, and the Coming of the Lord is at hand. Two voices are heard in the course of these bowls (vs. 5-7). The angel of the waters acknowledges the justice of the judgment and its cause. The voice from the altar represents the souls of the martyrs, whose prayers are now being answered (6:9-10). These plagues bring no repentance, but only deeper enmity to God (v. 9).

3. The Fifth Bowl (16:10-11). This judgment falls upon the throne of the beast, the political power of the world. "His kingdom was darkened": the light by which the subjects of the beast have been allured dies away, and men see the failure of their hopes. "They gnawed their tongues for pain": the system in which they had trusted breaks down, leaving them in misery and despair (Luke 21:25-26). And still there is no repentance on the part of the human race.

4. The Sixth Bowl (16:12-16). When this bowl is poured out two scenes take place.

(1) The Euphrates is dried up to prepare the way for "the kings that come from the sunrising" (v. 12). The east, or the sunrising, has been mentioned before as the seat of Divine authority and action (7:2). Therefore those who come from the sunrising must be agents of God. The Euphrates has appeared in a former vision as the seat of the paganizing power of the nations of the world (9:14). The drying up of the Euphrates is used in the Old Testament as symbolical of the Lord's preparation of a highway for the return of scattered Israel (Isa. 11:15-16). It would seem therefore that the kings from the sunrising represent His own redeemed people who are being prepared to share the throne with Christ (3:21). They are clearly to be distinguished from the kings in the next scene.

(2) The kings of the whole world, under demonic instigation from the dragon and the two great beasts, are gathered together "unto the war of the great day of God, the Almighty" (vs. 13-14). Here is an obvious symbol of the nations of the world being driven on by the self-interest of their national policies to the final judgment of God. Their gathering place is called Har-Magedon (A.V. Armageddon), which means the mount of Megiddo (v. 16). This name marks the plain in central Palestine where most of the great battles of the Old Testament were fought. Here Barak defeated Sisera and Gideon defeated the Midianites. Here Saul was defeated and slain by the Philistines and Josiah was defeated and wounded to death by the Egyptians. In interpreting this scene, the symbolical character of the Revelation must not be forgotten. This is no local battle-field, but a symbolical picture of uni-

versal war, and a prediction of God's final judgment upon the nations of the world. It is parallel with the appalling scene in Jer. 25:15-29.

Into the midst of this passage is thrust a parenthesis, which has no connection with the context (v. 15). It is a warning of the sudden and unexpected coming of the Lord. This is the only place in all the Revelation where such a warning is given; and it evidently means that the event will occur when the conditions portrayed in this vision are realized. The imagery is taken from the nightwatchmen in the Temple. If one of them should be seen without his outer garment, it would mean that he had been found asleep at his post and it had been taken from him.

5. The Seventh Bowl (16:17-21). This plague falls upon the air, the realm of Satan, "the prince of the power of the air" (Eph. 2:2). All else has been smitten; it only remains to smite the source of evil. The voice that came from the Throne, "It is done", corresponds with the cry that came from the Cross, "It is finished". In the one case it marked the climax of the first coming of Christ; in the other case it seems to mark the climax of His Second Coming. The event itself is not described, but the remainder of the passage gives a summary of its tremendous import.

The last bowl has brought us to the same point of time as the last trumpet, which announced the victory of the Kingdom of Christ over the kingdoms of the world (11:15). Chapter 16 ends with the same crisis as chapter 11. The remaining chapters of the book carry out the issues of that event. The angels who poured out the seven bowls remain upon the scene until the end of the Revelation (17:1; 21:9).

THE DOOM OF THE FOES OF CHRIST
(Chs. 17—20)

The visions which now appear set forth the circumstances relating to the Coming of Christ, and the ultimate consummation of His work of redemption. We are shown His foes being overthrown one by one, until at last Satan himself is eliminated, and death, "the last enemy" (1 Cor. 15:26), is abolished.

1. The Mystery of Babylon (Ch. 17). The judgment of Babylon, which has been announced twice already (14:8; 16:19), is now to be revealed. John is called to come and be shown "the judgment of the great harlot", a significant name for an apostate church (vs. 1-2). He is carried away into a wilderness, and sees a woman sitting upon a scarlet-coloured beast. The beast is that of 13:1, representing the political power of the world; and the whole appearance of the woman indicates the Church of Rome (vs. 3-6).

Her position on the beast symbolizes Rome's attitude toward political power. She seeks to manage it, and make it serve her interests. The woman is "arrayed in purple and scarlet": Rome's worldly pomp. She is "decked with gold": Rome's worldly wealth. She has the name "Mystery" on her forehead, claiming to be the Bride of Christ (Eph. 5:32). But her true name is, "The Mother of Harlots". She was "drunken with the blood of the saints, and with the blood of the martyrs of Jesus". This is more truly descriptive of the Roman Church than of the Roman Empire. She

has shed more innocent blood and put more Christians to death than any other institution in history.

As John wonders at the sight, the angel proceeds to tell him "the mystery of the woman, and of the beast that carrieth her". The details of the description are difficult and obscure, but as a whole they make up what is manifestly a composite picture of pagan and Papal Rome (vs. 7-14). History has confirmed and substantiated the parallel; for as time went on Papal Rome succeeded to the power of pagan Rome. The angel follows his account of the woman with a prediction of her ultimate destruction by the very powers with which she had been in league (vs. 15-17). Through them God would accomplish His will, and bring down His judgment upon her. Finally the angel identifies the woman with the great city of Rome itself, which was then the capital of the world (v. 18).

2. The Fall of Babylon (Ch. 18). Here the imagery changes, and Babylon is represented as a city. She now becomes a symbol of Satan's crowning achievement, the counterfeit of the Kingdom of God on earth. This he accomplished with the aid of his two great allies of ch. 13, who are referred to hereafter as the beast and the false prophet. It is an alliance of political power with religious apostasy. Babylon's fall is announced in terms taken from the Old Testament predictions of the desolation of ancient Babylon (vs. 1-3; Isa. 21:9; 13:20-22; Jer. 50:39; 51:37). The people of God are warned to come out of her, that they may have no fellowship with her sins, and no share in her punishment (vs. 4-8). This call for separation from the world rings all through the history of redemption. It is a summons to maintain aloofness of spirit in the midst of the world's business.

Then there comes a lamentation over Babylon's fall, in which the catastrophe is described as it affects the kings (vs. 9-10), the merchants (vs. 11-17), the sailors and shipmasters (vs. 17-19). The social and economic order of the world has been overthrown; the commerce and trade of the nations has been destroyed. All the laments are of a selfish character, indicating that all this world order has been ministering to human self-indulgence and luxury. A significant note comes in at the end of v. 13. It has trafficked in the "souls of men"; it has been destructive of spiritual life.

A very different effect is revealed in Heaven, which is called to rejoice that God has avenged His servants (v. 20). The suddenness and completeness of the fall of Babylon is emphasized by the threefold repetition of the phrase "in one hour" (vs. 10, 17, 19). The same thing is illustrated by a symbolic act on the part of the angel (v. 21), who then brings his prediction to an end with a dirge over Babylon of exquisite beauty and sublimity (vs. 22-24).

3. The Overthrow of the Beast and the False Prophet (Ch. 19). This is the main theme of the chapter. It begins with a triumph-song in Heaven over the fall of Babylon, a fourfold Hallelujah, in which the angels, the elders, and the living creatures all take part, representing the whole universe under the reign of the Lord God Almighty (vs. 1-6). Now that the harlot church has been judged and put out of the way, they rejoice that the marriage of the Lamb has come, and the true Bride has made herself ready for her union with Christ in glory (vs. 7-8).

This song of the marriage of the Lamb is the last of seven songs in the Revelation. The others are, the praise of the Creator (4:8-11), the praise of the Lamb (5:8-14), the song of redemption (7:9-12), the song of the Kingdom (11:15-18), the song of triumph over Satan (12:10-12), and the song of the victors on the glassy sea (15:3-4). The prospect of the bliss of the marriage supper overwhelmed John, and he fell down to worship the angel, who at once reminded him that the angels in Heaven are but fellow-servants with the followers of Jesus on earth (vs. 9-10). "They that are bidden to the marriage supper" are not to be distinguished from the Church. The redeemed are both the Lamb's guests and the Lamb's Bride.

At this point a scene is described of grand and appalling symbolism. A Rider upon a white horse comes out of Heaven with the angelic armies in His train (vs. 11-16). His whole appearance, and the statement that "in righteousness he doth judge and make war", indicate that we have here the coming of Christ with the angels of His power to render vengeance on His foes (1 Thess. 3:13; 2 Thess. 1:7-10). On His head were many crowns, and He is represented as having four names. He was called "Faithful and True", as having given a true and faithful revelation of God. He had a name written which no one knows but himself—His own inherent nature, which is beyond the capacity of man to understand. "His name is called, The Word of God": it is thus He is known to the Church. On His garment, where it fell over His thigh, a name was written that all could read: "King of kings and Lord of lords". It is thus He is to be known to the world.

The vision was accompanied by a proclamation, made by an angel standing in the sun (vs. 17-18). This was intended to mark the universal character of the judgment executed by the Rider on the white horse. His victory over the beast and the false prophet is described in the next scene (vs. 19-21). It results in the destruction of Satan's two great allies, which are both cast into "the lake of fire". This signifies the ultimate and complete elimination of the two organized agencies of the world which oppose the cause of Christ—a political system based on human self-will and self-interest, and a religious system usurping the function of the Saviour of men.

4. The Overthrow of Satan (Ch. 20). The arch-foe still remains to be judged. The main theme of this chapter is not the millennial reign of Christ, which is only an incident in the vision, but the final victory of Christ over Satan, and his ultimate doom. The Seer first beholds Satan bound, and consigned to the abyss from which he released the plague of demonism upon the earth (9:1-3), where he is imprisoned for a thousand years (vs. 1-3). Ever since he was cast out of Heaven at the Ascension, he has been waging war on earth against the followers of Christ (12:9-12; 1 Pet. 5:8). And now he is cast out of the world and banished for a time from the affairs of men. This clears the way for the reign of Christ over the earth, and the martyrs (6:9-11) and those who have come victorious through the conflict with His foes come to life again and reign with Him. This is the first resurrection (vs. 4-5).

As all the numbers in the Revelation are symbolical, so also is the number "a thousand". Ten is the number of the kingdoms of the world, or the manifestation of world power (13:1; 17:3, 12). Here it is raised to the third power, which gives it a divine character. The thousand years, therefore, means the age of God's reign upon earth, during which the cause of Christ will be triumphant. Nothing is said as to the nature of this period, nor is there any suggestion that Christ and His glorified saints will dwell on earth. They reign from Heaven. A blessing is pronounced upon those who have part in the first resurrection and are thus enabled to share in this reign (v. 6). This is the fifth of seven beatitudes in this book. It is distinguished from the other six by the addition of "holy" (1:3; 14:13; 16:15; 19:9; 22:7, 14).

At the end of this period, for some reason unexplained to us, Satan is to be released from his prison. He will gather the hosts of Gog and Magog against the saints of God (vs. 7-8). This symbolism is taken from Ezek. 38-39, where Gog and Magog represent nations on the utmost limits of the world. Here they probably represent spiritual hosts of wickedness, which Satan summons from the utmost limits of his world of evil for a final attack upon the Kingdom of God. The reign of Christ and His saints does not cease. The struggle is as brief as it is fierce. Fire from Heaven destroys the foes, and Satan's doom is sealed. He is cast into the lake of fire, where the beast and the false prophet are (vs. 9-10).

Then there comes a sublime and awful scene, which takes place before "a great white throne" (v. 11). The whole description implies that the final judgment of the wicked has come. It is an enlargement of 11:18. John saw "the dead, the great and the small, standing before the throne" (v. 12). These were "the rest of the dead" of v. 5, whose resurrection he proceeds to describe in detail (v. 13). "And books were opened"—the records of the lives and deeds of men. The sentence of the Judge is not arbitrary; it rests on evidence.

"And another book was opened, which is the book of life"—the roll of the citizens of the Kingdom of God. The other books would be vouchers, as it were, for the book of life. "Death and Hades were cast into the lake of fire" (v. 14). This means that all the results of Satan's work are eliminated from the world. John describes, in the language of symbolism, what Paul has already told us in direct words (1 Cor. 15:26, 54). When the judgment of the white throne is ended, all that are not enrolled in the Kingdom are consigned to the lake of fire; and this is "the second death" (v. 15). As there is a second and higher life, so there is a second and deeper death. As after that life there is no more death, so after that death there is no more life.

THE NEW HEAVEN AND THE NEW EARTH
(Chs. 21—22)

The long conflict is over, and the final judgment is passed. What the Revelation was intended to show to the servants of God has been accomplished. The Lamb has triumphed over all His foes. It now remains to reveal His union in glory with the Church, which has shared the conflict with Him. This blissful vision is set in the frame of the new heaven and the new earth.

1. The New Creation (21:1-8). When "the earth

and the heaven fled away" from the face of the Judge in the preceding vision (20:11), the way was prepared for "a new heaven and a new earth" to come into the Seer's view (v. 1). In this new world, "there was no more sea", for in John's mind the sea was associated with the restless nations. The metropolis of the new earth was not a new Babylon, but a new Jerusalem, built of heavenly material (v. 2). It was to be the dwelling-place of God, where He would have fellowship with men as His own people, and all the woe that sin had brought into the world would be done away (vs. 3-4). John heard a voice from the Throne announce an entirely new creation, which would be the final result of the Redeemer's work (vs. 5-6). In this new creation all the promises given to His people would be realized, and from it all evil would be banished (vs. 7-8).

2. The New Jerusalem (21:9-27). There is a striking parallel noted at once between this vision (vs. 9-10) and that of Babylon (17:1-3). Each vision is announced by one of the seven angels that had the seven bowls. There John was shown the great harlot: here he is shown the Bride, the Lamb's wife. There he was taken into a wilderness: here he is taken to a mountain. Evidently the intention is to mark the contrast between the apostate woman and the faithful wife. The vision of the new Jerusalem is of surpassing grandeur and beauty. The features of its symbolism are not to be taken literally, but are given us to brood over in wonder, till their mystic meaning comes stealing into our souls. They are profoundly significant of spiritual realities.

(1) Her outward appearance (vs. 11-14). The number "twelve", identifying the Church, occurs five times in these verses. The city shone with the glory of God, represented in the white brilliance of the jasper stone. With three gates on each side, the city was open to all the world.

(2) Her perfect measurements (vs. 15-17). The numbers here are all multiples of twelve. The city lay foursquare, and was a perfect cube, the same shape as the Most Holy Place in the tabernacle, where the symbol of God's presence dwelt.

(3) Her general structure (vs. 18-21). The description here reaches the sublimest heights of which human imagination is capable. It is a grand enlargement of the splendour of Zion described in Isa. 54:11-12. The twelve foundations of the city wall were precious stones; and John names them one by one, as his eye delights to dwell upon their loveliness. These are not architectural details, but symbolized spiritual realities. They are beautiful suggestions of grace and glory. Precious stones cannot be manufactured by man, but are formed in the crucible of the Creator out of ordinary earthly elements. The holy city is not the product of human efforts at reform, but is built of sinners saved by Divine grace. "The twelve gates were twelve pearls" —the only stone in all the list that comes from a stab of pain in a living creature. The way into the city is by the Cross.

(4) Her inward life (vs. 22-27). The Lamb is the centre of all the life and light within the city. He takes the place of sun and moon. No temple is needed, for God is worshipped and adored directly. "There shall be no night there", for there will be no sin or foe to lurk in the darkness. Some of the features here are drawn from Isaiah's prediction of the glory of Zion (60:3, 11, 19-20).

3. The New Paradise (22:1-5). The figure changes here, and the Garden of Eden blends with the New Jerusalem. The curse of the Fall and all its results have been removed, and the source and secret of life are now available to all. This is the meaning of the symbolism. The river of life and the street run side by side through the city, and trees of life grow there in rows, which never cease to yield their fruit. The closing feature of the vision brings its bliss to a climax. The servants of the Lamb see His face, and His name is on their foreheads. In the light of His glory and in the fellowship of His presence, they share His everlating reign.

4. The Conclusion (22:6-21). The Revelation has come to an end, and the angel, who was commissioned to show it to John (1:1), now confirms it in the name of Christ (vs. 6-7). So astounding was the closing vision that the Seer forgot the warning recently given him (19:10), and prostrated himself before the angel, and received from him the same rebuke (vs. 8-9). Then the voice of Christ is heard giving a final warning. When the judgments to be administered at His Coming have taken place, the state of the righteous and the unrighteous will be fixed for ever (vs. 10-12). This is followed by a statement summing up the message and the purpose of the whole book (vs. 13-15).

Jesus continues His testimony by repeating and emphasizing the purpose for which the Revelation was given (vs. 16-17), and uttering a solemn protest against wilful perversions of the teaching of the prophecy (vs. 18-19). The Lord sounds the keynote of the Revelation again in one final word, to which the Apostle adds the prayer of the Church (v. 20). There is nothing more to be said; and the book now closes with a brief benediction, indicating that it was intended to be read in the churches, like the Epistles (v. 21).

THE END